ISBN 978-0-266-04242-6
PIBN 11034391

# ARCHIVES OF MARYLAND

## PROCEEDINGS AND ACTS

OF THE

## GENERAL ASSEMBLY OF MARYLAND

SEPTEMBER, 1704—APRIL, 1706

PUBLISHED BY AUTHORITY OF THE STATE, UNDER THE DIRECTION
OF THE MARYLAND HISTORICAL SOCIETY

WILLIAM HAND BROWNE
*Editor*

BALTIMORE
MARYLAND HISTORICAL SOCIETY
1906

The Friedenwald Company
BALTIMORE, MD., U. S. A.

ROOMS OF THE MARYLAND HISTORICAL SOCIETY,

BALTIMORE, *July* 25, 1906.

*To the Maryland Historical Society:*

GENTLEMEN :

We have the honor to submit the Twenty-sixth Volume of the Maryland Archives, being the Proceedings and Acts of the General Assembly at the Sessions of 1704, 1705, and 1706.

Respectfully,

CLAYTON C. HALL,
HENRY STOCKBRIDGE, JR.,
BERNARD C. STEINER,
*Committee.*

# ARCHIVES OF MÅRYLAND.

The following volumes have been published :

## PREFACE.

The most important business of the session of Sept.–Oct., 1704, was the thorough revision of the laws, and enactment of what was nearly a complete code. The Governor and Assembly were on the most harmonious terms; interchanges of polite speeches and professions of esteem were frequent, and halcyon weather prevailed. That the urbane Seymour had, however, when he chose to use it, a rough side to his

## NOTE.

It should have been mentioned in the Preface that the Act for Regulating the Militia, referred to on p. 411, is merely a re-enactment, *verbatim*, of the Act on p. 269.

a fund to assist New York in her defensive measures against the French and Indians. New York, though notified that this fund was at her disposal, had never asked for it—an abstention, in the eyes of the Assembly, so unnatural and inexplicable, that it must be connected with some dark design. However, there the money was, and it was now proposed that it should be sent to England to be used in baffling New York's machinations.

The sessions of 1705 and 1706 present little that calls for remark. The conspiracy of Richard Clark and his accomplices, and the burning

# PREFACE.

The most important business of the session of Sept.–Oct. the thorough revision of the laws, and enactment of what w complete code. The Governor and Assembly were on the monious terms; interchanges of polite speeches and pre esteem were frequent, and halcyon weather prevailed. That Seymour had, however, when he chose to use it, a rough tongue, is shown by his objurgation of two Catholic priest been guilty of the enormity of saying mass in a chapel. ernor's bark was apparently worse than his bite, for we find l a bill suspending the prosecution of priests who should cele in private houses.

One thing that gave the Assembly much uneasiness wa from England that agents from New York were urging a bring all the colonies under that government. It is hardly that the Privy Council would have entertained such a propos mere possibility of it was alarming. Both Houses joined in to the Queen; but the Upper House pointed out that if an countermining was proposed, a sum of money must be pr necessary expenses; and to this the Lower House demurred. nious expedient was then proposed. In 1702 the Assembly a fund to assist New York in her defensive measures against and Indians. New York, though notified that this fund disposal, had never asked for it—an abstention, in the e Assembly, so unnatural and inexplicable, that it must be conr some dark design. However, there the money was, and i proposed that it should be sent to England to be used in ba York's machinations.

The sessions of 1705 and 1706 present little that calls f The conspiracy of Richard Clark and his accomplices, and t

*Preface.*

of the State house and Court house, seem to have made the Assembly nervous; but fuller particulars of this somewhat mysterious affair will be found in the Council Journal.

In 1706 Queen Anne's County was erected out of portions of Talbot and Kent.

This Legislature distinguished itself by its zeal for the advancement of trade. Apparently under an impression that by creating a town or port they could create the commerce to make it thrive, they erected more than forty, of nearly all which this act of 1706 remains the sole biography and epitaph.

Owing to a misunderstanding at the printing office, the paging of the text begins with page 25. No pages are wanting.

# PROCEEDINGS AND ACTS

OF THE

# GENERAL ASSEMBLY

# OF MARYLAND.

*At a Session held at Annapolis, September 5–October 3,* 1704.

CHARLES CALVERT, LORD BALTIMORE,

*Proprietary.*

JOHN SEYMOUR,

*Governor.*

———

THE UPPER HOUSE OF ASSEMBLY.

Maryland ss<sup>t</sup>
At a Council in Assembly begun and held at the Town and
Port of Annapolis in Ann Arundell County the fifth day of
September in the third year of the Reigne of our Sovn Lady
Anne by the grace of God of England Scotland France and
Ireland And the Dominions thereunto belonging Queen De-
fender of the Faith &c Annoq Domini 1704 and there con-
tinued until the 3<sup>d</sup> day of October next ensuing.

Present

His Ex<sup>cy</sup> Col John Seymour her Majest<sup>ics</sup>

Governour &c.

|  |  |  |
|---|---|---|
| The Honble | Tho<sup>s</sup> Tench Esq<sup>r</sup> | Lieu<sup>t</sup> Col William Holland |
|  | Col John Addison | James Sanders Esq<sup>r</sup> |
|  | Tho<sup>s</sup> Brook Esq<sup>r</sup> | Kenelm Cheseldyn Esq<sup>r</sup> |
|  | Col John Hammond | Col Thomas Ennals |

His Excy laid before the Board what he intended to say to
the Assembly upon their first meeting which was read as follows Viz<sup>t</sup>

M<sup>r</sup> Speaker & you Gent<sup>n</sup> Delegates

The Reasons why the last Sessions was so short and consequently so little of the publick Business finished I presume
can be no new things to this present Assembly, And as most
of her Majesty's Royall Instructions were postponed to this
meeting I cannot doubt of your Advice & ready concurrence
in those weighty matters so heartily recommended by her
most gracious Majesty the Queen to your Serious Consideration


Gentlemen

They shall be severally laid before you being thought by
her Majesty and her noble wise English privy Council to be
absolutely necessary and advantageous to your Country And
her Majestys Royall Sanction to the Laws revised and Enacted
now will Eternize the prudent Conduct of you.


Gent<sup>n</sup> Delegates

I dare assure you there cannot be any thing maturely Proposed for the real good and Prosperity of this Province but
her Majesty will assent to it with all the Cheerful Willingness

Original becoming the Royall Beneficence of so good a Queen.   And
Journal. am as sure will be displeased to find any Sly Insinuations
(that ill grounded Jealousies may foment to the disadvantage
of the publick) should render what her Majesty most graciously designed for your Welfare and happy Establishment
ineffectuall.

Gentⁿ as I am a very plain Dealer I would not have my
sincerity mistaken nor my good Intentions for your Service
interpreted Designing for I as much despise that or flattery
as you can abominate double dealing

Therefore I again recommend the honour and tranquillity
of your Country together with her Majestys Instructions to
your Considerations that the Unanimity of your Councils may
demonstrate your Steady Loyalty to her Majestⁱᵉˢ Government and the good wholesome Laws enacted this Sessions
may assure the whole World of your prudent hearty Concurrence in this critical juncture

Gentⁿ as I will never determine any thing of moment without laying it before her Majestⁱᵉˢ honble Council here for their
Advise and Decision I think myself obliged in honour and
Conscience to let the Representatives of the Province know
from Time to Time whatever is designed or Carryed on
against the true Interest of their Country.   Mʳ Speaker shall
for your Perusal have the best Information of the particulars
I can at present give and leave it to your wise Determination
if any Part of the Project ought to be made publick or till I
have the true account of the whole Contrivance by an Author
we must all rely on, in the Interim Cannot doubt but you will
think of some proper methods to obviate any clandestine
machination levelled against your Constitution

If your interest and Fortunes become so precarious to be
at the disposal of illnatured neighbourhood without your
approbation or Consent lay it not at my dore since I have
done the Duty of your Friend and Governour timely to
advertize you what is negotiating to your disadvantage   For
whilst I have the Honour to be distinguished by her Majesⁱⁱᵉˢ
Commission I would gladly have the province Support its
reputation of being independent from every thing but England and as nothing sure can be so dear to mankind as to let
the lasting ornaments of wise Industrious Progenitors be
transmitted to Posterity all prejudicial Innovations ought to
be avoyded with Care and Resolution

And since divine Providence has in a good measure Established Christianity here I cannot but take notice that the many
domestick Immoralitys within this province are great Scandals
to the Religion we profess and at this day you and our
European Friends are at such a vast Expence to maintaine.

There are others who bid defiance to all Magistracy and Laws Original Journal. which I hope will awaken you to amend what is defective in order to Suppress these unwarrantable Practices Scarce ever heard of in civilized Countries for if your Laws already made are of Force to curb these Disorders its a very great omission they are not vigorously asserted to punish these and all other known Vices by that Authority

Virtue and Religion are the true Ingredients to make any Country flonrish as a due obedience to the Laws is the best true Sign of honest good People, a character I would ever have you preserve that all mankind may know and value your Conduct Joyning heartily with me in Endeavours & wishes you may prosper many & many years

Gent<sup>n</sup> with all modesty I acquaint you nothing has made me uneasy since my Arrival but the Illness of my House and if you shall think I deserve no better Accommodation during my abode in the Province I must acquiesce with your sentiments and Endeavour to be Contented being Resolved never to ask for or expect what at any time you Judge unreasonable

I am very Confident there is no one here Present but believes there was an absolute necessity of Convening a new Assembly and since her Majesties Council thought this a proper Time to meet them I can never doubt but your Debates will be tempered with so discreet a Moderation and Candour this will be no long but an happy Sessions that our Enemies abroad may see we are unanimous and vigilant, our Friends at home know we are heartily Loyall, and the good people you represent thank you for your Loyalty to our Sov<sup>n</sup>, your Care of and ffidelity to your Country, with your unwearied Solicitudes and Endeavours to oppose all her Majesties Enemies whatsoever, and those likewise who shall ever pretend to disturb the peace welfare and Union of this Province under any Specious Pretence whatsoever

The dispatch of the many great Affairs before you will be a very generous ease to the Province and as true a Satisfaction to me being obvious to all considering psons what a Detriment it is to every Gent<sup>n</sup> met here on this occasion to be detained longer than the publick Service may reasonably require, and the charge of the Country I hope may not be an improper Consideration too upon your debates within the Compass your better Judgments may think necessary to bring this Sessions to an honourable Conclusion

Which was well approved of by the Board

Then came Kenelm Cheseldyn Esq<sup>r</sup> and Col Thomas Ennalls who being appointed of her Majesty's honourable

Original
Journal. Council had the oaths appointed by Act of Parliament instead
of the oaths of Allegiance and Supremacy and the oath of
Abjuration and Settling the Succession of the Crown which
they took and Subscribed and also the Test and then took
their Places at the Board

The Board believing a Sufficient appearance of the Delegates of Assembly were met at the House ordered that the
clerk of the Council go to the Court House and Speak to the
said Delegates to present themselves before his Excellency
the Governour   Whereupon the said Delegates came up and
acquainted his Excellency they were met to the number of
twenty nine according to the several Writts of Election, and
Desired to know his Excellency's pleasure if they should
proceed to Business or attend for a greater number to which
his Ex$^{cy}$ was pleased to say that he believed they were a Sufficient number and desired they would proceed to choose
their Speaker for that Time was equally precious to them as
to himself and her Majties honble Council after which they
departed

Then came the Members of the House of Delegates and
present Col William Dent for their Speaker who excused himself as unfitt for that Honour and Trust but his Ex$^{cy}$ was
pleased to say that it was only his modesty & Approved him as
Speaker after which he prayed free access to his Excys 'pson,
freedom of Debate and that if any mistake should happen he
would Impute it to his Weakness and then Departed to the
House

Maj$^r$ Greenberry M$^r$ Young and M$^r$ Muschamp from the
House to know if his Ex$^{cy}$ was pleased that the members who
had heretofore Sat in the last Assembly and qualifyed themselves by taking the Several Oaths required should now at
this their meeting take the same oaths againe, to which his
Ex$^{cy}$ said he was of opinion that they must take now those
oaths againe for that this was not another Session but another
General Assembly their Several trusts in the other being
ceased and New ones reposed in them: the said Gent$^n$ were
desired so to acquaint the House.

A Dedimus Potestatem under the great Seal of this her
Majties Province being prepared directed to the honourable
Thomas Tench Esq$^r$ and Col John Addison Thomas Brook
Esq$^r$ and Col John Hammond of her Majesties honble Council to Swear the Delegates and Representatives in this present
General Assembly.   The said Gent$^n$ were ordered to go down
to the House and Swear the Several Members which they did
and made report that they had administred the oaths to Col
William Dent Speaker of the House and the following mem-

bers viz^t George Muschamp Esq^r Major Will^m Aisquith, M^r
Tho^s Beale Cap^t Will^m Watts, M^r

| | | |
|---|---|---|
| Peter Watts | Col Tho^s Smyth | M^r Elias King |
| M^r William Frisby | M^r Jn° Wells | M^r Samuel Young |
| M^r Cha^s Greenberry | M^r Joseph Hill | M^r John Leach |
| M^r Robert Skinner | M^r John Mackall | M^r Tho^s Howe |
| Col James Smallwood | M^r Ja^s Phillips | Col Edw^d Dorsey |
| Col Ja^s Maxwell | Major W^m Barton | M^r Rob^t Tyler |
| M^r Sam^l Magruder | | |

Which they took and Signed with the Test
The Board adjourned till nine of the clock tomorrow morning.

Wednesday Sep^r 6^th 1704

The Council Sate, Present

His Excellency the Governour
Tho^s Tench Esq^r

The
Honble {
Col John Addison    Lieu^t Col William Holland
Thomas Brooke Esq^r    James Sanders Esq^r
Col John Hammond    Kenelm Cheseldyn Esq^r
Col Edw^d Lloyd    Col Thomas Ennals
}

Lieu^t Col James Maxwell and Major Greenberry come with M^r William Taylard whom they present to his Excy from the House as chosen to be their Clerk.

His Ex^cy was Pleased to admitt thereof and accordingly M^r Taylard was sworn in presence of the said members

Col Smallwood and M^r Young presented several members newly come to the House to be sworn viz^t M^r Rob^t Gouldesborough M^r Tho^s Greenfield Major John Taylor M^r Joseph Ennals and M^r John Hudson who had the oaths administred to them together with the Test which they signed according to Law

M^r Muschamp and Maj^r Taylor come from the House to acquaint his Exc^y that their House wait his Exc^ys Commands

M^r· Sanders and Col Ennalls sent to the House to acquaint them that his Ex^cy commands their attendance at the Council Board who Return and Say that they delivered their Message

Then came M^r Speaker and the members of the house of Delegates to whom his Exc^y spake as before concerted with her Majesty's honble Council

The Council adjourned for two Hours.

Post Meridiem The Council sat Present as in the morning.

His Exc^y being acquainted that M^r Joseph Holt Minister of William and Mary Parish in Saint Maries County and

Edward Hilliard Church Warden of the same Parish who was
lately snmmoned to appear at this Board to answer the said
Minister's Complaint for Locking him out of the Parish
Church of Saint George's are now attending

Ordered that they be called in With their evidences, but
his Exc^y being informed that the said Church Warden relyed
upon the Testimony of Some Gentlemen of that Parish and
County now sitting in the House of Delegates he was pleased
to Say he would not Send for any such particular members
without the Consent of the House after which his Exc^y was
informed that three of the members of the same House of
Delegates were coming to the Council Board but being met
and asked by the Clerk of the Council upon what occasion
they replyed that the House was informed that his Exc^y had
sent for them whereupon the said clerk assured them it was a
mistake and desired they would acquaint the House upon
which they went back and his Exc^y being told that this mistake had happen thro the said Edward Hilliard's inadvertent
folly His Exce^y is pleased to say he is not so Satisfyed for that
he rather believes he made use of his name and therefore desired the Advice of the Board what apprehensions they have of
this Action of the s^d Edward Hilliard and how he should be
dealt with on this occasion

The Gent^n of this Board say the said Edward Hilliard did
an indignity to this Board in presuming to carry such a
Message

M^r Cheseldyn says he is of opinion he did it ignorantly.

Edw^d Hilliard being called in is Severely reprimanded and
confessing what he did was unadvisely humbly begged pardon

M^r Tench and M^r Smith are sent to the House with the
following Message.

Gent.

Whereas his Exc^y is informed that one Edw^d Hilliard had
without any authority from his Exc^y or this Board made use
of his Exc^ys name to require three of the Honses members to
come before his Exc^y the Governour and Council, Gent. We
do assure you that the said Edward Hilliard did the Same of
his own head and that his Exc^y the Governor and this Board
did not ever in the least give any such Directions but will
always be very tender of the Rights and Priviledges of this
House of Delegates and therefore take this occasion to prevent any misapprehensions

Signed ᵽ order W Bladen Cl Council

The said M^r Tench and M^r Smith return and say they have
delivered the Message.

M^r Joseph Holt appeared before the Board and his Exc^y is restoring Original pleased to ask him if he had made publick his Exc^ys order for Journal. restoring him to his Function. To which he answered he had not shewn it to every body, but Some who desired had seen it and that he fully designed to have had it entered at the first regular Vestry but to Speak Truth it was out o'f his Mind

Ordered that Esq^r Tench Col Addison M^t Smith Col Lloyd and Col Ennalls hear M^r Holt and the Complaint against him and report the Same to his Ex^cy

The Board adjourns till nine of the clock to Morrow Morning

Thursday September the 7^th 1704

The Council Sate Present as Yesterday

Upon reading the following report of the Members of this Board appointed last night to Examine the Complaint against M^r Holt as follows viz

Sept 7^th 1704

In obedience to your Exc^ys Command we have heard M Joseph Holt Minister of William and Mary Parish in Saint Maries County and the Complaint of the Vestry of that Parish against him and we humbly Report to your Exc^y that upon hearing the whole matter we are of opinion that he hath so misbehaved himself since your Exc^ys Clemency upon his last Submission that he is not a person fitting to be further continued in the Ministerial function in that Parish or Else where which we humbly Submitt to your Excellencies better Judgment.

Thomas Tench    Robert Smith
John Addison    Edward Lloyd    Thomas Ennalls

Resolved the said M^r Holt be Suspended ab officio et Beneficio within this Province

And ordered the s^d M^r Holt be called in and told so

Ordered the s^d M^r Holt be paid the forty pounds of To:' bacco ℗ poll to this very Day being the Seventh of September

His Excellency the Governour and the Board desire the honble Kenelm Cheseldyn Esq^r to take Care of the Glebe and Secure the Library of that Parish

Came Col Francis Jenkins a member of this Board Who had the Oaths appointed to be taken instead of the oaths of Allegiance and Supremacy administred to him and the Oath

3

Original of Abjuration the which he Subscribed with the Test and then
Journal. took his place at the Board.

M^r Robert Gouldsborough M^r Thomas Frisby M^r James
Philips and M^r John Wells bring from the House of Delegates

By the House of Delegates Sep^r 7^th 1704.

In answer to a Message Sent to this House from his Ex^cy
the Governour and the honble Council by Thomas Tench and
Robert Smith Esq^rs Yesterday The House ordered that the
Thanks of this House be given to his Excellency for his kind
Expression of a tender regard he hath of the Liberties and
Priviledges of the members of this house expressed in the
said Message and they do humbly hope that his Excellency
will be pleased so continue the Same

Signed ⅌ order W Taylard Cl Ho. Del.

Came Lieut^t Col Smallwood and presented M^r Gerard
Foulke a Delegate for Charles County to whom were administred the oaths appointed to be taken instead of the Oaths of
Allegiance and Supremacy as also the Oath of Abjuration the
which he Subscribed with the Test. The same Col Smallwood brought with him the following Message.

By the House of Delegates Sep^r 6^th 1704

Upon reading and debating the Laws this house Nemine
Contradicente resolve it is absolutely necessary that the whole
body of the Laws be Revised and that it be now done accordingly

If therefore your Excellency and Council have any Thing
to offer on this Subject the House is ready to receive it

Signed ⅌ order W Taylard Cl ho Del

Lieut^t Col William Barton with five other Members bring
·from the House a bill for regulating ordinarys

M^r Greenfield and M^r Young present to this Board the
Members chosen to Serve for Somersett County Viz^t M^r
Joseph Gray M^r John Waters M^r John Jones and M^r John
Macclaster who after they had the usual and appointed oaths
administred to them and they had Subscribed the Oath of
Abjuration and Test withdrew

The Council adjourns till the Afternoon

Post Meridiem the Council Sate Present as before

M'' King Col Barton Col Thomas Frisby M'' Hill and Cap'' William Watts come with Col Thomas Smithson late Speaker of the House of Delegates and M'' William Stone to see them sworn which they were accordingly, And his .Ex'' and the Board desired the members of the house to return them Thanks for sending so many members with so worthy a ꝑson that has deserved so well of the Publick

His Ex'' desires the members of this Board to give him to morrow at nine of the Clock in writing what they have to propose for her Majesties Service, or the Interest and advancem'' of the Province

M'' King and M'' Foulke come from the house to desire the Lord Baltimores objections to the Land Law and the Law for limitting the Time for paym'' of obligations

Ordered the said Papers to be laid before the House & are accordingly sent by Col Jenkins

Came M'' William Stone from the house with the following ordinance viz''

By the House of Delegates Sep'' 7th 1704.

Whereas this House oftentimes do find it very difficult to get Paper and Parchm'' for Supply of the publick Business therefore thought fit and 'tis resolved by the House that M'' Samuel Young Treasurer of the Western Shoar send for a Quantity of Paper and Parchm'' out of England that is to Say the value of Six pounds Sterl. in parchment and four pounds in Paper for the publick use for which the said M'' Samuel Young shall be allowed

To which this House humbly prays the Concurrence of the hon''ᵇˡᵉ Council.

Signed ꝑ order W Taylard Cl Ho Del.

Which ordinance was assented to by her Majesties bouble Council and sent to the House by Lieu'' Col William Holland

The Board adjourned to Eight of the Clock to morrow morning

Fryday September the 8th 1704.

The Council Sate Present as yesterday

M'' Muschamp and M'' Beal come from the house to desire the Pensilvania Case stated about the bounds of this Province and Pensilvania which was given the said Gentlemen

Cap^t Watts and M^r Aisquith bring from the House the following Message

By the House of Delegates Sept 8^th 1704

The Committee for Elections and Privileges enters the house and reports that upon reading the within Indenture appeared all four Delegates therein appointed are duly and legally Elected but the Sheriff of Somersett County has not made any due and legal Return thereof as by Law he ought to do.

Which the Committee offers to the House for their Consideration

Upon reading the above Report of the Committee the House Concur therewith that the members are duly Elected and that the Sheriff has not done his Duty, that his failure is not wilful or prejudicial to the publick but only in a deficiency in not returning Separate Indentures for each Person therefore he is not lyable to the Penalty of the Act of Assembly, but however we pray he may be summoned to answer the neglect before his Excell^cy and Council &c.

Signed ꝑ order W Taylard Cl Ho Del.

Whereupon the following answer was sent to the House

By his Ex^cy the Governour and Council

The Houses Message relating to the omission or mistake of the Sheriff of Somersett County on the return of the Writt of Election was received at this Board and the said Sheriff will be cautioned of the like for the future

· Signed ꝑ order W Bladen Cl Council.

The honble Thomas Tench Esq^r John Addison Esq^r Thomas Brook Esq Robert Smith Esq^r are sent to the House with the following Message Viz.

Sept. 8^th 1704.

By his Ex^cy the Governour and Council in Assembly Your House being now settled and resolved upon revising the Body of Laws of this province We recommend unto Your Serious Considerations several of her Majesties royal Instructions laid before you the last Assembly viz:—

1. The raising of Supplys for defraying the publick Charge on which occasion you are to take especial Care that

all monies to be levyed be made lyable to be accounted for to her Majesty in England and her Lord high Treasurer and that no Imposition on liquors continue less than one Year but be indefinite without Limitation of Time (except for a temporary end which shall have its full effect within a certain time) that no Laws be reenacted except on urgent occasions but in no Case more than once without her Majesty's express Consent.

2. That all Planters and Christian Servants be well and fitly provided with Arms and that they be listed under good officers and when and as often as shall be thought fit mustered and trained whereby they may be in a better readiness for the Defence of the province and that they appear in Arms at all times as they shall be required upon which we do propose that this Assembly would oblige them who pretend for Conscience Sake they cannot bear Arms to Supply others with Horses and Arms.

3. That a Law be made to punish false musters mutiny and Desertion and for the better preserving good Discipline amongst Soldiers

4. That fitt Storehouses be settled throughout the province for keeping arms Ammunition and other publick Stores

5. That a general Survey be made of the whole province and of every County and of all Landing Places and Harbours & exact maps transmitted for England and that fortifications be erected at the publick Charge in which the cheerful Concurrence of the Assembly is not doubted

6. That Stocks be provided and publick Workhouses built in Convenient places for Employing poor and indigent people

7. That an Act be prepared to relieve the Creditors of persons becoming Bankrupt in England and having Estates in Maryland

8. Further you are desired to make Answer to the Lords of Trade and foreign Plantations Letter with the Lord Baltimores Objections to the two Acts of Assembly the one for ascertaining the Bounds of Land and the other for limiting the Time for payment of Obligations within this Province

9. Likewise it is recommended and proposed whether it may not be proper to make a Law to confirm all Proceedings since the Departure of his Ex^cy Col Blakiston to his present Excellency's Arrival and also of the last Assembly

10. That it be enquired by this Assembly and ascertained what Laws and Statutes of the Kingdom of England are in force in this province and that measures be taken to have the Several Acts of Parliament of every Sessions sent from England

11. That Encouragement be given to the Inhabitants of
this Province to Supply the same with Rum &c by Exempting
them being owners of Vessels (tho not Country built) from
the payment of the Duty of three pence ℔ Gallon

12. That a Law be made by the Assembly to prevent the
importation by Land of rum, wine, strong Liquors, beer, bread,
flour, and Horses from Pensilvania & that Encouragement be
given to Tillage by the Inhabitants

13. That this Province do throughly acquaint themselves
with the motions of the Piscattaway or Accokick Indians who
do not pay their Tribute as usual & take such methods upon
the Report of these Indians now Joining the Senecas in order
to war with the Tuskaroras both to discover their Strength
and Alliances & Likewise to provide for the better Security
of this Province and that all Alliances be settled with our
neighbour Indian

14. That Six County Courts in one year are thought too
many and therefore burthensome and Cause great County
Levys And whereas there being but two Provincial Courts in
the year the Delay of Justice is complained of, It is proposed
whether it would not be of Advantage to the Province and
the Trade thereof that in every year there be held four
Provincial Courts two for tryal and two for appearances all
which Courts would not continue much longer or be of much
greater Charge than the two at present now are and whether
the sitting of the County Courts Justices might not be better
regulated by taking Turns four at a Time being enough to
hold a Court Whereas there are Sometimes twelve at once
upon the Bench. That the Extravagancy of their Jurisdiction
be reasonably Limitted as to the sum and that Execution be
not limitted or stayed until after the tenth of May Yearly.

15. That the Act of Assembly for pleading Discount in
barr be Explained by some publick Vote or resolve of the
House being wofully mistaken by the Justices in Several
County Courts by which Practices it is feared that many Per-
jurys are introduced

16. That effectual measures be taken by this Assembly to
oblige Coopers and others setting up Tobᵒ Casks to comply
with and not exceed the Act of Assembly in the tare of those
Casks which are grievously Complained of by several Masters
of Ships and destructive to Trade Owners and Builders of
Vessels not knowing how to regulate them for Stowage and
by which means also her Majesties Governour is defeated of
great Part of the Revenue by the Act of Assembly and her
Majesties royal Instructions designed and alotted him.

17. That the Limitation of Actions on accounts is too
short so that the Creditor cannot be Civil to his Debtor for

fear of the Act which is desired by Several to be extended for one year more

18. That the Act of Assembly for punishing fornication and Adultery be Explained when a man's estate shall redeem his Body

19. That all County Levys and Vestries Accounts be yearly laid before the Governour and Council for their Inspection

20. That all Freemen be obliged to give a good Account of themselves how they gain their Livelyhoods or in default of being able to give such account the Justices of the County Court be impowered to place them out to work and make Corn at such Wages as to the said Justices shall seem reasonable.

21. That this Assembly would consider whether it would not be of publick Service to settle a publick Post of each side of the Bay between New Castle and Virginia

22. · That in the Act for Electing of Delegates a Clause be inserted to punish Persons having no right to Vote that disturb Elections and that the reasons may be enquired into why S$^t$ Mar$^{ies}$ City should send two Burghesses and if it were not fitt to Encourage this Town being the Seat of Government with that Privilege

23. And all protested Bills of Exchange should be Equal with Specialt$^{ies}$ and be recovered by Action of Debt.

Signed ꝑ order W Bladen Cl Council.

The Petition of M$^r$ Joseph Holt praying to be reheard was Read and rejected

The Board adjourns 'till three of the clock Afternoon

Post Meridiem the Council Sate Present as in the Morning Adjourns till nine of the Clock to Morrow Morning

Saturday September 9$^{th}$ 1704.

The Council Sate Present as Yesterday

Then was read the Petition of Cap$^t$ Richard Johnson who had surprized and brought in the Prize L'Ortolons praying some share thereof or Allowance thereout to which his Excellency was pleased to say he was very unwilling to dispose of any part thereof till better informed. Therefore her Majest$^{ies}$ Council did advise that the said Johnson should be creditted to the Value of two hundred pounds Sterl out of

Original the produce of the said Prize he giving good Security to re-
Journal. fund the same

M$^r$ Wells and M$^r$ Skinners brought up the petition of M$^r$ Joseph Holt to the House praying them to intercede with his Ex$^{cy}$ to restore him to his Benefice to which the following answer was sent back by Robert Smith Esq. and Col John Hammond Viz.


By her Majest$^{ies}$ honble Council in Assembly
September the 9th. 1704.

M$^r$ Joseph Holt's Petition with your Endorsement wherein we perceive upon his Importunity your Commiseration (not being fully acquainted with his Enormous life and Conversation) has induced you to give him more Credit than he can any ways pretend to, much less deserve, and so be Content to apply for his Restoration, has been read at this Board, and we acquaint you that altho his Ex$^{cy}$ is very willing to gratify the house in anything they can request yet we cannot be Content to advise his Ex$^{cy}$ to restore a person who has had so many warnings and yet notwithstanding his many Solemn Promises and assurances has so much scandalized his Function and prejudiced the Service of the church
Signed ꝑ order W Bladen Cl Coun:


Col Dorsey and four other members bring from the house the house's answer to his Excellenc$^{ies}$ Speech as follows viz.

To his Excellency the Governour.

The reason we did not sooner give answer to your Ex$^{cys}$ Speech was because we were desirous to have as full an house as could be had on so solemn occasion

We have received and carefully debated the Contents thereof and as we are well assured of her Majesty our gracious Queen's Goodness and Virtue in her unwearied Care and Protection of all her Subjects and the wise Constitution of her Governm$^t$ so we Esteem ourselves very happy in a Governour that imitates so glorious an Example for we cannot but observe thro' your plain Elegant Discourse a generous English Zeal for her Majest$^{ies}$ Service Joyned with a tender regard to the Welfare of this Province, And we do (and believe ever shall) Esteem ourselves Easy and Safe under your wise and just Administration and pray for your Continuance

We have perused and will in due Time Consider the Sev- <sup>Original</sup> eral Articles this day laid before us and we doubt not but <sup>Journal.</sup> your Ex<sup>cy</sup> (with due respect to those honble Gentlemen with you) will believe us the most proper and Capable to inform your Ex<sup>cy</sup> how far the present Constitution of the Province is able to comply therewith and that your Ex<sup>cy</sup> will be assured that nothing shall be omitted by us that with the Safety and good of our Country we can do.

We return you our hearty Thanks for the Intimation your Ex<sup>cy</sup> is pleased to give us of some design carrying on against us and beseech you to make more plain to our Speaker as you were pleased to say that we may take more suitable measures therein

We have resolved the Revising our Laws and what ever appears deficient therein shall be provided for Suppression of Vice and Immorality and we pray your Ex<sup>cy</sup> to give strict Charge to all Officers and Ministers thro your Government whose Duty it is to put the said Laws in vigorous Execution by Causing the same to be Strictly observed since good Laws without due Execution and observance are but dead Letters to no purpose

We hope your Ex<sup>cy</sup> is Satisfied that we do not trifle away our Time but do attend the business for which we came and we assure you that hitherto our Debates have been moderate and Candid and hope none is inclined to foment nor are we to receive any the least Suspicions and Jealousies of your Ex<sup>cy</sup> since both your words and Actions have given us such ample Assurance of your generous resolution of Governing us by the Laws protecting us in our rights and being ready to assent to any thing for the real Good and benefit of this Province, and we are Confirmed in opinion that the Honour of our Sovereign and Welfare of this Province are so inseparably annexed that they are never to be parted

Worthy S<sup>r</sup> we are deeply Sensible of your generous and just Carriage to us and hope you shall always find us a grateful modest and peaceable People, And as we pray for her Majest<sup>ies</sup> long and happy Reign, so we do for your Government over us

By the House of Delegates Sep<sup>r</sup> 8th. 1704
Signed p order W Taylard Cl ho Del.

The Board adjourned 'till eight of the Clock on Monday morning.

Monday Sep^r 11^th 1704

The Council Sate in Assembly present

His Excellency the Governour

| Col John Addison | William Coursey Esq^r |
| Thomas Brooke Esq^r | Kenelm Cheseldyne Esq^r |
| Robert Smith Esq^r | Col Francis Jenkins |
| Col John Hammond | Col Thomas Ennals |
| James Sanders Esq^r | |

His Ex^cy was pleased to lay before the Board the following
Letter of Col Ninian Beale viz.

Sep^r 9^th 1704

May it please your Ex^cy

I think it my Duty to render your Ex^cy an Account of the
late murder that has been Committed by the Heathen in Virginia at Potowmack Creek the last of October murdered one
man two women one Child and on Thursday last there came
one Indian from the mountains to the Eastern branch there
being a great many Indians hunting in those places and hal-
lowed over the Eastern branch to some other Indians at
Andrew Hamiltons they having a Cabbin there and the
Indian went over to see what he hollowed for and stayed a
matter of half an hour and returned and Told the said Ham-
bleton that they must all go to the mountains to morrow.
Which they are all in general gone.   May it please your Ex^cy
Ammunition is very scarce in these Parts.   No more but
your Excellency's humble Servant to Command whilst
       Sep^r 9^th 1704                           I am   Ninian Beale

These from Rock Creek

The last day of October mentioned in the s^d Letter is supposed to be a mistake and should be the last day of August.

Advised that his Ex^cy the Governour will write to Col Beale
to desire his utmost Care and Diligence to prevent any mis-
chief or disturbance in these parts and if any should happen
to give his Ex^cy and Col Addison the Speediest notice and
that if any Arms or Ammunition are wanting there upon Intimation Care will be taken to send what is requisite and that
he apply to Col Addison for any Ammunition.

The honble Col Thomas Ennalls presented to his Ex^cy and
the Council the complaint of M^r Henry Coursey a Nanticoke
Indian against M^r Peter Taylor of Dorchester County that
being indebted to the said Peter Taylor four bushells of Indian
Corn two buckskins and one Doe Skin in all of the Value of

Seven Doeskins he had for securing the paym<sup>t</sup> thereof pawned to the said Taylor one Belt of Peak to the Value of fifty Doeskins who has Converted it wholy to his own use tho the said Indian had tendered him pay and refuses to pay to the said Indian the forty three Doeskins due to the said Indian on ballance

Ordered that Col Ennalls caution the said Taylor to comply with the said Indian

His Ex<sup>cy</sup> was pleased to send the following Paragraph of a Letter to him by M<sup>r</sup> Smith and Col Hammond to the Speaker of the House of Delegates according to the Desire of the House viz<sup>t</sup>

### September the 11th. 1704

M<sup>r</sup> Speaker the Paragraph underwritten came in a Letter to me from an Eminent Merchant in London dated the 6th of February 1703/4

Sir I must by the by hint of a Design New York hath of making all the Colonies Tributarys to them in order to Support or rather enrich them and they seem to push the thing for the Half as to have a number to be chosen out of the Northern and Southern Governments to represent these Colonies and meet at New York instead of their own Assemblys and to have one Vice Roy and General of all the forces of the Continent and that of Virginia and Maryland &c to be dependents under them a Project to this Effect is Lodged with the Lords            John Seymour

The following Message sent to the House by Col Jenkins and M<sup>r</sup> Cheseldyne Viz.

### By his Excellency the Governour & Council

### Sep<sup>r</sup> 11<sup>th</sup> 1704.

Gentlemen By a good Providence and a cheerful Assistance of the Publick and other worthy Gentlemen The Church in this town is now in such forwardness that with the blessing of Almighty God we have proposed to have divine Service celebrated therein upon Sunday the 24<sup>th</sup> Inst<sup>t</sup> at which time the Sacrament will be administred, therefore to the End we may open the said Church with the greatest Solemnity we are capable of here in this remote part of the World we desire M<sup>r</sup> Speaker and the House of Delegates will Concur to accompany his Ex<sup>cy</sup> and this Board at the said Church at the Time af<sup>d</sup>      Signed ꝑ order W: Bladen Cl Coun.

Came M^r Greenfield and Lieut Col Maxwell and humbly
acquaint his **Ex^cy** that the House do comply with the said
message

Col Smith and four other members bring from the House
the following Message

By the house of Del^s Sep^r the 11th. 1704

This House returns your **Ex^cy** their humble thanks for the
Intimation you were pleased to give of a design forming
against our Constitution and your Explaining the same by a
message this day sent by the honb‍le Robert Smith and John
Hammond Esq^r and pray that you will always preserve the
same tender Regard of us which we will endeavour to deserve

Signed ꝑ order W Taylard Cl ho Del.

The Board adjourns for two Hours.

Post Meridiem the Council Sate Present

His **Ex^cy** the Governour

|  |  |  |
|---|---|---|
| The honb‍les | Col John Addison | Lieut Col W^m Holland |
|  | Thomas Brook Esq^r | James Sanders Esq^r |
|  | Robert Smith Esq^r | Kenelm Cheseldyne Esq^r |
|  | Col John Hammond | Col Thomas Ennalls |
|  | Col Francis Jenkins | William Coursey Esq^r |

His **Ex^cy** being informed that two Popish Priests to wit
William Hunter and Robert Brooke pursuant to the summons
from this Board attend to the Complaint against them made
and that M^r Charles Carrol a Lawyer accompanied them,
asks the Board if the said Priests ought to have their Council
with them who unanimously agree and say they should not

His **Ex^cy** Queries whether upon the Pretence of any Custom of Toleration from the first Settlem^t of this Province the
Actions of these Priests can pretend any justification who
say not

The said M^r William Hunter and M^r Robert Brooke appeared and are told on what occasion they were called before
his **Ex^cy** M^r William Hunter gives his **Ex^cy** many thanks for
the opportunity of appearing before his **Ex^cy** and says he is
very sorry for any annoyance in his Conduct as to his consecrating the Chappel he did not Consecrate it for that is an
Episcopal Function and that no body was present but himself
in his common Priests vestments and that neither under his
**Ex^cys** Eye nor in his presence but if any such thing was done
it was above fourteen months ago, and long before his **Ex^cys**

arrival M$^r$ Brook says he did say mass in the Court Time at the Chappel of S$^t$ Mar$^{ies}$ but found that others had formerly done so

Advised that this being the first Complaint the said M$^r$ Hunter & M$^r$ Brooke be severely reprimanded and told that they must not Expect any Favor but the utmost Severity of the Law upon any misdeameanour by them committed and being called in his Ex$^{cy}$ was pleased to give them the following Reprimand Viz.

Gentlemen

It is the unhappy Temper of you and all your Tribe to grow insolent upon Civility and never know how to use it and yet of all People you have the least reason for considering that if the necessary Laws that are made were let loose they are Sufficient to crush you and which (if your arrogant Principles have not blinded you) you must need to dread.

You might methinks be Content to live quietly as you may and let the Exercise of your Superstitious Vanities be confined to yourselves without proclaiming them at publick Times and in publick places unless you expect by your gawdy shows and Serpentine Policy to amuse the multitude and beguile the unthinking weakest part of them an Act of Deceit well known to be amongst you

But Gentlemen be not deceived for tho the Clemency of her Majest$^{ies}$ Government and of her gracious inclinations leads her to make all her Subjects Easy that know how to be so yet her Majesty is not without means to curb Insolence but more especialy in your Fraternity who are more eminently than others abounding with it, and I assure you the next occasion you give me you shall find the Truth of what I say which you should now do but that I am willing upon the earnest Sollicitations of some Gentlemen to make one tryal (and it shall be but this one) of your temper

In plain and few words Gentlemen if you intend to live here let me hear no more of these things for if I do and they are made good against you be assured I'll chastize you, and least you should flatter yourselves that the Severit$^{ies}$ of the Laws will be a means to move the pity of your Judges I assure you I do not intend to deal with you so I'll remove the Evil by sending you where you may be dealt with as you deserve

Therefore as I told you I'll make but this one Tryal and advise you to be civil and Modest for there is no other way for you to live quietly here.

You are the first that have given any disturbance to my Government and if it were not for the hopes of your better

Original demeanour you should now be the first that should feel the
Journal. Effects of so doing

Pray take notice that I am an English Protestant Gentleman and can never equivocate

After which they were discharged

The members of this Board taking under their Considera-·
tion that such use of the Popish Chappel of the City of Sᵗ
Marˡᵉˢ in St Marˡᵉˢ County where there is a protestant Church
and the said County Court is kept is both Scandalous and
offensive to the Government do advise and desire his Exᶜʸ the
Governour to give immediate orders for the Shutting up the
sᵈ Popish Chappel and that no Person presume to make use
thereof under any pretence whatsoever

Whereupon it was ordered by his Exᶜʸ the Governour that
the present Sheriff of St Marˡᵉˢ County lock up the sᵈ Chappel and keep the Key thereof.

Mʳ Young Mʳ Leech and Mʳ Mackal bring from the House
the following message Viz


By the House of Delegates Sepʳ 11ᵗʰ 1704

Upon the Subject in the last message touching the Design
forming against the Constitution of the Government resolved
that all possible means be used to prevent the same as being
levelled against her Majestˡᵉˢ Interest and the good of this
Country and therefore Ordered that a Committee be appointed
to consider the many Evils that would redound both to ·her
Majestˡᵉˢ Interest and the Welfare of this Province and that
his Exᶜʸ be pleased to join some of the bouble Council with
the Committee to consider and make Report and that his Exᶜʸ
would be pleased to join his Interest with ous to prevent the
same                Signed ℗ order W Taylard Cl ho Del.


Ordered that Mʳ Tench Mʳ Brooke Mʳ Smith Mʳ Cheseldyne
& Mʳ Coursey joine the Committee of the House so soon as
they are ready

The Bill for regulating ordinarˡᵉˢ Read and Sent down to
the House by Mʳ Smith and Mʳ Cheseldyne with this recommendation from the Board that in the Seventeenth Line of the
said Bill these words be after County (if her Majesty shall so
think fitt or otherwise as she shall be graciously pleased to
direct) and least the House should apprehend or have any
jealousy that this Board are desirous to have the said fines for
ordinary licences applyed otherwise than by the House proposed they are willing the Law be temporary for some small
time two years or less if the House think fit

Lieut' Col Thomas Smithsons Petition read setting forth Original that he was taken sick at a Sessions of Assembly held the Journal twenty third day of October last and has been at great Charges for Physick and Expences then having no business of his own but only to serve the Country and prayed to be reimbursed the said Charges and Expences

The said Petition being thought reasonable is recommended to the House of Delegates for their Consideration and Allowance

The Board adjourned till eight of the Clock to morrow morning

Tuesday Sep<sup>r</sup> 12th 1704

The Council Sate Present as yesterday

ꝑsent his Ex<sup>cy</sup> the Governour

| | | |
|---|---|---|
| The Honble | Thomas Tench Esq<sup>r</sup> <br> Col John Addison <br> Thomas Brook Esq<sup>r</sup> <br> Robert Smith Esq<sup>r</sup> <br> Col John Hammond <br> Col Francis Jenkins | L<sup>t</sup> Col William Holland <br> James Sanders Esq<sup>r</sup> <br> Kenelm Cheseldyne Esq<sup>r</sup> <br> Col Thomas Ennalls <br> William Coursey Esq<sup>r</sup> |

Col Thomas Ennals being indisposed has leave given him to go home

M<sup>r</sup> Charles Kilburne's petition for allowance for looking after the Guns and firing them on occasions as required read and referred to the House of Delegates

Thomas Hebbs Petition read and referred to the House of Delegates

Major Low M<sup>r</sup> Leech M<sup>r</sup> Eccleston and M<sup>r</sup> Thomas Frisby bring from the House a message in answer to the message by M<sup>r</sup> Coursey that the house has appointed them to join the members of the Council on the Subject proposed

To which was returned.

By his Ex<sup>cy</sup> the Governour and Council in Assembly
September the 12th 1704.

This Board Judging that the Conference yesterday desired by the House to Consider of what was therein proposed was of great moment to the Province did not appoint less than five of their members to join those of the House and therefore we desire that you'll add some more of your members to those you have already appointed to join with ours of this Board

Original and that they meet and go upon the said Conference at two of
Journal. the Clock in the Afternoon
Signed ℣ order W Bladen Cl Coun.

Major Lowe and three other members bring from the House
the following Message

By the House of Delegates Sep<sup>r</sup> 12<sup>th</sup> 1704

This House have read and Considered the message touch-
ing the Bill for regulating ordinar<sup>ies</sup> on the back of the bill
and if the making the Law for a short time as proposed by
the honble Council is thought of weight to move this House
to Consent to them additional words we hope may have as
Strong Effect to move your honour to Concur with the house
in leaving them out for so short Time for since by the Time
her Majest<sup>ies</sup> Pleasure can be known the Law will Expire and
'tis agreed that 'till then the fines arising shall be <sup>a</sup>pp<sup>lied</sup> to
the Count<sup>ies</sup> and therefore tis but saying what we all intend
to do and this method proposed is altogether new and that
Contained in the bill agreeable to all other Laws but not one
in the whole province having such a reserve nor can we suppose that her Majesty enjoyns any such reserve, but in what
shall be reserved to her Majest<sup>ies</sup> Governour and therefore this
House does earnestly pray the honble Council's Considerations and Concurrence with this House therein
Signed ℣ order W Taylard Cl ho Del.

The Council adjourns till the afternoon

Post Meridiem Council Sate Present as before.

Came M<sup>r</sup> Smallwood and M<sup>r</sup> Foulke and M<sup>r</sup> Delahide with
the following Bills to wit

A Bill for the publication of all Laws read the first time and
this board do believe parchment is very difficult to be got at
present and that good Paper is better in this Country

A Bill declaring that the altering or scratching out of the
mark of Tob° or altering the quality thereof after received
without lawful order or warrant shall be deemed and adjudged
felony read the first time

A Bill against Engrossing and regrating read the first Time

A Bill for limitation of certain actions for avoiding suits at
Law read the first Time

A Bill appointing Constables and what relates to their
offices read the first time

A Bill directing the manner of suing out Attachments read
the first time, and sent to the House by Col Hammond and
Col Holland together with William and John Sweatnam's petition and a bill to Impower the said William to Sell Land

M$^r$ Gray and M$^r$ Howe from the House present M$^r$ Richard
Jones a Delegate chosen for Ann Arundell County to be sworn
who took the Oaths and Subscribed the Oaths and Test &c

The Council adjourns 'till to morrow morning

Wednesday Sep$^r$ 13$^{th}$ 1704
The Council in Assembly sate Present as before

M$^r$ Waters M$^r$ Jones and M$^r$ Macclaster bring from the
House the following Message Viz.

By the House of Deleg$^s$ Sept$^r$ 3$^d$ 1704

The members upon your Invitation have intended with your
Excellency to View the Church and have taken notice of the
place you are pleased to be made for the Burgesses and Delegates to sitt in and we do very well approve of what your Ex$^{cy}$
has done and hold ourselves obliged to return you our hearty
thanks for your regard of us and for the Care and Trouble
you have been pleased to take in that affair and we desire you
to order a small door to be cut over against the Porch by the
Pulpit to give Air to the Church and when you see fit to add
a small Vestry room to it, and that in laying out the Church
Yard you will be pleased to enclose all the Graves within it
Signed ꝑ order W Taylard Cl Ho Del.

Came M$^r$ John Taylor and M$^r$ John Hudson and brought
up the Bill for publication of all Laws which the House insists
upon to be engrossed in parchment Saving those this present
Sessions to be sent to the Countys

The Board adjourns to three of the Clock in the Afternoon

Post Meridiem Council Sate Present as before

His Ex$^{cy}$ asking for the Petition of M$^r$ Cockshut M$^r$ Colebatch and M$^r$ Hall resolved by the Board that it be heard to
morrow morning

A Bill for publication of all Laws read with the resolve of
the House thereupon Endorsed that they insist on the Law
as already drawn but because Parchm$^t$ cannot now be had for
the Several Countys that good Paper for the present shall
Suffice and agreed to by this Board Provided that s$^d$ Resolve

Original
Journal. be inserted in the body of the Law as a Salvo and is returned
to the House by Col Addison

And is again brought from the House with the Salvo inserted by Col Barton.

Mr Thomas Frisby Mr Pearce Mr Dare bring up the other
Bills this day sent down to the House

Then came the members of the Council appointed to join
those of the House upon the Conference and made report of
what had been transacted there which was not by the Board
agreed conceiving that the Conferees had mistaken the Subject matter of the Conference proposed therefore ordered the
following Message be sent to the House viz.

### By the Council in Assembly Sepr 13. 1704

The report of the Committee appointed the 11th Inst{t} touching the Design forming against the Constitution of the
Government has been read at this Board and it is Conceived
that the Conferees have mistaken the Subject matter of the
Conference for want of having the same in Writing which by
the Houses message to this Board was to Consider the many
Evils that would thereby redound both to her Majest{ies} Interest
and Welfare of this Province therefore propose that full Instructions be given the said Conferees and that they meet
again on that Subject by eight of the Clock to morrow morning
Signed ꝑ order W Bladen Cl Coun.

Mr Tyler and Mr Magruder bring from the House the following message viz.

### Sepr 13th 1704
#### By the House of Delegates

·Resolved by this House that it is necessary for the Safety of
this Province that the Secretary who has the keeping of the
Records before his Entering into his office be obliged and
bound to preserve the Books in which the Records are contained in as good Condition as he receives them at his own
Charge and they be Visitted at every meeting of Assembly
and that if any Defect be in keeping the said Records to be
repaid and made good out of his own Estate and that the present Secretary give security as above to which the Councill's
Concurrence is prayed
Signed ꝑ order W Taylard Cl Ho Del.

The Board adjourns till nine of the Clock tomorrow morn{g}

Thursday Sep' 14. 1704

Council Sate Present as yesterday

A Bill directing the manner of suing out Attachments &c
read and passed the second time for Engrossing

A Bill for Limitation of Certain Actions for avoiding Suits
at Law read the second time & does pass for engrossing

A Bill against Regrators and Ingrossers read the second
Time & passed for Ingrossing

A Bill declaring the altering or Scratching out the mark of
Tobᵒ or altering the Quality thereof after received without
Lawful Order or Warrant shall be deemed felony read the
second time and passed for Engrossing with the addition of
these Words (or discovered) at the End of the Law

And A Bill for publication of all Laws read the third Time
and passed for Engrossing and sent to the house by Mʳ
Sanders & Mʳ Coursey

Ordered that a Copy of what his Exᶜʸ was pleased to say
to the Popish Priests be delivered Mʳ Coursey

The following Petition preferred and read at the Board


Maryland Sct.

To his Exᶜʸ the Governour and her Majestⁱᵉˢ honble Council of this Province

The Petition of Thomas Cockshutt Joseph Colebatch and
Henry Hall Clks Humbly Sheweth

That Whereas we are informed that Joseph Holt Clk for
some misdeameanours laid to his Charge has been lately suspended by your Exᶜʸ and this Honble Board ab officiis et
Beneficio which penalty we are perswaded in our Consciences
cannot be inflicted upon him by any Civil Power whatsoever
as such but only by his Bishop and that too according to the
Canons of our Church and only by Virtue of the Authority
Committed to him by Christ our Lord for our office as ministers
of Christ is purely Spiritual and therefore we cannot be deprived of it or the Exercise thereof by any Lay Person or Persons how great Soever without Sacrilegiously usurping upon
the Divine Authority Committed by Christ to his Church
which we hope is not designed by the late Suspension nor can
we see how Mʳ Holt could in Conscience Submitt to it if any
such Thing were intended thereby we therefore humbly beseech your Exᶜʸ and this honble Board that if the said Mʳ Holt
has transgressed the Laws he may be proceeded against as
they direct and not be interrupted in the Exercise of his Office
'till such time as by his Bishops Authority he may (as upon a
legal Enquiry he shall appear to deserve) be punished by sus-

Original
Journal.
pension deprivation or Deposition and your Petitioners shall forever pray &c.

Whereupon the said M^r Tho^s Cockshutt M^r Joseph Colebatch & M^r Henry Hall being called in his Ex^cy was pleased to say to them.

Gentlemen    Your inconsiderate Petition to my Self and her Ma^ties honble Council is a birth so untimely rash and monstrous that nothing but the ill digested Conceptions of your hot Brains could have begotten, let me tell you that Zeal in good men who are sure they are in the right is always Commendable but when it is otherwise to such men it becomes like the Chariot of the Sun lashed by the unskilful as well as unfortunate Phaeton and is equally dangerous to themselves as well as others and such a Zeal it is plain has infatuated you in charging my Self and this hon:ble Board with a Crime you Express not less than Sacrilegious in that I should oppress or derogate from the Authority of this Church in whose orthodox Faith and Principles I have been ever Educated and have always professed

Gentlemen    I Believe my Care and Protection of the Church since my Arrival in this Province have meritted better Returns from every of its Members than the ill usage you have treated me with in petitioning the House of Delegates as if there were a Necessity for a Barrier between the Rights of the Church and my Self and calling my Authority in Question But why should I mention or wonder at this part of your Folly when your Extravagance has Soared beyond the utmost Zenith. If my Self and her Majest^ies honble Council had Exceeded our Authority in M^r Holts suspension it would have become you first of all to have been certainly assured thereof and then it would not only have been mannerly but religiously Just in you with modesty (which is a Virtue I perceive you are unacquainted with) to have represented to me wherein you had presumed to have taken upon you so publickly to reprove your Elders and Superiors, for be assured while I have the honour to command herein this Province her Majesty Ever shall be Supreme Head and Governour of the Church here therefore repair to your Several Parish Charges and for the future have a Care How you Engage in such like Extravagancy least you give me occasion to use you as Contemners of Authority and Disturbers of her Majest^ies peace After which they withdrew.

M^r Robert Tyler brings from the House the Bill declaring it to be felony to scratch out the mark of Tob° or alter the Quality after received insisted on by the House without

Amendment which is agreed to by the Board and sent to the House by Mʳ Sanders.

The Board adjourns to three of the Clock in the Afternoon Past meridiem

The Council Sate Present as before

Mʳ Aisquith Mʳ Beale Capᵗ Watts and Mʳ Peter Watts bring from the House a bill for killing of Crows & Wolves.

A Bill providing what shall be Evidence to prove foreign and other Debts and to prevent vexatious and unnecessary suits at Law pleading discount in bar

A Bill for publication of Marriages

A Bill for the preservation of the several Harbours within this Province

A Bill for ascertaining the Expences of the Delegates of Assembly and Commisʳˢ of the County and provincial Courts

A Bill against excessive usury

A Bill relating to the Standard of English Weights and measures.

A Bill·for Settlement of an annual Revenue upon her Majestⁱᵉˢ Governour within this Province for the Time being

A Bill for advancement of Natives and Residents

A Bill declaring the Grantees of Land lying within the Indians land may have Action of trespass against such Persons as carry away Timber &c.

A Bill impowering Mʳ William Sweatnam to sell Lands

A Bill prohibiting Commissioners, Sheriff Clerks &c to plead as Attorneys.

The following Message to the House by Esqʳ Tench and Col Addison viz.

By the Council in Assembly Sepʳ 14th. 1704.

Whereas Mʳ Alexander Hall a Gentⁿ who has long served his Country and the Crown of England as an officer abroad in the wars and has the honour to be marryed to a relation of his Exᶜʸ the Governour, therefore in Compliment to his Exᶜʸ Came over into the Province with him and we desire he may be Capable of Serving her Majesty in some small Employment here in this Province notwithstanding the Act prohibiting the same Mʳ Hall being as we are informed a very honest Gentleman
Signed ꝑ order W Bladen Cl Coun.

The following Message brought from the House by Col Smith Mʳ John Watts & Mʳ Robert Skinner

Original
Journal.
By the House of Delegates Sep^r 14th 1704

The Committee of Aggrievances reported that the Lord Baltimore's Agents do exact four hund^d and Eighty pounds of Tob° for every hundred Acres and Refuse to give Patents for the Land till the Purchase mony be payed

Thereupon it was ordered that M^r Charles Carrol one of his Ldships Agents have notice to attend this House to shew by what Authority he requires the Same. And accordingly he appeared this morning and said he had such Instructions from the Lord Baltimore that he gave publick Notice thereof and he produced and gave in a Copy of such publick notice and says the reason why his Ldship requires two hund^d and forty pounds of Tob° more than usual was because one half of the fees due to his Lordship's officers on such Warrants and grants was taken from them and given to her Majest^ies Secretary but that if it may be thought fit to restore the Land records and the Fees to his Ldships Officers that additional two hund^d and forty pounds of Tob° shall be immediately taken of and no more required for the same and that the said Records shall be put into such Persons hands to keep as shall be from time to time approved on by his Ex^cy the Governour and Assembly and an oath & good security given for the faithful and careful keeping of them upon Consideration whereof It appears a great aggrievance to the good People of this Province and discouragement to the People of it to pay double price for their Land and almost double Fees for their Patents and since it is proposed to be remedyed and Sufficient Caution be given for Safe keeping the Records we humbly pray your Honours that a Conference may be had on this Subject and the Persons now Joyned in Conference upon the Business of New York may be Charged with this when the other is dispatched

Signed ᵱ Order W Taylard Cl Ho Del.

The said Gentlemen also bring up a bill for confirming to the Govern^r of this Province the antient Duty of three pence ᵱ Tonn on the Burthen of Ships and Vessels.

A Bill for Confirming the Proceedings of the several Courts from the Death of his Ex^cy Lionel Copley Esq^r late Governour of this Province until the Arrival of his present Ex^cy Governour Seymour.

Ordered that the said Bills lye on the Table to be read to morrow morning.

The Board adjourns to nine of the Clock to morrow morn^g

Friday Sep' 15th. 1704.     

The Council Sate Present as yesterday

Major Lowe from the house acquaints his Ex<sup>cy</sup> that the Conferees from the House are ready to join those of the Board.

Ordered that the members of this Board appointed go upon the Conference who accordingly went

Col Smallwood with three other members with M<sup>r</sup> Coursey a Delegate for Talbot County to see him sworn who took and Subscribed the Test and Oaths

M<sup>r</sup> Skinner and two other Members bring the following Bills from the House viz<sup>t</sup>

Bill declaring how naturalization Fees and of other private Laws shall be proportioned

Bill prohibiting importation of Bread &c from Pensilvania

Dowlin's petition to confirm Land &c.

Bill encouraging the Inhabitants to adventure their Ships &c

Bill appointing Court days

Bill ascertaining the Gauge of tobacco hogsheads

The following Message is sent to the House by Col Addison Col Hammond Col Jenkins M<sup>r</sup> Sanders and M<sup>r</sup> Cheseldyn

By his Ex<sup>cy</sup> the Governour & Council in Assembly

In answer to the houses message by M<sup>r</sup> Greenfield and five other members delivered to his Ex<sup>cy</sup> last night is sent you a Copy of her most Sacred Majest<sup>ies</sup> royal Instructions to his Ex<sup>cy</sup> the Governour and we Conceive that the Reasons of the said Instructions are very obvious for that if her Majesty shall be pleased to disassent to any particular Law or Laws the whole body of them thereby may not be repealed as having but one assent to the whole

Signed ꝑ order W Bladen Cl Coun.

Col. Maxwell and five other members bring up from the House their Concurrences to the Message about M<sup>r</sup> Alexander Hall and the following Message Viz.

By the House of Deleg<sup>s</sup> Sep<sup>r</sup> 15<sup>th</sup> 1704.

Tho we have hitherto been silent to one part of his Ex<sup>cys</sup> Speech touching the incommodiousness of your House    It has not been without a due Concern and hearty desire to do all that in us lyes to make our Actions acceptable to so good a Governour as you approve your Self to us

We have seen the restraint her Majesty has laid on your Exc<sup>y</sup> and how far she is pleased to permitt your Ex<sup>cy</sup> to accept and us to give

Original
Journal.

As to the Building of a House we are utterly incapable to perform the same and therefore 'tis fruitless to Attempt it

Your Ex^{cy} knows that out of the twelve pence ℗ H:hd to her Majesty for Support of Government she is graciously pleased to allow three pence ℗ Hhd for supplying the Coun-try with Arms and Ammunition and preserving the Same And we are informed that out of the same the Province is plentifully supplyed and that there is about one thousand pounds in Bank and the Stock increasing   We humbly move it to your Ex^{cy} if it may not be proper to address her Majesty to apply such part thereof as may be Spared from that use to the Building a House and whether your Ex^{cy} and Council will please to Join with us in such Address

And tho we are not able to build such House as proposed yet since her Majesty has been pleased to permitt your Ex^{cy} to accept and us to give Something in lieu of House Rent We will Examine our Ability and hope we shall be able to make some suitable Acknowledgments to the tender Regards you have shewn for us

We have Considered of the Several Articles and Proposals laid before us and so soon as the Clerk can draw them of the Journal your Ex^{cy} shall know the opinion of the House thereon

Signed ℗ order W Taylard Cl ho Del.


The twelve bills brought up yesterday by Cap^t Beale and other members Read and with several Endorsements Sent to the House by Col Lloyd and Col Holland

The two Bills brought up yesterday by M^r Greenfield and the five other members read and Sent to the house by Col Addison and M^r Sanders

The Board adjourns for two Hours


Post meridiem

The Board met Present as before

Came M^r Hudson with the Bill against transporting People away without Passes.

The Board adjourns to nine of the Clock to morrow morning


Saturday Sep^r 16th. 1704

The Council Sate Present as yesterday

Ordered that a Proclamation issue against all immoralities Sabbath breaking and Drunkenness prophane Cursing and Swearing to be read once a month for six months together

The Board adjourns till Monday morning nine of the Clock

Monday September 18<sup>th</sup> 1704 Present as on Saturday Original Journal.

At the Request of S<sup>r</sup> Thomas Lawrence Baronett principal Secretary of this Province who claims publick tobacco in the hands of M<sup>r</sup> Vincent Hemsley late high Sheriff of Talbott County and is by the said Hemsley refused to be paid the said M<sup>r</sup> Hemsley's Bond for the due ꝑformance of his Sheriff's office is by his Ex<sup>cy</sup> and this Board on the behalf of her Majesty assigned over unto the said S<sup>r</sup> Thomas Lawrence by him to be sued for the Recovery of the s<sup>d</sup> Tobacco.

M<sup>r</sup> Henry Coursey M<sup>r</sup> William Frisby and M<sup>r</sup> John Taylor bring from the House the following Bills.

A Bill for quieting Possessions Enrolling Conveyances &<sup>c</sup>

A Bill declaring the Grantees of Land Lying within the Indians' Land may have Action of Trespass against such ꝑsons as carry away Timber &<sup>c</sup>

A Bill for advancement of natives and Residents

A Bill prohibiting commissioners Sherrs &c to plead as Attorneys &<sup>c</sup>

A Bill ascertaining the Expences of the Delegates

A Bill for the preservation of the several harbours

A Bill Confirming all Proceedings at Law since the Death of Governour Copley to this Time

A Bill for killing Wolves and Crows

A Bill for publication of Marriages

A Bill relating to the standard of English weights and Measures

A Bill against excessive usury

A Bill to enable Col Edward Dorsey to sell Lands in Annapolis

A Bill Impowering William Sweatnam to Sell Lands

Which several Bills were read and with the sev<sup>l</sup> Endorsements sent down to the House by M<sup>r</sup> Cheseldyn & M<sup>r</sup> Coursey

The following bills which were brought from the house on Fryday last by M<sup>r</sup> Skinner and other two members of the house viz.

A Bill prohibiting the importation of Bread flower Beer &<sup>c</sup> from Pensilvania

A Bill prohibiting Masters of Ships and others from transporting away any ꝑsons without passes

A Bill for causing Grand and petite Jurors and witnesses to come to the Provincial and County Courts

A Bill declaring how Fees for Naturalizations and other private Bills shall be proportioned

A Bill to Encourage the Inhabitants of this Province to adventure their Ships more freely abroad &c.

A Bill ascertaining the Gauge of tobacco Hhds

A Bill for appointing Court Days

Were read and with the Several Endorsements sent to the
House by Col Lloyd and Mʳ Coursey

Major Greenberry & Mʳ Hill from the House to see Mʳ
Plater sworn to his Naval Officers accompts who accordingly
made oath thereunto

The Board adjourned to three of the Clock

Post Meridiem Council Sate Present as before

Mʳ Gerard Foulke from the House acquaints his Exᶜʸ that
the Sheriffs of Kent Charles and Talbot Countys have neglected to return their Lists of Taxables and therefore prays
that his Exᶜʸ would be pleased to send Expresses therefore
and Command the Sheriffs afᵈ immediately to appear and
answer their Contempt

Came Mʳ Hodson and Mʳ Jones and brought from the
House the following Bills vizᵗ

A Bill for laying an Impost on Rum Wine Spiritts and
Brandy from Pensilvania by or over Land

A Bill declaring the Division of Several Countys to be firm
and stable

A Bill for Settling an Annual Revenue on her Majestⁱᵉˢ
Governour

A Bill for causing Grand and petite Jurors to come to
Courts &c.

A Bill confirming the three pence ꝑ Tonn to the Governour

A Bill for quieting Possessions Enrolling Conveyances &c.

A Bill for laying an Imposition on Several Commodities
transported

Which bills were read the second time at the board and will
pass

Mʳ Skinner and Mʳ Leech bring from the house a Bill appointing Court Days &c.

A Bill prohibiting the Importation of Bread Beer Flower
&c from Pensilvania

A Bill prohibiting Masters of Ships &c from conveying Persons without Passes

A Bill Encouraging the Inhabitants of this Province to
adventure their Ships &c.

A Bill declaring how fees for naturalization and other private
Laws shall be proportioned

A Bill proportioning the Gauge of tobacco H:hds.

The above thirteen Bills brought by Mʳ Hodson and Capᵗ
Jones Mʳ Skinner and Mʳ Leech being read the second time
at this Board are sent down to the House by Mʳ Smith Col
Hammond Mʳ Cheseldyne and Mʳ Coursey

The following proclamation for punishing all Immoralities and prophaneness read & approved of viz: Original Journal.

By his Excellency John Seymour Esqʳ her Majesty's Capᵗ General and Governour in chief in and over this her Province of Maryland and the territorys thereto belonging and Vice Admiral of the same.

A Proclamation for preventing & punishing all immorality and Prophaneness.

Whereas we cannot but be deeply sensible of the great Goodness and Mercy of Almighty God in the peaceable and happy Enjoyments of his manifold Blessings to us in this Province under her most sacred Majestⁱᵉˢ immediate Government Therefore we ought in Gratitude to return our most humble and hearty thanks to him and Express the same by a Suitable Life and Conversation avoiding all occasions of offending so good and gracious a God by breaking our straite      of our Obedience & Duty to him and whereas nothing can prove a greater dishonour to a well obeyed Government where the Christian Faith is professed nor is likelier to provoke God to withdraw his mercy and blessings from us and instead thereof to inflict heavy and Severe Judgments upon this Province than the open & avowed practice of Vice Immorality and Prophaneness which amongst many men has too much prevailed here of late years to the high displeasure of Almighty God and the great Scandal of Christianity and the ill and fatal Examples of others who have been Soberly Educated and whose Inclination would lead them to the Exercise of Piety and Virtue did they not daily find such frequented and repeated instances of dissolute living Prophaneness & Impiety which has in a great measure been occasioned by the remissness and Neglect of the Magistrates not putting in Execution those good Laws which have been made for the Suppressing and Punishmᵗ thereof and by the ill Example of many in Authority to the Great Dishonour of God and Reproach of our holy religion

Wherefore and for that we cannot reasonably Expect the Increase or Continuance of the Blessings we Enjoy unless the like Evills be prevented for the Future I think my Self bound in Duty to God and the Care of her Majestⁱᵉˢ Subjects to me Committed during my Administration of Government here to take Effectual Course that Religion Piety and Good manners may Encrease and flourish in this Province  I have therefore by and with the Advice and Consent of her Majestⁱᵉˢ honble Council thought fit to Issue this my Proclamation, and do hereby publish and Declare that I will discountenance and most Severely punish all manner of Vice Immorality and Pro-

phaneness in all ᵽsons from the highest to the lowest degree
within this Province and particularly those who are in Authority or offices of Trust and do Expect that all such Persons
and others of Creditt and good Repute will to their utmost
Contribute to the discountenancing men of dissolute and de-
bauched Lives that they being reduced to shame and Contempt may be enforced the sooner to reform their ill Habits
and practices so that the displeasure of good Men towards
them may supply what the Law cannot wholly Prevent

And for the more effectual reforming such men who are a
discredit to the Province I do hereby strictly Charge and
Command all Justices Sheriffs Constables and other officers
both Ecclesiastical and Civil and other her Majesty's good
Subjects whom it may Concern to be very diligent and Strict
in the discovery and Effectual Prosecution and punishment of
all Persons who shall be guilty of Excessive drinking Blasphemy prophane swearing and Cursing Lewdness prophana-
tion of the Lords Day or other dissolute immoral and dis-
orderly Practices as they will answer it to Almighty God and
incur my utmost resentments

And for the more Effectual Discovery of the said Enormitys I
do hereby direct and require all her Majestᶦᵉˢ Justices of the
Peace to give Strict Charges at their respective Courts for
the due prosecution and punishment of all Persons that shall
presume to offend in any of the kinds afᵈ and also of all Persons
that Contrary to their duty shall be remiss or negligent in
putting the said Laws in Execution and that they do at their
grand Jury Courts Cause this my Proclamation to be publickly read in open Court immediately before the Charge is
given

And I do hereby further Charge and Command all and
every the ministers in his or their respective Parish Churches
or Chappels to read or Cause to be read this my Proclamation
at least six times in every year immediately after divine Service and to make and Stir up their respective Auditories to
the practice of Piety and Virtue and the avoiding of all Immoralities and Prophaneness

Given at the Town and Part of Annapolis this Sixteenth
day of Sepʳ in the third year of the reign of our Sovereign
Lady Anne by the Grace of God of England Scotland France
and Ireland and the Dominions thereto belonging Queen
Defender of the Faith &c.  Annoq Domini 1704.
God Save the Queen

And sent to the House of Delegates for their Perusal by
Col Addison and five other members of her Majestᶦᵉˢ hon:ble
Council

M^r Tho^s Frisby and Seven other members of the House bring the said Proclamation with the following Endorsement

By the House of Delegates Sep^r 18th. 1704

The within Proclamation was here read and approved of by the House who give their hearty Thanks to his Ex^cy for his pious Resolutions Contained therein and will concur to our utmost to Encourage and promote the same

Signed ꝑ order W Taylard Cl Ho Del.

The Board desires his Ex^cy to order the s^d Proclamation to be printed

The Board adjourns to nine of the Clock to morrow morning

Tuesday Sep^r 19th. 1704.

Council Sate Present as yesterday

Produced and read his Highness Prince George the Lord high Admirals orders to Cap^t George Rogers Commander of the Gasport to Return for England

And whereas the said Cap^t Rogers Expects her Majest^ies Ship Jersey under the Command of Cap^t Smith from new England will be ready to Join him at New York by the Eighth of October to Sail for England and does promise to take care of what Ships by that Time will Come under his Convoy from Virginia and Maryland It is therefore advised and Resolved by the Board that the Ships now ready to Sail and that can be got ready in time be cleared and permitted to Sail giving bond to Join the s^d Man of War at New York.

Came M^r Mackall and M^r Foulke with the resolves of the House upon several of her Majest^ies royal Instructions which were read and approved of by the Board.

Col Smallwood and diverse other members bring from the House the following Message Viz^t

By the House of Delegates Sep^r 19th. 1704.

By a paper read in the House we perceive what your Ex^cy was pleased to Say to two Popish Priests on the occasion there mentioned and as all your Actions so this in particular gives us great Satisfaction to find you generously bent to protect her Majest^ies Protestant Subjects her against the insolence and Growth of Popery and we are Cheerfully thankful to you for it

Signed ꝑ order W Taylard Cl Ho Del.

Original    Three Petitions from the Inhabitants between Chester and
Journal. the South Side of Sasafras Rivers of the other part of Kent
County on the South Side of Chester river and of part of Talbot County and Kent Island for a better Division and regulation of Kent Talbott and Cecil Countys and Erecting a new
County read and referred to the Consideration of the house
of Delegates

Read the Petition of the Inhabitants of Saint Paul's Parish
in Prince Georges County for dividing the said Parish  Ordered that the Petitioners agree where they would have it
divided and the measures will be used for the relief.  The
said Petition sent to the House of Delegates by Col Holland

Came M^r Hodson and M^r Ennalls with the following Message Viz.

By the House of Delegates Sep. 19^th 1704.

This House desire the hon:ble Council's answer to our last
Message touching the Bill for regulating ordinarys
Signed p order W Taylard Cl Ho Del.

Whereupon the following answer was sent to the House by
Col Addison Col Lloyd & Col Jenkins Viz.

By the Council in Assembly Sep^r 19^th 1704.

Your Message desiring our Reply to your answer about
the Bill for regulating ordinarys we received and propose that
your House would Join two or three of your Members with
M^r Smith and M^r Cheseldyn at two of the Clock this Afternoon to Consult and propose how the s^d Law should pass
Signed p order W Bladen Cl Council.

The Council adjourns 'till three of the Clock in the afternoon Post Meridiem

Council Sate Present

His Ex^cy the Governour

| | |
|---|---|
| Thomas Tench Esq^r | Col Edward Lloyd |
| Col John Addison | L^t Col William Holland |
| Robert Smith Esq^r | James Sanders Esq^r |
| Col John Hammond | Kenelm Cheseldyn Esq^r |
| Col Francis Jenkins | William Coursey Esq^r |

Came M^r Robert Skinner and brought up the bill for confirming the last Will and Testament of Charles Ashcombe and

John Winfell and desired the House might have Satisfaction given them in Passing the Bill
    Ordered that William Bladen inform the house therein
M$^r$ Muschamp and M$^r$ Thomas Frisby to inform his Ex$^{cy}$ that they are appointed to meet his Ex$^{cy}$ and the Gentlemen from this Board in reference to passing the Bill for regulating ordinarys
    They are told that the Gentlemen of the Council will Join them at M$^r$ Freemans
    Came M$^r$ Francis Dollahide and brought up the bill for laying an Imposition of nine pence $\mathfrak{p}$ Gallon on Rum Wine Spirits and Brandy from Pensilvania by and over Land Endorsed by the House that they insist upon the Bill as drawn Exclusive of the Amendment which was agreed to by the Board and the Bill the second Time read and sent to the House by M$^r$ Sanders.
    Then was read the representation of the Rector Governours and Visitors of the Free School praying allowance for the rent of Room for the publick Library from the third of May 1700 at the rate of twelve pound $\mathfrak{p}$ annum and also a Consideration for the rest of the house made use for the publick Service
    The said representation is referred to the Consideration of the House of Delegates and sent by Col Holland
    The Gentlemen of the Council appointed upon the Conference with the members of the House of Delegates to obviate the Designes of New York and also about the Land Records take their places at the Board & make the following reports viz.

### Sep$^r$ 1704

At a Conference appointed by his Ex$^{cy}$ the Governour Council and Assembly to consider of and advise and Lay before her Majesty such Reasons as may induce her Majesty to put a Stop to all Proceedings levelled against the Constitution of this Province by the Governour of New York
    1   It is Conceived by this Conference that if the Seat of Government be at New York it will not only be a means to allure and Entice many Tradesmen Artificers and others now among us who follow the Trade of Planting Tobacco here to desert this Province and fly to that of New York where they may follow their several Trades and Callings and gain to themselves more Ease and Advantage thereby lessening the Revenue of the Crown of England and also by these means we shall in a short time be Enabled to Supply us with such manufactures and other necessaries which we now have imported from England and inevitably destroy our Commerce with the same.

2. We do Conceive that New York having Power and Authority will upon all occasions Command from us such forces as they shall think fitt for the Safety and Strengthning themselves as will in great measure weaken this Province (now but thinly seated) and thereby leave the remaining part of the Inhabitants here open to the Incursions of the Common Enemy the Indians by whom we are invironed and many of them as near to us as those of New York who are often Committing murders on the Inhabitants here and have lately destroyed several Persons and having opportunity of Joyning with the Several Nations of Indians now among us to Effect their designs leaving us in a deplarable Condition the Lives of the Inhabitants greatly hazarded thereby and the Province in general in danger of being totally laid waste

3. That it will be very disadvantageous to the Inhabitants of this Province upon all occasions as Councills Assemblys General Courts and upon Appeals and Differences betwixt party and party to travel thither it being near four hundred miles distant from us and the ways unpassable in the Winter Season by Reason of the desert Roads violent Frosts, deep Snows and the difficulty in passing the Rivers and Bays so that the poorer Sort of People will not be able to undergo such great Charge and Fatigue and the richer to Avoid it will remove themselves and their Estates to England or other Parts and so tend to the ruin of the Tobacco Trade and Consequently lessen the Revenue of the Crown

4. That the Constitution of this Province to theirs is so disagreeable and of so different a nature both in Traffick and other Things that the Laws there composed Cannot be agreeable to the Trade and Affairs of the Country nor the Constitution of the Inhabitants thereof

It is humbly offered to the Consideration of the hon:ble House of Delegates whether it may be of Service to the Country that a certain summe of mony be raised and Lodged in the hands of some able Merchant or Merchants in London ready to be called out upon any occasion for the better Encouraging the persons negotiating this Affair and whether or no it may not be thought of Service to the Country that some person be appointed by the House and sent home with such Pacquetts for their more Safe and Speedy Conveyance

Signed ⅌ order Thoˢ Jones Cl Com.

By the Conference appointed by his Exᶜʸ the Governour and Council and Assembly to Enquire into some Aggrievances relating to the Land office and the Lord Baltimores Agents &c.

The Conferees having laid before them and read the Message of the House on this Subject and the order of his late

Majesty in Council in relation to the division of the Fees of that office between the said Lord Baltimore and S$^r$ Tho$^s$ Lawrence Secretary of Maryland do report as follows.

That it is Conceived proper that an Act or Ordinance of Assembly be drawn up passed and assented to by his Ex$^{cy}$ the Governour Council and Assembly that whatever Warrants for the future be Granted by his Ldships officers and assigned Either the whole or any part thereof to any Person that on the Return of the Certificate It shall and may be Lawful for him or them to demand a Grant thereof notwithstanding the Purchase mony be unpaid by the first taker up of the Warrant and that notice be given thereof to his Ldships Agents

That forasmuch as att present the Records of the Land office are much torn damnified and some part lost and that the offices for granting of Lands are now in two Several Persons Hands which ·were heretofore Entire and that by their being so divided occasions his Lordship the Lord Baltimore to double the Purchase of his warrants which we humbly Conceive a great Aggrieveance and pray her Majesty may be addressed for Remedy thereof

Signed ℗ order Tho$^s$ Jones Cl Conference

Which Several Reports were approved of & agreed to by this Board

Thé Council adjourns till nine of<br>the Clock to morrow morning

Wednesday September the 20th. 1704<br>Council Sate Present as yesterday

M$^r$ Smith and M$^r$ Cheseldyn return to the Board and report that the Conferees from the House had agreed to this Condition to the Bill for regulating of ordinaries that is to say in the Seventeenth Line after County these words (and we do humbly pray that her Majesty will be graciously pleased that the said Fines of twelve hundred pounds of tobacco and four hundred pds of tobacco be applyed to the uses as in the said Bill is desired) after which came the following Message from the House by M$^r$ Coursey M$^r$ Muschamp & M$^r$ Thomas Frisby

By the House of Delegates Sep$^r$ 20th. 1704.

The Clause proposed by the Conferees as it is made to take place cannot be brought in with good sense as it is there

5

Original worded but in regard we perceive it is their Resolve that the
Journal. Bill may pass in a Petitionary manner we are Content that it
be so and therefore Propose that it run thus

For the better regulating Ordinar^ies &c. for the future and
in pursuance of her Majest^ies royal Instructions for raising
further Supplys for defraying the publick Charge of this
Province to effect which the Burgesses and Delegates of
this General Assembly do humbly Pray that her Majesty will
be graciously pleased to grant that it may be Enacted &c.

Signed ꝑ Order W Taylard Cl H Del

Which is agreed by this Board

Cap^t Watts & M^r Leech bring up the following Bills. Viz

A Bill for the more Speedy Conveying of publick Letters
& Packetts and for defraying the Charge thereof

A Bill directing the manner of summoning and electing
Delegates to serve in succeeding Assemblys

A Bill Confirming purchases made by the Commissioners
of the Countys Courts for the uses of the Countys &c.

A Bill restraining the Extortions of Sheriffs Subsherr. and
Deputy Commissarys

A Bill for Amerciaments in the Provincial and County
Courts

A Bill for securing Persons' rights to Town Lands

A Bill confirming Titles of Land to Churches

A Bill for stay of Execution after the tenth of May yearly.

A Bill ascertaining the Bounds of a Certain Tract of Land
to the use of the Nanticoke Indians

A Bill ascertaining Damages on protested Bills of Exchange

A Bill impowering Commissioners of the County Courts to
levy and raise tobacco to defray the necessary charges of
their County's and Parishes

Col Edward Dorsey and Cap^t Beale from the house to see
Matthias Vanderheyden prove his Naval officers acc^t who
accordingly makes Oath thereunto

And the same Time William Bladen Naval officer of the
Port of Annapolis makes oath to the accounts of his Collection

M^r Young M^r Aisquith and M^r Ennals from the House to
see Col Dent sworn to his Naval officers accounts

The Council adjourns to the afternoon


Past Meridiem the Council Sate Present as in the morning

M^r Howe brings from the house the following Bills

A Bill for the naturalization of Otho Othoson

A Bill laying an imposition on Several Commodities Exported

A Bill declaring the Division of several Counties to be firm Original and Stable Journal.

The said Bills were read severally Endorsed and with these this day read sent to the house by Col Addison Col Ienkins Col Lloyd and M$^r$ Cheseldyn

Came Col Maxwell and M$^r$ Joseph Gray with the Bills providing what shall be good Evidence to prove foreign debts which is read and that Clause for pleading never demanded recommended to be as in the former Law and sent to the House by Col Hammond

The Board adjourns 'till nine of the Clock to morrow morning

Sep$^r$ the 21$^{st}$ 1704

Council Sate Present as yesterday

Col Ninian Beals Letter taken into Consideration it was ordered that Col Addison Col Beale and Col Smallwood acquaint the Piscattaway Indians that they make choice of an Emperour and present him to his Ex$^{cy}$ at Annapolis to be Confirmed and that at that Time it is Expected the Indians should pay their Tribute and renew their Articles.

Came M$^r$ Hodson and four other members and bring up the following Bills Engrossed.

A Bill ascertaining the Expences of the Delegates of Assembly

A Bill confirming all proceedings to this present Time

A Bill relating to the Standard of English Weights and Measures.

A Bill laying an imposition of nine pence ·P Gallon on Rum Wine and Spirits

A Bill prohibiting Commissioners Clerks Sheriffs and Deputy Clerks to plead as Attorneys

A Bill against Excessive usury

A Bill for the preservation of the several Harbours

A Bill declaring the Grantees of Land within the Indians Land shall have Action of Trespass against such as Carry away Timber

A Bill for publication of Marriages

A Bill against Ingrossers and Regrators

A Bill prohibiting Masters of Ships and others to transport or Convey away Persons out of this Province without Passes

A Bill Confirming to the Governour the Duty of 3$^d$ ℗ Tunn

A Bill for publication of all Laws

A Bill declaring it Felony to alter tobacco after received

A Bill appointing Constables and what relates to their office

A Bill for limitting Certain Actions for avoiding Suits at Law

A Bill for Settling an annual revenue on her Majestⁱᵉˢ Governour for the Time being

A Bill appointing Court Days

A Bill for advancement of Natives and Residents

A Bill to Enable Col Dorsey to Sell Lands

A Bill to Enable William Sweatnam to Sell Lands

A Bill for Quieting Possessions and Enrolling Conveyances

A Bill for killing Wolves and Crows

A Bill directing the manner of suing out Attachments

Which said twenty four Bills were read assented to and sent to the House by Col Hammond and Col Jenkins

The Council adjourns till the Afternoon

Post Meridiem Council Sate Present as in the Morning

Col Maxwell Capᵗ Beale and Capᵗ Philips bring the following bills from the House

A Bill for administration of Justice in the County Courts &c.

A Bill for Relief of Creditors against Bankrupts

A Bill for marking high ways

A Bill confirming the last Wills and Testaments of Charles Ashcombe John Whinfell and John Burnam

A Bill for appeals and Writts of Error

Major Lowe brings from the House what shall be good Evidence to prove foreign and other Debts

The Board adjourns to nine of the Clock to morrow morning

Fryday Sepʳ 22ᵈ 1704.

The Council Sate Present as yesterday

Mʳ Wells brings from the House the following bills

A Bill prohibiting Liquors to be carryed to Indian towns

A Bill imposing 3ᵈ ℗ Gallon on Rum

A Bill for recording all Laws

A Bill for securing merchants tobacco and others after received

A Bill for taking special Bayl &c.

Advised by the Council and ordered by his Exᶜʸ the Governour that Col John Hammond take into his Care and Custody the Prize of L'ortolent with the Cargo and by publick Sale dispose thereof to the best Advantage keeping the produce thereof in his Hands, and to be accountable for the same when his Exᶜʸ shall have Instructions out of England Concerning the same

The Council adjourns for two hours

Original
Journal. Post Meridiem Council Sate present as before and Adjourned till to morrow morning

Saturday Sep^r the 23^d

Council Sate Present as yesterday

Came M^r William Frisby and M^r Tyler to acquaint his Ex^cy the House was sitting if he had anything to Command or offer

Col Addison being indisposed had leave to go home

The several Bills brought by Col Maxwell M^r Lowe and M_r Wells read and sent to the House with the Endorsements by M^r Saunders and M^r Coursey

M^r Coursey brought up the Address to her Majesty about New York

M^r Gerard Foulk brought up the Bill for Appeals and Writts of Error insisted on by House as drawn

M^r Ennals brings up a Bill for settling Lands on Susannah Blainey &c

The Board adjourns till two of the Clock in the Afternoon

Post Meridiem

Council Sate and Adjourns till nine of the Clock on Monday Morning

Monday Sep^r 25^th 1704

The Council Sate Present

The Honble
| | |
|---|---|
| Thomas Tench Esq^r | L^t Col William Holland |
| Robert Smith Esq^r | James Sanders Esq^r |
| Col John Hammond | Kenelm Cheseldyn |
| Col Francis Jenkins | William Coursey Esq^r |
| Col Edward Lloyd | |

M^r Hodson and three other Members from the House bring the following Message Viz.

By the House of Deleg^s Sept^r 25^th 1704

This House are very well Satisfyed with the well composed Discourse preached by the Reverend Doctor Wotton at opening of the Annapolitan Church and think it highly worthy of the press which if your Ex^cy does we pray your Ex^ry to give Order for          Signed p order W Taylard Cl.

Which was assented to by the Council.

W Bladen Cl Coun.

The Board adjourns to Nine of the Clock to morrow morn.

Tuesday Sep^r 26th 1704

Council Sate Present as Yesterday

Came M^r Hill & Major Aisquith from the house with the following Bills.

A Bill for paym^t of Criminal fees &c.

A Bill for punishing the offences of Adultery and Fornication

A Bill requiring the Masters of Ships and Vessels to publish the rates of their Freight before they take tobacco on Board

A Bill for punishment of Blasphemy prophane Cursing and swearing

A Bill of Directions for the Sherriff's office and more easy payment of publick and County Levies.

Which Bills being read and Endorsed were sent to the House by M^r Sanders

The following Message sent to the House by M^r Tench M^r Smith Col Jenkins and Col Lloyd

By his Ex^cy the Governour and Council in Assembly
Sep^r 26th. 1704

Gentlemen

Your Message of the 15^th Inst^t touching an House to be built for her Majest^ies Governour being this day read at the Board his Ex^cy was pleased to declare that he would never Consent to appropriate that which was given for so publick a Benefitt to the Province as Supplying them with Arms and Ammunition of which they can never have too great a Store to his own private Accommodation and Advantage    Therefore we desire some other Measures may be taken to answer her Majest^ies royal Instructions either in Building such House or assigning to his Ex^cy the Governour a competent sum of mony for        thereof

Signed ℘ Order W Bladen Cl Coun.

M^r Coursey M^r Tho^s Frisby & M^r Tyler bring up the following bills viz.

A Bill for securing the Parochial Librarys &c.

A Bill for Encouragement of Tillage and Relief of poor Debtors

A Bill prohibiting the Abuses Committed by Woodrangers Original Journal.
and to prevent Multitudes of Horses.

A Bill for Imposition of $3^d$ ℘ $hh^d$ on tobacco for defraying the Publick Charge

A Bill for Encouragement of such Persons as will undertake to build Watermills

A Bill relating to Servants and Slaves

A Bill for rectifying the ill practices of Attorneys &c.

A Bill for regulating the Militia &c.

A Bill for Speedy Tryal of Criminals and ascertaining their punishment in the County Courts when prosecuted there

Which were read and Endorsed and sent to the house by Col Lloyd and M$^r$ Sanders.

Came M$^r$ Muschamp and three other Members from the house and brought up the following Bills

A Bill ascertaining the Gauge of Tobacco H:hds.

A Bill prohibiting the Importation of Bread Beer Flour &c

A Bill Confirming purchases made by the Commissioners of the County Courts

A Bill for restraining the Extortions of Sheriffs Subsheriffs &c.

A Bill for naturalization of Otho Othoson

A Bill to Encourage the Inhabitants of this Province to adventure their Ships and Vessels more freely abroad to import Rum &c.

A Bill declaring how Fees of Naturalization and other private Laws shall be proportioned

A Bill for Conveying of publick Letters and Packetts &$^c$

A Bill for Causing Grand and Petite Jurors & Witnesses to Come to Courts &c.

A Bill for Amerciaments in the Provincial & County Courts

A Bill for stay of Executions after the tenth day of May yearly.

A Bill ascertaining Damage on protested Bills of Exchange

A Bill ascertaining the Bounds of a certain tract of Land to the use of Nanticoke Indians

An Act directing the Manner of summoning & Electing Delegates and Representatives to Serve in succeeding Assemblys

An Act for regulating of Ordinarys &c.

A Bill impowering Commissioners of the County Courts to levy tobacco to defray the necessary Charges of their County's and Parishes

A Bill confirming Titles of Land given to Churches

A Bill declaring the Division of Several Countys within this Province

A Bill securing rights to Town Lands

up the following bills

l imposing 3ᵈ ᵱ Gallon on Rum & Wine 20 sh ᵱ poll
s and twenty shill ᵱ poll on Irish Servᵗˢ for defraying
lick Charge
l for recording Laws &c.
l prohibiting Liquors to be carryed to Indian Towns &c.
l for taking Special Bayle &c.
l for marking High Ways &c.
l Confirming the Last Will and Testament of Charles
be of Saint Marˡᵉˢ County Gent. decᵈ John Whinfel
n Burnam decᵈ
l for settling Lands on Susannah Blaney &c.
l for the better Administration of Justice in the County

l for relief of Creditors in England agᵗ Bankrupts
ll for securing Merchants and other's tobacco after
d
h were read and with the others brought up by Mʳ
mp assented to by the Council and sent to the House
Lloyd and Mʳ Sanders.
: Mʳ Coursey with the bill directing the Sherr. in their
hich was again read and sent to the house by Col
nd Mʳ Sanders
Council adjourns 'till to morrow morning


Wednesday Sepʳ 27ᵗʰ 1704
Council Sate present as yesterday
: Mʳ Samuel Young Mʳ Robert Tyler and Mʳ Joseph
and brought the following Message


By the House of Delegates Sepʳ 27. 1704.
)sed whether it may not be necessary for the ornament
ine's Church in Annapolis that the Pews appointed for
egates of Assembly may be built at the publick Charge
: flag stone may be sent for out of England to lay the

:fore resolved by the House that the Ground assigned
Gentlemen of the Assembly in the said Church be
h decent pewes as his Exᶜʸ the Governour shall please
: and shall be paid for out of the publick Treasure also
Samuel Young Treasurer for the Western Shoar send

for so much Flagg stone as will lay the Alleys at the Charge Original
of the publick also to which his Ex$^{cy}$ and Council's Concur- Journal.
rence is desired

Signed ꝑ order W Taylard Cl Ho. Del.

Which was assented to by the Council and sent down to
the house of Delegates by M$^r$ Sanders.

The Address to her Majesty about New York sent to the
House with the following Message by M$^r$ Tench & M$^r$ Coursey
viz.

By his Excellency and Council in Assembly
September the 27$^{th}$ 1704.

His Ex$^{cy}$ the Governour and Council have already addressed
her Majesty on this occasion therefore unless the House will
shew their nearer Concern by raising and Lodging Mony in
England to be made use of for negotiating this Matter more
Effectually neither his Ex$^{cy}$ nor this Board will Joyne in the
present Address proposed

Signed ꝑ order W Bladen Cl Council

The bill providing what shall be good Evidence to prove
foreign Debts was read and the Board do insist on the last
Clause being better Explained

The Bill for appeals and Writts of Error read and Endorsed
unless the House will agree to the Bill as proposed it will be
referred to the next Sessions of Assembly

The said two Bills sent to the House by M$^r$ Coursey

Came M$^r$ Henry Coursey from the House desiring to know
of the Board what they mean by Explaining the last Clause in
the Bill providing what shall be good Evidence to prove
foreign Debts &c And is told that this Board would not have
any thing but mony allowed in Discount

Came Major Lowe and brought up a bill to prevent the
Growth of Popery which was read in Council the first and
second time well approved of passed for Engrossing and sent
to the House by Col Ienkins and M$^r$ Cheseldyne.

Came M$^r$ Hodson and two other Members with the bill for
Appeals and Writts of Error desiring it might pass as drawn
being thought really beneficial to the Province and to Induce
the Board there to alledge that the Defend$^t$ will not be wholly
remediless but may have his Injunction in Chancery

The Bill is agreed to and sent to the House by M$^r$ Sanders

The Board adjourns till the Afternoon

Original
Journal.                    Post Meridiem Council Sate Present as before

Came M^r Muschamp M^r Tyler and brought from the House
the Address to her Majesty Endorsed


By the House of Delegates Sep^r 27^th 1704.

We have received your Honours Resolutions touching the
Address We confess we are something surprised to find that
your Honours after you had agreed with us on Reasons to be
Contained in it and had in your former Letter or Address
shewn at the Conference said that you believed the General
Assembly would proceed further on that Subject your Honours
should refuse to Joyne with us because we do not now raise
mony when your Honours know all the Account We have of
the design is but dark and uncertain and such as we are not
absolutely to rely on

We heartily wish we could Concur with your Honours in
all things for the good of this Province and we shall be always
as ready as any to raise mony where the necessity of the Province requires it which in this we Cannot perceive   Therefore
since we shall not say or do any thing in the name of the Province without your Honours in Conjunction neither shall we
meddle with this address unless your Honours Joyne with us

Signed ᵽ Order W Taylard Cl Del.


Came M^r Coursey and brought the following Message Viz.


By the House of Delegates
Sep^r 27^th 1704

The greatest Part of the Bills having passed your Honours
Assent and this House the next material matter offering to our
Consideration is settling the Law for regulating officers Fees
and therein of the charge of the Great Seal to the Laws of
this Province for the future on which we desire to know
whither your Honours think it most proper for the dispatch of
business to proceed by drawing the Bill or by Message and
Answer or by appointing a Conference with some of this house
and your Board in either of which or any other reasonable
Method we are ready to proceed

Signed ᵽ Order W Taylard Cl Ho Del.


M^r Eccleston and M^r Dollarhide bring up the Bill for providing what shall be good Evidence to prove foreign Debts

&ᶜ Explained by the House which was agreed to by the Board and sent to the House by Col Hammond with the following Message

### By the Council in Assembly Sepʳ 27ᵗʰ 1704

The message by Mʳ Muschamp and Mʳ Tyler this Afternoon we have observed and thereupon we do acknowledge we did Resolve the Address to her Maty in the name of the Province as absolutely necessary and agreed to the Reasons therein Contained and did really believe the General Assembly unanimously would have Joyned in it thinking those Accounts we had tho never so small and uncertain, Sufficient to caution us to stand upon our Defence and Avert such apparent Damages to the present well settled Constitution of our Country and upon the Conference did propose not only mony should be remitted to England but some trusty sensible person sent by this Assembly to negotiate this Affair which was referred to your Consideration but we find rejected

Therefore to what end should we frame addresses never to be Presented or Considered which without mony to accompany them to the Persons whose several hands and offices they pass through can expect no better Fortune or Countenance 'twas upon this score and no other we refused Joyning in the said Address and now assure you [we] wish your whole House had as deep a sense of this imminent Danger as we for then surely you would to preserve your Constitution do what is fitting and then his Exᶜʸ the Governour and this board will never refuse heartily to joyne with you in this address or any other for the Interest or advantage of the Province

Signed ᵱ order W Bladen Cl Council

The Board adjourns 'till to morrow morning


### Thursday Sepʳ 28th 1704

Council Sate Present as yesterday

Came Mʳ Coursey and Mʳ Tyler and bring from the House the following Message


### By the House of Delegates
### Sepʳ 28th 1704

The House according to two several Laws of this Province entering into Consideration of and settling the fees due on

Original
Journal. private bills passed this Sessions and what shall be allowd
for transcribing the Laws of last & this Sessions of Assemly
have agreed and proposed to allow his Ex⁰ as Keeper of ɩe
broad Seal for Every Copy of the Laws of last Sessions ɩf
Assembly four hundred pounds of Tobᶜ and for every Coy
of the Laws of this Sessions fifteen hundred pounds of To⁰
to be payed by the Countys for those sent to the Countys ad
by the publick for Copys sent for England and for the privaᵗ
we propose for the Keeper of the Great Seal Viz.

| | Tob° |
|---|---|
| Col Edwᵈ Dorsey's Seale to the Bill for Sel-ling Lands | 120 lb |

| | £ | s. | |
|---|---|---|---|
| To Mʳ Speaker his Fee | 2.. | 0.. | |
| To the Clerk of the House | 1.. | 0.. | |

| | Tob° |
|---|---|
| Mʳ William Swetnam his Seale to the Bill | 120 lb |

| | £ | s. | |
|---|---|---|---|
| To Mʳ Speaker | 4.. | 0.. | |
| To the Clerk | 2.. | 0.. | |

| | Tob° |
|---|---|
| Otho Othoson to the Seal to his Bill for naturalization | 120 lb |

| | £ | s. | |
|---|---|---|---|
| To Mʳ Speaker | 4.. | 0.. | |
| To the Clerk | 2.. | 0.. | |

| | Tob° |
|---|---|
| Mʳ Ashcomb to the Seal of the Bill for con-firming the Will | 120 lb |

| | £ | s. | |
|---|---|---|---|
| To Mʳ Speaker | 4.. | 0.. | |
| To the Clerk | 2.. | 0.. | |

| | Tob° |
|---|---|
| Mʳ Winfill t the Seal to the bill Confirming John Winfills Will | 120 lb |

| | £ | s. | |
|---|---|---|---|
| To Mʳ Speaker | 1.. | 0.. | |
| To the Clerk | 0.. | 10.. | |

| | Tob° |
|---|---|
| To the Seale of the Bill confirming Boarman's Will | 120 lb |

| | £ | s. | |
|---|---|---|---|
| To Mʳ Speaker | 1.. | 0.. | |
| To the Clerk | 0.. | 10.. | |

| | Tob° |
|---|---|
| Susannah Blaney for Seale to the Bill to Settle Land | 120 lb |

| | £ | s. | |
|---|---|---|---|
| To Mʳ Speaker | 1.. | 0.. | |
| To the Clerk | 0.. | 10.. | |

To all which this House prays the Concurrence of ɩ
honᵇle Councill

Signed p order W. Taylard Cl Ho Del.

To which the following Answer was sent to the house ɩ

By the Council in Assembly Sep' 28th 1704.

The Message this day about settling the Fees due for private bills and transcribing the Laws of the last and this present Sessions has been read and Considered by this Board and as to the first Proposal for Copys of the Laws for last Sessions which should then have been Settled we cannot Think a less reward due therefore than what has been usual that is to say one thousand p$^{ds}$ of Tob° ⅌ Copy as may appear by the County Levys this three or four years last past

That as to the Copys of this present Sessions we Cannot believe any Person will undertake to do them well for less than 2500 ℔ Tob° ⅌ Copy They being so many

Therefore desire so much may be allowed to the Keeper of the Great Seal to Enable him to get them Speedily transcribed as well to be Sent for England as to the County Courts

Thirdly as to the private Bills it being as absolutely necessary that the Sealed Copy thereof be sent to England as of other publick Laws we desire you will Explain whether you meant the Keeper of the great Seal should take one hund$^d$ and twenty pounds of Tob° for the original Law and the same for each Copy or but one hundred and twenty pounds of Tob° for all which is conceived unreasonably less than formerly was allowed to wit four hundred and Eighty pounds of Tob° for patent of Denization

We further observe to you that upon private Bills you have not taken any notice of any Fees to the Clerk of this Board who has as great Burthen of the Business of this Assembly as any other Clerk        Signed ⅌ order W Bladen Cl Coun.

M$^r$ Greenfield Col Peirce & Cap$^t$ Watts bring up a Bill for better Administration of Justice in probate of Wills &c which being read the first and second Time is sent to the House by Col Hammond and M$^r$ Sanders

Col Smallwood Col Peirce and M$^r$ Watts bring from the House the following message

By the House of Delegates Sep' 28$^{th}$ 1704.

We have Considered the last message by Kenelm Cheseldyne and William Coursey Esq' of this Day for settling of Fees on private Laws and transcribing the Body of the Laws and as to those of this Sessions we have by Examining Committee of Laws found they will be of greater Length than what we at first believed, and therefore are Willing to allow two thousand pounds of Tobacco for Every Copy and that is

Original private bills passed this Sessions and what shall be allowed
Journal. for transcribing the Laws of last & this Sessions of Assembly
have agreed and proposed to allow his Ex^cy as Keeper of the
broad Seal for Every Copy of the Laws of last Sessions of
Assembly four hundred pounds of Tob° and for every Copy
of the Laws of this Sessions fifteen hundred pounds of Tob°
to be payed by the Countys for those sent to the Countys and
by the publick for Copys sent for England and for the private
we propose for the Keeper of the Great Seal Viz.

| | | |
|---|---|---|
| Col Edw^d Dorsey's Seale to the Bill for Selling Lands } | Tob° 120 ℔ | |
| | £ s. | d. |
| To M^r Speaker his Fee | 2.. 0.. | 0 |
| To the Clerk of the House | 1.. 0.. | 0 |
| M^r William Swetnam his Seale to the Bill } | Tob° 120 lb | |
| To M^r Speaker | 4.. 0.. | 0 |
| To the Clerk | 2.. 0.. | 0 |
| Otho Othoson to the Seal to his Bill for naturalization } | Tob° 120 lb | |
| To M^r Speaker | 4.. 0.. | 0 |
| To the Clerk | 2.. 0.. | 0 |
| M^r Ashcomb to the Seal of the Bill for confirming the Will } | Tob° 120 lb | |
| To M^r Speaker | 4.. 0.. | 0 |
| To the Clerk· | 2.. 0.. | 0 |
| M^r Winfill to the Seal to the bill Confirming John Winfills Will } | Tob° 120 lb | |
| To M^r Speaker | 1.. 0.. | 0 |
| To the Clerk | 0.. 10.. | 0 |
| To the Seale of the Bill confirming Boarman's Will } | Tob° 120 lb | |
| To M^r Speaker | 1.. 0.. | 0 |
| To the Clerk | 0.. 10.. | 0 |
| Susannah Blaney for Seale to the Bill to Settle Land } | Tob° 120 lb | |
| | £. s. | d. |
| To M^r Speaker | 1.. 0.. | 0 |
| To the Clerk . | 0.. 10.. | 0 |

To all which this House prays the Concurrence of the
hon:b̶le Council

Signed ᵱ order W. Taylard Cl Ho Del.

To which the following Answer was sent to the house by
M^r Cheseldyne and M^r Coursey

By the Council in Assembly Sep^r 28th 1704.

The Message this day about settling the Fees due for private bills and transcribing the Laws of the last and this present Sessions has been read and Considered by this Board and as to the first Proposal for Copys of the Laws for last Sessions which should then have been Settled we cannot Think a less reward due therefore than what has been usual that is to say one thousand p^ds of Tob° ᵽ Copy as may appear by the County Levys this three or four years last past

That as to the Copys of this present Sessions we Cannot believe any Person will undertake to do them well for less than 2500 lb Tob° ᵽ Copy They being so many

Therefore desire so much may be allowed to the Keeper of the Great Seal to Enable him to get them Speedily transcribed as well to be Sent for England as to the County Courts

Thirdly as to the private Bills it being so absolutely necessary that the Sealed Copy thereof be sent to England as of other publick Laws we desire you will Explain whether you meant the Keeper of the great Seal should take one hund^d and twenty pounds of Tob° for the original Law and the same for each Copy or but one hundred and twenty pounds of Tob° for all which is conceived unreasonably less than formerly was allowed to wit four hundred and Eighty pounds of Tob° for patent of Denization

We further observe to you that upon private Bills you have not taken any notice of any Fees to the Clerk of this Board who has as great Burthen of the Business of this Assembly as any other Clerk          Signed ᵽ order W Bladen Cl Coun.

M^r Greenfield Col Peirce & Cap^t Watts bring up a Bill for better Administration of Justice in probate of Wills &c which being read the first and second Time is sent to the House by Col Hammond and M^r. Sanders

Col· Smallwood Col Peirce and M^r Watts bring from the House the following message

By the House of Delegates Sep^r 28^th 1704.

We have Considered the last message by Kenelm Cheseldyne and William Coursey Esq^r of this Day for settling of Fees on private Laws and transcribing the Body of the Laws and as to those of this Sessions we have by Examining Committee of Laws found they will be of greater Length than what we at first believed, and therefore are Willing to allow two thousand pounds of Tobacco for Every Copy and that is

the highest that ever we find allowed even when the whole
body has been revised and which we Cannot in reason advance
    As to the last Session Laws we have examined the Laws &
find the Proportion is sufficient and why your Honours propose 1000 lb Tob° because of Precedents and not as the Law
directs us then we should allow but one thous⁴ pounds of
Tob° for this Body which would be unreasonable but your
Honours know it is the true Intent of the Law that we and
you look to and not critical Exceptions which if we would
make use of we might scruple to allow any thing for last Sessions Laws because they were not allowed for then as the
Law directs but we mean nothing but what is honest and fair
and desire to be so understood and used
    To the private bills we mean the Persons to be answerable
for the same as the publick is for the publick ones
    And altho we shall not dispute the weight of Business that
lyes upon any Clerk believing Every one has Enough We
Desire to be Excused from increasing any ffees on private
bills at this Time more than what has been used before and
we do not find your Clerk (tho we have a respect for him)
ever allowed any ffees on private bills and hope you will not
press that matter any further but joyne with us in hearty Endeavours to dispatch the weighty matters in Hand
                    Signed ℘ order W Taylard Cl Ho Del.

    Mʳ Frisby and two other members bring from the House
the following Message Viz.


                By the House of Delegates
                    September the 28th. 1704
    We have Considered your Honours message by Col Ham-
mond and are Sorry your Honours will not join in the Address
Since you are pleased to say you think it necessary to prevent
an imminent Danger and we cannot believe our Agent has so
little value of us as to let it lye Dormant by him when we gave
him the assurance of paying what he disburses for us in laying
it before her Majesty which we always proposed to do
    Your Honours are pleased to say you have addressed her
Majesty on that subject and we doubt not but your Honours
expect it to take Effect and yet we have not heard of any sum
of Mony raised or person appointed to go with it, and we
hope this may go also if your honours please.  We again
humbly offer ourselves in the Addresses and we hope we shall
be discharged of any misfortune that may attend the non
addressing since we are ready to Joyne in it

The above was wrote before his Ex^cy commanded our At- tendance and what he was pleased to say we have Considered and with all due Respects to his Ex^cy we speak it we cannot surcease to recede and shall be glad if his Excellency will please to Joyne with us in the Address

Signed ꝑ order W Taylard Cl Ho Del.

The Board adjourns 'till to morrow morning eight of the Clock

### Fryday Sep^r 29th. 1704.

### Council Sate Present as before

Came M^r Hodson and M^r Taylor brought up the following Bills Viz.

A Bill for payment of Criminal ffees

A Bill for encouragement of such as will undertake to build Water mills

A Bill for the Imposition of three pence ꝑ Hhd on Tobacco to the Country &c.

A Bill for securing the Parochial Librarys

A Bill for punishing the offences of Adultery and Fornication

A Bill for providing what shall be good evidence to prove fforeign Debts.

A Bill relating to Servants and Slaves which were assented to by the Council and sent to the House by Col Hammond

M^r Young and M^r Hill bring from the House their answer to the Lord Baltemores objections against the Land Law thus Endorsed

### By the House of Delegates

September 29^th 1704.

The within reasons are offered by this House to the Lord Baltimore's objections to the Land Law and tho we are of opinion that the Land law ought to be revised so as to answer the reasonable part of his Lordships objections yet because of other great matters under present Consideration Time will not permitt so careful Examination as the same ought to be done with therefore we pray your Honours to Joyne with us in a small bill to Continue the same Law in force till next Sessions of Assembly when by God's Grace it may be revised as it ought to be and this we pray to the end that the Province in the meantime may not loose the Benefitt of the most useful and necessary part of the said Law

Signed ꝑ order W Taylard Cl ho Del.

Original   Col Smallwood brings from the House the following En-
Journal.   grossed Bills Viz.
A Bill ascertaining the height of Fences &c.
A Bill directing the Sheriffs in their offices and for the more
easy payment of the publick and County Levys
Which were assented to by this Board and sent to the
House by Col Hammond
The Board adjourns 'till the afternoon

Post Meridiem the Council Sate Present as before

Came M^r Mackall with two Engrossed Bills viz.
A Bill for rectifying the ill Practices of Attorneys &c.
A Bill requiring masters of ships to publish their freight
Which were assented to by her Majest^{ies} honble Council and
Sent down to the House by Col Jenkins and M^r Sanders
M^r Robert Skinner brought up a bill for continuing in force
the Act Entituled an Act for ascertaining the Bounds of Land
A Bill confirming the petitionary Act relating to ffree school
which were read the second time and sent to the House by
Col Jenkins & M^r Sanders with the following Messages

By the Council in Assembly Sep^r 29th. 1704

Gent.   You have considered your Message by W^m Frisby
Major Low and M^r Philips Concerning the address proposed
to her Majesty and your Dependance upon Col Blakiston and
have resolved to joyne with you in the s^d Address and doubt
not but his Ex^{cy} will be inclined thereto likewise Therefore
Propose that it be fairly transcribed
Signed p order W Bladen Cl Council.

By the Governour & Council in Assembly
Sep^r 29th. 1704

We doubt not but many Gentlemen among you are throughly
sensible of what value the honble M^r Blaythwaytes Friendship
may be to this Province in general he being the only Gentleman myself or Col Blakiston can apply to on any occasion for
the Ease or advantage of the Province therefore recommend
to your house that you would seriously Consider of the Reference last Assembly to this for settling some annual Salary
on the s^d M^r Blaythwayte as he is Auditor General and the
accounts of this Province must all pass through his Hands
Signed p order W Bladen Cl Coun.

The Scheme of officers Fees proposed to be retrenched being read at this Board his Ex<sup>cy</sup> is pleased to ask the Council whether it be reasonable to retrench any of the s<sup>d</sup> Fees who say the Fees are not greater than the service requires Save the Secretary's Fees for an Injunction an auditâ Querelâ and Writt of Enquiry of Damages which this Board are willing should be regulated as proposed

By his Ex<sup>cy</sup> the Governour and Council in Assembly
Sep<sup>r</sup> 29th. 1704.

Resolved by this Board that an Address be sent to her Majesty to Congratulate the Success of her arms under the Conduct of his Grace the Duke of Marlborough and that the Thanks of his Ex<sup>cy</sup> the Governour and this Board and the honble Assembly be given her Majesty for placing his Grace in that Station since the loss of his Majesty King William of glorious memory    Signed ꝑ order W Bladen Cl Council

The three last messages were sent to the House by Col Hammond Col Jenkins Col Lloyd and Col Holland

The following messages sent to the House by Col Hammond and M<sup>r</sup> Sanders

By the Council in Assembly Sep<sup>r</sup> 29th. 1704.

We have moved his Ex<sup>cy</sup> that whereas in the year 1702 the then Assembly did vote £300 sterl for the assistance of New York which summe was directed to be paid out of the publick Treasure of this Province to the order of that Government when sent for but for as much as the Government of New York has not yet thought fitt to send for that Sum of Mony we are induced to suspect they have greater designes against us and therefore desired his Ex<sup>cy</sup> would admitt the same sum to be remitted to M<sup>r</sup> John Hyde in England ready for that Service in Case the Lord Cornebury shall require the same otherwise that our Agent might make use of all or any part thereof to obviate any Machinati<sub></sub>ons by the said Government of New York against our Constitution if any such be prosecuted to which his Ex<sup>cy</sup> has been pleased to Assent Therefore we desire to have your Concurrence therewith signed ꝑ Order                             W Bladen Cl Coun

The House acquainted that the Board consent to regulate the ffee of four pounds of Tob° ꝑ Annum for Searches and

Original that four pounds of tob° be taken for the four years and two
Journal. pounds of tob° for every year
The Board adjourns 'till to morrow morning Eight of the
Clock

Saturday September the 30th 1704

Council Sate Present as yesterday

Came Mʳ Coursey from the House who says they are ready
to join his Exᶜʸ and this Board in the congratulatory Address
to her Majesty and desire such Address may be prepared

Mʳ Hodson Mʳ Ennalls Mʳ Stone bring up five Engrossed
bills Viz.

A Bill for punishmᵗ of Blasphemy prophane Swearing &c.

A Bill for continuing the Land Law &c.

A Bill for Speedy Tryal of Criminals &c.

A Bill for encouragement of Tillage and Relief of poor
Debtors &c.

A Bill Continuing the Petitionary Act relating to Free
School

A Bill to prevent the Growth of Popery which were assented
to by her Majestⁱᵉˢ hon:ble. Council

Mʳ Philips brings up a bill impowering a Committee to lay
the Levy which was read twice and passed for Engrossing and
sent to the House by Mʳ Sanders

Col Thoˢ Smith brings from the House

By the House of Delegates

September the 30th 1704

We having Settled the Journal of Accounts find therein
Tob° due to his Exᶜʸ for the great Seal and otherwise we
therefore Desire to know whether it will be more acceptable to his Exᶜʸ to have the Tob° in specie or mony for the
same out of the treasure of this Province at one penny ⅌ pound

And that since there is Mony in Bank and the publick Levy
like to be very high and hard upon the poorer sort we Propose to pay the honble Council and Delegates of this Session
some part of their hundred and forty pounds of Tob° ⅌ diem
in mony at one penny ⅌ pound if your Honours are pleased
to Concur with us therein which we desire because it is hard
to procure mony to bear our Expences here

Signed ⅌ order W Taylard Cl Ho Del

Mʳ Jones and Mʳ Magrowder bring from the house the following Message

By the House of Delegates Sep[r] 30th 1704

In answer to your Honours Message by Col Hammond Col Holland Col Jenkins and Col Lloyd touching the mony for New York Your Honours know that former Assemblys have addressed her Majesty on that Subject and said it should be ready when Called for and we do not know how soon it may be Called for there being but barely that sum (if so much) now in Stock and therefore we desire it may remain as it is and the Address presented as agreed on

Signed ꝑ order W Taylard Cl Ho Del.

By the Council in Assembly Sep[r] 30th 1704.

The Message by Thomas Smith proposing the Tob° due to the Keeper of the Great Seal, and some small Part of the Councills and Burghesses Salaries to be paid in mony has been considered by this Board and so no less Expectance of the Value of Tob° this year than the last and formerly when the Levy was payed in mony at 10[s] ꝑ Cent Tob° Wherefore we agree such paym[t] should be made at the Rate to wit 10[s] ꝑ Hundred w[t] Tob°    Signed ꝑ order W Bladen Cl Council.

By the Council in Assembly Sep[r] 30th 1704

Your Message by M[r] Jones and M[r] Magrowder is agreed to by this Board and we desire the Address may be sent up to be Signed

We have Sent the other Address to her Majesty of which we desire your Approbation or that you will amend the same as you think fitt

Signed ꝑ order W Bladen Cl Council

The two last Messages were sent to the House by Col. Hammond

M[r] Robert Tyler brings from the House the following Proposal

By the House of Delegates

Proposal made for regulating Attorny's Fees as follows

Attorny's Fees in the Provincial Court

|  | lb. Tob° |
|---|---|
| In Every common Action | 400 |
| Appeals and Writts of Error | 400 |
| Enjectment on Title of Land | 400 |
| Action of Account | 400 |

Original
Journal.
If Judġment to Acc$^t$ by Auditors more                400
On Arrest of Judgment                                  200
Appeale to the Governour and Council                   800
Fee in Chancery                                        800
Commissary's Court                                     400
In County Courts
In Action of Debt Bills Bonds           ⎫
Assumptions and Accounts Trespass       ⎬              100
and Battery                             ⎭
Bond above two Thous$^d$                               200
Actions of Debt upon Penal Statutes and Informations. 200
Actions upon the Case for Scandalous    ⎫
                                        ⎬              200
Words and Actions upon Escape           ⎭

By the House of Delegates September the 30th 1704

These are the Regulations proposed for the Attornys Fees wherein your Honours Concurrence is prayed that it may be Part of the Law for settling officers Fees
Signed ꝑ order W Taylàrd Cl Ho Del.

Which being read the following Answer was sent by M$^r$ Sanders

By the Council in Assembly Sep$^r$ 30th 1704

This Board are already sensible of a very good Law of this Province impowering the Justices to settle such Rules and Fees as they shall think reasonable and do believe such Justices are proper Judges therefore do allow only such as are reasonable neither have they ever heard of any Act of Parliam$^t$ settling Attorneys Fees in England but that they are always settled by the Discretion of the Court where such Attornys Practice          Signed ꝑ order W Bladen Cl Council.

Came M$^r$ Hudson and brought up the Bill for Administration of Justice in probat of Wills &c Engrossed which being assented to by this Board was sent to the house by Col Hammond M$^r$ Sanders & M$^r$ Cheseldyne

Major Low brings up the Bill for Limitation of officers Fees which was read at this Board the first and second Time and passed for Engrossing and sent to the House by Col Hammond

M$^r$ Greenfield and six other members bring from the House the Address to her Majesty about New York desiring it may be signed

Mʳ Coursey & six other members bring up the Congratula- tory address to her Majesty which being read and Approved is sent to the House to be transcribed

Col Maxwell and two other Members bring from the House the following Answer relateing to Esqʳ Blaythwaite

By the House of Delegates Sepʳ 30ᵗʰ 1704

We have again Considered the message touching the honourable William Blaythwayte Esq̔ʳ which was resolved the last Sessions and that is that the office was not Erected for our Benefitt nor are we Concerned to support it   The Crown that Created the office has annexed a suitable Sallary to it and that we are Sensible of we have a great honour for the Gent. since he is thought worthy of such eminent Employment and as his Exᶜʸ is pleased to say he is ready to receive applications for the Province and we hope while we behave ourselves good Subjects his Justice will Entitule us to his Countenance and any favour he shall be pleased to do us we shall not be backward in a suitable acknowledgemᵗ of

We wish your Honours knew the publick Stock because you please to press us to several Allowances that we have not mony to answer and therefore we pray your Honours to Inspect the same and then Consider whether we do not the utmost we Can

Signed ⱷ order W Taylard Cl Ho. Del.

The Board adjourns to Eight of the Clock to-morrow morning

Monday October the 2ᵈ 1704.

Council Sate Present as on Saturday

Mʳ Cheseldyne at his request have Leave to go home

The following Message sent to the House by Col Hammond

By the Council in Assembly October the 2ᵈ 1704

It is represented to us that by the bill on foot for Limitting officers Fees the Surveyours are Retrenched in theirs which was not observed when read at this Board we think the former Fees were agreeable to that offices Ingenuity and Trouble and notify the same to the House that the bill might be engrossed with the sᵈ oversight rectifyed

Signed ⱷ order W Bladen Cl Council.

Original    Major Low brings from the House a Bill of Repeale and a
Journal.    Bill declaring several Acts formerly made to be in force

Lawrence Hannin's Petition praying Leave to keep ordinary in the Port of Annapolis without paying fine for a Licence
brought from the House with their Assent and praying the
assent of this Board which is Granted

M^r King and M^r How bring from the House as follows


By the House of Delegates    October the 2^d 1704.

We have Examined the ffees on Resurveys as retrenched
and it seems to us the Retrenchment is not unreasonable but
Sufficient reward proposed to Encourage Art and Industry
and we hope your Honours will think so too on reading the
same, the Clause is thus Allowed Resurvey of 140 Acres the
same Fees as allowed on primitive Surveys and no more the
former Law was in that part found Excessive burthensome
and this Conceived but moderate and therefore doubt not your
Honours Concurrence to the Engrossed Bill which is now
ready to be sent up
                    Signed ꝑ order W Taylard Cl ho Del.


Sent by Col Jenkins to the House the following Resolve.


By the Council &c.

The Board resolve that the Sermon preached by M^r Cockshutt at the opening of the Church at Annapolis on Sunday
the 24th of September in the Afternoon be printed if the
House shall think fitt
                    Signed ꝑ Order W Bladen Cl Council.


Which was returned by Major Greenberry with the Houses
Concurrence

M^r Waters and M^r Magrowder bring up the addresses
signed

The Board adjourns till the Afternoon


Post Meridiem Council Sate Present as in the Morning

Came M^r Hudson with two Bills sent to the house in the
morning Engrossed which were assented to by her Majest^ies
honble Council

*The Upper House.* 87

By the Council in Assembly

October the 2ᵈ 1704

We put you in mind that now the Sessions is near a Conclusion we have not yet seen the Address proposed to her Majesty Concerning the aggrievance at present of Granting Lands in this Province
Signed ꝑ order W Bladen Cl Council.

Sent to the House with the above Bills assented to by Esqʳ Sanders
Came Mʳ Ennalls with the Houses answer thereto as follows

October the 2ᵈ 1704
By the House of Delegates

Upon reading the Message by the honbłe James Sanders Esqʳ relating to the Land Records &c this House Inspected their Journal and find a former Vote that for as much as many weighty Matters lay under Consideration   It was resolved the Consideration thereof be referred to next Session of Assembly        Signed ꝑ Order Wᵐ Taylard Cl Ho Del.

Came Col Smith and five other Members with the Journal of the Committee of Accounts and following Message Viz.

By the House of Delegates October the 2ⁿᵈ 1704

Conceived by this House that by any Command of the Queen or Law of this Province They are not bound to pay for any Copys of the Laws to be sent home
Nevertheless this House to shew the Honour they have to our Governour and to Settle this point for the future we will consent that what the Committee of Accounts have allowed shall pass for this Time and for the future no more than one original here and two Copys to be sent home shall be chargeable to the Province to which this House prays the Concurrence of the honbłe Council with which we Consent to the Journal
Signed ꝑ order W Taylard Cl Del.

Original
Journal.
M^r Taylard and four other members bring from the house the following message

By the House of Delegates
8ber 2^d 1704

May it please your Ex^{cy}
Having an entire Dependance that your Ex^{cy} has given us of your Resolutions to Govern us according to Law and Preserving us in our rights and Propert^{ies} and your Willingness to assent to what may be reasonably Proposed for the Ease and Welfare of this .Province we have proposed to present your Ex^{cy} with thirty Pounds yearly to defray the Charge of your house Rent while your Ex^{cy} Continues your Government and Residence in this Province which we Pray you to accept and understand us Candidly in all Things
Signed ꝑ order W Taylard Cl Ho. Del.

The Board adjourns 'till eight of the Clock to morrow morning

Tuesday October the 3^d 1704
Council Sate Present as yesterday

Major Greenberry M^r Leech and M^r James bring up the Bill for officers fees their limitation, & the following to agree to the said Bill

By the House of Delegates October the 3^d 1704

We have considered the reasonableness of the Surveyours Fees as regulated by the Bill and finding them most just and fitting cannot Consent to any alteration the former Settlement in that Point being Experienced to have been oppressive to the People and a great Aggrievance and Several Persons now in this Province that have been and are in that Employment being sensible of the Justice thereof are Content therewith and we pray your Honours to Consider of·and Concur with us that the Law may not be laid aside to the great Inconveniency of the Country
Signed ꝑ order W Taylard Cl ho Del.

Which is agreed to by the Board and the following Message thereon sent to the House by Col Lloyd.

By the Council in Assembly Octob^r 3^d 1704 Original Journal.

Your Message about the present regulating of Surveyors Fees is agreed to by this Board rather than Delay the Sessions
Signed ꝑ order W Bladen Cł Council

The Bill for officers Fees being assented to is returned to the House by Esq^r Tench

The following Messages sent to the House by Col Hammond and Coł Lloyd with the Journal of the Committee of Accounts by the Council &c.

The Message by Coł Smith and others with your Journal of the Committee of Accounts to which is Subscribed your Conditional Assent has been perused and Considered by this Board Whereupon we are sorry to find the little notice you take of what his Ex^cy was pleased so generously and frankly to tell you the other day that he would make no Bargaines desired not your Bounty but required your Justice wherefore if you think at ten shill ꝑ Cent We hereby let you know that we are not for any Allowance this Sessions to be made in mony but are Inclinable to advise his Excellency that the mony now in Bank be reserved for the Country's Service in greater Emergenc^ies. You are not willing to foresee your Allowance out of the three pence ꝑ hh^d for Arms of particular Sums is not within your province therefore ought to be Expunged
Signed ꝑ order W Bladen Cl Coun.

Which was answered by M^r Coursey and four other members thus.

By the House of Delegates 8^ber 2^d 1704

We have read and debated your Honour's Message and are sorry you are pleased to be so Tart upon us for doing what we Conceive to be our Duty to our Country and it is our rights and Priviledges we humbly suppose to debate and Consider of any publick tax to be laid upon the People as this of Sealing the Laws and Duplicates and we hope we have proposed it with all the Tenderness and Justice that can be reasonably Expected and with all due Submission to his Ex^cy and your Honours we cannot depart from it Therefore if your Honours are not pleased to joyne with us in apportioning the mony to help to lessen the Levy according to the Tenour of the Laws at the price first proposed to us and agreed to we Cannot help it and our Country Cannot impute it to us if you please to send the Journal We will regulate it in Tob° as soon as we can and lay it before your Honours if

Original there be any thing your Honours think unreasonable Please to
Journal. remark it that it may be Considered we do not pretend to
meddle with allowances for Country Arms cleaning as you
are pleased to suppose therefore it shall be Expunged
   We Expected kinder usage but shall content ourselves at
present without any other Remarks.
                    Signed ꝑ order W Taylard Cl Ho Del.

   To the foregoing answer was sent by Esq. Tench and four
other members of the House as follows.


                  By the Council in Assembly
                    October the 3ᵈ 1704.
   Upon reading your last Message we find we are mistaken
by the House as to the Sealing the Laws and Duplicates a
Dispute we never Expected to have been revived this Sessions as it seems to be by your Message with your Journal of
the Committee of Accounts therefore must observe to you that
either your Allowance on the said Journal are Just and fitting
to be made by this Assembly or otherwise we believe neither
your House or this Board would agree thereto and if it be
but in order to the payment of what is due from the publick
Wherefore was your Message requiring his Excellency's Confession to future Retrenchments Contrary to his Majestᶦᵉˢ Instructions for sending Sealed Duplicates of the Copy of the
Laws tacked like a Petitionary Bill nay a doubted Right you
have to the free use of her Majestᶦᵉˢ Great Seale to these
Duplicates or at least to be dispensed with in not complying
with that Injunction to Confirm which you have only your own
opinions we never designed or have Endeavoured but to have
cultivated a good understanding with your House and promote the Interest of our Country by readily agreeing to what
was fitting for us and therefore have avoided taking Notice of
several Messages from you Especially that of the 30th of
September Mʳ Coursey and six other members wherein you
seem either to question our understanding or Integrity
   The Allowances to this Board is but one Quarter in respect
to those to the Members of your House the mony raised by
Impost was always Intended by this Board to be disposed of
for defraying the publick Charge of the Country and we know
not how it could be better Employed and when we have assured you we do not regard our own Advantage in what is
allowed to us we may be allowed to tell you without any ill
usage that we wonder when you are sensible of the publick

Charge of the Country you should propose to transcribe so long a Journal of the Committee at this time a Day when the Sessions is so near a Conclusion, Therefore propose it be assented to as it now stands and as to the foregoing dispute this Agreement will not be Conclusive but the matter may be more Calmly and leisurely debated another Sessions

Signed ꝑ order W Bladen Cl Council

Major Taylor & M<sup>r</sup> Frisby bring from the house the Journal of the Committee of Accounts with the following Message

By the House of Delegates October 3<sup>d</sup> 1704

Since your Honours will not Consent to what we have here reasonably proposed as to Duplicates for the future we are Discharged from that Proposal and are obliged to assert our Priviledges to futurity. We cannot fill up the Bill without your Honours Assent to the Journal of Accounts since you have proposed it two ways and we now send it to the Intent your Honours may Endorse what your Result is

Signed ꝑ order W Taylard Cl Del.

Which being read the mony and Tob° Allowances in the said Journal of Accounts are assented to by the hon:ble Council and sent to the House by Col Jenkins

Came M<sup>r</sup> Elias King with three Engrossed Bills for apportioning the publick Levy this present which was assented to by the Council and sent by Col Hamond M<sup>r</sup> Sanders, and M<sup>r</sup> Coursey Who are ordered to acquaint M<sup>r</sup> Speaker and the House that his Ex<sup>cy</sup> is ready to receive them and pass the Bills agreed to this Sessions Came M<sup>r</sup> Speaker and the members of the House of Delegates and bring with them the following Bills Engrossed and Assented to as well by the House of Delegates as her Majesty's hon:ble Council.

1. An Act for quietting Possessions Enrolling Conveyances and securing the Estates of Purchasers
2. An Act for Settlement of an annual Revenue on her Majest<sup>ies</sup> Governour within this Province for the Time being
3. An Act appointing Court Days in each respective County within this Province
4. An Act against Ingrossers and Regrators
5. An Act for publication of Marriages
6. An Act for killing of Wolves and Crows
7. An Act for ascertaining the Expences of the Council and Delegates of Assembly Commissioners of the Provincial and County Courts of this Province.

Original
Journal.    8.   An Act to make valid good and Effectual all manner of
Process and Proceedings from the year 1692 till this Time
   9.   An Act relating to the Standards of English Weights
and Measures
   10.   An Act imposing 9ᵈ ꝑ Gal on Rum Wine Spiritts and
Brandy from Pensilvania and its Territorys into this Province
   11   An Act for limitation of Certain Actions for avoiding
Suits at Law
   12.   An Act for directing the manner of suing out Attachments and limiting the Extent of them
   13.   An Act against Excessive usury
   14.   An Act for the Preservation of Several Harbours and
Landing Places within this Province
   15.   An Act for declaring the Grantees of Land lying within the Indians Land may have any Action of trespass against
such Persons as Carry away Timber under pretence of having
bought the same of the Indians
   16.   An Act prohibiting Commissioners Sherriffs Clerks and
Deputy Sherrˢ to plead as Attorneys in the respective County
Courts where they bear office
   17.   An Act prohibiting Masters of Ships or other Persons
from transporting or Carrying away out of this Province any
Persons without passes
   18.   An Act confirming to the Governour the duty of 3ᵈ ꝑ
Ton on the Burthen of Ships and Vessels.
   19.   An Act for the Advancement of natives and Residents
of this Province
   20   An Act Enabling William Sweatnam of Talbot County
to sell Lands &c.
   21.   An Act Enabling Col Edward Dorsey to sell Lands
and Houses in Annapolis
   22.   An Act declaring the altering or scratching out the
mark of tobacco or altering the Quality after received Felony.
   23.   An Act for appointment of Constables and what relates to their office
   24.   An Act for publication of all Laws of this Province
   25.   An Act for recording all Laws in the Secretᵗʸˢ office
   26.   An Act to stay Execution after 10th of May yearly
   27.   An Act for Amerciaments in the Provincial and County
Courts
   28.   An Act Confirming Tithes of Land given to Churche's
use.
   29.   An Act for better Administ of Justice in the Court of
Chancʳʸ
   30   An Act imposing 3ᵈ ꝑ Gallon on Rum Wine &c.
Negroes and Irish Servants

31. An Act directing the manner of Electing and Sumon- Original
ing Delegates &c to Serve in succeeding Assembl^ies Journal.
32 An Act for ascertaining the Bounds given to the use
of the Nanticoke Indians
33. An Act ascertaining Damage on protested Bills
34. An Act for marking and making the heads of Rivers
and Creeks &c passable for Horse and Foot
35. An Act for taking Special Bayle &c.
36. An Act prohibiting the Inhabitants of this Province to
carry Liquors to Indian Towns
37. An Act regulating Ordinar^ies &c.
38. An Act securing Persons rights to Town Lands
39. An Act declaring the Division of Several Count^ies to
be firm and Stable
40 An Act for settling Lands on Susannah Blaney
41. An Act for confirming the last Will of Charles Ash-
comb John Whinfel and John Burnam
42. An Act for Impost on Several Commodit^ies Exported
43. An Act causing Jurors and Witnesses to come to Court
44. An Act for speedy Conveying publick Lett^rs and
Packetts
45. An Act impowering Comm^rs of County Courts to levy
tob° for defraying County and Parish Charges.
46. An Act securing Merch^ts Tob° and others after received
47. An Act for relief of Creditors in England ag^t Bankrupts
48. An Act restraining the Extortions of Sheriffs &c.
49. An Act for confirming purchases made by County
Courts
50. An Act declaring how naturaliz^n fees shall be paid
51. An Act for the Encouragement of the Traders of this
Province
52. An Act for natural^zn of Otho Othoson
53. An Act prohibiting Pensilvania Trade
54. An Act Ascertaining the Gauge of Tob° Hhds.
55. An Act to Encourage Persons to build Watermills
56 An Act laying Impost of 3^d ꝑ Hh^d for defraying publick Charges.
57. An Act providing Evidence to prove fforeign debts
58 An Act for securing Parochial Librar^ies
59. An Act for punishing Adultery and Fornication
60. An Act for paym^t of Criminal Fees
61. An Act relating to Servants and Slaves &c.
62. An Act ascertaining the height of Fences &c.
63. An Act for direction of Sherriffs &c.
64. An Act reviving the Land Law &c.

65.   An Act Encouraging Tillage &c.
66.   An Act for punishing of Blasphemy &c.
67    An Act reviving the Petitionary Act of Free Schools
68.   An Act to prevent the Growth of Popery
69    An Act for Speedy Tryal of Criminals &c.
70.   An Act for better Admin$^n$ of Justice in probat of Wills
&c.
71.   An Act for Appeals and Errors &c.
72.   An Act for ordering the militia &c.
73.   An Act commanding masters to publish freights
74.   An Act rectifying the ill Practices of Attorneys
75.   An Act for Limitation of officers Fees.
76.   An Act of repeale
77.   An Act declaring Sev$^l$ former Acts to be in force
78.   A Bill for apportioning the publick Levy
To every of which Bills his Ex$^{cy}$ was pleased to assent and
Enacted them into Laws by underwriting them Severally
Thus on Behalf of her Majesty &c
I will this be a Law
John Seymour

And likewise sealed them severally with the broad Seal of
this Province which being done his Ex$^{cy}$ was pleased to say
That he Thanked them for their Earnest endeavours in revising the Laws pursuant to her Majest$^{ies}$ royal Instructions
and hoped that these Gentlemen who were Magistrates and
Justices in their Several Count$^{ies}$ would take Care to see them
put in Execution
After which his Excell was pleased to prorogue them to the
fifth day of December next.
W Bladen   Cl Council.

# PROCEEDINGS AND ACTS

OF THE

# GENERAL ASSEMBLY

# OF MARYLAND.

*At a Session held at Annapolis, September* 5*–October* 3, 1704.

CHARLES CALVERT, LORD BALTIMORE,

*Proprietary.*

JOHN SEYMOUR,

*Governor.*

---

THE LOWER HOUSE OF ASSEMBLY.

Maryland ss
  Journal⸳⸳
September ⸳⸳
Lady Anne ⸳⸳
and Ireland ⸳
of our Lord ⸳
  The house ⸳
Writt of Ele⸳⸳
bearing date⸳
Lord 1704 ⸳
Severall an⸳ ⸳
them to ma⸳⸳
respective C
serve as De⸳⸳
aforesaid t⸳ ⸳
of Annapo⸳⸳
being on tw⸳⸳
appeard as ⸳
champ Es⸳⸳
Watts M⸳ ⸳⸳
M⸳ Thomas ⸳
Wells For ⸳
Charles Gr⸳⸳
For Calver⸳
Jn⸳ Macall ⸳
Dent Esq⸳ ⸳⸳
Edward Do⸳
For Talbot⸳ ⸳
chester Cou⸳⸳
Joseph E⸳⸳⸳
Thomas F⸳ ⸳
Georges C⸳⸳
Magruder.
  Upon ca⸳⸳
lowing Mem
rard Fouli⸳ ⸳
County ⸳⸳⸳
Hugh Eccl⸳⸳
feild Esq⸳ i⸳⸳
  Afterwar⸳⸳
that they f⸳⸳
M⸳ W⸳ De⸳⸳

Maryland ss. P. R. O.<br>B. T. Md.<br>Vol. 17.

Journall of the house of Assembly Begun the fifth day of September in the third Yeare of the Reigne of our Sovereigne Lady Anne by the Grace of God of England Scotland France and Ireland Queen defender of the faith &cᵃ And in the Yeare of our Lord One thousand Seaven hundred and four.

The house of Assembly being calld by Vertue of her Majestys Writt of Election issued out of the High Court of Chancery bearing date the Twenty fifth day of May in the Year of our Lord 1704 And direct'd to the Citty of Sᵗ Marys and the Severall and respective County's of this province Commanding them to make choice of Four sufficient and·Able men in each respective County and two for the Citty of Sᵗ Mary's afd to serve as Deputys and delegates for the said Citty and Countys aforesaid to be and personally appear at the Towne and porte of Annapolis upon the fifth day of Septembᵣ aboue recited being on tuesday in the Year of our Lord 1704 on Which day appeard as follows Vizt For Sᵗ Marys Citty George Muschamp Esqᵣ For Sᵗ Marys County Mᵣ Thoˢ Beale Mᵣ Wᵐ Watts Mᵣ Wᵐ Asquith and Mᵣ peter Watts For Kent County Mᵣ Thomas Smith Esqᵣ Mᵣ Wᵐ Frisby Mᵣ Elias King Mᵣ Jnᵒ Wells For Ann Arrundell County Samˡ Young Esqᵣ Majᵣ Charles Greenberry Mᵣ Iohn Hammond and Mᵣ Ioseph Hill For Calvert County Mᵣ Robert Skinner Mᵣ Iohn Leach Mᵣ Inᵒ Macall & Mᵣ Thomas How For Charles County Wᵐ Dent Esqᵣ Mᵣ Iames Smallwood For Baltemore County Coll Edward Dorsey Mᵣ James Phillips And Mᵣ Francis Dellahyde For Talbott and Somersett Countys none appear'd For Dorchester County Majᵣ John Taylor Mᵣ Iohn Hudson and Mᵣ Ioseph Ennalls For Cecill County Mᵣ Edward Blag Mᵣ Thomas Frisby Coll Wᵐ Peirce & Mᵣ Wᵐ Dare For Prince Georges County Mᵣ Wᵐ Barton Mᵣ Robert Tyler and Mᵣ Samˡˡ Magruder.

Upon calling over the same were found Wanting these following Members Mᵣ Iames Hay for Sᵗ Marys Citty Mᵣ Gerrard Foulk and Mᵣ Wᵐ Stone for Charles County Talbott County All wanting Somersett County All wanting Mᵣ Hugh Eccleston of Dorchester County and Thomas Greenfeild Esqᵣ for Prince George's County Wanting.

Afterwards it was concluded by the members then present that they Attend his Excy and Councill and that 'tis desir'd Mᵣ Wᵐ Dent on their behalfe Acquaint his Excy that pursuant

P. R. O.
B. T. Md.
Vol. 17. to her Majestys Writt there are Twenty nine Members mett And to know his Excys pleasure whither with that Number of Members they might proceed to Election of a Speaker in order to goe on business.

The house thereupon Attended his Ex^cy and Councill And the said M^r Dent having Acquainted his Ex^cy as Aforesaid whither they should proceed to the Choice of A Speaker Thereupon his Ex^cy was pleas'd to Signify he thought there were A Sufficient number to Compose A house to make choice of A Speaker which he. desird Might be Speedily done that they might proceed to dispatch business.

And thereupon the Members tooke their leave Withdrew and repaird to the Stadthouse And then those Members togeather with Baltemore County then Appearing proceeded to make choice of their Speaker And by a Gen^ll Vote Nemine Contradicente they made Choice of W^m Dent Esq^r their Speaker And plac't him in the Chaire Accordingly.

Which being done they repair'd to the Councill Chamber where they presented their Speaker to his Ex^cy the Governour Where M^r Speaker made a Short Excusatory Speech disabling himself by reason of some imperfections and humbly prayd his Ex^cy to direct the house to make choice of some more able memb^r of that house To Which his Ex^cy replied that he did very well Allow of their choice for Which he returnd his Ex^cy humble thanks for thinking him worthy the Execution of a place of so Great charge And trust promising him to use his Uttmost endeavour care and dilligence therein And so offerrd unto him in the name and on behalfe of the said house of Assembly that they might have their Accustomd and Usuall previledges Access to his Ex^cys person upon Urgent occasions and Free liberty of Speech w^ch was granted And his Ex^cy was pleasd to say he would send some of the Councill and Clerk' to see them Quallifyed and so soone as the house is setled he would Acquaint them the occasion of Calling this Assembly.

Thereupon the Speaker with the rest of the members repaird to their house where M^r Speaker returns them thanks for the honour done him in their choice promising them to discharge that great trust layd on him According to the best of his Abillity

Ordered that the house meet at the Stadt house every day during this Sessions by Eight A Clock in the Morning and Sitt till twelve And so from two ti'l six in the afternoone.

Propos'd Whither it be not necessary to know of his Ex^cy the Governour Whither those members that have Allready taken the oaths appointed by Act of parliam^t are enjoynd to take the same againe, thereupon

Resolved M$^r$ Sam$^{ll}$ Young M$^r$ Charles Greenberry and M$^r$ P. R. O.
George Muschamp attend his Ex$^{cy}$ and Councill to know their B. T. Md. Vol. 17.
pleasure therein

They returne and informe the house that his Ex$^{cy}$ was pleas'd to say that the severall members must take them All Anew It being A new Sessions of Assembly and According to the Custom of England in such cases.

The honoble Thomas Tench In$^o$ Addison Thom$^s$ Brooke and W$^m$ Holland Esq$^{rs}$ from the Councill togeather with M$^r$ W$^m$ Bladen their Clerk enters the house to Administer the Oaths which were tendered.

The honoble speaker George Muschamp Esq$^r$ M$^r$ W$^m$ Watts M$^r$ W$^m$ Aisquith M$^r$ Peter Watts Coll Thom$^s$ Smith M$^r$ W$^m$ Frisby M$^r$ Elias King M$^r$ Iohn Wells M$^r$ Sam$^{ll}$ Young M$^r$ Charles Greenberry M$^r$ Ioseph Hill M$^r$ Rob$^t$ Skinner M$^r$ Iohn Leach M$^r$ Iohn Macall M$^r$ Thom$^s$ Howe M$^r$ Iames Smallwood M$^r$ Edward Dorsey M$^r$ Iames Maxfeild M$^r$ Iames Phillips M$^r$ Francis Dollahyde M$^r$ Edward Blag M$^r$ Thomas Frisby Coll W$^m$ Peirce M$^r$ W$^m$ Dare M$^r$ W$^m$ Barton M$^r$ Rob$^t$ Tyler and M$^r$ Sam$^{ll}$ Magruder having taken the oath of Allegiance and Abhorrency and the oath of Abjuration and signe the same and test severally only M$^r$ Iohn Hamond A member for Ann Arrundell County refus'd the same.

M$^r$ Speaker having taken the chaire the rest of the members took their places Accordingly

The house adjourned till to morrow morning Nine A Clock.

## Wednesday Sept$^r$ 6$^{th}$ 1704

The house mett againe and being calld over were all present as Yesterday only M$^r$ Iohn Hamond who refus'd the oaths.

The house Nemine Contradicente made choice of W$^m$ Taylard to be their clerke and

Order'd that M$^r$ Charles Greenberry and Major Iames Smallwood goe with him to present him to his Ex$^{cy}$ and Councill that they may See him quallified.

They returne and Acquaint M$^r$ Speaker that they have seen the Clerke quallifyd And that his Ex$^{cy}$ was pleas'd to say he well approvd of their choice and would grant him A Commission

Orderd by the house that the Oath of Clerk of the Assembly taken by the said W$^m$ Taylard be here entred viz$^t$

I William Taylard doe swear that I will well and truely Execute the office of Clerke of the house of Delegates According to the best of my power Skill knowledge and Under-

P. R. O.
B. T. Md.
Vol. 17. standing and that I will make true and fair entrys of the
Severall proceedings in the house and fair Journal thereof
returne into the Secretary's Office According to law.
So help me God.

M^r Thom^s Greenfeild A member for prince Georges County
M^r Rob^t Gouldesborough of Talbott County   M^r Thomas
Beale of St. Marys County enters the house And M^r Iohn
Taylor M^r Iohn Hudson and M^r Ioseph Ennalls who had liberty
yesterday to take their ease being long on the Water alsoe
now enters the house and Orderd that Major Iames Small-
wood and M^r Sam^ll Young attend his Ex^cy and Councill to see
them take the oaths.
They returne and say they have seen them severally Sworne
And signe test and take the oath of Abjuration
Thereupon they tooke their place in the house.   Produced
A transcript of the Rules and orders of this house Which
being read And signed Is ordered to be sett up in the same
for the members thereof upon all occasions to peruse
Mooved by A member of this house on behalfe of M^r Richard
Dallam and some other Clerks formerly employd that they
being capeable may againe be employd on the like services
Therefore orderd that M^r Richard Dallam and M^r In^o Col-
lins Attend as Clerks on the Committee of Laws and likewise to
doe other Services of Writing as shall be by the house requird.
And likewise M^r Thomas Bordley is appoint^d Clerke of the
Comittee for Stating the publiq Accounts &c^a
Resolv'd that M^r Iames Wooten Minister of St. Anns par-
rish be desired to read prayers morning and evening in the
house of Delegates.
Resolvd that George Valentine be continued in the Office
of Serjeant Attendant to this house And that he cause the
Drum to be beaten and hoist the flagg at the Usuall times
And likewise Resolvd that Moses Adney be and is by the
house appointed doorkeeper.
Moov'd by A member of the house whither it be not necessary the foregoing officers be remind'd of their dutys
Thereupon Resolvd that George Vallentine and Moses
Adney be calld into the house, who appear'd and M^r Speaker
was pleasd to Acquaint them that the house had Continued
them in their Severall Offices Therefore Advis'd them that
forasmuch as they are privy to some proceedings in this house
not to devulge any the Secretts or debates thereof as they
would Answer it at their Perrills Which they promis'd Strictly
to observe & likewise the said Vallentine is put in minde of
keeping the Gate cleansing the towne ditch and keeping the

Towne fence in good repaire, the said M^r Valentine, made r. R. o, B. T. Md. Vol. 17. Answer that he will for the future use his endeavour to per- forme the same and do what els belongs to the duty of his office to the Sattisfaction of All persons Concernd.

M^r W^m Bladen Clk of the Councill' enters the house and delivers M^r Speaker the Severall Writts of Election (Somersett County only Excepted)

Orderd they be laid by till calld for

Order'd that George Muschamp Esq^r and M^r John Taylor Attend his Ex^cy in Councill to Acquaint him that M^r Speaker & the rest of the members are ready to Attend his Ex^cy when he please to comand them

They returne and say they deliverd their Message And that his Ex^cy was pleasd to signify to them that he should be ready to receive them in a Small time and that he would give the house notice thereof

Soone After the Honoble Iames Saunders Esq^r enters the house and Acquaint'd M^r Speaker that his Ex^cy required him and the rest of their Members to give their imediate Attendance on his Ex^cy at the Councill Chamber

Thereupon M^r Speaker and the rest of the members Attended his Ex^cy and Councill in the Councill chamber.

Then his Ex^cy was pleasd to signify to the house the reason of their being now calld togeather by speaking to them As follows viz^t

M^r Speaker and You Gent Delegates.

The reasons why the last Sessions was so short and Consequently so little of the publiq business finished, J presume can be no new things to this present Assembly And as most of her Maj^ts Royall instruccons were postponed to this meeting J cannot doubt of your Advise and ready concurrence in those weighty matters so heartily recomended by her Gracious Majesty the Queen to your Serious consideration

Gent, they shall be severally laid before you being thought by her Maj^ty and her noble wise English privy Councill to be Absolutely necessary And Advantageous to Your Countrey and her Maj^ts Royall Sanction to the laws revisd and Enacted now will eternize the prudent Conduct of you Gent delegates.

I dare Assure you there can't be any thing maturely proposed for the reall Good and prosperity of this province but her Ma^ty will Assent to it with All the Cheerfull Willingness becoming the Royall Beneficence of so good a Queen and am as Sure will be displeasd to finde any Slye insinuacons (that ill grounded Iealousys may foment to the disadvantage of the publiq) should rendér what her Maj^ty Graciously design'd for your wellfare and happy Establishment inefectuall.

P. R. O.  B. T. Md.  Vol. 17.

Gent   As I am a Very plain dealer I would not have my Sincerity mistaken nor my Good intentions for Your Service interpreted designing for I as much despise that or flattery as You can abominate double dealing.

Therefore I Againe recomend the honour and tranquillity of Your Country togeather with her Majestys Jnstruccons to your Consideration that the Unanimity of Your Councills may demonstrate your steddy Loyalty to her Majestys Government And the good Wholsome laws Enact'd this Sessions may Assure the whole world of Your prudent hearty concurrence in this Criticall Juncture.

Gent   J will never determine any thing of moment without laying it before her Maj⁺ˢ honoᵗ Councill here for their Advice and decision I think my self oblidgd in honour and Conscience to lett the representatives of this Province know from time to time whatever is design'd or carry'd on against the true interest of their Countrey:   Mʳ Speaker shall for your perusall have the best information of the perticulers I cann at p'sent Give, And leave it to your wiser determinacon, if any parte of the project ought to be made publiq till I have the true Account of the Whole contrivance by an Authority we must All rely on in the interim cannot doubt but You will think of some propper Methods to Obviate any Clandestine Machination levelld agᵗ Your Constitution.

If Your interest and fortunes become soe precarious to be at the disposall of an Jll Naturd neighbourhood Without Your Approbation or consent lay it not at my doore, since I haue done the duty of your friend and Governour truely to Advertise you what is negotiating to yoʳ disadvantage, for while I have the honoʳ to be distinguishd by her Maj⁺ˢ Comicon I would Gladly have the province support its reputation of being independant from everything but England, And as nothing sure cann be so deare to mankind as to lett the lasting ornaments of Wise industrious progenitors be transmitted to posterrity all prejudiciall Jnnovacons ought to be Avoided with care And resolution

And, Since A devine providence has in A good measure Established Christianity here I cannot but take notice that the many Domestick Imorallity's within this province are great Scandall to the Religion wee profess And at this day You and our European friends are at such a Vast expence to Maintayne, There are others who bid defyance to all Magistracy and laws which I hope will Awaken you to Amend what is defective in order to suppress these Unwarrantable practises Scarce ever heard of in Civillizd Country's for if Your laws allready made are of force to Curb these disorders Its A Very Great omission they are not Vigourously Asserted to punish these and P. R. O. B. T. Md. Vol. 17. All other known vices by that Authority. Vertue and religion are the true ingredients to make any Country flourish as A true obedience to the laws is the best true signe of honest Good people A Charracter I would ever have you preserve, that All mankind may know and Vallue yo<sup>r</sup> Conduct  o ning heartily with me in endeavours and Wishes You may prosper many and many Yeares.

Gent. With all Modesty I acquaint you that nothing has made me Uneasy Since my Arrivall in this province but the illness of my house And if you shall think I deserve noe better Accomodation during my Abode in the province ʝ must Acquiece with your Sentiments and endevour to be contented being Resolved never to ask for or expect what at any time You ludge Unreasonable.

ʝ am very confident there's no one here present but beleives there was An absolute necessity of Convening a New Assembly and Since her Majestys councill thought this A propper time to meet them I cann never doubt but Your debates will be temper'd with soe discreet a moderacon and candour this Will be no long but an happy Session that our enemy's abroad may See Wee are Unanimous and Vigilant, our freinds at home know Wee are heartily loyall And the good people you represent thanke you for your Loyalty to our Sovereigne, Your care of and fidellity to your County with your Unwearied Solicitudes and endeavours to oppose All her Majestys Enemy's whatsoever And those likewise who shall ever pretend to disturb the peace Wellfare and Union of this province under any specious pretence whatsoever.

The dispatch of the many Great Affaires before you will be A very Generous Ease to the province And as true A satisfaction to me being obvious to All considering persons what A detriment tis to every Gent mett here on this occasion to be detained longer then the publiq Service may reasonably require, And the charge of the Countrey I hope may not be an Impropper consideration to ripen your debates within the Compass Your better ludgments may thinke necessary to bring this Sessions to an honourable Conclusion

Which being ended M<sup>r</sup> Speaker and members having taken leave of his Ex<sup>cy</sup> and Councill) returnd againe to the house And M<sup>r</sup> Speaker having taken the chaire

ʝts orderd that his Ex<sup>cys</sup> Speech be read in the house.

Which being read its resolv'd that the consideration thereof be referrd till fryday next in the Afternoone.

Moov'd by A Member of this house that A Comittee of Election and privileidges might goe forth which was by the

P. R. O.
B. T. Md.
Vol. 17. house thought necessary And thereupon the house appointed
Coll Edward Dorsey M$^r$ W$^m$ Frisby M$^r$ Robert Gouldes-
borough M$^r$ Iohn Macall And M$^r$ Francis Dollahyde to be A
Comittee of Election and privileidges to Examine such matters
that come before them and make reporte thereof to the house.

M$^r$ Thomas Greenfeild Coll Iames Maxwell and M$^r$ Iohn
Wells are by the house appointed A Comittee to enquire
into the Agrievances of the province and are order'd to make
report to the house of their proceedings.

Resolvd by the house Nemine Contradicente that one and
twenty Members and M$^r$ Speaker shalbe sufficient to compose
A house to proceed upon business

The house Adjourn'd till two A Clock in the afternoon

Post Merediem

The house mett againe According to Adjournm$^t$ and being
calld over the members were p$^r$sent as in the morning.

Moov'd by a Member that the Iournall of last Assembly be
read to discover what referrences there are to this present
Assembly therefore Resolv'd that the Iournall of the last Sessions of Assembly held at Annapolis the 26 day of Aprill last
be read in the house upon reading thereof this house finde
Severall proposalls referrd to the consideracon of this Assembly Therefore have thought fitt they be now Consider'd And
for that purpose the house have order'd perticuler remarks to
be made of them to be laid before the house for their Consideracon

Order'd that the Gent Appointed for their Comittees goe
forth upon their business.

Upon reading and debating one referrence of last Assembly relating to revising the laws

The house Nemine Contradicente Resolves it. Absolutely
necessary that the whole body of laws be revisd And that
Message be sent his Ex$^{cy}$ to signify the same.

Bill regulating ordinary's and limitting the Number of them
&c$^a$ Deliverd to M$^r$ Watts who is order'd to carry the same to
the Clerke of the Comittee of Laws that it may be fairly transcribed, and ready to be laid before the house to morrow
morning.

The Severall Comittees enter the house.

M$^r$ W$^m$ Watts Acquaints M$^r$ Speaker that his Ex$^{cy}$ had
Comanded him M$^r$ Thomas Beale and M$^r$ Peter Watts to Attend him in Councill upon some matters that lye before them
Therefore prayd liberty of the house to give their Attendance
as Was requir'd, Which being granted they departed the house
but soone After returnd and tooke their places in the house.

Orderd that the message for revising the laws be prepard
against the morning which follows Viz^t

By the house of Delegates Sept^r 6^th 1704
Upon reading and debating the laws This house Nemine
Contradicente Resolves it is Absolutely necessary that the
whole body of the laws be revis'd and that it be now done Accordingly.   If therefore Your Ex^cy and Councill have any thing
to offer on this Subject this house is ready to receive it
Signd ꝑ order W^m Taylard Cl house Del

The honoble Thomas Tench and Robert Smith Esq^rs from
the Councill enters the house and delivers M^r Speaker the
following Message

By his Ex^cy the Govern^r & Councill in Assembly
Sept^r 6. 1704.
Gent   Whereas his Ex^cy is inform'd that one Edward Hilhard
had Without any Authority from his Ex^cy or this board made
use of his Ex^cys name to require three of the houses members
to Come from the house before his Ex^cy the Govern^r and
Councill   Gent Wee doe assure you that the said Hilhard did
the same of his owne head And that his Ex^cy the Govern^r and
this board did not ever in the least Give any such directions
but will Always be very tender of the rights and privileidges
of the house of Delegates And therefore take this occasion to
prevent any Misapprehensions.
Signd ꝑ order W Bladen Clk Coun

Which being read in the house It is Resolved the same be
Answerrd in the Morning.
The house Adjourns till to morrow morn Eight A Clock.

Thursday Sept^r 7^th 1704
The house mett againe and being All calld over were present as Yesterday.
M^r Gerrard Fowlke a member for Charles County enters
the house and its Orderd that Coll Iames Smallwood goe with
him to his Ex^cy to see him sworne.
He returnes and says he saw him take the oaths According
to Act of parliament and signe the test and oath of Abjuracon

P. R. O
B. T. Md.
Vol. 17. Orderd Mʳ Robert Gouldesbourough Mʳ Thomas Frisby Mʳ Iames Phillips & Mʳ Iohn Wells carry up to his Exᶜʸ and Councill the following message.

By the house of Delegates.
Septʳ 7. 1704

In Answer to A message sent to this house from his Exᶜʸ the Governour and the honoble Councill by Thomas Tench & Robert Smith Esqʳˢ Yesterday the house orderd that the thanks of this house be given to his Exᶜʸ for this kind Expressions of A tender reguard he hath of the libertys and privileidg's of the members of this house Exprest in the said Message. and they doe humbly hope that his Exᶜʸ will be pleasd to Continue the same.          Signd ℗ order
                                              W Taylard Cl ho: Del

They returne and say they deliverd their Message.
Moovd by a member that for-as-much as Mʳ Iohn Hamond A Delegate for Ann Arrundell County has Absolutely denied and refused the oaths Appointed by law & is Altogeather uncapeable to Serve in this house
Jt is therefore orderd that Mʳ Speaker issue his Warrant to her Majᵗˢ principall Secretary or his Dᵗʸ to make out A new Writt of Election for A member instead of Mʳ Hamond to serve in this Assembly.
Which Accordingly issued, and sent the honol Secretary or his Deputy by the hands of George Muschamp Esqʳ
Whoe returnes and says he deliverd the same.
Orderd by the house that Mʳ Samˡˡ Young one of her Majestys Iustices of the provinciall Court and A member of this house call before him George Vallentine Serjeant Attendant and Moses Adney door keeper And Admster· to them an oath that they or either of them shall not directly or indirectly declare or devulge any of the debates or Secretts of the house so long as they Continue in such offices.
Mʳ Young returnes into the house and says he has Admstred such oath to them
Bill for regulating ordinary's &cᵃ brought into the house.
Read the first time & endorsd that it doe pass and ·prayd that his Exᶜʸ the Governour & Councill will concurr therewith
          Signd ℗ order Wᵐ Taylard Clk. house· Del.

Sent up to his Exᶜʸ and Councill By Majʳ Wᵐ Barton Major Iohn Taylor Mʳ Robert Tiler Mʳ Samˡˡ Magruder Mʳ Ioseph Hill Mʳ Ioseph Ennalls and Mʳ Iohn Hudson

They returne and say they deliverd the same. Moov'd by P. R. O.<br>B. T. Md.<br>Vol. 17.
A member of the house that the towne pasture is still bur-
thened with Stocks of horses cattle hoggs sheep & goats to
the prejudice of the publiq Therefore its Advisd that the law
be revis'd And that such Addicon be made thereto as shall be
thought necessary to suppress the same

Therefore orderd that M<sup>r</sup> Sam<sup>ll</sup> Young and M<sup>r</sup> Ioseph Hill
prepare A bill to remedy the same and add such other
clauses thereto as shall be thought necessary, In order thereto
Severall heads were deliver'd.

The Comittee of Election and privileidges enters the house
and delivers M<sup>r</sup> Speaker A paper of Complaint against A
member of the house.

Upon Which Coll W<sup>m</sup> Peirce A member for Cecill County
was ordered to withdraw and Accordingly he did.

Thereupon orderd the following paper be read and entred
in this Iournall viz<sup>t</sup>, In A Iournall of the proceeding's of an
Assembly at Annapolis the 29 day of Iune Annoq Dni 1701
is Contain'd as followeth Viz<sup>t</sup>

The Iournall of the Comittee of Agrievances was read as
follows, It is offerrd as an Agreivance against the Sherriff of
Cecill County that the Sherriff made A returne in the Yeare
1697 which was Short of the list of taxables Given by the
Constables twenty three.

Alsoe in the Yeare 1698 was returnd Short as ꝑ the Constables List 22 Taxables and in the same Year did Add to the
lists ¾ of A pound of tob ꝑ poll.

In the Yeare 1696 was Allowd 2160<sup>l</sup> tob by the publiq to
the County towards boat-hire for bringing the Delegates of
that County to the Assemb whereof there was never any more
paid that Yeare then 720<sup>l</sup> tob.

Alsoe there was Allow'd to the County in the Yeare 1697
by the publiq 1440<sup>l</sup> tob whereof there was no Creditt given to
the County that Yeare by the Sherriff

Orderd that the Serjeant attendant bring to the barr Coll
W<sup>m</sup> Peirce who being examind in relacon to the matter of fact
Alledgd against him by the Comittee of agrievance acknowl-
edgd the same.

Resolved that the said Comittee of Agrievances call before
them the said W<sup>m</sup> Peirce and State the Account of the Publiq
and that he refund the same and be fined for his misfeazances
to the use of the publiq 1000<sup>l</sup> tobacco.

The Comittee of Agrievances orderd to enquire and finde
out what Coll Peirce had receiv'd on Account of the Publiq
more then what he had given Creditt Enters the house and
reports as follows. Wee have calld Coll W<sup>m</sup> Peirce before us
and doe finde he has recd the sume of 2556<sup>l</sup> tob for which he

P. R. O.
B. T. Md.
Vol. 17. is to be Accountable for to the publiq And Alsoe his fine according to the Afores⁴ order of the house And Also promisd to refund the ¾ part of A pound of tob ℔ poll Which he unjustly leavy'd to the County

A true coppy from the Iournall first above mentioned
                                        Wᵐ Taylard Cl h d

Which was Endorsed as followeth Vizᵗ


By the Comittee of priveleidg's & Elections
                    Septʳ 7ᵗʰ 1704.
It is humbly reported to the house that it is their opinion that the within paper relating to Coll Wᵐ Peirce doth not properly lye before this Comittee.
                    Signd ℔ order Rich⁴ Dallam Cl Com


Which said paper and the report of the Comittee thereon being here read Itt was humbly offerrd to the house by A member whither the said Coll Peirce be not disabled from sitting in the house being so Accriminated as is sett forth against him in the Aforesaid paper.

Therefore put to the Question whether he be quallifyed to sitt in the house or not And being carryd in the affirmative Its orderd by the house that the said Coll Peirce be desired to walk in

He appeard and Mʳ Speaker acquainted him with what was done in the house and so desir'd him to take his place.

The members of Somersett County vizᵗ Mʳ Ios: Gray Mʳ Iohn Waters Mʳ Iohn Iones Mʳ Inᵒ Maclaster enters the house & Orderd that Samˡˡ Young and Thomas Greenfeild Esqʳˢ Attend them to see them take the oaths &cᵃ before his Exᶜʸ and Councill.

They returne and say they saw them sworne signe the test and oath of Abjuration

Moovd by A member of the house that they proceed to read and debate the severall referrences of last Sessions

Resolvd they do proceed

As to the Sallary of ten pounds ℔ Cent Allowd Exʳˢ and Admʳˢ upon Accounts of their Admstration affaires being debated.

Its Resolved that the Allowance of tenn ℔ Cent Sallary shall be Allow'd upon noe Accounts Whatever but where it Shall appear that the Sums of money or tobacco be bona fide recd and paid And for such parte of the decds Estate that shall

remain After All debts and charges paid and disbursd And P. R: O.<br>B. T. Md.<br>Vol. 17.
Acco<sup>ts</sup> passed before the Comissary there shall be no such
duty Allowd but the remainder to be left intire for such as
shall have right to the same.

Resolvd it be Ascertaind by A law.

The house Adjournes till 2 A Clock Afternoon.

Post Merediem

The house mett againe being calld over were All p<sup>r</sup>sent as
in the morning

M<sup>r</sup> W<sup>m</sup> Stone A member for Charles Co<sup>ty</sup> enters the house.

The house being Informd that Coll Tho<sup>s</sup> Smithson A member of this house is come to towne Its Resolvd by the house
that in the gratefull remembrance of the many Eminent Services he has done to this province the whole house with the
Speaker will wait on him to his place in the house which was
done Accordingly

Orderd that M<sup>r</sup> Elias King M<sup>r</sup> Thomas Frisby M<sup>r</sup> W<sup>m</sup> Barton M<sup>r</sup> Ioseph Hill & M<sup>r</sup> W<sup>m</sup> Watts attend the honoble
Thomas Smithson Esq<sup>r</sup> and M<sup>r</sup> W<sup>m</sup> Stone to see them take
the oaths &c<sup>a</sup> before his Ex<sup>cy</sup> in Councill.

They returne and say they saw them sworne & signe the
test and oath of Abjuration & that his Ex<sup>cy</sup> thanks the house
for the house for the hono<sup>r</sup> done to so worthy a person as
Coll Smithson in sending soe many members of the house to
Attend him.

Then was read the following Lre directed to M<sup>r</sup> Speaker Viz<sup>t</sup>

M<sup>r</sup> Speaker

I haue kept my bed this tenn days with A Swelling in my
feet and knees w<sup>ch</sup> is the Cause of my Absence as soon as possibly I cann shall Attend my duty I hope my p<sup>r</sup>sent inabillity will
be Sufficient to excuse who am S<sup>r</sup>          Yo<sup>r</sup> humb Serv<sup>t</sup>

Tuesday 5<sup>th</sup> Sept<sup>r</sup> 1704                    Henry Coursy

Which being read in the house his excuse is Allowd of

Orderd that Coll Tho<sup>s</sup> Smithson M<sup>r</sup> Robt. Goldesborough
M<sup>r</sup> Charles Greenberry M<sup>r</sup> W<sup>m</sup> Stone and M<sup>r</sup> Elias King be
& are by the house appointed A Comittee of laws.

The referrence relating to the Conversion of the Indians
was read & referrd till the morning for consideracon

The proposall of last Session of making A law to suppress
popish preists and others from perverting her Maj<sup>ts</sup> Subjects
& bringing them over to the Church of Rome &c. was read
And the house finding it A matter highly to be considerd

P. R. O.
B. T. Md.
Vol. 17.
Resolvd that it be referrd till the Comittee of laws make their report upon the laws of England on that matter.

The peticon of Mʳ Charles Pye and the resolve thereupon with the referrence of last Assembly was read and debated.   &

Orderd by the house that the Comittee of laws prepare A bill for releife of the peticoner

Orderd the peticon be deliverd the Comittee for that purpose.

Moovd by A member of the house that the land law And the Lord Baltemores objections And the law limitting payment of obligacons be sent for and laid before the house.

Resolved they be sent for.

The referrence of last Assembly relating to the peticon of Mʳ Iohn Whittington for sale of Danˡ Toas land for payment of his Debts was here read But forasmuch as the peticoner does not appear to prosecute the same its further referrd.

The referrence relating to engrossing the laws in partchment Read and debated Resolvd the bills be engrost in partchment

Mʳ Young is desird by the house to treat with Mʳ Richard Dallam about purchasing of partchmᵗ from him for that use and reporte the same to the house.

And likewise resolvd the sd Young send for A quantity of paper and partchment to the Vallue of tenn pound Sterling for the publiq use And that an Ordnance for that purpose be drawne up and sent his Exᶜʸ for concurrence of the honob Councill wᶜʰ follows

By the house of Delegates
September 7. 1704

Whereas this house haue often times found it very difficult to gett paper and partchment for supply of the publiq business therefore thought fitt And its Resolved by the house that Mʳ Samˡˡ Young Trearer for the Westerne Sheare Send for A quantity of paper and partchment out of England that is to say the Vallue of Six pounds Sterling in partchment And four pounds in paper for the publiq use For wᶜʰ the sd Young shall be Allowd to wᶜʰ this house humbly prays the Concurrence of the honoble Councill

Signd p order
Wᵐ Taylard Cl h D

Sent up to his Exᶜʸ p Mʳ Wᵐ Stone
He returnes and says he deliverd the same.

The proposall of last Assembly relating to An Allowance to be made Mʳ Blathwaite Auditor Genˡˡ and referrd to the

Consideracon of this Assembly being here read and debated P. R. O
Its resolv'd that this house Concurrs with the opinion of the B. T. Md.
last Assembly that there is no reason to grant to such An Vol. 17.
officer any Allowance out of the publiq Stock of this province

Coll Francis Ienkins enters the house and delivers M$^r$ Speaker the land law And the law for limitting time for payment of obligacons And the Lord Baltemores observations thereon with other papers thereto relating and departed.

Proposd by A member of this house that some person or persons in England may be appointed to whom the publiq trearers may remitt such bills of Exchange as come to their hands for the publiq Stock soe that if such person or persons faile the trearers may be blameless.

Resolvd Nemine contradicente that such person be appointed And that Coll Nathan$^{ll}$ Blakistone (being agent for this province) be appointed to whom the trearers shall hereafter remitt the said bills.

The Comittee of Election and priveleid'ges enters the house and returns all the Indentures of the severall Countys and Citty of S$^t$ Mary's within this province Except Somersett County and reports that the members therein mencond are All duely Elected and returned And as for Somersett County the indenture is thus endors'd by the Comittee of Election and privileidges Sept. 7$^{th}$ 1704

Upon reading the within Indenture it appeares all the four delegates therein appointed are duely and legally Elected but the Sherriff of Somersett County has not made any due or legall returne as he ought to have done.

Which the Comittee offers for their Consideration

Which being read and debated, This house concurs therew$^{th}$ that the members are duely Elected and that the Sherriff has not done his duty but that his failure is not willfull or prejudiciall to the publiq but is A deficiency in not returning Separate Indentures from each person therefore he is not lyable to the penaltys of the Act of Assembly but however Resolved that this house pray his Ex$^{cy}$ that he may be sumoned to Answer his neglect before his Ex$^{cy}$ & Councill

And orderd A message be sent his Ex$^{cy}$ for that purpose and to be prepar'd against the morning.

Coll W$^m$ Holland from the Councill enters the house and delivers M$^r$ Speaker the ordnance for partchm$^t$ thus Endors'd

By the honob her Maj$^{ts}$ Councill
Sept. 7$^{th}$ 1704.

The honoble her Maj$^{ts}$ Councill Concurr with the Aboue resolve of the house          W Bladen Cl Councill.

The house Adjourns till to morrow morning 8 a clock

P R. O.
B. T. Md.
Vol. 17.

Fryday Sept[r] 8th 1704.

The house mett againe According to Adjournm[t] and being called over were All present as Yesterday.

Read what was done Yesterday.

The mocon of last night relating to the conversion of Indians now lyeing under debate of the house

Putt to the question whither the house shall proceed any further at present upon this mocon or not

Resolvd in the negative

Moovd by a member what care shall be taken to regulate the difference relating to the bounds of land betwixt the Inhabitants of this province and pensilvania.

Resolvd it be referrd to A further consideracon

M[n] Muschamp and M[r] Beale orderd to Attend his Ex[cy] & Councill to desire them to send to the house the papers relating to the case of pensilvania.

They returne with the Af[d] papers and present them to M[r] Speaker.

Orderd the following message relating to the returne of Somersett County Indentures be entred as foll[o]

By the house of Delegates Sept[r] 8. 1704

The Comittee of Election and priveleidges enters the house & reports that upon reading the Indenture it appeard All four Delegates therein appointed are duely Elected but the Sherriff of Somersett County has not made any due and legall returne thereof as by law he ought to doe.

Which the Comittee offers to the house for ther Consideration.

Upon reading the aboue report of the Comittee the house Concurr therewith that the members are duely Elected And that the Sherriff has not done his duty that his failure is not willfull or prejudiciall but only in A Deficiency in not returning Separate Indentures for each person Therefore he is not lyable to the penalty of the Act of Assembly but however wee pray that he may be sumoned to Answer the neglect before his Ex[cy] & Councill.

Signd p ord[r] W[m] Taylard Cl he D

Which being read was sent up to his Ex[cy] and Councill by by M[r] W[m] Watts and M[r] W[m] Aisquith.

They returne and say they deliverd their message.

M[r] Sam[ll] Young Enters the house and reports that he has treated with M[r] Dallam About the purchase of parchment And

that the said M<sup>r</sup> Dallam is willing to part with it for the Coun- P. R. O. B. T. Md. Vol 17.
treys service at the rate of 18<sup>d</sup> ꝑ Skinn which is agreed to by
the house.

The house make choice and doe appoint Coll Thomas
Smith M<sup>r</sup> Ioseph Hill and M<sup>r</sup> Iames Phillips A Comittee for
Stating the publiq Acco<sup>ts</sup>

W<sup>m</sup> Coursey Esq<sup>r</sup> from the honoble Councill enters the
house and delivers M<sup>r</sup> Speaker the following Message Which
was read & orderd to be entred Viz<sup>t</sup>

By his Ex<sup>cy</sup> the Gov<sup>r</sup> & Councill
Sept<sup>r</sup> 8<sup>th.</sup> 1704

The houses Message relating to the omission or mistake
of the Sherriff of Somersett County on the returne of the writt
of Election was recd at this board And the said Sherriff will
be cautiond of the like for the future.

Signd ꝑ ord<sup>r</sup> W Bladen Cl. Co.

The honob Thomas Tench Esq<sup>r</sup> Ino Addison Esq<sup>r</sup> Thomas
Brooke Esq<sup>r</sup> and Robert Smith Esq<sup>r</sup> from the honoble Councill enters the house and delivers M<sup>r</sup> Speaker the following
message.

Sept<sup>r</sup> 8<sup>th</sup> 1704
By his Ex<sup>cy</sup> the Govern<sup>r</sup> & Councill in Assembly.

Gent
Your house now being Setled and resolvd upon revising
the body of laws of this province Wee recomend unto your
Serious consideracon severall of her Maj<sup>ts</sup> Royall instruccons
layd before you the last Assembly Viz<sup>t</sup>

1.  The raising of Supplys for defraying the publiq charge
on which occasion you are to take Especiall care that All
moneys to be leavyd be made lyable to be Accounted for to
her Maj<sup>ty</sup> in England & her Lord High treārer And that no
Imposicon on liquors continue less then one whole Year but
be indefinite without limittacon of time (Except for A temporary end And which shall have its full Effect within A Certaine time) That no laws be reenacted Except on Urgent occasions but in no case more then once without her Majestys
Express Consent

2<sup>d</sup>  That All planters and Christian servants be well & fitly
provided with Arms And that they be listed under good officers And When and as often as Shall be thought fitt Musterd
and trayned whereby they may be in A better readyness for

8

P. R. O.
B. T. Md.
Vol. 17.
the defence of the province And that they appear at Arms at All times as they shalbe requird w^{ch} Wee do propose that this Assembly would oblidge those who pretend for Conscience sake they cannot bear Arms to supply others with horses and Arms

3. That A law be made to punish false musters Mutiny and desertion And for the better preserving Good discipline among Souldiers.

4. That fitt Storehouses be Setled throughout the Province for keeping Arms Amunicon and other publiq Stores.

5. That A Gen^{ll} Survey be made of the whole province and of every County and of All landing places and harbours And Exact mapps transmitted for Engl and that fortifications be erected at the publiq charge in Which the Cheerfull Concurrence of the Assembly is not doubted.

6. That Stocks be provided and publiq work-houses built in Convenient places for employing poore and indigent people.

7. That an Act be past to relieve the Credittors of persons becoming bankrupt in England and having Estates in Maryland.

8 Further you are desired to make Answer to the R Honoble the Lords of trade and Forreigne p̄tacons Letters with the Lord Baltemores objections to the two Acts of Assembly the one for Acertaining the bounds of land And the other for limitting the time for payment of obligacons within this province.

9. It is recomended and proposd whither it may not be propper to make A law to confirme All proceedings since the departure of Coll Blackistone to his present Ex^{cys} Arrivall and Alsoe of the last Assembly.

10^{th} That it be enquird by this Assembly and Acertain'd what laws and Statutes of the Kingdome of England are in force in this province And that measures be taken to haue the severall Acts of parliament of every Sessions Sent from England.

11 That encouragement be given to the inhabitants of this province to Supply the same with rum &c^{a} by exempting them (being owners of Vessells tho' not Countrey built) from the payment of the duty of 3^{d} p Gallon.

12. That A law be made by this Assembly to prevent the importacon by land of rume Wine Strong liquors beer bread flower and horses from pensilvania. And that encouragement be given to tillage by the Inhabitants.

13. That this province do throughly Acquaint th'mselves with the mocons of the piscattaway or Accokick Indians who do not pay their tribute as Usuall and take such measures

upon the reporte of those Indians now o ning the Senecas in
order to warr with the Insharora's both to discover their
Strength and Aliances And likewise to provide for the better
Securety of this province & that All Aliances be setled with
our neighbour Indians.

14.   That Six County Courts in one Yeare are thought too
many and therefore burthensome and cause Great County
leavys whereas here being but two provintiall Courts in A
Yeare the delay of Iustice is Complained of  It is proposed
whither it would not be of Advantage to the province and
the trade thereof.that in every yeare there be held four provinciall Courts two for tryalls and two for Appearances all
which Courts would not Continue much longer or be of much
greater charge then the two at p$^r$sent now are And whither the
Sitting of the County Court Iustices might not be better regulated by taking turns four at A time being enough to hold
A Court whereas there are some times twelve at once upon
the bench that the extravagancy of their Iurisdiction be reasonably limitted As to the sume And that Execution be not Stayd
Untill After the tenth of May Yearly.

15   That the Act of Assembly for pleading discount in barr
be explaind by some publiq Vote or Resolve of the house
being Wilfully mistaken by the Iustices in Severall County
Courts by which practise its feared many perjury's are introduced.

16.   That Effectuall Measures be taken by this Assembly to
oblidge Coopers and others setting up tobacco casq to comply
with and not Exceed the Act of Assembly in the tare of those
casq w$^{ch}$ are Greviously Complaind of by severall Masters of
Shipps and destructive to trade owners and builders of Vessells not knowing how to regulate them for Stowage And by
Which means Alsoe her Maj$^{ts}$ Governour is defeated of Great
parte of the revenue by the Act of Assembly and her Majesty's
Royall instruccons designed & Allotted him.

17.   That the limittacon of Actions on Account is too shorte
so that A Credittor cannot be civill to his Debtor for fear of
that Act which is desired by severall to be Extended for one
Yeare more.

18.   That the Act of Assembly for punishing fornication
and Adultery be explaind when a mans Estate shall redeem
his body.

19.   That All County leavys and Vestrys Accounts be
yearly laid before the Governour & Councill for their inspection

20.   That All freemen be oblidged to give A good Account
of themselves how they gaine their livelyhoods or in default
of their being able to give such Acco$^t$ the Iustices of the
County Court be empowred to place them out to worke and

make corne at such wages as to the said Iustices Shall seem reasonable.

21    That this Assembly would Consider whither it may not be of publiq service to settle a publiq post on each side the bay between Newcastle and Virginia.

22ᵈ    That in the Act for Electing of delegates a Clause be incerted to punish persons having no right to Vote that disturb Elections And that the reasons may be enquired into why Sᵗ Mary's should send two Burgesses And if it were not fitt to encourage this towne being the Seate of Gouernment with that privileidg

23.    And that All protested bills of Exchange should be equall with Specialtys and to be recoverd by Action of debt.

Signd ℗ order W Bladen Cl Co:

Which being read It is resolvd the same be referrd to the consideracon of a full house.

Moovd by A member of this house that the land records of this province are much torne and Abused and lye at A very loose rate and forasmuch as those records being the only Securety Wee have for our reall Estates

Its therefore prayd they may be inspected and that further care be taken of them for the future.

Thereupon orderd that Majʳ Inᵒ Taylor Mʳ Samˡˡ Young Mʳ Thomas Frisby and Mʳ Iohn Leach repair to the land office & view and Inspect the said records And reporte to the house and what condition they are in And What methods may be taken for there better Securety for the future

The house Adjournes till 2 A Clock afternoon

Post Merediem.

The house mett According to Adjournment and being Calld over were All psent as in the morning.

The house now proceeds to reading his Exᶜʸˢ Speech to this house at first opening the Sessions.

Which being read and debated.  It is Resolvd Nemine Contradicente that the same be answer'd in Generall, And its desird by the house that Mʳ Speaker and Mʳ Samˡˡ Young prepare Answer to the same against to morrow morning.

The house now taking under consideration the severall Articles of her Maᵗˢ Instruccons laid before them this day.

1ˢᵗ    Article for Raising Supplys to defray the publ charge &cᵃ Read and fully debated in the house.

Its Resolvd that what money has been raizd has been applyed and to be Applyed to help defray the publiq charge of

the province and Its been an ease to the poorer sorte of peo- P. R. O.
ple by laying it upon the richer the Same being very Small B. T. Md.<br>Vol. 17.
and the Sallary for Collecting Scarce Acceptable to any man,
And its utterly impracticable to be Accomptable to any other
person then has been us'd, Her Maj$^{ts}$ Gov$^r$ being allways upon the place And Sees how its disposed of so that this house
cannot without Apparent prejudice to the Countrey make any
other Alteracon in the method of Accounting for it then what
has been made.

2 & 3$^d$ Articles relating to the Militia and false musters
was likewise read and debated in the house and Jts Resolved
that the present law Stand with some small Alteracon Viz$^t$
that Xtian Negroe Slaves be not included in Musters.

The other Articles referrd to A further consideration

The house Adjourns till to morrow Morning Eight a Clock.


Saturday Sept$^r$ 9$^{th}$ 1704

The house Againe mett according to Adjournm$^t$ being Calld
over All were present as Yesterday only M$^r$ Thom$^s$ Greenfeild.

Read what was done Yesterday.

The house now proceed to debate the other Articles of her
Maj$^{ts}$ royall instructions. Viz$^t$

4. That fitt Storehouses be setled through the province &c$^a$
This Article has been fully Argued & debated.

Its resolvd the Country has noe need to be at such charge
there being Allready A Storehouse built in Annapolis for the
same purpose and provision made by law to Deliver the Arms
and Amunition to the Comanders of each respective Co$^{ty}$
whose Estates are lyable to answer for the same by the law
Allready made which wee thinke at p$^r$sent to be Sufficient

5. Article that a Gen$^{ll}$ Survey be made of the whole province &c$^a$ was also read & debated.

Resolvd that the Complying with this Article is Altogeather
impossible the bounds of the province not being knowne till
the lines of the prop$^{rys}$ be laid out And the whole province
is one entire landing place there being no rocks nor shelves
to hinder it

And the Erecting of fortifications is held impracticable because it cannot be able to answer the ends nor the Countrey
able to bear the burthen

6. Article that Stocks be provided and publiq work houses
built Read and debated.

The house Resolves that the greatest difficulty is in getting
people to work rather then finding work for people And that
the poore are Sufficiently provided for by law there being no

P. R. O.
B T. Md.
Vol. 17.

such thing as beggers goeing from doore to doore for want of employment    Therefore noe Occasion of such work house as proposed.

7$^{th}$    That An Act do pass for reliefe of Credittors ag$^t$ Bankrupts &c$^a$ being read

Its referrd to the Comittee of laws to inspect the laws of England and make their report to the house upon that Subject

8$^{th}$    Article referrd as Above

9    Article As to making A law to confirme all proceedings since Governo$^r$ Blakiston till this time

Resolved A bill be drawne for that purpose.

The other Articles of the instructions referrd for further consideration

Brought into the house the peticon of M$^r$ Joseph Holt Which was here read And orderd the same be entred on this Iournall viz$^t$

### Maryland Dies Saturnij 1704

To the honob W$^m$ Dent Esq$^r$ Speaker of the house of Delegates & the rest of the worthy Members of this honob Assembly convened at the port of Annapolis by his Ex$^{cy}$ In$^o$ Seymour Esq$^r$ her Maj$^{ts}$ Capt. Gen$^{ll}$ & Governo$^r$ of this province

The humble peticon of Joseph Holt late Minister of W$^m$ and Mary parrish in S$^t$ Marys county

Humbly Sheweth

That Whereas some complaints have been made to his Ex$^{cy}$ and the honob Councill of State which greatly reflect upon the conduct of yo$^r$ hono$^{rs}$ peticoner perticulerly as he is A minister of the Church of England, he is much concernd and greivd for the same and especially that his Ex$^{cy}$ has signified his displeasure soe highly against him as to declare him suspended he thinks it his duty to apply himself to this honob house hoping there to finde such a tender sence and compassion in the hearts of All the honoble Members as will commisserate his infelicitys And endeavour to Accomodate these unhappy differences that can noe ways be composed but by his owne submission to the censor of Authority which he humbly presumes to offer by your Hono$^{rs}$ mediation that his Ex$^{cy}$ would vouchsafe to restore him to his former Dignitys

Which extraordinary favours shall Allways be most thankfully Acknowledged And that which Still will be more Gratefull to ingenious Minds It shall lay an eternall obligacon upon your unworthy peticoner to walke more circumspectly According to his holy profession

And When he reaps the fruits of such an Excellent favour he shall not faile to returne all hearty thanks to your hono$^{rs}$

And be encouraged to persevere in the Churches Service P. R. O.<br>B. T. Md.
Wherein he will never forgett to pray for your honours happy- Vol. 17.
ness both in your owne persons and posterrity's whom God
long preserve in peace and tranquillity
Soe prayeth
Your most humble sincere<br>& obed<sup>t</sup> Serv<sup>t</sup> to Command<br>Ios : Holt
Which being read and debated
Its Resolved it be granted upon the peticoners humble
sence of his past Erro<sup>rs</sup> and the Strong Assureance he gives
of forsaking them and Amending his life this house are content to become humble Supplicants to your Ex<sup>cy</sup> for your
favour in making one tryall more of him in hopes that he will
make good in his future life and conversation what is promised
in his peticon which if he failes of that yo<sup>r</sup> Ex<sup>cy</sup> will Suspend
him for ever      Signd p order W<sub>m</sub> Taylard Cl h D.

Orderd it be sent up to his Ex<sup>cy</sup> by M<sup>r</sup> John Wells and M<sup>r</sup>
Robert Skinner
They returne and say they deliverd the same

M<sup>r</sup> Speaker brought into the house the Answer to his
Ex<sup>cys</sup> Speech by him prepar'd, Which was orderd to be read
and entred as followeth viz<sup>t</sup>

To his Ex<sup>cy</sup> the Govern<sup>r</sup>
S<sup>r</sup>
The reason wee did not sooner give Answer to yo<sup>r</sup> Ex<sup>cys</sup>
Speech was because wee were desireous to have as full a
house As could be had on so solemn an Occasion.
Wee have reced and Carefully debated the contents thereof and as Wee are well assured of her Maj<sup>ty</sup> our gracious
Queens goodness and virtue in her unwearyd care and protection of All her subjects and the wise constitucon of her
Government, so wee Esteem our selves very happy in a
Governour that imitates so glorious an Example for Wee cannot but observe through your plaine Elegant discourse A Generous English Zeale for her Maj<sup>ts</sup> service Ioyned with a tender
reguard to the welfare of this province And wee doe and
beleive ever shall Esteeme our Selves Safe and easy under
your wise and Iust Administracon And pray for your continuance
Wee have perusd, And will in due time consider the severall
Articles this day layd before us and wee doubt not but your
Ex<sup>cy</sup> (with due respects to those honoble Gent with you) will

P. R. O.  beleive us the most capeable and propper to informe your
B. T. Md.  Ex^cy how farr the present constitution of this province is Able
Vol. 17.  to comply therewith And that yo^r Ex^cy will be Assur'd that
nothing will be omitted by us that with the safety and good of
our Countrey Wee can doe.

Wee returne you our humble thanks for the intimacon yo^r
Ex^cy is pleasd to give us of some designe carrying on Against
us And beseech you to make the same more plaine to our
Speaker as you were pleas'd to say that we may take suitable
measures therein.

Wee have resolvd the revising our Laws and whatever
appeares deficient therein wilbe provided for Suppression of
Vise and imorality and wee pray your Ex^cy to give Strict
charge to all officers and Ministers through your Government
Whose duty itt is to putt the same laws in Vigorous Execution
by causing the same to be Strictly observed, since good laws
without due Execution & observance are but dead Letters to
noe purpose.

Wee hope your Ex^cy is sattisfyed that Wee do not trifle
away any time but doe Attend the business for Which wee
came And wee Assure you that hitherto our debates has been
moderate and candid And hope none is enclined to foment nor
are Wee to receive any the least Suspiccons or Iealousy of
your Ex^cy since both your words and Actions has given us
suce Ample Assureance of your Generous resolucons of
Governing us by the laws, protecting of us in our rights And
being ready to Assent to any thing for the reall benefitt of this
province And wee are well confirmd in opinion that the hono^r
of our Sovereigne and Welfare of this province are so inseper-
ably Annext that they are never to be parted.

Worthy S^r  Wee are deeply sencible of yo^r Generous and
Just carriage to us and hope you shall Allways finde us A
Gratefull peaceable and modest people And As Wee Pray for
her Maj^ts long and happy reigne soe wee doe for your Government over us.          Signd p order W^m Taylard Cl h D

By the house of Delegates
Sep^r 8 1704

Which being read and approved of by the house was sent
up to his Ex^cy and councill by M^r W^m Frisby Coll Edw^d
Dorsey M^r How M^r Gerrard Fowlke and M^r Francis Dellahyde.
They returne and say they delivered the same.

Rob^t Smith Esq^r from the honob Councill enters the house
and delivers M^r Speaker the peticon of M^r Ioseph Holt returnd
endorsd As followeth

By her Maj^ty^s honob Councill in Assembly

Sep^r 9 1704

P. R. O.
B. T. Md.
Vol. 17.

M^r Ioseph Holts peticon with your endorsment Wherein Wee perceive upon his Importunity's yo^r comisseration (not being fully Acquainted with his enormous life & conversation) has induced You to give him more credit than he can any wise pretend to, much more deserve and so be content to apply for his restoration has been read at this board And Wee Acquaint you that Altho' his Ex^cy is Very willing to gratifye the house in any thing they cann request Yet wee cannot be Content to Advise his Ex^cy to restore A person who has had so many Warnings And yet notwithstanding his many solemn promises and Assurances has soe much Scandalizd his function And prejudiced the service of the Church

Signd ꝑ order W Bladen Cl Coun

Which was here read and Resolved M^r Ioseph Holt the peticoner haue notice thereof

M^r George Valentine Serjeant Attendant ꝑ Permission enters the house and Complaines against Thomas Reynolds who by Vertue of Meane process out of the County Court at s. of one De hinoysa did seize & Arrest the said George during the sitting of this Assembly.

And soe orderd to withdraw.

Whereupon it was Resolvd that the matter of Complaint from an officer of this house is A breach of privileidge.

Therefore orderd that the Serjeant Attendant forthwith bring the said Thomas Reynolds to the barr of this house to Answer the premises.

Proposd by A member of this house that some care be taken for the encrease of Deare by restrayning the people from killing them in the Sumer time.

Which being debated,

The house is of opinion and thinks it not fitt to restrain the Indians from hunting being granted them by Articles of peace and therefore not to restraine the inhabitants

The house adjourns till 2 A Clock in the Afternoone.

### Post Merediem

The house met againe According to Adjournement And being called over were all p^rsent as in the morning.

Proposd by A member that forasmuch as Tanners in this province are Very prejudiciall to the Inhabitants by their making bad leather, Therefore its prayd that Measures may be taken to remedy it

Which being debated in the house

P. R. O.  Its Resolved that the mocon be sett aside at p'sent
B. T. Md.  The house now proceed to debating the Articles of Instruc-
Vol. 17.
cons &c<sup>a</sup>

10<sup>th</sup> Article in 2 parragraphs Viz<sup>t</sup> the first being required What Laws and Statutes of England are in force in this province &c<sup>a</sup> being here read.

Jts Resolved that this being A matter will take up so much time to be considerd of this Assembly because of many other Weighty matters now comes under consideration. But for that its A good Mocon and ought not to dye therefore Orderd that the honoble Thomas Smithson Esq<sup>r</sup> M<sup>r</sup> Robert Goulds-borough M<sup>r</sup> Henry Coursy and M<sup>r</sup> Nicholas Low or any two of them whereof the s<sup>d</sup> Thom<sup>s</sup> Smithson Esq<sup>r</sup> or M<sup>r</sup> Goulds-borough to be one to make inspection into the Statute laws of England. And from thence draw A Collection of What they thinke to be most practicable in this province To which purpose they are empowrd to employ A Clerk to Attend them & Appoint Suitable times for meeting And to make reporte to the next Sessions of Assembly of their proceedings there in for w<sup>ch</sup> they are to be consider'd.

As to the 2<sup>d</sup> pagraph of the tenth Article that measures be taken to have the Severall Acts of parliament of every Sessions Sent from England. Resolved that our Agent be desired to send into this province for our use such Acts of pliament as by that paragraph is required.

Moovd by A member whither it be not of Service to the Countrey to Continue Coll Nathan<sup>ll</sup> Blakiston our Agent as before.

Resolvd that Coll Nathan<sup>ll</sup> Blakiston be continued Agent pursuant to the Resolve of last Sessions.

The peticon of Xpher Goodhand decd now p'ferrd by his widdow and others was here read but

Forasmuch as M<sup>r</sup> Nathaniell Hinson is a party concernd having no notice thereof therefore

Orderd that Sumons goe forth to the sd Hinson to Appeare at the next Sessions of Assembly when & wheresoever it Shall be held that he may be heard in the premises if to him it Shall seem meet

And likewise orderd that notice thereof be given to M<sup>rs</sup> Goodhand.

The house Adjourns till monday Morning 8 A Clock.


Monday Sept<sup>r</sup> 11<sup>th</sup> 1704.

The house mett againe being calld over were present as on Saturday

M$^r$ Iames Hay A member for St. Marys Citty M$^r$ Nic° Lowe P. R. O. B. T. Md. Vol. 17.
A member for Talbot County and M$^r$ Hugh Eccleston for
Dorchester County enters the house.

Orderd that M$^r$ W$^m$ Aisquith and M$^r$ Peter Watts Attend
them to see them sworne in Counc$^{ll}$

They returne and say they have seen them sworne signe
the test & oath of Abjuration

Then was read what was done Yesterday.

The house now proceed to debate the following Article.

11 Article for encouragem$^t$ of Importacon of rum &c.
being read.

Its resolvd by the house that its proper to give encouragem$^t$
as proposd by this Article by Exempting the inhabitants of
this province (who shall buy or build Vessells) from some
duty's as others are lyable to Viz$^t$

1. Resolved the inhabitants be exempted from 3$^d$ ᵱ Gallon

2. That they be exempt from the duty upon negroes and
White Servants

3$^d$ And that All such Shipps & Vessells belonging to the
inhabitants shall pay but ½ Officers fees as others doe.

12. That A law be made for preventing the importacòn of
rum bread beer Flower &c. by land being debated.

Resolved by the house that beer bread English and Indian
Graine horses Mares & tobacco be totally prohibited to continue for three yeares.

Likewise Resolvd that A duty be layd upon rume Spirritts
wine and brandy.

Put to the Vote whither the duty shalbe Six pence or Nine
pence Sterling ᵱ Gallon

Carryd by Majority of Voices that it be 9$^d$ ᵱ Gallon

And resolvd that all duty's on pensilvania Comodity's shall
be paid in the Currant money of this province And that the
navall officers shalbe oblidg'd to receive the same in ready
money And that the Navall Officers take An oath to see this
law put in Execution

13. Relating to the Piscattaway and Accokick Indians was
read, And the house finding this Article wholly to relate to
his Ex$^{cy}$ the Govern$^r$ Therefore his Ex$^{cy}$ is desird to take such
measures therein as he shall thinke most proper to bring the
said Indians to payment of their tribute And to know What
their Alliances are.

The other Articles are referrd to A further consideration

Proposed by A member whither it be not Convenient to
make A law for encouragem$^t$ of tillage

Debated but referrd to A further Consideracon

The honob Robert Smith Esq$^r$ & Iohn Hamond Esq$^r$ enters
the house and delivers M$^r$ Speaker the following mess

P. R. O.
B. T. Md.
Vol. 17. M^r Speaker.

Sept^r 11^th 1704

The parragraph under written came in A letter to me from
an Eminent merchant in Lond Dated the 16 Feb^ry 1703/4
S^r I must by the by hint of A Designe new York hath of
making All the Collonys tributary's unto 'em in order to Support or rather to enrich them and they seem to push the thing
for the ¾ as to have A number to be chosen out of All the
Northern and Southerne Goverments to represent those Collonys and meet at New York instead of their owne Assemblys
and to have one Viceroy and Gen^ll of all the forces of the
Continent And that of Virginia & Maryland &c^a to be depen-
dants under them A project to this Effect is lodged with the
lords.                                                  In° Seymour

Resolvd thanks be given his Ex^cy for the Aboue intimacon
And that A Message be sent for that purpose.


By the house of Delegates 11 Sept^r 1704.

This house returne Your Ex^cy their humble thanks for the
intimacon You were pleasd to give of A designe forming
against our Constitucon and Your Explaining the same by the
message this day sent by the honoble Robert Smith and Iohn
Hamond Esq^rs and pray that you will Allways preserve the
same tender reguard for us Which wee'l endeavour to deserve.
Signd ꝑ order W^m Taylard Cl h D.


Which message being read was sent up to his Ex^cy by Coll
Smith M^r W^m Frisby M^r Iohn Wells M^r Ios, Hill & M^r Robert
Skinner.
They returne and say they deliverd their message
Coll Ienkins and Kenelm Cheseldyne Esq^r enters the house
and delivers M^r Speaker the following message


By his Ex^cy the Govern^r & Councill
Sept^r 11^th 1704

Gent
By a good providence And the cheerfull Assistance of the
publiq and other worthy Gent the Church in this towne is now
in such forwardness that (with the blessing of Allmighty God)
we have proposd to have devine Service cellebrated therein
upon Sunday the 24 Instant At w^ch time the Sacrament will be
Administred Therefore to the end wee may open the said

Church with the Greatest Solemnity Wee are capeable of here P. R. O.
in this remote parte of the world wee desire M^r Speaker and B. T Md.
the house of Delegates Will Concurr to accompany his Ex^cy Vol. 17.
And this board to the said Church at the time of Af^d
Signd ꝑ order W^m Bladen Cl Coun

Which being read is agreed to by the house and Resolved
they will Comply with whats desir'd.

Was read Againe the message brought from the Honoble
Councill by ‵Robert Smith and Iohn Hamond Esq^rs

Resolvd by the house that All possible means be us'd to
prevent the same as being levelld Against her Maj^ts Interest
And the good of this Countrey Therefore orderd that A Comittee be Appointed to consider the many Evills that would redound to her Maj^ts Interest and the Welfare of this province
And that his Ex^cy be prayd to o ne some of the honoble
Councill with the Comittee.

Orderd it be drawne up in A message to his Ex^cy for that
purpose which follows viz^t

By the house of Delegates Sept^r 11. 1704

Upon the Subject in the last message touching A designe
forming Against the Constitution of the Gouernment

Resolved that All possible meanes be used to prevent the
same being levelld against her Maj^ts Interest and the good of
this Countrey And therefore orderd that A Comittee be appointed to consider the many Evills that would redound both
to her Maj^ts interest and the Welfare of this province And that
his Ex^cy be pleasd to o ne some of the honoble Councill with
the Comittee to consider and make reporte And that his Ex^cy
would be pleasd to o ne his interest with ours to prevent the
same. Signd ꝑ order W^m Taylard Cl h D.

Which being read its orderd M^r Sam^ll Young M^r Iohn Leach
& M^r Macall carry the same to his Ex^cy and Councill.

Bill for appointing Constables &c.
Read the 1^st time and do pass.
The house Adjournes till 2 A Clock Afternoon.

Post Merediem

The house mett againe according to Adjournment being
Calld over were All present as in the morning.

Severall bills brought into the house were read

P. R. O.
B. T Md.
Vol. 17.
Bill taking away all Errors &c^a
Read & comitted for Amendment
Bill for Destroying of Crows
Read & comitted for Amendment
Bill directing the manner of Sueing out Attachments.
Read the first time and do pass.
Bill declaring the baptizing of negroes not to Manumitt or sett them free.
Read and Resolvd this bill in the very words be made A branch in the Act relating to Servants & Slaves.
Bill for publication of All laws
Read the first time and do pass
Bill for limittation of Accons.
Read the first time and do pass
Resolved that that the latter clause limitting the time for paym^t of Obligacons in A law Entituled an Act for securing Ex^rs & Adm^rs from double payment of debts and limitting the time for payment of obligacons be wholly left out as Impropper to the Utillity of this province.
Bill ag^t Engrossers and regraters
Read the 1^st time and do pass with the alteracon made.
M^r Young M^r Leach and M^r Macall returne and say they delivered their message.

The following peticon being brought into the house was orderd to be read.

To the Honoble the house of Delegates.
The humble peticon of Jn° Toas Gent Humbly Sheweth to your hono^rs that pursuant to A mocon made to the last Assembly by the Adm^rs of Dan^ll Toas yo^r pet^rs brother for a bill Empowring them to make Sale of the land whereof he died Seizd The said Assembly sent A Sumons to your peticoner in order to shew cause why the said bill should not pass That your peticoner in obedience to the said Sumons Attended this present Assembly since the first Sitting thereof, that true it is that dan^ll Toas decd Your peticoners brother dyed intestate Seizd of A Considerable Estate in fee simple whereby your pet^r is indesputably and apparently the said Dan^lls heire at law And humbly leaves it to your consideration if such an Act (if past be not Contrary to law and Iustice And to the great prejudice And ruine of your peticoner
May it therefore please yo^r hono^rs to put A stop to the said Act And to discharge yo^r petr^r from further Attendance upon the same &
As in duty bound shall ever pray &c

Which being read it is orderd by the house that nothing be P. R. O.
further proceeded upon the peticon of In° Whittington till he B. T. Md.
appeares himselfe and then the peticon of the said Toas to be Vol. 17.
considerd of

The peticon of Cecillia Allford read & Referrd till tomorrow
morning for consideracon

The house Adjourns till to morrow morning 8 A Clock.

Tuesday Sep<sup>r</sup> 12<sup>th</sup> 1704

The house mett againe being calld over were present As
Yesterday.

Read What was done Yesterday.

The house proceeds to debate the Articles &c<sup>a</sup> Viz<sup>t</sup>

14.  Article relating to the provinciall and Co<sup>ty</sup> Courts

Read and Resolvd Nemine Contradicente that the p'sent
Constitucon of our provinciall & County Courts are Sufficient

The latter part of the same Article relating to the stay of
Executions After the tenth of Aprill being read

Its Resolved that the limittacon for stay of Executions be
made After the tenth of may

15.  That the Act for pleading discount in barr be explain'd
&c. was read & referr'd to the consideration of the Comitee
of laws to explaine the same and make reporte thereof to the
house.

16  Relating to Coopers and the Gauge of tob hhds Being
read & Considerd

It is the opinion of the house that the laws allready provided
are Sufficient to remedy that evill

17  Article relating to limittacon of accons read

This Article is answerd by A vote Yesterday.

18  That the law punishing fornication and Adultery be
Explained when a mans Estate shall redeem his body

Read and referrd to the Comitee of laws who are desired
to explaine the same.

The mocon Yesterday for encouragem<sup>t</sup> of tillage was againe
considerd and.

Resolvd the Comitee of laws bring in a bill for that purpose

The honob Rob<sup>t</sup> Smith and Kenelm Cheseldyne Esq<sup>rs</sup> enters
the house And delivers M<sup>r</sup> Speaker A bill for regulating Ordnarys endorsd thus

By the Councill in Assembly<br>Sept<sup>r</sup> 12<sup>th</sup> 1704

The within bill for regulating ordnary's having been read
and Considered at this board Wee do propose that in the 17

P. R. O.
B. T. Md.
Vol. 17.
line of the said bill these words be added after County (if her
Maj^{ty} shall so think fitt otherwise if she shall so graciously
please to direct) And that you may not apprehend or haue any
Iealousy's that this board are desireous to haue the said fines
for ordnary lycenses applyd otherwise then as by the house it
is intended Wee are willing the law be temporary for some
Small time if the house thinke fitt

Signd p ord^r W^m Bladen Cl Councill

Peticon of Coll Thomas Smithson being brought into the
house and read is granted &

Orderd the Comittee of Accounts give Allowance as prayd.

The Message by Rob^t Smith & Kenelm Cheseldyn Esq^rs
being endorsd on the bill for regulating ord^rys &c. was read &
Answerd as follows Viz^t

By the house of Delegates
Sept^r 12. 1704

This house haue read and Considerd the message touching
the Bill for regulating ordnarys on the back of the bill And if
the making of the law for A Short time as proposd by the
honoble Councill is thought of weight to moove this house to
consent to them Addiconall words Wee hope may haue As
strong Effect to moove yo^r hono^rs to concurr with this house
in leaving them out for so short a time Since by the time her
Maj^ts pleasure can be knowne the law will expire And its
Agreed that till then the fines Arrising shall be applyd to the
Countys And therefore it is but saying what wee All intend to
doe And this method proposd is Altogeather new And that
Contained in the bill Agreeable to all other laws Not one in
the whole province having such A reserve as is here propos'd
Nor cann Wee see that her Majesty enjoyns any such reserve
but in what Shalbe offerrd to her Majesty's Governour And
therefore this house does Earnestly pray the honoble Councills
Consideration and Concurrence with the house therein

Signd per order W^m Taylard Cl h D.

Sent up by M^r Lowe M^r Ecclestone & M^r Frisby
They returne and say they deliverd the same.

M^r W^m Coursey from the Councill enters the house and
delivers M^r Speaker the following Message Viz^t

By his Ex<sup>cy</sup> the Gov<sup>r</sup> & Councill

P. R. O.
B. T. Md.
Vol. 17.

Sept<sup>r</sup> 11 1704

In answer to the message of M<sup>r</sup> Leach M<sup>r</sup> Young & M<sup>r</sup> Macall to desire his Ex<sup>cy</sup> to o ne some of the Members of this house to consider the evills that may redound to her Maj<sup>ts</sup> Interest and this province by the designe hinted to be formed against our Constitucon Orderd that M<sup>r</sup> Tench M<sup>r</sup> Brooke M<sup>r</sup> Smith M<sup>r</sup> Cheseldyn & M<sup>r</sup> Coursey Joyne the Comittee of the house so Soone as they are ready.

Signd ꝑ order W<sup>m</sup> Bladen Cl Councill.

Which being read Its Resolvd that M<sup>r</sup> Nicholas Lowe M<sup>r</sup> W<sup>m</sup> Frisby M<sup>r</sup> Iohn Leach and M<sup>r</sup> Hugh Ecleston joyne with the Members of the honoble Council on the Subject proposd and orderd to Attend them in the Afternoone.

Upon mocon made to the house on behalfe of Thomas Reading printer that he may be lycens'd to print his Ex<sup>cys</sup> Speech and the houses answer to the same. ·

Jts Resolvd he be lycensd so to doe likewise proposd that he may be constituted publiq printer to print all laws and other publiq matters Which being debated this house Resolves he be constituted printer first Giving bond with Securety to behave himselfe in that Office.

The Comittee of Agreivances enters the house and preferrs to the house A Iournall of their proceedings which was orderd to be entred.

By order of the house of Delegates.

A Comittee to enquire into the Agrievances of this province. The members appointed for the same are

> . Thom<sup>s</sup> Greenfeild Esq<sup>r</sup> ⎫
> Coll Iames Maxwell  ⎬
> M<sup>r</sup> Iohn Wells    ⎭

Which members met Accordingly and made choice of Thomas Greenfeild Esq<sup>r</sup> to be their Chairman and Appointed In° Collins to serve as Clerk:

Whereas by the information of A member of the honoble house of Delegates for Cecill County who applys to this Comittee as well on his owne behalfe as on the behalfe of this neighbours inhabitants of Cecill County it appeares that severall Gent not residing in the Aforesaid County have quarters and plantations there whereat they keep negroes Molattoes and other Slaves under such overseers who Allow them not only the privileidge of Gunns doggs and Amunicon but of using such their Instruments without the bounds of

P. R. O.
B. T. Md.
Vol. 17. their Ma^{rs} plantacons to the no Small damage of the neighbour-
ing Stocks of Cattle hoggs &c^a which he humbly conceives an
Agrievance to the Inhabitants Aforesaid

It being by this Comittee Considerd of and Judgd an inde-
niable Agrievance and very prejudiciall to the good people
inhabitants of the said County is humbly referrd to the consideration of the house of Delegates.

It is by this Comittee thought A great agreivance and
humbly offerrd to the house as such that therr is no law provided Against the frequent meetings & Assembly of Negroes
in this province w^{ch} proove very prejudiciall to the Countrey
by their plotts and ill contrivances ag^t their Masters &c^a at
Such their meeting's.

Upon the mocon of An honob member of the house it is
offerrd that the present method of having one provinciall
Court Justice, out of every County is not at all necessary it
causes A great charge to the province by the number of them
and enforce that many Unlearnd men are in that office to the
dishonour of her Maj^{ty} and that A Small Competent number
would Suffice who by her Maj^{ty} may be paid (As it Justly
ought to be) to the ease of the province And that such reasonable Sallary may be Allow'd to such Justices as may encourage
such industrious and studious persons as would endeavour to
quallify them selves for their Maj^{tys} Service the present method
being such as deterrs any judicious person even from owning
or pretending to any reading which prooves only a Snare to
entangle them in troublesome and unproffitable offices.

It is in humble manner offerrd as an Agreivance and prayd
that it may be enquird into why his Lopps officers make the
people pay four hundred & Eighty pounds of tobacco for A
Warrant of one hundred Acres of land Whereas his Lopps
order is but 240 or thereabouts as it is sayd.

It is likewise offerrd As A great Aggreivance to the publiq
that the charge of Cleaning and repairing the County Arms
is A Constant and durable charge to the respective County's
Therefore since the province is Allready well Supplyd with
Arms it would be A great ease to the County's that some part
of the three pence ꝑ hhd w^{ch} is assigned to the supplying of
Arms be applied to pay for the cleaning of them &c^a that each
respective County be Acquitt of such Yearly and Constant
charge                    Signd ꝑ order Ino Collins Cl Com

Which being read the house resolves to debate the same.

1^{st}   Relating to Negroes Carrying of Gunns &c^a
Read & Resolved that negroes and other slaves be not
permitted to carry any Gunns or other offensive weapon from

plantation to plantation being of from his Ma^rs land without P. R. O.
lycense from their Ma^rs If any such be found he is lyable to be B T. Md.
Vol. 17.
carry'd before a Iustice of peace and Whipd And his Gun and
other offensive Weapon to be forfeited to him that shall Seize
the same This to be Added to the Act of Servants & Slaves.
 2  Article being read and debated
This house resolves it noe Agrievance to the province.
 3^d  Article relating to the Number of the Iustices of the
provinciall Court being burthensome to the Countrey &c^a
This Article being read it is Resolved that application be
made to his Ex^cy the Governo^r to redress the same by those
that are Agreivd.
 4.  Article relating to land Warrants.
Read and is referrd for debate till to morrow in A full house
and orderd M^r Carroll haue notice to appeare here to morrow
to Answer such questions as may be proposed.
 5^th  Article relating to cleansing Arms.
Answerd by an ordinance made for that purpose.
The house Adjournd till 2 A Clock in the Afternoone.

### Post Merediem

The house met According to Adjournment and were present
as in the morning
Iames Sanders Esq^r from the Councill enters the house and
delivers M^r Speaker the foll message.

### By his Ex^cy the Govern^r & Councill in Assembly
### Sept. 12^th 1704

This board Iudging that the conferrence yesterday desir'd
by the house to consider of what therein was proposed was of
great moment to the province did appoint noe less then foure
of their members to  o  ne with those of the house And therefore wee desire you will Add some more of your members to
those you haue Allready Appointed to joyne with ours and
that they meet and goe upon the said Conferrence at two A
Clock in the Afternoone.
Which being read is Resolvd that Coll Edward Dorsey &
M^r Edward Blay be Added to the other members to  o  ne in
Conferrence & Orderd to attend the Gent of the Councill
The following peticons brought into the house was
orderd to be read
The peticon of Thomas Hebb read the consideration where-
of is referrd to the Comittee of Accounts for Allowance.
The peticon of Charles Kilburne read & referrd to the
Comittee of Acco^ts for Allowance

P. R. O.
B. T. Md.
Vol. 17. The peticon of the honob Thom<sup>s</sup> Smithson Esq<sup>r</sup> with the endorsement from the honoble Councill read & Granted orderd the Comittee of Accounts Give the Allowance as pray'd.
Bill for appointing Constables Ac<sup>a</sup>
Read the 2<sup>d</sup> time and do pass.
Bill declaring it to be fellony to Alter the quallity of tobacco.
Read the 2<sup>d</sup> time and doe pass.
Bill for publication of All Laws
Read the 2<sup>d</sup> time and do pass.
Bill for Appointing Constables &c<sup>a</sup>
Read the 2<sup>d</sup> time and do pass.
Bill for limittacon of Accons.
Read the 2<sup>d</sup> time & do pass.
Bill against engrossers & regraters.
Read the 2<sup>d</sup> time & do pass.
Bill directing the manner of Sueing out Attachments.
Read the 2<sup>d</sup> time
M<sup>r</sup> Sam<sup>ll</sup> Young is desired by the house to conduct M<sup>r</sup> Richard Iones into the house being A member chosen for Ann Arrundell County
Orderd the Comittee of agreivances goe forth upon their Comittees.
Bill for appointing Constables.
Bill declaring it to be fellony to Alter the quallity of tobacco.
Bill for publication of All Laws.
Bill ag<sup>t</sup> Engrossers and regraters.
Bill directing the manner of sueing out Attachments.
All read the 1<sup>st</sup> & 2<sup>d</sup> time and Sent up to his Ex<sup>cy</sup> and Councill p Coll Smallwood M<sup>r</sup> Fowlks and M<sup>r</sup> Dollahyde.
They returne and say they deliverd the bills .
The Indenture for M<sup>r</sup> Rich<sup>d</sup> Iones A member for Ann Arrundell County sent up to the Comittee of Elections to be considerd of
The peticon of Iohn Nicholls read & Referrd till to morrow for consideration
M<sup>r</sup> Thomas Reynolds being brought to the barr pursuant to an order of this house and being chargd with A breach of privileidge in arresting George Vallentine is now under debate & the said Reynolds and Vallentine orde'd to withdraw
Which matter being fully debated the house is of opinion that in reguard M<sup>r</sup> Reynolds did give the said Vallentine notice of his privileidge And did not pretend to Arrest him but with a reserve to his privileidge therefore is not guilty of A willfull breach of the privileidge of this house.
And therefore resolvd the s<sup>d</sup> Reynolds be dischargd and the Arrest declared Void.

Orderd M⁰ Reynells and M⁰ Vallentine be againe calld into P. R. O.
the house who appeard And M⁰ Speaker was pleasd to acquaint B. T. Md. Vol. 17.
M⁰ Reynolls what was done and likewise cautioned M⁰ Val-
lentine to take care to preserve the privileidges of this house
for the future.

M⁰ Sam¹¹ Young enters the house and brings w^{th} him M⁰
Rich^d Iones A member for Ann Arrundell County in the
stead of M⁰ Iohn Hamond.

The Comittee of Elections and priveleidges enter the house
and reports that M⁰ Richard Iones is duely Elected and returnd
a member to Serve for All County.

M⁰ Thomas How M⁰ Ioseph Gray orderd to Attend M⁰
Iones to see him Sworne.

They returne and say they saw him take the oaths appointed
&c & Signe the test & oath of Abjuration

Moovd by A member of the house that its yet unsetled how
· farr the limitts of Calvert County extends it Selfe towards S^t
Marys Charles and Prince Geo^e County's because of the River
of Petuxent and therefore prays that this Assembly determine
how farr the limitts of each place shall extend.

Proposd that each County shall extend it selfe to the Channell of the said River And that what Shipps shall ride in the
Channell of the said River may be Arrested by either County
that come at them

But it's desired that Calvert County shall Extend it Selfe to
high water mark of the Westerne side of the said River
thereupon.

Put to the question whither the Channell or highwater
marke shall be the bounds or not

Carryd by Majority of Votes that it be According to the
first proposall that the channell shall devide the bounds.

And Resolvd that All Countys devided by rivers take the
same measures to be recomended to the Comittee of laws to
Annex that Resolve to the law· for devision of County's

Bill declaring that Grantees of land lyeing within the
Indians land may have Accons of trespass against such persons
as Cutt timber of their land on pretence of having bought it

Read 1^{st} time and Comitted for Amendm^t

The peticon of Thomas Cockshute Ioseph Colebatch and M⁰
Henry Hall Ministers was here read but is

Referrd for consideration of A full house to mor morning
& orderd M⁰ Young give notice thereof to the peticoners

Bill prohibitting Com^{rs} Sherriffs &^{ea} to plead as Attorneys
Read the 1^{st} time

The house Adjourns till to morrow morning Eight A Clock.

P. R. O.
B. T. Md.
Vol. 17.

Wensday Sept$^r$ 13$^{th}$ 1704.

The house mett againe and p$^r$sent as Yesterday
Read what was done Yesterday.

Moovd by A member of the house that there was some
Misunderstanding in debate of the peticon of Thomas Smithson Esq$^r$ thereupon againe read and debated.

And resolvd by the house the Resolve yesterday thereupon
be Confirmed.

The peticon of M$^r$ Hale M$^r$ Cockshute M$^r$ Colebatch was
Againe read & orderd the peticoners enter the house. Who
appeare and upon some debate they were orderd to withdraw.

And the peticon being againe debated
Its Resolvd it be Wholly rejected.

The house now proceed to debate the other proposalls from
the honoble Councill.

19. Article relating to County leavys and Vestrys Acco$^{ts}$
Read and this house concurrs therewith &
Orderd A bill be prepar'd for that purpose

20. That All freemen be oblidged to give a good Account
of themselves &c$^a$ Read &
Resolvd by the house that the laws all ready made are
Sufficient

21. Article relating to publiq posts &c$^a$ Read & debat'd Jts
considerd that the present Weight of business at this time
will not Admitt of A full consideration thereof

Therefore referrd to consideration of next Assembly.

22$^d$ Article relating to the members of the Citty of S$^t$
Mary's Read & debated.

And orderd that the Charter for that Citty of S$^t$ Mary's be
laid before this house next Assembly and then further to be
considered.

Order'd by the house the foll message be sent up to his
Ex$^{cy}$ and Councill

By the house of Delegates Sept$^r$ 13$^{th}$ 1704.

The members upon your invitation haue Attended your
Ex$^{cy}$ to View the Church and haue taken notice of the place
you are pleasd to be made for the burgesses and delegates
to sitt in And wee do very well approove of what your Ex$^{cy}$
has done And hold our selvs oblidgd to returne you our hearty
thanks for your regard of us And for the care and trouble
you haue been pleas'd to take in that Affaire And wee desire
you to order A small doore to be .cut over against the porch
by the pullpit to give Aire to the Church And when you see

fitt to Add A small Vestry roome to it And that m laying out
the Church Yard You will please to inclose all the Graves with
in it.          Signd ℗ order W^m Taylard Cl ho Del

P. R. O.
B, T. Md.
Vol. 17.

Sent up by M^r Waters M^r Iones & M^r M^claster
They returne and say they deliverd the message
The Honoble Iohn Hamond & W^m Holland Esq^r enters
the house and delivers M^r Speaker the following Bills
Bill declaring it to be fellony to Alter the quallity of tobacco
etc. Endors'd Eod Die Read at the Councill Board the 1^st time
                    W. Bladen Cl Co:

Bill Against Engrossers & regraters.
Endorsd Eod die Read at the Councill board the 1^st time
                    W Bladen C Co.

Bill for limittacon of Actions Endors'd Eod Die Read at the
Councill board the 1^st time          W Bladen C Co.

Bill directing the manner of Sueing out Attachments &c^a
Endorsed Eod Die Read the 1^st time at the Councill board
                    W Bladen Cl Counc

Bill for Appointment of Constables Endors'd Eod die By
her Maj^ts Councill.
Read the first time & do pass          W Bladen Cl Co.

Bill for publication of All laws Endors'd Eod Die, Read at
the Councill board And it is observed that partchment is very
difficult to be gott at present And that good paper is better
in this Countrey.          W Bladen Cl Councill

Which endorsment was read in the house And Resolved
that this house insist upon the law as drawne but because
partchment Cannot now be had for the Severall Countys
Resolvd that good paper at p^rsent shall suffice W^ch said bill
with endorsment was sent up to his Ex^cy and Councill ℗ M^r
Iohn Taylor and M^r Hudson.
They returne and say they deliverd the same.
The peticon of In^o Sweatnam praying a bill Empowering
W^m Sweatnam to sell land
Read & Granted
And A bill brought in for that purpose Endors'd

P. R. O.
B. T. Md.
Vol. 17.
Sep' 12 1704

By the Councill in Assembly Read the 1ˢᵗ time
W Bladen Cl. Co.

Read the 1ˢᵗ time in the house and do pass.

The reporte of the Comittee of Agrievances brought into
the house, And being read its ordered the same be debated
Resolved they proceed thereupon.
First Agrievance read relating to riding horses &c.
Read and fully debated
Jt is Resolved that A bill be prepar'd to redress that Agreivance by Imposing a fine of 500ˡ tobacco one halfe to the
informer and the other halfe to the party Greiv'd togeather
wᵗʰ such damages as the party Greiv'd can make appear he
sustained And that this law be given in charge to All Grand
Iury's.
2ᵈ Article in the said report relating to freight
Read and Resolvd that A bill be prepared to remedy that
evill declaring that every Master of A Ship shalbe oblidgd
(before he take any tobacco on board) to sett up at the County
Court house in writing What freight he will goe at that voyage,
of which the Clerk is to take notice and enter upon Record
And any one that shall Shipp tobacco before such note of the
freight shall forfeit All such tobacco as shall be so shipt And
the Maʳ to forfeit twenty Shillings Sterling for every hogshead
he takes on board one halfe to her Maᵗʸ for the use of the
County where the tob Shalbe Shipt And the other halfe to the
informer And likewise that the Master of every Shipp thatt
send for tob to other County's Shalbe oblidgd to send A
Certificate of Notice given as Aforesaid And the Collectors
and Navall Officers within this province to procure A coppy
of Such law and Affix it in their offices.
The house Adjournes till 2 A Clock in the Afternoone.

### Post Merediem

The house met againe and present as in the morning.
By the Comittee Appointed to inspect and Veiw the land
records of Maryland &cᵃ
Jt is reported to the honob house of Delegates as followeth.
That its Absolutely necessary these foll books should be
Amended.
Libʳ D. S. Nº. F. The Alphabett to be repaired and new
transcribed.

Lib[r] D. Booke of Instruccons of which such parte as relates to land to be transcribed in A well bound booke and Alphabetted. P. R. O.
B. T. Md.
Vol. 17.

Lib : D. S. N°. B. to be Amended in A Small parte of the Alphabet w[ch] is torne.

Lib : L. So much thereof as relates to land to be transcribed as before.

Lib N S N° 2 to be coverd with ozenbriggs or buckerume aboue the binding.

Lib N S N° B : to be coverd as before.

Lib S D N° A to be mended in the Alphabett any to be transcribed in the letter F and to be mended Alsoe in the binding.

Lib[r] W C N 5 to be mended in the binding Alphabettd and Covered as before.

Lib[r] W C N° 4 to be mended & Coverd as before.

Lib[r] W C N° 3 the Alphabett to be transcribed to be mended in the binding and Coverd as before.

Lib W C N° 2 to be mended in the binding.

Lib C B N° 2 to be mended in the binding and cou'd as before.

Lib[r] W C from Anno 1675 to 1680 to be mended in the binding and Coverd as before

Lib[r] M M The Alphabett to be transcribed from the Lre H and the binding to be mended & coverd as before.

Lib[r] A booke formerly transcribd to be Examind by the orriginall

Lib[r] B the same

Lib[r] W S the Alphabett to be transcribd from the beginning & to be new bound or Well mended

Lib K K one leafe in the Alphabett Containing the Lres M & N to be mended & all the binding to be mended & Covered as before.

Lib[r] R M to be transcribd in A large Well bound book being A Small paper pamphlett.

Lib I I to be mended in the binding and Coverd as before

Lib[r] H H the Alphabett to be transcribd from the letter R to be mended in the binding And Coverd as before.

Lib[r] G G to be new bound.

E E to be mended in the leaves and Coverd as before.

Lib[r] D D to be mended in the Alphabetted binding & Coverd as before

F F to be mended and Coverd as before.

Lib[r] C C to be mended and Coverd as before

Lib[r] A A the Corners.of the Covers to be mended and in the binding and Coverd as before.

P. R. O.
B. T. Md.
Vol. 17. Lib' X to be new bound and the Alphabett of the letter M to be transcribed.

Lib' R to be new bound.

Lib' Q to be new bound.

Lib' I K to be new bound and Alphabetted and the first leafe to be transcribed.

Lib' H to be transcribd in A Well bound book.

Lib' R A Small pamphlett new markd to be transcribd & Alphabetted with some other small books in A well bound book. Which are All the books that want imediate repaire as it Seems to the Comittee

And its further offerd to the house by the said Comittee that its Very expedient and Wilbe much for the preservation of the said Records for the future that such benches or Desks be made for placing the same on as the new Register of the land office shall direct for that it appeares to the said Comittee that the boxes wherein· they are now kept Add more to their destruction then preservation and Serve only to wear them to peices.

The further consideration of which is referrd and Submitted to the house by the said Comittee.

Signd ꝑ order Th° Bordley Cl Com^ee

Which reporte being read and debated its Resolvd this house Concurr with the report of the Comitee And orderd that M' Sam'' Younge M' Charles Greenberry see the same Complyd with as requird And make report thereof to next Sessions of Assembly for which an Allowance to be made.

Orderd the foll message be sent his Ex^cy viz^t

Resolvd by this house that its necessary for the safety of this province that the Secretary who has the keeping of the records before his entring into his office be oblidgd and bound to preserve the books in which the records are Contained in As good Condition as he receives them at his owne charge And they be visited At meeting of every Assembly And that if any defect be in keeping the records to be repaird and made good out of his owne Estate And that the present Secretary Give Securety as Aboue to w^ch the Councills Concurrence is pray'd.          Signd ·ꝑ order W^m Taylard Cl ho Del.

Mooved by A member that A Clause in his Ex^cys Speech relating to building A house for her Maj^tys Gov' be read

Which was read and debated, And put to the Question whither the Countrey is at present in A Capacity of building a house for her Maj^ts Governo' as requird or not

Carryed in the negatiue.

But Resolvd as to An Allowance for house rent this house P. R. O. B. T. Md. Vol. 17. will further consider.

The honoble Coll In° Addison enters the house and delivers Mʳ Speaker

Bill for publication of All laws Endorsd thus By his Exᶜʸ the Govʳ & Councill Septʳ 13 1704

The resolve of the house on this bill is agreed to provided it be incerted in the body of the laws as a Salvo.

Signd ꝑ order Wᵐ Bladen Cl Councˡˡ

Bill declaring the maner of Sueing out Attachmᵗˢ

Bill declaring it to be fellony to Alter the Quallity of tobacco &cᵃ

Bill for limittacon of Certain Actions.

Bill Against Engrossers and Regraters

Bill for Appointment of Constables etᵃ Sent up to his Exᶜʸ and Councill by Mʳ Thomˢ Frisby Mʳ Wᵐ Dare and Mʳ peirce.

They returne and say they deliverd the bills

Bill for publication of All laws.

Read & Endors'd by the house Del Septʳ 13 1704

Read and Amended as proposed And Sent up to his Exᶜʸ and Councill ꝑ Mʳ Wᵐ Barton

He returns and says he deliverd the same.

Bill providing what shall be evidence to proove forreigne & other debts etc.

Read the first time.

The Comittee of Agreivances enter the house and reporte that the lord Baltemores Agents doe Exact 480ˡ tobacco for every hundred Acres of land And refuse pattents for the land till the purchase money be paid, thereupon it was

Orderd that Mʳ Charles Carroll one of his Lopps Agents haue notice to Attend the house to Shew by what Authority he requires the same &

Orderd that Mʳ Ioseph Hill give Mʳ Carroll notice to Attend the house to morrow morning

Bill for preservation of harbours &cᵃ

Read the first time.

Bill for publication of Marriages read the first time

The house Adjournes till to morrow morning 8 A Clock.

### Tuesday Septʳ 14ᵗʰ 1704.

The house met According to Adjournmᵗ and being calld over were present as Yesterday only Mʳ Thomas Greenfeild & Majʳ Wᵐ Barton absent

P. R. O.
B. T. Md.
Vol. 17. The honoble Iohn Hamond Esqʳ from the Councill enters the house and delivers the following message.


By the Councill in Assembly.
Septʳ 13 1704

The reporte of the Comittee appointed the 11ᵗʰ Instant touching the designe forming agᵗ the constitucoñ of this Government has been read at this board and its Conceived that the Conferrees haue mistaken the Subject matter of the sd Conferrence for want of having the same in writing Which by the houses message to this Board was to consider the many Evills that would thereby redound both to her Majᵗˢ Interests and Welfare of this province therefore propose that full instruccons be given them And that they meet againe on that subject by Eight of the Clock to morrow morning.

Signd ꝑ order Wᵐ Bladen Cl Coun


Which being read this house concurrs therewith & Orderd the members againe Attend the Gent of the Councill as desired.

Read what was done Yesterday

Propos'd by a member that the widdow of Coll Thompson putts into the Comittee of Accounts for Allowance of A bond of one Samˡˡ Scotts who dyed insolvent for payment of Dutys on Rum &c. which being referrd to this house by the Comittee of Accounts and Read and debated

Jts Resolved that forasmuch as Coll Thompson neglected the duty of his office in not taking good Securety his Estate is lyable to Answer for the same.

The peticon of Iohn Nicholls for Sale of Wᵐ Edmondsons land read and Resolvd it be granted and leave Given to bring in A bill Empowring Mʳ Nicholˢ Lowe Admʳ of the said Decd to sell land for payment of the debt with A Clause that the overplus if any when the debt paid be secured for the orphans to whom the land was Given And not to be taken or deemd Assetts in the hands of the Admʳ.

Bill relating to the Standard of English Weights & Measures.

Read the first time and do pass with Amendmᵗ

According to order of last night Mʳ Charles Carroll ꝑ Permission enters the house & being demanded why his Lopps Agents Exact 480ˡ tob for every Warrant for 100 Acres And refuse to give pattents for the land till the purchase money be paid he Answered he has such instruccons from the Lord

Baltemore And that he gave publiq notice thereof and he P. R. O. B. T. Md. Vol. 17.
produced and Gave in A Coppy of such publiq notice and says
the reason why his Lopp requires 240¹ more then formerly
was because one halfe of the fees due to his Lopps officers on
such Warrants and Grants was taken from them & Given to
her Maj$^u$ Secretary But that if it may be thought fitt to restore
the land records and the fees to his Lopps officers that Addiconall 240 shall imediatly be taken of and noe more required
and only such fees as were formerly requir'd for the same And
that the said Records shall be put in such persons hands to
keep as Shall from time to time be approovd of by his Ex$^{cy}$
and an oath and Good Securety Given for the faithfull and
carefull keeping the same.

Thereupon M$^r$ Carroll withdrew and this being debated
Orderd A message thereon be sent his Ex$^{cy}$

Bill to enable Coll Dorsey to sell land &c.

Read the 1$^{st}$ time and will pass with Amendm$^t$ and Orderd
Sam$^{ll}$ Dorsey haue notice.

Bill ag$^t$ Excessive Usury

Read 1$^{st}$ time.

The honob Robert Smith and W$^m$ Coursey Esq$^{rs}$ enters the
house and delivers M$^r$ Speaker the following bills.

Bill for declaring it to be fellony to Alter the Quallity of
tobacco Endors'd

By the Councill in Assembly
Sep$^r$ 14 1704

Read 2$^d$ time and Will pass for engrossing with the Amendment proposed          W$^m$ Bladen Cl Councill.

Bill against engrossers and regraters.
Endorsd Read the 2$^d$ time and past for Engrossing.
         W$^m$ Bladen Cl Counc.

Bill for Appointment of Constables Read the 2$^d$ time and
past for Engrossing          W Bladen Cl Co$^{ll}$

Bill for limittacon of Accons.
Endors'd Read the 2$^d$ time and past for Engrossing
         W Bladen Cl Councill

Bill directing the manner of Sueing out Attachments
Endors'd Read the 2$^d$ time and past for Engrossing
         W$^m$ Bladen Cl Coun

P. R. O.
B. T. Md.
Vol. 17. Bill declaring it to be fellony to Alter the Quallity of tob<sup>co</sup> againe read & Endorsd as follows.

### By the house of Del Sep<sup>r</sup> 14 1704

The house insists upon the bill as first drawne & Cannot Assent to the addicon Its A Sharp penalty & ought to be limitted to A Short time Especially considering that the party Greivd has remedy at the Comon law to recover his damages And therefore wee pray your honours Concurrence to the bill as drawne.          Signd ℗ order W<sup>m</sup> Taylard Cl ho Del

Sent up to his Ex<sup>cy</sup> and Councill by M<sup>r</sup> Robert Tiler He returns and says he deliverd the same
Bill for killing of Crows etc.
Read the 1<sup>st</sup> time in the house
Iames Saunders Esq<sup>r</sup> from the honoble Councill enters the house and delivers M<sup>r</sup> Speaker.
Bill declaring it to be fellony to Alter the quallity of tobacco endorsd.

### By the Gov<sup>r</sup> & Councill
### Sep<sup>r</sup> 14 1704

Read the 2<sup>d</sup> time and past for engrossing with the Amendment proposed.          W Bladen Cl Counc

Bill for publication of All laws endors'd

### By the Gov<sup>r</sup> & Councill Sep<sup>r</sup> 14 1704

Read the 2<sup>d</sup> time and past for engrossing.
          W Bladen Cl Coun

Bill for expences of Del<sup>s</sup> and Commissioners Read in the house the first time and do pass.
Bill for advancement of the natives and residents of this province.
Read in the house the first time.
Bill declaring that the Grantees of land lying within the Indians may haue Actions of trespass
Read the first time.
Bill Ascertaining nauall officers and Collecters fees.
Read & Comitted for Amendm<sup>t</sup>
Bill for Settlement of an Annuall Revenue on her Maj<sup>ts</sup> Governour

Read the first time and do pass. P. R. O.<br>B. T. Md.<br>Vol. 17.
Bill prohibitting Commissioners & Sherriffs to plead as Attorneys
Bill for publication of Marriages
Bill providing what shalbe evidence to proove forreigne & other debts.
Bill for preservation of Harbours.
Bill for Ascertaining Delegates and Com$^{rs}$ Expences.
Bill for killing Woolves and Crows.
Bill against Excessive Usury.
Bill relating to the Standard of English Weights and Measures.
Bill for Setlem$^t$ of an Anuall revenue on her Maj$^{ts}$ Governour.
Bill ag$^t$ purchasing timber of the Indians.
Bill for Advancement of the Natives.
Bill empowring W$^m$ Sweatnam to sell land.
The Aboue bills Were sent up to his Ex$^{cy}$ & Councill by M$^r$ Thomas Beale M$^r$ W$^m$ Aisquith M$^r$ W$^m$ Watts and M$^r$ Peter Watts
The house Adjourns till 2 A Clock Afternoone.


Post Merediem

The house met According to Adjournment were calld over and present as in the Morning only Calvert County members
The message relating to the land records read and
Orderd to be sent up to his Ex$^{cy}$ and Councill.
Coll Thomas Smith M$^r$ Iohn Wells M$^r$ Robt. Skinner are orderd to carry the same w$^{ch}$ follows viz$^t$


By the house of Delegates
Sept$^r$ 14 1704

The Comittee of Agreivances reported that the Lord Baltemores agents do Exact 480$^l$ tob for every 100 Acres and refuse to give pattents for the same till the purchase money be paid  Thereupon it was orderd that M$^r$ Charles Carroll one of his Lopps Agents haue notice to Attend this house to show by What Authority he requires the same and Accordingly he appeard this morning and said he had such instruccons from the Lord Baltemore that he gave publiq notice thereof and he produced and Gave in A Coppy of such publiq notice and says the reason why his Loop requires 240 more then formerly was because one halfe of the fees due to his Lopps officers on such Warrants and grants was taken from them and given to her

P. R. O.
B. T. Md.
Vol. 17. Maj^ts Secretary but that if it may be thought fitt to restore the land records and the fees to his Lopps officers that Addiconall 240 shall be imediatly taken of and no more required and only Single fees as formerly requird for the same And that the said Records shall be put into such persons hands to keep As shall from time to time be approovd of by his Ex^cy the Governour and Assembly And an oath and good Securety given for the faithfull and carefull keeping of them, upon consideration whereof it Appears A great Agreivance to the good people of this province and discouragement to the people of it to pay double price for the land and Allmost double fees for the pattents and since its proposed to be remedied and sufficient Caution given for safe keeping the Records Wee humbly pray your honours that A Conferrence may be had upon this Subject and the persons now Ioynd in Conferrence upon the business of New York may be chargd with this when that other is dispatcht        Signd ⱷ order W^m Taylard Cl h D.

Bill confirming to the Governo^r of this province the antient duty of 3^d ⱷ tonn
Read the first time.
Bill to make Vallid in law all process and proceedings &c^a
Read the 1^st time
Bill prohibitting M^rs of Shipps from transporting persons without passes
Read the first time.
M^r Thomas Beale M^r W^m Watts M^r Will^m Aisquith and M^r Peter Watts enters the house & say they deliverd their bills in the morning sent by them.
The foll Message read and approovd of & orderd to be sent up to his Ex^cy & Councill

By the house of Delegates
Sept^r 14 1704.

Upon examination of the severall Rolls of the laws of this province made in the severall Sessions of Assembly Wee finde that from the first Setlement of the province to the revolucon and from thence to the last Session of Assembly the Severall Acts in each Sessions of Assembly was Annexd togeather and seald with one Great Seale of the province And with the Royall Assent to the same were Allways understood to be sufficient but in the last Session of Assembly Wee finde that each perticuler bill was Sealed with the great Seale and the Royall Assent to every one singly and apart from the other which Wee are Sencible will encrease the charge of the province Especially considering the great number of laws that is P. R. O.<br>B. T. Md.<br>Vol. 17. like to pass this Sessions of Assembly.

Therefore wee humbly pray your Ex$^{cy}$ to lett us know if there be any Absolute necessity of passing the laws Separately and with the charge of the great Seale to every of them or that the great Seale Affixing to All of them in one body with the Royall Assent at the end of each Session may be sufficient as has been used heretofore the granting whereof (if it may be) will lessen the charge of this province.

Sent up to his Ex$^{cy}$ and Councill by M$^r$ Thomas Greenfeild M$^r$ John Leach M$^r$ Iohn Macall M$^r$ Thomas How Coll Iames Smallwood and M$^r$ Gerrard Fowlks And the bill confirming to the Governour the Antient duty of 3$^d$ ℔ tonn

Bill to confirme all proceedings at law &c$^a$ to this time.

Proposed by A member that forasmuch as the Reg$^r$ of the Commissarys Court and the severall Deputy's are not enjoynd by any law to performe their dutys in such offices which being debated

Jts Resolvd that A law be prepar'd to enforce them to their dutys under A penalty.

And the Comittee of laws are desired to inspect the law for Admtracon of Iustice in probatt of Wills &c$^a$ and report to the house What Amendments Are necessary

The house Adjourns till to morrow morning 8 A Clock.

## Fryday Sept$^r$ 15 1704

The house met againe According to Adjournment.

Being calld over were All p$^r$sent as yesterday

Read what was done Yesterday.

Orderd the Gent appointed to o ne in Conferrence About the New York Affaires attend the Gent of the Councill

Proposd that forasmuch as that business is of A High Concerne to this province there be more members to o ne.

Thereupon Resolved that M$^r$ Sam$^{ll}$ Young & M$^r$ Thomas Greenfeild be Added to the members of this house upon that Conferrence and are orderd to withdraw.

The house proceed to reading the bills

Dowlins peticon and bill for Setling land &c$^a$

Read the 1$^{st}$ time.

Bill for Sumoning Grand & Pettit Iuro$^{rs}$.

Bill for Setling fees for Naturallization and other private bills

Bill prohibiting the importacon of bread.

Bill Appointing Court days.

Bill Encourageing to Venture Shipps etc.

All the foregoeing bills were read in the house the first time.

P. R. O.
B. T. Md.
Vol. 17. Thomas Tench and Iohn Hamond Esq$^{rs}$ enters the house and delivers the following Message.

By the Councill in Assembly
Sep$^r$ 14 1704

Whereas M$^r$ Alexand$^r$ Hall a Gent who has long Servd his Countrey and Crowne of England as an officer Abroad in the Warrs And has the hono$^r$ to be Marryd to A relation to his Ex$^{cy}$ the Governour therefore in Complement to his Ex$^{cy}$ came over into the province with him And Wee desire he may be capable of Serving her Maj$^{ty}$ in Some Small employment in this province notwithstanding the Act prohibitting the same the said M$^r$ Hall being as Wee are credibly informed A very honest Gent        Signd ꝑ order W Bladen Cƚ Council

Which being read this house readily concurr therewith and orderd the same be endorsd and returnd his Ex$^{cy}$ in Councill.

Bill Ascertaining the Gage of tob hogsheads
Read the 1$^{st}$ time and do pass w$^{th}$ Amendm$^t$

M$^r$ Thomas Frisby orderd to Attend M$^r$ Coursey a member for Talbott County into the house.

He enters the house with the said M$^r$ Frisby Accordingly.

Bill Quieting possessions read the 1$^{st}$ time & Comitted for Amendment

Orderd that M$^r$ Iames Smallwood M$^r$ Tho$^s$ Frisby and M$^r$ Iohn Macall and M$^r$ Thomas Beale Attend M$^r$ Coursey to see him Sworne.

They returne and say they saw him Sworne & Signe the test and Abjuration

Bill declaring fees on private Acts etc.

Bill prohibitting the importation of bread &c$^a$.

Bill and peticon òf Dowlins to Confirme land.

Bill Appointing Court days.

Bill Ascertaining the Gauge of tob hogsheads.

Sent up to his Ex$^{cy}$ and Councill ꝑ M$^r$ Robt Skinner M$^r$ Tiler and M$^r$ Magruder.

They returne and say they deliverd the bills.

The Comittee of Agrievances enters the house & delivers the reporte.   orderd to be entred.   vizt.

It is humbly offerrd that the exporting Iron out of this province is A great Agreivance.

Jt is humbly offerrd as A great aggreivance to the inhabitants of the back plantacons who by reason of their remoteness from the Water haue not the Advantage of landing places for their Goods or Rolling houses to lay their tobacco in till the same be fetched on Board the Shipps but are forct to make P. R. O. B. T. Md. Vol. 17. use of other persons landing places and Altho the the party's agreivd haue offerrd to the owners of such land where such landing places are the full Vallue for so much thereof as wou'd be sufficient for such remote inhabitants to build A Store house to lay their goods in the owners thereof Absolutely deny to gratify their reasonable desires in the premises.

Jt is humbly therefore prayd that some method be taken for the releife of persons so Aggreivd by compelling the s^d owners to Sell or dispose of A sufficient quantity of such land by A Iury according to the method used for purchasing Church or towne lands or otherwise to the Iudicious opinions of the house shall seem most meet

It is further represented that of late Severall persons living neer the heads of Rivers where the same are Narrow make and cause to be made wares for ketching fish Cross those rivers thereby hindring the passage of boats &c. to those landings which they could formerly Easily come to, to the great prejudice of persons residing at the Uttermost heads of such rivers by obstructing their boates to pass and repass as Aforesaid.

The Striking of Fish in or neer Somersett County is thought A great agreivance.      Signd p order In° Collins Cl

Which being read the house proceed to debate the same

1. Parragraph ag^t Exportacon of Iron, being debated is Allowd of to be an Agreivance.

2. Parragraph relating to Store houses Is likewise Allowd to be an Agreivance, And Resolvd it be remedy'd by A law.

And being proposd how farr Masters of Shipps and Sailors shalbe oblidgd to roll their tobacco

Put to the question whither it shall be A mile or two miles from landing places.

Carryd by the Majority of Votes it shall be put one mile.

The following Message being read was Agreed to by the house and orderd to be entred.

### By the house of Delegates Sep^r 15^th 1704

Though Wee haue been hitherto Silent to one part of his Ex^cys Speech touching the incomodiousness of yo^r house it has not been without A due Concerne and hearty desire to do all that in us lyes to make our Actions Acceptable to so good A Governo^r as you haue approovd Your Selfe to us.

Wee have seene the restraint her Maj^ty has laid on yo^r Ex^cy and how farr she is pleased to permitt yo^r Ex^cy to Accept and us to give.

P. R. O.
B. T. Md.
Vol. 17.
As to the building A house wee are utterly uncapable to performe the same and therefore its fruitless to Attempt it

Yo$^r$ Ex$^{cy}$ knows that out of the 12$^d$ ℗ hhd to her Maj$^{ty}$ for Support of Government she gratiously pleasd to Allow 3$^d$ ℗ hhd for supplying the province with Arms and Amunition and preserving the same And Wee are informd that out of the Same the province is plentifully Supplyed And that there is About A thousand pounds in bank and the Stock increasing Wee humbly mooue it to yo$^r$ Ex$^{cy}$ if it may not be propper to address her Maj$^{ty}$ to apply such parte thereof as may be spard from that Use to the building A house and whither your Ex$^{cy}$ and Councill will please to o ne with us in such address.

And though Wee are not Able to build Such house as proposed Yet since her Maj$^{ty}$ has been pleased to permitt your Ex$^{cy}$ to Accept and us to give Something in liew of house rent Wee will Examine our Abillity And Wee hope shalbe able to make some Suitable acknowledgment to the tender regards you haue Showne for us.

Wee haue considered of the Severall Articles and proposalls laid before us And so soone as the Clerke cann draw them off the Iournall Your Ex$^{cy}$ shall know the opinion of this house thereon                    Signd ℗ order W$^m$ Taylard Cl ho Del

Which being read orderd that Coll Maxwell M$^r$ Dollahyde M$^r$ Ioseph Gray M$^r$ Iohn Waters M$^r$ Iohn Iones and M$^r$ In$^o$ Maclaster carry the same togeather with this houses concurrence with the message relating to M$^r$ Hall to his Ex$^{cy}$ & Counc$^{ll}$

They returne and say they deliverd the same.

3$^d$ Parragraph of the reporte of the Comittee of Agreivances relating to Wares and hedges Sett up in Rivers & Creeks to the Great hazard of boates &c$^a$    Read & debated.

Resolvd that no hedges nor wares be sett up in any Creeks or Rivers belowe any landing places And that the same be remedied by A Clause to be Added to the Act for preservation of harbours &c$^a$

4$^{th}$ The Aggreivance relating to Striking fish Read and debated.

Jt is Resolvd its no Aggreivance to the province.

W$^m$ Holland & Edw$^d$ Lloyd Esq$^{rs}$ Enters the house and delivers the following bills.

Bill providing What Shalbe Evidence to proove forreign & other debts.

Bill prohibitting Commissioners &c. to plead as Attorney's

Bill for publication of Marriages.

Bill for preservation of Harbours.

Bill Against Excessive usury.
Bill empowring W$^m$ Sweatnam to sell land.
Bill relating to the Standard of Weights and Measures.
Bill Setling An Annuall revenue on the Governo$^r$
Bill for killing Woolves and Crows &c.
Bill declaring Grantees of land lying within the Ind$^{ans}$
All which foregoeing bills were endorsd Viz$^t$

P. R. O.
B. T. Md.
Vol. 17.

By the Councill Sept$^r$ 15$^{th}$ 1704.
Read the 1$^{st}$ time and do pass          W$^m$ Bladen Cl Co.

Bill Ascertaining the expences of Delegates &c$^a$

Endorsd Sept$^r$ 15 1704
Read in Councill the first time and recomended that the
Sallary of Councello$^{rs}$ be incerted.          W Bladen Cl Coun

Bill for Advancement of Natives etc.

Endorsd Sept$^r$ 15 1704
Read & will pass with Amendment   W Bladen Cl Counc

Coll In$^o$ Addison and Iames Saunders Esq$^r$ enter the house
And delivers M$^r$ Speaker the following bills.
Bill to make Vallid All manner of process &c$^a$

Endorsd Sept$^r$ 15$^{th}$ 1704   By the Councill
Read and will pass with Amendm$^t$   W Bladen Cl Coun

Bill confirming to the Gov$^r$ the duty of 3$^d$ ℘ tonn
Endorsd Read in Councill & will pass.   W Bladen Cl Co.

Orderd the foregoing bills be read in the house in the
afternoone
M$^r$ Sam$^{ll}$ Dorsey According to order Enters the house ℘
permission And being demanded by M$^r$ Speaker if he had
any thing to Say why A bill should not pass for Sale of land
etc.   He answerd that forasmuch as it is Entaild And he a
party concernd Could not Consent to it Unless the money
that shalbe raizd by Sale thereof or so much thereof as he is
Concernd with be paid and deliverd to him
Jt was declard by Coll Dorsey that it was Allways so
intended.

P. R. O.
B. T. Md.
Vol. 17. Upon w$^{ch}$ termes the said Sam$^{ll}$ Dorsey is willing the bill Should pass and he withdraws.   And the Bill read the 2$^d$ time and doe pass.

The house Adjournes till 2 A Clock in the Afternoone.

Post Merediem.

The house met againe being calld over were All present as in the morning.

The Comittee withdraws.

The house proceeds to read the following bills.

Comittees Sent for in.

Bill for Advancement of Natives etc.

Read 2$^d$ time with Amendm$^t$ proposd & do pass.

Bill for providing A Standard etc.

Read 2$^d$ time and do pass.

Bill prohibitting Commissioners &c. to plead as Attorneys.

Read the 2$^d$ time and pass.

Bill for publication of All Marriages

Read the 2$^d$ time and do pass.

The Comittee of laws enters and delivers the foll paper

Sep$^r$ 15$^{th}$ 1704

By the Comittee of laws

The proposall of last Sessions of making A law to Suppress popish preists and others from perverting her Majestys Subjects &c$^a$ And the house having found it A matter highly to be considerd of referrd to this Comittee to make their reporte.

The Comittee doth humbly reporte that Wee haue perusd the Acts of parliament made in the latter Yeares of W$^m$ the third of happy memory do find none of those to haue such relation to this province as to be effectuall to prevent the evill Mentioned.          Signd p order Richard Dallam Cl

Which being read in the house and debated.

Jts Resolvd Nemine Contradicente that A bill be prepared to remedy the Evill etc.

Resolvd that the preists of Rome be wholly prohibitted from baptizing any And from perswasion and perverting any of her Majesty's Subjects to the supsticon of the Church of Rome Referrd for a bill to be prepared.

Bill for preservation of Harbours.

Read the 2$^d$ time Amended and passes with Amendm$^t$.

Bill prohibitting All Masters of Shipps from Conveying out of the province et$^a$.

P. R. O.
B. T. Md.
Vol. 17.

Read the 1ˢᵗ time Yesterday.
The Aforegoing bills Sent up by Mʳ Hudson.
He returns and says he deliverd the same.
Bill for killing Woolves and Crows.
Read the 2ᵈ time and do pass.
Bill declaring the Grantees of land lyeing within the bounds
of Indians &cᵃ.
Read the 2ᵈ time and do pass.
Bill to make good and Effectuall in law All process
Read the 2ᵈ time with the Amendment proposed & made
and do pass.
Bill empowering Wᵐ Sweatnam to sell land.
Read the 2ᵈ time and do pass.
Bill for preservation of all harbours &cᵃ.
Read the 2ᵈ times & Amended with the Addiconall clause
and do pass.
Bill declaring the Grantees of land &c.
Bill for quieting possessions.
Bill Ascertaining the Expences of Councilʳˢ.
Bill relating to the Standard.
Bill for publication of Marriages
Bill for killing Woolves etc.
Bill to make good & Effectuall all process.
Bill empowring Wᵐ Sweatnam to sell land.
Bill for preservation of harbours.
Bill Against Excessive Usury.
Bill for Advancement of the Natives.
Bill prohibitting Commissioners &c. to plead.
Bill to enable Colt Dorsey to sell land.
All sent up to his Exᶜʸ and Councill by Mʳ Henry Coursey
Mʳ Wᵐ Frisby & Mʳ Iohn Taylor
Proposed that forasmuch as to morrow being A day ap-
pointed for the Vissitors of the Free Schoole to meet and
some members must give their Attendance there.
Jts therefore put to the vote whither the house Meet to
morrow or Adjourne till monday morning
Carryd by Majority of Votes that the house Adjourne till
monday morning thereupon
The house Adjourn'd till monday morning 8 A Clock.


Monday Sepʳ 18ᵗʰ 1704.
The house mett According to Adjournment
Being calld over were p'sent as on fryday only Mʳ Green-
field & Mʳ Blay.
Read what was done Yesterday.

P. R. O.
B. T. Md.
Vol. 17. M$^r$ Henry Coursey M$^r$ W$^m$ Frisby and M$^r$ Iohn Taylor enters the house and say they deliverd to his Ex$^{cy}$ and Councill the bills Sent by them on fryday last

Bill providing what shalbe evidence to prooue Foreigne and other debts &c$^a$. being read & debated

Jts orderd it be left for further consideration

Iohn Addison Iohn Hamond Francis Ienkins James Sanders And Kenelm Cheseldyne Esq$^{rs}$ enters the house & delivers the following Message.

By his Ex$^{cy}$ the Gov$^r$ & Councill in Assembly
Sept$^r$ 15$^{th}$ 1704

In Answer to the houses Message by M$^r$ Greenfield and five other members deliverd to his Ex$^{cy}$ the last night is Sent You herewith A Coppy of her Most Sacred Majestys Royall instruccons to his Ex$^{cy}$ the Governour And Wee conceive that the reason of the said Instruccon to his Ex$^{cy}$ the Governour is Very obvious for that if her Majesty shalbe pleasd to disassent to any perticuler law or laws the whole body of them may not be thereby repealed as having but one Assent to the whole.

Signd ꝑ order W Bladen Cl Co.

The coppy of her Maj$^{ts}$ Royall instruccons to his Ex$^{cy}$ the Governour that came with the aboue Message, You are to transmitt Authentick coppys of All laws statutes and ordinances that are now made and in force Which haue not Yet been sent or which at Any time hereafter shalbe made or Enacted within our province Each of them Seperately under the publiq Seale unto us and our Commissioners for trade and plantacons within three Moneths or by the first opportunity After there being Enacted togeather with duplicates thereof by the next Conveyance upon paine of our highest displeasure And the forfeiture of that Yeares Sallary wherein you shall at any time upon any pretence whatsoever omitt

In° Seymour.

The peticon of Iosiah Wilson brought into the house and read Viz$^t$.

To the honoble house of Delegates

The humble peticon of Iosiah Wilson Sheriff of prince Georges County.

Sheweth

That one Thomas Hart a Convict before the provinciall Court was in September 1703 comitted into your peticoners

Custody for All fees due to Your peticon<sup>r</sup> and other officers P. R. O.
an Acco<sup>t</sup> of which is berto Annexd And Altho by the sd pro- B. T. Md.
vinciall Court an order was made that in case the said Harts Vol 17.
former Master paid not his Criminall fees and Accepted his
Service for the same Yo<sup>r</sup> peticoner should keep the said Hart
without Jmprisonm<sup>t</sup> fees from that time till the next County
Court for prince Georges County in November foll<sup>o</sup> And then
present the said Hart to the Iustices of that Court to be
Adjudg'd or disposed of as they thought fitt for sattisfaction
of the fees. But the said Harts Ma<sup>r</sup> one George Iones Absolutely refused to pay the fees And denied to Accept the
Service of the said Hart And the Iustices of prince Georges
County refus'd Any ways to intermeddle therein so that the
said hart lyes Still in yo<sup>r</sup> peticoners Custody And is A great
burthen and charge to him not being capable of Getting his
livelyhood.

Your peticoner therefore most humbly pray's the direction
of this honoble Court for his releife in the premises And that
by an order of this house he and other Officers may be paid
their Iust fees out of the publiq

And will ever pray etc.

### Thomas Hart D<sup>r</sup>

|  | lb | tob |
|---|---|---|
| To Iosiah Wilson 228 days Imprisonm<sup>t</sup> fees | | 4560 |
| To Comittment 100 Ferriage ouer two Rivers 8<sup>s</sup> | | 180 |
| To M<sup>r</sup> Attorney Gen<sup>ll</sup> | | 400 |
| To the Secretary | | 400 |
| To the Sherriff of AA<sup>ll</sup> County and ⎱ Cryer of the provinciall Court ⎰ | | 1060 |
| | | 6600 |

Which being read and debated in the house This house haue
Againe Resolvd that the Aboue fees be paid by Prince Georges
County At laying their next leavy and that the neglect thereof
will be taken as contempt to the Authority of this house.

And that An ordinance be prepar'd and sent up to the honob
Councill for their concurrence to that Purpose Viz<sup>t</sup>

### By the house of Delegates
### Sep<sup>t</sup> 22 1704

Upon reading the proceeding of this house and the returne
of the Iustices of prince Georges County this house are of
opinion that the said County ought to haue paid the said Fees
by Vertue of the af<sup>d</sup> order And now haue Againe Resolved
that the said County pay the same the neglect whereof will be

P. R. O.
B. T. Md.
Vol 17.
taken a Contempt to the Authority of this Assembly To w^{ch} the concurrence of the Honoble Councill is prayd.

Signed ꝑ order W^m Taylard Cl house Del

Edward Lloyd and W^m Coursey Esq^{rs} enter the house and delivers the following bills.
Bill prohibitting Importation of bread beer etc.
Bill Causing Grand and pettit Iuro^{rs} to come to Co^{rt}.
Bill prohibitting Masters of Shipps & other Vessells from transporting persons without passes.
Bill declaring how fees for private Acts shalbe proporcond
Bill to encourage inhabitants to Adventure Shipps etc.
Bill Ascertaining the Gage of tobacco hogsheads.
Bill Appointing Court days.
All endorsed thus Sept^r 15 1704.
Read in Councill the first time

W Bladen Cl Coun.

Orderd the Aboue bills be read in the house in the Afternoon
The house proceed to read the following bills.
Bill declaring the devision of severall Countys etc.
Read the 1^{st} time and do pass.
Bill laying an Imposicon of 9^d ꝑ Gallon on rum &c^a
Read the 1^{st} time and do pass.
Bill laying an Imposicon on severall Comodity's
Read 1^{st} time and do pass.
Bill for Setlement of An Annuall Revenue upon her Maj^{ts} Governour
Read the 2^d time and do pass.
Bill for reliefe of Credittors in England ag^t bankrupts
Read the first time & Comitted for Amendm^t
Bill Confirming to the Gov^r of this province the duty of 3^d ꝑ tonn
Read the 2^d time and do pass.
M^r Sam^{ll} Young and M^r Ioseph Hill orderd to attend the Councill to see M^r plater proove his Navall officers Accounts.
They returne and say they saw it done.
The peticon of Iane Crafts Widdow praying an Allowance for the foundacon of the Church
Read in the house and debated.
Jts Resolvd it be rejected.
Kenelm Cheseldyne Esq^r enters the house and delivers M^r Speaker the following bills.
Bill empowring W^m Sweatnam to sell land Endorsd Sept^r 18 1704   Read the 3^d time and do pass for engrossing.

W^m Bladen Cl Councill

Bill to Enable Coll Edward Dorsey to sell land &c[a]      P. R. O.<br>B. T. Md.<br>Vol. 17.
Endorsd Sept[r] 18. 1704.   Read and Agreed to by the Coun-
cill for engrossing                     W[m] Bladen Cl Co[ll]

Bill ag[t] Excessive Usury.
Bill relating to the Standard of Weights & meas[rs]
Bill for Publication of Marriages.
Bill for Killing of Woolves & Crows.
Bill to make Vallid & Effectuall all process.
Bill for preservacon of harbours.
Bill for Ascertaining the Councill[rs] & Del Expences.
Bill to prohibitt Comiss[rs] & Sherriffs to plead as Attorneys.
Bill for Advancement of the Natives etc.
Bill declaring that the grantees of land lying within the Indians may haue Accons of trespass etc.
All which Bills were Endorsd as Aboue.
And orderd they be sent up to the Comittee by George Muschamp to be engrosst
Bill for quieting possessions brought from the Councill endors'd Sept[r] 18 1704.
Read in Councill the 1st time          W[m] Bladen Cl Co.

A proposall relating to the Examiner Generalls Office being brought into the house was orderd to be read which follows Viz[t]
To the honoble the house of Assembly now sitting.
It is humbly proposd that the Examiner Generalls Office being found by Experience to be of great Utillity to the good people of this province since the same was Erected inasmuch as it prevents Seuerall mischeifs and inconveniences dayly discoverd to the Great damage of severall people in the old Surveys made before that office was sett up that the fees thereof be incerted Among other officers fees by law Establisht Which will be A great incouragement to the Examiner for the time being to be very Carefull in All matters relating to that office Whereas on the Contrary as the fees are now precarious and only Setled by the Lord prop[ry] and his Councill there can not be had a man fitt for the place that Will Accept of it the present Examiner being upon laying downe his place unless he may haue some Assurance of his fees
Its humbly Submitted to the honoble house wherein Are knowne to be now sitting severall persons of Good Skill in the mathematicks what fees the pains to be taken in that office may Iustly deserve Especially in intricate Surveys which haue many Courses &c[a]
Which being read the house is off opinion that Such an Office is necessary.

P. R. O.
B. T Md.
Vol. 17.
And thereupon is referrd to the Comittee of laws to pre-
pare A bill to Setle the fees.

The house Adjournes till 2 A Clock in the Afternoone.

### Post Merediem

The house met Againe being calld over were present as in the morning.

Mʳ Iohn Taylor orderd to goe up to some of the offices for A printed body of laws.

He returns and says that there is none perfect but what belongs to the County Court office And that Mʳ Bordley the Clk refused to send it

Upon which he was orderd to goe to said Bordley and Acquaint him that the house comands the laws Imediatly to be sent

Mʳ Taylor comes againe into the house & says he has been with Mʳ Bordley and Acquainted him with the Comand of the house but he still refused the Sending it.

Whereupon orderd the Serjeant Attendant imediatly bring the said Mʳ Bordley before the Barr of this house to Answer his Contempt

Soone after the said Bordley togeather with the Serjeant enter the house &

Mʳ Speaker was pleasd to acquaint him of his contempt to the house in disobeying their Comands And was orderd to withdrawe

Then this house fully considerd and debated the same And upon his Submission, it is agreed to be acquitted.

Mʳ Bordley appeares againe and Orderd he bring downe the body of law belonging to the County.   Which he did and deliverd it to Mʳ Speaker and upon his Submission he was discharg'd.

Upon reporte of the Comittee of Accoᵗˢ that Kent Charles & Talbott County Sherriffs haue not returnd their lists of taxables.

Orderd thereupon that Mʳ Gerrard Fowlkes Attend his Exᶜʸ & Acquaint him that this house prays his Exᶜʸ to send Expresses for the lists And Comand the Shrffs forthwith to Appeare And Answer their Contempt

Bill declaring the devision of Severall County's.

Bill laying An Imposicon on Severall Comodity's.

Bill laying An Imposicon of 9ᵈ ℘ Gallon on rum

Bill for quieting possessions and enrolling Conveyances.

Bill Confirming to the Governoʳ the duty of 3ᵈ ℘ tonn

Bill for calling Grand & Pettit Iuroʳˢ.

Bill for Setling A revenue on her Majᵗˢ Govʳ for the time being

Which sd bills Were sent up to his Ex$^{cy}$ and Councill p M$^r$ Iohn Hamond and M$^r$ Richard Iones.

They returne and say they deliverd the bills.

The house proceed to reading the following bills.

Bill Ascertaining the Gauge of tob hogsheads.

Bill to encourage the Inhabitants to send shipps Abroad.

Bill declaring how fees for private Acts be proportioned.

Bill prohibitting Ma$^{rs}$ of Shipps transporting p$^r$sons without passes.

Bill prohibitting the Importacon of bread etc.

All read the 2$^d$ time and Sent up to his Ex$^{cy}$ & Councill p M$^r$ Iohn Leach and M$^r$ Robt Skinner.

They returne and say they deliverd them

Iohn Addison Iohn Hamond Edward Lloyd Francis Jenkins Iames Sanders and Kenelm Cheseldyne Esq$^{rs}$ enters the house and delivers M$^r$ Speaker A proclamation for preventing and punishing Imorallity & prophaness.

Which was here read and orderd to be thus endors'd.


### By the house of Del Sept$^r$ 18 1704

The within proclamation was here read and Approovd of by the house who give their hearty thanks to his pious resolucons conteynd therein And will Concurr to our Uttmost to promote & encourage the same.

Signd p order W$^m$ Taylard Cl ho Del.

Which proclamation and endorsment was returnd to his Ex$^{cy}$ and Councill by M$^r$ Tho$^s$ Frisby M$^r$ Iames Hay M$^r$ Ioseph Gray M$^r$ Iohn Waters M$^r$ Iohn Maclaster M$^r$ Iohn Iones M$^r$ W$^m$ Barton and M$^r$ Thomas Beale.

They returne and say they deliverd the same.

The house Adjournes till to morrow morning 8 A Clock.


### Tuesday 19$^{th}$ Sept$^r$ 1704.

The house met againe According to Adjournm$^t$ & being calld over were present as Yesterday.

Read what was done Yesterday.

The Gent Members Appointed to consider New Yorke Affaire And the members of the house likewise Attending the Conference About Setling the land records &c. are orderd to Attend the conferrences this morning who withdrew Accordingly.

The Bill for prohibition of bread beer &c. came into the house and upon debate made It was resolvd the same be

P. R. O.
B. T. Md.
Vol. 17. Amended And sent up to his Ex$^{cy}$ by M$^r$ Henry Coursey to pray his Ex$^{cy}$ that the same be Allowd of and may pass for engrossing.

M$^r$ Coursey returnes with the bill & says his Ex$^{cy}$ & Councill were pleasd to Agree to the amendment of the said bill and Orderd it be engrossed.

Robert Smith Esq$^r$ from the Councill enters the house and delivers M$^r$ Speaker the following bill Viz$^t$

Bill Confirming the last Will and testament of Charles Ascom of St Marys County

Endorsd Sept$^r$ 18 1704   Read 1$^{st}$ time in Councill
W$^m$ Bladen Cl


Bill prohibitting Importacon of bread beer etc.

Endorsd Read in Councill the 2$^d$ time and past for engrossing                     W$^m$ Bladen Cl Co.


Bill for quieting possessions endorsd as Aboue.

Bill Confirming to the Gov$^r$ the duty of 3$^d$ ᵱ tonn endorsd as Aboue

Bill causing Grand & pettit Iuro$^{rs}$ & Witnesses to come to Co$^{rt}$

Endorsd as Aboue.

Bill for Setlement of An Annuall revenue upon her Maj$^{tie}$ Governour.

Endorsd as Aboue.

Bill laying an Imposicon on Severall Comoditys Exported.

Endorsd as Aboue.

Bill laying an Imposicon of 8$^d$ ᵱ Gallon on rume &c.

Endorsd Sept$^r$ 18 1704

Read in Councill the first time & proposd that the Impost be 12$^d$ ᵱ land & 6$^d$ water             W$^m$ Bladen Cl Co.


Bill declaring the devision of severall Countys

Endorsd Sept$^r$ 18 1704

Read in Councill and will pass        W$^m$ Bladen Cl Co.


Bill to encourage the Inhabitants to Adventure Shipps & Vessells Abroad.

Endorsd Sept$^r$ 18 1704

Read the 2$^d$ time in Councill and past for engrossing.
W$^m$ Bladen Cl Co.


Prohibitting Masters of Shipps and others from transporting persons without passes.

Endorsd Sept[r] 18 1704
Read in Councill the 2[d] time and past for engrossing.
W Bladen Cl Coun

P. R. O.
B. T. Md.
Vol. 17.

Bill declaring how fees for naturallization and other private Acts shall be proportiond.
Endorsd Sept[r] 18 1704
Read in Councill the 2[d] time & past for engrossing.
W[m] Bladen Cl Co.

Bill Ascertaining the Gauge of tob hhds
Endorsd as Aboue.
Bill Appointing County Court days, endorsd as aboue.
Then was brought into the house and read the foll paper w[ch] his Ex[cy] was pleased to say to some Romish preists &c[a]

Gent
Its the unhappy temper of you and All yo[r] tribe to growe Insolent upon Civillity And never know how to use it And Yet of All people You haue the least reason For considering that if the necessary laws that are made were lett loose they are Sufficient to Crush You And w[ch] (if Your Arrogant principles haue not blinded Your Understanding) You must needs dread.
You might methinks be Content to live quietly as you may And lett the exercize of yo[r] Superstitious Vanity's be confined to Your Selves, without proclaiming them at publiq times And in publiq places unless you Expect by your Gawdy Shews and Serpentine pollicy to Amuse the Multitude and beguile the unthinking part of them An Art of deceipt well knowne to be Among You But Gent be not deceiv'd for tho the Clemency of her Maj[ts] Government And of her Gratious inclination leads her to make All her Subjects Easy that know how to be so Yet her Maj[ty] is not without means sufficient to Curb insolence in All but more Especially in Your fraternity who are more Eminently soe then others Abounding with it And I Assure You the next occasion you give me You shall feele the truth of what I say Which You should now doe but that I am willing upon the Earnest Sollicitations of some Gent to make one tryall more (And it shalbe but this one) of yo[r] temper:
In plain and few words, Gent if you intend to live here lett me hear no more of these things, for if I doe And they are made Good Against you be Assured Ile chastise Yoe And least You should flatter yo[r] selves that the Severrity of the laws will be a means to moove the pitty of Your Iudges I Assure you I dont intend to deale soe with You. Ile remoove

P. R. O.
B. T. Md.
Vol. 17. the Evill by sending You where you may be dealt with as You
deserve.

Therefore as I told you I'le make but this one tryall And
Advise you to be Civill and modest for their is noe other
way for you to live quietly here.

You are the first that have Given any disturbance to my
Government And if it were not for the hopes of Your better
demeano$^r$ you should now be the first that Shou'd feel the
Effect of soe doeing.

Pray take notice that I am an English protestant Gent And
that I can never equivocate.

This is A Coppy of What his Ex$^{cy}$ the Govern$^r$ was pleasd
to say to the two popish preists upon their being presented
for Saying Mass publiqely at the Citty of St Mary's when the
County Court was sitting And for consecrating A popish
Chappell.                              W$^m$ Bladen Cl Coun

Which being read Its orderd by the house the following
Message be sent.

By the house of Delegates Sept$^r$ 19 1704.

By A paper read in this house wee perceive what Your Ex$^{cy}$
was pleasd to say to the two popish preists on the occasion
there mencond, And as All yo$^r$ Actions, so this in p'ticuler
gives us great Sattisfaction to find you Generously Resolvd
to protect her Maj$^{tys}$ protestant Subjects here against the
insolence and Growth of popery and· wee are cheerefully
thankfull to you for it
                      Signd p order W$^m$ Taylard Cl ho Del

The Seuerall Resolves of the house ·upon the severall
Articles of her Maj$^{ts}$ Instruccons And other proposalls laid
before this house Read in the house and sent up to his Ex$^{cy}$
and Councill by M$^r$ Iohn Macall and M$^r$ Gerrard Fowlks.

They returne and say they deliverd them

The message relating to the popish preists abouesd was
Sent up to his Ex$^{cy}$ and Councill by Coll Iames Smallwood
Coll W$^m$ Barton M$^r$ Iohn Macall M$^r$ Ino. Wells M$^r$ Tho$^s$ Frisby
M$^r$ Iohn Maclaster & M$^r$ Robert Tyler

They returne and say they deliverd the same

Moovd by A member of this house that for the ease of the
inhabitants of this province in payment of their publiq Taxes

they shall have liberty to pay it in money at A Certaine price P. R. O. B. T. Md. Vol. 17. to be Setled And by A certaine day in each Year to the Sherriff of each County And the Sherriff to pay the same Againe to those who have right to the same And At the same rate.

And likewise the 3ᵈ ₱ hhd to be paid by Maʳˢ of Shipps to the Navall Officers, shalbe by them answerable to the publiq in ready money, Currant Coyne of the province, and not by bills of Exchange.

Its resolvd the same is A good Mocon and orderd the Committee of laws prepare A bill for that purpose.

Moovd likewise by A member that some measures be taken that A mans Goods may redeem his body out of prison

Resolvd A bill be prepared.

The peticon of Iosiah Wilson read in the house and debated.

The house finding it to be for an Allowances of Imprisonment ffees it is noe ways incumbent on the Countrey to pay by the law of the province And Alsoe of A dangerous consequence Therefore is rejected.

Orderd the following Message be entred Vizᵗ

By the house of Delegates Septʳ 19ᵗʰ 1704

This house desire the honoble Councills Answeir to our last Message touching the bill for regulation of Ordnary's.

Signd ₱ order Wᵐ Taylard Clk house Del.

The foregoeing Message sent up to his Exᶜʸ and Councill by Mʳ Ioseph Ennalls And Mʳ Iohn Hudson.

They returne and say they deliverd the same.

Coll Holland enters the house and delivers Mʳ Speaker the following peticons and some bills.

Which bills is referrd till Afternoone for reading.

The peticon of the Inhabitants of Cecill County for deviding their County

The Peticon of the Inhabitants of Kent County on the South side Chester River for division of their County.

And the Peticon of the inhabitants of Talbott County for devision of their County.

Severally endorsd thus.

By his Exᶜʸ the Govʳ & Councill Sepʳ 19ᵗʰ 1704

This peticon referrd to the consideracon of the house of Delegates                                    Wᵐ Bladen Cl Coun

11

Vhich said Severall peticons and endorsments thereon was
1 and debated And the house finding Matters of A great
ight & Moment lye before them.
'herefore Resolvd the Consideration of the Severall peticons
be referrd till next Sessions of Assembly.
'he peticon of the Freeholders and inhabitants of St Pauls
rish in Prince Georges County. was read & debated And
Resolvd that the four delegates for that County in this
nt Gen^ll Assembly togeather with M^r Robert Bradley and
fames Stoddard be and Are Appointed to make A devision
1 Ascertaine the bounds to the equall Advantage of the
rishioners as may be and to reporte the same to the house
t Sessions of Assembly.   And then the house Will further
ceed.
'he house Adjournes till 2 A Clock in the Afternoon

### Post Merediem

'he house met againe according to Adjournment, being
ld over were present as in the morning.
'he foll Message brought into the house by In° Addison
l Francis Ienkins Esq^rs.
)rderd to be entred Viz^t.


By the Councill in Assembly Sept^r 19^th 1704

Your Message desireing our reply to yonr Answer About
  bill for regulating ordnary's wee receivd And propose
t Your house would Appoint two or three of yo^r members
oyne with M^r Smith and M^r Cheseldyne of this board at
> of the Clock this Afternoone to consult and propose how
  said law should pass.
                 Signd p order W Bladen Cl Councill.

Read and orderd to be endors'd

         ,

By the house of Delegates Sept^r 19^th 1704

/I^r George Muschamp and M^r Thom^s Frisby by the house
  appointed to  o ne in conferrence with the Gent of the
ıncill proposed.    Signd p ord^r W^m Taylard Cl h D.


3ill prohibitting the Importacon of bread beer et^c
)rderd to be read Againe with the amendment made and
pass for engrossing.
3ill for quieting possessions and Enrolling Conveyances.

Bill Confirming the duty of $3^d$ ℔ tonn.

P. R. O.
B. T. Md.
Vol. 17.

Bill Causing grand and Pettit Iur$^{ors}$ to come to Courts.

Bill Setling An Annuall revenue on the Governour.

Bill to encourage the Inhabitants to Venture their Shipps

Bill prohibitting Ma$^{rs}$ of Shipps and other from transporting persons out of the province.

Bill Declaring how fees for Naturallization and private Acts shall be proporcond.

Bill Ascertaining the Gage of tob° hogsheads

Bill Appointing Co$^{ty}$ Court day's.

Bill prohibitting importation of bread beere &c$^a$

All read and past for engrossing & endorsd thus.

Signd ℔ order W Bladen Cl Coun

Sent up to the Comittee of laws to be engrosst by M$^r$ W$^m$ Watts.

He returns and says he deliverd the bills.

Bill Confirming the last Wills & testaments of Charles Ascomb In° Winfell and In° Burnham

Read and orderd to be endorsd as foll Viz$^t$

By the house of Delegates Sept$^r$ 19$^{th}$ 1704

This bill being read this house do declare that as for Burnham's Will this house haue knowledge of and Are willing to pass, And As for the others this house Wou'd know by What Authority it was brought in being Alltogeather Strangers to it

Signd ℔ order W$^m$ Taylard Cl ho Del

Sent up ℔ M$^r$ Rob$^t$ Skinner

Orderd M$^r$ Iames Phillips call M$^r$ Bladen into the house, Who Appeares, And proposd to him if he would Accept of tenn pounds Sterl in full Sattisfaction of All Millitary Commissions that shall Issue during the p$^r$sent Governours Continuance in Comanding in this province

M$^r$ Bladen Accepts of the same. but Resolved that this, be no president for the future.

M$^r$ Rob$^t$ Skinner returns and say's he delivered his Ex$^{cy}$ & Councill the bill for confirming Ascombs Winfells & Burnhams Wills.

Bill laying Imposicon on Severall Comoditys.

Read the 2$^d$ time.

M$^r$ W$^m$ Bladen Clerk of the Councill ℔ permission enters the house And Acquaints M$^r$ Speaker that he is ready to give him Sattisfaction About bringing in the Bill for confirming

P. R. O.  Ascombs Will etc. in order thereto deliverd Severall papers
B. T. Md.  &c. . Thereupon further consideration is referrd till to morrow
Vol. 17.  morning.

Bill for laying an Imposicon on Severall Comoditys
Exported
Read the 2ᵈ time and do pass. .
Bill laying Imposicon on rum etc.
Endors'd Whither it might not be 12ᵈ ℗ Gallon by land &
6ᵈ water.                                    W Bladen Cl Co.

And by the house Endorsd thus this house doe insist upon
the bill as it is drawne exclusive of the Amendment proposd
by the Councill.
    Sent up to his Exᶜʸ and Councill by Mʳ Francis Dollahyde.
" He returns and says he deliverd the same.
Bill declaring the devision of Severall County's
Read 2ᵈ time and do pass.
Bill for releife of Credittors in England Against bankrupts.
Read the 2ᵈ time with Amendment And Againe Committed
for Amendment with A clause proposed.
    Iames Sanders Esqʳ from the honoble Councill enters the
house and delivers Mʳ Speaker the following bill.
Bill laying Imposicon of 9ᵈ ℗ Gallon on rum
Endorsd read & Agreed to by the Councill and do pass for
engrossing.            ·          W Bladen Cl Councill.

Sent up to the Comittee of Laws by Mʳ Inᵒ Waters to be
Engrost
He returnes & says he deliverd it
Wᵐ Holland Esqʳ enters the house and brings from the
Councill the following representation

Maryland ss.

        By the Rector Govʳ & Visitors of the Freeschoole
                    Sepʳ 16ᵗʰ 1704

Jt is humbly represented to his Exᶜʸ the Governour her
Majᵗˢ honoble privy Councill and the Genˡˡ Assembly that
According to Agreement by us made the 3ᵈ day of May 1700
With A Comittee of the house of Delegates for A Roome in
the Freeschoole to place the library in from that time to the
third Instant the Sume of Fifty two Pounds Sterling for rent
for the said Library roome is due And further Wee do represent that the other parte of the schoole hath been before that

time and ever since usd for the publiq Service for Which Wee
pray A reasonable Allowance.

Signd ꝑ order W Bladen Cl Libr Scool

Which was endors'd
By his Ex^cy the Gov^r & Councill
Sep^r 19 1704

The within representation referrd to the consideracon of the house of Delegates.
Signd ꝑ order W^m Bladen Cl Counc

Which being read Its orderd that M^r In^o Waters goe & desire his Ex^cy that the Agreement made may be laid before this house to morrow And the house will further consider thereof
The house Adjourns till to morrow morning 8 A Clock.

Wednesday Sep^r 20^th 1704

The house mett According to Adjournement being calld over were present as Yesterday
Read What was done Yesterday.
Severall bills brought into the house by the Comittee of laws. Were orderd to be read Viz^t
Bill empowering the Commissioners of the County Courts to raise tob to defray the necessary charge of the Countys and Parrishes.
Bill Ascertaining damages on protested bills of Exchange
Bill Ascertaining Land to the use of the Nanticoke Ind^as
All read the 1^st & 2^d time & ꝑ Speciall order do pass.
The honob W^m Coursey Esq^r enters the house and delivers
M^r Speaker
Bill for stay of Executions after the 10^th of May.
Bill to Confirme titles to land Given to churches.
Bill Securing rights to Towne land.
Bill for Amercements in the prov^ll and County Courts.
Bill for confirming purchases made by the Commission^rs of County Courts.
Bill for restraining the Extortions of Sherriffs
Bill for directing the manner of Electing & Sumoning Del^s
Bill for conveying publiq pacquetts.
The foregoing bills were read the first and Second time and by Especiall order passt And Sent up to the Councill ꝑ M^r W^m Wallis And M^r Iohn Leach.

P. R. O.
B. T. Md.
Vol. 17. The Gent Appointed by the house to Conferr About the bill for regulating ordinarys et* enters the house and upon their report the following message was ordered to be Sent up.


By the house of Delegates Sep[r] 20th 1704

The clause proposed by the Conferrees as it is made to take place cannot brought in with good Sence as it is there Worded but in reguard Wee perceive it is their Resolve that the bill may pass in A peticonary maner Wee Are content it be soe, And therefore wee propose that it runn thus

For better regulating ordinarys &c* For the future and in pursuance of her Maj[tr] Royall Instruccons for raising further Supplys for defraying the publiq charge of this province To effect which the Burgesses and Delegates of this present Gen[ll] Assembly Doe humbly pray that her Maj[ty] will be gratiously pleasd to grant that it may be Enacted And be it Enacted etc.

Signd ꝑ order W[m] Taylard Cl h D

Which being read Was sent up to the Councill ꝑ M[r] Henry Coursey M[r] George Muschamp and M[r] Frisby.

They returne and delivers M[r] Speaker the Bill for regulating ordnary's &c*. Endorsd thus.


By the Councill in Assembly Sep[r] 20th 1704

The report of the Conferrees upon this bill And the houses Message thereupon haue been read And the latter is Agreed to

Signd ꝑ order W Bladen Cl Counc

The Gent of the Conferrencc Appointed by his Ex[cy] the Gov[r] Councill and Assembly to enquire into the Agrievances relating to the land Office & the Lord Baltemores Agents.

The conferrees having laid before them and read the message of the house on this Subject And the order of his late Maj[ty] in Councill in relation to the devision of the fees of that office between my Lord Baltemore and S[r] Thomas Lawrence Barron[tt] Sec[ry] of Maryland doe reporte as foll[o]

That it is Conceivd propper that An Act of Assembly or ordinance be drawne up past And Assented to by his Ex[cy] the Gov[r] and Councill & Assembly that what ever Warrants for the future be granted by his Lopps Officers And Assigned either the whole or any parte thereof to any other persons that on returne of the Certificate it Shall be lawfull for him or them to demand A Grant thereof Notwithstanding the purchase

money be unpaid by the first taker up of the Warrant And
that Notice thereof be Given to his Lopps Agents.

That forasmuch as at p'sent the records of the land Office are much torne damnifyed & some part lost And that the Offices for Granting of lands are now in the hands of two Severall persons Which were heretofore intire And that theire being so devided Occasions his Lopp the Lord Baltemore to double the purchase of his Warrants Which Wee humbly conceive to be A Great Agrievance And pray her Maj^{ty} may be Addrest for remedy thereof

Signd ꝑ order Th Iones Cl Com^{ee}

Which reporte was here read in the house & in reguard the Great & Weighty Matters lyeing before the house At this time therefore Resolvd the further consideration thereof be referrd to the next Sessions of Assembly.

Then the house Adjournd till 2 A Clock in the Afternoone.

### Post Merediem

The house met againe According to Adjournment, And being Calld over were All present as in the Morning.

Was brought into the house the foll bill Orderd to be read.

Bill for Naturallization of Otho Ottherson

Read the 1^{st} and 2^{d} time and do pass,

Bill declaring the Devision of Countys' et^{a}

Bill laying An Imposicon on Severall Comodity's etc. Sent up to the Councill.

The Message last night relating to the rent of the Free schoole was Againe read And the Agreement as was desired layd before the house being read And fully debated. It is Resolvd this house is willing to pay the rent Agreed upon for the Use of the Whole house without any further charge to this time.

And proposd that forasmuch As the ends of the Free schoole has Appeard hitherto not to be Answerrd.

Resolvd that it be referrd to the Consideration of the next Sessions of Assembly What further measures shall be taken to perfect so good A worke.

The peticon of St Pauls Parrish in Prince Georg's County With endorsment was deliverd to M^r Magruder.

M^r Tho^s Greenfeild M^r W^m Aisquith And M^r Robert Skinner are desired to take the bill for confirming Wills etc. With the Wills & other papers relating to it And withdraw to consider Whither the house can pass that bill With Safety And make reporte thereof to the house.

Bill for regulating Ordinarys etc.

P R. O.
B. T. Md.
Vol. 17.

Read the 2ᵈ time and pass with Amendmᵗ for Engrossing. Sent up to the Councill ᵱ Mʳ Coursey and Mʳ Muschamp. They returne and say they deliverd it

Bill providing What shalbe evidence to proove Forreigne Debts &cᵃ

Read the 2ᵈ time with the Amendment made and do pass. Sent up to the Councill by Mʳ Iames Maxwell.

. He returnes and Says he.deliverd the same.

Coll Iames Maxwell Mʳ Thomas Beale Orderd to Attend Mʳ Vanderheyden Navall Officer to see him proove his Accounts before the Councill.

They returne and say they haue seen him and Mʳ Wᵐ Bladen prooue their Navall Officers Accounts.

Orderd Mʳ Young Mʳ Aisquith and Mʳ Ennalls goe and See Coll Dent proove his Navall Officers Accounts.

Who returne And say they haue seen it done.

Bill for limittacon of Actions Engrost And Endorsd Vizᵗ Read & Assented to by the house of Dels.

Bill Directing the manner of Sueing out Attachmˡˢ Endors'd Read & Assented to by the house of Delegates.

Bill Against Engrossers and regraters

Bill for Publication of Marriages

Bill for killing of Woolves & Crows.

All endorsd as aboue & Signd        Wᵐ Taylard Cl h D

The house Adjournes till to morrow Morning Eight A Clock.

### Tuesday [sic] 21ᵗʰ Septʳ 1704

The house mett Againe According to Adjournment being calld over were All present as Yesterday only Mʳ Wᵐ Barton sick.

The Gent appointed to inspect the Will of Mʳ Charles As-comb of St Mary's County And In° Winfell of Calvert County reporte as followeth.

By the Comittee for inspecting the Wills of Charles As-comb & of Ino Winfell decd.

Jt is humbly reported to the honob house of Delegates by Mʳ Thomas Greenfeild Mʳ Wᵐ Aisquith And Mʳ Robt. Skinner Members Especially Appointed for the Inspection Afd that upon the perusall of the said Wills they Are by them Adjudged And verily beleivd to be the last Wills of the said Charles As-comb & Iohn Winfell but that they finding to the same Wills the. Evidence of one or two Wittnesses to Corroborate the Vallidity of the same in law which is referrd to the Considera-tion of the house.        Signd ᵱ order In° Collins Clk

Upon reading and debating of which reporte Resolvd that the Will of the said Iohn Winfell be Recorded in the office for probatt of Wills.

Then the bill was read the 2$^d$ time & do pass w$^{th}$ the Amendments made.

Resolvd that the persons to whose use private Bills pass be oblidged to make sattisfaction And the publiq be no ways chargd therewith

Orderd Message be prepard and Sent his Ex$^{cy}$ relating to the foregoing Resolves.

The honob In$^o$ Addison Francis Ienkins Edw$^d$ Lloyd And Kenelm Cheseldyne Esq$^{rs}$ from the Councill enters the house And delivers M$^r$ Speaker the following bills.

Bill directing the Manner of Electing delegates.

Bill for purchases made by the Com$^{rs}$ for the use of their Co$^{tys}$

Bill restraining the Extortion of Sherriffs.

Bill for Amercements etc.

Bill for Securing rights to towne lands &c.

Bill Ascertaining Damages on protested bills etc.

Bill Ascertaining the bounds of the Nanticoke Ind$^{as}$ Land.

Bill empowring the Com$^{rs}$ of the County Courts to raise tobacco to defray their Charges.

Bill Confirming titles to land Given to churches.

Bill for Naturrallization of Otho Ottherson

Bill laying An Imposicon on Severall Comodity's.

Bill declaring the devision of Severall Countys.

Bill for conveying publiq Lres

Bill for regulating ordnarys etc.

all Endorsd Sept$^r$ 20 1704

Read in Councill and past for engrossing.

W$^m$ Bladen Cl Co.

Alsoe A bill for Stay of Executions After the tenth day of May.

Endors'd Eod Die

Read in Councill and will pass the words Mayor Recorder or any two of the Aldermen of the Citty of St Mary's being left out for this Board know noe Comicon or Authority Granted or confirmd by her Majesty for the holding that Court

W Bladen Cl Co.

Which being read the house concurrs therewith and the bill do pass with Amendment

Bill imposing 9$^d$ ⅌ Gallon on rum

P. R. O.
B. T. Md.
Vol. 17.
Bill Ascertaining Expences of Comissioners etc
Both read & Assented to by the house of Del^s

W^m Taylard Clk.

The honob Iohn Hamond Esq^r from the Councill enters the house And delivers M^r Speaker
Bill providing what Shalbe evidence to prooue forreigne & other debts          Endorsd Eod Die.

Read in Councill And recomended that the Clause Giving the Defendant Costs upon the Issue not demanded be left As it was in the former law for that if the defendant has paid parte of the debt he can't plead that and take Advantage of Noe Demand made.          W^m Bladen Cl Council

Bill to make Good Vallid & Effectuall All process
Bill Setling A Standard of W^ts and Measures.
Bill prohibitting Ma^rs of Shipps and others from transporting persons without passes.
Bill Confirming the duty of 3^d ℔ tonn
Bill Ag^t Excessive Usury.
Bill for preservation of Harbours
Bill declaring the Grantees of Indians land.
Bill prohibitting Com^rs &c. to plead &c^a
Bill for quieting possessions.
Bill declaring Altering tobacco to be fellony.
Bill Appointing Constables &c^a.
Bill for Setling an Anuall Revenue on the Gov^r
Bill for Appointing Court day's.
Bill for Advancem^t of Natives and residents.
Bill Enabling W^m Sweatnam to Sell land.
Bill Enabling Coll Dorsey to Sell land.
All which foregoing Bills Were read and Assented to by the house of Delegates.          W Taylard Cl.

M^r Iohn Hudson M^r Robert Skinner M^r W^m Aisquith And M^r Thomas Beale Sent up to his Ex^cy & Councill with the foregoeing Endors'd
Bills read this day. and the other five Engrost bills read last night
They returne and say they deliverd the same.
The house Adjourns till 2 A Clock Afternoone.

Post Merediem

The house mett According to Adjournnm^t were calld over and present as in the morning.

Bill for Releife of Credittors.
Read the 2ᵈ time wᵗʰ Amendmᵗ and do pass.

P. R. O.
B. T. Md.
Vol. 17.

The reporte of the Conferrence relating to New York Affaires Was read and orderd to be entred Vizᵗ.

By the Conferrence appointed for the Affaires of New York.

1ˢᵗ It is conceivd that if the Seat of Gouᵉnment be at New York it will not only be A means to Allure and entice Many trades men Artificers And others Now among us Who follow the trade of planting here to desert this province And fly to that of New Yorke where they may follow their Seuerall trades & Callings and Gaine to themselves more ease and Advantage, thereby lessening the Revenue of the Crowne of England And Alsoe by these Meanes they will in A Short time be Enabled to Supply us with Such Manufactory's and other necessary's which now Are Imported from England & inevittably destroy our Comerce with the same.

2 Wee conceive that New York having power and Authority will upon All Occasions Comand from us such forces as they Shall think fitt for the Safety and Strengthning themselves as Will in A great Measure weaken this province (Now but thinly Seated) And thereby leave the remaining parte of the Inhabitants here open to the incursions of our Comon Enemy the Indians by whom Wee are Environ'd And many of them As neere to us as those at New Yorke who are often Comitting Murthers on the Inhabitants here And haue lately destroyd severall persons And having opportunity also of o ning with the Severall Nations of Indians residing among us to Effect their designes leaving us in a deplorable Condition the lives of the Inhabitants Greatly hazarded thereby And the province in Generall in danger of being totally laid Waiste.

3ᵈ That it will be very disadvantageous to the inhabitants of this province upon All occasions As of Councills Assemblys Genˡˡ Courts And upon Appeales and differences between party and party to travell thither being neere 400 Miles distant from us And the ways impassable in the Winter Season by reason of the desert road's Violent frosts deep Snows and Rivers And bay's to pass over Soe that the poorer sort of people will not be Able to undergoe so Great A charge and fatigue. And the Rich to Avoid it will remoove themselves & Estates to England or other parts And so tend to the ruine of the tobacco trade And Consequently lessen the Revenue to the Crowne.

4 That the Constitucon of this province to theirs is of so disagreeable And different A nature both in traffick and other things that the laws there compos'd cannot be Agreeable to the trade and Affaires of this Countrey nor the Constitucon of the inhabitants of this province.

P. R. O.
B. T. Md.
Vol. 17.
Jt is humbly offerrd to the consideration of the house of Delegates Whither it may not be of Service to the Countrey that A Certaine Sume of money be raisd & lodgd in the hands of some Able Merchant or Merch[ts] in England ready to be calld out upon any such occasion for the better encouragement of the persons negotiating this Affaire And whither or no it may not be thought of Service to the Countrey that some person be appointed by the house And sent home with such pacquetts for their more Safe and Speedy Conveyance.

Signd p order Th Iones Cl Conf

Which reporte being read and debated to the first parte thereof this house Concurrs with the Conferrence & ·

Resolvd that An Address to her Ma[ty] may be prepar'd, but As to the last Clause this house thinke there's no Occasion of raising Money at this time for negotiating that Affaire And for the same reason no Occasion of sending Any person home As by that last Article in the reporte is proposed.

Bill for limitting A time After w[ch] no grant or pattent shall be made upon Certificates Ascertaining What time Quiett possession Shall make A title.

Read the 1st time and put to the Question whither the bill shall lye for further consideration or be rejected.

Carryd by Majority of Voices that the same be rejected.

Bill for marking highways &c.

Bill for better Admstration of Iustice of Co[ty] Co[rts] both read the 1st and 2[d] time and by Especiall order do pass. & the bill for Appeals & regulating Writts of Erro[r]

Bill for releife of Credittors against Bankrupts

Sent up to the Councill by M[r] Iames Maxwell M[r] Iames Phillips and M[r] Thomas Beale.

togeather with the following Message.

By the house of Delegates
Sept[r] 21st 1704

This house haue Considerd the charge of the Great Seale &c[a] and upon debate thereof haue come to the following Resolves.

1    1 20[l] tob is the true and propper fee Setled by law on the Great Seale for passing any bill As Coming under the Gen[ll] Clause in the last part of the parragraph in the Act for Officers fees.

2[d]    that the same fees Wee are content be Allowd the great Seale for such Bills as shall pass this or future Assemblys out of the publiq Stock Except private bills made for private

Advantages Where the partys for whom such bill passes are to pay Such fees As the Sessions Agree to according to Another law made for that purpose. P. R. O<br>B. T. Md.<br>Vol. 17.

3ᵈ  That one Seale to the Whole body of laws to be sent to each County is Sufficient And that there is no need to Seale them seperately.

To those Wee pray the Concurrence of the honoble Councill to prevent any dispute or Misunderstanding for the future.

Signd ꝑ order Wᵐ Taylard Cl ho Del.

They returne and say they deliverd the bills and Message.

Coll Inº Hamond & Coll Francis Ienkins enters the house And delivers Mʳ Speaker the following Engrosst bills Vizᵗ.

Bills for Quieting possessions
Bill for Setling an Anuall revenue on the Governoʳ
Bill Appointing Court days.
Bill Against Ingrosssers and regraters.
Bill for publiq Marriages.
Bill for killing Woolves & Crows.
Bill Ascertaining Councilloʳˢ Expences.
Bill to make Effectuall in law All Process.
Bill for Setling A Standard of Wᵗˢ and Measures.
Bill Imposing 9ᵈ ꝑ Gall on Rum.
Bill for limittation of Actions.
Bill directing the manner of Sueing out Attachmᵗˢ.
Bill Against Excessive Usury
Bill for preservation of harbours.
Bill declaring the Grantees of Indians land.
Bill prohibitting Comʳˢ & Sherriffs to plead as Attorneys
Bill prohibitting Mʳˢ of Shipps etc. to transport persons without passes.
Bill confirming to the Govʳ 3ᵈ ꝑ tonn
Bill for Advancemᵗ of Natives etc.
Bill Enabling Wᵐ Sweatnem to sell land.
Bill Against Altering the marke or quallity of tobº.
Bill Appointing Constables.
Bill for publication of All laws.

Endorsd Septʳ 21 1704

Read and Assented to by her Majᵗˢ honoble Councill
Wᵐ Bladen Cl Co.

Bill providing What Shalbe evidence to prooue Forreigne debts.

Read the 2ᵈ time with Amendment And orders that Mʳ Nicholas Lowe carry the sd bills up to his Exᶜʸ And Councill And Acquaint their honoʳˢ with the Amendment.

P. R. O.
B. T. Md.
Vol. 17.
He returnes and Sayes he deliverd it

The house Adjournes till to morrow morning Eight A Clock.

### Fryday Sept$^r$ 22$^d$ 1704

The house mett Againe And being Calld over were present As Yesterday.  & Maj$^r$ W$^m$ Barton Sick Yesterday enters the house.

Read What was done Yesterday.

The reporte of the Conference relating to New York Affaires with the Endorsment Was sent up by M$^r$ Iohn Taylor to the Comittee of laws who is desired to prepare An Address to her Maj$^{ty}$ upon the matters proposed.

The following bills from the Comittee of laws brought into the house & orderd to be read.

Bill prohibitting liquors to be carryd to Indian townes

Bill for securing Merch$^{ts}$ and other tob$^o$ After receivd.

Bill for recording All laws.

Bill Imposing A duty on rum negroes and Irish Serv$^{ts}$ Read the first & 2$^d$ time and by Especiall order do pass.

Sent up to the Councill p M$^r$ Iohn Wells.

He returnes and says he deliverd the bills.

The honob Thom$^s$ Tench Ino Addison Robt Smith Kenelm Cheseldyne And W$^m$ Coursey Esq$^{rs}$ enters the house and delivers M$^r$ Speaker the following Message.

### By the Councill in Assembly Sept$^r$ 22$^d$ 1704

In Answer to the houses Message by Coll Maxwell and others this board doe Agree to the first Article that 120$^l$ is the true and propper fee setled by law on the Great Seale for passing any bill As Coming under the Gen$^{ll}$ Clause in the law.

Orderd it be entred on the Iournall of the house.

The house Adjourns till 2 A Clock in the afternoon

### Post Merediem

The house met Againe and were p$^r$sent as in the morning.

Brought into the house the following Engrost bills Viz$^t$ Orderd they be read.

Engrost bill restrayning the Extortions of Sherriffs &c$^a$

Engrost bill Confirming purchases made by Com$^{rs}$ of the respective Countys.

Engrost bill prohibitting Importation of bread.

Engrost bill Ascertaining the Gauge of tob hhds

P. R. O.
B. T. Md.
Vol. 17.

Engrost bill declaring how fees for Naturalliza[n] & other private Acts Shalbe proporcond.

Engrost bill Encourageing the Inhabit[ts] to Venture Shipps

Engrost bill for Naturallization of Otho Ottherson

Engrost bill for causing Grand & pettit Iuro[rs] & Wittnesses to Come to Courts.

Engrost bill for the more Speedy Conveyance of publiq pacquetts

All Endorsd read & Assented to by the house of Delegates.

Iames Sanders and W[m] Coursey Esq[rs] enter the house & Delivers M[r] Speaker the following Bills.

Bill for taking Speciall bayles.

Bill Securing tob After recd

Bill for recording the laws.

Bill Imposing 3[d] p Gallon on liquors etc.

Bill prohibitting liquors to be carryd to Ind[a] townes.

Bill to confirme the last Will of Ascom & others

Bill for marking highways.

Bill for releife of Credittors ag[t] Bankrupts.

All Seuerally endorsd Eod Die.

Read in Councill And past for engrossing.

Alsoe A bill for better Admtracon of Iustice.

W[m] Bladen Cl Co.

### Endors'd Sept[r] 22[d] 1704

This Bill read & Will pass with the Amendment of the Title of the Act　　　　　W Bladen Cl Councill

Which bill was read with the Amendment in the Title and Agreed to by the house and do pass.

All which bills were Sent up by M[r] Muschamp to be Engrost.

He returns and says he deliverd the bills

Bill for Appeales and Writts of Erro[r]

Endorst the house insist on the bill as drawne.

Sent up to the Councill by M[r] Gerrard Fowlks.

M[r] Henry Coursey brought in An Address to her Majesty Read in the house and Approovd of and Sent up to the Councill p M[r] Coursey.

He returns And says he deliverd the same

Engrost bill for Stay of Executions After the 10th May Yearly.

Engrost bill for Amercem[t] in the prov[ll] & Co[ty] Courts

Read And Assented to by the house of Del

Bill for Setlement of land on Susanah Blaney.

Read 1st and 2[d] time and do pass.

Sent up to the Councill p M[r] Ioseph Ennalls.

P. R. O.
B. T. Md.
Vol. 17.
He returns And says he deliverd the same
Engrost bill Ascertaining the bounds of the Nanticoke Ind[s]
Read & Assented to by the house.
Engrost bill Ascertaining damages on protests.
Read & Assented to by the house.
The house Adjournd till 2 A Clock in the Afternoone.

### Post Merediem

the house met againe According to Adjournm[t] being calld
over Were p[r]sent as in the Morning.
The house proceed to reading the Engrost bills.
Engrost bill for Securing persons rights to towne lands.
Engrost bill declaring the devision of Severall Countys
Engrost bill Confirming land to churches.
Engrost bill Empowring Com[rs] of the County Courts to
leavy and raise tob.
Engrost bill for regulating Ordinary's.
Engrost bill directing the manner of Electing Delegates.
All read & Assented to by the house of Delegates.
Engrost bill laying an Imposicon on Sev[ll] Comoditys.
Read & Assented to by the house of Delegates.
The house Adjourns till Monday Morning 8 A Clock.

### Monday Sept[r] 25[th] 1704

The house met againe According to Adjournm[t] being calld
over were p[r]sent as on Saturday.
Read What was done on Saturday.
The honob Iames Sanders Esq[r] enters the house & delivers
M[r] Speaker the following bills.
Bill for Appeales & Writts of Erro[r] Endorsd thus.

### By the Councill in Assembly Sept[r] 25[th] 1704.

This board think that the prohibitting the liberty of Appeales for fear of some litigious persons making ill use thereof May be A means to deprive many honest Men who Are
injurd by Illegall Iudgm[ts] of what the law Allows to witt A
Review thereof & of Which of right ought not to be denied
them however Wee Agree with the house that such Appeale
be not less for then 20[l] Sterling or 4000[l] tob.
Signd p order W Bladen Cl Counc

Bill for Setling land on Susan[a] Blaney.
Endorsd Read in Councill the 1st and 2[d] time and do pass
for Engrossing                                    W Bladen Cl Counc

Sent up by M<sup>r</sup> Goldesborough to be engrost
Bill providing Evidence to prooue forreigne Debts
Endors'd By the Councill in Assembly Sept<sup>r</sup> 25<sup>th</sup> 1704
Read the 2<sup>d</sup> time and its wisht for preventing pjurys the last
clause of this bill might be conformable to the former law thats
to say Money or tob paid to be proovd and Allow in discount
W<sup>m</sup> Bladen Cl Counc.

P. R. O.
B. T. Md.
Vol. 17.

Bill for Appeales and Writts of Erro<sup>r</sup> was read with the
Endorsment from the Councill And orderd it be Endors'd
thus Viz<sup>t</sup>

By the house of Del 25<sup>th</sup> Sept<sup>r</sup> 1704

This house Still insists upon the bill as before drawne from
which this house will not receed.
Signd p order W<sup>m</sup> Taylard Cl h D

Sent up to the Councill p M<sup>r</sup> Henry Coursey.
He returns and says he deliverd it
Bill providing What Shalbe Evidence to prooue Forreigne
& other debts. Endorsd thus Viz<sup>t</sup>

By the house of Delegates.
Sept<sup>r</sup> 25<sup>th</sup> 1704

The former law was found to be A great inducem<sup>t</sup> to perjury And Wee hope this Will prevent it therefore Wee insist
on the bill as drawne.
Signd p order W<sup>m</sup> Taylard Cl h D.

Sent up to the Councill by M<sup>r</sup> Iohn Hudson
He returns and Says he deliverd the same
Bill relating to Servants And Slaves.
Read the 1<sup>st</sup> time.
The house Adjournd till 2 A Clock in the Afternoone.

Post Merediem.

The house mett Againe According to Adjournment being
calld over All were present as in the morning only Maj<sup>r</sup> W<sup>m</sup>
Barton sick with the Gripes.
Moovd by A member that forasmuch as Maj<sup>r</sup> Barton is now
Sick of the Gripes he might haue leave to go home for re-
couery Which was granted And leave Given him

12

P. R. O.    Proposd Whither it be not Advisable to haue the Sermon
B. T. Md.  preachd Yesterday at first opening the Church of Annapolis
Vol. 17.   printed.

Resolvd A message be prepard And sent for that purpose
Viz[t]

### By the house of Del Sept[r] 25 1704

This house are Very well Sattisfyd with the well Compos'd discourse preached by the Reverend D[r] Wooten at opening the Annapolis Church And think it highly worthy of the press which if Your Ex[cy] does, Wee pray Yo[r] Ex[cy] to give order for the same.            Signd p order W[m] Taylard Cl h D.

Sent up to his Ex[cy] and Councill by M[r] Iohn Hudson Hugh Ecleston and Iohn Iones.

They returne And Say they deliverd the same.

The house Adjourns till to morrow morning 8 A Clock.

### Tuesday 26th Sept[r] 1704:

The house mett Againe According to Adjournment And were present as on Yesterday only Coll Dorsey Sick with A feavour.

On his behalfe it was moovd that he may have leave to go home Which was granted.

Severall bills brought into the house orderd to be read Viz[t]
Bill for punishm[t] of privateers and pyrats.

Read the 1st time and resolvd theres no Occasion of such bill therefore rejected.

Bill for encouragem[t] of Tillage & releife of poore D[rs]

Read the 1st time And Approovd of with A Clause to be put in that the Severall Comodity's be Merchantable And Well Securd And packt in good Caske.

Sent up to the Comittee of laws by M[r] Henry Coursey; to have Such Clause Added.

Bill for requiring Masters of Shipps to publish the rate of freight &c[a]   Read the 1st time.

Bill for Punishment of Adultery and fornicacon
Bill for Punishment of Blasphemy etc.
Read the 1st time.

Bill for payment of Criminalls fees.
Read the 1st & 2[d] time & do pass.

Bill for direction of the Sherriffs office.
Read the 1st time and doe pass.

The foregoing bills Sent up to the Councill by M[r] Ioseph Hill & M[r] W[m] Aisquith.

P. R. O.
B. T. Md.
Vol. 17.

They returne and say they deliverd them
Bill for Speedy tryall of Criminalls etc.
Bill for regulating the Millitia.
Read the 1ˢᵗ & 2ᵈ time And by Especiall order do pass.
Put to the Question in whom the property of Stollen goods remaine And to whom the same shall be deliverd After conviction
Referrd to the Consideration of next Assembly

By his Exᶜʸ the Govʳ & Conncˡˡ
Septʳ 26 1704
Gent   Your Message of the 15 Instant touching An house to be built for her Majᵗˢ Governoʳ being this day read at the Board His Exᶜʸ was pleasd to declare that he could never Consent to Appropriate that Which was Given for soe publiq A benefitt to the province, As the Supplying them with Arms and Amunition (of which they cann never haue too great A Store) to his owne private Accomodacon and Advantage Therefore wee desire that Some other Measure may be taken to Answer her Majᵗˢ Royall instructions either in building such house or Assigning to his Exᶜʸ the Governoʳ A competᵗ Sume of Money for rent thereof.
Signd ℗ order W Bladen Cl Co.

Which Message was brought from the Councill by the honob Thoˢ Tench Francis Ienkins Edward Loyd Esqʳˢ. And being read in this house Resolvd it be referrd for further Consideration
Bill rectifying the ill practises of Attorneys.
Bill relating to Servants and Slaues.
Bill for encouragemᵗ to build Water mills.
Read the 1ˢᵗ & 2ᵈ time & ℗ Especiall order do pass.
Bill Against horse raceing on Saturdays.
Being read And debated in the house.
Put to the Question Whither it pass or be rejected.
Carryd by Majority of Votes it be rejected.
But the latter clause in the Same being good & Necessary It is Resolvd that it be Added to another law.
Bill Imposicon of 3ᵈ ℗ hogshead etc.
Read the 1ˢᵗ time & passt
Bill prohibitting the Abuses of Woods rangers
Read the 1ˢᵗ time and do pass.
Bill for encouragemᵗ of Tillage.
Bill for Securing parrochiall library's
Read the 1ˢᵗ and 2ᵈ time And do pass.

P. R. O.
B. T. Md.
Vol. 17.

Sent up to his Ex^cy & Councill by M^r Henry Coursey M^r Thomas Frisby and M^r Robert Tyler.

They returne and say they deliverd them

The house Adjournd till 2 A Clock Afternoon

## Post Merediem

The house met Againe And being calld over were present as in the morning.

The foll Engrosst bills Assented to by the house were sent up to the Councill by M^r Muschamp M^r Haẏ M^r Iones & Maj^r Maxwell Viz^t

Bill empowring the Co^rs of County Courts to raise tob°

Bill regulating ordnary's.

Bill Confirming titles to land Given to churches.

Bill directing the Manner of Electing delegates.

Bill for devision of Severall County's.

Bill Securing rights to towne lands.

Bill laying An Imposicon on Severall Comoditys Exported.

Bill restraining the Extortion of Sherriffs etc.

Bill Confirming purchases made by County Courts

Bill prohibiting the Importacon of bread beare &c.

Bill Ascertaining the Gauge of tob hogsheads.

Bill declaring fees for private Acts etc.

Bill Encourageing the inhabitants to Venture Shps

Bill for Naturallization of Otho Ottherson

Bill Causing Grand And Pettit Iuro^rs to Come to Co^rts

Bill for conveying publ Lres

Bill for Stay of Executions &c.

Bill for Amercements in the prov^ll & Co^ty Courts.

Bill Ascertaining the bounds of Nanticoke Ind^as land

Bill Ascert^g damage on protested bills of Exchange.

The Gent returne & say they deliverd the bills.

The following Engrost bills brought into the house were read Examind & Endorsd.

Bill Securing Merch^ts And others tob°

Bill for releife of Credittors Against bankrupts.

Bill for Admtracon of Iustice in Severall Courts

Bill for Setling Land on Blaney.

Bill Confirming the last Will & testam^t of Ascomb &c.

Bill for Marking high ways.

Bill for taking Speciall bayles

Bill prohibitting the inhabitants to carry liquors to Ind^a townes

Bill for recording All laws.

Bill imposing 3^d p Gall on liquors 20^s on Negroes & 20^s on Irish.

All Which bills Were Endorsd, read & Assented to by the house of Delegates And sent up to the Councill ᵱ Mʳ Henry Coursey Mʳ Iames Hay & Mʳ Thomˢ Frisby.

They returne and say they deliverd the bills

The honob Iames Sanders Esqʳ enters the house and delivers Mʳ Speaker the following bills Vizᵗ.

Bill for Punishment of Blasphemy.

Bill requiring Mastʳˢ of Shipps to publish their freight

Bill for Punishment of Adultery and fornication

Bill for Paymᵗ of Criminalls fees

Severally thus Endorsd Vizᵗ.

Read in Councill the 1ˢᵗ & 2ᵈ time and do pass for Engrossmᵗ

W Bladen Cl Co.

Sent up to the Comittee of laws ᵱ Mʳ Goldsborough to be Engrost

Alsoe A bill for directions of Sherriffs and payment of leavys etc. Endorsed thus.

Eod Die. Read the first time in Councill And Approovd of so farr as directing the Sherriffs office But as to paying the leavys in money this house cannot consenc to give the Sherriff so Great An Advantage over the publiq officers & Credittors As by the law seems to be Granted them

Signd ᵱ order W Bladen Cl Co.

Bill for restraining the Growth of popery &cᵃ.

Read the 2ᵈ time and Orderd that there be A provision made for the children of preists turning protestants And to prohibitt All others from turning papists. Recomended to the Comittee of laws to Add this Clause to the bill.

Bill for direction of Sherriffs & payment of leavys in money &c.

Read the 1ˢᵗ time And here debated

The bill was Againe Sent up to the Councill ᵱ Mʳ Henry Coursey who is orderd to desire the Councill to Explaine What publiq Officers Are meant in the Endorsment of the bill.

The house Adjourns till to morrow morning 8 A Clock.

Wensday Septʳ 27ᵗʰ 1704

The house mett Againe According to Adjournmᵗ being Calld over were pʳsent as Yesterday.

Read What was done Yesterday

Proposd Whither it might not be necessary for the ornamᵗ of St Anns Church in Annapolis that the pews Appointed for

P. R. O.
B. T. Md.
Vol. 17. the Delegates of Assembly may be built At the publiq charge And that flag stone may be sent for out of England to lay the Alley's.

Resolvd by the house that the ground Assignd for the Gent of the Assembly in the sd Church be built with Decent pews As his Ex$^{cy}$ the Governo$^r$ shall please to direct And Shall be paid for out of the publiq treasure.

Alsoe that M$^r$ Sam$^{ll}$ Young trearer for the Westerne Sheare Send for so much smooth flagg stone As will lay the Alley's At the charge of the publiq Alsoe.

Which resolve was orderd to be drawne up & Sent his Ex$^{cy}$ and Councill for their Concurrence

Which was done and Sent up by M$^r$ Sam$^{ll}$ Young M$^r$ Ioseph Ennalls And M$^r$ Rob$^t$ Tyler.

The honoble Coll Edward Lloyd and Iames Sanders Esq$^r$ enters the house And delivers M$^r$ Speaker the following Engrost bills.

Bill for taking Speciall bayles etc.

Bill prohibitting liquors to be carryd to Ind$^a$ townes.

Bill empowring Com$^{rs}$ of the County to raise tob to defray the charges

Bill Causing Iurors & Wittnesses to come to Courts.

Bill for Speedy Conveying publiq letters &c.

Bill Securing p$^r$sons rights to towne land.

Bill decl devision of Severall Countys

Bill for Setling land on Sus$^a$ Blaney.

Bill Confirming the Wills of Ascomb & others.

Bill declaring fees for private Acts

Bill encourageing the inhabit$^{ts}$ to Venture their Shipps.

Bill for Naturallization of Otho Ottherson

Bill to restraine the Extortion of Sherriffs & others

Bill Confirming purchases made by Com$^{rs}$ of Countys &c.

Bill Imposing 3$^d$ p Gallon on rum & Wine &c.

Bill Confirming titles of land to the use of Churches &c.

Bill for Stay of Executions After the 10$^{th}$ May.

Bill for Amercem$^{ts}$ in prov$^{ll}$ & County Courts.

Bill for Marking highway's.

Bill for regulating ordnary's.

Bill for Securing Merchants and others tob$^o$.

Bill for releife of Crs in England Ag$^t$ bankrupts

Bill prohibitting the Importation of bread beer &c.

Bill Ascertaining the Gauge of tob hogsheads.

Bill laying an Impost on Sev$^{ll}$ Comoditys

Bill directing the Manner of Electihg Delegates.

Bill for Admtration of Iustice in Sev$^{ll}$ Courts.

Bill for Ascertaining the bounds of Nanticoke Ind$^a$ Land

Bill Ascertaining damages on protested bills &c.

Bill for recording All laws.
All which bills were Severally Endorsd.

P. R. O.
B. T. Md.
Vol. 17.

Sept$^r$ 26$^{th}$ 1704
Read and Assented to by her Maj$^{ts}$ honob Councill.
W$^m$ Bladen Cł Counc.

The honob Iames Sanders Esq$^r$ enters the house and delivers
M$^r$ Speaker the Ordinance About the pews Endorsd thus
Eod Die   Read & assented to by his Ex$^{cy}$ & her Maj$^{ts}$
honoble Councill.                    W$^m$ Bladen Cl Councill.

The honob Edw$^d$ Lloyd and Iames Sanders Esq$^{rs}$ enters the
house and delivers the following bills.
Bill directing the Sherriffs office &c.
Bill for Securing the parochiall library's
Bill for encouragem$^t$ of tillage &c.
Bill for relelfe in Abuses of Woods rangers.
Bill for encouragem$^t$ of building Water mills.
Bill relating to Servants & Slaues.
Bill rectifying the ill practises of Attorney's.
Bill regulating the Militia
All severally endorsd Sept$^r$ 26$^{th}$ 1704
Read in Councill and past for engrossing.
                                        W$^m$ Bladen Cł Co.

Orderd M$^r$ Iohn Waters carry the sd bills up to the Comittee of laws to be engrost
Bill for Speedy tryall of Criminalls
Endors'd Read in Councill the first time And thought that
the fine on the County Clk for not Certifying the former conviction in Another County Which he is Ignorant of is hard.
                        Signd ꝑ ord$^r$ W Bladen C Coun.

Read with Amendm$^t$ And Approovd of by the house:   Sent
up to the Councill ꝑ M$^r$ Geo. Muschamp.
He returns and says the Councill Agreed to the Amendm$^t$
Sent up to the Comittee to be engrost.
The honob Thom$^s$ Tench and W$^m$ Coursey Esq$^{rs}$ enters the
house And delivers M$^r$ Speaker the Address to her Maj$^{ty}$
Endorsd thus.

By his Ex$^{cy}$ the Gov$^r$ & Councill.
Wee haue Allready Addrest her Maj$^{ty}$ on this Occasion
therefore Unless the house will Shew their neer Concerne by

P. R. O.
B. T. Md.
Vol. 17.
raising And lodgeing Money in England to be made use of
for this Matter more Effectually Negotiating Neither his Ex^cy
nor this board Will o ne in the p^rsent Address proposd.

Signd ꝑ order W^m Bladen Cł Counc


W^m Coursey Esq^r enters·the house and delivers M^r Speaker the bill for Appeales & Writts of Erro^r  Endorsd Sept^r
27^th 1704
By the Councill in Assembly, Unless the house will Agree
to the bill as proposed by this board to be referrd to the next
Sessions of Assembly.                    W^m Bladen Cł Co.


Bill providing What Shall be evidence to proove Forreigne
Debts &c.
Endorsd Sept^t 27^th 1704


By the Councill in Assembly.
We insist that the last Clause be explained.
W^m Bladen Cl Co.


Sent up Againe by M^r Henry Coursey to the Councill to
Know in What Manner they would haue it Explained.
Bill to prevent Growth of popery.
Read the 1^st time.
And Sent up to the Councill ꝑ M^r Nic Lowe.
He returns And says he deliverd the bill
The Adress to her Maj^ty relating to New York Affair being
under debate, & the Endorsm^t of the Councill thereon
Jts put to the question whither the Address shalbe p^rsented
in the name of the house without Conjunction w^th the Councill
or not
Carryd by Majority of Votes that this house will not proceed
of themselve's.
The honob Francis Ienkins And Kenelm Cheseldyne Esq^rs
enters the house and delivers M^r Speaker    The bill to prevent Growth of popery.
Endorsd Eod Die   Read the 1^st & 2^d time and is Well Approovd of And past for engrossing.    W^m Bladen Cl Co:


Which  Was Againe read in the house and past for En-
grossing.
The endorsm^t of the Councill upon the bill for Appeales &
Writts of Erro^r were Again read & Orderd to be thus endors'd
Viz^t

By the house of Delegates
Sept<sup>r</sup> 27 1704

P. R. O.
B. T. Md.
Vol. 17.

This house desire your hono<sup>rs</sup> to Consider the Good that this Act has done by 9 or 10 Years use Without Any Complaint Against it As Also that in Appeale or Writt of Erro<sup>r</sup> the Superiour Court cannot review the Iustice of the fact As You Seem to be of Opinion but only the Erro<sup>rs</sup> in law And its too true that for a Nicety in law many a Iust Iudgment has been ouerthrowne Since the Countrey is not capable to come up to the rules of the laws of England in the regularrity of their proceedings for Want of Abillity both in Iudges And Officers And Wee haue no Statute of Jeofailes to help us.

Consider Alsoe wee pray, that if A man is Wrongd in Iustice or Equity in any Iudgment Aboue 1200: the Court of Chancery can releife him And that Answers the Supposition of Yo<sup>r</sup> hono<sup>rs</sup> of Want of right or Iustice to any person for A Iust debt

And With Submission wee hold this law as drawne Absolutely necessary for the Welfare of this province Which carrys no other designe then to restraine litigious persons for Catching Advantages by the Strict Rules of the law which Wee are not Able to Comply with And therefore Wee Earnestly desire Yo<sup>r</sup> hono<sup>rs</sup> Consideration And Concurrence to A law so much for the Good of the province. Which if Wee can't obtaine Wee haue done our dutys And shall say no more.

Signd p order W<sup>m</sup> Taylard Cl h D.

Sent up to the Councill by M<sup>r</sup> Iohn Hudson M<sup>r</sup> Ioseph Ennalls M<sup>r</sup> Francis Dollahyde.

They returne and say they deliverd the same.

The house Adjourns till 2 A Clock in the Afternoone.

### Post Merediem

The house met Againe were calld over and present as Yesterday.

M<sup>r</sup> Rich<sup>d</sup> Iones A member for Ann Arrundell County made Application to the house that he might Go home being ill with the Gripes Which is granted he tooke his leave & withdrew.

The house proceed to proportion the fees for coppys of the laws And private bills.

Resolvd that 1500<sup>ll</sup> tobacco be Allowd for every Coppy of the laws this Sessions and 400<sup>l</sup> tob for each Coppy of the laws last Sessions.

Iames Sanders Esq<sup>r</sup> enters the house & delivers M<sup>r</sup> Speaker the bill for Appeales & Writts of Erro<sup>r</sup>.

P. R. O.
B. T. Md.
Vol. 17.
Endorsd Eod Die    By the Councill.
All the houses desire Wee do agree to the bill being willing
to trust to your Iudgments therein      W<sup>m</sup> Bladen Cl Co.

Read and Sent up to the Comittee for engrossment ᵱ M<sup>r</sup>
George Muschamp.
The house proceeds to Setle the fees for private bills

|  | | | lb. tobo. |
|---|---|---|---|
| Coll Dorsey for the Seale to the private bill to Sell land. | | | 1 20 |
|  | l. | s. | d. |
| To M<sup>r</sup> Speaker his fee | 2. | o. | o. |
| To the Clk of the house | 1. | o. | o. |
| M<sup>r</sup> W<sup>m</sup> Sweatnam for Seale to his private bill | | | 1 20 |
| M<sup>r</sup> Speaker | 4. | o. | o. |
| To the Clerk of the house | 2. | o. | o. |
| Otho Ottherson for Seale to his bill for Naturallizaon | | | 1 20 |
| To M<sup>r</sup> Speaker | 4. | o. | o. |
| To the Clerk of the house | 2. | o. | o. |
| M<sup>r</sup> Ascomb for Seale to the bill to confirm the will | | | 1 20 |
| To M<sup>r</sup> Speaker | 4. | o. | o. |
| To the Clerk of the house | 2. | o. | o. |
| M<sup>r</sup> Winfels Seale to confirme the will | | | 1 20 |
| To M<sup>r</sup> Speaker | 1. | o. | o. |
| To the Clerk of the house | o. | 10. | o. |
| Bill for Confirming In° Burnams Will to the house | | | 1 20 |
| To M<sup>r</sup> Speaker | 1. | o. | o. |
| To the Clerk of the house | o. | 10. | o. |
| Susan<sup>a</sup> Blaney to the Seale to the bill to sell land | | | 1 20 |
| To M<sup>r</sup> Speaker | 1. | o. | o. |
| To the Clerk of the house | o. | 10. | o. |

Read the following Message prepared.


·By the house of Delegates Sept<sup>r</sup> 27<sup>th</sup> 1704
Wee haue recd Your hono<sup>rs</sup> resolutions touching the
Address Wee confess wee are Something Surprizd to finde
that yo<sup>r</sup> honours after you had agreed with us on reasons to
be containd in it And had in your former Letter or Address
Showne at the Conferrence, said that you beleived the Gen<sup>ll</sup>
Assembly would proceed further on that Subject Your hon<sup>rs</sup>
should refuse to  o ne with us because wee do not now raise

Money when yo<sup>r</sup> hon<sup>rs</sup> know All the Account wee haue of the P. R. O.<br>B. T. Md.<br>Vol. 17. designe is dark and Uncertaine And such As Wee Are not Absolutely to relye on

Wee heartily Wish Wee could Concurr with yo<sup>r</sup> hono<sup>rs</sup> in All things for the Good of the province And Wee shall be Allways as ready as any to raise money Where the necessity of the province requires it which in this wee cannot perceive.

Therefore since Wee shall Not say or do Any thing in the Name of the province without Your hono<sup>rs</sup> in Conjunction Neither shall wee medle with the Address without Your hono<sup>rs</sup> o ne with us.      Signd ꝑ order W<sup>m</sup> Taylard Cl house.

Sent up to his Ex<sup>cy</sup> ahd Councill ꝑ M<sup>r</sup> George Muschamp & M<sup>r</sup> Robt. Tyler with the Address and the Aboue Message Endorst upon the same.

They returne and say they deliverd the same.

Orderd the foll Message be prepar'd Viz<sup>t</sup>.

### By the house of Delegates Sept<sup>r</sup> 27<sup>th</sup> 1704.

The Greatest part of the bills having past Yo<sup>r</sup> hono<sup>rs</sup> Assent And this house the next Materiall Matter offerring to our consideration is Setling the law for Regulation of Officers fees And therein of the charge of the Great Seale of the laws of this province for the future On Which wee desire to know whither yo<sup>r</sup> hono<sup>rs</sup> think it most proper for the dispatch of business to proceed by drawing the bill or by Message & Answer. or by Appointing A Conferrence with some of this house and Your board either of Which or in any other reasonable method Wee are ready to proceed in.

Signd ꝑ order W<sup>m</sup> Taylard Cl house.

Which being read and debated is Approovd of & Orderd that M<sup>r</sup> Henry Coursey And M<sup>r</sup> Iames Maxwell carry up the same to his Ex<sup>cy</sup> & Councill.

They returne and say they deliverd the same.

The bill providing What Shalbe Evidence to prooue Forreigne & other debts &c. read And orderd to be thus Endorsd.

### By the house of Del Sept<sup>r</sup> 27<sup>th</sup> 1704

The last Clause is Explaind And the clause is to restrain the Extravagant Manner of mens prooving Accounts by their owne oaths which has introduced too much perjury in the province And Which Yo<sup>r</sup> bono<sup>rs</sup> Complaind on At the beginning

P. R. O.
B T. Md.
Vol. 17.

of this Session And desird that it might be explaind tho by the endorsment on this bill Yo<sup>r</sup> hono<sup>rs</sup> seem to desire the former law Againe however if this Explanation, agrees Not to your desire be pleasd to explaine it in yo<sup>r</sup> owne way that this house may Consider thereof.

Signd ᵽ order W<sup>m</sup> Taylard Cl house

Which being read was Sent up by M<sup>r</sup> Coursey to the honob Councill.

Who returns and says he deliverd it

The honob In° Hamond Esq<sup>r</sup> Enters the house and delivers M<sup>r</sup> Speaker the Bill providing What Shall be Evidence to prooue forreigne And other Debts.   Endorsd As follows.

Sept<sup>r</sup> 27<sup>th</sup> 1704

Read in Councill Agreed to And past for engrossing
W<sup>m</sup> Bladen C Co.

Which being read, orderd M<sup>r</sup> George Muschamp Carry up the bill to be Engrost

Orderd A Message be prepard to be sent up to the Councill to morrow Morning relating to the debate.   & Setling fees for private bills &c<sup>a</sup>

The house Adjourns till to morrow Morning Eight A Clock.

Thursday 28<sup>th</sup> Sept<sup>r</sup> 1704

The house mett Againe According to Adjournment being calld over Were All p<sup>r</sup>sent as Yesterday.

Read What was done Yesterday.

The Message prepard upon the Resolves of the house proporconing the fees for private bills, orderd it be read

The house According to two Severall laws of this province entring into consideration of and Setling the fees due on private bills past this Sessions And What Shalbe Allowd for transcribing the laws of last And this Sessions of Assembly haue Agreed and propose to Allow his Ex<sup>cy</sup> as keeper of the broad Seale for every coppy of the laws of last Session 400<sup>l</sup> tob And for every coppy of the laws of this Session 1500<sup>l</sup> tob to be paid by the County's for those sent to the County's And by the publiq for the Coppy's sent for England And for the private laws wee propose for the Keeper of the Seale Viz<sup>t</sup>

ᵽ Ord<sup>r</sup> W Taylard Cl h D

[ll. tob.] P. R. O.
B. T. Md.
Vol. 17.

| | l. | s. | d. | |
|---|---|---|---|---|
| Coll Dorsey for Seale to the bill for Setling land | | | | 1 2 0 |
| To Mr Speakers fee | 2. | 0. | 0. | |
| To the Clerk of the house | 1. | 0. | 0. | |
| Mr Wm Sweatnam for the Seale to his private bill | | | | 1 2 0 |
| To Mr Speaker | 4. | 0. | 0. | |
| To the Clerke | 2. | 0. | 0. | |
| Otho Otterson for the Seale to his bill | | | | 1 2 0 |
| To Mr Speaker | 4. | 0. | 0. | |
| To the Clerk | 2. | 0. | 0. | |
| Mr Ascom for Seale to the bill to confirme the Will | | | | 1 2 0 |
| To Mr Speaker | 1. | 0. | 0. | |
| To the Clk of the house | 0. | 10. | 0. | |
| Mr Winfell for Seale to the bill to confirme the Will to the Keeper | | | | 1 2 0 |
| To Mr Speaker | 1. | 0. | 0. | |
| To the Clerk | 0. | 10. | 0. | |
| To Seale to the bill for Burnams Will | | | | 1 2 0 |
| To Mr Speaker | 1. | 0. | 0. | |
| To the clerke of the house | 0. | 10. | 0. | |
| Susannah Blaney for Seale to the bill to Sell land | | | | 1 2 0 |
| To Mr Speaker | 1. | 0. | 0. | |
| To the Clerke of the house | 0. | 10. | 0. | |

To All Which this house prays the concurrence of the honob Councill.

Signd p order Wm Taylard Cl house Del

Read & Approovd And Sent up by Mr Coursey Mr Tyler and Mr Phillips.

They returne and say they deliverd their Message.

Coll Ino Hamond Enters the house And delivers Mr Speaker the following Message.

### By the Councill in Assembly Sept. 27th 1704

The Message by Mr Muschamp And Mr Tyler this Afternoone Wee haue observd And thereupon Wee do Acknowledge Wee did resolve the Address to her Majty in the Name of the province As Absolutely necessary And Agreed on the reasons therein containd And did really beleive the Genll Assembly would Unanimously haue  o nd in it thinking those

P. R. O.
B. T. Md.
Vol. 17. Accounts Wee had tho never so Small & Uncertaine Suffi-
cient to Caution us to Stand upon our defence And Avert
Such Apparent prejudice to the p'sent well Setled constitucon
of our Countrey And upon the conferrence Wee did propose
Not only that Money should be remitted to England but some
trusty Sencible person Sent by this Assembly to negotiate this
Affaire Which was referrd to yo' Consideration but Wee finde
reject'd Therefore to what end Shou'd Wee frame Addresses
never to be presented or considerd of Which without money to
Accompany them to the persons whose sever" hands and Offices
they must pass through cann Expect No better fortune or
Countenance twas upon this Score And no other Wee refused
to Ioyn in the Address And now Assure You that Wee Wish
yo' Whole house had As deep A Sence of this eminent danger
as Wee haue, for then Surely You would do what is fitting to
preserve Yo' constitucon And then his Ex^cy the Gov' and this
board will never refuse heartily to  o ne With You in this
Address or any other for the Interest & Advantage of the
province.            Signd p order W^m Bladen Cl Counc^ll

Read and referrd for further consideration.
The following Engrost bills brought into the house Viz^t.
Bill for punishing Adultery and fornication
Bill for payment of fees from Criminalls
Read & Assented to by the house of Dels.
Bill for Admtracon of Iustice in probatt of Wills
Read the 1^st and 2^d time and do pass.
Sent up to the Councill p M^r Tho^s Greenfeild M^r W^m Peirce
& M^r W^m Watts Who returne and say they deliverd the same.
The house Adjournd till 2 A Clock in the Afternoone.

Post Merediem
The house met According to Adjournm^t and being calld
over were present as in the morning.
Proposd by A member whither Indians brought from other
Countrey's and Sold As Slaves here Are to be Accounted so,
Since the law is not full in that point
Resolvd they be Accounted so if sold for such which is
referrd to the Consideration of next Assembly
The honob Thomas Smithson Esq' from the Comittee of laws
enters the house and brings with him the land laws
with the lord Baltemores Exceptions And this houses Answer
to it. Which was read And orderd to be considerd of to
morrow.
Kenelm Cheseldyne & W^m Coursey Esq^rs Enter the house
and delivers M^r Speaker the following message Viz^t.

By the Councill in Assembly Sept<sup>r</sup> 28 1704     P. R. O.
B. T. Md.

The Message this day About Setling the fees due for private Vol. 17. bills And transcribing the laws of the last and this p'sent Sessions has been Considerd by this board And as to the first proposall for coppy's of the laws of the last Sessions Which should then haue been setled Wee cannot thinke A less reward due therefore then what has been Usuall that is to say 1000<sup>l</sup> tobacco ℔ Coppy as may appear by the County leavys these three or four years last past

That as to the coppys of this p'sent Session's Wee cannot beleive Any persons Will Undertake to doe them Well for less then Two thousand five hundr'd ℔ coppy they being so many Therefore desire so much may be Allowd to the keeper of the Great Seale to Enable him to gett them Speedily transcribed As Well to be sent to England As to the County Courts.

3<sup>d</sup>   As for the private bills it being as Absolutely necessary than Sealed Coppys thereof be sent for England as of other publiq laws Wee desire you to explaine whither you meant the keeper of the Great Seale should take 120<sup>l</sup> tob for the orriginall law And the same for each coppy or but 120<sup>l</sup> tob in All which is conceivd Unreasonably less then formerly was Allways Allowd to witt 480<sup>l</sup> tob for A Pattent of Denization.

Wee further observe to you that upon private bills You haue not taken notice of Any fees to the Clerk of this board Who has As great A burthen of the business of this Assembly as Any other Clerk.     Signd ℔ order W<sup>m</sup> Bladen Cl Co.

Which being read in the house and debated Its proposd Whither the coppy of Each body of laws for this Sessions of Assembly be Vallued & paid by the publiq And Countys At the rate of 2000 or 1500<sup>l</sup> tob.

Put to the Question Whither 2000 or 1500.

Carryd by Majority of Votes that Each coppy of the body of laws made this Sessions be Vallued at 2000<sup>l</sup> tob

But this house do insist possitively upon 400<sup>l</sup> tob for the laws made last Sessions.

And Resolv'd the severall Coppys for the Co<sup>tys</sup> And them to be sent for England be paid for Accordingly.

As to that Clause relating to the Clerk of the Councill for Allowance of fees on private bills

Read and debated.

And resolvd that forasmuch as this house cannot find any p'sident heretofore for the same Therefore thought fitt to give no Allowance.

Upon which orderd the following Message be sent up to the Councill Viz<sup>t</sup>.

P. R. O.
B. T. Md.
Vol. 17.

By the house of Delegates Sept[r] 28th 1704

Wee have Considerd the last Message by Kenelme Cheseldyn and W[m] Coursey Esq[rs] of this day for setling the fees on
private laws And transcribing the body of laws And As to
those of this Sessions Wee haue by Examining the Comittee
of laws found they will be of Greater length then What Wee
at first beleived And therefore are willing to Allow 2000[l] tob
for every coppy And thats the highest that euer wee find
Allowd Even when the Whole body has been revised which
Wee cannot in reason Advance.

As to the last Sessions laws Wee haue Examind the laws
and finde the proporcon is Sufficient; and why Your hono[rs]
propose 1000 because of presidents when there is A plain law
directory in the point Wee cant Imagine And if your bono[rs]
would haue them presidents And not the law direct us then wee
should Allow but 1000 for this body which wou'd be unreasonable but Yo[r] hono[rs] know it is the true intent of the law that
Wee and You look to and Not Criticall Exceptions Which if
Wee wou'd made use on wee might Scruple to Allow any
thing for last Sessions laws, but Wee Meane nothing but What
is honest And fair And desire to be so understood and Used.

To the private bills we meane the persons to be Answerable
for the same As the publiq is for the publiq bills.    And Altho
wee Shall not dispute the Weight of business that lyes upon
any clerk beleiving euery one has enough

Wee desire to be excus'd from increasing any fees on private
bills At this time more then what has been used before And
Wee do not finde Yo[r] Clerk (tho Wee haue A respect for him)
ever Allowd any fees on private bills And hope you will not
press that Matter Any further but o ne with us in hearty
endeavo[rs] to dispatch the Weighty Matters in hand.

Signd p order W[m] Taylard Cl h D.

Which being read and Approovd of was sent up to his Ex[cy]
and Councill by M[r] Iames Smallwood M[r] W[m] Watts & M[r] W[m]
Peirce.

They returne and say they deliverd the same.

The honob In° Hamond Esq[r] enters the house And delivers
M[r] Speaker

Bill for admtration of Iustice in probatt of Wills &c[a]

Endorsd Eod die.    Read the 1st and 2[d] time and do pass
for engrossment                          W[m] Bladen Cl Co.

Sent up to the Comittee of laws to be Engrost
The following Message orderd to be read Viz[t].

By the house of Delegate Sept<sup>r</sup> 28<sup>th</sup> 1704

P. R. O.
B. T. Md.
Vol. 17.

Wee haue considerd Your hono<sup>rs</sup> Message by Coll Hamond and Are sorry yo<sup>r</sup> hono<sup>rs</sup> will not ͦne in the Address Since You are pleasd to say You think it necessary to prevent Any Eminent danger And Wee cannot beleive our Agent has so little Vallue of us As to let it lye dormant by him when wee Give him the Assurance of paying What he disburses for us in laying it before her Majesty Which wee Allways proposd to doe.

yo<sup>r</sup> bono<sup>rs</sup> are pleas'd to say You haue Adrest her Maj<sup>ty</sup> on that Subject And wee doubt not but Your honours Expect it to take Effect And Yet wee haue not heard of Any Sume of money raisd or any person Appointed to goe with it And wee hope this may Goe alsoe If Yo<sup>r</sup> hono<sup>rs</sup> please Wee Againe humbly offer our Selves in the Address And hope Wee shall be discharg'd of any Misfortune that may Attend the Non Addressing since Wee are ready to ͦne in it

The Aboue was Writt before his Ex<sup>cy</sup> commanded our Attendance And what he was pleasd to say we haue Considerd And with all dutifull respect to his Ex<sup>cy</sup> wee Cant see cause to receed And Shalbe Glad if his Ex<sup>cy</sup> will please to ͦne with us in the Address.

Signd ᵽ order W<sup>m</sup> Taylard Cl h Del.

Orderd the foregoeing Message be sent up to the Councill by M<sup>r</sup> W<sup>m</sup> Frisby M<sup>r</sup> Nicholas Low And M<sup>r</sup> Iames Phillips.

They returne and say they deliverd the same.

The house Adjournd till to morrow morning 7 A Clock.

### Fryday 29<sup>th</sup> Sept<sup>r</sup> 1704.

The house Againe met According to Adjournment being calld over were present As Yesterday.

Read What was done Yesterday.

The following Engrost bills brought into the house and orderd to be read.

Bill for Securing the parrochyall library's

Bill for Imposicon of 3<sup>d</sup> ᵽ hhd on tob<sup>o</sup>

Bill relating to Servants And Slaves.

Bill for Encouragem<sup>t</sup> of building Water mills.

The provideing Evidence to prooue forreigne debts.

The Aboue Engrost bills being read & Assented to by the house were Sent up to the Councill by M<sup>r</sup> In<sup>o</sup> Hudson and M<sup>r</sup> Iohn Taylor.

They returne & say they deliverd the same.

13

P. R. O.
B. T. Md.
Vol. 17. The honoble In° Hamond enters the house and delivers M^r Speaker the following Message.


By the Councill in Assembly Sept^r 29^th 1704

Wee haue considerd the houses Message last night by Coll Smallwood and others and Agree to the Sume of 2000^l tob for each Coppy of the laws this Sessions As Alsoe to the fees Setled for private bills as Explained by yo^r Message but finding the house under A mistake About such fees to our Clerke desire it may be better considerd And he Allowd Equally with yours.                    Signd ᵱ order W^m Bladen C Co.


The Lord Baltemores objections to the land law And the houses Answer to the same was Againe debated And orderd to be thus Endorsed.   & Sent to the Councill Viz^t


By the house of Delegates Sept^r 29^th 1704

The within reasons is offerrd to this house in Answer to the Lord Baltemores Objections to the land law And tho Wee are of opinion that the said law ought to be Revis'd so As to Answer the Ld Baltemores reasonable objections Yet because of the other great Matters under p^rsent consideration time Will not Admitt, so çarefull Examination as the same ought to be done with Therefore Wee pray yo^r hono^rs to o ne with us in A Small bill to continue the same law in force till next Sessions of Assembly when by Gods grace it may be revisd As it ought to be And this wee pray to the end that the province may not in the meane time loose the benefitt of the Usefull And Necessary part of the said law.
                    Signd ᵱ order W^m Taylard Cl h D.


Which Was Read approovd of And sent up to the Councill ᵱ M^r Sam^ll Young And M^r Ioseph Hill
They returne And say they deliverd the same
Proposd by A member of the house for the more Ease in the Administration of Iustice to the inhabitants of this province
    1^st   That the province be devided in two Circuits Viz^t the Westerne And Easterne Shoare.
    2^d   That four Iudges be Appointed for each Circuit
    3^d   That care and provision be made to support the Iudges.
    4   That the County Courts be Abridged And limitted in their Iurisdiction

5   That Writts of Error may lye from these two Corts to the
Governour And Councill

P. R. O.
B. T. Md.
Vol. 17.

All of which is prayd may be referrd to the next Sessions of
Assembly.

The following Engrost bills brought into the house Vizt.

Engrost bills for directions of Sherriffs in their office

Engrost bill Ascertaining the height of fences.

Both read and endorsd Assented to by the house of
Delegates.

Sent up to the Councill by Coll Iames Smallwood.

He returns and says he deliverd the same.

The house Adjourns till 2 A Clock Afternoon

### Post Merediem.

The house met According to Adjournmt being Calld over
were present as in the morning

The following Engrost bills brought into the house.

Engrost bill for rectifying the ill practise of Attornys.

Engrost bill requiring Mars of Shipps to publish the rates of
freight

Read & Assented to by the house of Delegates And Sent
up to the Councill ᵱ Mr Ino Macall

He returnes And Says he deliverd the same.

Bill for Rattifying the peticonary Act relating to the.Free-
schoole.

Bill Continueing in force the Act Ascertaining the bounds
of land.

Read the 1st & 2d time and do pass

And Sent up to his Excy and Councill ᵱ Mr Robert Skinner.

He returns and Says he deliverd the same.

The honob Francis Ienkins And Iames Sanders Esqrs enter
the house and delivers the following Engrost bills.

Engrost bill requiring Mars of Shipps to publish the rate of
freight.

Engrost bill ratifying the ill practise of Attorneys.

both Endorsd Read & Assented to by the honoble Councill.

Wm Bladen Clk Councill.


Wm Holland & Kenelm Cheseldyne Esqrs enters the house
and delivers the following Message.


By the Councill in Assembly Septr 29th 1704.

Gent

Wee haue considerd your message by Mr Wm Frisby Major
Lowe and Mr Phillips Concerning the Address propos'd to her

P. R. O.
B. T. Md.
Vol. 17. Maj^{ty} and Your dependance on Coll Blakistone And haue resolvd to ο ne with You in the said Address And doubt not but his Ex^{cy} will be inclind thereto likewise therefore proposed that it be fairly transcribed

Signd ꝑ order W Bladen Cl Co.

Which being read orderd the same be transcribed.   And is Sent up to the Comittee of laws for that purpose.

The following Engrost bills brought into the house and orderd to be read.

Eng^{t} bill for Appeals & Writts of Erro^{r}

Engrost Bill for regulating the Millitia.

Read And Assented to by the house of Delegates.

Part of the Iournall of Accounts read And the rest to be read to morrow.

The honoble In° Hamond Esq^{r} Francis Jenkins Edward Lloyd and W^{m} Holland Esq^{rs} enters the house and delivers M^{r} Speaker the following Message.

By his Ex^{cy} the Governo^{r} & Councill in Assembly.
Sept^{r} 29^{th} 1704.

Resolvd by this board that An Address be sent her Maj^{ty} to Congratulate the Success of her Armes under the Conduct of his Grace the Duke of Marlborough And that the thanks of his Ex^{cy} the Gov^{r} this Board And the Gen^{ll} Assembly be Given her Maj^{ty} for placeing his Grace in that Station since the loss of his Maj^{ty} King William of Glorious Memory.

Signd ꝑ order W^{m} Bladen Cl Concil

Read And Resolvd An address be prepared and this other Message Viz^{t}

By the Gov^{r} & Councill in Assembly
Sept^{r} 29^{th} 1704.

Wee doubt not but many Gent Among you are throughly Sencible of What Vallue the honob M^{r} Blathwaits Freindship may be to this province in Gen^{ll} being the only Gent my self or Coll Blakistone can apply to on any occasion for the Ease or Advantage of the province Therefore recomend to the house that You would Seriously consider of the referrence last Assembly to this for setling some Annuall sallary on the sd M^{r} Blathwait As he is Auditor Generall thro' whose hands the Accounts of this province must pass

Signd ꝑ order W Bladen Cl Council

Read And referrd for further consideracon

Also was brought by the same Gent the following Message.

P. R. O.
B. T. Md.
Vol. 17.

By his Ex$^{cy}$ the Gov$^r$ & Co: in Assembly.
Sept$^r$ 29$^{th}$ 1704

The Scheeme of Officers fees proposd to be retrenchd being read At the board His Ex$^{cy}$ is pleasd to Ask the Councill whither it be reasonable to retrench any of the said fees Who say that the said Fees are not Greater then the Service requires. Save the secretary's fees for An Injunction An Audita Querela and Writt for enquirey of Damages.

Which this board Are Willing should be regulated As proposed.                    Signd ꝑ order W$^m$ Bladen Cł Councill

Which was Also read And the Consideration thereof referrd till to morrow.

The house Adjourns till to morrow morning Seaven A Clock.

### Saturday Sept$^r$ 30$^{th}$ 1704

The house Met Againe According to Adjournement being Calld over were All present as Yesterday only Coll Smithson

Brought into the house Severall Engrost bills Viz$^t$

Bill declaring· the Act intituled An Act Ascertaining the bounds of land.

Bill for encouragem$^t$ of Tillage &c$^a$

Bill for punishing Blasphemy and prophane Swearing

All Read And Assented to by the house of Deł$^s$

The honob W$^m$ Holland and Iames Sanders Esq$^{rs}$ enters the house And delivers the following Message.

### By the Councill in Assembly Sept$^r$ 29$^{th}$ 1704

Wee haue moovd his Ex$^{cy}$ that Whereas in the Yeare 1702 The then Assembly did Vote 300$^l$ Sterling for the Assistance of New Yorke Which Sume was directed to be paid by the publiq treasurers of this province to the order of that Gouernment When Sent for But inasmuch as the Gouernment of New York has not Yet thought fitt to Send for that Sume of money Wee are induced to Suspect they haue Greater designes against us And therefore desired his Ex$^{cy}$ would Admitt the said Sume should be remitted to M$^r$ Iohn Hyde in England ready for that Service in case the Lord Cornberry shall require the same Otherwise that our Agent might make

P. R. O.
B. T. Md.
Vol. 17. use of All or any parte thereof to Obviate Any Machynations by the said Gouernment of New York Against our pʳsent Constitution if any Such be prosecuted To which his Exᶜʸ has been pleasd to Assent Therefore wee desire to haue Your Concurrence therewith.       Signd ꝑ order Wᵐ Bladen Cl Co.

Read and Resolvd this house will Consider.
Engrost bill Against the Growth of popery
Engrost bill declaring the peticonary Act relating to the Freeschoole to be in force
Engrost bill for Speedy tryall of Criminalls.
Read & Assented to by the house of Del

Wᵐ Taylard Cl

The foregoing Engrost bills sent up to his Exᶜʸ & Councill by Mʳ Hudson Mʳ Ennalls & Mʳ Stone
They returne and say they deliverd the bills.
Bill Empowring A Comittee to lay & Assess the publiq leavy.
Read the 1ˢᵗ and 2ᵈ time and by Speciall Order do pass.
And Sent to the Councill by Mʳ Iames Phillips.
He returns And says he deliverd the bill.
The following Message read Vizᵗ

By the house of Delegates Septʳ 30ᵗʰ 1704
Wee having Setled the Iournalls of Accounts finde therein tob due to his Exᶜʸ for the Great Seale & otherwise Wee therefore desire to know Whither it Will be most Acceptable to his Exᶜʸ to haue the tob in Specie or Money for the same out of the treary of this province at 1ᵈ ꝑ pound And that Since there is money in bank And the publiq leavy like to be very high And hard upon the poorer Sort of people Wee propose to pay the honob Councill and Delegates of this Sessions Some Small parte of their 140ˡ tob ꝑ day in Money at 1ᵈ łe if Your honoʳˢ Are pleasd to concurr with us therein Which Wee desire because its hard to procure money to bear Expences here.       Signd ꝑ order Wᵐ Taylard Cl h D.

Which being read is sent up to the Councill by Mʳ Thomas Smith.
He returnes and says he deliverd the same.
The engrost bill for admstration of Iustice in probatt of Wills &ᶜᵃ
Brought into the house and Endorsed.

Read And Assented to by the house of Del[t]
The Message of last Night by Coll Holland & others relating to the money for New York read Againe this morning
and debated & Resolvd the foll Message be sent in Answer
to the same.

P. R. O.
B. T. Md.
Vol. 17.

### By the house of Delegates Sept[r] 30th 1704.

In Answer to your hono[rs] Message by Coll Hamond.  Coll
Loyd  Coll Ienkins touching the money for New York Yo[r]
hono[rs] know that former Assemblys haue addresst her Maj[ty]
on that Subject and said that it Shoud be ready When Calld
for And Wee dont know how soone it may be calld for there
being but barely that Sume (if so much) Now in Stock And
therefore Wee desire it may remaine As it is And the Address
prosecuted As Agreed on
Signd p order W[m] Taylard Cl h D.

Which Was read And Sent up to the  Councill by M[r] Sam[ll]
Magruder and M[r] Iohn Iones.
They returne & say they deliverd it
Bill for Admstration of Iustice in probatt of Wills &c. being
Engrost & Read and Assented to by the house of Delegates,
Sent up to the honob Councill p M[r] Iohn Macall And M[r] Iohn
Hudson
They returne and say they deliverd the Bill.

Proposall made for Regulating Attorneys fees as foll[o]

### Attorneys fees in provintiall Court

| | le tob |
|---|---|
| In every Comon Action | 400 |
| Appeale and Writt of Erro[r] | 400 |
| Ejectment or Title of land | 400 |
| Accon of Account | 400 |
| If Iudgment to Account by Audito[rs] more | 400 |
| On Arrest of Iudgment | 200 |
| Appeale to the Gov[r] & Councill | 800 |
| Fee in Chancery | 800 |
| Comissarys Court | 400 |

### In County Courts.

| | |
|---|---|
| In Accons of Debt bills bonds Assumpcons & Account trespass & battery | 100 |
| Bond Aboue 2000 | 200 |
| Actions of D[t] upon penall Statutes or informa | 200 |
| Actions of the case for Scandalous words and Actions upon Escape | 200 |

P. R. O.
B. T. Md.
Vol. 17.

By the house of Delegates
Sept^r 30^th 1704

These are the regulations proposd for Attorneys fees
Wherein Your hono^rs Concurrence is prayd that it may be
made parte of the law for Setling Officers fees

Signd ꝑ order W^m Taylard Cł h D

Read & Sent up to the Comittee by M^r Robt. Tyler
He returns And Says he deliverd the same.
The honoble Iames Sanders Esq^r Enters the house and
delivers M^r Speaker the following Message Viz^t

By the Councill in Assembly Sept^r 13 1704

This board are Allready Sencible of A very good law of
this province Empowring the Iustices to Setle such rules and
fees as they think reasonable And do beleive such Iustices are
propper Iudges therefore doe Allow only such as Are reasonable Neither haue Wee Ever heard of any .Act of Parliam^t
Setling Attorneys fees in England but that they are Allways
Setled by discretion of the Courts Where such Attorneys
practise          Signd ꝑ order W^m Bladen Cl Counc

Which was read in the house.
Bill for Apporconing the publiq leavy etc.
Bill for limittacon of Officers fees.
Read the 1^st and 2^d time & by Especiall order do pass
The house Adjourne till 2 A Clock in the Afternoone.

Post Merediem.

The house met Againe According to Adjournm^t being calld
over were p^rsent as in the morning.
The honob Coll In° Hamond and Kenelm Cheseldyn Esq^r
enters the house And delivers M^r Speaker 2 Messages And
the Address to her Sacred Majesty Viz^t

By the Councill Sept^r 30 1704

Your Message by M^r Iones and M^r Magruder is Agreed to
by this board And Wee desire the Address may be sent up
to be signd    Wee haue sent the other Address to her Majesty
of Which Wee desire Your Approbation And that you would
Amend the Same if You think fitt.

Signd ꝑ order W^m Bladen Cł Counc

The Address upon the Success of her Maj^{tys} Victorious P. R. O. B. T. Md. Vol. 17.
Arms &c. Read Amended And then Approovd of by the
house & sent up to the Councill by M^r Coursey togeather with
the following Message.

### By the Councill in Assembly Sept^r 30 1704

The Message by Coll Smith proposing the tob due to the
Keeper of the Great Seale And some Small parte of the
Councills & Burgesses Sallarys to be paid in Money has been
considerd by this board And so noe less Expectance of the
Vallue of tob this Yeare then the last And former When the
leavy was made in money At the rate of 10ˢ ℗ cent Wherefore
Wee Acquaint You that You Agreed such payments be made
At the rate Viz^t 10 ℗ Cent
Read & the house will consider:
Signd ℗ order W^m Bladen Cl Co.

The Address to her Sacred Majesty upon New Yorke
Affaire brought into the house Engrost Being read & Sent up
to the honob Councill by M^r Thomas Greenfeild M^r Iohn Iones
M^r Robert Tyler M^r Magruder for their hono^rs first to Signe
the Address.
They returne and say they deliverd it
M^r Coursey returnes from the Councill And brings with him
the Address which he carryd, Orderd it be Engrost
Iohn Hamond and Kenelm Cheseldyne Esq^rs Enters the
house & bring with them the following Engrost bills.
Engrost bill for Admtration of Iustices for probatt of Wills
&c^a.
Engrost bill for Tryall of Criminalls.
Engrost bill to prevent the Growth of popery.
Engrost bill confirming the freeschoole.
Engrost bill for encouragem^t of releife of poor D^rs.
Engrost bill for confirming the land law.
Engrost bill for punishing Blasphemy & prophane Cursing
&c^a
Which said Bills were severally Endorsd Viz^t.

### Sept^r 30^th 1704

Read And Assented to by her Maj^{ts} honob Councill
W^m Bladen Cl

The Message relating to the honob W^m Blathwait Esq^r of
Yesterday Again read and debated.

P. R. O.
B. T. Md.
Vol. 17. Resolvd that the following Message be Sent in Answer thereto Viz$^t$

By the house of Delegates Sept$^r$ 30 1704
Wee haue Againe considerd the Message touching the honoble W$^m$ Blathwait Esq$^r$ which was resolved once last Sessions And that is that the Office Was not Erected for our benefitt nor are Wee Concernd to Support it, the Crowne that Created the Office has Annexd A Suitable Sallary to it And that Wee are Sencible of Wee haue A great honour for the Gent Since he is thought worthy of such Eminent Employment And as his Ex$^{cy}$ is pleased to say is ready to receive Applications for the province And Wee hope While wee behave our Selves as Good subjects his Iustice will intitle us to his Countenance And Any favour he shall be pleasd to doe us Wee shall not be backwards in Suitable Acknowledgments.

Wee Wish Your hono$^{rs}$ knew the publiq Stock because You are pleasd to press us to Severall Allowances that wee haue not Money to Answer therefore Wee pray Yo$^r$ hono$^{rs}$ to inspect the Same And then consider Whither Wee do not the Uttermost Wee cann.        Signd p order W$^m$ Taylard Cl h D

Which being read was Approovd of by the house And Sent up to the Councill by M$^r$ W$^m$ Aisquith M$^r$ Iames Maxwell & M$^r$ Gerrd Fowlk.

They returne and say they deliverd the same
Iames Sanders Esq$^r$ enters the house and brings with him the Address, Which was Sent to be Engrost.

The honob In$^o$ Hamond Esq$^r$ enters the house and delivers the bill for limittacon of Officers fees.

Endors'd.  Read & Assented to by her Maj$^{ts}$ honoble Councill.                      W$^m$ Bladen Cl Co.

Orderd the following Message be entred.  Wee haue considerd Yo$^r$ hono$^{rs}$ Message touching paying tob at 1$^d$ p $^{ll}$ And that You think it of 10$^s$ p Cent Vallue.

Wee see by the reasons Yo$^r$ hono$^r$ Gives that You doe not beleive it Worth 10$^s$ now but hope it will and that Against All prospect

However in hono$^r$ to his Ex$^{cy}$ our Governo$^r$ Wee Agree it be so taken And it shall be Accordingly so Calculated.

By the house of Delegates Sept$^r$ 30 1704
              Signd p order W$^m$ Taylard Cl h

Sent up to his Ex$^{cy}$ and Councill by M$^r$ Henry Coursey M$^r$ Iohn Hudson M$^r$ Robt Skinner and M$^r$ W$^m$ Stone

They returne and say they deliverd the Message P. R. O.<br>B. T. Md<br>Vol. 17.
Bill for repeale of laws. Read the 1ˢᵗ & 2ᵈ time and by
Especiall order do pass for Engrossing.

Then was the Address to her Majⁱʸ relating to New York Affaires brought into the house and Signed by Mʳ Speaker and Severall Members & Sent up to the Councill ᴘ Mʳ Henry Coursey.

The Message About building A house for the Govʳ was Againe read & debated.

And is referrd till monday morning for further consideration.

Propos'd who should Signe the Letter the hono Coll Blakiston Agent for the province

Resolvd Nemine Contradicente that the honob Speaker Signe the same in the name and on behalfe of the whole house.

The house Adjournes till Monday morn 7 A Clock.

Monday 2ᵈ October 1704.

The house mett Againe According to Adjourᵗ being calld over were present as on Saturday only Mʳ Goldsborough

Read What was done Yesterday.

Mʳ Speaker was pleasd to informe the house that he did in the Name and on behalfe of the house Signe the Address to her Majⁱʸ And the letter Which was approovd of & orderd to be entred on the Iournall.

Bill declaring Severall Acts of Assembly formerly made to be in force.

Read the 1ˢᵗ & 2ᵈ time & do pass.

The Message relating to building A house for her Majⁱˢ Govʳ or Giving Allowance for house rent

Againe read & debated

Put to the Question whither an Allowance be Given for rent or not

Carryd in the Affirmative that there be in Allowance made.

Bill for Repeals &c.

Read 1ˢᵗ & 2ᵈ time and do pass

Bill declaring severall Acts to be in force.

Sent up the Councill ᴘ Mʳ Nichᵒ Lowe.

He returns and says he deliverd the same

Iohn Hamond Esqʳ from the honob Councill enters the house and delivers Mʳ Speaker the following Message.

By the councill in Assembly octob 2ᵈ 1704.

Its represented to us that by the bill on foot for limitting officers fees the surveyoʳˢ are retrenchd in theirs which was

P. R. O.
B. T. Md.
Vol. 17. not observd when read At the board Wee thinke the former fees were agreeable to that office Ingenuity and trouble and Notify the same to the house that the bill may be engrost with the oversight rectifyed.

Signd ꝑ order W^m Bladen Cł Co.

Which being read in the house and debated was Answerrd As follows Viz^t

By the house of Delegates October 2^d 1704

Wee haue Explaind the fees on resurveys as retrenchd and it Seems to us the retrenchm^t is not unreasonable but sufficient reward proposd to encourage Art and Industry And Wee hope yo^r hono^rs will think so too on reading the same the clause is thus Allowed.

Resurvey of 140 Acres or under 400^l tob Any q^ty Aboue 140 Acres the same fees as is Allowed on primitive Survey's and no more the former law was in that part found Excessive burthensome And this Conceivd but moderate And therefore doubt not Yo^r hono^rs Concurrence to the Engrost bill Which is now ready to be sent up.

Signd ꝑ order W Taylard Ch D

Read in the house Approovd of & Sent to the Coun ꝑ M^r King & M^r Howe.

They returne and say they deliverd the same.

Put to the question Whither the Allowance for house rent proposd be 30^l or 20^l.

Carryd by Majo^ty of Voices that 30^l ꝑ Annum be Allowd his Ex^cy for house rent

The engrost dupplicates of the Address brought into the house with the Coppy of the Lre to Colł Blakiston Which was Sent up to the Councill by M^r Henry Coursey.

He returnes and says he deliverd the same.

Upon reading the bill for Officers fees: proposed by A member that the Executo^rs & Adm^rs of Officers that do any thing Contrary to this Act be included in the penalty.

2^d That Noe Execution issue for officers fees After Yeares.

3^d That noe Execution be Granted any officer for fees till Oath made y^t the Seuerall Services Are performed for w^ch they are chargd And that to be certifyd by the party that Signes Execution for them

The consideration whereof is referrd to the next Sessions of Assembly.

The honob Francis Ienkins Esq$^r$ Enters the house & delivers M$^r$ Speaker.
P. R. O.
B. T. Md.
Vol. 17.

The bill for repealls &c.

Bill declaring Severall Acts to be in force, both Endorsd thus, By the Councill in Assembly. October 2$^d$ 1704 Read the 1$^{st}$ & 2$^d$ time And do pass for engrossm$^t$

W$^m$ Bladen Cl Co.

And likewise deliverd the follow Message.

Resolvd that the Sermon preached by M$^r$ Cockshute At opening the Church at Annapol the 24$^{th}$ of September in the Afternoone be printed if the house thinke fitt

Signd p order W$^m$ Bladen Cl Counc

Which being read the house Concurrs therewith

Endorsd so, And sent up to the Councill by M$^r$ Greenberry He returns and says he deliverd the same.

The honoble Francis Ienkins Esq$^r$ enters the house and delivers M$^r$ Speaker the engrost Address And letter to Coll Blakiston Signd p the honob Councill &

Orderd M$^r$ Speaker Signe the same on behalfe of the whole house, which was done Accordingly.

Engrost bill declaring Severall Acts to be in force

Engrost bill for repeale of Severall laws. both Read & Assented to by the house of Delegates.

The dupplicates of the Addresses to her Maj$^{ty}$ & the coppy of the letter to Coll Blakistone sent up to the honoble Councill by M$^r$ In$^o$ Waters & M$^r$ Sam$^{ll}$ Magruder.

They returne and say they deliverd the same.

The house Adjourns till 2 A Clock in the Afternoon

Post Merediem

The house met According to Adjournment and being Calld over were All p$^r$sent as in the morning.

Engrost bill for Appeales &c. And the bill declaring Severall Acts to be in force Sent up to the honob Councill by M$^r$ Iohn Hudson for their Assent

He returns and Says he deliverd the bills

The honoble Iames Sanders Esq$^r$ enters the house and delivers M$^r$ Speaker the following Engrost bills

Bill for repeale of some laws.

Bill declaring Severall Acts to be in force both Engrost and Endorsd as follows.

October 2$^d$ 1704

Read and Assented to by her Maj$^{ts}$ honob Councill.

W Bladen Cl Councill.

P. R. O.
B. T. Md.
Vol. 17.
He likewise brought the following message

By the Councill in Assembly
October 2ᵈ 1704

Wee do put You in minde that now the Sessions is neer A Conclusion Wee haue not Yet Seen the Address propos'd to her Majesty concerning the p'sent Agrievance of Granting lands in the province.    Signd ꝑ order Wᵐ Bladen Cl Co.

Which being read Resolvd it be Answerd as follows.

Octob 2ᵈ 1704   By the house of Delegates.

Upon reading the message ꝑ the honoble Iames Sanders Esqʳ relating to the land records &c.   This house inspected their Iournall And find A former Vote that forasmuch as many Weighty Matters lay under consideration it was Resolved the consideration thereof be referrd to next Sessions of Assembly.
Signd ꝑ order Wᵐ Taylard Cl ho

Sent up to the Councill ꝑ Mʳ Ioseph Ennalls & Mʳ Wᵐ Aisquith.
They returne and say they deliverd the same.
Engrost bill for regulating Officers fees
Read & Assented to by the house of Delˢ
The Iournall of the Comittee of Accounts Read & Assented to And Endorsd as follows.

By the house of Delegates Octobʳ 2 1704

Read and Approovd of According to the proposicon herewith sent          Signd ꝑ order Wᵐ Taylard Cl ho Del

Orderd the following Message be sent up with the Iournall of Accounts

By the house of Del Octobʳ 2ᵈ 1704

Conceivd by this house that by any Comand of the Queene or law of the Countrey they are not bound to pay for any coppy's of the laws to be sent home.
Nevertheless to shew the honoʳ this house haue to our Govʳ And to settle this point for the future Wee'l consent that

What the Comittee of Acco$^{ts}$ haue Allowd Shall pass for this P. R. O.
time And for the future no more then one orriginall here and B. T. Md.
two Coppys to be sent home Shalbe chargeable to the province. Vol. 17.
To which this house prays the Concurrence of the honoble
Councill with which wee consent to the Iournall.

Signd ꝑ order W$^m$ Taylard Cl h D.

Which being read was Sent up to the honob Counc$^{ll}$ with
the Iournall of Accounts by M$^r$ Thomas Smith & others
 They returne and say they deliverd the same
 The foll Message ordred to be entred.

By the house of Del$^s$ Octob 2 1704.

 May it please yo$^r$ Ex$^{cy}$
Having an Entire dependance on the Assureances yo$^r$ Ex$^{cy}$
has Given us of Your resolucons to Governe us According to
law And preserving us in our rights & property's And Your
Willingness to Assent to What may be reasonably proposed
for the ease And Welfare of the province Wee haue propos'd
to p$^r$sent Yo$^r$ Ex$^{cy}$ with thirty pounds in money Yearly to defray the charge of your house rent while Yo$^r$ Ex$^{cy}$ continues
this Gou$^r$nment Which wee pray You to Accept And Understand us candidly in All things

Signd ꝑ order W$^m$ Taylard Cl h Del

 Read and Approovd of by the house & sent up to his Ex$^{cy}$
by M$^r$ Iohn Taylor Edw$^d$ Blay Francis Dollahyde Io$^n$ Iones and
In$^o$ Waters.
 they returne and say they deliverd their Message.
 Upon reading the Act for limittacon of Officers fees it was
orderd the following Message be Sent up.

By the house of Delegates octob 3$^d$ 1704

 Wee haue Considerd the reasonableness of the Surveyo$^{rs}$
fees as regulated by the bill and finding them most Iust And
fitting cannot consent to any Alteration the former Setlement
in that point being Experienced to haue been oppressive to
the people And A great Agreivance And Severall persons
Now in this house that haue been and are in that Employment being Sencible of the Iustice thereof are content therewith and Wee pray Your honours to consider of and concurr
with us that the law may not be laid Aside to the Great in-
convenience of the Countrey.

Signd ꝑ order W$^m$ Taylard Cl h D

P. R. O.
B. T. Md.
Vol. 17. Read & approovd of by the house & orderd it be sent up to the Councill to morrow Morning.

The house Adjourns till to Morrow morning 8 A Clock.

## Tuesday 8$^{ber}$ 3$^d$ 1704.

The house mett againe According to Adjournm$^t$ being calld over were present as Yesterday.

The Engrost bill for regulating Officers fees Endorsd. And the Message prepard last night relating to it were Sent up to the honoble Councill by M$^r$ Charles Greenberry M$^r$ In$^o$ Iones & M$^r$ Iohn Leach

They returne and Say they deliverd the same.

The Honoble Iohn Hamond Edward Lloyd Esq$^{rs}$ enters the house and delivers M$^r$ Speaker the following Message Viz$^t$

By the Councill in Assembly Octob 3$^d$ 1704

The message by Coll Smith and others with your Iournall of Comittee of Accounts to which is Subscribed your Condiconall Assent has been perused & Considerd by this board Whereupon wee are Sorry to finde the little notice you take of What his Ex$^{cy}$ was pleasd so Gratiously and Frankly to tell you the other day that he would make noe bargaines desired not yo$^r$ bounty but requird Your Iustice Wherefore if you thinke Wee haue Courted Your condescention in Allowing of tobacco at 10$^s$ $\maltese$ Cent Wee hereby lett you know that wee are not for any Allowance this Sessions to be made in money but are inclinable to Advise his Ex$^{cy}$ that the money now in banke be reservd for the Countrey Service on Greater emergency's You are not Willing to forsee, Your Allowance out of the three pence $\maltese$ hhd for Arms of particuler Sums is not within Your province therefore ought to be expunged.

Signd $\maltese$ order W Bladen Cl Counc.

Which being read this house Resolves they will consider

The Honoble Edward. Lloyd Esq$^r$ enters the house and delivers M$^r$ Speaker the following message

By the Councill in Assembly 8$^r$ 3$^d$ 1704

Yo$^r$ Message 'About the present proposed regulacon of Surveyo$^{rs}$ fees is Agreed to by this board rather then delay the Sessions.        Signd $\maltese$ order W$^m$ Bladen Cl Co:

The Aboue Message by Coll Hamond & Coll Lloyd read P. R. O.<br>B. T. Md.<br>Vol. 17. and debated Resolvd it be Answerd by the following Message viz[t]

By the house of Delegates   October 3[d] 1704

Wee haue read and debated Your hono[rs] message and are Sorry you are pleasd to be so tart upon us for doeing what wee Conceive to be our duty to our Countrey And it is our right and privileidge Wee humbly suppose to debate and consider of any publiq tax upon the people as this of Sealing the laws And duplicates is And wee hope wee have propos'd it with All the tenderness & Iustice that can reasonably be Expected and with all due Submission to his Ex[cy] And Your hono[rs] Wee cannot depart from it

Therefore if Your honours are not pleas'd to o ne with us in apportioning the money to help lessen the leavy According to the tenour of the laws at the price you first proposd to us And agreed to Wee cant help it And our Countrey can't impute it to us If you please to send the Iournall Wee will Regulate it in tobacco as soon as Wee cann And lay it before Yo[r] hono[rs] if there be any thing you think Unreasonable please to remarke it that it May be considerd.   .

Wee do not pretend to medle with the Allowances for Countrey Arms cleansing as You are pleasd to Supose therefore it Shall be expunged.

Wee expected Kinder usage.but shall Content our selves at p[r]sent without any other remarks.

Signd p order W[m] Taylard Cl h D

Which being read and approovd of by the house And Sent up to the Honoble Councill by M[r] Henry Coursey M[r] Sam[ll] Young M[r] Charles Greenberry M[r] In[o] Taylor & M[r] Thomas Beale.

They returne and say they deliverd their Message.

The honob Thomas Tench Esq[r] In[o] Hamond Esq[r] Rob[t] Smith Esq[r] and Edward Lloyd Esq[r] enters the house & delivers M[r] Speaker the Iournall of the Comittee of Accounts with the following Message viz[t]

By the Councill in Assembly octob the 3[d] 1704

Upon reading Yo[r] last Message wee find wee are mistaken by the house as to the Sealing the laws and Duplicates.  A dispute wee never expected to haue been reviv'd this Sessions as it Seems to be by yo[r] Message with the Iournall of the

14

P. R. O.
B. T. Md.
Vol. 17.

Comittee of Accounts Therefore must now observe to you that either the Allowances on the said Iournall are Iust and fitting to be made by this Assembly or otherwise Wee Beleive neither yo' house nor this board Would Agree thereto Wherefore was yo' Message requiring His Ex^{cys} concession to future re- trenchments contrary to her Maj^{tys} Instruccons for Sending home Seal'd duplicates of the coppys of the laws Enacted here tachd like a peticonary bill. nay rather an undoubted right You haue to the free use of her Maj^{ts} Great Seale for those duplicates or at least to be dispensd with in not complying with that Injunction to confirme which you haue only yo' owne opinions.

Wee never designd or haue endeavourd but to cultivate a good Understanding with your house & promote the interest of the Countrey by readily agreeing to what was fitting for us And therefore have Avoided taking notice of Severall Messages from you Especially of that of the 30^{th} of Sept' by M' Coursey And Six other Members of your house Wherein you Seem either to question our integrity.

The Allowance to this board is but one quart' in respect to those to the Members of Your house the money raisd by Imposts was allways intended by this Board to be disposed of for defraying the publiq charge of the Countrey and Wee know not how it could be better applyed And when wee haue Assurd you that wee do not reguard our owne Advantage in what is Allowd to us Wee may be Allowd to tell you without any ill Usage that wee wonder (When you are Sencible of the publiq charge) you should propose to transcribe so long A Iournall of the Comittee of Accounts at this time A day when the Sessions is so neer A Conclusion Therefore propose it be Assented to as it now stands And as to the foregoing dispute this Agree- ment will not be conclusive but the matter may more calmly & leizurely be debated Another Sessions.

Signd p order W^m Bladen Cl Co.

Which being read and debated was Answerd as foll


By the house of Delegates
Octob 3^d 1704

Wee would Avoid All disputes or Multiplicity of Messages but cannot depart from our privileidges. What ever is Setled by law on the publiq charge is A Iust debt but the number of Duplicates is not so Setled And What Wee are willing to do now is to the intent to Setle for the future to prevent disputes which Wee are not willing to entaile on those that Comes

After And wee are troubled to see Yoᵣ Honours wrest our P. R. O. B. T. Md. Vol. 17.
words as tho' wee claimd the use of the Great Seale for nothing,
Wee haue not said or done any thing to deserve such A construction Wee hope.

If Wee proposd to transcribe the Iournall it was in complyance with yoᵣ honoᵣˢ resolution to haue Allowances in tobacco
And Wee did not Expect to be reprimanded for it.

Wee do not reflect on yoᵣ honoᵣˢ Understanding or integrity
And wish that Every where All reflections was Avoided.

. Wee desire Your honoᵣˢ interprett our good meaning aright
and to concurr with us that Wee may proceed to Compleat
this Sessions.          Signd ꝑ order Wᵐ Taylard Cl.

Which was read and approovd of by the house & Sent up
to the honob Councill by Mᵣ Charles Greenbery Mᵣ Iames
Smallwood Mᵣ Wᵐ Frisby Mᵣ Inᵒ Iones Mᵣ Iames Maxwell.

They returne and say they deliverd it
The house Adjournd till 2 A Clock in the Afternoone.

### Post Merediem.

The house mett againe being calld over were present as in
the morning.

The honoble Thomas Tench Robt Smith Iames Sanders
Francis Ienkins and Wᵐ Coursey Esqᵣˢ enters the house and
delivers Mᵣ Speaker the following Message.

### By the Councill in Assembly October 3ᵈ 1704

Gent  Wee haue Acquainted you with what wee cann say
upon the Subject of last Message which Matters Shall never
be drawne into president  the laws proposed Are all agreed to
Therefore wee desire You will Get the bills ready that this
day may end with this present Sessions
          Signd ꝑ order Wᵐ Bladen Cl Co.

Which was read in the house.
Orderd the foll Message be sent up.

### By the house of Del   October 3ᵈ 1704

Since Yoᵣ bonoᵣˢ Will not consent to what wee haue so
reasonably proposd As to duplicates for the future Wee are
dischargd from that proposall and are obligded to Assert our
privileidges to futurity.  Wee cannot fill up the bills without

P. R. O.  yo' bono'' Assent to the Iournall of Accounts since you haue
B. T. Md'
Vol. 17.  proposed it two ways and Wee now send it to the intent Your
hono'' may endorse w' your result is,

signd ℗ order W<sup>m</sup> Taylard Cl house

Which was read and approovd of and sent up to the honoble
Councill by M' Iohn Taylor and M' Tho' Frisby togeather
with the Iournall of Accounts
They returne and say they deliverd the same.
The honoble Francis Ienkins Esq' enters the house & de-
livers M' Speaker the Iournall of the Comittee of Accounts.
Endorsed to the tob Accounts thus.

By the Councill in Assembly Octob 3<sup>d</sup> 1704
Assented to by her Maj<sup>ts</sup> honob Councill

W<sup>m</sup> Bladen Cl

And the money Accounts was likewise endorsd.

By the Councill in Assembly Octob 3<sup>d</sup> 1704
Assented to by her Maj<sup>ts</sup> honoble Councill.

W<sup>m</sup> Bladen Cl Co.

Bill for Apporconing the publiq leavy
Read & Assented to by the house of Delegates.
Sent up to the Honob Councill ℗ M' Elias King.
He returnes and says he deliverd the same.
Bill for limittacon of Officers fees.
Bill for repeale of some laws.
Bill declaring Severall former laws to be in force.
Which bills Engrost were sent up to be Seald by M' W<sup>m</sup>
Stone and M' In° Macall.

By the house

Since Wee haue made Many concessions in order to End
disputes as to coppys or duplicates of the laws for the future
and prayd the Councills Concurrence but in returne thereof
haue had nothing but reprimands indecent & unparliamentary
Expressions which for the sake of our Countrey wee will not
Spend more time or money to debate and resent But resolve
that What Wee haue Asserted is our undoubted right And
that no money is or cann be raisd on the publiq or the Countrey to pay for Duplicates or coppys of the laws Seald to be
sent for Engl but such as Shall be with consent of the

Countrey by their Representatives and that what is now consented unto is in honour to his present Ex<sup>cy</sup> our Governour
and not to be drawne into any president for that the publiq is
not lyable to the charge of any duplicates or coppys to be sent
to England for the future tho consented to now.

Which being read was Approovd on by the house and
orderd to be recorded on this Iournall.

Resolvd that the Severall County Courts pay 120$^l$ of tob$^o$ for
the Seale to the whole body of laws to be sent them.

And four hundred pounds of tobacco for transcribing the
laws made last Sessions And two thousand pounds of
tobacco for the laws made this Sessions to be paid out of the
County leavy's.

Memd that forasmuch as there are Six private Acts and two
other bills for which there has been an Allowance made ouer
& Aboue what was due Therefore Resolvd the same be refunded to the Countrey next Sessions.

In$^o$ Hamond Esq$^r$ from the honoble Councill enters the
house and delivers M$^r$ Speaker the bill for Apportioning the
publiq leavy. Endorsd.

Read & Assented to by the Councill & house of Del$^s$

M$^r$ Sam$^{ll}$ Young and M$^r$ Charles Greenberry Order'd to see
the Clerk make such regulations in the Iournall as haue been
proposed.

Moovd by the Clerk of this house that forasmuch as Extraordinary Services haue been done by him the last and this
Sessions of Assembly and likewise duplicates to be by him
and at his charge prepared to be sent for England Which was
not heretofore done by any Clerke Therefore prays an Allowance for the same and that the sallary may be Advanced for
the future to support that office

Resolvd the consideration thereof be referrd till next
Assembly.

Orderd the following Addresses be entred on the Iournall
viz$^t$

By the Burgesses and delegates of her Maj$^{ts}$ Province of
Maryland.

To the Queens most Excell$^t$ Majesty Most Gracious Sou-
ereigne.

His Ex$^{cy}$ In$^o$ Seymour Esq$^r$ our p$^r$sent Govern$^r$ having had
some Advices of A designe sett on foot by some persons
unknowne to him or us to Address yo$^r$ Maj$^{ty}$ & lay downe
some Method for Altering the present constitution of this
Government so happily Established under yo$^r$ Maj$^{tys}$ imediate
Comand by subjecting us to the Gou$^r$nm$^t$ of New York or in
some measure making this dependant on that Was pleasd to
lay the same before us at the opening of this Sessions at Which

P. R. O.
B. T. Md.
Vol. 17. as Wee are infinitely oblidgd to his Ex$^{cy}$ so Wee are Extreemly surprisd as knowing how greatly prejudiciall the same will be, not only to Your Maj$^{ts}$ Interest but to the happyness and tranquility of this Your Maj$^{ts}$ poore enoyd province in these and many other instances Viz$^t$

1$^{st}$   Its conceivd that if the Seat of Gou$^r$nment be at New Yorke it will not only be A means to Allure and entice many trades men Artificers and others now Among us who follow the trade of Planting tobacco here to desert this province And fly to that of New Yorke where they may follow their Severall trades and callings & gaine to themselves more ease and Advantage, thereby lessening the revenue of the Crowne of England, But Also by those means they will in A Short time supply us with such Manufactarys and other necessary's which now are imported from England And inevitably destroy our Comerce with the same.

2.   Wee conceive that New York having power & Authority Will upon All occasions Comand from us such forces as they shall thinke fitt for the Safety and Strengthning themselves w$^{ch}$ will in A great measure weaken this province (now but thinly Seated) And thereby leaue the remaining parte of the inhabitants here open to the incursions of our Comon Enemys the Indians by whom Wee are environd And many of them as neere to us as those of New Yorke and often committing Murthers on the Inhabitants here, having lately destroy'd severall persons and Cannot want opportunity's also of Ioyning with the severall nations of Indians residing Among us to Effect their designes leaving us in A deplorable condition the lives of the inhabitants Greatly hazarded thereby and the Whole province in danger of being totally laid waiste.

3$^d$   That it will be very disadvantageous to the inhabitants of this province upon All occasions as of Councills Assemblys Gen$^{ll}$ Courts &c.   And upon appeales and differences between party and party to travaile thither it being neere 400 Mile distant from hence And the ways not passable in the winter Season by reason of the desert roads Violent frosts Deep Snows And Rivers and bays to pass over.   so that the poorer sort of people will not be able to Undergoe so great charge and fatigue And the Richer to Avoid it will remooue themselves & Estates to England or other parts which will tend to the ruine of the tobacco trade and Consequently lessen the Revenue of the Crowne.

4.   That the constitucon of this province to theirs is of so differrent and disagreeable a nature both in traffick and other things that the laws there composed cannot be agreeable to the trade and Affaires of this Countrey nor the constitution of the inhabitants of this province.

P. R. O.
B. T. Md.
Vol. 17.

Many more Wee Coud insert and What Wee here haue humbly offerrd are most undoubted truths Which Wee Most humbly hope Yo<sup>r</sup> Sacred Majesty Will never p<sup>r</sup>mitt to be Experienced But that Your Majesty Will in Your princely wisdome be pleasd to detect the contrivance and finally Stopp the designe That without Any opportunity to plead for Our owne & Your Maj<sup>ts</sup> Interest wee may not be given up to any other Gouernment then such as Your Majesty has Allready Establishd ouer us which will encourage the industrious reso- lucons of us And our posterrity to approoue our Selvs in euery thing.

Yo<sup>r</sup> Maj<sup>ts</sup> Most faithfull most obedient & loyall Subjects.

Signd ꝑ the honob Councill and house of Delegates.

To the Queens most Excellent Maj<sup>ty</sup>

The humble Address of your Maj<sup>ts</sup> most dutifull & Loyall Subjects the Gouerno<sup>r</sup> Councill and Gen<sup>ll</sup> Assembly of Your Maj<sup>ts</sup> province of Maryland.

Most Gracious Sovereigne.

Wee your Maj<sup>ts</sup> Most dutifull and loyall Subjects having A deep sence of your Maj<sup>ts</sup> most benigne and Gratious protection to us here as well as yo<sup>r</sup> Constant and tender reguard of and to the welfare of All your Maj<sup>ts</sup> Good Subjects in Gen<sup>ll</sup> cannot thinke that our silence can be Suitable to the Warme influences Wee feele of yo<sup>r</sup> princely vertues & piety by and Under which wee haue [un]interrupted And Compleat enjoyment of All that can be neer or dear to us Our religion most illustriously countenanced by your most Glorious Example and our propertys supported And Secured by yo<sup>r</sup> unerring wisdom & Constant Iustice therefore since it has been observ'd in all Ages that by the true piety and vertue of princes and rulers great blessings haue been deriv'd downe to their people & Subjects who are as wee haue the Greatest reason to Acknowledge our Selves happy in such A case Wee humbly beg leaue to con- gratulate the Glorious Successes of her Maj<sup>ts</sup> Victorious Arms under the conduct of his Grace the Duke of Marlborough Your maj<sup>ts</sup> most faithfull Subject and Generallissimo by Ex- pressing our most Earnest Ioy that Allmighty God has touchd Your Royall breast to make choice of so Valliant & Wise A leader to Succeed the loss of his late Majesty of Ever Glorious memory Not only to the lasting honour of Yo<sup>r</sup> Maj<sup>ty</sup> And the English nation but the defence and Supporte of all yo<sup>r</sup> Allies and Confederates Against the Comon Enemey Wherefore as our duty oblidges and our gratitude lead us to returne our most hearty thanks to Allmighty God for his Continuall preservation & prosperrity of Yo<sup>r</sup> most Sacred & his Royall

P. R. O.
B. T. Md.
Vol. 17. highnesses most Illustrious persons soe wee shall neuer omitt
our earnest and dayly prayers for the Continuance of All these
and other his Mercys & blessings And that After A long And
Glorious reigne never to be forgotten in this World for your
unexampled pyety Noble Vertuous and Constant Adherence
& Supporte of and to the church As by the law Established
and Your Royall care and preservation of Your good And
loyall Subjects You may attaine Everlasting Ioy And fellicity
in the world to come

Which Address being read and Approovd of Was Signd by
Mr Speaker on behalfe of the house of Delegates. And
likewise

Signd by his Ex^cy and Councill.

Orderd the following letter be entred Viz^t

Annapolis 30^th Sept^r 1704
Sr

Wee haue nothing to add beyond what was Contain'd in the
Lre from last Assembly A coppy whereof you haue inclosed
only to desire Your care and Assistance in laying our Enclos'd
Address before her Majesty And Using your utmost Efforts to
put a Stop to the designe, And what fees You Expend in the
necessary dispatch of the same shall be punctually paid by us
Wee are Streightned in time at p^rsent Wee recomend the
Contents of the Enclosed And that to your care and freindship
and subscribe.

Yo^r most faithfull humble Servants.

Signd on behalfe and by order of the house of Delegates
W^m Dent Speaker

Orderd the said Addresses and letter be forthwith sent to
Coll Blakiston our Agènt in England.

And that Duplicates thereof be likewise prepared to follow
them

The honob Coll Iohn Hamond enters the house & Acquaints
Mr Speaker that his Ex^cy was ready to receive him & the
whole house at the Councill Chamber in order the Conclude
this Session

Thereupon the house Adjournd to the Councill Chamber.

Where Mr Speaker deliverd to his Ex^cy the following
Engrost bills Viz^t

An Act for quieting possessions & enrolling Convey.

An Act for Setlement of An Annuall Revenue upon her
Maj^ts Governour in this province.

An Act Appointing Court days in each respective County's
within this province.

An Act Ag^t Engrossers and regraters.

An Act for publication of Marriages.

An Act for killing of Woolves and Crows.

P. R. O.
B. T. Md.
Vol. 17.

An Act Ascertaining the Expences of Councello^n & Delegates of Assembly Com^rs of the Com^rs and County Courts of this province.

An Act to make Valid Good & Effectuall in law All mañer of process and proceedings from the Yeare 1692 to this time.

An Act relating to the Standard of English Weights & Measures

An Act Imposing 9^d ⅌ Gallon on rum Spirritts wine and brandy Imported by land from pensilvania into this province

An Act for limittacon of Certaine Actions for Avoiding Suites at law.

An Act directing the mañer of Sueing out Attachm^ts in this province And limitting the Extent of them

An Act Against Excessive Usury.

An Act for preservation of Severall harbours and landing places in this province.

An Act declaring the Grantees of land lyeing within the Indians land May haue Actions of trespass.

An Act prohibitting Com^rs Sherriffs & Clerks to plead as Attorneys in the Severall County Courts.

An Act prohibitting Masters of Shipps & Vessells & others from transporting or carrying Away any p^rsons out of this province without passes.

An Act Confirming to the Gov^r of this province the duty of 3^d ⅌ tonn upon the burthen of Shipps & Vessells.

An Act for Advancement of the Natives and residents of this province.

An Act Enabling W^m Sweatnam of Talbott County Devisee of Rich^d Sweatnam decd to sell land.

An Act enabling Coll Edw^d Dorsey to Sell land & houses &c.

An Act declaring the Altering or Scratching out the marke of tob or Altering the quallity After recd to be fellony.

An Act for Appointment of Constables and What relates to their Office.

An Act for publication of All laws within this province.

An Act for recording all laws in the Secretarys office and transmitting the Iournall of the house of Assembly in the same.

An Act for Stay of Executions After the 10^th of May Yearly.

An Act for Amercements in the provinciall & Co^ty Courts

An Act Confirming titles to land Given to the use of Churches.

An Act for the better Admstration of Iustice in the high Court of Chancery & other Courts of this province.

P. R. O.    An Act Imposing $3^d$ ℔ Gallon on rum Wine $20^s$ ℔ poll on
B. T. Md.  Negroes & Irish servants.
Vol. 17.
An Act directing the manner of Electing & Sumoning Delegates.

An Act Ascertaining the bounds of A certaine tract of land to the use of the Nanticoke Indians.

An Act Ascertaining What damage shalbe Allowd on protested bills of Exchange.

An Act for marking highway's.

An Act for taking Speciall bayle in the Severall Countys.

An Act prohibitting the inhabitants of this province or any others to carry liquors to the Ind^a townes.

An Act for regulating ordnary's.

An Act for Securing p^rsons rights to towne lands.

An Act declaring the devision of Severall Countys &c

An Act for Setling lands on Susanna Blaney.

An Act Confirming the last Will & testament of Charles Ascomb In° Winfell and In° Burnham

An Act for laying·An Imposicon on Severall Comoditys Exported out of this province.

An Act Causing Grand & Pettit Iuro^rs & Wittnesses to Come to Courts.

An Act for the more Speedy conveying publiq Letters & paquetts and defraying the charge thereof

An Act empowring the Com^rs of the County Courts to leavy and raise tob to defray the necessary charges of their Countys and parrishes.

An Act for Securing Merchants and others tob After recd

An Act for releife of Credittors in England Against Bankrupts

An Act for restrayning the Extortion of Sherriffs Sub Sherriffs and deputy Commissary's.

An Act Confirming purchases of the Com^rs for their respective Countys.

An Act declaring how fees for private bills and Naturallizations shallbe proporcond.

An Act to encourage the inhabitants of this province to Venture their Shipps and Vessells more freely Abroad

An Act for Naturallization of Otho Ottherson

An Act prohibitting the Importacon of bread beer flower &c^a from pensilvania or Elswhere into this province.

An Act Ascertaining the Gauge of tob hogsheads.

An Act to encourage such p^rsons as will undertake to build Watermills.

An Act laying Impost of $3^d$ ℔ hogshead to defray publiq charges.

An Act providing What Shalbe evidence to proove forreigne & other debts &c  P. R. O. B. T. Md. Vol. 17.

An Act for Securing the pochyall Library's &c

An Act for punishing the offences of Adultery & fornication.

An Act for payment of fees from Criminall persons

An Act relating to Servants and Slaves.

An Act Ascertaining the height of fences.

An Act directing the Sherriffs in their office & more easy payment of the publiq & County leavy's

An Act Entituled An Act Ascertaining the bounds of land to be in force.

An Act for encouragem$^t$ of Tillage and releife of poore Debtors.

An Act for punishment of blasphemy prophane Swearing & Cursing.

An Act relating to the Free shoole.

An Act to prevent the Growth of popery in this province.

An Act for Speedy tryall of Criminalls in the County Courts.

An Act for the better Admstracon of Iustice in probatt of Wills

An Act for Appeales and regulating Writts of Erro$^r$.

An Act for ordering and regulating the Millitia.

An Act requiring Ma$^{rs}$ of Shipps &c$^a$ to publish the rates of their freight &c$^a$

An Act for rectifying the ill practises of Attorney's

An Act for limittacon of Officers fees.

An Act for repeale of Certaine laws.

An Act declaring Severall Acts of Assembly formerly made to be in force

An Act for Apportioning the publiq leavy.

To each bill Aforesaid his Ex$^{cy}$ was pleased to Assent by Endorsing them Severally thus.

### October 3$^d$ 1704

On behalfe of her Sacred Maj$^{ty}$ &c I will this be A law

Jo: Seymour

And likewise Sealed them Severally with the broad Seale of the province Which being soe endorsd & Sealed. His Ex$^{cy}$ was pleased to Acquaint the house that he thought it Convenient for her Maj$^{ts}$ Service to prorogue them till the 5$^{th}$ day of December next And they were Accordingly prorogued

W Taylard Clk of the house of Delegates

Examined by me Alex$^r$ Hall Deputy Secretary

# ACTS

Maryland ss.

Att a Session of Assembly Begun and held at the Town and port of Annapolis in Ann Arundell county the 5<sup>th</sup> day of September in the third year of the Reigne of our Sovereigne Lady Anne by the Grace of God of England Scotland France and Ireland Queen Defender of the faith &c<sup>a</sup> and in the year of our Lord one thousand seven hundred and four.

## Were Enacted the Laws following

An Act directing the Manner of Suing out Attachments in this Province and limitting the Extent of them. For Settling the Manner of proceedings on Attachments and limitting the Extent of them and providing what shall be levyed on Attachments and Executions.

Be it enacted by the Queens most excellent Majesty by and with the Advice and Consent of her Majestys Governour Councill and Assembly of this Province and the Authority of the same that from hence forth no Attachment shall issue out of any Court of this Province before a Writt or Sumons be first made out upon which Writt if the party Defendant be an Inhabitant or Resident within this province and the Sheriff shall return a Non est Inventus one other Writt or summons shall thereupon in manner aforesaid issue forth against the said Defendant And if the Sheriff shall upon the second Writt or summons return a Non est Inventus likewise An Attachment p. 2 shall and may in manner and forme hereafter sett down be awarded And in Case any Writt or summons shall issue forth of any of her Majestys Courts within this Province against any person or persons absent out of this Province in such case upon the Returne of a Non est Inventus by the Sheriff on such Writt or sumons and the party plaintiff his leaving with the Attorny of such Absent Defendant (if he hath left an Attorny a Copy of his Declaration or short Notes expressing the Cause of Accon or if he hath left no Attorny then the Plaintiff leaving a Copy of the said Declaration or short Note expressing the true Cause of Accon at the house where the said Defendant absent die last reside or dwell and making such proof of his Accon as the said respective Courts shall think fitt It shall and may be lawfull for the Iustices of the said Courts to award an Attachment against the Goods Chattells and Creditts of the said absent Defendant so as aforesaid prosecuted and not appearing to the said Accon which are or shall be in the hands and possession of any person or persons whatsoever (yea) even in the Plaintiffs own hands for the Defendants use in this

Province. In which said Attachments there shall be a Clause comanding the Sheriff of the Respective Countys at the time of the executing the said Attachments to make known to each person or persons in whose hands and possession the said Goods Chattells & Creditts so as aforesaid in their hands attach'd are should not be Condemn'd and Execution thereof had and made as in other Cases of Recoverys and Judgments given in Courts of Record Att which day of Return of the said Attachment if the said Defendant shall not then appear nor the Garnishee in whose hands the af$^d$ goods Chattells and Creditts of the Defendant were attachd to shew Cause to the Contrary the respective Courts shall and may condemn the said Goods Chattells and Creditts so as aforesaid attachd and award Execution thereof to be had and made by capias ad Satisfaciendum fieri facias or otherwise as in other Judgments he The said Plaintiff so prosecuting as aforesaid giving good and sufficient Security before the Justices of each respective Court to and for the use of the said defendant so as aforesaid being not found within this province to make restitution of the said goods Chattells or Creditts so as aforesaid Condemn'd or the Value thereof if the Defendant so as aforesaid prosecuted shall at any time within one year and a day to be accounted from the said Attachment awarded come in and either in person or by Attorny appear to the said original accon and make it appear that the said plaintiff hath been and is Satisfyed and paid the Debt or demand in the said Accon or shall otherwise in Court discount or barr the said plaintiff of the same or any part thereof which said Condemnation and Execution of the said Goods Chattells or Creditts of the said Defendant in the hands of the Garnishee or Garnishee as aforesaid had and made shall be sufficicent and pleadable in barr by the said Garnishee or Garnishees in any Accon brought against him or them by the said Defendant for the same.

Provided allways that no Sheriff shall levy by way of Execution as aforesaid against any the said Garnishee or Garnishees any more than the plaintiffs Debt and Cost nor against any Garnishee or Garnishees than what the said Plaintiff in the said Accon shall make appear to the said respective Courts to be of the said Goods Chattells and Creditts of the said Defendant in each respective Garnishee or Garnishees hands together with such Costs only as the Garnishee or Garnishees shall put the plaintiff to by denying him or themselves to be indebted unto such Defendant and contesting the same. Provided also that no Sheriff in any County within this province shall by any Attachment or any other Execution had upon such Attachment or by any other Execution whatsoever levy seize or take

L. the goods and chattells of any the Inhabitants of this province so farr as to deprive them of all livelyhood for the future but that Corn for necessary Maintenance Bedding Guns Ax pott and Labourers necessary tools and such like houshold implements and ammunition for subsistance shall be protected from all Attachments and executions whatsoever.

Provided also that such as shall be found by positive proof or other Circumstances wilfully to absent themselves into the woods or elsewhere from the Sheriffs sight whereby they cannot be found to be brought to tryall and such also as shall be absent by Flight or proscription out of this Province to be averr'd upon oath shall have no benefitt of any favourable Interpretation of this Law.

4   And be it enacted by the Authority aforesaid that from henceforth any person or persons having obtain'd a judgment in any Court of this Province or that shall hereafter obtain any Judgment in any Court of this Province against any person or persons it shall and may be lawfull to and for the said Plaintiff in the said Judgment at his will and pleasure instead of any other execution without those previous requisites as above in this act prescribed and directed to take out an Attachment against the goods Chattells and Creditts of the said Defendant in the said Judgment in the said plaintiffs own hands or in the hands of any other person or persons whatsoever which said attachment shall likewise have the Clause aforesaid comanding the Sheriff of the said County to whom it shall be directed at the time of Executing the said Attachment to make known to each person or persons in whose hands & possession the said Goods Chattells and Creditts of the absent Defendant shall be attachd that he or they be and appear at the respective Courts at the day of the returne of the said Attachments to shew cause (if they have any) why the said Goods Chattells and Creditts so as abovesaid in their hands attachd should not be condemn'd & execution thereof had and made as in other Cases of Recoverys and Judgments given in Courts of Record Att which day of the returne of the said Attachmen- if the s^d Defendant shall not then appear nor the said **Garnti** shee in whose hands the Goods Chattells and Creditts of the said Defendant were attach'd to shew sufficient cause to the contrary the said respective Courts shall and may Condemn the said Goods Chattells and Creditts aforesaid so as aforesaid Attachd and award Execution thereof to be had and made either by Capias ad Satisfaciendum fieri facias or otherwise as the said Plaintiff might have had against the Defendant himself on the Judgement aforesaid which said Condemnation & Execution of such goods Chattells and Creditts of

the said Garnishee as aforesaid had and made shall be Suffi- Lib. L. L.
cient and pleadable in Barr by the said Garnishee or Garni- No. 64.
shees in any Accon ag$^t$ him or them by the said Defendant
for the same

| | | |
|---|---|---|
| September 20$^{th}$ 1704 | Maryland Octob 3$^d$ | Sept. 20$^{th}$ 1704 |
| Read and assented | 1704 | Read and assented |
| to by the house of | On behalf of her | to by her Ma$^{tys}$ |
| Delegates | Ma$^{ty}$ &c I will this | hon$^{ble}$ Councill |
| Signd p Ord$^r$ | be a law | W Bladen Cl Concil. |
| W. Taylard Clk. | Jo. Seymour | |

An Act of Directions for the Sheriffs Office in this province p. 5
and for the more easy payment of the publiq & County Levys.

Be it enacted by the Queens most excellent Majesty by and
with the Advice and Consent of her Majestys Governour
Council and Assembly of this Province and the Authority of
the same That no Sheriff under Sheriff or Deputy Sheriff shall
seize any Tobacco unshipt or Seize or mark any Merchants or
others Tobacco received markt and nailed for any Cause
whatsoever but only for Levys. And the severall Sheriffs
are hereby impowered to break the lock of any Tobacco house
or other houses where Tobacco is or shall be secured with
designe to prevent the said Sheriff from Seizing such Tobacco
for publiq Levys and any sheriff so Seizing or marking any
hogshead or Hogsheads of Tobacco containing more than
what is justly due to the publiq for Levys without making
Satisfaction to the person to whom such Tobacco doth belong
as by giving Creditt or Suffering him to take the Overplus
out of such Hogshead of Tobacco at the Choyce of the party
paying or owing the same shall pay for every such Default
the Sume of two thousand pounds of Tobacco one half to her
Majesty her heires and Successors for support of Government
the other half to the party grieved to be recovered in any Court
of Record of this province by action of Debt bill plaint or
Information wherein no Essoyn proteccon or Wager of Law
to be allowed.

And if it Shall so happen that at any time any Sheriff shall
seize any Hogshead of Tobacco which shall weigh more than
such levy or Levys shall amount unto if the remaining part
due to the party or partys from whom they shall receive such
levy or levys be the greater Quantity then and in every such
Case the Sheriff or Sheriffs shall take out of the said Hogshead
such quantity or quantitys of Tobacco due to him for such levy
or levys and the said Hogshead And the remaining part of the
Tobacco shall be and remaine with the party or partys paying

the same But if the remaining part of such Hogshead of Tobacco so seized as aforesaid and belonging to the party or
partys paying the same shall be the less Quantity than is due
to the said Sheriff or Sheriffs for leavys as aforesaid then and
in every such Case the Owner or Owners of such Tobacco
shall take out the Overplus of such Tobacco and the Hogshead with the remaining part shall belong to such sheriff or
Sheriffs receiving.

And be it further enacted by the Authority aforesaid by and
with the Advice and Consent aforesaid That no Sheriff or
Sheriffs within this Province shall require ask for demand or
receive of or from any person whatsoever any ffees or reward
for Serving any Writt Warrant or precept from the Governour
and Councill or from any justice of peace or for Summoning
any Grand jury or for Summoning any pettit Jury in Criminall
Causes or for Summoning or Subpaing any Witness or Witnesses
in Criminall Causes against any person or persons prosecuted
in any of the Courts of this province as a Criminall or for
executing of any Judgment given against a Criminall but in
all such Cases the severall Sheriffs shall and are hereby injoyn'd and required to execute and performe the several things
aforesaid ex officio and every Sheriff offending shall forfeit the
Sume of one thousand pounds of Tobacco for every such
Offence the one half thereof to her Majesty her beires and
successors for the support of the Government of this province
and the other half thereof to the party grieved to be recovered
in any Court of Record of this province by action of Debt bill
plaint or Information wherein no Essoyn Protection or wager
of Law to be allowed.

And whereas many Litigious persons have and for the future
may comence Accons of trespass upon the Case rather out of
Spite and Malice than any reall Cause of Accon and not setting forth in the Originall Writt the Cause of such accon and
yet lay Damage to a vast sume to deter persons from being
baile for prevention whereof for the future.

Be it enacted by the Authority Advice and Consent aforesaid that in all Actions of trespass upon the Case where damages are laid to be above four thousand pounds of Tobacco if
no Declaration be sent with the Writt expressing the true
Cause of Accon the Sheriff shall not require a baile bond exceeding the sume of eight thousand pounds of Tobacco altho'
the Damage be laid in the Writt for any greater sume whatsoever and any Sheriff offending herein shall forfeit the sume of
four thousand pounds of Tobacco the one half thereof to her
Majesty her heires and Successors for the support of Government the other half to the party grieved to be recovered in

any Court of Record of this province by Accon of Debt bill
plaint or Information wherein no Essoyn protection or Wager
of Law to be allowed.

And to the end that publiq Creditors may be speedily
Satisfyed their Debts due from the publiq

Be it enacted by the Authority Advice and Consent aforesaid That every publiq Creditor within this Province shall be
at his Eleccon to make application to the Governour of this
Province for the time being to put such Sheriffs Bond or Bonds
in suite or otherways may imediately have an Action of Debt
against such Sheriff in the County where the ffact ariseth for
such publiq Tobacco as shall be due to such Creditor.

And to the end that no Officer or other person may be
surprized or injustly molested either upon the Account of
payment or Collection of publiq dues,

Be it likewise enacted by the Authority aforesaid by and with
the Advice and Consent aforesaid that any person or persons
having publick Tobacco due to them or ffees in any Sheriffs
hands to collect and that do not Signify to such Sheriff or
Sheriffs their dependance and resolution of making use of the
same on or before the five and twentieth day of December in
the year the same shall be due to him or them shall not have
take or demand any benefitt or Advantage by this Act allowed
for that present year and so every year successively nor shall
the Sheriff of any respective Countys levy by way of Execution
any publick dues or officers ffees upon the body goods or
Chattells of any the Inhabitants of this province except they
have made a demand thereof at or before the twentyeth day of
January for that present year And so every year successively.

And be it also enacted by the Authority Advice and Consent
aforesaid that any Sheriff within this province having in his
hands publick Officers ffees to collect shall not presume to levy
by Execution upon the body goods and Chattells of any the Inhabitants of this province any ffees to him comitted to collect
where the Person or Persons from whom such ffees appear to
be due produce the former Sherriffs Receipts or otherways
make appear the same to be paid under forfeiture and penalty
of trible the sume executed to the party or partys grieved to
be recovered with Cost in any Court of record within this
province by bill plaint or information wherein no essoyn
protection or wager of Law to be allowed.

And forasmuch as Sheriffs bonds have of late years been
usually taken in the County Courts for the better conveniency
of Sheriffs getting security without any Certain forme thereof
· prescribed

Be it therefore enacted by the Authority Advice and Consent aforesaid That all Sheriffs bonds hereafter to be taken

throughout this Province shall be made in manner and forme
following (that is to say)

Maryland ss.  Know all men by these presents That wee A.
B. &ᶜᵃ of the County of——in the province aforesaid are holden
and firmly bound unto our Soveraign Lady Anne &c in the full
sume and Just quantity of—pounds of good sound Merchantable leaf Tobacco and Casq to be paid to her said Majesty her
heires and Successors To the which payment well and truly to
be made wee bind ourselves and either of us and either of our
heires Executors and Administrators Joyntly and severally for
the whole and in the whole firmly by these presents seald with
our Seals and dated the—day of—in the—year of her Majestys
reign Annoq Dmi &c.

The Condition of the above obligation is such that if the
above bounden A. B. do well and truly serve her said Majesty
her heires and Successors in the Office of High Sheriff of
the County of——within the Province aforesaid And also shall
render unto her said Majesty and other her Officers a true
faithfull and perfect Account of all and singular her said Majestys Rights and dues and to her Officers a true and Just account
of their ffees that he shall or may be entrusted with by her
Majestys Governour and other her Officers within this Province
to receive and collect and his Account to her said Majesty her
heires and Successors and to her and their Governour there
for the time being for the ffines and forfeitures & other dues
belonging to her said Majestys Governour As also his Accoᵗ
of all ffees dues and Summs of Money or Tobacco for levys
P. 9 or ffees due to any her Majestys Officers & other good people
within this Province shall pass an Account of by the tenth day
of Aprill next ensuing the date hereof and in all other things
as Sheriff of the County of        shall behave himself well and
honestly towards all persons according to the best of his power
skill and knowledge Then this obligation to be voyd and of no
Effect or else to stand in full force strength and vertue.

Which said bond taken in forme aforesaid if by the County
Court the Comissioners thereof shall transmitt the same into
the Secretarys Office together with all former Sheriffs bonds
by them taken and the said Comissioners are hereby required
and injoyn'd to take new security yearly and every year of
such Sheriffs so long as they shall continue in the said Office
having especiall regard not to admitt any person to be security
as aforesaid but such as are good and Substantiall ffreeholders
within their Countys and also to make the Obligation of such
bond so to be taken from any sheriff answerable to the publiq
charge of their respective Countys.

And for incouragement of such persons now bearing or that shall hereafter bear the Office of Sheriff and who shall punctually comply with the publiq Creditors It is also hereby further enacted by the Authority Advice and consent aforesaid that it shall and may be lawfull for her Majestys Governour for the time being where no just complaint is made against such Sheriff to continue and make good their Comission for the time and terme of three years Successively but no longer.

And be it further enacted by the Authority advice and Consent afores$^d$ that from and after the end of this present Session of Assembly every person or persons within this province which are taxable within the severall and respective Countys thereof shall and may by force and vertue of this Act at any time or times between the laying of the County Levy and the five and twentyeth day of December then next ensuing pay his or their levy or levys in mony or so much thereof as he or they shall please or think fitt after the rate of one penny per pound for Tobacco And the severall and respective Sheriffs of this Province are required by this Act to receive the same accordingly. Provided allways that when such person or persons shall pay mony instead of Tobacco for his or their levy or levys as aforesaid and shall not pay & discharge the whole sum of Tobacco with which he or they stand charged for his or their levys by mony but shall leave some part thereof still due & owing in Tobacco such part so left due in Tobacco shall not be so broken that the Sheriff cannot receive the same p. 10 intire in a Hogshead or Hogsheads the Quantity of five hundred pounds of Tobacco being so accounted.

And be it Enacted by the Authority aforesaid by and with the Advice and consent aforesaid That the severall Sheriffs of the severall and respective Countys within this Province shall and may after the end of this Sessions of Assembly by force and vertue of this Act pay and discharge proportionably to what he shall receive in money and not more Officers ffees and allowances made to any Person or persons whatsoever in the publiq or County Levys in mony after after the rate of one penny per pound for Tobacco Provided allways that when such Sheriff or Sheriffes shall pay mony instead of Tobacco to any person for his allowance in the publiq or County levy and shall not pay and discharge the whole summe of Tobacco due to such person in mony at the rate aforesaid but shall leave some part thereof still due & owing in Tobacco then and in every such Case such part left due & owing in Tobacco shall not be so broken that the party or partys cannot receive the same intire in a Hogshead or Hogsheads.

This Act to continue for three years or to the end of the next Generall Assembly which shall first happen.

| | |
|---|---|
| September 29<sup>th</sup> 1704 | September 29<sup>th</sup> 1704 |
| Read and assented to by | Read and assented by her |
| the house of Delegates. | Majestys honourable Councill |
| W. Taylard Clk. | W Bladen Cl Concil |
| house Del. | |

Maryland Octob 3ᵈ 1704

On behalf of her Majesty &c I will this be a law.

Jo: Seymour

An Act for the encouragement of such persons as will undertake to build Watermills.

Dayly Experience sheweth that the want of Watermills is the true Cause that Husbandry in tilling the Ground & for Sowing of wheat and barley is but coldly prosecuted tho the Advantage thereby in raising the Stock of neat Cattle be great and for as much as most part of the places fitt for Setting p. 11 up of Watermills are already in the hands of persons under age or unable to be at the Charge of building a Watermill or else such as are wilfully obstinate in forbidding and hindring such persons as would purchase the said places fitt for building watermills and sett them up to the encrease of our trade and Navigation much to the publiq Damage of the province. Be it enacted by the Queens most excellent Majesty by and with the Advice and Consent of her Majestys Governour Councill and Assembly of this Province and the Authority of the same that if any person or persons from and after the publication hereof shall desire to sett up a Watermill upon any Land next adjoyning to any Runn of Water within this Province not being the proper possession or ffreehold of such person or persons nor leas'd to them to the Intent thereon to sett a Watermill they shall purchase a Writt out of Chancery directed to the sheriff of the County where such land lyeth requiring him by the Oath of twelve men of his County to enquire what damage it would be to her Majesty or others to have a Mill sett up in such place as aforesaid The fform of which writt followeth viz. Anne by the Grace of God of England Scotland France and Ireland Queen Defender of the ffaith &c To the Sheriff of A. County Greeting Wee Comand you that by the oaths of twelve Honest and lawfull men of the County by whom the truth of the Matter may be better known You dili-

gently inquire if it be to the damage of us or others if wee Grant Lib. L. L.
N. N. of N County twenty Acres of land lying at N. in the No. 64.
County aforesaid viz.   tenn Acres on one side such Runn and
tenn acres on the other side of such Runn of Water together
with liberty to take fall cutt down and carry away either by
Land or water any Wood or Timber fitt for building a Mill
other than Timber fitt to Splitt into Clapboards upon any the
lands next adjoyning to the said twenty Acres of Land lying
on each side of the said Runn of water att N. N. aforesaid in
the County aforesaid And if it be to the damage and prejudice
of us or others then to what Damage and prejudice of us and
to what damage and prejudice of others and of whom and in
what Manner and how and of what value they are by the year
according to the true value thereof now before any other improvement of the said twenty Acres of Land and who are the
present possessors of the said twenty Acres of Land and what
lands and Tenements remain to the present possessor over
the said twenty acres.   And if the said Land remaining to
the present Possessors over the said twenty Acres will Suffice
to uphold their Mannour viz.   The sixth part of their Mannour p. 12
allotted them by the Conditions of Plantations for the Demesne
as before the alienation so as the County by the Alienation
aforesaid in default of the present possession more than was
wont be not charged and grieved and the Inquisition thereupon
openly and distinctly made to us in our Chancery under the
Seale and the Seals of them by whom it was made without
delay send &c² Upon return of which Writt in Case the person
or persons who by the said Inquest shall be found to be the
true Owners and Possessors of the land fitt to build a Mill
upon shall refuse to build a Mill thereon within one year from
that day to be computed and reckon'd and give Security the
same building to prosecute and finish within two years after
the said Beginning or laying the ffoundation as aforesaid for
the publiq good of the Province it shall and may be lawfull for
her said Majesty her heires or Successors or for their Chief
Governour here for the Time being from time to time to grant
any such twenty Acres of Land fitt to build a Water mill upon
as aforesaid together with free Egress and Regress to the said
Water mill either by Land through any mans land next
adjoyning or else by water together with liberty to fall any
Timber for building the said Water Mill other than board
Timber fitt to Splitt or cleave into Clapboards for any time or
Term not exceeding eighty years then next to come under the
yearly rent of the land then by the oath of twelve men by
vertue of the writt aforesaid return'd to be paid to the Owner
of the said land so found and return'd as aforesaid Which said
Grant from her said Majesty her heires and Successors or from

the Governour here for the time being as aforesaid shall be good and available in law to the Grantee as aforesaid for any term of years not exceeding eighty years as aforesaid ag$^t$ all persons whatsoever any Law Custom or Usage heretofore had made or us'd within this Province to the Contrary notwithstanding.

Provided allways that before any Person or Persons whatsoever shall have such Grant to build a Water mill as aforesaid he or they shall enter into bond to her said Majesty with two Sufficient Suretys in the Sume of fifty thousand pounds

p. 13 of Tobacco with Condition to begin to build the said Watermill within one year then next to come and the building to prosecute and finish within two years after such beginning.

And for the great advantage that is already found to the Province in generall by the Mills already built some of which do stand upon lands whereof the Title is doubtfull for want of due forme of the Conveyance or of the last wills and testaments by which the lands have been conveyed or devised to the builders of such Mills.

Be it therefore enacted that all & every such person or persons as aforesaid who have built Mills shall and may have Writt or Writts as aforesaid to enquire of the true yearly value of the land where such Mill doth stand and of tenn Acres of land on each side of the said runn as aforesaid and upon return of such Writt as af$^d$ shall have a grant from her Majestys Chief Governour here as aforesaid for any term not exceeding eighty years and yearly rent returne as aforesaid to be paid to the right owner of the said land as aforesaid Any Law or Usage to the contrary hereof in any wise notwithstanding.

And be it enacted by the Authority aforesaid that from and after the publication hereof no person or persons whatsoever having or that shall hereafter have obtain'd any Grant for any Lands whereof such person or persons are not the real Owners or Possessors thereof and whereupon he she or they have already built or shall hereafter build a water mill as this law hath before directed shall have any right title or Claime to any Land granted for any time or terme whatsoever after such Mill by him or them already built as aforesaid or that shall hereafter be built shall be casually broke or gone to decay as aforesaid other than two years for the new erecting building finishing and repairing of such mill as aforesaid but that in all and every Case where any person or persons that have already built or that shall hereafter build any Water mill which are or that hereafter shall be broke or gone to decay as aforesaid and shall not within two years after the Publication hereof or within two years after such mill shall become broke or gone to decay as aforesaid cause the same to be new builded repaired

and finished as aforesaid it shall and may be lawfull for the Lib. L. L.
reall Owner or Owners of such land to such person or persons No. 64.
so granted as aforesaid to reenter upon the same and in Case
such person or persons shall refuse or deny to give the Owner p. 14
or Owners of his Land as aforesaid peaceable and Quiett
possession thereof such Owner or Owners shall and may recover his right to the same by Ejectment or otherwise as the
law directs any thing in this Act contain'd to the contrary notwithstanding.

And for prevention of the abuse frequently comitted by
persons keeping Water mills by taking excessive Tole.

Be it therefore enacted by the Authority aforesaid by and
with the Advice and Consent aforesaid that from and after the
publication hereof as aforesaid no master owner Miller or
other person properly belonging to or otherwise owning any
Mill within this province shall ask demand or receive for
grinding any Quantity or Quantitys of Indian Corne or Wheat
whatsoever above the Sixth part of every Bushell of Indian
Corn and eighth part of every Bushell of Wheat by him or
them so ground as aforesaid upon penalty and forfeiture of one
thousand pounds of Tobacco one half to the use of her Majesty
her heires and Successors for the Support of Government and
the other half to him or them that shall inform or sue for the
same to be recovered in the respective County Courts by accon
of Debt bill plaint or information wherein noe Essoyn Protection or wager of Law to be allowed any other act usage or
custom to the Contrary notwithstanding.

Provided allways that if any person upon encouragement
of former Acts hereby repeald have begun to build any Mill
they shall still have all those advantages that they might have
had by such Act hereby repealed as if the former Act or Acts
were still in force.

September 29<sup>th</sup> 1704      Sept<sup>r</sup> 29<sup>th</sup> 1704.
Read and assented to by the      Read and assented to by
house of Delegates      her Maj<sup>tys</sup> honble Councill.
W Taylard Clk HD.      W Bladen Cl Concil.

Maryland 3<sup>d</sup> October Anno Dmi. 1704.
On behalf of her Majesty &c I will this be a Law.
Jo. Seymour.

An Act declaring that the Altering or scratching out of the p. 15
mark of any Tobacco or altering the Quality thereof after
received without lawfull order or Warrant shall be deem'd
and adjudg'd ffelony.

Be it enacted by the Queens most excellent Majesty by and
with the Advice and Consent of her Majestys Governour

Lib. L. L.
No. 64.
Councill and Assembly of this province and the Authority of
the same that the altering or scratching out of the Mark of
any Tobacco received and paid in Hogsheads or altering or
changing the quality of Tobacco in Hogsheads so received
and paid either by uncasing or otherwise without lawfull
warrant in writing under the hand of such person who received
the same or for whose use the same was received and paid be
deem'd and adjudged ffelony And whosoever shall be found
guilty thereof by confession or by verdict of twelve men in any
Court of Record within this Province shall have Judgment to
restore four fold to the party greived and stand in the pillory
two hours during the Court time with his Offence fairly
written in paper and placed on the back of such convict person.

Provided that no person be prosecuted upon this Act after
one year and a day from the time of the Fact committed.

September 21ˢᵗ 1704                 September 21ˢᵗ 1704
Read and assented to by        Read and assented to by
the house of Delegates          her Majestys honᵇˡᵉ Councill
W Taylard Clk house Del.         W Bladen Cl. Concil.

Maryland October 3ᵈ 1704
On behalf of her Majesty &c I will this be a Law.
Jo: Seymour.

An Act for the publication of all Laws within this Province
To the end that no person may be ignorant of the Laws of
this province  Be it enacted by the Queens most excellent
Majesty by and with the Advice and Consent of her Majesty's
Governour Council and Assembly of this Province and the
Authority of the same that from hence forward all the Acts
p. 16 that shall pass from this and all the Succeeding Assemblys
shall be from time to time fairly transcribed into parchment
and by writt under the great Seale of this Province from time
to time by the Chancellour for the time being to the Sheriff of
each respective County to be transmitted and Commandment
to them in the said writts shalbe given the said Acts in their
Severall and respective Countys at their next County Court
to publish and proclaime to be firmly observed and kept.

And be it further enacted by the Authority aforesaid that
every severall and respective County shall from time to time
pay to the Chancellour for the time being for such Transcript
of the Laws so much Tobacco as by the said Generall Assembly in which the said Laws are made shall be assess'd and
allowed.

Provided allways that because there is not parchment now
to be had in this Province for transcribing the Laws of this

present Sessions to be sent to the Countys that for this Ses- Lib. L. L.
sions only good paper shall be accepted to transcribe the <sup>No. 64.</sup>
several Laws in

| September 21<sup>st</sup> 1704 | September 21<sup>st</sup> 1704. |
|---|---|
| Read and Assented to by | Read and Assented to by her |
| the house of Delegates | Majestys honble Councill. |
| W Taylard Clk house Del. | W Bladen Cl Concil. |

Maryland October the 3 1704
On behalf of her Majesty &c I will this be a Law.
Jo: Seymour.

An Act declaring severall Acts of Assembly formerly made to
be in force.

Be it enacted by the Queens most excellent Majesty by and
with the Advice and Consent of her Majestys Governour
Council and Assembly of this Province and the Authority of
the same That the severall and respective Acts of Assembly
heretofore made and enacted (that is to say) One Act Intituled
An Act for erecting Ann Arundell and Oxford Towns into p. 17
Ports and Towns one other Act of Assembly Intituled An Act
for punishment of Persons suborning Witnesses and Comitting
willfull and corrupt perjury One other Act Intituled An Act
for sanctifying and keeping holy the Lords day comonly called
Sunday One other Act Intituled An Act concerning Indians One
other Act Intituled an Act for the present Security of the
frontier plantations from the Incursions and Violence of Indians
One other Act Intituled an Act prohibitting trade with the
Indians for any fflesh dead or alive except Dear or Wild fowle
One other Act intituled for quietting differences that may
arise between his Majestys Subjects within this province and
the severall Nations of Indians of what places soever and every
Clause matter or thing therein containd is hereby declared to
be and remaine in full force and Effect to all Intents Constructions and purposes whatsoever to the end of the next
Sessions of Assembly this present Sessions not having leizure
fully to consider thereof.

| October 2<sup>d</sup> 1704 | October 2<sup>d</sup> 1704 |
|---|---|
| Read and Assented to by | Read and Assented to by her |
| the house of Delegates | Majestys honourable Councill. |
| W Taylard Clk h D. | W Bladen Cl Concl. |

Maryland October 3<sup>d</sup> 1704
On behalf of her Majesty &c I will this be a Law.
Jo: Seymour.

Lib. L. L. An Act for the better Administration of Justice in Probatt of
No. 64.    Wills and granting Administrations Recovering of Legacys
and securing filiall portions.

Whereas for due Administration of Justice it is most
necessary that the Wills of all Persons may be duly proved and
Letters of Administration of the Estates of all persons dying
without wills may be granted to such persons who have the
best right to succeed thereto and all legacys Speedily recovered
and filial portions and orphans Estates duly secured and
easily obtain'd according to the true Intent of the laws here-
p. 18 tofore made now in force or hereafter to be made.

Be it enacted by the Queens most excellent Majesty by and
with the Advice and Consent of her Majestys Governour
Councill and Assembly of this Province and the Authority of
the same that the Judge or Comissary Generall for probatt of
Wills and granting Administrations shall hold his Court once
in two months at the least or oftner as the Case shall require
and therein shall proceed according to the law of England now
in force or to be hereafter in force within twelve months after
such Laws shall be publishd in the Kingdom of England if
pleaded before him saving in such Cases as by this present
Act is provided and that it shall and may be lawfull for the
Iudge for probatt of Wills to prove any last will within this
Province altho: the same concern Titles of Land any Law
usage or Custom of England to the Contrary notwithstanding.

And to the end that all filiall portions may be secured to the
Children of all persons dying intestate and legacys paid to of
making wills Be it likewise enacted by the Authority aforesaid
by and with the Advice and consent aforesaid ffirst that the
Judge for probatt of Wills and granting Administrations shall
call all Executors and Administrators to Account for the Estate
of all persons deceased within twelve months next after Administration comitted And if any Administrator shall faile to
give an Account within the time aforesaid being lawfully thereunto cited That then the said judge if he see just cause may
revoke the first Letters of Administration to such Administrator comitted and shall grant Administration de bonis non
Administratis to some other person as in his discretion he shall
think fitt Which said Administrator duly appointed shall give
Security as all other Administrators do and shall sue and implead the former Administrator before the judge aforesaid for
an Account of the Estate of the Intestate And in Case it shall
appear to the Judge aforesaid that the former Administrator
hath wasted and imbezelled the Estate of the Intestate then the
Judge shall assign the bond entered into by the former Administrator and his Security unto the latter Administrator to be
p. 19 relieved against them for such Wasting or embezileing.

· And be it farther inacted by the Authority aforesaid by and with the Advice and Consent aforesaid that when a full Account is made by any Administrator of any Intestates Estate the Judge aforesaid shall make distribution of the Surplusage of such Estate in manner and forme following (that is to say) One third part of the said Surplusage to the wife of the Intestate and all the residue by equall portions to and amongst the Children of such persons dying Intestate and such persons as legally represent such Children in Case any of the said Children be then Dead other than such Child or Children (not being heir at Law) or who shall have any Estate by the Settlement of the Intestate or shall be advanc'd by the Intestate in his life time by portion or portions equall to the share which shall by such Distribution be allotted to the other Children to whom such Distribution is to be made.

And in Case any Child (other than the heir at law) who shall have any Estate by Settlement from the said Intestate or shall be advanced by the Intestate in his life time by portion not equall to the Share which will be due to the other Children by such distribution as aforesaid then so much of the Surplusage of the Estate of such Intestate to be distributed to such Child or Children as shall have any Land by Settlement from the Intestate or were advanc'd in the life time of the Intestate as shall make the Estate of all the said Children equall as near as can be estimated but the heir at law notwithstanding any Land that he shall have by descent or otherwise from the Intestate is to have an equall part in the distribution with the rest of the Children without any Consideration of the value of the land which he hath by descent or otherwise from the Intestate.

And in case there be no Children nor any legall representatives of them then one Moyety of the said Estate to be allowed to the wife of the Intestate the residue of the said Estate to be distributed equally to every of the next of Kindred of the Intestate who are in equall degree and those who legally represent them (provided there be no representatives admitted among Collateralls after brothers and sisters Children) and in Case there be no wife then all the said Estate to be distributed equally to and amongst the Children and in Case there be no Child then to the next of Kindred in equall degree of or unto p. 20 the Intestate or their legall representatives as aforesaid and in no other Manner whatsoever.

And after such division or distribution made by the Judge aforesaid the Judge shall transmitt the Account thereof to the severall and respective Justices of the County Courts where the said Estates shall be and remaine And if any part thereof belong to an orphan who is capable of choosing his Gardian

Lib. L. L.
No. 64.

such orphan shall be called to Court and shall then and there Choose his Guardian into whose hands the said orphans Estate shall be comitted but if such orphan be not at- age then the Justices aforesaid shall put the persons Lands goods and Chattells of the said Orphan into the hands of such person or persons as they shall think fitt and take a bond with two sufficient Suretys in the names of the Orphans themselves for the securing and delivering of the said Estate to said Orphans or their guardians when thereunto lawfully called according to the rules and directions hereafter by this Act prescribed and not otherwise Which rules shall be rules not only for the Justices of the County Courts to proceed by in taking the Accounts of Guardians or Trustees for Orphans but also for the Judge for Probatt of Wills and granting Administrations in the Account of Administrators and bare executors to the benefitt of others nor shall the Judge give any other allowances to any Administrator or Administrators upon his or their Accounts but for debts bona fide owing from the deceased and really paid or secured to be paid by the severall and respective Administrators.

1st No Negro or other Slave shall be sold or disposed of by any Administrator for payment of Debts or otherwise reserved for the Administrators own use in Satisfaction of any debts due to the said Administrator nor any Execution Served upon any Negroes or other Slaves so long as there shall be other goods of the deceased Sufficient to Satisfy the Just Debts of the deceased but shall be kept upon the hazard of the Estate and imploy'd for the benefitt of the Creditors and Orphans (if any be) during the first year at the end of which the Administrator is to account for the Estate and the profitts of such slaves shall be assetts to the Creditors and dividable between the wife and Children or relations of the said deceased if there be no Creditors And the Judge for probatt of wills upon passing p. 21 the Account by such Administrator shall allow him his reasonable Charges.

2d That no account be allowed for diett Cloths physick or Education to any Administrator or guardian to any orphan against the Estate of the Intestate or against the filial part of any Child comitted to any Guardian or other persons intrusted by the County Court but the said Orphan shall be maintained and educated by the interest of their estate and the increase of their stocks so farr forth as their said Interest and increase will extend but if the Estate be so small as that it will not extend to a free education of such orphans then such orphans shall be bound apprentices to some handy craft trade or other person at the discretion of the County Courts untill they arrive to the age of twenty one years except some Kinsman or relation or

some other Charitable person will maintain them for the
increase of the small Estate they have without any dimunition
of the principall which shall allways be delivered to the orphans
at the years hereafter in this Act limitted and appointed then
such Kinsman relation or other Charitable person is thereby
obliged to performe the same as is by this law before injoyn'd
and to be ascertain'd by the County Courts.

Provided allways that no orphan shall be put into the hands
of any person of Different Judgment in religion to that of the
Deceased parents of the said orphans.

3   That all Cattle horses and Sheep shall be return'd in kind
by the Guardian or other persons intrusted with orphans
Estates (that is to say) so many Cattle horses and Sheep as
were delivered to the Guardians or Trustees of the Orphans.

4.  That all mony plate rings and Iewells be preserved and not
used by the Guardians or Trustees and delivered in kind to
the Orphans when they come to age and that all Houshold
Stuff and Lumber be appraised in mony and not otherwise
and the value thereof paid to the orphans as aforesaid, either
in mony Sterling according to the Appraisment or in Tobacco
at the then price currant and in Case any difference shall arise
what shall be the price currant at the day of payment limitted
in the bond taken, the Justices of the County Court where the
Orphans Estate doth lye shall then determine what shall be
the price currant.

5   That every Male orphan shall be of full age to receive his
Estate from his guardian at the age of twenty one years and
not before but in case any person by his last will and Testament doth appoint any person to be his Executor or executrix
that is full Seventeen years of age that person so appointed
shall be adjudged to be of Sufficient age to be Executor or p. 22
Executrix and if such Executor or Executrix be under the age
of Seventeen years the Administration shall then be comitted
to such other person as the Judge for probatt of wills and
granting Administrations shall approve of durante Minoritate
and so to the Profitt use and behoof of the Infant Executor or
Executrix and not otherwise nor in any other Manner And for
as much as the right to Administration of the goods of persons
intestate may fall upon persons under the age of Seventeen
years It is hereby declared that as they are within like reason
so are within like law with Infant Executors.

6   That every female orphan shall be accounted of full age to
receive her Estate at the age of Sixteen years or day of Marriage which shall first happen       .

7   That all Negroes and other Slaves after the Transmitting
the Estate to the County Courts as aforesaid shall be praised
to the Guardian or Trustees and be preserved by them and be

dians or Trustees use and enefitt
ives and of the like ability obody
hans out of their increase if ny be
w limitted and if any of th said
otherwise impotent or belamd and
make the originall Stock goo as to
body that then they shall bargain
unty Courts and the guardias or
orphans so much mony or Tobacco
all adjudge the Orphans sock of
value than they were at the me of

Estate unto the Severall and respective Justices of the County
Courts where the Estate shall lye to the end the said justices
may enquire whether the Administrator hath by fraud or otherwise neglected to recover the same or hath received and never
accounted for the same and shall with the residue of the said
Estate comitt the said Desperate Debts to the care of the said
Guardians or other Trustees by them imploy'd and shall yearly
and every year call the said Guardians to Account for the same
and duly inspect what of the said Debts they have received or
might have received and if the said Guardian or trustee fálle
to give in his Account yearly or by fraud or Covin neglect or
forbear to receive the same the said Guardian or trustee shall
stand and be accountable for every such Debts by them received
and not accounted for or neglected or forborn to be recovered
under the penalty of five hundred pounds of Tobacco each
Justice present in Court one half to her Majesty the other half
to the Informer or that shall sue for the same.

10   That the justices of the County Court take able and Sufficient security for Orphans Estates and inquire yearly of the
Security and if there be just cause that they require new and
better Security and if upon refusall to give new and better
security to remove the orphans Estates out of their hands and
farther that the Justices of the County Courts shall yearly in
June Court inquire by a Jury of good and lawfull men to be
Sumoñd out of the Severall Hundreds of the County not
under the Number of twelve who upon their oaths shall inquire, the forme of which oath is hereby exprest viz—Whether
the orphans be kept Maintain'd and educated according to
their Estates and whether apprentices are taught their Trade
or rigorously used and turn'd to common labour at the Ax
and How instead of learning their Trades.

And if they find that Orphans are not maintain'd and educated according to their Estates or Apprentices neglected to
be taught their trades upon pretence that the last year is
enough to learn their trade that they remove them to other
guardians and Masters And in Case the jury find that any
apprentice is not taught his trade but put to other labour as
aforesaid the County Court shall condemn the Master of such
apprentice to make the Apprentice such Satisfaction as in
Justice his years of labour or Other work shall deserve.

11   That the Justices of the County Courts cause the Condition of the bonds they take of Guardians or Trustees of orphans
Estates be exactly drawn to the Act and recorded in the County
Court And the Indentures for apprentices likewise that it may
duly appear to the judges whether Guardians Trustees and
Masters do right and justice to Apprentices and to the Country that the justices do right between them and to that end

employed to the said Guardians or Trustees use and benefitt and the like number of Slaves and of the like ability of body be return'd to the said orphans out of their increase if any be at their full age by this law limitted and if any of the said Slaves be grown aged or otherwise impotent or belamed and that the increase will not make the originall Stock good as to the Number and ability of body that then they shall be again appraised by the said County Courts and the guardians or trustees shall pay to the orphans so much mony or Tobacco as the County Courts shall adjudge the Orphans stock of Negroes then to be of less value than they were at the time of their first appraisment and delivery of their said slaves to the said Guardians or Trustees but in Case no guardian or other person will upon those terms accept of those Slaves then it shall and may be lawfull for the said Severall and respective County Courts to put the said Slaves out upon other terms to any other person so that the said originall stock of Slaves be not sold nor any of their increase but in the best Manner preserv'd for the orphans till they come to their severall ages by this Act limitted & appointed to the intent they may have their first Stock made good to them in number value and ability of body if it may be.

8   That all Servants for years be likewise return'd in kind to
p. 23 the orphans at their full age (that is to say) the same number at the same age and sex and by like number of years to serve and of the same ability of body as near as can be estimated as the Servants were when received by the guardian or Trustees.

And to the end that after Distribution made as aforesaid the acco[t] thereof may not be neglected to be transmitted to the Severall and respective Justices of the County Courts as before is directed

Be it enacted by the Queens most excellent Majesty by and with the Advice and Consent aforesaid that if such judge for probatt of Wills Commissary or Commissarys Generall shall not within two months after distribution made as aforesaid transmitt the account thereof as before by this Act is directed to the severall and respective Justices of the County Courts where the Estate shall be and remaine he or they shall forfeit and pay to our Sovereign Lady the Queen her beires and Successors the sume of tenn thousand pounds of Tobacco of which one moyety for the support of Government of this Province the other moyety to him or them that shall sue for the same by action of Debt bill plaint or information wherein no Essoyn protection or wager of Law to be allowed.

9   Whereas every Administrator in an Inventary inserteth what Debts are Sperate and what Debts are desperate the Judge for probatt of Wills shall transmitt those desperate Debts of the

Estate unto the Severall and respective Justices of the County
Courts where the Estate shall lye to the end the said Justices
may enquire whether the Administrator hath by fraud or otherwise neglected to recover the same or hath received and never
accounted for the same and shall with the residue of the said
Estate comitt the said Desperate Debts to the care of the said
Guardians or other Trustees by them imploy'd and shall yearly
and every year call the said Guardians to Account for the same
and duly inspect what of the said Debts they have received or
might have received and if the said Guardian or trustee faile
to give in his Account yearly or by fraud or Covin neglect or
forbear to receive the same the said Guardian or trustee shall
stand and be accountable for every such Debts by them received
and not accounted for or neglected or forborn to be recovered
under the penalty of five hundred pounds of Tobacco each
Justice present in Court one half to her Majesty the other half
to the Informer or that shall sue for the same.

10   That the Justices of the County Court take able and Suf- p. 24
ficient security for Orphans Estates and inquire yearly of the
Security and if there be just cause that they require new and
better Security and if upon refusall to give new and better
security to remove the orphans Estates out of their hands and
farther that the Justices of the County Courts shall yearly in
June Court inquire by a Jury of good and lawfull men to be
Sumoñd out of the Severall Hundreds of the County not
under the Number of twelve who upon their oaths shall inquire, the forme of which oath is hereby exprest viz—Whether
the orphans be kept Maintain'd and educated according to
their Estates and whether apprentices are taught their Trade
or rigorously used and turn'd to common labour at the Ax
and How instead of learning their Trades.

And if they find that Orphans are not maintain'd and educated according to their Estates or Apprentices neglected to
be taught their trades upon pretence that the last year is
enough to learn their trade that they remove them to other
guardians and Masters And in Case the Jury find that any
apprentice is not taught his trade but put to other labour as
aforesaid the County Court shall condemn the Master of such
apprentice to make the Apprentice such Satisfaction as in
Justice his years of labour or Other work shall deserve.

11   That the Justices of the County Courts cause the Condition of the bonds they take of Guardians or Trustees of orphans
Estates be exactly drawn to the Act and recorded in the County
Court And the Indentures for apprentices likewise that it may
duly appear to the Judges whether Guardians Trustees and
Masters do right and Justice to Apprentices and to the Country that the Justices do right between them and to that end

that they cause the Clark of their County to present the Jury
with a list of the Orphans and apprentices of their County
every June Court.

12 And for better ascertaining what Sallary shall be allowed
Executors and Administrators upon their Account of Administration by the Comissary Generall of this province for the
pain and trouble hazard and adventures in administring
Estates.

Be it enacted by the Authority aforesaid by and with the
p. 25 advice and Consent aforesaid that for every sume or Summs
of mony or Tobacco bona fide received or paid by Executors
or Administrators the Comissary Generall shall allow the Executors or Administrators the Sallary of Tenn per Cent.

And be it further enacted by the Authority aforesaid by and
with the Advice and Consent aforesaid that if the Residuary
legatees of any person or persons dying in this Province and
making a will or the next of Kindred to any pson or psons
dying intestate in this Province and who ought to have the
residue of such deceased persons Estate do dwell in England
or other parts of her Majestys Dominions out of this Province
so that the Executor or Administrator convert the Residue of
all the reall and personall Estate (after Debts and legacys here
paid) into mony or other Effects for the best advantage of the
persons to whom due and returns the same to such Residuary Legatees or kindred as aforesaid that then the Comissary
Generall shall allow to such Executor or Administrator the
usuall Sallary allowed by Merchants to their Factors viz. tenn
per Cent.

And whereas it sometimes happens that persons of great
dealing dying in this Province leave their books very imper-
fect so that it cannot be exactly known what Debts are due
upon such books unless the Executor or Administrator take the
paines to carry about such books from one Supposed Debtor to
another to state Accounts which many times proves a very considerable toyle to the Executor or Administrator and requires a
very great deale of trouble and Charge and many times there
appear Discounts or defeazances or receipts to barr such book
Debts or the Debtors where the accounts are old are are insolvent or the like and the Executors or Administrators for such
their great pains and diligence have hitherto had noe allowance.

Therefore least it should be a discouragement to Executors
and Administrators that having no Sallary therefore they
should neglect for sparing of paines to improve the Testators
or other Estates—

Be it enacted by the Authority Advice and Consent aforesaid that where the Executor or Administrator can fairly

make it appear to the Comissary Generall that he hath had such Considerable toile as aforesaid and no benefitt hath arisen to him thereby to recompence his said toyle It may be lawfull to and for the Comissary generall to allow such Executor or Administrator something in the whole for such pains and desperate Debts at the discretion of such Comissary Generall not exceeding five pounds sterling per Cent. on any p. 26 one Mans Estate.

But for such part of the deceasd's Estate that shall remaine (after all Debts and Charges paid and disbursed and account past before the Comissary Generall) to Residuary Legatees or other Legatees or next of Kindred and delivered to them in Specie without traversing the Estate and converting it into mony or Tobacco for that purpose there shall be no Sallary allowed any usage Custom or former Act of Assembly to the contrary notwithstanding.

And further in regard by the Judges or Comissary Generall for proving of wills and granting Administrators Comission there is a saving to all persons their right of appeale from the sentence of the said Judge to the Chief Governour of this province for the time being.

Be it enacted by the Authority aforesaid by and with the Advice and consent aforesaid that all and every person and persons appealing from the Sentence of the said Judge shall within fifteen days at the farthest after such sentence enter his appeale before the said Governour and within fifteen days more petition the Governour of this province for the time being to examine the Sentence of the said Judge or appoint such other person or persons as he shall think fitt to hear and determine the same whose sentence shall be finall without other appeale repeale or review

Be it enacted by the Authority aforesaid by and with the Advice and Consent aforesaid that the Comissary generall of this province or other person that shall from time to time be appointed as Judge or Judges in Testamentary Causes for granting Administrations shall from time to time and at all times during his or their Continuance in such Office Constitute ordain and appoint some able and Sufficient person of good repute and a freeholder in every respective County within this Province to take the probatt of any last Will and Testament of any persons either Nuncupative or in writing even though the same be concerning titles of land and likewise the granting of any Administration of the goods and Chattells of persons dying intestate in the respective County or Countys where each person or persons so appointed shall reside and inhabitt which said person in each respective County of this Province so appointed as aforesaid shall and p. 27

may take the proof of any will whatsoever as aforesaid of any
person as aforesaid within the County as aforesaid and grant
Letters Testamentary upon the Same And likewise grant Administration to any person or persons whatsoever that right
has to the Administration of any person deceased within the
County where he dwelleth as aforesaid But if any Contest or
dispute shall arise between any persons concerning the right
to Administrations or executorship the same shall be decided by the Comissary Generall or Judge in Testamentary
Causes and not by such person appointed in each County as
aforesaid neither shall such person grant Administration or
take the probatt of such will till such time as such dispute or
difference shall be decided & determin'd by the proper Judge
thereof and Certificate from such Judge of the same And such
person so appointed as aforesaid shall and is hereby allowed
as a ffee for granting such letters of Administration as aforesaid Swearing the Administrators and appraisors as for the
probatt of any will and Swearing the Executor or Executrix
and letters Testamentary the sume of one hundred and fifty
pounds of Tobacco to be paid by such person or persons requiring Administration or Letters Testamentary as aforesaid
unless the Estate be so small as the Inventary of such Estate
doth not amount unto tenn pounds Sterling there shall be
paid to such person so appointed for such letters of Administration or Letters Testamentary as aforesaid the sume of fifty
pounds of Tobacco and no more and then and in every such
Case the Comissary Generall shall have no ffees.

And be it enacted by the Authority aforesaid by and with
the Advice and Consent aforesaid that all Guardians of Orphans that shall have any real Estates Lands with the Orphan
or Orphans to whom the same belong comitted to them other
than such whom the Testator in his life time by his last will
and Testament hath otherwise ordered and disposed off within
one month after taking upon him or her the Guardianship of
such orphan or orphans shall with one Comissioner of the
said County where the land lyeth and two other persons of
good repute and well Skilled in building and plantation
Affaires neither of them being akin indebted or otherwise
interested in either Orphan or guardian enter into the lands
and plantation to such Orphan or Orphans belonging and
p. 28 view the dwelling houses and Out houses Lands Orchards
and ffences that are upon the said plantation And then and
there the said two persons so qualifyed as aforesaid shall take
their corporall oaths upon the holy Evangelist by the said
Comissioner to be Administred that according to the best of
their Skill and Judgment they will make a Just Estimate
of the Annuall value of the said lands and plantation and

what Dwelling houses Outhouses & Orchards are upon the same and what repair they are in What part of the said Land the said Guardian may be farther permitted to clear upon the said plantation as well to raise the yearly rent so valued as aforesaid as also toward his yearly Charge in keeping the said dwelling houses Out houses Orchards and ffences in repair and So by him to be left Allways having a regard to leave a proportionable part both for quality and quantity of uncleared Land for the benefitt and advantage of the orphans or heir when at age to possess the said Land or Plantation as also the Orphans Maintenance out of the same where the profitts of personall Estates be not sufficient to maintain him or them and the Same to certify under their hands and Seals attested by the Comissioner so administring the oaths as aforesaid to the County Court next ensuing after such view so had and made as aforesaid and there to remain upon Record untill the said Orphan or heir come to age Which Certificate so entred and remaining upon record as aforesaid shall be sufficient evidence in law for the said Orphan or Orphans to recover double Dañiages in an Accon of Wast by them to be brought when at age for any Wast Sale or destruction comitted or done in any of the premisses other than what the persons have Certifyed and thought necessary with due respect had to all Circumstances and matters aforesaid.

And to the end as well the Guardian and Guardians aforesaid as the other persons mencoñd and appointed to Value the land as aforesaid may not faile to do their duty.

Be it enacted by the Authority aforesaid by and with the Advice and Consent aforesaid that every Guardian or Guardians of any Orphan or Orphans that shall for the future neglect within one month after entring upon his or their p. 29 Guardianship aforesaid to do and performe what is by this Act required shall forfeit the Suñie of five thousand pounds of Tobacco—And any two psons in the said County living being thereunto demanded that shall effect or neglect what is by this Act required of them to do & pform shall forfeit the sume of five hundred pounds of tobacco each one half thereof to our Sovereign Lady the Queen her heires and Successors for the use of such orphans the other half to the informer or him or them that will sue for the same to be recovered in any Court of Record in this Province of all and every such persoñ that shall so as aforesaid refuse or neglect to performe what is by this Act required.

And whereas it has been doubted whether in valuing or estimating the said Orphans lands and plantations in this Act mencoñd the Quitt rents to the Lord of the same are not to be

Lib. L. L.   considered and allowed for as well as reparations & other
No. 64.   things in this Act mention'd.

It is hereby further enacted and declared that the said Quitt
Rents ought and are hereby declared and enjoyn'd to be
Considered deducted and allowed upon the yearly value oɪ
the said land and the Guardian to pay the same.

And that any Guardian aforesaid that shall neglect after
such allowance made of the same in the value of the said
Land and hath not paid such Quitt rent as aforesaid shall forfeit to the Orphan when at age fourfold the value of such
rents that he left in Arrears at the full age of such Orphan to
be recovered by accon of Debt bill plaint or information
wherein no Essoyn protection or wager of Law to be allowed.

And be it further Enacted by the Authority aforesaid by
and with the Advice and Consent aforesaid that the Comissioners of each County Court within this province by vertue
of this Act shall have power from time to time and at all
times hereafter upon presentment of the Orphan Iury or
other information given to them of such Sale wast or destruction made done or comĩtted upon any Orphans reall Estate
by any such Guardian by legall Warrant to cause the said
Guardian to appear before them in the County Court and if
upon Examination thereof the said information be Sufficiently
proved that the said Guardian shall answer the Damage of
such Wast by him comĩtted contrary to the law when orphans
come to age that then the said Commissioners do require the
said Guardian to give Sufficient Security to make Satisfaction
to the said Orphan or Orphans when at age as aforesaid and
upon refusall thereof as the said Orphan or orphans (if at age
to choose his or their Guardian) shall elect and if not then
p. 30   such other as the Comissioners shall think meet being willing
to take the same who shall enjoy the said land or Plantation
comitting no Wast and performing all such Matters and
things at his entry thereupon as by this Act required untill the
said Orphan comes to age And the said person so Chosen or
by the Justices put in possession as aforesaid shall in the
name and to the use of such Orphan bring his Action of
Wast against the former guardian for the damages by him
Comĩtted and the Commissioners of each respective County
are hereby obliged to give the same in Charge every June
Court to the said orphan Jury under the penalty of sixteen
hundred pounds of Tobacco one half thereof to her Majesty
her heires and Successors for the Support of Government the
other half to him or them that shall sue for the same to be
recovered in the Provincial Court by bill plaint or information
wherein no Essoyn protection or wager of Law to be
allowed.

And be it further Enacted by the Authority aforesaid by and
with the Advice and Consent aforesaid that the Severall and
respective Deputy Comissarys which are and shall be in the
Severall and respective Countys within this Province shall and
are hereby sufficiently authorized and impowered to pass
audite and allow all such accounts as shall come before them
relating to dead mens Estates wherein they have granted letters of Administration or Letters Testamentary not exceeding fifty pounds Sterl. and to transmitt such Accounts within
two Months to the Comissary Generalls Office at Annapolis
under the penalty of two thousand pounds of Tobacco one
half to her Majesty for the Support of Government and .the
other half to such party that shall pass such Account and to
transmitt the same to the Comissary Generall for which passing such Account the said Deputy Comissary shall be allowed
as a ffee the Sume of fifty pounds of Tobacco and no more
And if such Deputy Comissary as aforesaid shall exact de-
maud or receive of any person whatsoever more than is by
this law for executing such his Office allowed him he shall be
lyable to such pains aud penaltys as are included in a certain
Act for limitting Officers ffees in this province but in case it
shall so happen that any person or persons having any interest or claime in Such Estates shall make any objections to the
legality or Justice of any Article or Articles contained in the p. 31
said Accounts then the said Deputy Comissarys are forthwith
to mark such Articles and transmitt the Account with all
papers thereto belonging unto the Comissary Generall before
whom all partys are to appeare and defend their Interest.

And whereas many men have bequeath and devised or hereafter may bequeath or devise to their wives by their last Wills
a Considerable part of their personall Estate intending no
doubt but not expressing that such bequest or devise should
be in full of such wives part portion or third part of the Testators Estate and yet such wives widows and relicts have not
only claim'd such bequest and devise as legacys but have farther claim'd their part of the remaining Estate of their deceased husbands,

Be it further Enacted by the Authority aforesaid by and
with the advice and Consent aforesaid that in such Case where
the Testator bequeaths & devises a Considerable part of his
personall Estate to his wife and it appears not in any part of
his will or Codicill that he intended the said Devise as a legacy
to his wife only and that she might nevertheless have her
third part of his remaining estate that it shall be at the election of such wife widow or relict within forty days inclusive to
make her Election before the Judge for probatt of wills or the
respective Deputy Commissarys in each respective County

whether she will be content with such devise or will have
her thirds and release the Devise and if she make Choice to
have what is so bequeathed or devised to her then by that
Choice she shall be for ever barred from claiming her third
part aforesaid And if she renounce what is so bequeathed and
devised she shall then have her third part aforesaid and be
barred of her devise but shall not claime or have both.

Provided allways that such part of the personall Estate or
Estates be lyable to pay the Debts of the deceased as other
part of the Estate is or ought to be

And if such wife widow or relict have any part of her Husbands land or reall Estate of Inheritance devised to her by her
husband and that it do not appear by any part of the will that
he intended her such part of his reall Estate aforesaid and a
Dower out of the rest of his reall Estate besides Then it shall
be lawfull for such wife widow or relict to make her election
as aforesaid within the time aforesaid whether she will accept
of such devise or of the third part of all her husbands reall
Estate of which she is indowable and if she accept of her devise she shall be forever debarr'd of her Dower out of the
rest of the Testators reall Estate aforesaid And if she accept
of her Dower then such acceptance shall be adjudged a full
recompence of her devise aforesaid and Land so devised as
aforesaid to such wife widow or relict shall be allways intended
to be but for life Except it be expresly devised forever or to
such woman and her heires or to such woman and her Assigns.

And be it further Enacted by the Authority Advice and
Consent aforesaid that every woman who since the twenty
seventh day of June One thousand six hundred ninety
nine having had any part of her husbands personall Estate
given or devised to her by her husband in his last will and
testament or Codicill and having no part of her said husbands
land or reall Estate devised to her shall by such bequest and
devise of any part of the personall Estate except so mencond
in such Will or Codicill aforesaid be debarr'd of her Dower
of his land but that if no Dower be assign'd her she may notwithstanding the said Act now demand or sue for her Dower
and the mean profitts thereof if she have been defac'd contrary to the tenour of this Act.

Provided allways that if any married woman shall have any
Estate settled upon her by Joynture or other settlement before Marriage such Joynture or Settlement shall barr her of
her Dower of her husbands lands yet it shall be lawfull for
her to accept what her husband shall by his last will and Testament devise her

And whereas many Orphans have greatly Suffered by the
Second marriages of such widows who having Estates in

possession by will or right of Administration either by such widows while sole or their husbands during the Coverture the same have been wasted and imbezelled and if the woman dye the said husband refuses to render an Account of such Estate alledging that he is neither Executor or Administrator to his wife nor of her former husband Where as at Comōn law a woman Covert Executrix can do no Act to prejudice her husband all such Act during the same being void without his Consent, he not preventing such Wast when in his power ought to answer for the same.

Be it therefore Enacted by the Authority aforesaid by and with the Advice and Consent aforesaid that for every such Wast by such Second husband during the Coverture such husband shall account for the same and be lyable to be sued for the said Estate due to such Orphan by such orphan if at age or if under age by his guardian as well as the Security or together with his wife if living and if the Security be insolvent then by himself and also for all wast comītted by his wife before Marriage if sued during the Coverture. And whereas orphans of persons dying intestate by the Good provision of this law in committing them to the care of the County Court to inspect the good Condition of their Securitys and good usage as aforesaid are by experience found to be in better Condition in respect of both than the orphans of Testators whose Executors hitherto have rarely given any Security and that the Security they have Given many times proves insolvent.

Be it therefore Enacted by the Authority aforesaid by and with the Advice and Consent aforesaid that the Judge for probatt of wills shall hereafter take good and Sufficient Security of all Executors and Administrators to the use of any orphan or orphans in any will mencoñd and not solely to their own use for the true performance of such last will and Testament according to law and the intent of the Testator & the Justices of the Svrall County Courts shall at the same time that they by a Jury Enquire of the good usage and condition of the Security of other orphans also enquire of these & if they find the security like to be insolvent or the orphans ill used to transmit the same to the Judge for Probat of Wills for the time being to be releived according to Law & the Testators intent and for the more Speedy Administration of Justice to orphans Legatees & others in her Majestys Court for probatt of wills and granting Administrations which hath hitherto by tedious methods used in Chancery before the Judges Sentence in the said Court can take effect the methods of England being at present not practicable here been often delayed.

Lib. L. L.    Be it therefore Enacted by the Authority aforesaid by and
No. 64.    with the Advice and Consent aforesaid that every person or
persons that shall not after sentence given in the said Court
against him or them within fifteen days after such Sentence
enter his appeale with the said Judge from such Sentence
and within fifteen days more procure an examination thereof
by a Court of Delegates nor in the meantime comply with
the sentence of the said Judge it being sent to them under
the hand and Seale of the said Judge nor given in Security
to perform the same and oath made of the refusall thereof It
shall and may be lawfull to and for the said Judge to issue
forth of the said Office under his hand and Seale an attachment against the bodys of the said persons so refusing and
him or them to imprison untill he or they Satisfy or comply
with the said Sentence or give in good Security to do the
p. 34 same. This law not to barr the said Judge to proceed
against persons not complying with Sentences given before
the making of this Act according to the former usage and
custom to compell them to the same

And whereas orphans and Creditors are many times injured
by the low Appraisements and undervaluing of the Estates
of the deceased therefore

Be it Enacted by the Authority aforesaid by and with the
Advice and Consent aforesaid that when any executor or Administrator doth appraise the Estate of the deceased he shall
give notice of such his appraisment and call together two of the
next akin of the said deceased and two of the Creditors of
the said deceased if any there be who shall be present at the
said Appraisment with the sworn appraisors and shall certify
to the Comissary or his Deputy under their hands that they
were present at the appraisment and do approve thereof
And if any Executor or Administrator return an Inventary
without such Certificate as aforesaid the said Judge or his
Deputy in each respective County in this Province shall not
accept or receive the same into his or their Office or Offices.

And be it further Enacted by the Authority aforesaid by
and with the Advice and Consent aforesaid that from and
after the publication hereof no person or persons being Executors or Administrators of any Estate within this province
shall be lyable to pay or Satisfy debts contracted out of this
province of what nature or quality soever (Debts due to her
Sacred Majesty her beires and Successors only excepted)
before Debts due within this province from the Estate or
Estates of any person or persons deceased shall be paid and
Satisfyed If such Executor or Administrator shall have
assetts in his her or their hands Sufficient to pay and Satisfy
the same such Executors and Administrators having respect

to the quality of the Debts due within this province as aforesaid unless the Creditor or Creditors of the deceas'd being
present residing out of this province as aforesaid on any
Accon or Accons by him her or them brought against such
Executors or Administrators as aforesaid upon any Debt or
contract of a higher Nature than those contracted within this
province as aforesaid be it by Statute Merchant or of the
Staple Judgments bond or otherwise do upon Tryall Sufficiently make it appear that such Executor or Administrator
had due knowledge and Cognizance thereof upon due proof p. 35
thereof as aforesaid if such Executors or Administrators
shall have paid Debts of an inferiour Nature not recovered
against them by due Course of Law or suffered Judgment
to go against them for any such Debt as aforesaid without
pleading such Foreign Debt in stay of Judgment such Executor or Administrator not having Assetts in his her or their
hands sufficient to pay the Debt as aforesaid and Satisfy the
same the Court before whom such Action shall be brought
shall give Judgment and award Execution against such
Executors or Administrators de bonis proprijs to such Creditor or Creditors as aforesaid as the law in that case directs
Anything in this present Act to the Contrary thereof in any
wise notwithstanding

September 30<sup>th</sup> 1704          September 30<sup>th</sup> 1704

Read and assented to by    Read and Assented to by her
the house of Delegates     Majestys honourable Councill
W Taylard Clk h.D.         W Bladen Cf Concil.

Maryland October 3<sup>d</sup> 1704

On behalf of her Majesty &c I will this be a law

Jo. Seymour.

An Act for the marking of Highways and making the heads
of Rivers Creeks Branches and Swamps passable for Horse
and foot.

Whereas it is thought Convenient and very much for the
benefitt of the Inhabitants of this province that Roads and
paths be marked and the heads of Rivers Creeks and
branches be made passable.
Be it therefore enacted by the Queens most excellent Majesty by and with the Advice and Consent of her Majestys
Governour Councill and Assembly of this province and the

Authority of the same that all publick and Main Roads be
hereafter Clear'd and well Grubbd fitt for travelling twenty foott
wide and good and substantiall Bridges made over all heads
of Rivers Creeks Branches and Swamps where need shall require at the discretion of the Justice of the County Courts.

And for the better ascertaining what is or shall be deemed
publick roads.

Be it likewise enacted by the Authority aforesaid that the
Justices of the County Courts shall sett down and ascertain in
their Records once every year what are the publick Roads of
their respective Countys and appoint Overseers of the same
And that no person whatsoever shall alter or Change any such
publick roads without the leave or license of the Governour
and Councill or Justices of the County Courts upon penalty
of five hundred pounds of Tobacco.

And if any Overseer so appointed should neglect to clear
the roads so as aforesaid he shall be fin'd five hundred pounds
of Tobacco in Cask and every labourer that shall refuse to
serve and obey the Overseer and every Master of Servants
that being Sumon'd or Warn'd shall refuse to send all his
Taxable Male Servants to the Overseer aforesaid he or they
shall be fined (that is to say) every labourer one hundred
pounds of Tobacco and the said Master for every Servant
warned and not sent one hundred pounds of Tobacco And
the Clerk of the County is hereby obliged to issue out warrants to the Overseers appointed upon penalty of one thousand
pounds of Tobacco and the Sheriff of each respective County
are to deliver the same to the severall and respective overseers appointed as aforesaid ex officio on penalty of one thousand pounds of Tobacco in Casq the one half of all which
ffines shall be employ'd and disposed of towards the Defraying the County Charge in such manner as the Comissioners
of each respective County shall in their Discretion think convenient the other half to him or them that shall inform or sue
for the same to be recovered in her Majestys Name for the use
aforesaid by bill plaint or information in any Court of Record
within this province wherein no Essoyn protection or wager of
Law to be allowed.

And that all the roads that lead to any fferrys Court house
of any County or to any Church or leading through any
County to the part of Annapolis shall be marked on both
sides the road with two notches if the road lead to Annapolis
the road that leads there at the leaving the other road shall
be marked on the face of the tree in a Smooth place cutt
for that purpose with the Letters A. A. sett on with a pair of
Marking irons and Couloured and so with two Notches all
along the Road and where at any place it leaves any other

Road it shall be again distinguished with the mark aforesaid on the Face of the tree with a pair of marking irons and colored as aforesaid And any road on the Eastern Shore in Talbot County that leads to the part of William Stadt at the entring into the same and upon parting with or dividing from any other road shall be marked on the fface of a tree in a Smooth place cutt for that purpose with the Letter W and so with two notches all along the Road And the roads that leads to any County Court house shall have two notches on the trees on both sides of the road as aforesaid and another Notch at a distance above the other two And any road that leads to a Church shall be marked at the entrance into the same and at the leaving any other road with a Slipe Cutt down the fface of the tree near the ground and any road leading to a fferry and dividing from the other publiq roads shall be marked with three notches of equali Distance at the entrance into the same and these rules and methods the severall Justices of the County Courts Shall from time to time give in Charge to the Overseers of the highways by them to be appointed for that purpose who are likewise injoynd carefully and strictly to observe and performe the same under the penalty aforesaid.

And where any Road shall lead through any Seated plantation or old fields,

Be it Enacted by the Authority aforesaid by and with the Advice and Consent aforesaid that the severall and respective Overseers within their severall and respective precincts do sett up posts so many as may be perceived from one to the other which posts shall be marked and notched according to the place they lead to as before in this Act for the marking and notching of Roads have been appointed And that the posts of all gates through which any such roads shall lead as aforesaid be marked and notchd as aforesaid under the penalty aforesaid anything in this Act to the contrary notwithstanding. And that the said Overseers shall from time to time as often as occasion shall require fell all Dead trees on each side of all Main roads where limbs hang over to prevent any damage p. 38 that may happen by their falling on travellers.

September 26. 1704      September 26th 1704
Read and Assented to by      Read and assented to by her
the house of Delegates.      Matys honourable Councill
                           W Bladen Cl Concil.

Maryland October 3d 1704
On behalf of her Majesty &c I will this be a Law.
                          Jo : Seymour.

L. L.    An Act prohibitting all Masters of Shipps or Vessells or any
. 64    other persons from transporting or conveying away any
person or persons out of this province without passes.

Be it enacted by the Queens most excellent Majesty by and
with the Advice and Consent of her Majestys Governour
Councill and Assembly of this Province and the Authority of
the same that from and after the publication hereof any person or persons whatsoever intending to depart this Province
shall first give notice of his her or their intended departure
by setting up his her or their Names at the Secretarys Office
the full Space of three months that if in the time aforesaid no
person shall underwrite the said person or persons so setting
up his or their respectivé name or Names as aforesaid It shall
be then lawfull for the Governour Keeper of the great Seale
or Secretary of this Province for the time being to sign a pass
to any such person or persons to depart this province for
which the party shall pay to the person signing the same the
sume of two shill. and six pence sterl And if any person or
persons upon any Suddain or emergent occasions are necessitated to depart this Province not having Sett up his her or
their Names at the Secretarys office aforesaid Then such Person or Persons giving goǫd and sufficient Security to the
Governoᵣ Keeper of the great Seale or Secretary to discharge
and pay all Debts and Accounts whatsoever due and owing
P. 39    from the said person to any of the Inhabitants of this Province
Then the said ·Person or Persons may have a pass as aforesaid.

And be it further enacted that any Masters of Shipps or
Vessells or other persons whatsoever that shall transport or
convey out of this Province by land or water any ffreeman
being indebted by bill bond account or otherwise to any Inhabitant thereof without such pass under the hand of the Governour Chancellour or Secretary aforesaid shall be lyable to
Satisfy all such Debts Ingagements and damages to the person or persons to whom such Debts or Damages respectively
shall be due within this Province except the samé be otherwise Satisfyed or that the Transporter or Conveyer away of
such person or persons procure such person' or persons to return again in one Month after whereby he may be lyable to
Justice here And every such person as aforesaid as shall transport or convey away out of this province any Servant or Servants being Servants here by Condition for wages Indenture
or Custom of the Country shall be lyable for to pay and Satisfy unto the Master or Owner of such Servant or Servants
so carryed away all such Damages as he or they shall make
appear to be justly due to such Master or owner for want of
such Servants as the Court before whom such Cause shall be
try'd shall think fitt.

And whereas severall ill minded people inhabitting and re- siding at the head of the bay have com̃only sett persons over the head of the bay and Susquehannah River being either Felons Debtors or runnaway Servants from the more remote parts of this Province for some small Advantage they have in buying or getting such mony goods or apparell as such persons so absenting or flying from Justice aforesaid have with them generally money goods or Apparell by them feloniously purloin'd from their Masters and other Owners by which means they may more easily travell to any other Government in retardation of Justice and to the great Dam̃age of such Creditors Master or Owners aforesaid.

Be it therefore Enacted by the Authority aforesaid by and with the Advice and Consent aforesaid that from and after the publication hereof no person or persons inhabitting or being at the head of the bay or in any other part of this Province shall transport or convey or cause to be transported or convey'd over Susquehannah river aforesaid or any other part of the bay above the North side of Sassafras River on the East- p. 40 ern Shore of the bay or over Potomack or Pocomoke rivers into the Colony of Virginia not having passes so procured as aforesaid or a Certificate from under the hands of two Justices of the Peace of the County where such person or persons intending to travell shall inhabitt And the County Seale affixed thereto Certifying the ffreedom of such persons And that he she or they are Clear to the best of their knowledge from any ingagements impeding their travelling as aforesaid on penalty of answering all such debts or damages to Creditors Masters or other Owners of Servants to be recovered as by this Law is provided against such as shall actually sett them out of this Province.

And be it further Enacted by the Authority Advice and Consent aforesaid that whatsoever person or persons shall from henceforth intice transport or privately carry or send away out of this Province any Apprentice hired or other Servants or Slaves belonging to any Inhabitant in this Province shall for every such Offence forfeit and pay to the Imployer or owner of such Apprentice hired or other Servants or Slave treble damages and Costs to be adjudged by the Justices of each respective County Court or the Justices of the Provincial Court for the time of such apprentices hired or other Servants or Slaves unlawfully being transported or carried away as aforesaid

September 21ˢᵗ 1704      September 21ˢᵗ 1704

Read and Assented to by      Read and Assented to by her
the house of Delegates      Majestys honᵇˡᵉ Councill
W Taylard Cl h.d      W Bladen Cl Council

Lib. L. L.
No. 64.

Maryland October 3ᵈ 1704

On the behalf of Her Maᵗʸ &c I will this be a Law

Jo: Seymour

An Act relating to Servants and Slaves.

p. 41     Whereas there have been severall Acts provided against servants Runnaways which have hereto proved ineffectual in regard they do not sufficiently provide incouragement for such Person or Persons Inhabitants of this Province as should seize such runaways or Servants by this Act deemed Runaways therefore for the better discovery seizing and apprehending such runaways

Be it Enacted by the Queens most excellent Majesty by and with the Advice and consent of her Majestys Governour Councill and Assembly of this province and the Authority of the same that from and after the publication hereof no Servant or Servants whatsoever within this Province whether by Indenture or according to the Custom of the Country or hired for wages shall travell by Land or water tenn Miles from the house of his her or their Master Mistress or Dame without a Note under their hands or under the hand of his or their Overseer if any be under the penalty of being taken for a runaway and to Suffer such penaltys as are hereafter Provided against Runaways

And it is hereby further Enacted by the Authority advice and consent aforesaid that any Servant or Servants unlawfully absenting him her or themselves from his her or their said Master Mistress Dame or Overseer shall serve tenn days for every one days absence and shall Satisfy or pay to his her or their Master Mistress or Dame all such Costs and Charges as shall be laid out and expended by his her or their Master Mistress or Dame for their taking up by Servitude to be adjudged when Such Master Mistress or Dame shall bring their said Servant before the Justices of the Provincial or County Court where the Owner Master Mistress or Dame or Overseer of such Servant shall live during the Sitting of the Court, be it before or after the expiration of such Servants first time of Servitude by Indenture or otherwise.

And be it further Enacted by the Authority advice and consent aforesaid that any person or persons whatsoever that shall wittingly or willingly entertain any such Servant or Servants unlawfully absenting him her or themselves as aforesaid shall be fin'd five hundred pounds of Tobacco for every night or twenty four hours that such person or persons shall give entertainment to such Servant or Servants unlawfully absenting him her or themselves as aforesaid the one half to her Majesty her beires and Successors for the Support of Government the other half to the informer or him or them that shall sue for the same to be recovered in any County Court of this Province by accon of Debt bill Plaint or Information wherein no Essoyn Protection or wager of law to be allowed.

And for the better discovery of Runaways It is hereby further Enacted by the Authority advice and Consent aforesaid that any Person or Persons whatsoever within this Province travelling out of the County where he she or they shall reside or live (without a pass under the Seale of the said County) for which they are to pay tenn pounds of Tobacco or one Shilling in mony such person or persons if apprehended not being sufficiently known or able to give a good account of themselves shall be left to the discretion and Judgment of such Magistrate or Magistrates before whom such person or persons as aforesaid shall be brought to Judge thereof And if before such Magistrate such person or persons so taken upp shall be deem'd and taken a Runaway or runaways he she or they shall suffer such Fines and penaltys as is hereby provided against Runaways.

And for the better encouragement of all persons to Seize and take up such Runnaways It is hereby further Enacted by the Authority Advice and Consent aforesaid that all and every such person or persons as aforesaid seizing or taking up such Runaways travelling without passes as aforesaid not being able to give a Sufficient Account of themselves as Aforesaid shall have and receive two hundred pounds of Tobacco to be paid by the Owner of such runaway so apprehended and taken up And if such Runaway or Runaways be not Servants and refuse to pay the same he she or they shall make Satisfaction by Servitude or otherwise as the Justices of the Provincial or County Courts where such person Shall be so apprehended and taken up shall think fitt.

And further for the better discovery and incouragement of our neighbour Indians to seize apprehend or take up any runaway Servants and bring them before a Magistrate they shall for a reward have a Matchcoate paid him or them or the value thereof which said reward to be paid and Satisfyed by the County where such person shall be apprehended and such runaway to reimburse the said County by Servitude or otherwise as the Justices of the Provincial or County Court shall think fitt.

And be it further Enacted by the Authority Advice and p 43 Consent aforesaid that at what time soever any of the said persons runaways shall be seized by any person or persons within this province such person or persons so apprehending or Seizing the same shall bring or cause him her or them to be brought before the next Magistrate or Justice of the County where such Runaway is apprehended who is hereby impowered to take into Custody or otherwise him her or them to secure and dispose as he shall think fitt untill such person or persons so Seized and apprehended shall give Sufficient Security to answer the premisses the next Court that shall first ensue in the said County which Court shall secure such person or persons till he or they can make Satisfaction to the Party that shall so apprehend or Seize such runaways or other pson as by this Act is required Except such pson shall make Satisfaction as aforesaid before such Court shall happen and that notice may be conveniently given to the Master Mistress Dame or Overseer of runaways taken up as aforesaid the Comissioners of the Countys shall forthwith cause a Note of the Runaways name so Seized and apprehended as aforesaid to be sett up at the next adjacent County Courts and at the Provincial Court and Secretarys office that all persons may view the same and see where such their Servants are and in whose Custody.

And furthermore for ascertaining what each Servant according to the Custom of the Country shall have at the expiration of their Servitude Bee it Enacted by the authority Advice and Consent aforesaid that every Man Servant shall at such time of expiration of his as aforesaid have allowed and given him one new hatt a good suite (that is to say) Coat and breeches either of Kersy or broad cloth one new shift of white Linnen one new pair of ffrench fall Shooes and stockings two hoes and one Ax and one Gunne of twenty shillings price not above four foot by the barrell nor less than three and an half which said Gunn shall by the Master or Mistress in the presence of the next Justice of the peace be delivered to such ffreeman under the penalty of five hundred pounds of Tobacco on such Master or Mistress omitting so to do and the like penalty on the said ffreeman selling or disposing thereof within the Space of twelve months the one half whereof to our Sovereign Lady the Queen the other to the informer. All women Servants at the expiration of their servitude as aforesaid shall have all owed and given them a Wastcoate and Petticoate of new half thick or pennistone a New shift of white Linnen shoes and stockins a blew apron two capps of white linnen and three barrells of Indian Corne

And be it further Enacted by the Authority Advice and p. 44 Consent aforesaid that no person whatsoever shall trade barter Comerce or any ways deale with any Servant whether hired or indented or Slave belonging or appertaining to any inhabitants within this province without leave or lycense first had and obtain'd from such Servants Master Mis- tress dame or Overseer for his so doing under the penalty of two thousand pounds of Tobacco the one half thereof to her Majesty her heires and Successors for the Support of Government the other half to the Master Mistress or true Owners of such goods So purloyn'd bartered or Conveyed away when proved by sufficient Witness or Confession of the party to be recovered in any Court of Record of this Province by accon of Debt bill plaint or Information wherein no Essoyn protection or wager of Law to be allowed.

And be it further Enacted by the Authority Advice and Consent aforesaid that if the Goods so traded or bartered as aforesaid shall exceed the Sume of one thousand pounds of Tobacco then the party or partys whose goods shall be imbezelled or bartered away as aforesaid shall have his Accon at law for the damage sustaind against the person or persons so offending dealing or bartering for the same anything in this Act to the contrary in any wise notwithstanding And in Case such person or persons so offending shall not be able to Satisfy the same then such person or persons shall be bound over by some one Justice of the peace and put in Security either to appear at the next provinciall or County Court where upon Conviction by Confession or Sufficient Witness the offender shall be punished by whipping on the barebacks with thirty stripes.

And for the ascertaining and limitting Servants times of Servitude Be it Enacted by the authority Advice and Consent aforesaid That whosoever shall transport any Servant into this Province without Indenture such Servant being above the age of twenty two years shall be obliged to Serve the full space and term of five years if between eighteen and twenty two without Indentures Six years if between fifteen and eighteen without Indentures seven years if under fifteen without Indentures shall serve till he or they arrive at the full age of twenty two years.

And be it further Enacted by the Authority advice and Con- sent aforesaid that all Servants transported out of Virginia into this Province shall Compleat their time of Servitude here which they ought to have served in Virginia and no more

And be it further Enacted by the Authority Advice and Consent aforesaid that every Master Mistress Dame Assignee or Trustee whatsoever owning or keeping any such Servants as aforesaid whether by vertue of Transportation purchase or otherwise shall within six Months after the receiving such Servants into their Custody within this Province except he she or they Claime but five years service of such Servants bring the said Servants into the respective County Courts where

17

they do inhabitt and every of the said Courts are hereby
authorized to Iudge and determine of the age of such Servants so bought & Cause the same to be entred upon record
And every owner as aforesaid neglecting or refusing to bring
such Servant or Servants before the Court as aforesaid shall
not only stand to the determination of the Court but also forfeit the sume of one thousand pounds of Tobacco to the
Queen her heires and Successors for the support of Government And if any Master or Servant aforesaid be greived with
the determination of the Court he shall within the time determin'd for their Service produce an Authentick Certificate of
such Servants age and shall have remedy to the ages afore
mencoñd.

And for as much as Disputes have formerly arose at what
time Servants time of Servitude whether by Indenture or
otherwise should comence Be it enacted by the Authority
advice and Consent aforesaid that all servants transported
into this Province whether by Indenture or otherwise and so
bound or adjudg'd as aforesaid shall comence their time of
Service from the first Anchoring of the Vessell within this
Province provided that the Vessell tarry not above fourteen
days after her Entry within the Capes and her first Ancharage
in this Province and all the days such Shipp or Shipps shall
tarry in Virginia above fourteen shall be adjudged part of the
service of such Servant which shall be afterward brought into
Maryland and there sold Any Law Usage or Custom to the
contrary notwithstanding.

And be it also Enacted by the Authority Advice and Consent aforesaid that every Indenture made by any Servant during the time of Service by former Indenture or Judgment of
the County Court according to the tenour of this Act shall be
void and not any ways oblige any Servant for longer time
p. 46 than by his first Indenture or Judgment of the Court shall be
limitted and appointed

And be it further Enacted by the Authority Advice and Consent aforesaïd that for all such runnaway Servants or Slaves
that shall be apprehended and taken up in the Province of
Pensilvania or Colony of Virginia and from thence brought
into this Province and delivered to a Magistrate of the County
into which they shall be brought the person for so doing shall
have paid and allowed him by the Master or Owner of such
Runaway four hundred pounds of Tobacco and Casq or forty
shiłł in mony upon his producing a Certificate from the Justice
or Sheriff of the Delivery of such Runaway Except Servants
or Runaways brought from Accamack into Somersett County
for such only two hundred pounds of Tobacco or twenty Shillings and the like from that side of Virginia next the River

Potomack for which said Suͫe or Suͫs paid such runaway
shall make Satisfaction when free by Service or otherwise
more than the ten days for one as the Court shall adjudge
But if such person so apprehended brought and delivered as
aforesaid be a freeman and refuse to pay such Suͫe or
Suͫes of Tobacco or mony then and in such Case the Magistrate before whom he shall be brought shall forthwith coͫitt
the said person so refusing to prison till he give sufficient
Security or make full Satisfaction by Servitude or otherwise.

And be it further Enacted by the Authority aforesaid that
if any Master or Mistress of any Servant whatsoever or overseer by order or consent of any such Master or Mistress shall
deny and not provide Sufficient Meat drink lodging and Cloth-
ing or shall unreasonably burthen them beyond their strength
with labour or debarr them of their necessary rest and sleep
or excessively beat and abuse them the same being sufficiently proved before the Justices of the County Courts the said
Justices have hereby full power and Authority for the first
and second offence to levy such ffine upon such Offender as
to them shall seem meet not exceeding one thousand pounds
of Tobacco to the use of her Majesty her heires and Successors for the Support of Government and for their third Offence
to sett such Servant so wrong'd at liberty and free from Servitude—

And be it also further Enacted by the Authority aforesaid p 47
that all Negroes and other Slaves already imported or hereafter to be imported into this Province and all Children now
borne or hereafter to be borne of such Negroes and Slaves
shall be slaves during their Naturall lives—

And for as much as many people have neglected to baptize
their Negroes or Suffer them to be baptized on a vain Appre-
hension that Negroes by receiving the Sacrament of Baptism
are manumitted and sett free

Be it hereby further declared and enacted by and with the
Authority Advice and Consent aforesaid that no Negro or
Negroes by receiving the holy Sacrament of Baptisme is
hereby manumitted or sett free nor hath any right or title to
freedom or Manumission more than he or they had before any
law Usage or Custom to the contrary notwithstanding

And be it further enacted by the Authority aforesaid that
any White woman either free or a Servant that shall Suffer
herself to be begott with Child by a negro or other slave or
free Negro such Woman so begott with child as aforesaid if
free shall become a Servant for and during the term of Seven
years If a Servant shall finish her time of servitude together
with the daͫage that shall accrew to such person to whom
she is a Servant by occasion of any Child or Children begotten

as aforesaid in the time of her servitude as aforesaid and after
such Satisfaction made shall again become a Servant for and
during the term of Seven years aforesaid and if such begetter
of such Child as aforesaid be a free Negro he shall become a
servant for and during the term of Seven years aforesaid to be
adjudged by the Justices of the County Court where such ffact
is comitted according to this law in the Clause made and provided against such Servants as have bastards And the Issues
or Children of such unnaturall and inordinate Copulations
shall be Servants until they arrive at the Age of thirty one
years and any white Man that shall begett any Negro woman
with Child whether ffree woman or Servant shall undergo the
same penaltys as white women all which times of Servitude by
this Act imposed upon the persons having so offended to be
disposed of or imployed as the Justices of such County shall
think fitt the produce whereof shall be Appropriated towards
the relief of the poor.

p. 48    And be it further Enacted by the Authority aforesaid that
any Servt Woman having a bastard Child and not able Sufficiently to prove the party chargd to be the begetter of such
Child in every such Case the mother of such Child shall
be only lyable to Satisfy the damage so sustain'd by servitude or otherwise as the Court before whom such Matter is brought shall see Convenient; provided that where
the Mother of any such Child as aforesaid do prove her
Charge by Sufficient Testimony of Witnesses confession of
the party Charged or pregnant Circumstances agreeing with
her Declaration in her extremity of her pains or throws of
travell and her oath taken by some Magistrate before the
time of her delivery of every such bastard Child or after her
delivery then the party Charg'd if a Servant shall satisfy half
the said Damage If a freeman shall Satisfy the whole Damage by Servitude or otherwise as the Court before whom such
Matter is brought as aforesaid shall think fitt And if any such
Mother as aforesaid be able to prove by such Testimony or
confession of the party Charged that he being a Single person and a ffreeman did before the begetting of such Child
promise her Marriage that then he shall be at his Choice
either to perform his promise to her or recompence her abuse
according as the Court before whom such Matter is brought
shall adjudge—

And be it further enacted by the Authority Advice and Consent aforesaid that after the end of this Sessions of Assembly
It shall and may be lawfull for the Provincial and County
Courts of this Province to hear and determine any Complaints
between Masters and Servants by way of petition to give
Judgment and award execution for the same and that upon
appeale or Writt of Error brought upon the same from any

County Court of this Province to the Provincial Court or from the Provincial Court to the Governour and Councill no such Judgment shall be revert'd for want of Judicial process or that the same was not tryed by a Jury or any matter of forme either in the Entry or giving Judgment Provided it appears by the record that the Defendant was legally Sumoñd and not condemnd unheard.

And be it further Enacted by the Authority aforesaid that Servants imported into this Province or any Servant that binds himself for years within this Province or any bound out by the County Courts of this Province that if any Matter of Dispute arises either in relation to their Indentures Contracts or wages or any other Matter of Difference between the said Masters and Servants the same shall be tryed heard and determined by Petition as aforesaid any Law Statute or Usage to the Contrary notwithstanding—

And be it enacted by the Authority Advice and Consent aforesaid that no Negro or other Slave within this Province shall be permitted to carry any Gunn or any other Offensive Weapon from off their Masters land without lycense from their said Master And if any Negro or other Slave shall presume so to do he shall be lyable to be carryed before a Justice of Peace and be whipt and his Gunn or other Offensive Weapon shall be forfeited to him that shall seize the same and carry such Negro so offending before a Justice of peace.

And be it enacted by the Authority aforesaid by and with the Advice and Consent aforesaid that from and after the end of this Sessions of Assembly any Servant or Servants whatsoever within this Province that shall feloniously take or purloine his or their Master Mistress or Dames goods or Chattells under the value of one thousand pounds of Tobacco shall be adjudg'd ffelons And being thereof lawfully convict in any County Courts of this Province shall be adjudg'd to pay four times the value of such goods so purloin'd to his or their Master Mistress or Dame which he she or they shall make good by servitude after the expiration of the first time of Service and shall also suffer such pains of whipping or pilloring as the Justices before whom such Matter is brought shall adjudge.

September 29<sup>th</sup> 1704      September 29<sup>th</sup> 1704

Read and Assented to by    Read and Assented to by her
the house of Delegates       Ma<sup>tys</sup> hon<sup>ble</sup> Councill
W Taylard Clk hD.         W Bladen Cl Concil.

Maryland Oct. 3<sup>d</sup> 1704

On behalf of her Majesty &c I will this be a Law

Jn° Seymour

Lib. L. L. No. 64.

P. 49

An Act for Quietting of Possessions Enrolling Conveyances and Securing the Estates of Purchasers—

Forasmuch as a good and beneficiall law Intitul'd an Act for Quietting of Possessions was made the twenty Seventh day of March Anno Domini one thousand six Hundred seventy and one in this Province which by the use thereof hath been found very much conducing to the benefitt of the said Province.

Be it therefore enacted by the Queens most excellent Majesty by and with the Advice and consent of her Majestys Governour Councill and Assembly of this Province and the Authority of the same that all Sales Gifts and Grants at any time before the thirteenth day of Aprill One thousand Six hundred Seventy and four (and not after) of any Lands Tenements or Hereditaments within this Province by any Person or Persons whatsoever that had right to sell give or Grant such lands Tenements or Hereditaments made by writing only with or w'hout seale shall for ever hereafter be accounted good and available in Law to barr the heires of such Vendors Donors or Granters any Error in the forme only of such writing to the contrary notwithstanding.

And for as much as divers Assignments of Patents written on the back side of such Patent for land are now worne out and also other Sales in paper either worne out or quite lost for which the purchase mony hath been bonâ fide paid.

Be it further Enacted by the Authority Advice and Consent aforesaid That all Sales Gifts or Grants at any time before the said thirteenth day of Aprill One thousand Six hundred Seventy four made by persons that right had as aforesaid If either the sale Gift Grant or payment bonâ fide can be paid by Witnesses such Sale Gift or Grant shall forever hereafter be accounted good and available in law to barr the heires of such Vendors Donors or Grantors or any person claiming Dower from such Vendor donor or Grantor Any Law usage or Custom to the contrary thereof notwithstanding.

And be it further Enacted by the Authority Advice and Consent aforesaid That all Sales and Grants of any Lands p. 51 Tenements and Hereditam'ts made by deed Indenture and inrolled since the said thirteenth day of Aprill one thousand six hundred seventy four or that hereafter shall be so made and inrolled shall be good and available in Law without Livery of Seizin

And whereas in the year of our Lord One thousand six hnndred seventy four and in the fourty second year of the year of the Dominion of the right honourable Cecilius Lord Baron of Baltimore a very good Law was made whereby it was enacted by his said Lordship by and with the Advice and Consent of the upper and lower houses of the then General

Assembly That no Mannours Lordships Lands Tenements and <sub>Lib. L. L.</sub> Hereditaments whatsoever within this Province should alter <sup>No. 64.</sup> pass or Change from one to another (as by the said Act relation being thereunto had more at large doth appear) except the same were acknowledged and inrolled as in the said law directed.

Be it therefore hereby declared and enacted by the Authority Advice and Consent aforesaid that whatsoever Deed or Deeds Conveyance or Conveyances during the Continuance of the said law were enrolled by vertue of the said law within the time therein limitted are and shall be taken and adjudged to be Effectual in Law according to the purport intent and meaning of such Deed or Deeds Conveyance or conveyances Inrolled. And if any Deed or Deeds Conveyance or Conveyances made during the Continuance of that Act were seald and delivered but not inrolled according to the Intent of the said law It is hereby Enacted and declared that nothing hath passed by such deed or deeds Conveyance or Conveyances not enrolled as aforesaid the repeale of the said Act notwithstanding

And whereas at an Assembly held at the City of Saint Marys on the tenth day of May Anno Domini One thousand six hundred ninety and two in the fourth year of the reign of our late Sovereign Lord and Lady King William and Queen Mary of blessed Memory An Act for the Enrollment of Conveyances and Securing the Estates of purchasers was then made whereby it was Enacted. That no Mannors Lands Tenements or Hereditaments whatsoever within this Province shall pass alter or Change from one to another whereby the Estate of Inheritance or ffreehold &c<sup>a</sup> shall take Effect &c as by the said Law (relation being thereunto had) more at large doth p. 52 appear Except the Deed or Deeds Conveyance or Conveyances by which the same were intended to pass as aforesaid Alter or Change from one to another were acknowledged and inrolled as the said Law directs—

Be it hereby Enacted and declared by the Authority Advice and Consent aforesaid that whatsoever Deed or Deeds Conveyance ar Conveyances during the Continuance of the said last mencoñd Act were enrolled by vertue thereof within the time therein limitted are and shall be taken and adjudged to be Effectual in law according to the purport Intent and meaning of such Deed or Deeds Conveyance or Conveyances enrolled And if any Deed or Deeds Conveyance or Conveyances made during the Continuance of that Act were seal'd and delivered but not inrolled according to the Intent of the said law It is hereby Enacted and declar'd that nothing hath passed by such Deed or Deeds Conveyance or Conveyances not inrolled as aforesaid the Repeale of the said Act notwithstanding.

And for the better ascertaining a way and Method for Conveying of Mannors Lands Tenements and Hereditaments for the future and for the avoiding the abuses and deceipts by Mortgages—

Be it Enacted by the Queens most excellent Majesty by and with the Advice and Consent aforesaid that from and After the publication hereof No Mannors Lands Tenements or Hereditaments whatsoever within this Province shall pass alter or Change from one to another whereby the Estate of Inheritance of ffreehold or any Estate for above seven years shall be made to take Effect in any Person or persons or any use or trust except the Deed or Conveyance by which the same shall be intended to pass alter or Change the same be made by writing indented and seald and the same to be acknowledged in the Provincial Court or before one Justice thereof or in the County Court or before two Justices of the same where such Mannours Lands Tenements or Hereditaments do lye and inrolled within six Months after the date of such writing Indented as aforesaid. And for the Caption of such acknowledgment there shall be paid to the party or partys taking
p. 54 the same One shilling and no more. And the Clerk shall well and truly inroll such Deed or Conveyance in a good Sufficient book in ffolio to remaine in the Custody of the Clerk of the same Court for the time being amongst the Records of the same Court and that the same Clerk shall on the back of every such deed in a full legible hand make an Indorsment of such inrollment and also of the ffolio of the book in which the same shall be Inrolled and shall to such Indorsment sett his hand. Provided allways and be it further Enacted by the Authority aforesaid that when the Grantor or Grantors Bargainor or Bargainors of such lands Tenements or Hereditaments shall live remote from either the Provincial Court or County Court where the land lyeth It shall and may be lawfull for such grantor or Bargainor to acknowledge the same in the County where such Bargainors liveth and a Certificate of such acknowledgment under the hand of the County Clerk and under the Seale of the same County of such acknowledgment shall be taken deemed reputed and be as good and valid as if the same had been acknowledged either in the Provincial or County Court where such land lyeth and be a sufficient Warrant for such County Clerk where the land lyes to inroll the same And if any such grantor or bargainor of any Land or Tenements as aforesaid shall happen to be out of this Province within any of her Majestys Dominions at the time of the ensealing such Writing or Writings indented so as the same cannot be acknowledged as is before directed or inrolled within the time for that purpose herein before limitted That in

every such Case such lands or Tenements as aforesaid shall be acknowledged by letter of Attorny well and Sufficiently proved either in the Provincial or County Court where such lands or Tenements lye or before one Justice of the Provincial Court or two Justices of the County Court as aforesaid and be inrolled as aforesaid anything herein before Contain'd to the Contrary thereof notwithstanding—

And be it further Enacted by the Authority aforesaid that every such Writing indented to be acknowledged and Inrolled P. 55 as aforesaid shall have relation as to the passing and Conveying of the Premisses and the Estate and Estates thereby Passd or intended to be passed and Conveyed by and from the day of the Inrollment of the same and not from the day of the date thereof and shall at all times be Construed and taken more favourably and beneficially for the benefitt and advantage of the Grantee or Grantees and more strongly for the barring the Grantors therein to be named and according to such Intents as by the words thereof shall appear to have been the true intent of the partys thereunto altho: the same be not so firmly drawn as is used in England where the Advice ot Councill learned in the law may be easily had.

Provided allways that if any ffeme Covert be named a party Grantor in any such Writing indented the same shall not be in force to debarr her or her heires except upon her acknowledgment of the same and the person or persons taking such her Acknowledgment shall examine her privatly out ot the hearing of her husband whether she doth make her acknowledgment of the same willingly and freely and without being induced thereunto by fear of threats of or used by her husband or fear of his Displeasure And the Person or Persons so examining her shall in a note or Certificate of the said Caption of the said acknowledgment certify her Examination and acknowledgment thereupon and that such Certificate be likewise enrolled upon record in which Case and by such acknowledgments and Certificates ffeme Coverts shall be barr'd and not othcrwise anything herein contained to the contrary Notwithstanding

Provided allways and be it Enacted by the Authority aforesaid by and with the Advice and Consent aforesaid That where any Acknowledgment or Acknowledgments of any Deed or Deeds Conveyance or Conveyances by them that right had to grant bargain and sell any Mannors Lands Tenements or Hereditaments within this Province have been made during p. 56 the Continuance of any the former recited Act of Assembly before one Justice of the Provincial Court or before one or two of the Councill and enrolled according to the Direction ot the fformer Acts shall be good and effectual in the Law to all

Lib. L. L.
No. 64. Intents Constructions and purposes whatsoever.   Anything in this Act contained to the contrary thereof in any wise notwithstanding.

| September 21 : 1704. | September 21ˢᵗ 1704 |
|---|---|
| Read and Assented to | Read and assented to by her |
| by the house of Delegates | Majestys honᵇˡᵉ Council. |
| W Taylard Clk h Del. | W Bladen Cƚ Conciƚƚ |

Maryland October 3ᵈ 1704

On the behalf of her Maᵗʸ &c I will this be a Law

Jnᵒ Seymour

An Act for the Speedy tryall of Criminalls and ascertaining their punishments in the County Courts when prosecuted there.

Whereas many Acts of Assembly have been heretofore made against Thieving and Stealing which at this present are not Sufficient to prevent the Comitting those Crimes or to punish them when Comitted.

Be it therefore Enacted by the Queens most excellent Majesty by and with the Advice and Consent of her Majestys Governour Councill and Assembly of this province and the Authority of the same That it shall and may be lawfull to and for the severall Justices of the County Courts of this Province
P. 57 to hold plea of adjudge and in lawfull Manner determine all thieving and Stealing of any goods or Chattells whatsoever not being above the value of one thousand pounds of Tobacco (Robbery Burglary and house breaking excepted) and every person or persons legally convicted of any such theiving and stealing (Except before excepted) by Testimony of one or more sufficient Evidence not being the party Grieved before any such County Court as aforesaid shall and may cause to be punished by paying fourfold of the value of the goods so theived or stolen as aforesaid to the party or partys greived thereby and by putting in the pillory and whipping so many stripes as the Court before whom such Matter is tryed shall adjudge (not exceeding forty) Which Court shall allways adjudge the value of the goods so theived and Stolen as aforesaid And if any such person so convicted have not sufficient goods and Chattells or be a servant whereby he is incapable to have goods & Chattells to Satisfy and pay the said ffourfold in every such Case such person or persons shall receive the Corporall punishment as aforesaid and Satisfy the ffourfold and ffees of Conviction by servitude.

And be it hereby Enacted and declared that the time of Service of a ffree person convict as aforesaid not having goods and Chattells as aforesaid shall com̃ence from the time of his Conviction as aforesaid And the time of Service of a Servant convict as aforesaid shall com̃ence at the expiration of such time of Servitude to which at the time of his Conviction he stood bound Which time of Servitude for Satisfaction for the stolen goods and ffees accrued as aforesaid shall be adjudged by such County Court either to the party Grieved or any other Person the Court shall order such convict to that will then and there pay or secure to be paid ffourfold and Costs aforesaid at the discretion of the Court And if any person or persons shall receive or take part of such stollen goods or assist the person so stealing as aforesaid to make away or Conceale them being legally convicted as aforesaid shall suffer the same Corporall pains with the party stealing as aforesaid Any law Statute usage or Custom to the Contrary notwithstanding.

And if any person or persons having been once Convicted of any such theiving and stealing (except before excepted) and shall after be again presented for theiving & stealing of any goods or Chattells said to be above the value of twelve pence it shall not be tryed and determined by any County p. 58 Court but the partys presented upon such presentment shall be proceeded against in the Provincial Court as a ffellon for Simple fellony But shall not be punished by death but only by paying the fourfold branding with a hott Iron or such other corporall punishment as the Court shall adjudge saving life and such presentment shall be by the Clerk of every such County Court imediately sent to the then next Provincial Court together with a transcript of his former Conviction If such Conviction was in the same Court where the presentment aforesaid shall be or otherwise made knowne to the Attorney Generall in what other Court such former Conviction was if to him knowne under the penalty of ffive hundred pounds of Tobacco to our Sovereign Lady the Queen her heires and Successors for the Support of Government and the Partys Witnesses against such ffelon if in Court at the time of such presentment shall be bound over to give Evidence as aforesaid or otherwise if not in Court an Account of their Names and places of dwelling be sent the Attorny Generall to be sumoñd against the then next Provincial Court in order to such tryall And the party presented if in Court to be bound over also by due Course of Law to answer such presentment or if not in Court proceeded against by due Course of Law as aforesaid.

And be it further Enacted by the Authority Advice and Consent aforesaid that any person or persons whatsoever that shall Kill any Unmarked Swine above three· Months old if not upon his or their own land or not in Company with his or their own Stock shall and is hereby adjudged a Hogstealer And shall be lyable to restore fourfold and suffer such corporall pains as against the first Offence in this Act is mencoñd.

And to prevent any Person or Persons concealing or disfiguring the Mark of any swine killed as aforesaid

Be it further Enacted by the Authority Advice and Consent aforesaid that any person or persons killing any such unmarkt Swine in the woods or else where and shall wilfully disfigure the mark or cutt off the Eare of such Swine so as to conceale the true and reall marke or whether it were marked or not shall p. 59 be deem'd and adjudgd a Hogstealer within the perview of this Act and shall suffer accordingly.

And to prevent the abuseing Hunting or Worrying of any Stock of Hoggs Cattle or Horses with Doggs or otherwise.

Be it Enacted that if any person or persons whatsoever that have been Convicted of any the Crimes aforesaid or other Crimes of evill ffame and dissolute living that shall shoot Kill or Hunt or be Seen to carry a Gunn upon any persons land whereon there shall be a Seated Plantation without the Owners leave having been once before warned shall forfeit and pay one thousand pounds of Tobacco One half to our Sovereign Lady the Queen her heires and Successors the other half to the party Grieved or those who shall sue for the same to be recovered as aforesaid.

And the better to imprint the Pains and Penaltys of this Law into the Minds of all Sorts of People and to prevent the Comitting any such crimes & Offences aforesaid

Be it also Enacted that this Act shall be publiqly read four times a year in every Parish Church of this Province at the time of a full Congregation either before or after Service by the Clerk or reader of such Church under the penalty of One thousand pounds of Tobacco forfeiture to our Sovereign Lady the Queen her heires and Successors for the use of the Parish to be paid or recovered of every such Clerk or reader so neglecting.

And be it Enacted by the Authority Advice and Consent aforesaid that every Clerk of the severall and respective County Court of this Province be and are hereby obliged ex officio to deliver unto the severall Clerks of their Parishes within their Countys a fair Copy of this Act for publishing and reading as aforesaid.

September 30th 1704

Read and Assented to by the house of Delegates
W Taylard Clk h.d.

September 30th 1704

Read and Assented to by her Majestys hoñble Councill.
W Bladen Cl Concil.

On behalf of her Majesty &c I will this be a Law

Jo : Seymour.

An Act for the Ordering and regulating the Militia of this p. 60
Province for the better Defence and Security thereof.

Be it Enacted by the Queens most excellent Majesty by and
with the Advice and Consent of her Majestys Governour
Councill and Assembly of this Province And the Authority of
the same That from and after the end of this Sessions of
Assembly the Militia of this Province shall be Mustered train'd
and exercised according to these Instructions and directing
following (that every Colonell Major or Captain of ffoot
allready comissionated or hereafter to be Comissionated by his
Excellency the Governour of this Province for the time being
shall have power to enlist such and so many Inhabitants
within this Province not hereafter Excepted in their Severall
and respective Divisions between sixteen and sixty years of
age as they shall think fitt by as equall proportions of the
Sayd Inhabitants and possibly they came to be of the Militia
or Train bands of this Province which said persons so enlisted
they shall exercise Muster and traine in and at such places and
at such certain times as to them shall seem meet or the service
safety or Defence of this Province shall require or as his
Excellency the Governoʳ of this Province for the time being
shall see cause to Order And that every such Colonell Major
or Captaine shall give Notice or Sumons upon every Training
or Mustering to every person so enlisted as aforesaid within
his respective Division orˈ Limitt at the head of his Company
or at the house of the party by an Officer of his Company or
Warrant under his hand to appear at such time and place as
he shall appoint for such training or mustering and that if any
man after such Notice given and Sumons as aforesaid shall
neglect to appear at the time and place appointed, as aforesaid
or that shall refuse when he hath so appeared to be enlisted
into the Militia and train band aforesaid or that being so
enlisted shall from time to time as he shall be Sumoñd or
warñd as aforesaid to appear and bring with him one good
Serviceable Gunn fix'd with six shotts of powder shall for
every such Offence (if a ffreeman) forfeit and pay the Suñe p. 61
of one hundred pounds of Tobacco and if a Servant letted or
hindred by his Master Mistress or Overseer then such Master
Mistress or Overseer to forfeit and pay the like Suñe of one
hundred pounds of Tobacco for every such Servant so letted
or hindred as aforesaid for the use of the ffoot Company to

purchase Drums and Colours and other Necessarys for the Company as the Comander shall direct.

Provided that this Clause be not construed to Countenance any Officer to press Arms or Amunition for any further Expedition or Service from training out that upon all such Occasions they shall be supply'd out of the County Magazine or store all which fforfeitures shall be adjudged heard and determin'd by such Colonell Major or Captain of any foot Company as aforesaid and account thereof kept in writing by the Clark of such Company which said Colonell Major or Captain of such Company as aforesaid is hereby authorized and impowered to award execution against the goods and Chattells of such persons so refusing neglecting or failing as aforesaid and that upon occasion of all such Execution the respective Clerks and Sheriffs of each respective County within this Province shall issue out and Serve Execution without any ffee or reward. And for the settling of Horse fforces That a Captain of each respective County for making up of his troop Elect and enlist his number of Men out of the Inhabitants of the said County according to such Instructions as he shall from time to time receive from the Governour of this Province for the time being Provided allways that such Troopers shall ride their own Horses And that no person shall be a Trooper without he be Owner of a good Serviceable Horse which shall pass Muster And that such Troopers in Consideration of their great pay hereafter to be allowed be bound and obliged to fjnd themselves with good able and sufficient ffurniture for the Horses and likewise to find themselves with Swords Carbines Pistolls Holsters and Amunition And if any Troopers shall neglect or refuse upon notice given them as aforesaid (to the foot) to appear at Musters at the time and place appointed as aforesaid by each respective Captain of .Horse accounted as required as aforesaid shall forfeit and pay the summe of one hundred pounds of Tobacco to be levyed as aforesaid to the use of the Troop (for p. 62 the purchasing of Trumpetts and Colours and other necessarys as the Comander shall think fitt And that all such Troopers for and in Consideration aforesaid at all such times as they are out arranging shall find their own Provisions but when in Actuall service to be found Provisions at the Charge of this Province to be paid by the Publiq And if it shall happen that any Troopers Horse should be Killed in the Service then the said Trooper to be paid for the said horse by the Publiq and not otherwise ffourthly that all persons in holy orders Delegates Magistrates and Constables shall in their proper persons be exempted from being compelled to muster and train either in horse or ffoot during such time as they Officiate or bear such Offices as aforesaid Provided that such Clause shall <sub></sub>Lib. L. L. not extend to Such persons as Already have or hereafter shall No. 64. accept of Comissioners for Military Service from the Governour of this Province for the time being so as to discharge such Persons from their respective Charges mention'd in such their Severall and respective Comissions.

And be it Enacted that all Negroes and Slaves whatsoever shall be exempted the duty of training or any other Military Service. That the pay for the Officers and Souldiers of the horse and foot aforesaid be not other than is hereafter mencond and for no longer time than such Officer or Officers shall be in Actuall Service viz. To every Colonell of ffoot two thousand pounds of Tobacco per Month. To a Major of ffoot twelve hundred pounds of Tobacco per month. To a Captain of ffoot one thousand pounds of Tobacco per month To a Lieutenant of ffoot Seven hundred pounds of Tobacco per month To an Ensign six hundred pounds of Tobacco per Month To a Serjeant four hundred pounds of Tobacco per month To a Corporall four hundred pounds of Tobacco per Month To a Drummer four hundred pounds of Tobacco per Month. To every private Souldier three hundred pounds of Tobacco per Month To every Major Generall Chief Comander in the ffield three thousand pounds of Tobacco per Month and that every Colonell of Horse have two thousand three hundred pounds of Tobacco per Month A Major of horse have fifteen hundred pounds of Tobacco per Month a Captain p. 63 of horse to be allowed thirteen hundred pounds of Tobacco per Month A Leiutenant of Horse to be allowed one thousand pounds of Tobacco per Month To a Cornett nine hundred pounds of Tobacco per Month To a Quarter Master seven hundred pounds of Tobacco per Month To a Corporall Seven hundred pounds of Tobacco per Month To a Trumpeter Seven hundred pounds of Tobacco per Month To every private Trooper Six hundred pounds of Tobacco per Month And that all these rates and allowances for such Officers and Souldiers aforesaid shall be allowed and paid and no more and the Month before mention'd be accounted computed and reckon'd according to Kallendar and noe otherwise. And to the Intent that whensoever it shall appear to the Chief Governour of this Province for the time being or his Councill to be necessary to raise forces for the Suppressing any fforeign Invasion or Domestick Insurrection or Rebellion or any ware with any Indians that the said Officers and Souldiers may be duly paid according proportions aforesaid And all other Charges and Management of such War may be duly paid and discharged without which this Province cannot be defended and Secured.

Be it Enacted by the Authority aforesaid that from henceforth all such necessary Charges of such Warr and Souldier pay
as aforesaid shall be payd discharged and defray'd by a Publiq
Levy by an equall Assessment upon the Taxables of this Province by the Consent of the ffreemen of this Province by their
Representatives in a Generall Assembly or out of the publiq
Treasury of this Province and no otherwise whatsoever.

And to the Intent that the Inhabitants of this Province may
not be abused by having their goods and provisions prest by
loose and idle persons who many times abuse their Comissions
and the people.

Be it further enacted by the Authority advice and Consent
that from henceforth the Comissioners of each respective
County shall yearly and every Year viz. Between the twenty
ninth day of September and the twenty fifth day of December
Nominate and appoint two honest and substantiall Men of their
Countys to be presse Masters for the year ensuing And if any
p. 64 one dye or depart the County or be lame or Sick within that
time that then the next Justice of the peace to nominate and
appoint one other in his stead that if occasion require they and
no other shall impress Victuals & other things given them in
Charge to be passd by Warrant from his Excellency the Gov-
erno^r in Chief for the time being And if any other but press-
masters so appoynted shall presume upon pretense of any
power as a press Master to Seize take press or Carry away any
goods or Comoditys of any the Inhabitants of this Province
shall pay to the persons greived treble the value of the Goods
and Comoditys so as aforesaid unjustly pressd.

Provided that no pressmaster or any person or persons
whatsoever shall presume at any time to Seize press or Carry
away from the Inhabitants resident in this Province any Arms
or Amunition of any kind whatsoever upon any duty or Service
or upon any Account whatsoever any law Statute or usage to
the contrary hereof in any wise notwithstanding.

And be it likewise Enacted by the Authority aforesaid that
the Comissioners of any County Court within this Province
who shall not between the seven and twentyeth day of September and the five and twentyeth day of December in each
respective year by precept from the County Court Signd by
the County Court Sign'd by the Clerk by the Court nominate
and appoynt such and so many press Masters for every County
as aforesaid shall each of them forfeitt and pay unto her
Majesty. for the Support of Governm^t the sume of five hundred pounds of Tobacco And such Press Masters who shall be
so nominated and appointed as aforesaid by such precepts as
aforesaid to him or them directed and shall thereupon refuse
or neglect to serve and truly perform and execute the said

Office and Place of Pressmaker shall forfeit and pay unto her Majesty for Support of Government for every time he or they so nominated and appointed shall refuse to serve as aforesaid the sume of five hundred pounds of Tobacco.

And for the more or better encouragement of such Souldiers as shall in the time of Warr adventure in the Service of the Country and Defence thereof against Indians or others.

Be it Enacted by the Authority aforesaid that the booty Prize Passage or Plunder or any Indian or other Seized or taken Prisoner shall by the Comander be equally divided and distributed amongst the Slaves by a Division or distribution to be made by the Poll. And for the incouragem$^t$ of such Souldiers as shall Adventure their Lives in the Service and Defence of this Province and for the Provision of Some reasonable Pensions to be for the future Settled on such Souldiers as shall happen to be maim'd or rendred incapable to gett a livelyhood for themselves or ffamily

Be it enacted by the Authority aforesaid that every Person th$^t$ shall adventure as a souldier in any Warr or Defence of this Province and shall therein happen to be maimed or receive hurt so as to be rendred incapable of getting a livelyhood as aforesaid shall according to his disability receive yearly pension to be raised out of the Publiq Levy of this Province for the time being of such Disability and every Person Slaine in the Service of this Province leaving behind him a wife and Children shall also be allowed a Competent Pension to the wife during her Widowhood and the Children till they be of years able to gett their living or be put out Apprentices And that this Pension be yearly paid and allowed out of the fifty thousand pounds of Tobacco ℔ annum to be raised by the Governour of this Province for the time being or the Councill as in this Act is hereafter Provided in the Intervalls of Assemblys the party Petitioning for such pension and allowance procuring a Certificate from the County Court where he she or they live that he she or they are Objects of Charity and deserve to have such Pension and allowance.

And be it further Enacted by the Authority aforesaid That if upon any foreign Invasion any person or persons whatsoever (except before excepted) that shall be press'd or be an enlisted Souldier within this Province shall upon the Comand of his Officer being a Captain at the least obstinately refuse to appear and serve in Arms for the Necessary Defence of this Province such Person or Persons so obstinately refusing to appear and serve in Arms as aforesaid shall upon Certificate thereof under Such Officers hands as aforesaid to the next Justice of the Peace of the County where such party liveth be proceeded against in Manner following (that is to say) the

18

Lib. L. L.
No. 64. same Justice of Peace to whom such Certificate shall be made shall Imediately issue out a Warrant to the Constable of the Hundred where such party liveth to apprehend him and bring him before himself or some other Justice of the Peace of the same County there to render a Sufficient excuse if any he hath for such his refusall or Non appearance as aforesaid And if the Justice of Peace shall not find the excuse of such party in such case to be reasonable and Sufficient then he shall imediately Comitt such person to the Custody of the Sheriff of such County there to remain untill he shall find Surety to appear at the next Provincial Court to be held for this Province there to be proceeded against according to the due Course of Law and if thereupon he Shall be Convict of such his Obstinate refusall or disobedience as aforesaid he shall be fin'd and imprison'd according to the Directions of the Justices of the Provincial Court And for the prevention of the great Charge of Annuall Assemblys who may meet for no other occasion but to lay the Publiq Levy in time of peace.

Be it Enacted by the Authority aforesaid that the Governour and Councill during the Intervalls of Assemblys for the defraying and payment of the small Charge of this Province be and are hereby impowered to assess the same equally to be levyed upon all the Inhabitants of this Province for the defraying the said Small Charges in time of peace as aforesaid any thing in this Act to the Contrary notwithstanding. Provided allways and it is the true intent and meaning of this Act the said Sumes for the small Charges of this Province so to be assessd by the Governour and Councill upon the Inhabitants of this Province as aforesaid shall not exceed in any one year the Sume of fifty thousand pounds of Tobacco And the Disbursements of the said Tobacco to be Accounted for at the next Generall Assembly after the raising and disbursing the said Tobacco as aforesaid.

And be it further Enacted by the Authority aforesaid that all Souldiers hereafter to be imploy'd in any Publiq Service within this Province be paid in the respective Countys where the said Souldiers live   This Act to Endure for three years and to the end of the next Sessions of Assembly after the end of the said three years.

<table>
<tr><td>September 29<sup>th</sup> 1704</td><td>October 2<sup>d</sup> 1704</td></tr>
</table>

|  |  |
|---|---|
| September 29th 1704 | October 2d 1704 |
| Read and Assented to by the house of Delegates | Read & assented to by her Ma^tys hon^ble Councill |
| W Taylard Clk h D. | W Bladen Cl Con. |

Maryland October 3<sup>d</sup> 1704.

On behalf of her Majesty I will this be a Law.

Jo: Seymour

An Act for laying an Imposition on Severall Commoditys ex- <sup>Lib. L. 1.</sup> ported out of this Province. <sup>No. 64.</sup>

Be it Enacted by the Queens most excellent Majesty by and with the Advice and Consent of her Majestys Governour Councill and Assembly of this Province and the Authority of the same that from and after the publication hereof no person or persons whatsoever inhabiting or residing within this Province Shall export any ffurrs or Skinns within this Act hereafter mencoñd and express'd but what he she or they shall pay unto her Sacred Majesty her heires and Successors to be imploy'd towards the Maintaining of a ffree Schoole or Schooles within this Province the severall dutys and imposts hereafter following (that is to say) for every Bear Skinn Nine pence sterling for Beaver four pence per Skinn for otter three pence ꝑ Skin for wild Cats, foxes, Minks wethers and calves Skins one penny half penny ꝑ Skin for musk rat four pence ꝑ dozen for Raccoons three farthings ꝑ Skin for Elk Skins twelve pence ꝑ Item for Deer Skinns drest or undrest four pence per Skinn for young bear and Cub Skinns two pence per Skinn And that all non Residents from and after the publication hereof that Shall export out of this Province any ffurrs or Skinns herein before mention'd and exprest Shall for every Skinn or ffurr by him exported of what nature or quality soever being comprized within this Act pay unto her Majesty her heires and Successors for the use aforesaid double the duty by this Act appointed to be paid by persons inhabiting or residing within this Province as aforesaid The Same Severall Impositions to be collected by the Severall and respective Navall Officers within this Province which said Navall Officers <sup>p. 68</sup> shall once a year render an Account of the said Imposition to the Publiq Treasurers of the Province for the time being who shall and are hereby Authorized and impowered to receive the same and render an Account thereof to the Generall Assembly of this Province To the uses Intents and purposes aforesaid.

And to the end the Severall Impositions may be justly and duly paid without ffraud or Deceipt

Be it enacted by the Authority Advice and Consent aforesaid That any person or persons whatsoever Exporting any ffurrs or Skinns out of this Province shall at or before Shipping on board of such Vessell in which such Skinns or ffurrs shall be exported as aforesaid render upon oath an Account of the Nature Quantity and Quality of the said Skinns by him her or them exported as aforesaid and whether the same be his her or their proper goods and Comoditys or the goods and Comoditys of any other Person or Persons then whether he she or they to whom they properly belong as aforesaid be Inhabitants or Residents of this Province as aforesaid which

said Oath shall be Administred by the severall and respective
Navall Officers or their Deputys thereunto especially appointed
And if any person or persons whether Inhabitants or non residents shall put on board any ship or other Vessel any ffurrs
or Skinns for which he she or they shall not have paid the
Imposition aforesaid or given good and Sufficient Caution for
the same to the Navall Officer of the Port or place from whence
such ffurrs or Skinns shall be shipp'd as aforesaid or to his
Deputy for the time being and a Certificate from under the
hand of such Navall Officer or his Deputy produce for the
payment or Caution by him given for payment of the Imposition aforesaid he she or they so offending shall forfeit and
loose all his her or their ffurrs and Skins so Shipped as aforesaid One half thereof to her said Majesty her heires and Successors for the use aforesaid the other half to him or them
that shall informe or sue for the same to · be recovered by
Action of Debt bill Plaint or Information wherein noe Essoyn
proteccon or Wager of Law to be allowed.

p. 69 And that the Master of any Shipps or Vessell that shall
willingly or knowingly take on board his said Ship or Vessell
any Skinns or ffurrs as aforesaid for which the party or partys.
Shipping the same shall not produce a Certificate as aforesaid
being thereof lawfully convict shall forfeit and pay the sum̄e
of five thousand pounds of Tobacco One half thereof to her
Sacred Majesty her beires & Successors for the uses aforesaid
the other half to him or them that shall informe or sue for the
same to be recovered as aforesaid.

And that the Severall and respective Navall Officers of the
severall and respective Ports may and are hereby Authorized
and Impowered when and as often as he or they shall think
fitt to enter into any Shipp or Vessell trading to and from this
Province and into any house warehouse or other building and
open any Trunk Chest Casq or ffardle and to search to make
in any part or place of such shipp or Vessell houses or buildings as aforesaid where such Navall Officer shall suspect any
furrs or Skinns to be as aforesaid for which no Account is
given or duty paid as aforesaid and upon finding any such
ffurrs and Skinns unqualified for exportation as aforesaid them
to Seize and have Condemn'd as by this law is before directed.

And be it further enacted by the Authority aforesaid and
with the Advice and Consent aforesaid that from and after the
publication hereof as aforesaid All persons not being Inhabitants of this Province exporting out of the same any Pork
Beef or Bacon shall pay unto her Sacred Majesty her heires
and Successors for the use in this Act before mencoñd and
expressd the severall impost following (that is to say) for
dryed beef and Bacon twelve pence the hundred weight and

so proportionably for any Greater or lesser quantity And for Pork and beef undryed twelve pence the barrell to Contain two hundred weight And that no undryed beef and pork be exported out of this Province but in Casq as aforesaid which said Severall impositions shall be Collected and gathered by the severall and respective Navall Officers who shall be accountable for the same as aforesaid And have full Authority to enter any Ship or Vessell as aforesaid and to make search for any such goods as aforesaid in such Method and manner as in this Act is before mention'd and expressed. And if any person or persons being non-residents as aforesaid shall put on board any Shipp or Vessell any Beef Bacon or Pork for which he she or they shall not have a Certificate as aforesaid or that ship on board any Beef or Pork that is undryed not being in Casq as aforesaid such person or persons so offending shall forfeit and loose all his her or their Meat so Shipped as aforesaid One half to her Majesty her heires and Successors to the use aforesaid and the other half to the informer to be recovered as aforesaid. And every Master of a Ship or Vessell that shall wittingly or knowingly take on board his said Shipp or Vessell any Beef Bacon or Pork contrary to the true intent and Meaning of this Act being thereof legally convict shall forfeit and pay the sume of five thousand pounds of Tobacco One half thereof to her said Majesty her heires and Successors for the use aforesaid the other half to the Informer or him or them that shall sue for the Same to be recovered as aforesaid And for the better understanding what persons shall be adjudged Non Residents It is hereby declared and Enacted by the Authority Advice and Consent aforesaid That all persons whatsoever trading to and from this Province shall be adjudged deem'd and taken as Non Residents and not having a Seated Plantation of Fifty Acres of Land at the least where he she or they with their ffamily (if any) have resided for and during the space of one whole year and that within the time and terme of twelve Months before any benefitt Claim'd by vertue of this Act or that hath or hereafter shall have an house in some Port or Towne as his or their proper ffreehold being forty foot in length and twenty foot in breadth with two brick Chimneys to the same wherein he she or they shall have resided for and during the space of one whole year as aforesaid And that no such person or persons trading to & from this Province having houses in any Towne or Porte within the same whereby he she or they may claime any benefitt or freedom in this Act given to the Inhabitants thereof shall have hold or enjoy such benefitt & privilege as aforesaid any longer than he she or they or his her or their ffamily shall in such Port and Towne actually inhabitt and reside.

Provided Allways and it is the true intent and Meaning of this Act that no Person or Persons whatsoever as shall trade directly to England to this Province as aforesaid be deem'd construed reputed or taken as foreigners but shall all and every such Person or Persons so trading directly from England to this Province as aforesaid have free liberty in the Exportation of any Skinns or Furrs whatsoever or in the Exportation of any Meat dryed or undryed equall with the Inhabitants of this Province paying such dutys and impositions for the said Severall and respective Coṁoditys as this Law hath imposed upon the Inhabitants aforesaid and no More.

And be it also further Enacted by the Authority aforesaid by and with the Advice and Consent aforesaid that one former Act of this Province Intituled An Act for laying an Imposition upon Severall Coṁoditys exported out of this Province be and is hereby repeal'd. Provided allways and it is the true intent and Meaning of this Act that no Person or Persons whatsoever having in any part transgressd against the aforesaid Law during the time it was in force being as yett undiscovered or unprosecuted for the same or under present prosecution for the same shall have and receive any benefitt or advantage by the Repeale thereof but that upon the prosecution or Discovery of such Person or Persons so having offended as aforesaid the said law shall be pleadable in any Court within this Province wherein any plaint or information is or shall be brought against such person or persons as aforesaid And the Judgmᵗ thereupon given by the Justices of the said Court as the nature of the Cause shall require in as full and ample manner as tho: the said Law at the time of the rendring such Judgment were then actually in force Anything before moncoñd or recited to the Contrary hereof notwithstanding.

| September 23ᵈ 1704. | September 26ᵗʰ 1704. |
|---|---|
| Read and Assented to by the house of Delegates. | Read & Assented by her Maᵗʸˢ honᵇˡᵉ Councill |
| W Taylard Clk hD. | W. Bladen Cl Con. |

Maryland October 3ᵈ 1704.

On behalf of her Maᵗʸ &c I will this be a law.

Joᵒ Seymour

p. 72 An Act for the Encouragement of Tillage and releif of poor Debtors.

Be it enacted by the Queens most excellent Majesty by and with the Advice and Consent of her Majestys Governour

Councill and Assembly of this Province and the Authority of
the Same that every Person or Persons Inhabitants of this
Province who after the end of this Sessions of Assembly shall
be indebted to any Person or Persons whatsoever inhabitants
of this Province in any Sume or Sums of mony or Quantitys
of Tobacco by Bond bill Book Debt or Account or that shall
have any Judgment or Judgments given and entred against
them in any Court of Record within this Province It shall and
may be lawfull for such Debtor or Debtors respectively to pay
and discharge themselves from such Debts and Judgments
when they have not the Specie for which the said Judgments
are given by the severall things following being of the Growth
and production of this Province (that is to say) Beef in well
Seasoned Casq tared and the Tare on the head sett Merchantable and well Saved at three half pence per pound Pork in
well seasoned barrells or other Casq Tared and the tare on
the head sett Merchantable and well saved at two pence per
pound. Bacon at three pence half penny per pound Dryed
beef at three pence per pound Wheat at three shillings six
pence per Bushell Oats at two shill per bushell Barley at two
shill per Bushell Indian Corn at one shilling Eight pence per
Bushell pease at three Shillings six pence per Bushell Beans
at three shillings six pence per Bushell and the prizes of the
aforesaid Comodity shall be rated in tob° at the rate of one
Penny ꝑ Pound as they are before rated and the Creditor and
Creditors of such Debtor & Debtors are by this act Enjoyned
and required to accept and take such Comodities or any of
them of their Debtor or Debtors in full discharge of the said
Debts and Judgments if tendred and paid at any one Convenient place in the County.

And be it further Enacted by the Authority Advice and
Consent aforesaid that in Case any Creditor or Creditors who
shall have Judgment or Judgments against any Debtor or p. 73
Debtors and shall refuse to accept and take from his or their
Debtor or Debtors such Comodity being of the growth of this
Province as aforesaid in Satisfaction of the Judgment or Judgments aforesaid But shall sue out Execution against the Debtor
or Debtors upon the Judgment or Judgments aforesaid and
imprison the Debtor thereon then it shall and may be lawfull
to and for the Sheriff in whose Custody the Debtor is And
such Sheriff is by this Act requir'd to receive and take of such
Debtor his prisoner the severall Comoditys aforesaid or so
many of them being of the Growth of this Province as the said
Debtor his prisoner shall offer to him to the full value of the
Debt and Costs and shall forthwith sett at large and discharge
the said Debtor from his imprisonment. And such Creditor
or Creditors shall have noe other Action against such Sheriff

Lib. L. L.  but for the Comoditys so as aforesaid received paying to the
No. 64.   Sheriff his ffees for taking the said Comoditys

Provided that this Act nor anything therein contain'd shall
be Adjudged to Extend to Merchants Adventurers who trade
from England hither nor to the payment of any bill or bills of
Exchange between Planters and Merchants but in all such
Cases they shall be as they were before the making of this
Act Anything in this Act to the contrary thereof in any wise
notwithstanding.

This Act to continue for three years and to the end of the
next Sessions of Assembly After the three years.

|  |  |
|---|---|
| September 30<sup>th</sup> 1704 | September 30<sup>th</sup> 1704 |

September 30<sup>th</sup> 1704          September 30<sup>th</sup> 1704

Read & Assented to by      Read and Assented to by her
the house of Delegates       Maj<sup>tys</sup> honble Councill.
W Taylard Cł hD.           W Bladen Cł Council.

Maryland October 3<sup>d</sup> 1704.

On behalf of her Ma<sup>ty</sup> &c I will this be a Law

Jo· Seymour

p. 74 An Act for the relief of Creditors in England ag<sup>t</sup> Bankrupts
who have imported any Goods into this Province not
accounted for

Be it Enacted by the Queens most excellent Majesty by and
with the Advice and Consent of her Majestys Governour
Councill and Assembly of this Province And the Authority of
the same that if any person who is become bankrupt in England and hath imported into this Province any Cargo of goods
and Merchandizes and the same Consigned to any his ffactor or
Agent in this Province who hath not accounted or shall not
have accounted for such Cargo to his principall (that is to say)
to the Bankrupt aforesaid before an Accon of Account be
brought against such ffactor or Agent by the Comissioner of
Bankrupt or before a legall demand made to have Account of
such Cargo to the said Com<sup>r</sup> by the Agent ffactor or Attorny
of such Comissioner that the Com<sup>rs</sup> of Bankrupts by vertue
of this Act may compell such Factor or Agent to Account to
them as he should have done to the Principall And the Comissioners of Bankrupt shall be adjudged deem'd and taken to
have the same right to such Goods and Cargo and the produce
of the same as they have to any the Goods and Wares of the
sayd Bankrupt in England.

Provided allways that no such Comission shall be put in Use Lib. L. L.
or executed before such ffactor of such Comissioners of Bank- No. 64.
rupts put in good Security to Satisfy the Debts contracted in
this Province by such Bankrupt Merchant his ffactor or ffactors
under the Creditt of such Cargoe or Cargoes of goods imported
which are hereby suppos'd to be all such Debts as shall be
contracted by such Bankrupt Merchant his Factor or ffactors
after Importation of such Cargo or Cargoes

<table>
<tr><td>September 26<sup>th</sup> 1704</td><td>September 26<sup>th</sup> 1704</td></tr>
</table>

| September 26th 1704 | September 26th 1704 |
|---|---|
| Read and assented to by | Read & assented by her |
| the house of Dell. | Ma<sup>tys</sup> honble Councill |
| W Taylard ClhD. | W Bladen Cl. Con: |
| | [Seal] |

Maryland October 3<sup>d</sup> 1704

On behalf of her Ma<sup>ty</sup> I will this be a Law

Jo: Seymour

An Act imposing Nine pence per Gallon on Rumm Spiritts p. 15;
Wine and Brandy imported by Land from Pensilvania into
this Province.

Be it enacted by the Queens most excellent Majesty by and
with the Advice and Consent of her Majestys Governour
Council and Assembly of this Province and the Authority of
the same that from and after the end of this present Sessions
of Assembly the Importer or Importers of Rume Spiritts Wine
and Brandy from Pensilvania and the Territorys thereto
belonging by Land shall for every gallon of the said Liquor
imported into this province by Land pay unto the Queens
Majesty her heires and successors for defraying the Publiq
Charges of this Province to be Collected by the Navall Officer
of Cecill County District for the time being or his Sufficient
Deputy the Sume of Nine pence Sterl Currant Mony of this
Province in ready mony And shall bring the same into this
Province to the place comonly called Bohemia Landing and to
no other under Penalty of Forfeiting to the Queens Majesty
her heires and Successors all such before mentioned Liquors
which shall be brought to any other place or the value thereof
in ready money One Moyety of the s<sup>d</sup> Forfeiture to the Queens
Majesty her beires and Successors for the Support of the
Government of this Province the other Moyety to the Informer
to be recovered in any Court of Record in this Province by
Accon of Debt bill plaint or Information wherein noe Essoyn
protection or wager of Law to be allowed.

And to the end that the said Nine pence per Gallon may be exactly paid and Collected

Be it enacted by the Authority Advice and Consent aforesaid that before the said Liquors shall be Waterborn in Cheasopeak Bay the Importer or Importers shall make Entry thereof upon oath with the Navall Officer of Cecill County District of the Number of Casqs and the Contents thereof which oath the said Navall Officer by vertue of this Act shall have Authority to Administer and of the full Contents the Navall Officer may abate twenty per Cent for Leakage & other Damage to be sustain'd.

And be it further Enacted by the Authority Advice and Consent aforesaid that if the Importer or Importers aforesaid after he hath brought the said Liquors to Bohemia Landing aforesaid shall put the same Liquors on board any Vessell in Cheasopeak Bay or any the Rivers Creeks or Harbours thereto
p. 76 belonging before the duty aforesaid shall be paid in ready mony as aforesaid That then the Importer or Importers shall forfeit the said Liquors or value thereof in ready mony to the uses aforesaid to be recovered as aforesaid

And be it further Enacted by the Authority aforesaid that when the Importer and importers aforesaid have made fair Entry as afores^d and paid the duty as aforesaid in ready mony as aforesaid that then the Navall Officer shall give the said Importer a Permitt to carry the same to any River Creek or Harbour or Port or place of this Province to make Sale of the same.

Provided always that if any Person or Persons shall import any the Liquors aforesaid from Pensilvania aforesaid in Sloops or other Vessells by Sea through the Capes of Cheasopeak into this Province that then such importer or Importer shall only pay the Duty of three pence p Gallon as others do And after the same Manner as is mencond in a Certain Act of Assembly of this Province Intituled An Act imposing three pence per Gallon on Rum and Wine and twenty Shillings per poll for Negroes for raising a Supply to defray the publiq Charge of this Province and twenty Shillings per poll for Irish Servants to prevent the Importing too great a Number of Irish papists into this Province.

And be it further Enacted by the Authority Advice and Consent aforesaid That the Navall Officer aforesaid for the said Duty of nine pence per gallon aforesaid shall account to the Publiq Treasurer of the Eastern Shore and the Publick Treasurer of the Eastern Shore Shall Account to the Generall Assembly of this Province in manner and form as is mencond in the aforesaid Act Intituled An Act imposing three pence per gallon on Rum and Wine and twenty Shillings per poll

for Negroes for raising a Supply to defray the publiq Charge Lib. L. L.
of this Province and twenty shillings per poll for Irish Ser- No. 64.
vants to prevent the Importing too great a Number of Irish
Papists into this Province.

And lastly Bee it Enacted that the said Navall Officer shall
make oath before his Ex<sup>cy</sup> the Governour or whom the Governour shall impower to Administer such oath that the said
Navall Officer shall use his uttmost power and diligence to
cause this Act effectually to be put in Execution and A Certificate of Such oath taken shall be entred upon the Councill
Book

September 21<sup>st</sup> 1704      Sept<sup>r</sup> 21<sup>st</sup> 1704

Read & Assented to by      Read and Assented to by her
the house of Dell.      Ma<sup>tys</sup> hon<sup>ble</sup> Councill
W Taylard Clk h D.      W Bladen Cl Concil.

Maryland October 3<sup>d</sup> 1704

On behalf of her Ma<sup>ty</sup> &c I will this be a Law

Jo: Seymour [Seal]

An Act for the better Administration of Justice in the high P. 77
Court of Chancery Provinciall and County Courts Speedy
Recovery of Debts directing how small Debts shall be
recovered and for the more easy obtaining of execution
against persons absenting from the Countys where the
Judgments were obtained against them.

Be it Enacted by the Queens most Excellent Majesty by
and with the Advice and Consent of her Majestys Governour
Councill and Assembly of this Province and the Authority of
the same that the Justices of the Severall and respective
County Courts do with all Convenient Speed after the Publication of this Act at the Costs and Charges of their respective
Countys purchase and procure the Statute Books of England
to this Time and Daltons Justice of the Peace where they are
not already procured for the use of their respective County
Courts.

Be it Enacted by the Authority aforesaid that the Justices of
each respective County Court by force and vertue of this Act
may make such rules and orders from time to time for the
well Governing and regulating their said Courts and the
Officers and Suitors thereof as to them in their Discretion
shall seem Meett and under such ffines and forfeitures as they
shall think fitt not exceeding one hundred pounds of Tobacco

Lib. L. L. for any one Offence All which ffines shall be to her Ma^ty
No. 64.  towards the defraying the County Charge.

And be it further enacted by the Authority aforesaid that
every Debt or Debts of Mony or Tobacco due to any person
being above the sume of two hundred and not above the
sume of tenn thousand pounds of Tobacco and being above
the Sume of Sixteen Shillings and eight pence and not
above the sume of fifty pounds Sterl in mony whereof
the Plaintiff is desirous of a Speedy recovery ag^t the Defendant his Debtor in the County Courts he shall proceed
against such Defendant in Manner and forme following (that
is to say) at the same time that the Plaintiff Sues out his Writt
against the Defendant he shall file with the County Clerk his
Declaration thereon And the Clerk shall make a Copy of the
said Declaration and deliver the same to the Sheriff with the
Writt and if the Sheriff can serve the said Writt upon the
Defendant [with] the Copy of the Plaintiffs Declaration eight
days before the Returne of the said Writt then the Defendant
shall be obliged by vertue of this Act to go to tryall with the
Plaintiff the same Court in which the Writt is return'd and
p. 78 shall not have any Imparlance and the Justice of the respective
County Courts are impowered by this Act to give Judgment
against the Defendant in Case of his Refusall to plead or
Answer as they might do in Case of a legall tryall had before
them except in some very extraordinary Cases or Accidents at
the Discretion of the said Justices.

And be it further enacted by the Authority aforesaid that
no County Court within this Province shall hold plea or have
Iurisdiction for the hearing and determining of any Accon or
Accons whatsoever wherein the reall Debt or Damages do not
exceed two hundred pounds of Tobacco or sixteen shillings
and eight pence in mony But that in all such Cases it shall and
may be lawfull for any ·one Justice of peace of each respective
County wherein the  Debtor doth reside to try hear and
determine the Matter of Controversy between the Creditor
and the Debtor and upon the full Hearing of the Allegations
of both partys shall give Judgment accordingly and if need
be shall award Execution by Fieri facias or Capias ad Satisfaciendum directing the same to the Sheriff of the County
wherein the Debtor shall be resident and such Sheriff is
required by this Act to execute such Writt exofficio (saving
allways to such Sheriff ffees for Imprisonment.

And be it further Enacted by the Authority aforesaid by
and with the Advice and Consent aforesaid that in all Actions
which shall at any time after the end of this Sessions of
Assembly be sued or prosecuted in the County Courts of this
Province wherein upon tryall it doth appear to the  Court that

the Just ballance doth not exceed two hundred pounds of Tobacco or Sixteen shillings & eight pence in mony the Plaintiff shall be NonSuited.

And be it further Enacted by the Authority aforesaid that in all Actions which shall at any time after the end of this Sessions of Assembly be sued or prosecuted in the Provincial Court of this Province and upon tryall it doth appear to the Court that the Iust ballance of the Debt or thing in Demand is under fifteen hundred pounds of Tobacco or six pounds five shill in mony the Plaintiff shall be Nonsuited.

And be it Enacted by the Authority aforesaid that her P. 79 Majestys high Court of Chancery within this Province shall not hear try Determine or give relief in any Cause Matter or thing wherein the Originall Debt or Damages doth not amount to twelve hundred & one pounds of Tobacco and five pounds and one penny in mony.

And be it Enacted by the Authority aforesaid that when any Person or Persons against whom any Judgment or Judgments shall be given in any County Court of this Province shall fly or remove him or themselves out of the County and Jurisdiction of that Court where such Judgment or Judgments shall be given That then and in every such Case the Plaintiff or Plaintiffs in every such Judgment or Judgments for the more easy obtaining the fruit and effect of such Judgment shall and may take the Transcript of the Record of such Judgment under the Seale of the Court where the said Judgment shall be obtain'd and lay the same before the Justices of the County Court where the said Defendant or Defendants shall happen to be which Transcript shall be entred upon the Record of such County Court and the Justices of Such County Court shall by vertue of this Act award execution against the Defendant or Defendants by Capias ad Satisfa. ciendum ffieri facias or Attachment for the Debt or Damage with the Costs in the Judgment mencoñd together with such Additional Costs as shall be expended in such Court where such execution shall be awarded without suing out any writt of Scire facias.

| September 26th 1704 | Septr 26th 1704 |
|---|---|
| Read and Assented to by the House of Delegates W Taylard Clk hD. | Read and Assented to by her Matys honble Councill W Bladen Cl Concil |

Maryland October 3d 1704

On behalf of her Majesty &c I will this be a law

Jo: Seymour

Lib. L. L.  An Act for Appeals and regulating Writts of Erro$^{rs}$
No. 64.

p. 80     For as much as the Liberty of Appeals and Writts of Erro$^r$ from the Judgment of the Provincial and County Courts of this Province is found to be of great use and benefitt to the good people thereof

Be it therefore Enacted by the Queens most excellent Majesty by and with the Advice and Consent of her Majestys Governour Councill and Assembly of this Province and the Authority of the same that no Execution upon any Judgment obtain'd either in the Provincial or County Courts or other inferiour Courts of Record within this Province shall be stay'd or delayed or any Supersedeas upon such Judgment granted or issued forth upon any Appeale or Writt of Error from any such Court or Courts of Record as aforesaid to the Court before whom such Appeale ought to be brought or before whom such Writt of Erro$^r$ ought to be heard tryed and determined unless such person or persons in whose name such Appeale or Writt of Erro$^r$ shall be made or brought as aforesaid or some other in his her or their behalf shall imediately upon making such Appeale or suing out such Writt of Error as aforesaid enter into bond with sufficient Suretys such as the Justices of the Court by whom Judgment shall be given as aforesaid or the Keeper of the Seale for the time being to whom Application shall be made for such Writt of Erro$^r$ as aforesaid shall approve of in double the Sume recovered by such Judgment obtain'd as aforesaid, with Condition that if the party Appellant or party suing out such Writt of Erro$^r$ as aforesaid shall not pursue the Direccons in this Act hereafter mencond at the next Court ensuing before whom such Appeale or Writt of Erro$^r$ ought to be tryed as aforesaid and prosecute the same with Effect and also Satisfy and pay to the said party his heires Ex$^{rs}$ Administrators or Assigns in Case the said Judgm$^t$ shall be affirm'd as well all and Singular the Debts damages and Costs adjudged by the Court before whom such Accon from whose Judgment shall be made or thereon a Writt of Error brought as aforesaid shall have been originally tried as also all Costs and damages that shall be awarded at the Court before whom such Appeale or Writt of Erro$^r$ shall be heard tryed and determin'd as aforesaid Then the said Bond to be and remain in full force and vertue otherwise of none Effect.

p. 81     And be it Enacted by the Authority aforesaid by and with the Advice and Consent aforesaid that no Person or Persons whatsoever against whom any Judgment shall be given in any County Court of this Province wherein the debt or damages for which such Judgm$^t$ shall be given shall have any Appeale

Lib. L. L.
No. 64.

or Writt of Erro' from the said County Courts or other inferiour
Courts of Record to the Provincial Court wherein the Debt or
Damages recovered do not amount unto the sume of six
pounds sterl or twelve hundred pounds of Tobacco And that
no person or persons whatsoever against whom any Judgment
shall be given in the Provincial Court of this Province wherein
the Debt or Damages recovered shall not exceed the sume
ffifty pounds sterl or Tenn thousand pounds of Tobacco shall
be allowed any Appeale or writt of Error to the Governour
and Councill of this Province but the Judgment of the Justices
of the said Courts by whom such Judgment shall be given as
aforesaid and thereupon entred shall be definitive for any such
Debt and damages as aforesaid any Law usage or Custom to
the contrary notwithstanding

And be it further Enacted by the Authority Advice and
Consent aforesaid That the Method and rule for prosecution
of Appeals and Writts of Erro' shall for the future be in manner and forme as is hereafter mencoñd and expressd (that is
to say) the party appealing or suing out such Writt or Erro' as
aforesaid shall procure a transcript of the full proceedings of
the said Court from whence such appeale shall be made or
against whose Judgment a Writt of Erro' shall be brought as
aforesaid under the hand of the Clerk of the said Court and
Seale thereof and shall Cause the same to be transmitted to
the Court before whom such Appeale or Writt of Error is or
ought to be heard tryed and determin'd as aforesaid And also
in the same Court file in writing according to the rule of the
said Court such Error in the proceedings as the Plaintiff in the
Writt of Erro' shall think fitt to Assigne or such Causes or
reasons as he or they had for making the said Appeale or
suing out such Writt of Erro' as aforesaid upon which Transcript the said Court to whom such Appeale shall be made, or
before whom such Writt of Erro' shall be brought as aforesaid
shall proceed to give Judgment.

And be it further Enacted by the Authority Advice and
Consent aforesaid That all Appeals made in manner aforesaid
shall be Admitted aud allowed of by the Superiour Court to
whom such Appeals shall be made as aforesaid in nature of a
Writt of Erro' And that every Clark of a Court shall at the
time of the sitting of that Court to which they respectively p. 82
belong and when any Appeale shall be demanded to enter a
Memorandum of such demand as well in his or their Journall
as in the ffair Records of the proceedings of such Court and
that no Clerk of a Court do refuse or delay upon request of
any Appellant as afd to write and make out a Transcript of
the whole proceedings as aforesaid under his hand and the
Seale of the Court as aforesaid upon penalty to pay the

respective Damages which such appellant shall sustain by such refusal or delay as aforesaid the said party paying or securing to be paid such respective Clerk his Just fees for the same according to Law.

And be it Enacted by the Authority Advice and Consent aforesaid that all Appeals or Writts of Error tryable before the Governour and Councill If it so shall happen that the former Judgment given shall be by the said Governour and Councill affirm'd such a determination shall be final and without any further review unless such Judgment shall exceed the sume of three hundred pounds sterl or the Sume of sixty thousand pounds of Tobacco then and in every such Case the party against whom such Judgment shall be given may appeale to the Queen and Councill in England.

And be it further Enacted by the Authority Advice and Consent aforesaid that all and every person and persons that shall Conceive him or themselves relievable in Equity from any Judgment given or about to against him in the Provincial or County Court aforesaid shall exhibit His bill and proceed in Chancery before any Appeale be entred or prosecuted before the Governour and Councill and not afterward and that all such persons as conceive themselves grieved by any decree in Chancery shall be at liberty to exhibit his prayer to the Governour and Councill to review and examine the same and that the Judgment Sentence or decree of such Court of Review shall be final as aforesaid unless as aforesaid the originall Debt or damages exceed three hundred pounds sterl or sixty thousand pounds of Tobacco as aforesaid then and in every such Case an Appeale to the Queen and Councill as aforesaid.

And be it further Enacted by the Authority Advice and Consent aforesaid that all appeals or Writts of Error already made and brought or hereafter to be made or brought before the Governour and Councill shall and may be heard by the said Governour and Councill out of Assembly time anything in the same with any other former Law or Practice to the contrary notwithstanding.

And for that it may so happen that the Governour of this Province for the time being may hereafter be concern'd in an Appeale made or writt of Error brought from the Judgment of the Provincial and County Court or the Governour and Councill aforesaid or be otherwise indisposed or absent.

be it therefore Enacted by the Authority Advice and Consent aforesaid That it shall and may be sufficient in every such Case for the Councill only to Hear and determine such matters of Controversy whereof the Eldest of the Councill in Commission being then present shall preside whose Judgment there-

upon shall be definitive except before entrenched in as full and
ample manner as though the said Governour were then actually
present and presiding Anything in this Act to the Contrary
notwithstanding

Sept 28. 1704                          Sept 29th 1704.

Read and Assented to             Read and Assented to by her
by the House of Delegates       Matth hon:ble Councill
        W. Dyland &c I D.              W. Bladen G: Cancl.

Maryland October 3d 1704.

In neme of her Maty &c I will this be a Law
                                              Jo: Seymour


An Act imposing three pence per Gallon on Rume and
Wine Brandy and Spirits and twenty shill per pole for
Negroes for raising a Supply to defray the Publiq Charge
of this Province and twenty Shillings per poll on Irish
Servants to prevent the Importing too great a number of
Irish Papists into this Province.

Be it enacted by the Queens most excellent Majesty by and
with the Advice and Consent of her Majestys Governour
Councill and Assembly of this Province and the Authority of
the same that from and after the publication hereof All
Masters of Ships and Vessells or others importing Irish
Servants into this Province by Land or by Water at the time
of their Entry shall pay unto the Naval Officer for the time
being belonging to each Port or place where they make their
Entry the summe of twenty Shill sterl per poll towards the
Defraying the publiq Charges of this Province for every Irish
Servant so imported on penalty and forfeiture of five pounds
sterling for every Servant so concealed at the time of his
Entry aforesaid the one half thereof to be appropriated to the
uses aforesaid the other half to the informer or him or them
that shall sue for the same to be recovered in her Matys name
in one Court of Record within this Province by action of Debt
bill Plaint or information wherein noe Essoin protection or
Wager of Law to be allowed.

And be it further Enacted By the Authority Advice and
Consent aforesaid that for every Negroe imported into this
Province either by land or Water The Importer or Importers
of such Negroe or Negroes shall pay unto the Naval Officer
aforesaid the summe of twenty shill Sterl per poll for the use
aforesaid on penalty and forfeiture of five pounds Sterl per

L. L.
64.
respective Damages which such appellant shall sustain by such refusall or delay as aforesaid the said party paying or securing to be paid such respective Clerk his Just ffees for the same according to Law.

And be it Enacted by the Authority Advice and Consent aforesaid that all Appeals or Writts of Erro$^r$ tryable before the Governour and Councill if it so shall happen that the former Judgment given shall be by the said Governour and Councill affirm'd such a determination shall be finall and without any further review unless such Judgment shall exceed the sume of three hundred pounds sterl or the Sume of sixty thousand pounds of Tobacco then and in every such Case the party against whom such Judgment shall be given may appeale to the Queen and Councill in England.

And be it further Enacted by the Authority Advice and Consent aforesaid that all and every person and persons that shall Conceive him or themselves releivable in Equity from any Judgment given or obtain'd against him in the Provincial or County Courts aforesaid shall exhibitt His bill and proceed in Chancery before any Appeale be entred or prosecuted before the Governour and Councill and not afterward and that all such persons as conceive themselves greived by any decree in Chancery shall be at liberty to exhibitt his prayer to the Governour and Councill to review and examine the same and that the Judgment Sentence or decree of such Court of Review shall be finall as aforesaid unless as aforesaid the originall Debt or damages exceed three hundred pounds sterl or sixty thousand pounds of Tobacco as aforesaid then and in every such Case to Appeale to the Queen and Councill as aforesaid.

p. 83    And be it further Enacted by the Authority Advice and Consent aforesaid that all appeals or Writts of Error allready made and brought or hereafter to be made or brought before the Governour and Councill shall and may be heard by the said Governour and Councill out of Assembly time anything in the same writt any other former Law or Practice to the contrary notwithstanding.

And for that it may so happen that the Governour of this Province for the time being may hereafter be concern'd in an Appeale made or writt of Erro$^r$ brought from the Judgment of the Provinciall and County Court to the Governour and Councill aforesaid or be otherwise indisposed or absent.

Be it therefore Enacted by the Authority Advice and Consent aforesaid That it shall and may be sufficient in every such Case for the Councill only to Hear and determine such matters of Controversy whereof the first of the Councill in Comission being then present shall preside whose Judgment there-

upon shall be definitive (except before excepted) in as full and Lib. L. L.
ample manner as though the said Governour were then actually No. 64.
present and presiding Anything in this Act to the Contrary
notwithstanding

<table>
<tr><td>Sept<sup>r</sup> 29. 1704</td><td>Sept<sup>r</sup> 29<sup>th</sup> 1704</td></tr>
<tr><td>Read and Assented to</td><td>Read and Assented to by her</td></tr>
<tr><td>by the house of Delegates</td><td>Ma<sup>tys</sup> hon<sup>ble</sup> Councill.</td></tr>
<tr><td>W Taylard Clk h D.</td><td>W Bladen Cl Concl.</td></tr>
</table>

Maryland October 3<sup>d</sup> 1704
On behalf of her Ma<sup>ty</sup> &c I will this be a Law.

Jo: Seymour

An Act imposing three pence per Gallon on Rumē and
Wine Brandy and Spiritts and twenty shill per pole for
Negroes for raising a Supply to defray the Publiq Charge
of this Province and twenty Shillings per poll on Irish
Servants to prevent the Importing too great a number of
Irish Papists into this Province.

Be it enacted by the Queens most excellent Majesty by and p. 84
with the Advice and Consent of her Majestys Governour
Council and Assembly of this Province and the Authority of
the same that from and after the publication hereof All
Masters of Ships and Vessells or others importing Irish
Servants into this Province by Land or by Water at the time
of their Entry shall pay unto the Navall Officer for the time
being belonging to such Port or place where they make their
Entry the sumē of twenty Shill sterł per poll towards the
Defraying the publiq Charges of this Province for every Irish
Servant so imported on penalty and forfeiture of five pounds
sterling for every Servant so concealed at the time of his
Entry aforesaid the one half thereof to be appropriated to the
uses aforesaid the other half to the informer or him or them
that shall sue for the same to be recovered in her Ma<sup>tys</sup> name
in any Court of Record within this Province by accon of Debt
bill Plaint or information wherein noe Essoyn protection or
Wager of Law to be allowed.

And be it further Enacted By the Authority Advice and
Consent aforesaid that for every Negro imported into this
Province either by land or Water The Importer or Importers
of such Negroe or Negroes shall pay unto the Navall Officer
aforesaid the sumē of twenty shill Sterł per poll for the use
aforesaid on penalty and forfeiture of five pounds Sterł per

19

Lib. L. L.
No. 64.
respective Damages which such appellant shall sustain by such refusall or delay as aforesaid the said party paying or securing to be paid such respective Clerk his Just ffees for the same according to Law.

And be it Enacted by the Authority Advice and Consent aforesaid that all Appeals or Writts of Error tryable before the Governour and Councill if it so shall happen that the former Judgment given shall be by the said Governour and Councill affirm'd such a determination shall be finall and without any further review unless such Judgment shall exceed the sume of three hundred pounds sterl or the Sume of sixty thousand pounds of Tobacco then and in every such Case the party against whom such Judgment shall be given may appeale to the Queen and Councill in England.

And be it further Enacted by the Authority Advice and Consent aforesaid that all and every person and persons that shall Conceive him or themselves releivable in Equity from any Judgment given or obtain'd against him in the Provincial or County Courts aforesaid shall exhibitt His bill and proceed in Chancery before any Appeale be entred or prosecuted before the Governour and Councill and not afterward and that all such persons as conceive themselves greived by any decree in Chancery shall be at liberty to exhibitt his prayer to the Governour and Councill to review and examine the same and that the Judgment Sentence or decree of such Court of Review shall be finall as aforesaid unless as aforesaid the originall Debt or damages exceed three hundred pounds sterl or sixty thousand pounds of Tobacco as aforesaid then and in every such Case to Appeale to the Queen and Councill as aforesaid.

p. 83    And be it further Enacted by the Authority Advice and Consent aforesaid that all appeals or Writts of Error allready made and brought or hereafter to be made or brought before the Governour and Councill shall and may be heard by the said Governour and Councill out of Assembly time anything in the same writt any other former Law or Practice to the contrary notwithstanding.

And for that it may so happen that the Governour of this Province for the time being may hereafter be concern'd in an Appeale made or writt of Error brought from the Judgment of the Provinciall and County Court to the Governour and Councill aforesaid or be otherwise indisposed or absent.

Be it therefore Enacted by the Authority Advice and Consent aforesaid That it shall and may be sufficient in every such Case for the Councill only to Hear and determine such matters of Controversy whereof the first of the Councill in Comission being then present shall preside whose Judgment thereupon shall be definitive (except before excepted) in as full and ample manner as though the said Governour were then actually present and presiding Anything in this Act to the Contrary notwithstanding

|  |  |
|---|---|
| Sept$^r$ 29. 1704 | Sept$^r$ 29$^{th}$ 1704 |
| Read and Assented to | Read and Assented to by her |
| by the house of Delegates | Ma$^{tys}$ hon$^{ble}$ Councill. |
| W Taylard Clk h D. | W Bladen Cl Concl. |

Maryland October 3$^d$ 1704

On behalf of her Ma$^{ty}$ &c I will this be a Law.

Jo$^:$ Seymour

An Act imposing three pence per Gallon on Rumē and Wine Brandy and Spiritts and twenty shill per pole for Negroes for raising a Supply to defray the Publiq Charge of this Province and twenty Shillings per poll on Irish Servants to prevent the Importing too great a number of Irish Papists into this Province.

Be it enacted by the Queens most excellent Majesty by and with the Advice and Consent of her Majestys Governour Councill and Assembly of this Province and the Authority of the same that from and after the publication hereof All Masters of Ships and Vessells or others importing Irish Servants into this Province by Land or by Water at the time of their Entry shall pay unto the Navall Officer for the time being belonging to such Port or place where they make their Entry the sumē of twenty Shill sterl per poll towards the Defraying the publiq Charges of this Province for every Irish Servant so imported on penalty and forfeiture of five pounds sterling for every Servant so concealed at the time of his Entry aforesaid the one half thereof to be appropriated to the uses aforesaid the other half to the informer or him or them that shall sue for the same to be recovered in her Ma$^{tys}$ name in any Court of Record within this Province by accon of Debt bill Plaint or information wherein noe Essoyn protection or Wager of Law to be allowed.

And be it further Enacted By the Authority Advice and Consent aforesaid that for every Negro imported into this Province either by land or Water The Importer or Importers of such Negroe or Negroes shall pay unto the Navall Officer aforesaid the sumē of twenty shill Sterl per poll for the use aforesaid on penalty and forfeiture of five pounds Sterl per

Lib. L. L.    poll for every Negro kept back or unaccounted for to be
No. 64.    apply'd for the uses aforesaid to be recovered as aforesaid.

And be it further Enacted by the Authority aforesaid by
and with the Advice and Consent aforesaid that from and
after the publication hereof All Masters of Shipps or other
Vessells that shall either by Land or Water import any Rum
Brandy Spiritts or Wine into this Province shall pay unto the
Navall Officer aforesaid where they make their entry the Sume
of three pence per Gallon for every Gallon of Rume Brandy
Spiritts or Wine so imported into this Province as aforesaid
to be applyd to the uses aforesaid (Liquors from England
allways excepted)

And be it further Enacted by the Authority Advice and
Consent Aforesaid that no Rume Brandy Spiritts or Wine
upon which the Dutys aforesaid are assessd shall be landed
or putt on Shore out of any Shipp or other Vessell which shall
import the same or any other without due Entry thereof with
p. 85    the Officer thereby appointed (upon oath of the said person or
persons importing any of the said Liquors) for Collecting the
same in the Port or place where such liquors shall happen to
be imported as aforesaid or before the duty due and payable
for the same be satisfyed or Secured to be satisfyed, and a
Warrant for the landing thereof be Sign'd by the Officer for
that purpose appointed upon pain and perill that all such
Liquors landed and putt on Shore contrary to the true intent
and Meaning of this Act shall be forfeited and lost on the full
value thereof one half to be appropriated towards the defraying of the Publiq Charge of this Province and the other half
to the Informer or him or them that Shall Sue for the Same to
be recovered as aforesaid in any of her Majestys Courts of
Record within this Province by Accon of Debt bill plaint or
information wherein no Essoyn Protection or Wager of Law
to be allowed.

And for the better encouragement of all Masters Merchants
Owners and other Persons whatsoever to make due Entrys
and payment of the Dutys Rates and impositions raised by
this Act in Consideration of Leackage and other damage the
Officer is hereby Authorized and impower'd to make allowance and abatement of twenty gallons in every hundred
Gallons of all such liquors so to be duly entred as aforesaid
And the Officers hereby appointed for collecting and gathering the dutys aforesaid shall and are hereby impowered upon
any Suspicion of ffraud or Deceit by any Importer Owner or
Proprietor of any such liquors in concealing and not making
due entry of the same to go and enter on board any Shipp or
Vessell or into any house or Ware house on Shore and
from thence to Seize bring on Shore or Secure all such liquors

for which the dutys aforesaid are not duly paid or Secured to be paid as aforesaid And that the said Officers and their Deputys may freely stay and remain on board untill the goods are delivered and discharged out of the said Ship or Vessell and all Officers as well Military as Civill of this Province and all Masters and Officers of Ships are hereby required and enjoyn'd to be aiding and assisting to such Navall Officers in discharging of their Duty aforesaid for all which the said Officers and others assisting them shall be saved and kept harmless by vertue of this Act.

And be it further Enacted by the Authority Advice and Consent afd that all such Navall Officers shall give good Security to the Governour of this Province for the time being and shall take the Severall Oaths well and faithfully to gather the Impost so arising by vertue of this Act or any Clause herein contain'd and adjust and faithfully to account twice a year and to give and render to the Publiq Treasurers of this for the time being Authorized for receiving the said Impost for which the said Treasurers shall have for their Sallary four pounds per Cent. who are to give good Bond for the same to be accountable and render an Account to the next Meeting of the Assembly to be by them disposed of towards the defraying of the Publiq Charge of this Province.

And be it further Enacted by the Authority Advice and Consent aforesaid that every Master of a Ship or other Vessell at the time of his Entry of such Shipp or Vessell wherein such Liquors shall be imported as aforesaid shall render upon oath an Account of the Quantity and Quality of Liquors aforesaid And the severall and respective Navall Officers within this Province for the time being shall at the time of their Entry of such Shipp or Vessell as aforesaid take good and Sufficient Security in her Majestys Name for the payment of the Imposition aforesaid to such use and purpose and in such manner and forme as by this Act is appointed all which dutys arising by such impositions upon liquors as aforesaid shall be collected and gathered by the Navall Officers in their severall and respective districts for which they shall have for their Sallary eight pounds per Cent and no more.

Provided allways that if any Importer of Rume or Wine into this Province after the end of this Sessions of Assembly and within three months after his Arrivall and such his report made to the Navall Officer or such other Officer legally impowered as aforesaid to take the same as aforesaid, shall export any of the said Rum Brandy Spiritts or Wine by him imported as aforesaid It shall and may be lawfull for every such importer by way of Debenture or drawback mony to stay and detain three fourth parts of such Imposition Allways pro-

Lib. L. L. vided that the said Exporter who desireth the benefitt of the
No. 64. said Debenture or drawback shall declare on his Corporall
Oath to be Administred by the said Officer on the Holy
Evangelists that the said Rume Brandy Spiritts or Wine by
p. 87 him desired to be exported is part of the said Rum Brandy
Spiritts or Wine by him imported and made report thereof as
aforesaid.  This Act to endure for three years or to the end of
the next Sessions of Assembly which shall next happen after
the end of the said three years.

<table>
<tr><td>Sept<sup>r</sup> 26<sup>th</sup> 1704</td><td>Sept<sup>r</sup> 26<sup>th</sup> 1704</td></tr>
</table>

Sept<sup>r</sup> 26<sup>th</sup> 1704                           Sept<sup>r</sup> 26<sup>th</sup> 1704

Read and assented to by   Read and Assented to by her
the house of Delegates          Ma<sup>tys</sup> hon<sup>ble</sup> Councill
W Taylard Clk h. D.              W Bladen Cl Concil.

Maryland October 3<sup>d</sup> 1704.

On behalf of her Ma<sup>ty</sup> &c I will this be a law

Jo : Seymour

An Act Impowering the Comissioners of the County Courts
to levy and raise Tobacco to defray the Necessary Charges
of their Countys and parishes.

Be it Enacted by the Queens most excellent Majesty by and
with the Advice and Consent of her Majestys Governour
Councill and Assembly of this province and the Authority of
the same That for the future it shall and may be lawfull to and
for the Severall and respective Comissioners of the Severall
and respective County Courts within this Province at their
severall and respective County Courts to be held for their
said Countys upon examination had before them of the Publiq
Charges of their Severall and respective Countys and allowances by them made of the same to levy and raise Tobacco for
payment and Satisfaction of the severall and respective County
Charges and the Sheriffs Sallary for Collecting thereof by an
equall Assessment of the Taxable persons of the said severall
Countys any former Law Act Usage or Custom to the Contrary in any wise Notwithstanding.

And be it further Enacted by the Authority Advice and
Consent aforesaid that the Clark of each respective County
p. 88 within this Province shall keep Account of such Tobacco
levyed and how disposed of in a fair book apart from other
Matters and a true copy thereof under the hand of the respective County Clark and under the Seale of the said County by
the said County Clerks be yearly and every year transmitted to

the Governour and Councill of this Province before the tenth day of March next ensuing after the laying of the levy for their Inspeccon.

And be it further Enacted by the Authority Advice and Consent aforesaid that if any Clerk of any County Court aforesaid shall neglect to transmitt a Copy of such accounts as aforesaid before the tenth day of March as aforesaid yearly and every year he shall forfeit and pay to our Sovereign Lady the Queen her heires and Successors the Summe of one thousand pounds of Tobacco One half to her Majesty her heires and Successors for the Support of Government the other half to the Informer or him or them that will sue for the same to be recovered by Action of Debt bill plaint or Information in any Court of Record of this Province wherein noe Essoyn protection or Wager of Law to be allowed.

And for purchasing Register Books and for repairing of Churches it is pray'd that it may be Enacted and

Be it Enacted by the Queens most excellent Majesty by and with the Advice and Consent of her Majestys Governour Councill and Assembly of this Province and the Authority of the same that when and as often as the necessity of each respective parish shall require Repaires or Supplys the Vestrymen and Church wardens thereof shall apply themselves to the Iustices of the County Courts at the time of the laying the County Levy who upon the Necessity appearing to them shall and are hereby impowered to raise by an equall Assessment by the poll on the Inhabitants of such respective parish such Sums of Tob° as by the said Justices shall be adjudged necessary to Supply the occasions aforesaid over and above the County levy not exceeding the Sume of tenn pounds of Tobacco per poll in one year which Sume so raised shall be Collected and p. 89 Gathered by the Sheriff of the same County and paid to the Vestrymen of each respective Parish or Parishes at the rate of five ₚ Cent for his Sallary.

And be it further Enacted by the Authority Advice and Consent aforesaid that where there is no Minister Resident in the Parish the Vestrymen of each respective parish in this Province shall keep a fair Account of the Disposition of the forty pounds of Tobacco ₚ Poll levyed in their Parish according to the Act Intituled An Act for Establishment of Religious Worship &c : and also of the tenn pounds of Tobacco per poll to be levyed and raised by vertue of this Act and a true Copy thereof under the hands of such principall Vestryman or four of his brethren of longest standing shall yearly and every year be transmitted to the Governour and Councill of this Province before the tenth day of March for their inspection.

294 *Assembly Proceedings, Sept. 5–Oct. 3, 1704.*

Lib. L. L.
No. 64.

And be it further Enacted by the Authority Advice and Consent aforesaid that if the Principall Vestryman and four of his brethren shall neglect to transmitt a Copy of such account as aforesaid before the tenth day of March as aforesaid yearly and every year they shall forfeit and pay to our Sovereign Lady the Queen her heires and Successors the Sume of one thousand pounds of Tobacco one half to her Majesty for Support of the Government the other half to the Informer or him or them that will sue for the same to be recovered by accon of Debt bill plaint or Information in any Court of Record of this Province wherein no Essoyn proteccon or Wager of Law to be allowed.

<table>
<tr><td>Sept<sup>r</sup> 23<sup>d</sup> 1704</td><td>Sept<sup>r</sup> 26<sup>th</sup> 1704</td></tr>
<tr><td>Read and assented to by the<br>house of Delegates<br>W Taylard Clk hD</td><td>Read and assented to by her<br>Ma<sup>tys</sup> hon<sup>ble</sup> Councill<br>W Bladen Cl Concil.</td></tr>
</table>

Maryland October 3<sup>d</sup> 1704
On behalf of her Ma<sup>ty</sup> &c. I will this be a Law
Jo : Seymour

p. 90 An Act directing the Manner of Electing and Sumoning Delegates and Representatives to serve in Succeeding Assemblys.

Forasmuch as the Cheifest and only ffoundation and Support of any Kingdom State or Comonwealth is the providing Establishing and Enacting good and wholesome Laws for the good rule and Government thereof and also upon any necessary and Emergent occasion to raise and Levy money for the defraying the Charges of the said Government and defence thereof neither of which according to the Constitution of this Province can be made ordain'd Establishd or raised but by and with the Consent of the ffreeman of this Province by their severall delegates and Representatives by them freely nominated Chosen and Elected to serve for their Severall Citys and Countys in a Generall Assembly. And for as much as the Safest and best rule for this Province to follow in Electing such Delegates and Representatives is the presidents of the proceedings in Parliaments in England as near as the Constitution of this Province will Admitt. The Governour Council and Delegates of this present generall Assembly do humbly pray that it may be enacted and

Be it enacted by the Queens most excellent Majesty by & with the Advice and Consent of her Majestys Governour

Lib. L. L.
No. 64.

Councill and Assembly of this Province and the Authority of the same that for the future when and as often as his Excellency the Governour of this Province for the time being shall upon any Accidents and urgent affair of this Province think fitt to call and Convene an Assembly and to send Writts for Eleccon of Burgesses and Delegates to serve in such Assembly the form of the said Writt shall be as followeth.

Anne by the Grace of God of England Scotland France and Ireland Queen Defender of the ffaith &c To the Sheriff of A. County Greeting These are to Authorize and impower p. 91 you imediately upon receipt hereof to call together four or more Comissioners of your County with the Clerk who are hereby required to sitt as a Court and during the sitting by vertue of your Office to make or Cause to be made publiq Proclamation thereby giving Notice to all the ffreemen of your said County who have within your said County a freehold of fifty Acres of Land or a Visible Estate of forty pounds Sterl at the least requiring them to appear at the next County Court to be holden for your County at a certain day within a reasonable time after such Proclamation made for Electing and Choosing of Deputys and Delegates to serve for your County in a Generall Assembly to be holden at the Port of Annapolis the        day of        att which time of Proclamation aforesaid the said ffreemen so required to appear or the Major part of such of them as shall then appear shall and may and are hereby Authorized and required to Elect and Choose four severall and sufficient ffreemen of your County each of them having a Freehold of ffifty Acres of Land or Visible Estate of forty pounds sterl at the least within your County And you shall give to each of them severally and respectively by four severall and respective Indentures under their hands and Seals to be Deputys and Delegates for your County at the said next Generall Assembly to do and Consent to those things which then by the favour of God shall happen to be ordain'd by the Advice and Consent of the great Councill of this Province Concerning such occasions and Affaires as shall relate to the Government State and defence of this Province But wee will not in any Case that you or any other Sheriff in our said Province be Elected. Which said Indentures shall be between you the said Sheriff of the one part and the said ffreemen electing of the other part And shall bear date the same day upon which the said Election shall be made and that upon such Election you the said Sheriff shall so soon as conveniently may be Certify and transmitt to the Chancellour of this Province for the time being one part of the said Severall and respective Indentures Close seald up under your hand and Seale and directed to the Governour of this Province and also to the

Chancellour and the other part of the said Indentures you are to keep for your Justification Witness our trusty and well beloved John Seymour Esq. our Capt. Generall and Chief Governour of this our Province at Annapolis &c.

And be it further Enacted by the Authority aforesaid that two Citizens to serve in the said Assembly for the City of Saint Marys shall be nominated Elected Chosen and appointed by the Mayor Recorder Alldermen and Comon Councill as heretofore hath been usuall

And be it further Enacted by the Authority aforesaid that the aforesaid four Delegates to be Elected in the respective County within this Province and the two Citizens of the City of Saint Marys be and are hereby bound and oblig'd to attend the time and place of the Meeting of such Assembly without any further Writt or Sumons to be to them sent under the Penalty of Such ffines as shall be by the house of Assembly imposed upon them unless upon Sufficient Excuse to be admitted by the said house of Assembly their absence be dispens'd withall Any Law Statute Usage or Custom to the contrary notwithstanding.

And be it also further Enacted by the Authority aforesaid that any Sheriff that shall refuse and neglect to make return of the delegates so Elected by Indenture as aforesaid before the day of Sitting of such Assembly or that shall make any undue or illegall returns of such elections shall for every fault be find two hundred pounds Sterl the one half to her Majesty her heires and Successors for the Support of Government and the other half to the Informer or them that shall sue for the same to be recovered in any Court of Record in this Province wherein no Essoyn Protection or wager of Law to be allowed.

Provided Nevertheless that this Act or anything herein contain'd shall not extend to be Construed to exclude any County or Countys City or Citys Burrough or Burroughs hereafter by her Majesty her heires or Successors to be erected and made within this Province from the liberty of such Election of Delegates and Representatives as is before express'd But that such p. 93 Writt as aforesaid shall upon calling every Generall Assembly for this Province for the future issue to the Sheriff of every such County when the same shall be erected and made into a County as aforesaid and to the Mayor Recorder and Alderman of every such City or Burrough Comanding such Sheriff or Mayor recorder and Aldermen to Cause four ffreemen of the said County and two freemen of the said City or burrough Qualifyed as in the said Writt is expressed to serve as Delegates and Representatives of the same County City or Burrough in the Generall Assembly then next ensuing Which said ffour Delegates for every such County and two for the City

and Burrough shall from henceforth be reputed and esteem'd Lib. L. L.
to be Members of the house of the Generall Assembly of this No 64.
Province anything in this Act to the Contrary in any wise
notwithstanding.

Provided also that no Ordinary Keeper within this province
during the time of his Keeping Ordinary shall be Elected
Chosen or Serve as a Deputy or Representative in the said
Generall Assembly so to be hereafter called convened and
appointed as aforesaid.

Sept<sup>r</sup> 23<sup>d</sup> 1704

Read and Assented to by
the house of Dellegates
W Taylard Cl hD

September 23<sup>d</sup> 1704

Read and Assented to by her
Majestys hon<sup>ble</sup> Councill
W Bladen Cl Council.

Maryland October 3<sup>d</sup> 1704.

On the behalf of her Ma<sup>ty</sup> I will this be a Law

Jo: Seymour

An Act to make Valid good and effectual in the Law all Manner of process and proceedings in the severall Courts of
this Province from the year One thousand six hundred
ninety to the year One thousand six hundred ninety two
and also from the Death of Lyonell Copley Esq. late Governor of this Province to the Arrivall of ffrancis Nicholson
Esq<sup>r</sup> Governour thereof and from the demise of his late
Ma<sup>ty</sup> King William the third to this present time.

Be it enacted by the Queens most excellent Majesty by and p. 94
with the Advice and Consent of Ma<sup>tys</sup> Governour Councill and
Assembly of this Province and the Authority of the same that
all Writts Pleas Process Indictments Informations Bills Suites
Accons Judgments decrees and Sentences awarded of or Concerning any Matter or thing whatsoever which was sued or
prosecuted to Judgment in any of the Courts of Record Chancery Admiralty or Comissarys Courts within this Province at
any Time or Times since the first day of Aprill in the year of
our Lord one thousand six hundred and ninety to the tenth
day of May One thousand six hundred ninety two And all
Writts Pleas process Bills Suites Accons Indictments Informations Judgments Decrees and Sentences awarded of or concerning any Matter or thing whatsoever which was sued or
prosecuted to Judgment in any of the Courts of Record Chancery Comissarys and Admiralty Courts within this Province at
any time or Times from the death of his Excellency Lyonell
Copley Esq<sup>r</sup> late Governour of this Province to the Arrivall of

the Cred^r that hath arisen due to the Debtor since the passing
such bill or bond or after such Assumpcon as aforesaid which
he desires may be discounted t shall and may be lawfull for
the Justices before whom such Matter shall be depending upon
good proofe made of such Acount to cause the same altho:
of a less or inferiour Nature to be discounted in Court and
give Judgment thereupon aginst the Defendant for so much
only as shall be remaining to he Plaintiff with Costs of Suite
Provided the ballance exceed vo hundred pounds of Tobacco
or sixteen Shillings and eight Pence in the County Courts and
fifteen hundred pounds of Tbacco or six pounds five shill
Sterl in the Provincial Courts otherwise the Plaintiff shall be
non suited as by other Laws ae provided.

And for the further Dec.ration what shall be taken &
allowed for Evidence to prove such Bills or Bonds

Be it enacted that the oath f one or more of those persons
that Subscribed as Witnesses ϶ such bill or Bond made before
one Justice of the Provincial Court or two Justices of any
County Court of this Provire in their respective Countys
shall be evidence to prove the Debts in the Provincial or any
County Courts of this Provinc if Sworne in Court Provided
nevertheless that if the Defedant will traverse such proofe
and put it on the County for proofe it shall be allowed him so
to doe.

And be it likewise Enacted by the Authority aforesaid that
an Account of goods sold wrk done mony lent and such
other Articles as lyes properly n Account and Sworne to by
the Plaintiff in any Accon brought or by the Defendant in his
Defence or discount of all o part of the Plaintiffs Claime,
before such Justice or Justices s aforesaid And that noe part ᴾ 99
or parcell thereof is paid othe than what is taken notice of in
the said Oath shall be receivedas evidence to prove the fact in
any Court of this Province rovided that any Plaintiff or.
Defendant in any Accon againt whom such oath is given for
Evidence shall be at his liberty o traverse such oath by giving
Evidence any other than himslf against it to invalidate the
same And the Court or Jury tht tryes the Cause shall Judge
by that which appears to them he fullest and fairest Evidence

September 29^th 1704           September 29^th 1704
Read in the house of Dele-   Read and assented to by her
gates and Assented to        Majestys hon^ble Councill
W Taylard Clk hD             W Bladen Cl Concil.

Maryland Ocober 3^d 1704
On behalf of her Ma^ty &c I vill this be a law.
                              Jo: Seymour

Lib. L. L. Chancellour and the other part of the said Indentures you are
No. 64. to keep for your Justification Witness our trusty and well
p. 92 beloved John Seymor Esq. our Capt. Generall and Chief Governour of this our Province at Annapolis &c.

And be it further enacted by the Authority aforesaid that two Citizens to serve in the said Assembly for the City of Saint Marys shall be nominated Elected Chosen and appointed by the Mayor Recorer Alldermen and Common Councill as heretofore hath been usuall

And be it further Enacted by the Authority aforesaid that the aforesaid four Delegates to be Elected in the respective County within this Province and the two Citizens of the City of Saint Marys be and are hereby bound and oblig'd to attend the time and place of the Meeting of such Assembly without any further Writt or Summons to be to them sent under the Penalty of Such fines as shall be by the house of Assembly imposed upon them unless upon Sufficient Excuse to be admitted by the said house of Assembly their absence be dispens'd withall Any new Statute Usage or Custom to the contrary notwithstanding.

And be it also futher Enacted by the Authority aforesaid that any Sheriff that shall refuse and neglect to make return of the delegates so Elected by Indenture as aforesaid before the day of Sitting of such Assembly or that shall make any undue or illegall retrns of such elections shall for every fault be find two hundre. pounds Sterl the one half to her Majesty her heires and Sucessors for the Support of Government and the other half to th Informer or them that shall sue for the same to be recover'd in any Court of Record in this Province wherein no Essoyn Protection or wager of Law to be allowed.

Provided Nevertheless that this Act or anything herein contain'd shall not extnd to be Construed to exclude any County or Countys City or Citys Burrough or Burroughs hereafter by her Majesty her heres or Successors to be erected and made within this Province from the liberty of such Election of Delegates and Representatives as is before express'd But that such
p 93 Writt as aforesaid shall upon calling every Gene-all Assembly for this Province or the future issue to the Sheriff of every such County whereithe same shall be erected and made into a County as aforesaid and to the Mayor Recorder and Alderman of every such City or Burrough Commanding such Sheriff or Mayor recorder ad Aldermen to Cause four ffreemen of the said County and vo freemen of the said City or burrough Qualifyed as in th said Writt is expressed to serve as Delegates and Representatives of the same County City or Burrough in the Generall Assembly then next ensuing Which ffour Delegates fo every such County and two ...

and Burrough shall from henceforth e reputed and esteem'd Lib. L. L. to be Members of the house of the Generall Assembly of this No 64. Province anything in this Act to th Contrary in any wise notwithstanding.

Provided also that no Ordinary Keper within this province during the time of his Keeping Olinary shall be Elected Chosen or Serve as a Deputy or Roresentative in the said Generall Assembly so to be hereaftr called convened and appointed as aforesaid.

Sept' 23ᵈ 1704

Read and Assented to by
the house of Dellegates
W Taylard Cl hD

:ptember 23ᵈ 1704

Reacand Assented to by her
Mjestys hon^ble Councill
V Bladen Cl Council.

Maryland October ₃ 1704.

On the behalf of her Ma'ʸ I will thi be a Law

Jo: Seymour

An Act to make Valid good and effecial in the Law all Manner of process and proceedings ii the severall Courts of this Province from the year One housand six hundred ninety to the year One thousand ix hundred ninety two and also from the Death of Lyonel Copley Esq. late Governor of this Province to the Arrivll of ffrancis Nicholson Esq' Governour thereof and from he demise of his late Ma'ʸ King William the third to this>resent time.

Be it enacted by the Queens most eccellent Majesty by and p. 94 with the Advice and Consent of Ma'ʸ' iovernour Councill and Assembly of this Province and the Auiority of the same that all Writts Pleas Process Indictments Iformations Bills Suites Accons judgments decrees and Senter.cs awarded of or Concerning any Matter or thing whatsoe:r which was sued or prosecuted to Judgment in any of the 'ourts of Record Chancery Admiralty or Comissarys Courts 'ithin this Province at any Time or Times since the first day f Aprill in the year of our Lord one thousand six hundred nd ninety to the tenth day of May One thousand six hundrd ninety two And all Writts Pleas process Bills Suites Accons Indictments Inform- tions Judgments Decrees and Senteres ʔ˙˙ cerning any Matter or thing what˙˙ prosecuted to Judgment in a˙˙ cery Comissarys and Adm˙˙ any time or Times fro˙˙ Copley Esq' late G˙˙

his Excellency Francis Nicholson Esq$^r$ Governour thereof shall be good and effectuall in the law to all Intents Construccons and purposes whatsoever any discontinuance of process or other Defects in the said proceedings notwithstanding

And be it further Enacted by the Authority Advice and Consent aforesaid that all Writts Pleas Process Accons bills Suites Indictments informations Iudgments Decrees and Sentences given or awarded of and Concerning any Matter or thing whatsoever which was sued or prosecuted to Judgment in any of the Courts of Record Chancery Comissarys and Admiralty Courts within this province at any time or times - from the demise of his late Majesty King William the third of blessed Memary to the end of this Sessions of Assembly Notwithstanding the want of any Jurisdiction or Authority in the said Courts shall be good and effectual in the law to all Intents Constructions and purposes whatsoever

Provided allways that this Act or anything therein Contain'd shall not be Construed to extend to take away such Errors in Law as shall or may arise upon in issuing of Process Mis-
P. 95 pleading and Erroneous rendring of Judgment in poynt of Law but in all such Cases the partys greived may have their Writt or Writts of Erro$^r$ upon such erroneous Judgments as they might have had before the making of this Act.

September 21$^{st}$ 1704                    September 21$^{st}$ 1704

Read and assented to by        Read and assented to by her
the house of Delegates.        Ma$^{tys}$ hon$^{ble}$ Councill
W Taylard Clk hD.              W Bladen Cl Concil.

Maryland October 3$^d$ 1704
On the behalf of her Majesty &c I will this be a Law
J$_o$ : Seymour

An Act providing what shall be Evidence to prove fforeign and other Debts and to prevent Vexatious and unnecessary Suites In law And pleading discounts in barr.

Be it Enacted by the Queens most excellent Ma$^{ty}$ by and with the Advice and Consent of her Majestys Governour Council and Assembly of this Province and the Authority of the same That all Debts of Record whether by Judgment Recognizances Deed Enrolled and upon Record the Exemplification thereof under the Seale of the Courts where the said Judgment was given or was Recorded shall be a Sufficient Evidence to prove the same And that all other Debts by bonds

bills Accounts or otherwise that shall from or after the publication hereof be sent hither to be putt in suite against any person
whatsoever living or residing within this Province shall be
proved by the Oaths of the Witnesses thereunto before a
Notary Publiq or other Officer lawfully Authorized thereunto
of the County or place wheresoever it shall happen the said
Bonds or Bills shall be sent from, Att which time and before
which Publiq Notary or other Publiq Officer shall be present
the Creditors who shall then likewise before such Publiq
Notary or other publiq Officer of the place soe Authorized
upon his Corporall Oath declare that the said Debt or any
part thereof saving what the said Creditor gives Creditt for is
not Satisfyed or that there are not any other Accounts between
the said Creditor and Debtor by which the said Creditor may
be likewise indebted to the said Debtor to the value of the
said Debt or any part thereof for any Matter or thing accrued
since the date of the said bond bill or Instrument or whether
the said Creditor hath not given to the said Debtor any Release
for the same to be sent together with the proofe from under
the hands and Seals of the said Publiq Notary or other Publiq
Officer thereunto appointed which if the Creditor shall refuse
or neglect to performe or Doe then the said Matter or thing
by the said Publiq or other Officer so by them Certifyed as
aforesaid shall not be received as Evidence to prove the said
Debt and if the said Creditor be dead and his Executor or
Administrator sue such bond Bill Account or otherwise sue any
Debtor for the same the Executor and Administrator in like
manner before such Notary Publiq or other Officer for that
purpose appointed shall sett forth and declare upon their oath
whether or noe they have not heard the Creditor in his life
time acknowledge that Debt or any or what part thereof to be
Satisfyed or whether or not upon sight of the Creditors books
writing or Accounts they have not seen Creditt given to the
Debtor since the day of the making the said bills bonds or
beginnings of the Accounts so sued for, all w$^{ch}$ in like Manner
is to be Certifyed by the Publiq Notary or other Off$^r$ thereunto
appointed under his hand and Seale to be sent along to this
Country together with the Testimony of the Witnesses that
have testifyed to the said Bonds Bills Accounts, or otherwise,
All which if the said Executor or Administrator refuse or neglect to do then the said Matter &c thing by the Publiq Notary
or other Officer appointed as aforesaid Certifyed shall not be
received in Evidence for valid against the Debtor

And be it Enacted by the Authority aforesaid that all and
every the Attorny and Attorneys who shall be employ'd in the
Prosecution of such Suites shall put in Security to pay the
Defendant all such Costs and Charges as shall be by the

Lib. L. L.  Defendant in that Case expended in Case the Plaintiff be Cast
No. 64.  in Suite.

p. 97  And to the end that no honest Debtor who hath not fledd
from the place or County where he Contracted his Debt nor
wilfully absconded himself or fledd from Justice shall be Surprized by unnecessary and vexatious Suites at Law

Be it Enacted by the Authority Advice and Consent aforesaid that no person whatsoever residing or trading in or to
this Province their Ex^{rs} Adm^{rs} Agents ffactors or Assigns
shall for any Sum or Sums of Tobacco or money due or owing
to him by account upon book or otherwise (and for which the
Debtor hath not past his hand and Seale to such his Creditor)
sue and implead such Debtor his Executors or Administrators
in any Court of Record within this Province unless he shall
first demand and require the same of such Debtors proper
person or otherwise at the habitation or place of Residence
of the said Debtor in the County where he shall dwell (to
prove which Demand the Creditors or demandants own oath
shall be Sufficient) And if the Debtor be not at home to be
spoke with then such Demandant shall have a Note under the
hand of such Creditor or demandant or those he shall empower
to receive the same what time and to whom the same shall be
paid And if thereupon the same be not paid accordingly then
it shall and may be lawfull for such Creditor to sue and
implead such his Debtor and recover against him all such
Costs and Damages as upon legall tryall in any Court of this
Province having Cognizance of the Cause shall be adjudged
as before the making of this Act but in Case any Person or
Persons shall sue and implead such his Debtor as aforesaid
without making demand as aforesaid and the Debtor plead
that the Debt was never demanded by such Plea the Debtor
shall be taken to Admitt the Plaintiffs Declaration to be good,
and shall only put the demand in issue which issue if the
Plaintiff do not o ne then the Pl^t shall be taken to have made
no demand and shall only have Judgment for his Damages
And shall loose all his own Costs and if the Plaintiff Joyn in
issue upon demand and it be found against him then the
Plaintiff shall loose his own Costs and pay Costs of such tryall
to the Defendant Yet the said Plaintiff shall have Judgment to
recover his Debt or Damages which he sues for, or so much
thereof as appears due upon ballance.

p. 98  And be it further enacted that if any Debtor or Debtors be
sued by any Creditor or Creditors for any Sume or Sumes of
Money or Tobacco due upon the Debtors assumption or due by
bill or bond under the hand and Seale of the Debtor and the
Debtors confess the Assumpcon and acknowledge his Act or
Deed but saith further that he hath an Account of his Own against

the Cred<sup>r</sup> that hath arisen due to the Debtor since the passing Lib. L. L. such bill or bond or after such Assumpcon as aforesaid which No. 64. he desires may be discounted it shall and may be lawfull for the Justices before whom such Matter shall be depending upon good proofe made of such Account to cause the same altho : of a less or inferiour Nature to be discounted in Court and give Judgment thereupon against the Defendant for so much only as shall be remaining to the Plaintiff with Costs of Suite Provided the ballance exceed two hundred pounds of Tobacco or sixteen Shillings and eight Pence in the County Courts and fifteen hundred pounds of Tobacco or six pounds five shill Sterl in the Provincial Courts otherwise the Plaintiff shall be non suited as by other Laws are provided.

And for the further Declaration what shall be taken & allowed for Evidence to prove such Bills or Bonds

Be it enacted that the oath of one or more of those persons that Subscribed as Witnesses to such bill or Bond made before one Justice of the Provincial Court or two Justices of any County Court of this Province in their respective Countys shall be evidence to prove the Debts in the Provincial or any County Courts of this Province if Sworne in Court Provided nevertheless that if the Defendant will traverse such proofe and put it on the County for proofe it shall be allowed him so to doe.

And be it likewise Enacted by the Authority aforesaid that an Account of goods sold work done mony lent and such other Articles as lyes properly in Account and Sworne to by the Plaintiff in any Accon brought or by the Defendant in his Defence or discount of all or part of the Plaintiffs Claime, before such Justice or Justices as aforesaid And that noe part P. 99 or parcell thereof is paid other than what is taken notice of in the said Oath shall be received as evidence to prove the fact in any Court of this Province Provided that any Plaintiff or. Defendant in any Accon against whom such oath is given for Evidence shall be at his liberty to traverse such oath by giving Evidence any other than himself against it to invalidate the same And the Court or Jury that tryes the Cause shall Judge by that which appears to them the fullest and fairest Evidence

September 29<sup>th</sup> 1704      September 29<sup>th</sup> 1704

Read in the house of Dele-      Read and assented to by her
gates and Assented to      Majestys hon<sup>ble</sup> Councill
W Taylard Clk hD      W Bladen Cl Concll.

Maryland October 3<sup>d</sup> 1704

On behalf of her Ma<sup>ty</sup> &c I will this be a law.

Jo : Seymour

Lib. L. I.,  An Act for the Confirming Titles of Land given to the use of
No. 64.    the Churches and Severall Chappells within this Province
Impowering the Comissioners of the respective Countys
and the Vestrys of the respective Parishes to take up Certain parcells of Land for the use of the same.

Whereas severall pious and well disposed persons have
given and granted Unto the respective Parishes whereto they
do belong Certain parcells of Ground for the use and benefitt
of a Church and Church-yard which said Land through the
neglect of the Vestrys who by an Act of Assembly of this
province made at a Sessions of Assembly held at the Port of
Annapolis the twentyeth day of July Anno Domini One
thousand six hundred ninety and Six Intituled An Act for the
Service of Allmighty God and establishment of the Protestant
Religion were Capacitated and Impowered by the names of
the principall Vestryman and the rest of his brethren Vestry-
p. 100  men of such parish to take and receive any Deed of Gift for
the same Notwithstanding the Charges of the respective
parishes in building Churches or Chappells thereon is like to be
lost or the Title thereunto very disputable for want of such Deed
of gift or Conveyance inrolled and recorded as by an Act of
Assembly is required the first Donors or grantors thereof
being dead and the heires of such Donors or Grantors either
refusing to make over such Land as aforesaid or under age
not capable of so doing.

Be it therefore Enacted by the Queens most excellent
Majesty by and with the Advice and Consent of her Majestys
Governour Councill and Assembly of this province and the
Authority of the same that all such lands as have formerly
been given to the use of any Church or Chappell and for
which the Donors or Grantors thereof in their life times have
not made a deed of Gift for the same or otherwise refuse so to
do and in Confidence of whose promise the parish have been
at the Charge of erecting and building their Churches thereon
be and remaine to the use of the parish for ever against all
Claims and pretensions of Claims made or that hereafter shall
be made by such Donors or Grantors or his or their beires
Executors or Assigns as firmly and absolutely as if the same
had been made over by Deed of gift Grant or otherwise
inrolled and recorded as aforesaid.

And to the end it may be known what Lands have been so
given to the use of any Church or Chapple aforesaid and
made over and Confirmed by deed of gift or Grant as aforesaid The Grand Jury in each respective County within this
Province next after the publication of this Act shall have in
Charge to enquire by what Titles such lands whereupon the

severall Churches or Chappells aforesaid within their respective parishes and in their precincts are held and to render an Account thereof to the Court who are hereby Impowered where any such lands shall appear to be given and not confirm'd as aforesaid in open Court to examine Witnesses in perpetuam rei Memoriam and the same Cause to be recorded in the County Records which shall be deem'd adjudged and taken in all Courts of Record within this Province as Sufficient proof of the Donation or Grant as also to the Quantity of Acres given or Granted as aforesaid And in Case it shall appear upon such Examination that Lands have been given for the use of any Church Chappell or Churchyard as aforesaid but the Quantity thereof not mention'd by the Donors or Grantors thereof as aforesaid That then and in every such Case the Vestry of the respective parish where such Gift or Grant hath been made and the Quantity not ascertain'd as aforesaid may demand and take of such lands for the use of the Church and thereto adjacent two Acres and no more which they shall Cause to be Surveyed and Staked out and make returns of two Certificates thereof One of which must be recorded in the County Court and the other in the high Court of Chancery there to be registered inperpetuam rei Memoriam as aforesaid.

And be it further Enacted by the Authority aforesaid by and with the Advice and Consent aforesaid that where the Vestry of any Parish within this Province have or shall think Convenient to place either Church or Chappell of Ease within their respective Parishes for the better Conveniency of their parishioners but the Owner or Owners of such Land Chosen out and appointed by such Vestry as aforesaid for the use of their parish aforesaid either refuse to make Sale thereof or are unreasonable in his or their Demands for the same or otherwise incapacitated by nonage non sanæ Memoriæ or beyond the Seas That then and in every such Case the respective Vestrys of the respective parishes shall apply themselves to the Comissioners of the County Court whereto they belong Upon whose Application the said Comissioners shall forthwith grant their warrants to the Sheriff of their County thereby requiring him at a certain day and time to be by them nominated and appointed to impannell a Iury of Substantiall ffreeholders next adjacent to the Land in quest aforesaid which said Comissioners and Jury aforesaid shall proceed in all things as by another Act of Assembly (Intituled An Act Impowering the Comissioners of the severall and respective Countys to take up and purchase land for their County Court houses) they are directed not exceeding two Acres as before in this Act mencoñd and expressed. Any thing in this Act or any other ordain'd to the Contrary notwithstanding.

Lib. L. L.
No. 64.

Sept<sup>r</sup> 23<sup>d</sup> 1704.

Read and Assented to by
the house of Delegates
W Taylard Cl. h.D.

Sept<sup>r</sup> 26 1704.

Read and assented to by
her Ma<sup>tys</sup> hon<sup>ble</sup> Councill
W Bladen Cl. Concil.

Maryland Octob. 3<sup>d</sup> 1704
On behalf of her Ma<sup>ty</sup> &c. I will this be a Law

Jo: Seymour

p. 102 An Act Declaring that the Grantees of Land lying within the Indians land may have Action of Trespass against such persons as Cutt Timber off their Land on pretence of having bought the same of the Indians.

Be it hereby Enacted and declared by the Queens most excellent Majesty by and with the Advice and Consent of her Majestys Governour Council and Assembly of this Province and the Authority of the same that the falling Mawling and carrying away of Timber or purchasing or receiving any Timber by any person or persons upon pretence of having bought the same of the Indians or upon any unlawfull pretence whatsoever on or from off any Lands within the bounds of the Indians Land whereof any other person or persons have in Him her or them the Fee be Judg'd deem'd and Accounted a Trespass And whosoever shall purchase or receive ffall Maule or Carry away Timber as aforesaid shall be deem'd and adjudg'd Trespassers and shall be lyable to Accon or Accons of trespass And the persons greived shall and may recover their Damages accordingly as if the Grantee or Pattentee aforesaid did actually occupy & enjoy such land And had improved it. Any Law Act of Assembly or Usage to the Contrary notwithstanding.

Sept<sup>r</sup> 21<sup>st</sup> 1704

Read and Assented to by
the house of Delegates.
W Taylard Cl hD

Sept<sup>r</sup> 21<sup>st</sup> 1704

Read and Assented to by her
Ma<sup>tys</sup> hon<sup>ble</sup> Councill
W Bladen Cl Concil.

Maryland Octob 3<sup>d</sup> 1704
On the behalf of her Majesty &c I will this be a Law

Jo. Seymour

p. 103 An Act for regulating of Ordinarys.

For the better regulating of Ordinary Keepers and Inholders within this Province for the future And inpursuance of her Ma^{tys} royall Instructions for raising further Supplys for defraying the publiq Charge of this Province To Effect which the Burgesses and Delegates of this present Generall Assembly do humbly pray that her Majesty will graciously be pleas'd to grant th^t it may be enacted and

Be it enacted by the Queens most excellent Majesty by and with the Advice and Consent of her Majestys Governour Councill and Assembly of this Province and the Authority of the same That from and after the publication hereof The Justices of each County be and are hereby empowered and Authorized from time to time as often as need shall require to grant Licenses to such person and persons as they shall think fitt to be ordinary Keepers and Inholders for the keeping of Ordinarys and Houses of Entertainment so long time and in such and so many places within their severall and respective Countys for the ease and Conveniency of the Inhabitants Travellers and Strangers as to them respectively shall seem meet. For which lycenses the said persons that shall be so lycens'd to keep Ordinary as aforesaid shall at the time of his and their taking such Lycenses enter into Recognizance to our Sovereign Lady the Queens Majesty to pay unto her Majesty towards the Defraying· the Charge of the County the Severall and respective Summs following that is to say ffor every Lycense to keep Ordinary in the Citty of Saint Marys Towns or Ports of Annapolis or Williamstad^t or at any County Court house within this Province the Sume of twelve hundred pounds of Tobacco and four hundred pounds of Tobacco at every other place within this Province for every year such person shall keep Ordinary as aforesaid to the use aforesaid for which said Lycense and Recognizance the party or partys taking the same shall pay to the Clark of each respective County Court the sume of Sixty pounds of Tobacco and no more.

And be it further Enacted by the Authority aforesaid that the Justices of the severall County Courts Be and are hereby authorized & Impowered at their severall County Courts in the months of January and August yearly and every year having Sumon'd each respective Ordinary Keeper within their respective Countys then and there to sett and assess the Rates and prizes of all Liquors and other Accomodations whatsoever by them the said Ordinary Keepers to be vended for the year ensuing and so yearly and every year. Which rates and prizes of all liquors so to be sett and assessd limitted and appointed by the Justices aforesaid shall be by their severall and respective Clarks Transcribed and sett up at their Severall and respective County Courts in some publiq Places there that every person or persons may peruse the same the Copy

of which table of prices of Liquors and accomodations every
Ordinary Keeper within each County are hereby obliged to
transcribe fairly and keep the same sett up in the most publiq
place of their houses for the perusall of all persons that
receive any Ordinary Accomodations from them under the
Penalty of one thousand pounds of Tobacco to her Majesty
her heires and Successors to be applyd to the use of the
County where such ordinary keeper shall live to be sued for,
on non payment thereof in her Majestys name for which
Summons and table of prizes every Ordinary Keeper shall pay
to such Clark the sume of forty pounds of Tobacco and no
more, And every Ordinary Keeper or Inholder that shall after
the setting up and Assessing the Rates and Prizes aforesaid
directly or indirectly take exact demand or receive for the
price and pay for any such liquors or other Accomodations for
which the Rates and Prizes shall be assessd and sett as aforesaid
of any person or persons whatsoever above the Rates and
prizes so sett and assessd as aforesaid shall for every such
Account sued for taken or received forfeitt and pay the sume
of five hundred pounds of Tobacco One half thereof to her
Majesty her beires and Successors for the use of the County
& the other half to him or them that shall informe or sue for
the same and loose every such Debt or Account sued for
taken or received so unjustly Charged exacted and demanded
the said fforfeitures to be recovered in any Court of Record
within this Province by bill Plaint or Information wherein noe
Essoyn Protection or Wager of Law to be allowed.

And be it further enacted by the Authority aforesaid that
every Ordinary Keeper or Inholder so to be Lycensed as
aforesaid shall within six Months after granting their respec-
p. 105 tive Lycenses be hereby obliged to provide and Maintaine if
they keep Ordinarys at the Court house in any County or the
Town and Port of Annapolis and Williamstad⁴ aforesaid six
good and substantiall beds Over and above what is for their
Own ffamily use with Sufficient Warm Covering for the same
together with Accomodation of Oats Hay and straw for Litter
and Indian Corne with stabling for twenty Horses at least
And if any Ordinary be kept at any other place or part of the
County than at the Court house such Ordinary Keeper shall
within the time aforesaid be provided with four spare bedds
with Covering and Sufficient stabling and Provender for six
horses at least under the Penalty of five hundred pounds of
Tobacco One half thereof to her Majesty her heires and Successors for the use of the County the other half to him or
them that shall informe or sue for the same to be recovered
by bill Plaint or Information wherein noe Essoyn protection or
Wager of Law to be Allowed.    Provided allways that no

person or persons so licens'd or to be licensd to Keep Ordinary as aforesaid shall during the time of such their Keeping
Ordinary be delegates or Justices of the Peace for any County
within this Province.

And be it further Enacted by the Authority aforesaid that if
any Ordinary Keeper shall keep evill rule in his house upon
Complaint made thereof to the Justices of the County Court
of such ordinary Keepers Misbehaviour or Keeping evill rule
in his house the said Justices of the County Courts are hereby
Authorized and Impowered to Suppress such ordinary Keeper
and Call in such Lycense.

And be it further Enacted by the Authority aforesaid that
any Ordinary Keeper disabled or Supprest as aforesaid or any
other person that shall presume to keep Ordinary without
Lycense first had and obtaind as aforesaid shall for every
Month he or they shall Keep Ordinary as aforesaid fforfeitt
and pay two thousand pounds of Tobacco and so proportionable for a longer or shorter Time that any persons shall sell
Liquors or doe contrary to this Law One half to her Majesty
her heires and Successors for the use aforesaid and the other
half to him or them that shall sue for the same to be recovered
in any Court of Record in this Province by bill plaint or Information wherein noe Essoyn protection or wager of Law to be
allowed

And be it further enacted by the Authority aforesaid that no
person or persons Inhabitting within this Province not having
lawfull license shall sell by retaile any Syder Quince Drink or p. 106
other strong Liquors to be drank in his her or their Houses or
about his her or their Plantations upon forfeiture of every
time he she or they shall be legally Convict thereof the sume
of one thousand pounds of Tobacco One half thereof to her
Majesty her heires and Successors for and towards the Defraying
the County Charge where such forfeiture shall become due
and the other half to the Informer or to him or them that shall
sue for the same to be recovered in any Court of Record
within this Province by Accon of Debt Bill Plaint or Information wherein noe Essoyn protection or Wager Law to be
allowed.

And be it farther enacted by the Authority aforesaid by and
with the Advice and Consent aforesaid that no person or persons whatsoever so lycens'd to Keep Ordinary as aforesaid
shall refuse to Creditt any person Capable of giving a Vote
for Election of Delegates in any County within this Province
to the value of four hundred pounds of Tobacco per Annum
for any Accomodation by him vended whereof any such persons so capacitated as aforesaid shall have occasion of or
require to be accomodated withall under the Penalty or ffor-

feiture of four hundred pounds of Tobaccò by each Ordinary Keeper so refusing to Creditt such person as aforesaid One Moyety thereof to her Majesty her heires and Successors for and towards the Defraying the County Charge where such fforfeiture shall become due the other Moyety to the Informer or him or them that shall sue for the same to be recovered as aforesaid.

And whereas it hath been found prejudiciall to the Inhabitants of this Province That Ordinary Keepers and Inholders have frequently Entertain'd divers freemen and loose persons a great time tipling at their houses as well to the great damage of many persons as their Own ruine.

Be it therefore enacted by the Authority aforesaid by and with the Advice and Consent aforesaid that it shall not be lawfull for any Such ordinary Keeper or Inholder to Keep such Ordinary or house of Entertainment untill they have entered into Recognizance before the Justices of each respective County granting Such Licenses with two Sufficient Suretys to the value of twenty pounds Sterl that they shall not entertain any ffreeman or other loose person in their houses above twenty four hours (Court times excepted) unless such person be Capable to give his vote for a Delegate in the said County or
p. 107 that he be retain'd as a servant to the said Ordinary Keeper or Inholder any Law Usage or Custom to the Contrary notwithstanding

And whereas dayly Experience shews the great prejudice to the Owners and Masters of Merchant Ships and Vessells trading into this Province by Ordinary Keepers entertaining of Saylors and others to such Shipps and Vessells belonging and trusting and encouraging them to continue tipling in their houses to the prejudice of Trade within this Province preventing and impeding the dispatch of such Ships and Vessells and very often when such Saylors have spent their Wages in such Ordinary occasions and induces them to run away and desert the Shipps and Vessells whereto they belong ffor the prevention whereof

Be it enacted by the Queens most excellent Majesty by and with the Advice and Consent of her Majestys Governour Councill and Assembly of this Province and by the Authority of the same that no Ordinary Keeper whatsoever within this Province shall presume to Harbour or Entertaine such Saylors to the neglect of their Service to their respective Comanders and prejudice to the dispatch of any Shipp or Vessell thereby undr the pain and penalty of being Suspended from keeping such Ordinary. And that no Ordinary Keeper whatsoever shall credit any such Saylor for more than five shillings during any one voyage under the penalty of loosing his Debt and

being fin'd to our Lady the Queen her heires and Successors
the Sume of five pounds Sterl whereof one half to the
informer the other half to the Vestry of such parish where
such Ordinary Keeper shall live towards the Defraying the
Parish Charge to be recovered in any Court of Record of this
Province by bill plaint p$^r$ Information wherein no Essoyn proteccon or Wager of Law to be allowed.

And Lastly tis hereby Enacted by the Authority aforesaid
by and with the Advice and Consent aforesaid that the Justices
of the Provincial Court and the Justices of the respective
County Courts shall give this Act in Charge to the severall Grand
Jurys and to their severall and respective Constables in their
said Countys to inquire into the breach of this Act and into all
Disorders comitted in the said Ordinarys and present the same
if any be to the severall Courts to be Examin'd and punished
according to Law. This Act to endure for three Years and to
the end of the next Sessions of Assembly which shall first
happen after the end of the said three Years.

| September 23$^d$ 1704 | September 26$^{th}$ 1704 |
|---|---|
| Read and assented to by | Read and assented to by her |
| the house of Delegates. | Majestys bon$^{ble}$ Councill |
| W Taylard Clk h.D. | W Bladen Cl Concil. |

Maryland October 3$^d$ 1704     p. 108

On behalf of her Majesty &c I will this be a Law.

Jo : Seymour

An Act ascertaining the Heighth of ffences To prevent the Evill
occasion'd by the Multitude of Horses and restraining Horse
Rangers within this Province.

Be it Enacted by the Queens most excellent Majesty by and
with the Advice and Consent of her Majestys Governour
Council and Assembly of this Province and the Authority of
the same that all Inclosures by ffences or otherwise within the
Intention of this Act hereafter mencond shall be five foot high
and that from and after the first day of May next till the tenth
day of November next and so yearly and every year all Owners
of any Horse Horses, Mares Colts and Geldings shall and are
hereby obliged to keep all such Horse or Horses Mares Colts
or Geldings within good & Sufficient Inclosures ffenced
Grounds or pastures Upon the pains and penaltys hereafter
following

And be it further Enacted by the Authority aforesaid by and
with the Advice and Consent aforesaid that if the Owner or
Owners of any such Horse or Horses Mares Colts or Geldings

as aforesaid shall omitt to take up drive in and keep up all
such Horses Mares Colts or Geldings as are before mencoñd,
or intended by default whereof any such Horses Mares Colts
or Geldings shall break into the pastures Corn-fields or other
Inclosures of any Inhabitant within this Province within the
time by this Act limitted aforesaid the said Owner or Owners
thereof having notice or warning thereof given him her or
them two severall times by the party grieved and notwithstanding the Owner or Owners of such Horse or Horses
Mares Colts or Geldings as aforesaid shall neglect to performe
what is by this law injoynd and required that then it shall and
may be lawfull for the person so grieved & damnifyed to shoot
Kill or Destroy all or any such Horse or Horses Mares Colts
& Geldings as aforesaid.

Provided allways that no person whatsoever tho: greived or
Damnifyed shall presume to shoot Kill or Destroy any such
Horse or Horses as aforesaid except upon his her or their proper
Inclosed Ground within his her or their lawfull possession by
lease for years yearly rent or other lawfull tenure upon the
penalty of paying the Owner thereof the full value of such
Horse Gelding Mare or Colt so Kill'd or Destroyd to be
Recovered by Accon of Trespass or Action on the Case in
any County Court of this Province.

And be it further enacted by the Authority aforesaid that if
the Owner or Owners of any Such Horse or Horses Mares
Colts or Geldings shall not be known to the party or partys
greived or damnifyed as aforesaid he she or they so greived
shall and are obliged with two Sufficient Evidences to take
Notice of the Colour Naturall and Artificiall Marks of any such
Horse Mare Colt or Gelding in writing and the same to affix
and sett up at the most publiq place within the County where
such Damage as aforesaid shall happen to be done for the
Space of one whole Month Att the end of which no Owner
appearing It then shall and may be lawfull for the partys
greived to shoot kill or destroy the said Horse or Horses upon
his her or their Lands as aforesaid.

And bee it further Enacted by the Authority aforesaid by and
with the Advice and Consent aforesaid That whosoever shall
unlawfully and without the Knowledge and Consent of the
Owner take another Mans horse Mare or Gelding and the
same keep one hour in his Possession and such horse Mare or
Gelding shall without Consent aforesaid occupy in any Labour
or travell shall not only pay Damages to the Owner but shall
forfeit and pay the Sume of five hundred pounds of Tobacco
One half to the Informer the other half to the party grieved to
be recovered in any County Court of this Province by Accon of
Debt bill plaint or Information wherein no Essoyn protection
or Wager of Law to be allowed.

And for as much as divers Complaints are made of the Abuses Comitted by such persons that have obtain'd Comissions from the Governour to range the Woods and fforrests after Wild Neat Cattle and Horses it is pray'd that it may be Enacted and

Be it Enacted by the Queens most excellent Majesty by and with the Advice and Consent of her Majestys Governour Councill and Assembly of this Province and the Authority of the same that it shall not be lawfull for any person after the p. 110 end of this Sessions of Assembly to make application to the Governour for the time being to grant a Comission to range as aforesaid except such person produce a Certificate from under the hand of the Justices of the County Courts where the said person is to range setting forth that he is of good ffame.

And be it further Enacted by the Authority aforesaid by and with the Advice and Consent aforesaid that no person Comissionated as aforesaid shall depute any person as a Deputy to range the woods and fforrests after Cattle and Horses as aforesaid except such person be likewise approved of by the Justices of the County in which he is to range as a Deputy.

And for as much as it is necessary to declare at what age Horses Mares and Cattle shall be deem'd wild

Be it Enacted by the Authority aforesaid by and with the Advice and Consent aforesaid that it shall not be lawfull for any Ranger within this Province to take up and Mark or otherwise dispose of any unmarkt horse Mare Bull or Cow which shall not exceed the age of three Years Any Law Usage or Custom to the Contrary Notwithstanding.

And be it further Enacted by the Authority aforesaid by and with the Advice and Consent aforesaid that the Justices in each respective County within this Province shall yearly and every year at their County Courts in the months of November and March during the Continuance of this Act cause it to be read in open Court and likewise give it in Charge to the Grand Jurys to enquire of any breaches thereof comitted by Wood rangers in that County.

And be it further enacted by the Authority aforesaid by and with the Advice and Consent aforesaid that no person whatsoever shall presume to range in the woods or fforrests after wild Neat Cattle or Horses without a lycense from his Excellency the Governour in Chief for the time being under the penalty of ffive thousand pounds of Tobacco for every such before mencoñd wild Creature that every such unlycens'd Ranger shall kill take or Convey away alive or dead One half to Our sovereign Lady the Queen her heires and successors the other half to the Informer or him or them that shall sue for the same by Action of Debt bill Plaint or Information in any

Court of Record in this Province wherein no Essoyn Protection or Wager of Law to be allowed This Act to endure three years and to the end of the next Sessions of Assembly which shall first happen after the three years.

| September 29th 1704 | Septr 29th 1704 |
|---|---|
| Read and Assented to by the house of Dell. | Read and Assented to by her Majestys honble Councill |
| W Taylard Clk h.D. | W Bladen Cl Concil. |

Maryland October 3d 1704

On Behalf of her Majesty &c I will this be a Law.

Jo: Seymour.

An Act for settlement of an Annual Revenue upon her Majestys Governour within this Province for the time being.

Whereas by an Act of Assemby formerly made Intituled An Act for providing a Support for the Lord Proprietary of this Province and likewise a Supply for defraying the publiq Charge of Government It was by the said Act publish'd and declared that from and after the first day of September then next ensuing there should be rais'd levyed Collected and paid to the said Lord Proprietary the sume of two shillings Sterl for every Hogshead or Quantity of a Hogshead of Tobacco which should be at any time thereafter Shipped in any Shipp or Vessell to be exported out of this Province on Condition that his said Lordship should receive his Rents and ffines for Alienacon of Lands in good sound Merchantable Tobacco when tendred at the rate of two pence per pound for one Moyety of the said Imposition the other Moyety by the said Act rais'd to be employ'd towards Maintaining a Constant Magazine and defraying other publiq and necessary Charges of the Government And whereas former Assemblys upon strict inquiry made into the Premisses did find his said Lordship had not only been very Deficient and at Small Charges and Expences in maintaining a Magazine as aforesaid but that this Province hath been obliged to defray all publiq Charges arising for the Support of Government by way of an equall Assessment upon the Inhabitants thereof the severall Provisoes in the afore recited Act to the Contrary Notwithstanding And whereas also his said Lordship the aforesaid Moyety of two shillings p. 112 per Hogshead under pretext of Maintaining a Magazine as aforesaid (untill the time of their late Majestys King William and Queen Mary taking this Province under their imediate protection) did Convert to his own use to the Impoverishing of

the Country and Defraud of the Publiq and being incapacitated
of complying with what by the said Act for the said Moyety
of two shillings per hogshead is required

Be it therefore enacted by the Queens most excellent Majesty
by and with the Advice and Consent of her Majestys Governour Councill and Assembly of this Province And the
Authority of the same that the said one Shilling per hogshead
for the Defraying the Charges of Government aforesaid as
well for such Shipps or Vessells as have already Clear'd before
the making of this Act as for such remaining in this Province
be rais'd levyed Collectd and payd unto our Sovereign Lady
the Queens most excellent Majesty her heires and Successors
for the Support of her Government for the time being in and
over this her Majesty's Province aforesaid And the Territorys
to the same belonging for every hogshead and quantity of an
hogshead of Tobacco which hath been for and during the time
af$^d$ or which hereafter shall be at any time Shipp'd in any
Shipp or Vessell to be exported out of this Province or any
the Territorys Islands Ports Rivers Creeks or Places thereunto
belonging as aforesaid.

And be it further enacted by the Authority aforesaid by and
with the Advice and Consent aforesaid that the said Duty and
Imposition shall be from time to time paid and Satisfyed by the
Master or Masters of every such Shipp or Vessell respectively
in which any such Tobacco shall be exported upon his or their
Clearing or taking out his or their Dispatch or Dispatches for
every such respective Shipp or Vessell and before the Departure of such Shipp or Vessell coming into this Province shall
at their first Arrivall here and before their loading on board
any goods or Comoditys of the Growth production or Manufacture of this province give good and Sufficient Security to
his Excellency or to the Officer thereunto especially appointed
for the payment of the said Duty or Imposition accordingly.

Provided allways and it is the true Intent and Meaning
hereof that this Act nor anything herein contain'd shall be
Adjudged Construed reputed or taken (any thing herein
express'd to the Contrary Notwithstanding) to disanull or
make void his Lordships Right to the other Moyety of the
said Two Shill per Hogshead to be paid in Consideration of
his rents and Alienation money in Tobacco at two pence per
pound during the term of his Naturall life (but that the same
be kept and hereby preserved to his Lordship in as full and
ample manner as by the said Law is expressed or intended)
or in the least to discharge his Lordship of Receiving the Rents
aforesaid at two pence per pound as by the said Act is injoyn'd
during also the terme of his Naturall life nor to discharge his
Lordship from Accounting for the Arrears of the one Shilling

Lib. L. L.
No. 64.

per hogshead for Supporting the Government and providing Arms and Ammunition but that He be obliged to all the aforesaid Matters and Things as fully and strongly as if the said Law were in full force.

And be it further enacted by the Authority aforesaid That every Master of a Ship or Vessell as aforesaid at the time of his Clearing shall upon oath declare the Quality and Quantity of his loading And that the Navall Officer by the Governour aforesaid appointed for the time being shall and is hereby Impowered to Administer the said Oath and in Case the said Master shall refuse the said oath or upon Suspicion of having goods on board for which he hath not clear'd It shall be lawfull for the said Navall Officer to enter on board any such Shipp or Vessell and the same to search for any such goods as aforesaid any thing in this Act before mencon'd notwithstanding.

<table>
<tr><td>September 21<sup>st</sup> 1704</td><td>Sept<sup>r</sup> 21<sup>st</sup> 1704</td></tr>
</table>

|  |  |
|---|---|
| September 21$^{st}$ 1704 | Sept$^r$ 21$^{st}$ 1704 |
| Read and assented to | Read and Assented to by her |
| by the house of Delegates | Majestys honourable Councill |
| W Taylard Clk h.D. | W Bladen Cl Concil. |

Maryland October 3$^d$ 1704

On the behalf of her Majesty &c. I will this be a Law

Jo. Seymour

Vide this Act recorded afterwards in folio 409.

p. 114 An Act prohibitting the Importation of Bread Beer fflower Malt Wheat other English or Indian Grain or Meale Horses Mares Colts or ffillys or Tobacco from Pensilvania & the Territorys thereto belonging.

Be it Enacted by the Queens most excellent Majesty by and with the Advice and Consent of her Majestys Governour Councill and Assembly of this Province and the Authority of the same that from and after the end of this Sessions of Assembly it shall not be lawfull for any person or persons whatsoever to import or Cause to be imported from the Province of Pensilvania or the Territorys thereto belonging or from any other Plantation or Province or Colony on this Continent in America into any part of this province by land or by water any Quantity or Quantitys of Bread beer fflower Malt Wheat or other English or Indian Grain or Meale Horse or Horses Mare or Mares nor any Colt ffilly or Tobacco. (Except Tobacco from Virginia to this place for loading Shipps) On pain and

Penalty that whosoever shall import contrary to this Act any Lib. L. L. the Things aforesaid shall loose and forfeitt the same One half No. 64. to her Majesty her beires and Successors for the Support of the Government of this province the other half to him or them that shall Seize or give Information of the same whereby they may be seized.

And be it further Enacted by the Authority aforesaid by and with the Advice and Consent aforesaid that every Justice of peace in this Province in proper County and every Navall Officer and Collector in or out of his District and every Constable or Constables in his or their Severall and respective Hundred and every Church Warden or Church Wardens in his or their severall and respective Parishes by vertue of their Offices and this Act may lawfully Seize in the Day time such goods and things as they find imported contrary to this Act And if any Private person being none of the Officers aforesaid shall discover any such Goods or things so unlawfully imported he shall inform the next Justice of the peace who is hereby injoyn'd and Com̄anded under the penalty of one Thousand p. 115 pounds of Tobacco to be forfeited to the use aforesaid to direct a precept to the next Constable or Constables of such Hundred where such things are Supposed to be Conceald thereby Com̄andıng at the request of such Informer to make Search for such things as aforesaid unlawfully imported where such Informer shall direct And the same having found to seize and secure for the use of her Majesty and Informer aforesaid And the same to keep for tenn days In which Time if the Owner thereof or person in whose possession found do not cause the same to be replevin'd and find sufficient Securitys to return the Goods If it be found they were unlawfully imported then the Officer that seized them shall deliver the said Goods to the Sheriff who is hereby Injoynd to make sale of them for the use of her Majesty and the Informer or Seizer.

And be it further enacted by the Authority aforesaid that the Onus probandi shall be on the part of him that Causes the same to be replevin'd to make it appear in any Court of Record in this Province that such things seized as aforesaid are not lyable to seizure as aforesaid which if he. do he shall be Quitt and carry his Goods away But if he do not the Seizer shall have Judgment to have the Goods and things so by him Seized return'd One half thereof to be delivered to the Informer and the other half to remain in the Custody of the Sheriff for the Queens use This Act to endure for three Years or to the end of the next Generall Assembly which shall first happen.

| September 23ᵈ 1704 | September 26ᵗʰ 1704 |
|---|---|
| Read and Assented to by the House of Delegates W Taylard Clk hD | Read and assented to by her Majestys honourable Council W Bladen Cl Concil. |

Maryland October 3ᵈ 1704
On behalf of her Majesty &c. I will this be a Law.
Jo. Seymour

p. 116 An Act for Limitation of Certain Actions for avoiding suites at Law.

Forasmuch as Nothing can be more Essentiall to the Peace and Tranquillity of this Province than the Quietting the Estates of the Inhabitants thereof and for the Effecting of which no better Measures can be taken than a Limitation of Time for the Comencing such Accons as in the Severall and respective Courts within this Province are brought from the time of the Cause of such Accon accruing

Be it Enacted by the Queens most excellent Majesty by and with the Advice and Consent of her Majestys Governour Councill and Assembly of this Province and the Authority of the same that all Actions of Trespass Quare Clausum fregit All accons of Trespass Detinue such over or Replevin for taking away goods or Chattells All Accons of Account Con-tract Debt Book or upon the Case other than such Accounts as Concern the Trade of Merchandize between Merchant and Merchant their ffactors & servants which are not Residents within this Province All Actions of Debt for lending or Con-tract without Specialty all Actions of Debt for Arrearages of Rents all Accons of Assault Menaces Battery Wounding and Imprisonment or any of them shall be sued or brought by any person or persons within this province at any Time after the end of this present Generall Assembly shall be Comenced or sued within the time and Limitation hereafter expressd and not after (that is to say) The said Accons of Accounts And the said Accons for Debt Detinue and Replevin for Goods and Chattells and the said Accons for trespass Quare Clausum fregitt within three years ensuing the Cause of such Action and not after and the said Actions on the Case for words and accons of Trespass of Assault Battery wounding and Impris-onment or any of them within one year from the time of the Cause of such Accon accruing and not after.

And be it further Enacted by the Authority aforesaid that if any person Intituled to any the Accon or Accons aforesaid shall be at the time of any such Cause of Accon accruing within the age of one and twenty years ffeme: Covert non Compos Mentis Imprison'd or beyond the seas that then such person or persons shall be at liberty to bring the same Accon or Actions within the time as is before limitted after their coming to or being of full age sound Memory at large or return'd from beyond seas as other persons having no such Impediment might or should have done.

And fforasmuch as divers disputes formerly arose whether Persons absenting the Province or wandring from County to County untill the time by the late Act for the reasons and purposes aforesaid Limitted and allowed were expired should have any benefitt thereby and different Iudgments given thereon in the severall and respective Countys within this Province for that the said Act was altogether silent.

Be it therefore Enacted by the Authority aforesaid that from and after the Publication hereof No person or persons whatsoever absenting themselves out of this Province or that shall remove from County to County after any Debt Contracted whereby the Creditor or Creditors may be at an uncertainty of finding out the said person or persons or his or their Effects shall have any benefit by the Limitation or Restriction in this Act Specifyed.

Provided allways that it is the true Intent and Meaning hereof that this Act or Anything herein Contain'd shall not be Construed Reputed or taken to prejudice or Debarr any person removing himself or ffamily from one County to another for his Conveniency or any person leaving this Province for the time and terme in this Act Limitted from the benefitt thereof he leaving Effects Sufficient and known for the payment of his Just Debts in the hands of Some person or persons who will assume the payment thereof to his Creditors any thing in this Act contain'd to the Contrary hereof in any wise notwithstanding.

And be it further Enacted by the Authority aforesaid by and with the Advice and Consent aforesaid that no bill Bond Judgment Recognizance Statute Merchant & of the Staple or other Specialty whatsoever shall be good & pleadable or admitted in Evidence against any person or persons of this Province after the Principall Debtor and Creditor have been both dead twelve years or the Debt or thing in Accon above twelve years Standing.

September 20<sup>th</sup> 1704    September 21<sup>st</sup> 1704

Read and Assented to by the    Read and Assented to by her
house of Dellegates p<sup>r</sup> Ord<sup>r</sup>    Majestys hon<sup>ble</sup> Councill
W Taylard Cl h.D.    W Bladen Cl Concil.

Maryland Octob. 3ᵈ 1704

On behalf of her Majesty &c I will this be a Law

Jo : Seymour

p. 118 An Act for the more Speedy Conveying of Publiq Letters and Pacquetts of this Province and Defraying the Charge thereof.

Forasmuch as severall of the Inhabitants of this Province have been formerly Subject to great and Manifest Inconveniencys by reason of pressing of Horses under pretext of Carrying and Conveying of Publiq Letters and Pacquetts for prevention whereof and that due Care may be taken for the future that all Publiq Letters and Pacquetts relating to her Majesty or the Publiq Service of this Province be securely and expeditiously Conveyed according to their Directions the Delegates of this Present Generall Assembly do pray that it may be Enacted and

Be it enacted by the Queens most Excellent Majesty by and with the Advice and Consent of her Majestys Governour Councill and Assembly of this Province and the Authority of the same. That the Sheriff of each respective County is hereby injoyn'd and Commanded to take care of all publiq Letters and Pacquetts and expeditiously to convey them according to their Directions to the next Sheriff or Undersheriff of the Adjacent County. And for the Encouragement of the Severall and respective Sheriffs and their Diligence in their Conveying such Publiq Letters and Pacquetts That they may be allowed the severall Summs hereafter exprest to be laid in the publiq Levy of this Province viz. To the Sheriff of Ann Arundell County—fifteen hundred pounds of Tobacco who is hereby obliged to Convey all such Letters and pacquetts as are directed and must go over to the Eastern Shore to Kent Island and there to be Delivered to the Sheriff of Talbot County or his Deputy To the Sheriff of Talbot County fifteen hundred pounds of Tobacco who is hereby also obliged to Convey all such Letters and Pacquetts as are directed to the Port of Annapolis to the said port To the Sheriff of Kent County eight hundred pounds of Tobacco who is also hereby obliged to Convey all such Letters and Pacquetts as are directed to the Port of Annapolis to Kent Island and deliver them to the Sheriff or p. 119 Undersheriff of Talbot County Except he convey them a more ready and expeditious Way to Annapolis who is also hereby obliged to Convey all such Letters and Pacquetts to the Port of Annapolis as aforesaid To the Sheriff of Cecill County one thousand pounds of Tobacco who is allso Obliged to convey all such Letters and Pacquetts as are directed to the North

Lib. L. L.
No. 64.

ward to the Town of Newcastle upon Delaware To the Sheriff of Dorchester County Eight hundred pounds of Tobacco To the Sheriff of Sumersett County five hundred pounds of Tobacco To the Sheriff of Calvert County Eight hundred pounds of Tobacco To the Sheriff of Prince Georges County one Thousand pounds of Tobacco To the Sheriff of Saint Marys County Eight hundred pounds of Tobacco To the Sheriff of Charles County one thousand pounds of Tobacco To the Sheriff of Baltemore County eight hundred pounds of Tobacco Which said Severall and respective Sums of Tobacco Shall be annually allow'd and paid to the Sheriffs as aforesaid in Consideration whereof the Sheriffs of the Said Severall and respective Countys shall defray all such Charges as shall accrue by reason of Conveying any such Letters or Pacquetts Any former Law Usage or Custom to the contrary Notwithstanding.

And be it further enacted by the Authority aforesaid that any Sheriff Under Sheriff or Deputy that shall neglect or Delay the Speedy Conveying of any such Letters or Pacquetts shall forfeit and pay to her Sacred Majesty for every Such Offence the Sume of five hundred pounds of Tobacco One half to the Informer or him or them that will Sue for the same and the other half to be imploy'd for the Defraying the County Charge where any such neglect shall happen, to be recovered in any of her Majestys Courts of Record within this Province by Accon of Debt wherein no Essoyn proteccon or wager of Law to be allowed

And be it further Enacted by the Authority aforesaid that all such Publick Letters and pacquetts be indorst for her Majestys Service and with the persons name that send them. And if any person or persons whatsoever shall at any time after the publication of this Act presume to Endorse any Letter or Letters pacquett or pacquetts so as aforesaid which are not for the Publiq Service He or they shall forfeit and pay for such Offence five hundred pounds of Tobacco to be recovered in Manner aforesaid This Act to endure for three years or to the end of the next Session of Assembly which shall first happen. p. 120

|  |  |
|---|---|
| September 23<sup>rd</sup> 1704 | September 26 : 1704 |
| Read and Assented to by the house of Dellegates<br>W Taylard Clk. h.D. | Read and assented to by her Majestys honourable Councill<br>W Bladen Cl. Concil. |

Maryland October 3<sup>d</sup> 1704
On behalf of her Majesty &c. I will this be a Law.

Jo.: Seymour

An Act for the Recording of all the Acts of Assembly of this Province in the Secretarys Office as also Transmitting of the Journall of the house of Delegates into the said Office.

Be it Enacted by the Queens most excellent Majesty by and with the Advice and Consent of her Majestys Governour Councill and Assembly of this Province and the Authority of the same that all the Act of Assembly which shall be enacted this present Sessions and all the Succeeding Sessions of Assembly shall within tenn Days after the end of each Sessions be transmitted into the Secretarys Office And the Secretary for the time being shall upon receipt of the said Acts into his Office cause the said Acts to be entred upon Record in a very fair legible hand and in a good Substantiall book bound with leather or parchment Cover with large Margents and also Alphabett the said book in good order and Affix the Seale of his Office thereto And the Clerk or Clerks that do record the said Acts shall make oath before the Governour of this Province for the time being or before one of her Majestys Councill or two of the Justices of the Provincial Court that he or they have carefully examin'd the Record of the said Acts by the p. 121 Originall Acts which have past the great Seale all which shall be done within Six Months Successively after the end of each Session.

And in Case the Secretary shall not pursue the Directions of this Act but shall make default he shall forfeit the summe of Tenn thousand pounds of Tobacco for every such neglect The one half thereof to her Majesty for the Support of the Government of this Province and the other half to him that will sue for the same to be recovered in any Court of Record within this Province by the Bill Plaint or Information wherein no Essoyn protection or Wager of Law to be allowed.

And be it Enacted by the Authority aforesaid that the Clerk of the house of Delegates for the time being shall transcribe the Journall of the said house into a fair book and in a good fair and legible Character within two Months after the end of each Sessions and shall transmitt the same so transcribed into the Secretarys Office there to remain And the Secretary is required by this Act to receive the same accordingly And the Clerk making default shall forfeit five hundred pounds of Tobacco for every Offence the one half to her Majesty for Support of the Government of this Province and the other half to him that will sue for the same.

And be it enacted by the Authority aforesaid by and with the Advice and Consent aforesaid that the Secretary shall be allowed for recording the said Acts in the publiq Levy so much as the Generall Assembly shall think the said Secretary shall reasonably deserve.

September 26<sup>th</sup> 1704     September 26<sup>th</sup> 1704   
Read and Assented to by     Read and Assented to by her
the house of Delegates     Majestys hon<sup>ble</sup> Councill
W Taylard Clk h.D.     W Bladen Cl. Concil.

Maryland October 3<sup>d</sup> 1704
On behalf of her Majesty &c. I will this be a Law.

Jo : Seymour

An Act for the punishment of Blasphemy Prophane Swearing p. 122
and Cursing

Be it Enacted by the Queens most excellent Majesty by and
with the Advice and Consent of her Majestys Governour
Councill and Assembly of this Province and by the Authority
of the same that from and after the end of this present
Sessions of Assembly if any person or persons whatsoever
within this Province shall blaspheme God (that is to say) Curse
him or deny Our Saviour Jesus Christ to be the Son of God
or shall deny the holy Trinity The ffather Son and holy Ghost
or the Godhead of any of the three persons or the Unity of
the Godhead or shall utter any Prophane words concerning the
holy Trinity or any of the persons thereof for his her or their
first Offence shall be bored through his her or their Tongue
and fined the Sume of twenty pounds Sterling to her Majesty
to be applyd to the defraying of the Charge of the County
where such Offence shall be comitted to be levyed upon his
her or their goods or Chattells Lands or Tenements And if
Such Offender or Offenders shall not have any Goods or
Chattells Lands or Tenements whereby the said ffine may be
levyed as before is directed then such Offender or Offenders
shall Suffer six Months Imprisonment of his her or their bodys
without Baile or Mainprize. And for every second Offence
whereof such Offender or Offenders shall be legally convict he
she or they shall be Stigmatized by burning in the forehead
with the Letter B. And be fin'd by the Court where he she or
they shall be Convicted forty pounds Sterl to the Queens
Majesty to be Applyd to the uses aforesaid to be levyed as
aforesaid And if such Offender or Offenders shall not have
any Goods or Chattells Lands or Tenements whereby the said
ffine may be levyed as before is directed then such Offender p. 123
or Offenders shall suffer Imprisonment of his her or their
bodys for the Space of one whole year from the Time of his
her or their Conviction or Convictions without Baile or Mainprize And for every third offence whereof Such Offender or
Offenders shall be legally Convict he she or they so offending

21

Llb. L. L.
No. 64.

shall be adjudged ffelons and Shall Suffer pains of Death as ffellons without any Benefitt of Clergy.

And be it Enacted by the Authority Advice and Consent aforesaid that any Person or Persons whatsoever that shall after the end of this Sessions of Assembly prophane Swear or Curse either in the presence or hearing of any Justice of the peace or other head Officer or that shall be Convict thereof by the oath of one Witness or by his own Confession before any one Justice of the peace or other head Officer shall forfeitt and pay for Such Offence the Sume of five shillings and in Case of Non payment thereof the Justice of peace before whom Such Conviction shall be shall make his Warrant to the next Constable to levy the same by distress and sale of the Offenders Goods rendring to him the Overplus and such Constable shall render Account thereof to the County Justices at the time of laying the County Levy And in Case the Constable shall refuse to obey and Execute the Comand or Warrant of any Justice of the Peace or Head Officer as aforesaid then such Constable shall forfeitt and pay the Sume of five Shillings to be levyed as aforesaid to the use aforesaid. And in Case the Severall Offenders aforesaid shall not have wherewith to pay the said ffines then such person or persons shall be punish'd by setting in the Stocks for the Space of one hour or Whipping.—

And Be it further Enacted by the Authority aforesaid by and with the Advice and Consent aforesaid that if any person or persons shall prophanely Swear or Curse in any Court house during the sitting of any Court and shall be thereof Convict informe aforesaid he she or they so offending shall imediately

p. 124 forfeit and pay the Sume of tenn shillings to be levyed as aforesaid to the use aforesaid or shall be sett in the Stocks two hours.

Provided allways that noe person shall be prosecuted upon this Act for Prophane Cursing and Swearing unless the same be proved and prosecuted within tenn days after the Offence Comitted.

And be it Enacted by the Authority aforesaid by and with the Advice and Consent aforesaid that every Justice of the peace or Head Officer before whom such Conviction of Swearing and Cursing shall happen to be shall receive the forfeitures aforesaid and shall give Account thereof at the time of the laying of Each County Levy.

|  |  |
|---|---|
| .  September 30<sup>th</sup> 1704 | September 30<sup>th</sup> 1704 |
| Read and Assented to | Read and Assented to by her |
| by the house of Delegates. | Majestys hon<sup>ble</sup> Councill |
| W Taylard Cl hD. | W Bladen Cl Concil |

Maryland October 3ᵈ 1704

On behalf of her Maᵗʸ &c I will this be a Law

Jo : Seymour

### An Act against Ingrossers & Regraters

Forasmuch as the Offences of fforestalling Ingrossing and Regrating are found Mischeivous and prejudicial to the Inhabitants of this Province.

Be it Enacted by the Queens most excellent Majesty by and with the Advice and Consent of her Majestys Governour Councill and Assembly of this Province and the Authority of p. 125 the same that whatsoever person or persons that from and after the publication hereof shall Ingross or gett into his her or their hands or Possession by buying Contracting or promise taking within this Province any goods or Merchandizes whatsoever or Servants to the Intent to sell the same again within the space of six months and the same or any part thereof shall within that time sell again for ready Tobacco or for Tobacco to be paid the shipping happening at the time of such first Sale or for Tobacco to be Shipp'd for payment or securing the payment of any bill or bills of Exchange or for ready mony or bills of Exchange to be drawn for payment of the said Goods Merchandizes or Servants with Intent to avoid the penalty by this Act hereafter provided and imposed or the said Goods Merchandizes or Servants shall transport out of this Province shall be accepted reputed and taken for an unlawfull Ingrosser and Regrater and shall Suffer such pains penaltys and forfeitures as are hereafter expressd Any Law Statute Usage or Custom to the Contrary thereof in any wise notwithstanding.

And be it enacted by the Authority aforesaid that if any person or persons from and after the publication hereof offend in any of the things before recited and being thereof duly convicted by Confession of the party or the oaths of two Witnesses before the Justices of the Provincial Court or the Justices of the County Courts for the time being where the Offences were Comitted shall for his her or their first Offence have or suffer Imprisonment for the Space of two Months without bayle or Mainprize And shall also loose and forfeit the value of the goods Merchandizes or Servants so by him or them bought or had. And if any person or persons lawfully convicted as aforesaid of or for the second offence Every Such person or persons so offending shall have and Suffer for his or their second Offence Imprisonment for the Space of one half year without Bayle or Mainprize and shall loose double the value of all the Goods Merchandizes or Servants so by him or them bought or had as aforesaid.

And be it further enacted by the Authority aforesaid that if any person or persons being lawfully Convicted as aforesaid of or for the second offence and shall again offend the third time and be thereof lawfully convicted that then every person for the third Offence shall be sett in the Pillary in the City Town or in the full County where he shall then Inhabitt and dwell and loose and forfeit all the goods and Chattells he or they have to their own use And also be Comitted to prison there to remain during the term of one whole year. The one Moyety of all which fforfeitures to be to our Sovereign Lady the Queen her heires and Successors for the Support of the Government of this Province and the other Moyety thereof to the Informer or him or them that shall sue for the same by Action of Debt bill plaint or Information in any Court of Record within this province wherein no Essoyn proteccon or Wager of Law to be allowed.

Provided that this Act nor any thing therein Contain'd shall not debarr or be Construed to debarr or hinder any person or persons Whatsoever within this Province by or out of any goods or Merchandizes by him or them so bought or purchas'd as aforesaid to Satisfy and pay unto any workman or Servant the hire or wages of him or them due for any work or Service whatsoever.

|  |  |
|---|---|
| September 20<sup>th</sup> 1704 | September 21<sup>st</sup> 1704 |

September 20<sup>th</sup> 1704               September 21<sup>st</sup> 1704
Read and Assented to               Read and Assented by her
by the House of Delegates          Majestys hon<sup>ble</sup> Councill
          W Taylard Cl hD               W Bladen Cl Concil.


Maryland October 3<sup>d</sup> 1704.
On the behalf of her Ma<sup>ty</sup> &c I will this be a Law.
Jo: Seymour

p. 127 An Act for stay of execution after the tenth of May yearly

Whereas many of the Inhabitants of this Province are and have been exceedingly grieved and burthen'd by executions laid upon them for Tobacco in Summer time when 'tis not possible for them to procure Tobacco for the payment and Satisfaction of their Creditors by means whereof they are oftentimes kept in prison a long time and thereby disabled from making and tending their Cropps to the great prejudice if not ruine of many the Inhabitants of this Province being thereby left destitute of any Means to Satisfy their Creditors for prevention whereof for the future

Be it enacted by the Queens most excellent Majesty by and with the Advice and Consent of her Majestys Governour

Councill and Assembly of this Province and the Authority Lib. L. L. of the same that after the tenth day of May in any Year no No. 64. Execution shall issue out of any Court of this Province against the body or Goods of any Person or Persons Inhabitting within this Province till the tenth day of November next or untill the tenth day of November in any year ensuing for any Debt or Debts or upon any Accon Judgment or Judgments sued had or recovered against the Inhabitants of or within this Province in the Provincial or any County Courts of this Province for any Cause Matter or thing whatsoever Provided such person or persons against whom any such Judgment is obtain'd together with two other persons such as the Justices shall approve of come before one Justice or more of the Provincial Court or two Justices or more of the Respective County Courts where such Judgment is obtain'd as aforesaid and shall confess Judgment for his Debt and Costs of Suite adjudged with stay of execution till the tenth day of November next for this present year or untill the tenth day of November in any other year next following and thereof procure Certificate under the hand of the same Justice or Justices before whom such Judgment shall be Confessd and such Certificate shall be a Sufficient Supersedeas to the Sheriff to forbear serving execution upon the body or Goods of the person so obtaining such Certificate. And if the party be taken in execution before such Certificate be produced then such Certificate being obtain'd afterwards as aforesaid shall be a sufficient Supersedeas to the Sheriff to Release of such p. 128 person out of prison upon that Execution the party paying or giving Security to such Sheriff for his due ffees for that Imprisonment And the Justice or Justices before whom such Judgment shall be confessed as aforesaid shall return the Judgment so confessd to the Clerk of the respective Court where the first Judgment was obtain'd to be entred upon Record for which entry the Clerk shall receive as a ffee five pounds of Tobacco and no more And that after the said tenth day of November it shall be lawfull to take out Execution upon the Judgment confessd as aforesaid without any Scire facias or any other delay against either the principall or the Security or all or either of them for such Judgment so confess'd as aforesaid any Law usage or Custom to the Contrary in any wise notwithstanding

September 23ᵈ 1704      September 26ᵗʰ 1704

Read and assented to by the    Read and assented to by her
house of Delegates           Maᵗʸˢ honᵇˡᵉ Councill
W Taylard Clk hD          W Bladen Cl Concil.

Maryland Ctob
On behalf of her Majesty &c I

An Act for killing of Wolve an
Be it Enacted by the Quees m
with the Advice and Consot
Councill and Assembly of th. Pr
the same that every person hat
wolf to any of the Justices & pe

Bill shall be allo'ed from the County where any such Crows
were killed the 3ume of Six pounds of Tobacco And the
Justice of peace before whom such Crows head shall be
brought shall Cuse the Bill to be Cutt of to prevent the
deceit of twice o1oftener paying therefore And shall give to
the person bring:g the same a Receipt therefore which Receipt shall be Sfficient Authority for the person Claiming
thereby to demad at the Next Levy Court so much Tobacco
as the Crows hads amount to at the rate aforesaid to be
rais'd levyed an( paid as aforesaid. This Act to continue
for and during te term of two whole years and to the end
of the next Sesion of Assembly which shall happen thereafter.

September o^th 1704     September 21^st 1704     p. 130
Read and Assentd to by the     Read and assented to by her
house of Dlegates     Ma^tys hon^ble Councill
W Tajard Cl hD.     W Bladen Cl Concil.

Maryland October 3^d 1704
On behalf of hr Majesty &c I will this be a Law
Jo. Seymour

An Act for Secuing Merchants and others Tobacco after they
have receivedt.

Be it Enacted y the Queens most excellent Majesty by and
with the Advic and Consent of her Majestys Governour
Councill and Asembly of this province and the Authority of
the same that fom and after the publication hereof every
House Keeper nd Inhabitant within this Province having a
Plantation wheron he maketh or Causeth to be made any
Tobacco shall bild and erect or otherwise fitt up and make
ready a good tijht house with a good Door Lock and Key
upon every planition where such Tobacco is made as aforesaid and Sufficint to Contain the Tobacco made on every
plantation.

And be it furter Enacted by the Authority aforesaid that
every Inhabitantbr House Keeper as aforesaid having a Plantation whereon h maketh or Causeth to be made any Tobacco
as aforesaid and nat shall pay away and dispose of any Tobacco
to any MerchantMaster of Shipp Saylor or any other person
whatsoever shallnotwithstanding such disposure or payment
secure and kee the said Tobacco as he would do his own
proper Goods fr and during the space of one whole year
Comencing fromthe time the Tobacco was received as aforesaid And if anyTobacco so received as aforesaid for want of

Maryland October 3ᵈ 1704

On behalf of her Majesty &c I will this be a Law.

Joᵗ Seymour

### An Act for killing of Wolves and Crows

Be it Enacted by the Queens most excellent Majesty by and with the Advice and Consent of her Majestys Governour Councill and Assembly of this Province And the Authority of the same that every person that shall bring the head of a wolf to any of the Justices of peace in any County within this Province shall be allowed two hundred pounds of Tobacco from the County where the Wolf shall be Killed And that such Justice of peace to whom the wolves head shall be brought shall Cutt out or Cause to be Cutt out the Tongue p. 129 and Cutt or Cause to be Cutt off the Ears of such Wolves head to prevent the deceit of twice or oftner paying for the same.

And be it further Enacted by the Authority Advice and Consent aforesaid that it shall and may be lawfull to and for the severall Justices of the severall and respective Countys within this Province and they are hereby Authorized Impowered and required yearly and every year at the time of laying the County levy to raise and assess by an equall assessment upon the Taxables of the said County such Sum or Sums of Tobacco as to the Justices of the severall and respective Countys shall seem meet and Convenient and such sums of Tobacco raised as aforesaid shall lay out and dispose of for the purchasing of Duffells or Matchcoates and when the same are purchasd shall deliver to such and so many persons residing Convenient to the Indians as the Justices aforesaid shall think fitt who shall render an Account to the said Justices at the next laying of the Levy how such Matchcoats delivered him or them have been disposed of & what part thereof remains in his her or their possession or hands.

And be it further Enacted by the Authority aforesaid that such person or persons having such matchcoats delivered as aforesaid be and are hereby required to deliver to any Indian or Indians for every Woolves head not having been paid for before One Matchcoat containing two yards of Duffells and give a true Account of the same at the next Levy Court as aforesaid to the Justices aforesaid and shall mark such woolves heads as aforesaid to prevent deceit as aforesaid.

And be it further Enacted by the Authority Advice and Consent aforesaid that every person that shall bring or Cause to be brought to any of the Justices of the peace in any County within this Province the head of a Crow with a perfect

Bill shall be allowed from the County where any such Crows Lib. L. L.
were killed the Sume of Six pounds of Tobacco And the No. 64.
Justice of peace before whom such Crows head shall be
brought shall Cause the Bill to be Cutt of to prevent the
deceit of twice or oftener paying therefore And shall give to
the person bringing the same a Receipt therefore which Receipt shall be Sufficient Authority for the person Claiming
thereby to demand at the Next Levy Court so much Tobacco
as the Crows heads amount to at the rate aforesaid to be
rais'd levyed and paid as aforesaid. This Act to continue
for and during the term of two whole years and to the end
of the next Session of Assembly which shall happen thereafter.

<table>
<tr><td>September 20<sup>th</sup> 1704</td><td>September 21<sup>st</sup> 1704</td><td>p. 130</td></tr>
</table>

|  |  |
|---|---|
| September 20<sup>th</sup> 1704 | September 21<sup>st</sup> 1704 |
| Read and Assented to by the | Read and assented to by her |
| house of Delegates | Ma<sup>tys</sup> hon<sup>ble</sup> Councill |
| W Taylard Cl hD. | W Bladen Cl Concil. |

Maryland October 3<sup>d</sup> 1704

On behalf of her Majesty &c I will this be a Law

J<sub>o.</sub> Seymour

An Act for Securing Merchants and others Tobacco after they
have received it.

Be it Enacted by the Queens most excellent Majesty by and
with the Advice and Consent of her Majestys Governour
Councill and Assembly of this province and the Authority of
the same that from and after the publication hereof every
House Keeper and Inhabitant within this Province having a
Plantation whereon he maketh or Causeth to be made any
Tobacco shall build and erect or otherwise fitt up and make
ready a good tight house with a good Door Lock and Key
upon every plantation where such Tobacco is made as aforesaid and Sufficient to Contain the Tobacco made on every
plantation.

And be it further Enacted by the Authority aforesaid that
every Inhabitant or House Keeper as aforesaid having a Plantation whereon he maketh or Causeth to be made any Tobacco
as aforesaid and that shall pay away and dispose of any Tobacco
to any Merchant Master of Shipp Saylor or any other person
whatsoever shall notwithstanding such disposure or payment
secure and keep the said Tobacco as he would do his own
proper Goods for and during the space of one whole year
Comencing from the time the Tobacco was received as aforesaid And if any Tobacco so received as aforesaid for want of

Lib. L. L.  such house as aforesaid should be damnifyed or stole the
No. 64.  person neglecting to provide such house shall make Satisfaction to the party that received the same.

p. 131    Provided allways that nothing in this Act contain'd shall be Construed Meant & intended to make any Inhabitant or House Keeper lyable to any Damage which shall or may happen to any Tobacco left with him to keep secure through any other Casualty whatsoever.

And be it Enacted by the Authority aforesaid by and with the Advice and Consent aforesaid that any person or persons whatsoever Merchants or others within this province that have at any time within twelve Months last past Received Markd or Naild or for the future shall receive Mark or Nail any Hogshead or Hogsheads of Tobacco within this Province of any person or persons Debtors within the same and which hath been paid and delivered to them for Satisfaction of their said Debts and Such merchants or others have upon receipt marking and nailing such hogshead or hogsheads of Tobacco delivered up their bills or other security to their respective Debtors of their said Debts or if the said Merchants or others have given releases or Discharges to their said Debtors of the said Debt And that before the said Merchant or others could remove the said Hogshead or Hogsheads of Tobacco from the said Debtors Tobacco houses if any Sheriff shall Come and seize such Tobacco so markd and naild as aforesaid that then and in every such Case if the party refuse to make and give to the said Creditors some other full Satisfaction for their said Debts It shall and may be lawfull for any two of her Majestys Justices of the respective Countys within this Province upon due proof thereof made before them of the said Debt and Sheriffs seizure as aforesaid And the party Debtor refusing to make that full Satisfaction to their Creditors for their said Debts at the said Creditors request to award him Execution with Costs such Costs not exceeding One hundred pounds of Tobacco against the body goods and Chattells of Such Debtor to be executed by the Sheriff for Satisfaction of the Creditors Just Debt and Costs as aforesaid in as full and ample Manner as if the Debt were recovered by due Course of Law.

| September 26th 1704 | September 26th 1704 |
|---|---|
| Read and Assented to by the house of Delegates | Read and Assented to by her Majestys honble Councill. |
| W Taylard Cl h.D. | W Bladen Cl. Concil. |

Maryland October 3d 1704

On behalf of her Majesty &c I will this be a Law.

Jo : Seymour

An Act for the taking Speciall bayle in the Severall Countys Lib. L. L. No. 64. p. 13. of this Province upon Accons and Suites depending in her Majestys Provincial Court.

For the Greater Ease and Benefitt of all persons inhabitting or residing within this Province in taking recognizances of Special bayle in all Accons & Suites depending or to be depending in her Majestys Prov¹ Court of this Province.

Be it Enacted by the Queens most excellent Majesty by and with the Advice and Consent of her Majestys Governour Councill and Assembly of this Province and the Authority of the same that when Speciall Bayle is required in the Provinciall Court by the Plaintiffs Attorny at the Calling over the Appearance Doggett And that the Court does Rule that Speciall bayle shall be given And the party against whom the rule is that he shall give Speciall Bayle be present The party Defendant shall then and there give Speciall bayle in open Court and shall be deem'd to be in the Custody of the Sheriff that arrested him in that Accon till he give Speciall bayle as aforesaid But if the said party Defendant be not able at the said provincial Court then and there to procure such Speciall bayle yet the said party shall be and remain in the Custody of the same Sheriff that arrested him and by him in Safe Custody kept and guarded and Carried back into the County where the Defendant was arrested and there in Safe Custody kept till he can procure such Speciall bayle But if such party against whom such Rule is made that Speciall Bayle shall be given be not present at the said Provinciall Court then the Sheriff of that County where the said party Defendant was arrested may and shall by vertue of such rule aforesaid for Speciall bayle to be given take the said party into his Custody again and him keep till he can procure Speciall bayle according to rule of Court.

And for the greater Ease of Making and taking Recognizances of such Speciall bayle it shall and may be lawfull for one of the Justices of the Provincial Court of this Province or president of the County Court to take and receive all and every such Recognizance or Recognizances of Bayle or bayles p. 133 as any person or persons shall be willing or desirous to acknowledge or make before him in his County in any Accon or suite depending or hereafter to be depending in the said Provincial Court which Recognizance shall be taken in such Manner and forme as followeth viz.

John Doe Plaintiff } You A. B. and C. D. and either of
against } you do undertake for the said Richard
Rich<sup>d</sup> Roe Defend<sup>t</sup> } Roe Defendant in          pounds of
Tobacco to be levyed on your and either of your Lands &

Tenements Goods & Chattells to the use of the said John Doe
the Plaintiff upon Condition that if the said John Doe do
obtain Judgment in an Accon of Debt or Trespass upon the
Case depending in the Provincial Court against the said
Richard Roe the Defendant that then the said Richard Roe
shall pay the Condemnation or deliver himself to the prison
of our Sovereign Lady the Queen or you will do it for him.
They acknowledge themselves to be Content therewith this
day of           before me.
    To the honourable Justices of the Provincial Court Which
said Recognizance of Bayle or Bayle prizes so taken as aforesaid shall be transmitted to the Justices of the said Provincial
Court sitting when and where such Action or suite shall be
depending. Which Recognizance or Recognizances of Bayle
prizes so taken as aforesaid the said Court shall receive upon
payment of such ffees as have been received for the taking of
Such Speciall bayle by the Officers of the said Court and shall
be of like force and effect as if the same were taken de bene
esse before the Justices of the Provinciall Court during their
sitting for taking of every such Recognizance or **Recogniz-**
ances of Bayle or Bayle prizes such Justice of the Provincial
Court or President of the County Court that shall take such
bayle shall receive only the Sume of five shill and no more.
    And be it further Enacted by the Authority aforesaid that
the Justices of the Provincial Court shall make such Rules and
orders for the Justifying of such bayles and making the same
absolute as to them shall seem Meet so as the Cognizor or
Cognizors of such Bayle or Bayles be not compelled to appear
in person in the Provincial Courts to Justify him or themselves.
p. 134     And it is hereby further Enacted by the Authority aforesaid
that such Justices of the Provincial or County Court before
whom any Recognizance of Bayle may happen to be taken
such Justice have and power is hereby given Him to examine
the Suretys upon oath touching the value of their respective
Estates if occasion shall require Any Law Usage Custom or
Practice Notwithstanding.

| September 26th 1704 | September 26th 1704 |
|---|---|
| Read and Assented to by | Read and assented to by her |
| the house of Delegates | Majestys honble Councill |
| W Taylard Clk hD. | W Bladen Cl Concil. |

Maryland October 3d 1704

On the behalf of her Majesty &c I will this be a Law.

Jo : Seymour

An Act ascertaining the Gauge of Tobacco Hogsheads.

Be it enacted by the Queens most excellent Majesty by and
with the Advice and Consent of her Majestys Governour
Councill and Assembly of this Province and the Authority of
the same that what person or persons soever shall make or
Cause or Suffer to be made for his use any Tobacco hogshead
or Hogsheads which shall exceed forty Eight Inches in length
of the stave and thirty two Inches in the head to be measur'd
or shall make or cause or Suffer to be made for his own use
any Tobacco Hogshead or Hogsheads under the size of forty
six inches in length and thirty inches in the head and the
same hogsheads or any of them shall pack full of Tobacco
shall forfeit and pay the sume of one hundred pounds of Tobacco Of which one half to her Majesty her heires and Successors for the Support of the Government of this Province
and the other half to him or them that complaine of the same
and Cause the same to be proved and such Complaint shall
be made to one or more Justice or Justices of the peace next p. 135
adjoyning who upon such Complaint shall issue out a warrant to the Constable of the Hundred to bring before him or
them the person or persons ag^t whom such Complaint is
made and the Witnesses which the Complainant shall name
which Justice or Justices shall have full authority by vertue
of this Act to hear and Determine the matter and if the
Complainant shall prove his Complaint before the Justice or
Justices aforesaid by his own oath & the oath of one Sufficient Evidence beside or Confession of the party the said
Justice or Justices of peace shall make out warrant to the
Sheriff to levy the same by Distress and sale of the Goods
and Chattells of the party having so offended and to pay the
Moyety to the said Complainant as aforesaid and the other
Moyety for the Queens use to Certify to her receiver Generall
or the Governour for the time being.

And if any Person or persons as aforesaid shall pack or
Cause or Suffer to be packt full with Tobacco any Green or
not well Season'd Tobacco Hogshead or Hogsheads and the
same pay away and be thereof Convict in manner aforesaid
He or they shall forfeit for every Hogshead or Hogsheads so
packt and paid away as aforesaid the sume of one hundred
pounds of Tobacco as aforesaid to the uses aforesaid to be
recovered as aforesaid.

And be it further enacted that if any person or persons
shall after the tenth day of December next ensuing pay or
tender to pay any packt Hogshead of Tobacco whereof the
full weight of the empty Hogshead or the full weight within
five pounds over or under is not Cutt and markt on the Bulge

of the Casq and be thereof Convict in manner aforesaid he or they so convict as aforesaid shall forfeit for every Hogshead or Hogsheads not having the weight sett thereon as aforesaid the Sume of one hundred pounds of Tobacco as aforesaid to the uses aforesaid to be recovered as aforesaid.

And for the better ascertaining what Tare shall be allowed upon Tobacco Hogsheads

Be it Enacted that the Receiver of any Hogshead of Tobacco shall pay and allow to the Owner or Owners thereof for each Hogshead received the Sume of forty pounds of Tobacco deducting the same out of the Gross weight of each hogshead markt on the bulge and no more Any other Act to the Contrary notwithstanding.

Septemb$^r$ 23$^d$ 1704            September 26$^{th}$ 1704
Read and assented to by      Read and assented to by her
the house of Dell.           Majestys hon$^{ble}$ Councill
W Taylard Cl h D.                W Bladen Cl Concil.

Maryland Octob$^r$ 3$^d$ 1704
On behalf of her Ma$^{ty}$ &c I will this be a Law
Jo : Seymour

p. 136 An Act for the Securing persons rights to Town Lands

Whereas it is represented to this Generall Assembly that severall persons of this Province and others that have taken up lotts in severall Town Lands laid out and Surveyed for Towns according to the Directions of severall Laws of this province heretofore made (that is to say) One Law made at a Generall Assembly held at the Ridge in Ann Arundell County the second day of October One Thousand Six hundred Eighty three Intituled an Act for Advancement of Trade and the other Act made at a Generall Assembly held at the City of Saint Marys the first day of April Sixteen hundred Eighty four Intituled an Additionall and Supplementary Act to the Act for Advancement of Trade and the other Act made at a Generall Assembly held at the City of Saint Marys the twenty seventh day of October One thousand six hundred Eighty six Intituled a farther Additionall Act to the Act for Advancement of Trade and the Supplementary Act of the Same And one other Act made at a Session of Assembly begunn and held at the Citty of Saint Marys the twenty first day of September Anno Domini Sixteen hundred Ninety four Intituled an Act for Erecting Ann Arundell and Oxford Towns into ports and Towns as by the severall Acts of Assembly remaining upon Record in the Secretarys Office of this Province may appear

And notwithstanding the severall persons who relying and depending upon the benefitts and priviledges in the said Laws granted have taken up Lotts in the said Towns entered them and paid for them or were ready to pay for them as the Law directed and have built and improv'd thereon Yett they are now threatned disquietted and disturbed by the persons Claiming rights to the said Lands upon pretence that because that the said Acts are since repeald The Titles of such takers up builders and Improvers are destroy'd and dye with the said Acts of Trade contrary to the true sense and rationall Construction of the same Laws or any other of like Nature. To prevent therefore and take of all such unnecessary Doubts and Scruples thereof

Be it Enacted by the Queens most excellent Majesty by and with the Advice and Consent of her Majestys Governour Councill and Assembly of this province and the Authority of the same that all and every person or persons that during the Continuance of the before mencoñd Acts of Assembly did take up pay for or tendred or were ready to pay for any Lott or Lotts of Land in any Town land laid out and allotted for Town lands by the former Laws or any of them and of the same lott made due entry and hath built and improved upon the same and followed the Directions of the above mencoñd Laws they the said person and persons so taking up entring building upon and following the direcoñs of the said Laws their heires and Assigns shall have hold and enjoy a good sure indefeazable Estate of Inheritance in fee Simple of in and to every such lott and lotts of Land so taken up and built on as aforesaid (according to the said Laws and directions) to them and their heires forever as fully freely and amply to all Intents and purposes as if the said former laws were still in full force and had never been repeald.

Provided allways that where any person or persons that hath or have so taken up built and improved and hath not paid the price sett upon the same that every such person is hereby injoyn'd to pay the said value of the said lott to the owner & Claimer of the land upon demand without fraud or Covin.

September 23<sup>d</sup> 1704      September 26<sup>th</sup> 1704

Read and Assented to by the    Read and assented to by her
house of Dellegates      Majestys hon<sup>ble</sup> Councill
W Taylard Clk h. Ɔ.      W Bladen Cl Concil.

Maryland October 3<sup>d</sup> 1704

On behalf of her Ma<sup>ty</sup> &c I will this be a Law

Jo: Seymour

An Act for rectifying the ill practices of **Attornys** of this Province And ascertaining the Attorney **Generalls** and Clark of Indictments ffees.

Be it Enacted by the Queens most excellent Majesty by and with the Advice and Consent of her Majestys Governour Councill and Assembly of this Province and the Authority of the same that after the end of this Sessions of Assembly no process for any Criminall Matter or other Misdemeanour shall p. 138 issue out of any of the Courts of this province against any person or persons whatsoever without a presentment be first found against the said person or persons by the Grand Jury unless by a special order of Court And if the Attorney.Generall or any other Attorny of the Provincial Court shall issue forth process against any person or persons and no presentment or order of Court appears upon Record to Justify the same the said Attorney so offending shall forfeit any pay for such his Offence the sume of ffive thousand pounds of Tobacco the one half to her sacred Majesty her heires and Successors towards the Defraying of the publiq Levy of this Province the other half to the party Greived or to him or them that shall Inform or sue for the same to be recovered in the Provinciall Court of this province by bill Plaint or Information And if any Clerk of the Indictments in any County Court of this province or any other Attorny practicing in the said Courts shall Issue forth process against any person or persons for any Criminall Matter or Misdemeanour without a presentment be first found by the Grand Jury against the said person or persons or Speciall order of Court appearing upon Record to Justify the same the said Clerk of Indictments or other Attorny so offending shall forfeit and pay for such his Offence the Sume of two thousand five hundred pounds of Tobacco the one half to her Majesty her heires and Successors towards the defraying the County levy the other half to the party greived or to him or them that shall informe or sue for the same to be recovered in the respective County Courts of this Province where such Offence was Comitted by Accon of Debt bill plaint or Information wherein no Essoyn protection or wager of Law shall be allowed. Neither shall the party so offending have any Appeale or writt of Errorᵗ but the Judgment of the County Court shall be definitive therein. And if the Clerk of the Provincial Court of this Province or any of the Clerks of the County Courts of this province shall issue out process in Criminall Causes without an order for the same under the hand of an Attorny practising in the said Court or Courts to Justify the same the said Clerk or Clerks so offending shall be lyable to the same fforfeitures and penltys of Attorneys soe offending and the said forfeitures to e recovered as aforesaid and go to the use aforesaid.

And be it further Enacted by the Authority aforesaid that ne Attorney Generall of this Province shall not recover nor eceive any ffee for any Navigation bond put in suite either rhere the Certificate was before the suite of the said Lands odged in the Secretarys office of this Province or where it ann be prov'd that he knew there was such Certificate eturn'd neither shall the said Attorney Generall Receive or ave any ffee for any bond for Countrey dues where the said ond appears not to be forfeited and if the said Attorney ienerall after the end of this Sessions of Assembly shall sue ny bond taken contrary to Act of parliament or any bond iken for Country dues and noe bills of Exchange appearing rotested nor noe other ffailure to forfeit the said bond, or rhere the said Certificate is returned into the said Secretarys )ffice appointed for keeping the same any of which Cases ppearing to the Provinciall Court the said Attorney Gen- rall shall not only loose his ffees but pay the Secretarys ffees nd what other Charges the party hath been at in defending ie same to be adjudged by the Provinciall Court.

And whereas severall persons have been sued in her Ma- estys Name for a Certain sume without ever mentioning for rhat the said bond was taken so that the persons do not now what Courses to take or who to apply y'selves to.

Be it Enacted by the Authority aforesaid that when any Vritt is issued forth upon a Navigation Bond taken in her Iajestys Name it shall be endorsed on the backside as follow- th (for whom the person was bound and in what year if a heriffs Bond) at whose request and prayer it was sued or ond taken in any of her Maj'ys Offices in this province it hall be endorsed at whose request it was sued, and for want f such Endorsement the writt shall Abate, and the party ireived shall recover his Costs against the Attorny that sued orth the said Writt.

And be it enacted by the Authority aforesaid by and with ie Advice and Consent aforesaid that whensoever the Grand ury in their respective County Courts of this Province shall iake a Presentment of the breach of any the Laws of this rovince save only the Act for speedy tryall of Criminalls nd ascertaining their punishment in the County Courts when rosecuted there if the party or partys presented Confess is or their Crime and Submitt to the Court then the Clerk f the Indictments shall have one hundred pounds of Tobacco or his ffee and no more But if the Clerk of Indictments raws a Bill of Indictment upon the said presentment or the arty traverses such presentment or Bill of Indictment and

... purge himself upon the Country for myself thereof Then the Clerk of the Indictments shall have two hundred pounds of Tobacco for his fee

September 20th 1704

Read and Assented to by the house of Delegates
    W Taylard Cle: h: D

September 29th 1704

Read and Assented to by her Majestys hon'ble Councill
    W Bladen Cl: Concil

Maryland October 3d 1704

On behalf of her Maj'ty this I will this be a Law
    Jo: Seymour


An Act for securing the Parochiall Libraryes of this Province

Bee it Enacted by the Queens most excellent Majesty by and with the Advice and Consent of her Majestys Governour Councill and Assembly of this Province and the Authority of the same That the Libraryes appointed for the severall and respective parishes within this Province shall be and remain in the hands and possession of the Minister of the Parish If there be any Minister actually inducted into and Incumbent in the said parish during his Residence in the said parish who is by law Ana obliged to keep and preserve the said Library take Care and Management and to be accountable for the same to the Governour Councill and Assembly as often as required

And to that purpose the said Minister shall pass two Receipts for the said Books inserting when they are and the title page of the same One receipt to be by the Vestry of the said Parish transmitted to the Governour and Councill and the other to remain with the Vestry of the said parish to be entred in their Register book And the said Vestry are hereby obliged to View the said Librarys twice in the year and inspect the same

And in Case the said Vestrys shall not or at least four in number at Eleven meeting view the said Librarys twice

And if it so happen that the Theave and any Damage or Imbecillment thereof they shall reconvenient Cause Satisfaction for the same to be made by Action at Deor to be brought against the said Minister his Executors or Administrators for the full value of such books as are or shall be wanting to be Confirmed & brought by the Vestrymen of such respective parish where such Damage and imbecillment shall happen who by this Act are impowered to bring their Special Action without their personal Vestrymen.

And in Case any Minister having the Charge of such Library shall be removed from his Charge he shall Deliver the said Library to the Vestry of the said Parish and make Satisfaction or reparation if any Damage or What suffered before his Departure not to the said parish Except by fire or such unavoidable Accident Or in Case of the Death of any such Minister having the Charge of such Library the Vestry of such Parish shall immediately take the said Library into their Custody and keeping and pass their Receipt for the same as above directed and shall in all points be answerable for the same except by fire or such like Accident as aforesaid.

And for the better preserving and securing the said Libraries It shall and may be lawful for his Ex'ce the Governour in this Province for the time being to appoint one or more Visitors of the said Libraries within this Province to report on the Estate of them or his Ex'ce the Governour and Council and they may make order or orders where any Disorder is about the said Libraries or to their Doors or the Effectual preserving of them.

September 20th 17—.
Read and Assented to
by the house of Burgesses.
W Bryant Clk. H. D

September 20th 17—.
Read and Assented to by her
Majestys Hon'ble Council
W Bassett D. Council

Virginia Octobr 5th 17—.
On behalf of her Majesty &c. I will that this be a Law.
E. Nottnor.

An Act restraining the Extortions of Sheriffs Sub Sheriffs and the Deputy Collectors.

Whereas there have been divers great Complaints from Several parts of this Province to the General Assembly of Severall Sheriffs Sub Sheriffs and Clerks of Comissaries of their Exacting and exporting great Sums of Tobacco above what the said lawfull fees warranted by the Act of Assembly of this

putts himself upon the Country for tryall thereof Then the Clerk of the Indictments shall have two hundred pounds of Tobacco for his ffee

September 29<sup>th</sup> 1704          September 29<sup>th</sup> 1704

Read and Assented to by          Read and Assented to by her
the house of Delegates          Majestys hon<sup>ble</sup> Councill
W Taylard Clk h D          W Bladen Cl Concil.

Maryland October 3<sup>d</sup> 1704

On behalf of her Maj<sup>ty</sup> &c I will this be a Law

Jo: Seymour

An Act for securing the Parochial Librarys of this Province.

Bee it Enacted by the Queens most excellent Majesty by and with the Advice and Consent of her Majestys Governour Councill and Assembiy of this Province and the Authority of the same that the Librarys appointed for the severall and respective parishes within this Province shall be and remain in the hands and possession of the Minister of the Parish (if there be any Minister actually inducted into and incumbent in the said parish) during his Residence in the said parish who is by this Act obliged to keep and preserve the said Library from Wast and imbezellment and to be accountable for the same to the Governour Councill and Assembly as often as required.

And to that purpose the said Minister shall pass two Receipts for the said books Inserting what they are and the title page of the same One receipt to be by the Vestry of the said Parish transmitted to the Gov'nour and Councill and the other to remain with the Vestry of the said 'pish to be entred in their Register book And the said Vestrys are hereby obliged to Visitt the said Librarys twice in the year and inspect the same.

And in Case the said Vestrys shall not (or at least four of them of Eldest standing) visitt the said Librarys twice in the year as by this Act is required the whole Number of Vestrymen shall forfeit and pay the Sume of fourteen hundred pounds of Tobacco one Moyety to her Majesty her heires and p. 141 Successors for the Support of Government the other Moyety to the Informer or him or them that shall sue for the same in any Court of Record in this Province by Accon of Debt bill plaint or Information wherein no Essoyn protection or Wager of Law to be allowed. And the Onus probandi shall lye on the part of the Vestry to make it appear that they have Visitted the Librarys as by this Act they are obliged.

And if it so happen that the Vestry find any Damage or Imbezillment thereof they shall require and Cause Satisfaction for the same to be made by Accon of Debt to be brought against the said Minister his Executors or Administrators for the full value of such books as are or shall be wanting to be Com̅enced & brought by the Vestrymen of such respective parish where such Dam̅age and imbezillment shall happen who by this Act are impowered to bring their Speciall Accon without their principall Vestryman.

And in Case any Minister having the Charge of such Library shall be removed from his Charge he shall Deliver the said Library to the Vestry of the said Parish and make Satisfaction or reparacon if any Damage or Wast suffered before his Departure out of the said parish (Except by ffire or such unavoidable Accident) Or in Case of the Death of any such Minister having the Charge of such Library the Vestry of such Parish shall immediately take the said Library into their Custody and keeping and pass their Receipt for the same as above directed and shall in all points be answerable for the same (except by ffire or such like Accident as aforesaid)

And for the better preserving and securing the said Librarys It shall and may be lawfull for his Ex^cy the Governour of this Province for the time being to appoynt one or more Visitors of the said Librarys within this Province to report the true Estate of them to his Ex^cy the Governo^r and Councill that they may make order to cause every one Concern'd about the said Librarys to do their Dutys to the Effectual preserving of them.

| | |
|---|---|
| September 29^th 1704 | September 29^th 1704 |
| Read and Assented to | Read and Assented to by her |
| by the house of Delegates | Majestys hon^ble Councill |
| W Taylard Clkh.D. | W Bladen Cl Concill. |

Maryland October 3^d 1704

On behalf of her Majesty &c I will this be a Law.

Jo: Seymour

An Act restraining the Extortions of Sheriffs Sub Sheriffs and Deputy Com̅issarys.

Whereas there have been divers Great Complaints from Severall parts of this Province to this Generall Assembly of Severall Sheriffs Sub-Sheriffs and Deputy Comissarys of their Exacting and extorting great Sum̅s of Tobacco above their due and lawfull ffees ascertaind by the Act of Assembly of this

22

Province from Severall of the Inhabitants of this province And tho: the Laws of this Province have inflicted a severe penalty upon any Officer that shall Charge and receive more than his due ffees Yet the said Officers have most cunningly and craftilly evaded the said Laws by taking bills or writings obligatory without ever delivering any Account Sign'd under their hands as the Law directs so that the party greived cannot Sufficiently prove the said Extortion and so is left without remedy, for Prevention whereof

Be it enacted by the Queens most excellent Majesty by and with the Advice and Consent of her Majestys Governour Councill and Assembly of this Province and the Authority of the same that no Sheriff Subsheriff or Deputy Comissary within this Province after the publication of this Act in their severall and respective Countys wherein they dwell shall take any Bond bill or any other writing obligatory of any person or persons upon any pretence whatsoever without endorsing the Account on the back of the said bond bill or writing obligatory for which the same was pass'd And if any Sheriff Subsheriff or Deputy Comissary within this Province shall during the time that he remains in his place or Office upon any pretence whatsoever take any bond bill or Writing obligatory without endorsing the Account on the back of the said bond bill or writing Obligatory as aforesaid by which it may appear upon what Consideration the same was taken the said bill bond or p. 143 writing obligatory shall be void and of no Effect And the Officer and Officers that took the same shall loose his Debt and forever be debarr'd of suing another Action for the recovery of the same any Law Statute or Usage to the Contrary in any wise notwithstanding.

And that whereas the said Officers are prohibitted from taking bills upon any pretence whatsoever during the time they remain in Office to the Intent the said Officers may receive no damage by the Act of Assembly for Limitation of Accons.

Be it further enacted by the Authority aforesaid that the time the said Officers remaine in Office shall not be reckon'd or Accounted in the Act of Limitation. And that whereas it hath been the practice of severall Sheriffs of this province where a person hath been in prison at the suite of two or three severall persons or hath lain for the satisfaction of two or more severall Judgments for the Sheriff to Charge twenty per Day for each Accon or Judgment, for prevention whereof

Be it Enacted by the Authority aforesaid that if any Sheriff after the publication of this Act shall exact and take any more than twenty pounds of Tobacco per Day of any prisoner tho: he lyes for the Satisfaction of severall Judgments he shall be lyable to the pains and penaltys of a Certain Act of Assembly Lib. L. L. No. 64. for settling Officers ffees.

| September 23ᵈ 1704 | September 26ᵗʰ 1704 |
|---|---|
| Read and Assented to by the house of Delegates W Taylard Clk h.D. | Read and Assented to by her Majestys honᵇˡᵉ Councill W Bladen Cl Concill |

Maryland October 3ᵈ 1704
On the behalf of her Majesty &c I will this be a Law.
                                                        Jo⁚ Seymour

An Act for ascertaining the bounds of a Certain tract of Land ᵖ· ¹⁴⁴ to the use of the Nanticok Indians so long as they shall occupy and live upon the same.

It being most Just that the Indians the Ancient Inhabitants of this Province should have a Convenient dwelling place in this their Native Country free from the Incroachments and Opressions of the English more especially the Nanticoke Indians in Dorchester County who for these many years have lived in peace and Concord with the English And in all Matters in obedience to the Government of this province. Wee the Burgesses and Delegates of this present Generall Assembly therefore do pray that it may be Enacted and

Be it Enacted by the Queens most excellent Majesty by and with the Advice and Consent of her Majestys Governour Councill and Assembly of this Province and the Authority of the same that all the land lying and being in Dorchester County And on the North side of Nanticoke River butted and Bounded as followeth Beginning at the Mouth of Chickawan Creek and running up the said Creek bounded therewith to the head of the Main branch of the same And from the head of the said Main branch with a line drawn to the head of a branch issuing out of the Northwest ffork of Nanticoke known by the Name of ffrancis Andertons branch and from the head of the said branch down the said Andertons branch bounded therewith to the Mouth of the same where it falls into the said Northwest ffork And from thence down the aforesaid Northwest ffork bounded therewith to the Main River and so down the main River to the Mouth of the aforesaid Creek shall be confirmed and assured and by vertue of this Act is confirm'd and assur'd unto to Panquash and Armotoughquan and the people under their Gov'nmᵗ or Charge and their beires and ᵖ· ¹⁴⁵ Successors forever any Law Usage Custom or Grant to the Contrary in any wise Notwithstanding to be held of the Lord

Lib. L. L.   Proprietary and his heires Lord Proprietary or Lords Proprie-
No. 64.   tarys of this Province under the yearly rent of one Bever Skinn
to be paid to his said Lordship and his Heires as other Rents
in this Province by the English us'd to be paid

Provided allways that it shall and may be lawfull for any
person or persons that hath formerly taken up and obtain'd
any Grants from the Lord Baltemore for any Tracts or parcells
of Land within the aforesaid Boundarys upon the Indians
Deserting or leaving the said land to enter occupy and enjoy
the Same anything in this Law to the Contrary notwithstanding.

And be it further Enacted by the Authority aforesaid that it
shall not nor may be lawfull for the Lord Baltemore to ask
have or demand any Rent or Service for any of the said Tracts
or Dividends as may or have been taken up as aforesaid within
the said Indians Boundarys untill Such time that the takers up
or Owners afores^d do enjoy or possess the same Any Law
usage or Custom to the Contrary notwithstanding.

September 23^d 1704         September 26^th 1704
Read and Assented to by      Read and Assented to by her
the house of Delegates.      Majestys hon^ble Councill
W Taylard Clk hD.            W Bladen Cl Concil.

Maryland October 3^d 1704.
On behalf of her Majesty &c. I will this be a Law
J₀ : Seymour

### An Act to prevent the Growth of Popery within this Province.

Be it Enacted by the Queens most Excellent Majesty by and
p. 146  with the Advice and Consent of her Majestys Governour
Councill and Assembly of this Province and the Authority of
the same that whatsoever Popish Bishop Priest or Jesuite shall
baptize any Child or Children other than such who have
Popish Parents or shall say Mass or exercise the ffunction of a
Popish Bishop or Priest within this Province or shall endeavour
to perswade any of her Majestys Leige people of this Province
to embrace and be reconciled to the Church of Rome and
shall be thereof legally Convict shall forfeit the sume of fifty
pounds Sterling for every such Offence the one half thereof to
our Sovereign Lady the Queen her heires and Successors for
the Support of the Government of this Province and the other
half thereof to him or them that will sue for the same to be
recovered in any Court of Record within this Province by bill
Plaint or Information wherein no Essoyn Protection or Wager
of Law to be allowed and shall also Suffer six Months imprisonment of his or their body or bodys without bayle or Mainprize.

And be it further Enacted by and with the Advice Consent Lib. L. L. and Authority aforesaid that if any Popish Bishop Priest or No. 64. Jesuit after such Conviction aforesaid shall say Mass or Exercise any other part of the Office or ffunction of a Popish Bishop or Priest within this Province or if any Papist or Person making profession of the Popish Religion shall keep Schoole or take upon themselves the Education Government or Boarding of Youth in any place within this Province such person or persons being thereof lawfully convicted that then every such Person shall upon such Conviction be transported out of this Province to the Kingdom of England together with his Conviction in order to his Suffering such pains and penaltys as are provided by the Statute made in the Eleventh and twelfth year of the reign of his late Majesty King William the third Intituled An Act for the further preventing the Growth p. 147 of Popery. And to the end that the Protestant Children of Popish Parents may not in the life time of such their parents for want of fitting Maintenance be Necessitated in Complyance with their parents to embrace the Popish Religion contrary to their own Inclination,

Be it Enacted by the Authority aforesaid by and with the Advice and Consent aforesaid that from and after the end of this Sessions of Assembly if any such parent in order to the Compelling such his or her Protestant Child to Change his or her Religion shall refuse to allow such Child a fitting Maintenance Suitable to the degree and Ability of such parent and to the Age and Education of Such Child then upon Complaint thereof made to the Governour of this Province or the Keeper of the Great Seale it shall be lawfull for the said Governour or Keeper of the Seale to make such order therein as shall be agreeable to the Intent of this Act.

| | |
|---|---|
| September 30<sup>th</sup> 1704 | September 30<sup>th</sup> 1704 |
| Read and assented to by | Read and Assented to by her |
| the house of Delegates | Majestys hon<sup>ble</sup> Councill |
| W Taylard Clk hd. | W Bladen Cl Concil. |

Maryland October 3<sup>d</sup> 1704

On the behalf of her Ma<sup>ty</sup> &c I will this be a Law.

Jo: Seymour

An Act for the punishing the Offences of Adultery and ffornication.

Be it enacted by the Queens most excellent Majesty by and with the Advice and Consent of her Majestys Governour

Lib. L. L.
No. 64.

p. 148

Councill and Assembly of this Province and the Authority of the same that after the end of this Session of Assembly whosoever shall directly or indirectly entertain or provide for or cause to be entertained or provided for any lewd woman or women or that shall frequent her or their Company after that Admonition to him or them be given by the Minister or the Vestry or the Church Warden or Church Wardens of the Parish where such person or persons shall inhabitt shall be adjudged a ffornicator or Adulterer as the Case shall be and shall suffer such Penaltys as by this law is hereafter appointed.

And be it further enacted by the Authority Advice and Consent aforesaid that every person or persons that shall Comitt ffornication and be thereof Convict in the Provincial or County Court either by Confession or Verdict of twelve men shall be fin'd thirty shillings or six hundred pounds of Tobacco by the Justices before whom such Conviction shall be to the Queens Majesty for the Support of the County Charge.

And be it enacted by the Authority Advice and Consent aforesaid that every person or persons that shall Comit Adultery and shall be thereof Convict either by Confession or Verdict of twelve men in the Provincial or any of the County Courts of this Province shall be fin'd by the Justices before whom such Conviction shall be three pounds sterling or twelve hundred pounds of Tobacco to the Queens Majesty her heires and Successors towards defraying such County Charge as aforesaid And in Case the said Offenders or any of them shall not have wherewith to pay the severall ffines by this Act Imposed then the said Offenders shall be adjudged to suffer Corporall Punishment by whipping upon his or their bare bodys till the blood do appear, so many stripes, not exceeding thirty nine as the Justices before whom such Conviction shall be adjudged

Provided that this Act shall not be Construed to extend as to the ffine to Women who have Bastards and do refuse to discover the ffather or Begetter of such bastard Children But that in such Cases it shall be in the discretion of the Justices before whom such woman or Women shall be Con-

p. 149

victed either to take the ffine by this Act appointed or to award Corporall punishment Anything in this Act before to the Contrary notwithstanding.

September 28th 1704

Read and assented to by the house of Delegates
W Taylard Clk hD.

September 29th 1704

Read and Assented to by her Matys honble Councill
W Bladen Cl Concil.

Maryland October 3ᵈ 1704

On the behalf of her Majesty &c I will this be a Law

Jo: Seymour

Lib. L. L.
No. 64.

An Act for the Appointment of Constables and what relates
to their Office

Be it enacted by the Queens most excellent Majesty by and
with the Advice and Consent of her Majestys Governour
Councill and Assembly of this Province and the Authority
of the same that the Justices of peace in every respective
County of this Province at the first County Court held after
Michaelmas shall appoint Constables in each Hundred of the
severall and respective Countys  And the said Constables
so appointed shall before they enter into that Office take the
severall and respective Oaths appointed to be taken by all
Officers by the Acts of Assembly of this province and the
oath of Constable in forme following (that is to say)

You A. B. shall well and truly serve our Sovereign Lady
the Queen in the Office of a Constable  You shall see and
Cause that her Majestys peace be well and duly kept according to your power you shall Arrest all such persons as in
your presence shall Com̃it any Riott ffray or other breach of
her Majestys peace  You shall do your best endeavour upon
Complaint to you made to seize all ffelons Barretors Riotters
or persons riotously Assembled  And if any such Offender
shall make any Resistance with fforce you shall levy Hue and
Cry and pursue them untill they be taken  You shall do your
best Endeavour that Hue and Cry be duly raised and pursued
against Murtherers Thieves and other ffelons and fugitive
servants and the laws and Orders against Vagabonds and
such other Idle persons coming within your Limits be duly
put in Execution  At your County Courts Coming you shall p· 150
present all offenders done against the severall Acts made for
the Suppressing of Drunkenness and also true presentment
make of all Bloodshedds affrays outcrys Rescues and other
Offences Comitted against her Majestys peace within your
Limitts you shall well and truly execute all precepts and
Warrants to you directed from the Justices of Peace of this
County or Higher Officers and you shall well and truly
according to your power Knowledge and Ability do and
execute all things belonging to the Office of a Constable so
long as you shall Continue in this Office.

So Help you God.

And if the person or persons so appointed shall before any
Justice of the peace refuse to take the severall Oaths afore-

said or shall refuse to provide a Sufficient person to Supply
his place by serving in the said Office and taking the Oaths
aforesaid that then such person so refusing shall be fin'd to
her Majesty in the Sume of ffive hundred pounds of Tobacco
towards the Defraying the publiq Charge of that County
and that such Justice of peace before whom such refusall
shall be made shall issue his Warrant to the Sheriff to levy
the said ffine by distress and Sale of the Goods and Chattells
of such person fin'd as aforesaid returning to him the Overplus which said Sheriff is hereby impowered and required to
levy the same accordingly and render Account thereof to the
Justice of peace of that County at the time of laying the
County Leavy.

And be it Enacted by the Authority aforesaid by and with
the Advice and Consent aforesaid that every Constable shall
on or before the twentyeth day of June in every Year respectively repair in person to every house or Habitation within
his hundred and there require of the Master Mistress Dame
or other Chief person of the ffamily a true List from under
their hand of all their Taxable persons they and every of them
have within their respective ffamilys out of which list the said
Constables shall make two fair lists under his hand and one
he shall send to the Sheriff of the County and the other he
shall present to the next County Court to be sett up and
if in Case any Master Mistress or Dame or other Chief persons of a ffamily shall refuse or deny to give such List or in
their Absence leave at their dwelling houses or Quarters such
a List and Account of their Taxable persons of their severall
ffamilys or in the said Account shall conceale any Taxable
p. 151 person or persons in his or their ffamily for every such Offence
or not giving a true List and Account of them to the Constables by the Time required and for every taxable person by
them Conceald shall forfeit and pay the Sume of five hundred
pounds of Tobacco for every such Offence one half thereof
to her Majesty her heires and Successors for the Support of
Government the other half to the Informer or him or them
that will sue for the same to be recovered in any Court of
Record of this Province wherein no Essoyn protection or
wager of Law to be allow'd

<table>
<tr><td>September 21<sup>st</sup> 1704</td><td>September 21<sup>st</sup> 1704</td></tr>
</table>

September 21<sup>st</sup> 1704      September 21<sup>st</sup> 1704
Read and assented to by the    Read and assented to by her
house of Delegates      Majestys hon[ble] Councill
W Taylard Clk hD.      W Bladen Cl Concil.

Maryland October 3<sup>d</sup> 1704

On the behalf of her Majesty &c I will this be a Law.

Jo. Seymour

An Act requiring the Masters of Shipps and Vessells to publish the rates of their ffreight before they take any Tobacco
on board.

Be it enacted by the Queens most excellent Majesty by and
with the Advice and Consent of her Majestys Governour
Councill and Assembly of this Province and the Authority of
the same that every Master and Comander of a Shipp or other
Vessell that purposes to export Tobacco on ffreight shall before
he take any such Tobacco on board his said Shipp or Vessell
publish in Writing by a Note under his hand which he shall
Cause to be affix'd on the Court door of that County where
his said Shipp shall ride at Anchor at what rate he will receive
Tob° upon freight ᵖ Tonn on board his said Shipp for that
intended Voyage which Note the Clerk of the County shall
enter upon Record.·

And be it further enacted by the Authority aforesaid that
whatsoever Merchant or other inhabitants of this Province
shall put any Tob° on board any Shipp Sloop or boate belonging to a Shipp on ffreight before such Master of such Shipp
hath sett up such Note as aforesaid he shall forfeit and loose
all such Tobacco so Shipt on board such Shipp sloop or boate
or the full value thereof in mony Whereof one half to her
Majesty for Support of the Government of this Province the
other half to him or them that will sue for the same to be
recovered in any Court of Record in this Province by Accon
of Debt bill plaint or Information wherein no Essoyn protection
or Wager of Law to be allowed.

And be it further enacted by the Authority aforesaid that if
any Master Comander of Shipp or other Vessell as aforesaid
shall take any such Tobacco on board his Shipp or Vessell
before he hath publish'd such Note as aforesaid he shall forfeit
for every such hogshead the Sume of twenty shillings to the
uses aforesaid to be recovered as aforesaid.

· And be it further Enacted by the Authority aforesaid that
every Master & Comander of Shipp or Vessell as aforesaid
that shall send any Sloop or other Craft to another County to
fetch Tobacco to be put on board his Shipp or Vessell on
freight shall send by the Skipper or Master of such Sloop or
other Craft a Certificate under the hand of the Clerk of that
County where such Note of freight was publish'd as aforesaid
Certifying the rate of his freight and publication thereof as
aforesaid under the penalty of forfeiting forty shillings sterl to
the uses aforesaid to be recovered as aforesaid And the Collectors and Navall Officers shall at the Charge of the County
where such Collectors and Navall Offʳˢ inhabitt procure Copys
of this Law for each Copy whereof the said County Clerk shall
have tenn pounds of Tobacco and no more and affix the same

in their Office or Offices on or before the tenth day of December next ensuing under the penalty of forty Shillings Sterl to be for such neglect forfeited and paid to the uses aforesaid to be recovered as aforesaid.

<table>
<tr><td>September 29<sup>th</sup> 1704</td><td>September 29<sup>th</sup> 1704</td></tr>
</table>

September 29$^{th}$ 1704              September 29$^{th}$ 1704
Read and assented to by the        Read and assented to by her
  house of Delegates.        ·        Majestys honourable Councill
      W Taylard Clk hD.                  W Bladen Cl. Concil.

Maryland October 3$^d$ 1704

On behalf of her Majesty &c I will this be a Law.

Jo : Seymour

p. 153 An Act for Appointing Court Days in each respective County in this Province

To the Intent that Court days may be ascertain'd and that the Comissioners within their respective Countys may know when to Attend

Be it Enacted by the Queens most excellent Majesty by and with the Advice and Consent of her Majestys Governour Councill and Assembly of this Province and the Authority of the same that for the ffuture St Marys Baltemore and Dorchester County Courts shall be held the first Tuesday in September November January March June and August and Ann Arundell Charles Somersett and Cecill Countys the second Tuesday in September November January March June and August And for Calvert and Talbot Countys the third Tuesday in Sep$^r$ Nov$^r$ Jan$^{ry}$ March June and August And for Kent and Prince Georges Countys the fourth Tuesday in September November January March June and August

And be it Enacted by the Authority aforesaid by and with Advice and Consent aforesaid that any two Justices of the Severall and respective County Courts whereof one of them to be Quorum shall have full power and Authority by vertue of this Act when and as often as need shall require to adjourne the said County Court and process and proceedings therein depending to such short time after as they shall see Convenient.

September 21$^{st}$ 1704              September 21$^{st}$ 1704
Read and Assented by        Read and Assented to by her
  the house of Delegates.        Majestys hon$^{ble}$ Councill
      W Taylard Clk hD.                  W Bladen Cl Concil.

Maryland October 3$^d$ 1704

On the behalf of her Ma$^{ty}$ &c. I will this be a Law.

Jo : Seymour

An Act for laying an Imposition of three pence per Hogshead Lib. **L, L.** on Tobacco for defraying the publiq Charge of the province. No. 64.

Be it Enacted by the Queens most excellent Majesty by and with the Advice and Consent of her Majestys Governour Councill and Assembly of this Province and the Authority of p. 154 the same that from and after the end of this Sessions of Assembly A Duty or Imposition of three pence for every Hogshead of Tobacco and the like duty of three pence for every ffive hundred pounds of Tobacco Containd in Chest box or Case on all Tobacco that shall be exported out of this province by Land or Water be rais'd Levyed and paid to her Majesty towards the defraying the Publiq Charge of this Province by all Masters of Shipps or other Vessells Trading into this province in ready Mony and to be Collected by the Navall Officer of the Port or District where such Ships or Vessells shall Clear.

And the said Navall Officers are directed and required by this Act to receive the Same in ready Mony accordingly and the said Officers shall account and pay for the said Imposition of three pence per hogshead And the three pence for every five hundred pounds of Tobacco contain'd as above in ready money to the Treasurers of this province who are hereby required to render account thereof and pay the same in ready Mony to the Generall Assembly.

And be it farther Enacted by the Authority aforesaid by and with the Advice and Consent aforesaid that the said Imposition of three pence per Hogshead and the three pence for every five hundred pounds of Tobacco contain'd as abovesd shall be appropriated by the Generall Assembly of this Province towards the paying of the publiq Charge thereof And to no other use whatsoever

And be it further enacted and declar'd by the Authority aforesaid by and with the Advice and Consent aforesaid That if any Tobacco should by any Casual Means be lost after the Imposition paid That then and in all such Cases the Owner or ffreighter of all such Tobacco shall have free liberty to freight and shipp off the like Quantity again without paying the said Imposition.

This Act to Continue for three years or to the end of the next Sessions of Assembly which shall first happen after the said three Years.

| September 29th 1704 | September 29th 1704 |
| --- | --- |
| Read and assented to by the house of Delegates. | Read and assented by her Majestys honble Councill |
| W Taylard Clk hD. | W Bladen Cl Concil. |

Maryland October 3ᵈ 1704.

On behalf of her Maᵗʸ &c I will this be a Law.

Jo : Seymour

p. 155 An Act prohibitting the Inhabitants of this Province or any others from Carrying Liquors to Indian Towns.

Be it enacted by the Queens most excellent Majesty by and with the Advice and Consent of her Majestys Governour Councill and Assembly of this Province and the Authority of the same that from and after the publication hereof any person or persons whatsoever inhabitting or trading into this Province that shall presume to carry any Liquors whatsoever to any Indian ffort or Town or within three Miles of any such ffort or Town and shall Vend or dispose of the same to any Indian or Indians whatsoever Such person or persons shall forfeit the Sum of five thousand pounds of Tobacco One half thereof to our Sovereign Lady the Queen her heires and Successors towards the Support of Government the other half to him or them that shall informe or sue for the same to be recovered in any Court of Record within this Province wherein no Essoyn Protection or wager of Law to be allowed.

<table>
<tr><td>September 26ᵗʰ 1704</td><td>September 26ᵗʰ 1704</td></tr>
<tr><td>Read and assented by the house of Delegates.<br>W Taylard Clk hD</td><td>Read and assented to by her Maᵗʸˢ honᵇˡᵉ Councill<br>W Bladen Cl Concil.</td></tr>
</table>

Maryland October 3ᵈ 1704

On behalf of her Maᵗʸ &c I will this be a Law.

Jo: Seymour

An Act prohibitting Comissioners Sheriffs Clerks and Deputy Clerks to plead as Attorneys in their respective County Courts.

Be it enacted by the Queens most excellent Majesty by and with the Advice and Consent of her Majestys Governour Councill and Assembly of this Province and the Authority of the same that no person being in the Comission of peace No Sheriff or Deputy Sheriff Clerk or Deputy Clerk of those Courts wherein they bear office shall plead as Attornys for or p. 156 in behalf of any person or persons on Penalty of fforfeiting three thousand pounds of Tobacco for every such Offence whereof such Offender shall be found Guilty one half thereof to her Majesty her **heires** and Successors for the Support of Government of this Province the other half to the Informer or him or them that shall sue for the same to be recovered in any Court of Record within this Province by bill Plaint or Information wherein no Essoyn protection or Wager of Law to be allowd

<table>
<tr><td>Septemb 21<sup>st</sup> 1704.</td><td>September 21<sup>st</sup> 1704</td></tr>
</table>

| Septemb 21st 1704. | September 21st 1704 |
|---|---|
| Read and assented to by the house of Delegates | Read and assented to by her Maties honble Councill. |
| W Taylard Clk hD | W Bladen Cl Concil. |

Maryland October 3<sup>d</sup> 1704

On the Behalf of her Majesty &c I will this be a Law.

Jo : Seymour

An Act to encourage the Inhabitants of this Province to Adventure their Shipps and Vessells more freely abroad to import Rum Sugar Negroes and other Comoditys.

Be it Enacted by the Queens most excellent Maj<sup>ty</sup> by and with the Advice and Consent of her Majestys Governour Councill & Assembly of this Province and the Authority of the same that no Shipp or Vessell built in this Province whereof all the Owners shall be Actuall Residents of this province And that no Shipp or Vessell English or Plantation built purchas'd enjoy'd and held by Owners which are all Residents of this Province nor the Owners thereof shall be lyable to pay the duty of three pence per Gallon for rum imported in such Shipp or Vessell mencofd in one Act of Assembly Intituled An Act Imposing three pence per Gallon on Rum and Wine and twenty Shillings per pole for Negroes for raising a Supply to defray the publiq Charge of this province and twenty shillings per poll on Irish Servants to prevent the Importing too great a Number of Irish papists into this Province nor to pay the Duty of twenty shillings for every p. 157 Negro imported mencofd in the aforesaid Act but from those Dutys aforesaid And from the Duty of three pence per Tonn payable to the Governour of this Province for the time being shall be fully and Clearly Exempted Any fformer Act or Acts of Assembly to the Contrary notwithstanding.

And be it Enacted by the Authority aforesaid that such Owner or Owners of such Shipps or Vessells as aforesaid shall for entring and Clearing pay no more but half so much ffees to the Navall Officers and Collectors with whom they

Lib. L. L. Enter and Clear as other Owners of other Shipps not belong-
No. 64. ing to the Inhabitants of this Province are lyable to pay Any
former Act or Statute to the Contrary notwithstanding.

|                          |                          |
|--------------------------|--------------------------|
| Sept$^r$ 23$^d$ 1704.    | Sept$^r$ 26$^{th}$ 1704  |
| Read and Assented to by  | Read and assented by her |
| the house of Delegates.  | Ma$^{tys}$ hon$^{ble}$ Councill. |
| W Taylard Clk hD         | W Bladen Cl Concil.      |

Maryland October 3$^d$ 1704.

On the behalf of her Maj$^{ty}$ &c$^a$ I will this be a Law.

Jo : Seymour.

An Act impowering a Comittee to lay Assess and Apportion
the public Levy of this present year Seventeen hundred and
ffour.

Whereas this present Generall Assembly have for the
defraying the publiq Charges of this province to this third
day of October Anno Dmi. Seventeen hundred and four rais'd
a Certain Sume of Tobacco and mony amounting to the Sume
of three hundred thirty six thousand seven hundred ninety
four pounds of Tobacco & ffourteen hundred thirty four pounds
Eight Shillings and nine pence half penny in Mony but by
p. 158 reason more publiq Charges may arise and grow due before
the usuall and accustom'd time of payment which is the tenth
day of October yearly untill which time to continue the whole
Assembly sitting for that occasion only would be very Chargeable and troublesome to the whole province in Generall for
the prevention whereof.

Be it enacted by the Queens most excellent Majesty by and
with the Advice and Consent of her Majestys Governour
Councill and Assembly of this Province and the Authority of
the same that Colonel Thomas Smith a Delegate for Kent
County M$^r$ Samuel Young M$^r$ Joseph Hill and Majo$^r$ Charles
Greenberry for Ann Arundell County together with Colonell
John Hamond of her Majestys honourable Councill or the
Major part of them shall be and appear at the Town of
Annapolis sometime as to them shall seem Convenient between
the second day and last day of October Instant then and there
to lay and assess what further Charges may accrew which to
them shall justly appear to be due from the publiq not exceeding the Sum of ffifty thousand pounds of Tobacco and one
hundred pounds in mony more than what is already raised and
likewise to Apportion order and pay out of the publiq Treasury

of this province so much mony as shall appear by the Journall Lib. L. L.
of Accounts of the last and this present Sessions of Assembly No. 64.
to be due together with what the said Comittee shall further
Allow according to the Limitation and Intent of this Act to
the severall persons to whom the same shall be due according
to former usages for paying the publiq Charge and a fair
Journall of all their proceedings to be delivered to the Clerk
of the Assembly for satisfaccon of all persons therewith
concerned.

<table>
<tr><td>Oct. 3<sup>d</sup> 1704.</td><td>Octob. 3<sup>d</sup> 1704</td></tr>
</table>

Oct. 3$^d$ 1704.

By the house of **Dellegates**
Read and Assented to.
W Taylard Cl hD.

Octob. 3$^d$ 1704

˙Read and assented to by her
Ma$^{tys}$ hon$^{ble}$ Councill.
W Bladen Cl Concil.

October 3$^d$ 1704.
On behalf of her Ma$^{ty}$ &c. I will this be a Law.
Jo : Seymour.

An Act against excessive Usury. p. 15

Be it enacted by the Queens most excellent Majesty by and
with the Advice and Consent of her Majestys Governour
Councill and Assembly of this Province and the Authority
of the same That no person or persons whatsoever within
this Province Whether Inhabitant or fforeigner upon any
Contract from and after the end of this present Sessions of
Assembly shall exact or take directly or Indirectly for Loane
of any Moneys Wares or Merchandizes or other Comoditys
whatsoever to be paid in money above the value of Six pounds
for the forbearance of one hundred pounds for one year
And so after that rate for a greater or Lesser Sume or for a
larger or shorter time. Nor shall any person or persons
whatsoever within this Province as aforesaid from and after
the time aforesaid Exact and take directly or indirectly for
Loane of any Tob° Wares Merchandizes or other Comoditys
for one year to be paid in Tobacco or other Comoditys of this
province above the value of eight pounds of Tobacco for the
forbearance of one hundred pounds of tobacco and after that
rate for a greater or lesser Sume or for a longer or shorter
time And that all bonds Contracts and assurances whatsoever
made After the time aforesaid for payment of any principall
money or Tobacco Goods or Comoditys aforesaid to be lent
or covenanted to be perform'd upon or for any Usury whereupon or whereby there shall be reserved above the rate of six
pounds in the hundred for mony as aforesaid or above eight

Lib. L. L.  pounds in the hundred for Tobacco or other goods & Comod-
No. 64.  itys as aforesaid shall be utterly void And that all & every person and persons whatsoever which after the Time aforesaid
shall upon any Contract to be made take accept and receive
by ways or Means of any Corrupt Bargain Loane Exchange
Chivezance shift or Interest of any Wares Merchandizes or
other thing or Things whatsoever or by any Deceitfull Ways
or Means or by any Covin Instrument or Deceitfull Conveyance for the forbearance or giving day of payment for one
whole year of and for their mony Tobacco goods and Comoditys aforesaid above the Sume of mony or Quantity of Tobacco aforesaid for the forbearance aforesaid shall forfeit and
p. 160  loose for every such Offence the treble value of the mony
Tobacco Wares Merchandizes or other things so lent bargain'd
sold exchang'd and shifted as aforesaid   The one half of the
said ffine and fforfeiture to our sovereign Lady the Queen
her heires and Successors for the Support of this Government the other half to him or them that shall sue for the same
to be recovered in any Court of Record of this Province by
Accon of Debt bill plaint of Information wherein no Essoyn
protection or wager of law to be allowed.

<table>
<tr><td>Sept<sup>r</sup> 21<sup>st</sup> 1704</td><td>September 21<sup>st</sup> 1704</td></tr>
</table>

Sept<sup>r</sup> 21<sup>st</sup> 1704      September 21<sup>st</sup> 1704
Read and Assented to by the   Read and Assented to by her
house of Delegates.      Ma<sup>tys</sup> hon<sup>ble</sup> Councill
W Taylard Clk hD      W Bladen Cl Concil.

Maryland October 3<sup>d</sup> 1704
On the behalf of her Ma<sup>ty</sup> &c I will this be a Law.
Jo: Seymour

An Act ascertaining the Expences of the Councellors Delegates of Assembly and Comissioners of the Provincial and
County Courts of this Province
For the ascertaining limitting and allowing unto the severall and respective Councellors Deputys and Delegates that
serve or shall serve in the Generall Assemblys of this Province
and of the severall and respective Comissioners of the Provincial and County Courts of this Province such Sum and
Sums of Tobacco as is hereby thought necessary and Sufficient
for their Defraying their Charges in attending such Assemblys & Courts.
Be it enacted by the Queens most excellent Majesty by and
with the Advice and Consent of her Ma<sup>ties</sup> Gov<sup>r</sup> Councill and
Assembly of this province and the Authority of the same that
all such Councillors be allowed the Sume of one hundred and

hfty pounds of Tobacco per day and the Delegates and Bur- <sub></sub> Lib. L. L. No. 64.
gesses of Assembly shall be allowed the sume of One hundred
and forty pounds of Tobacco per day during the time they
shall attend such Assemblys and no more (besides their Itin- p. 161
erant Charges) to be paid and allow'd them out of the publiq
Levy of this province And the Severall and respective Com^rs
of the Provincial Courts for the defraying their Charges and
expences during the time they shall sitt in & attend such
Courts the Sume of one hundred and forty pounds of Tobacco
per day and no more (besides their Itinerant Charges) to be
paid them likewise out of the Publiq Levy of this Province
as aforesaid And the severall Comissioners of the County
Courts shall be allowed for the defraying of their expences
during the Time they shall sitt in and attend such Courts as
aforesaid the Sume of Eighty pounds of Tobacco per day
and no more which Sume of Eighty pounds of Tobacco as
af^d the said Com^rs of the County Courts are hereby Impowered to Assess and leavy where such Comissioners shall serve
as aforesaid for the defraying the Expences aforesaid And no
more.

Provided allways And it is the true Intent and Meaning
of this Act that where any Justices of any County Court
being a full Court or above the Number of seven shall agree
together in Court sitting and Consent to lessen any Allowance
hereby given or if it be to take the same totally of it shall
and may be lawfull to such full Court to lessen and take off
any part of the Allowance hereby given and settled to the
Comissioners of the said County Courts and entring such
Rule in the Record shall for that year be an absolute Law
and rule for every Justice of that County Court as to their
Expences And it shall not be lawfull to collect or Raise any
more tobacco for defraying the County Courts Justices Expences than so much as by such Consent and rule shall be
limitted and agreed on as aforesaid And if they see fitt to
make the same rule or such other as they shall agree on as
aforesaid one in every year any thing herein to the Contrary
notwithstanding.

September 21. 1704              September 21. 1704
Read and Assented to by the    Read and assented to by her
house of Delegates             Ma^ties hon^ble Councill
W Taylard Clk hD               W Bladen Cl Concil.

Maryland October 3^d 1704
On the behalf of her Ma^ty &c. I will this be a Law.
Jo: Seymour

23

Lib. L. L. An Act relating to the Standard of English Weights and
No. 64.    Measures

p. 162    Whereas there is now a Standard of Weights and Measures
agreeable to the Standard of Weights and Measures in her
Majestys Exchequer in England settled with in the severall
Countys of this Province.

Be it enacted by the Queens most excellent Majesty by and
with the Advice and Consent of her Majestys Governour
Councill and Assembly of this Province and the Authority of the
same that all persons whether Inhabitants or fforeigners shall
repair and bring their Stillards with which they weigh and
receive their Tobacco to the Standard yearly and every year
to be tryed Stamp'd and Numbred for which they are to pay
to the person keeping the Standard One shill for every time
such Stillards shall be tryed and stampt as aforesaid And every
person or persons that shall have their Bushell half Bushell
peck Gallon bottle Quart and pint if they make use of the same
or any of them in buying or selling by tryed and Stampt at the
Standard aforesaid Except such of the Measures aforesaid as
come out of England and are there Stampt for w<sup>ch</sup> they shall pay
for the Stamping the aforesaid Measures Six pence apiece.

And whosoever shall presume to sell by any dry Measures
without first having the said Measures tryed and Stampt at the
Standard shall forfeit the Sume of ffive hundred pounds of
Tobacco.

And whosoever likewise shall presume to weigh and receive
Tobacco by stillards have not within one year past from such
weighing and receiving been try'd and Stampt at the Standard
shall forfeit One thousand pounds of Tobacco The one half of
which fforfeitures to be to her Majesty her heires and Successors towards the Defraying the Charge of the County where
the Offender shall dwell or Reside And the other half to the
Informer or Informers to be recovered in any Court of Record
of this Province by bill plaint or Information wherein no Essoyn
proteccon or Wager of Law to be allowed.

And if any Person or Persons shall refuse to pay any Tobacco
p. 163   or by such Stillards try'd and Stamp'd as aforesaid and shall
thereby compell the Owner to have them try'd over again
within the year If the Stillards are true such person so refusing
or compelling as aforesaid shall pay for the new Stamping but
if not the Owners of the Stillards to pay for the same.

|                          |                          |
|--------------------------|--------------------------|
| Sept<sup>r</sup> 21. 1704 | Sept<sup>r</sup> 21. 1704 |
| Read and assented to by the | Read and Assented to by her |
| house of Delegates | Ma<sup>tys</sup> hon<sup>ble</sup> Councill |
| W Taylard Clk hD. | W Bladen Cl Concil |

Maryland October 3ᵈ 1704

On the Behalf of her Maᵗʸ &c. I will this be a Law.

Jₒ : Seymour

An Act for Publication of Marriages.

Be it Enacted by the Queens most excellent Majesty by and with the Advice and Consent of her Majestys Governour Councill and Assembly of this Province And the Authority of the same that all persons who desire Marriage shall apply themselves either to a Minister Pastor or Magistrate for the Contracting thereof.

And be it further enacted by the Authority aforesaid by and with the Advice and Consent aforesaid that all persons within this Province intending Marriage shall make publication thereof either at the Church Chappell County Court or Meeting house next where they dwell and that at such time when such Church Chappell or Meeting house shall be full and thereby capable to take Cognizance thereof And that it shall and may be lawfull upon Certificate had from the Minister pastor or County Court where such publication shall have been made three weeks after the said publication for either Minister Pastor or Magistrate (where no Minister can be had) to Joyn in Marriage such persons aforesaid and if any person shall presume to contract marriage without such Publication made and Certificate thereof had as aforesaid or without particular Lycense from the Governoʳ for the time being do privately within the Limitts of this Province contract Marriage every person so Contracted or marryed shall be lyable to a ffine of one thousand pounds p. 164 of Tobᵒ And every such Minister Pastor or Magistrate Joyning in Marriage any persons without such Publication or lycense or any ways infringing this Act shall be lyable to a ffine of ffive thousand pounds of Tobacco the one half of the said ffines to our Sovereign Lady the Queen her heires and Successors for the Support of the Government of this Province And the other half to the Informer to be recovered by bill plaint accon of Debt or Information in any Court of Record wherein no Essoyn protection or wager of Law to be allowed.

And be it further enacted by the Authority aforesaid by and with the Advice and Consent aforesaid That all Ministers Pastors and Magistrates who according to the law of this Province do usually Joyne people in Marryage shall Joyn them in Manner & forme as is sett down and expressd in the Liturgy of the Church of England Which being finishd the Minister Pastor or Magistrate shall say I being hereunto by law Authorized do pronounce you lawfull man and wife.

Lib. L. L. No. 64. And be it further Enacted by the Authority Advice and Consent aforesaid that the Minister Pastor or Magistrate by vertue of this Act is impowered to ask Demand and receive from the partys so marryed or Joynd together the Sume of one hundred pounds of Tobacco and no more.

September 20th 1704

Read and Assented to by the house of Dell.
W Taylard Clk hD.

Septembr 21st 1704

Read and Assented to by her Matys honble Councill.
W Bladen Cl Concil.

Maryland October 3d 1704.

On the behalf of her Maty &c. I will this be a Law
Jo: Seymour

An Act ascertaining what Damages shall be allowed upon protested bills of Exchange.

Be it enacted by the Queens most excellent Majesty by and p. 165 with the Advice and Consent of her Majestys Governor Councill and Assembly of this Province and the Authority of the same that there shall not be allowed to any person or persons whatsoever having Just Cause to implead any person or persons whatsoever living or residing within this Province upon any bill of Exchange drawn for any Sum or Sums of Mony whatsoever payable in England or elsewhere and brought in here protested more than the Sum of twenty pounds per Cent. Damages over and above the Debt sued for and recovered together with ordinary Costs of Suite Any Law Statute Usage or Custom to the Contrary Notwithstanding.

And be it further enacted by the Authority aforesaid that if any person or persons draw any bill of Exchange upon any Person or Persons or Society and Company in England or elsewhere out of this Province And the same be protested and the Protested bills be return'd into this Province within four Years after the date of Such bills That then the Debt occasion'd by the non acceptance or nonpayment of such bills shall be accounted a Debt of equall Nature with any Specialty And in payment of Debts by Executors or Administrators be preferr'd before any other Debt which is not under hand and Seale such executor or Adminr having timely Notice of such protested bills of Exchange Any Usage or Custom to the Contrary notwithstanding.

Sept<sup>r</sup> 23<sup>d</sup> 1704.

Read and Assented to by the
house of Delegates
W Taylard Clk hD.

Sept<sup>r</sup> 26<sup>th</sup> 1704

Read and assented to by her
Ma<sup>tys</sup> honble Councill.
W Bladen Cl Concil.

Lib. L. L.
No. 64.

Maryland October 3<sup>d</sup> 1704.
On the behalf of her Majesty &c I will this be a Law.

J<sub>o</sub>: Seymour

An Act Declaring how ffees for Naturalization and other pri- p. 166
vate Laws shall be proportion'd.

Whereas divers Complaints have been made that severall
persons have Exacted and taken imoderate ffees of Persons for
private bills for prevention whereof for the ffuture.

Be it enacted by the Queens most excellent Majesty by and
with the Advice and Consent of her Majestys Governour
Councill and Assembly of this Province and the Authority of
the Same that the ffees to be taken by the severall Clerks and
Officers belonging to the Assembly for Naturalization and
other private laws be such as shall be allowed and adjudg'd by
the respective Assemblys when and where such persons shall
be Naturalized and Such bill passd and that no person whatsoever presume to demand or exact any more ffees of any such
persons Naturaliz'd or for whom such private Act shall pass
than what are so allow'd and to be allowed under the penalty
of two thousand pounds of Tobacco to every ·such person
exacting or extorting more than what is or shall be allowed
by such Assembly Assessing the ffees as af<sup>d</sup> The said fforfeiture
to be recovered in any Court of Record of this Province by
Action of Debt bill plaint or Information wherein no Essoyn
Protection or Wager of Law to be allowed, the one half to her
Majesty for the Support of the Government of this Province
the other half to the party grieved.

Sept<sup>r</sup> 23<sup>d</sup> 1704

Read and Assented to by the
house of Delegates
W Taylard Clk hD.

September 26<sup>th</sup> 1704

Read and Assented to by her
Ma<sup>tys</sup> hon<sup>ble</sup> Councill
W Bladen Cl Concil.

Maryland October 3<sup>d</sup> 1704
On the behalf of her Ma<sup>ty</sup> &c I will this be a Law

J<sub>o</sub>: Seymour

Lib. L. L.
No. 64.
p. 167 An Act for Amerciaments in the Provincial and County Courts.

Whereas many Suits are arisen upon ffrivolous occasions by Litigious Persons for prevention wherof for the future.

Be it Enacted by the Queens most excellent Majesty by and with the Advice and Consent of her Majestys Governour Councill and Assembly of this Province and the Authority of the same that all persons Whatsoever that are cast in any Cause be they Plaintiff or Defendant shall be Amerced beside the Damage and Costs in the Provincial Court fifty pounds of Tobacco to be employd as the Governour and Councill shall think fitt and in the County Courts thirty pounds of Tobacco to be employ'd and disposed of towards defraying the County Charge in such Manner as the Comissioners of each respective County shall think fitt.

And for the due Collection thereof

Be it Enacted by the Authority aforesaid that the Clerk of the Provincial Court and the severall County Courts keep an exact Account of the Amerciaments and deliver or send the same to the severall Sheriffs of the particular Countys who are hereby required to collect the same with the levy and are accordingly impowered for default of payment to make distress and Comanded not to return any arrears except in Cases of Executors or Administrators who cannot pay without orders, and

Be it further Enacted that the Clerk of the respective Courts give unto the Chief Judge of such Court a List of the Amerciaments that Court imposed.

| September 23 : 1704 | September the 26th 1704 |
|---|---|
| Read and assented to by the house of Delegates | Read and assented to by her Matys honble Councill |
| W Taylard Clk hD. | W Bladen Cl Concil. |

Maryland October 3d 1704.

On the behalf of her Majesty &c. I will this be a Law.

Jo: Seymour

p. 168 An Act confirming purchases made by the Comissioners of the respective Countys by vertue of a fformer Act of Assembly Intituled An Act impowering the Comissioners of each respective Countys to purchase Land for use of their respective Courts &c.

Whereas at a Generall Assembly held at the Port of Annapolis the twenty sixth day of May One thousand six hundred Ninety seven a Certain Act of Assembly was made Intituled An Act impowering the Comissioners of each respective County to purchase lands for the use of their respective Courts which is now executed.

Be it Enacted by the Queens most excellent Majesty by and with the Advice and Consent of her Majestys Governour Councill and Assembly of this Province and the Authority of the same, that what purchases of Lands the Comissioners had made according to the said Act for the use of the respective Countys and recorded within the severall and respective County Courts whereunto they properly belong shall be a perpetual Barr against him or them from whom the land was purchasd and against all persons Claiming by from or under him her them or any of them forever.

And be it further enacted by the Authority af$^d$ that the Lott whereon the Court house of Dorchester now stands and the Tenement thereon remain to the use of that County forever as by the last paragraph of the said Act is more at large exprest.

<table>
<tr><td>Septemb$^r$ 23 : 1704</td><td>September 26$^{th}$ 1704</td></tr>
<tr><td>Read and Assented to by the house of Delegates</td><td>Read and assented to by her Majestys hon$^{ble}$ Councill.</td></tr>
<tr><td>W Taylard Clk hD.</td><td>W Bladen Cl Concil.</td></tr>
</table>

Maryland October 3$^d$ 1704

On behalf of her Ma$^{ty}$ &c. I will this be a law.

Jo: Seymour

An Act Repealing all former Acts of Assembly heretofore made saving what are hereby excepted.

Be it enacted by the Queens most excellent Majesty by and with the Advice and Consent of her Majestys Governour Councill and Assembly of this Province and the Authority of the same that all and every Act and Acts of Assembly of this Province made or Enacted at any time before the Session of Assembly begun and held at the Port of Annapolis the twenty Sixth day of Aprill One thousand and Seven hundred and four Except the Act Intituled an Act for the Establishment of Religious Worship within this Province according to the Church of England and for the Maintenance of Ministers and Except the Act for keeping good rules and orders in the Port of Annapolis and which are not revived saved and Enacted this Present Session of Assembly be and

Lib. L. L. No. 64. are hereby repealed and made void saving allways to all and every person or persons whatsoever was and is his and their rights and benefits which he or they had by the former Acts of Assembly Anything in this Present Act contain'd to the Contrary notwithstanding.

October 2ᵈ 1704

Read and assented to by the house of Delegates
W Taylard Clk hD.

Octobʳ 2ᵈ 1704

Read and Assented to by her Maᵗʸˢ honᵇˡᵉ Councill
W Bladen Cl Concil.

Maryland October 3ᵈ 1704

On behalf of her Maᵗʸ &c. I will this be a Law.

Jo: Seymour

p. 170 An Act Confirming to the Governour of this Province the duty of three pence per Tonn upon the burthen of Ships & Vessells.

Whereas the Governours of this Province have heretofore had and enjoy'd a Duty of three pence per Ton of the burthen of all Ships and Vessells trading into this Province.

Be it therefore enacted by the Queens most excellent Majesty by and with the Advice and Consent of her Majestys Governour Council and Assembly of this Province and the Authority of the same that the severall and respective Masters of all Ships of Vessells trading and Coming into this Province of what burthen soever shall at the time of entring Such Ships and Vessells as aforesaid pay unto the Governour of this Province for the time being three pence per Tonn for every Tonn of burthen the said Shipp or Vessell shall be off or give good Caution to the Navall Officer with whom he or they shall enter for payment thereof. All such Shipps or Vessells as are bonâ fide built in or belonging to the people of this province excepted.

September 21. 1704

Read & assented to by the house of Delegates
W Taylard Clk hD.

Septʳ 21ˢᵗ 1704

Read and assented to by her Maᵗʸˢ honᵇˡᵉ Councill
W Bladen Cl Concil.

Maryland October 3ᵈ 1704

On the behalf of her Maᵗʸ I will this be a Law

Jo: Seymour

An Act declaring the Act Intituled An Act ascertaining the Lib. L. L. bounds of land to be in force. No. 64.

Be it enacted by the Queens most excellent Majesty by and with the Advice and Consent of her Majestys Governour p. 171 Councill and Assembly of this Province and the Authority of the same that the Act of Assembly made at a Generall Assembly begun and held at the Porte of Annapolis the twenty seventh day of June in the year of our Lord one thousand Six hundred ninety nine Entituled An Act ascertaining the bounds of Land and every Clause Matter or thing therein Contain'd is hereby declared to be and remaine in full force and effect to all Intents Constructions and purposes whatsoever to the end of the next Sessions of Assembly this present Sessions not having leisure fully to Consider thereof.

|  |  |
|---|---|
| Sept<sup>r</sup> 30<sup>th</sup> 1704 | Septemb<sup>r</sup> 30<sup>th</sup> 1704 |
| Read and Assented to by the | Read and Assented to by her |
| house of Delegates | Ma<sup>tys</sup> hon<sup>ble</sup> Councill |
| W Taylard Clk hD. | W Bladen Cl Concil. |

Maryland October 3<sup>d</sup> 1704

On the behalf of her Ma<sup>ty</sup> &c I will this be a Law

Jo: Seymour

An Act declaring the Peticoñary Act relating to the ffree-holders to be in force.

Bee it enacted by the Queens most excellent Ma<sup>ty</sup> by and with the Advice and Consent of her Ma<sup>tys</sup> Governo<sup>r</sup> Councill and Assembly of this Province and the Authority of the same that the Petitionary Act of Assembly for founding and Establishing ffree-Schools within this Province made at a Generall Assembly of this Province begun and held at Annapolis the first Day of July in the year of our Lord One thousand six hundred Ninety Six directed to his most excellent Majesty and every branch Clause and Paragraph thereof is hereby declared to stand and be in full force power and vertue to all Intents Construccons and purposes whatsoever.

|  |  |
|---|---|
| September 30<sup>th</sup> 1704 | September 30<sup>th</sup> 1704 |
| Read and Assented to by the | Read and Assented to by her |
| house of Delegates. | Ma<sup>tys</sup> hon<sup>ble</sup> Councill |
| W Taylard Clk hD | W Bladen Cl Concil. |

                        Maryland October 3ᵈ 1704.
           On the behalf of her Maᵗʸ &c I will this be a Law.
                                                    Jo: Seymour

p. 172 An Act enabling William Sweatnam of Talbot County Gent
       Devisee of Richard Sweatnam dec'd to sell Sixteen hundred
       and twenty four Acres of Land.

    Whereas Capt. Richard Sweatnam late of Talbot County
deceased by his last will and Testament duly proved and
recorded in the Office of the Judge for probatt of Wills and
granting Administrations &c did devise unto his son William
Sweatnam four thousand seven hundred and fifty seven acres
of Land party of which were these following tracts called
and Containing as herein exprest (to witt) Abington two
hundred Acres, Bodwell two hundred and fifty Acres Downs
fforrest three hundred Acres Bridgwater three hundred Acres
Hacton two hundred and fifty Acres Moorfields one hundred
and twenty four Acres and Browns Lott two hundred Acres
in all sixteen hundred and twenty four Acres lying in Talbot
and other Countys which by the said Will were entail'd on
the said William Sweatnam and the beires of his body and in
default thereof to his brother John Sweatnam and the heires
of his body both which sons of the said Capᵗ Richard Sweatnam that is to say William and John Sweatnam are now living
and have issue of their bodys lawfully begotten And have
apply'd to this Generall Assembly that in regard the said
sixteen hundred and twenty four Acres of Land are fforrest
land and at present of little or no Advantage to the said
William Sweatnam or in any Considerable time likely to be
so but that the rents thereof will in a Small time Surmount
the value of the said lands there being now due therefore to
the right honourable the Lord Proprietary one hundred and
forty pounds sterl.  The Burgesses of this Generall Assembly
do pray that it may be Enacted and
    Be it Enacted by the Queens most excellent Majesty by and
with the Advice and Consent of her Majestys Governour
Councill and Assembly of this Province and the Authority of
the same that the said William Sweatnam for the reasons
aforesaid be and is hereby Empowered (notwithstanding
p. 173 such entaile by the last Will and Testament of the said Capᵗ
Richard Sweatnam or any other Law Statute or Usage to the
Contrary) to sell or other wise dispose of the aforesaid tracts
of Land called Abington Bodwell Downs fforrest Bridgwater Hacton Moorefields and Browns lott containing sixteen hundred and twenty four Acres of Land to any persons

whatsoever their heires and Assigns who by vertue of this Lib. L. L.
Act and the Grant and Conveyance of the aforesaid severall No. 64.
tracts of Land or any part of them by the said William
Sweatnam to them their heires and Assigns shall forever have
hold occupy and enjoy to them their heires and assigns for
ever a good Size and indefeazable Estate of Inheritance in
ffee simple The force and effect of the said Will of the said
Captain Richard Sweatnam or any Law Statute or usage to
the Contrary in any wise notwithstanding.

|  |  |
|---|---|
| September 21. 1704 | September 21st 1704 |
| Read and Assented to by the | Read and Assented to by her |
| house of Delegates. | Majestys honble Councill |
| W Taylard Clk hD. | W Bladen Cl Concil. |

Maryland October 3d 1704.
On the behalf of her Maty &c. I will this be a Law.

Jo: Seymour

### An Act for settling of Lands on Susanna Blaney &c.

Whereas David Blany late of Talbot County in the Province of Maryland deceasd did by his last will and Testament
give devise and bequeath unto Susanna Blaney daughter of
the said David and to her heires for ever a Certain tract
of Land being part of two tracts of Land the one called
Wisbitch and the other Poplar Hill containing in all fifty
Acres lying on the east side Back Wye River in Talbot
County for which said tract of Land the said David Blaney
had bargain'd and fully paid to one Benjamin Blackleach
of Cecill County in the Province aforesaid whereupon the
said Blackleach past his obligation for Conveyance of the
same But the said David unhappily dying before the said
Blackleach had Conveyed over the said Lands and Katherine the relict and Executrix of the said David afterwards
intermarrying with one William Alderne of Talbot County
aforesaid which said Aldern contrary to many solemn promises made in behalf of the said Susanna prevaild with the p. 174
said Blackleach to convey the said land to himself and his
heires and assigns for ever and upon so doing delivered the
said Blackleach his Obligation past to the said Blaney as
aforesaid yet notwithstanding the aforesaid Conveyance of
the aforesaid lands He the said Alderne constantly promised
that he would either by Will or Deed give or Convey the said
lands to the said Susanna But being since dead Intestate and

Lib. L. L.
No. 64. w^{th}out passing any Deed therefore the said Katherine in behalf of the said Susanna humbly prays that it may be Enacted and

Be it enacted by the Queens most excellent Majesty by and with the Advice and Consent of her Majestys Governour Councill and Assembly of this Province and the Authority of the same that the Estate of the said William Alderne his heires or Assigns therein so unjustly gain'd cease and deter-mine and that the said ffifty Acres of Land with all the Tenements Hereditaments and appurtenances thereto be-longing or in any wise appertaining be settled and Vested in the said Susanna Blaney her heires and assigns for ever any Claime of the said Benjamin Blackleach his heires or Assigns or any Law statute usage or Custom to the Contrary in any wise notwithstanding.

|  |  |
|---|---|
| September 26^{th} 1704 | Septemb. 26^{th} 1704 |
| Read and assented to by the house of Delegates. | Read and assented to by her Ma^{tys} hon^{ble} Councill |
| W Taylard Cl hD. | W Bladen Cl Concll. |

Maryland October 3^{d} 1704

On the behalf of her Ma^{ty} &c I will this be a Law.

Jo. Seymour

An Act confirming the last wills and Testaments of Charles Ashcome late of Saint Marys County Gent^{n} deceasd and of John Whinfell of Calvert County planter deceased and likewise of John Burnam late of Talbot County deceasd.

p. 175 Be it enacted by the Queens most excellent Majesty by and with the Advice and Consent of her Majestys Governour Councill and Assembly of this Province and the Authority of the same that the last Wills and Testaments of Charles Ash-come late of Saint Marys County Gent deceased being in ffavour of his Children and the last will and Testament of John Whinfell late of Calvert County Planter deceased being in favour of his son Jonas Whinfell and each and either of the said last wills and Testaments shall be good and effectual in Law to all Intents Constructions and purposes whatsoever to pass the said Lands therein mencoñd and to pass Vest and settle the severall Estates of Inheritance therein expressed to be devised to the severall persons and their Heires therein mencoñd according to the Intent of the Testators notwith-standing that the said Wills were only publishd and declar'd

in the presence of two Witnesses whereas more by Law are Lib. L. L. No. 64.
required thereto Any Law Statute or Usage to the contrary in
any wise notwithstanding.

And be it further Enacted by the Authority Advice and
Consent aforesaid that the last will and Testament of John
Burnam late of Talbot County deceased shall be good and
effectual in the law to all Intents purposes and Construccons
whatsoever and shall be sufficient to pass the Lands therein
mencoñd and to Vest and settle the ffee simple thereof in
Samuel Dowlin his heires and assigns forever according to the
Intention of the said Will any Inability by Nonage in the
Testator notwithstanding.

And that the Will of the said John Whinfell having not yet
been entred upon Record in the Comissarys office be now
received and recorded in the said Comissarys Office and
accepted and taken at all times as the Will of the said John
Whinfell

<table>
<tr><td>September 26<sup>th</sup> 1704</td><td>September 26<sup>th</sup>1704</td></tr>
<tr><td>Read and Assented to by the<br>house of Delegates<br>W Taylard Cl hD.</td><td>Read and assented to by her<br>Ma<sup>tys</sup> honb<sup>le</sup> Councill<br>W Bladen Cl Concil.</td></tr>
</table>

Maryland October 3<sup>d</sup> 1704

On the behalf of her Ma<sup>ty</sup> &c I will this be a Law.

Jo: Seymour

An Act to enable Colonell Edward Dorsey to sell some entaild p. 176
Lands and houses in the Port of Annapolis for the use of
his Children.

Whereas Colonell Edward Dorsey has represented to the
Generall Assembly that he has built in the Town and Port of
Annapolis severall houses which he afterwards entaild upon
his Children and that the said Houses are now and have been for
a Considerable time untenanted whereby they are in a Ruinous
Condition and will in a little time be quite decay'd and totally
lost to the said Children with whose Conveniency it does not
consist to reside in the same themselves but could in Case the
said Intaile were cutt of dispose of the same to some advantage wherefore it was prayd that An Act might be pass'd in
favour of the s<sup>d</sup> Children that the said Entaile may be Cutt off
And the said Edward impowered to make Sale of the said
houses for the benefitt and advantage of his said Children.

September 2⁺ 1704
Read and Asseted to by
the house of Deleates
W Taylar Clk hD.

September 26ᵗʰ 1704
Read and Assented to by her
Maᵗʸˢ honᵇˡᵉ Councill
W Bladen Cl Concll.

!aryland October 3ᵈ 1704
On the behalf o her Majesty &c I will this be a Law.
Jo : Seymour

The Seale of th Secretaries Office
affixed hereunto n the behalf of
Sʳ Thomas Laurene Baronᵗ Secreʸ

ꝑ me
Th Bordley Clk of the
Secretaries office.

Lib. L. L.    Be it therefore enacted by the Queens most excellent Majesty
No. 64.    by and with the Advice and Consent of her Majestys Governour
Councill and Assembly of this Province and the Authority of
the same  That the said Entaile shall be and is hereby forever
Cutt off And the said Colonell Edward Dorsey hereby Empowered to make unto any purchaser or purchasers of any or
all the said Houses and lotts of Ground thereunto belonging
a good firm Estate of Inheritance in ffee Simple for such Consideration as such purchasers and he shall agree upon (the
said Entaile or any thing therein contain'd to the Contrary
notwithstanding.

And that the purchase mony arising by the sale of all or
any the said houses and Lands shall be  paid and delivered to
such Child or Children to whom the said houses or Lands
belonged by vertue of the same Entaile.

September 21 : 1704           September 21. 1704

Read and assented to by the     Read and assented to by Her
house of Delegates.           Ma^{ty*} hon^{ble} Councill
W Taylard Clk hD            W Bladen Cl Concil.

Maryland October 3^d 1704.

On the behalf of her Ma^{ty} &c I will this be a Law.

Jo : Seymour

p. 177 An Act for Naturalization of Otho Othason of Cecill County.

Be it enacted by the Queens most excellent Majesty by and
with the Advice and Consent of her Majestys Governour
Councill and Assembly of this Province and the Authority of
the same that Otho Othason of Cecill County Planter born in
the Province of Pensilvania of parents from Guelderland in
Holland shall from hence forth be adjudg'd reputed and taken
as one of her Majestys Naturall borne Subjects of this Province And that he by the Authority aforesaid be enabled and
adjudg'd to all Intents and purposes to demand Challenge ask
have hold and enjoy any Lands Tenements Rents and Hereditaments to which he might any ways be Entituled as if he
were a free and Naturall born Subject And also be enabled to
prosecute Maintain avow Justify and defend all Manner of
Accons Suites Pleas Plaints and other demands whatsoever as
liberally frankly freely fully and lawfully as if he had been a
Naturall borne Subject within this Province Any Law statute
usage or Custom to the Contrary notwithstanding.

Lib. L. L.
No. 64.

September 23ᵈ 1704
Read and Assented to by
the house of Delegates
W Taylard Clk hD.

September 26ᵗʰ 1704
Read and Assented to by her
Maᵗʸˢ honᵇˡᵉ Councill
W Bladen Cl Concil.

Maryland October 3ᵈ 1704
On the behalf of her Majesty &c I will this be a Law.
Jo : Seymour

The Seale of the Secretaries Office
affixed hereunto on the behalf of
Sʳ Thomas Laurence Baronᵗ Secreᵗʸ

p me
Th Bordley Clk of the
Secretaries office.

Lib. L. L.
No. 64.
Be it therefore enactedy the Queens most excellent Majesty by and with the Advice ad Consent of her Majestys Governour Councill and Assembly f this Province and the Authority of the same  That the said :ntaile shall be and is hereby forever Cutt off  And the said :olonell Edward Dorsey hereby Empowered to make unto ay purchaser or purchasers of any or all the said Houses and otts of Ground thereunto belonging a good firm Estate of Ineritance in ffee Simple for such Con. sideration as such purqasers and he shall agree upon (the said Entaile or any thig therein contain'd to the Contrary notwithstanding.

And that the purchæ mony arising by the sale of all or any the said houses ancLands shall be  paid and delivered to such Child or Childre to whom the said houses or Lands belonged by vertue of te same Entaile.

<table>
<tr><td>September 21 . 174</td><td>September 21. 1704</td></tr>
<tr><td>Read and assented toy the<br>house of Delegats.<br>W Taylard Cc hD</td><td>Read and assented to by Her<br>Ma'y' honᵇˡᵉ Councill<br>W Bladen Cl Concil.</td></tr>
</table>

Maryand October 3ᵈ 1704.

On the behalf of hc Ma'y &c I will this be a Law.

Jo : Seymour

p. 17: An Act for Naturalizaon of Otho Othason of Cecill County.

Be it enacted by thQueens most excellent Majesty by and with the Advice and Consent of her Majestys Governour Councill and Assembl of this Province and the Authority of the same that Otho Oiason of Cecill County Planter born in the Province of Pensvania of parents from Guelderland in Holland shall from hece forth be adjudg'd reputed and taken as one of her Majests Naturall borne Subjects of this Province And that he byhe Authority aforesaid be enabled and adjudg'd to all Intent and purposes to demand Challenge ask have hold and enjoy ny Lands Tenements Rents and Hereditaments to which t might any ways be Entituled as if he were a free and Nattall born Subject And also be enabled to prosecute Maintain aow Justify and defend all Manner of Accons Suites Pleas laints and other demands whatsoever as liberally frankly freel fully and lawfully as if he had been a Naturali borne Subjet within this Province Any Law statute usage or Custom tohe Contrary notwithstanding.

September 23d 1704
Read and Assented to by
the house of Delegates
W Taylard Clk hD.

September 30th 1704
Read and Assented to by her
Maty Honble Councill
W Bladen Cl Councill

Maryland October 3'1704
On the behalf of her Majesty &c I wl this be a Law.
Jo Seymour

The Seale of the Secretaries Offi
affixed hereunto on the behalf of
Sr Thomas Laurence Baron' Secre

I hereby Certify that is
Secretaries Offire

# PROCEEDINGS AND ACTS

OF THE

# GENERAL ASSEMBLY

# OF MARYLAND.

*At a Session held at Annapolis, Dec.* 5-9, 1704.

CHARLES CALVERT, LORD BALTIMORE,
*Proprietary.*

JOHN SEYMOUR,
*Governor.*

---

THE UPPER HOUSE OF ASSEMBLY.

24

Mary l:

Annaṛ
ber in
Ann by
Ireland
1704.

and Go

This
eral A:
that Pu
Board ⱱ
this pre
Advice
thereto.
Prem

Hon:.ᵇˡᵉ

meetin
Counci
Provinc
to Con
stances
being b
lating o

At a Council in Assembly held at the Town and Port of
Annapolis in Anne Arundel County the fifth Day of Decem-
ber in the third · year of the reign of our Sovereign Lady
Ann by the Grace of God of England Scotland France and
Ireland Queen Defender of the Faith &c. Annoq Domini
1704.

### Were Present

His Excell John Seymour Esq<sup>r</sup> her Majesty's Cap<sup>t</sup> General
and Governour in chief

|                          |                          |
|--------------------------|--------------------------|
| Thomas Tench Esq<sup>r</sup> | Col Edward Lloyd |
| The hon<sup>ble</sup> Tho<sup>s</sup> Brook Esq<sup>r</sup> | L<sup>t</sup> Col W<sup>m</sup> Holland |
| Col John Hammond | Ja<sup>s</sup> Sanders Esq<sup>r</sup> |

This being the Day appointed for the meeting of the General Assembly pursuant to his Excellency's Proclamation to
that Purpose his Excellency was pleased to communicate to the
Board what he intended to say to them upon the opening of
this present sessions as followeth & desired them to give their
Advice what they thought proper to be left out or added
thereto.

Premising to and thus bespeaking the Council

Hon:<sup>ble</sup> Gentlemen

I Thank God We have so good Weather at this present
meeting whereby all the Gentlemen of her Ma:<sup>tys</sup> hon<sup>ble</sup>
Council as also those of the house of Delegates of this
Province have the opportunity of being Present here in order
to Consult advise and Redress the present unhappy Circumstances this Province lyes under of our publick Court House
being burnt with several of our Laws especially that for regulating our Militia so absolutely necessary that it would be the
greatest neglect and folly not to Endeavour reenacting thereof
Whereupon so much depends the preservation & defence of
the Country

I must acquaint you that upon the 21<sup>st</sup> of October last with
the advice of the Gent. of her Ma:ty's Council then present I
thought fitt upon the pressing occasion to Convene the
Assembly upon the 21<sup>st</sup> of November and accordingly issued
Proclamations to the several Countys for Convening them
But afterwards finding that it was doubted by some whether it
might not be irregular to have them meet sooner than this

U. H. J. Day the Time they were first Prorogued to. I offered it to
three of her Majesty's hon:ᵇˡᵉ Council being all I could then
get to advise with. Who gave me their best Advice and that
upon the greatest Reason that since it was doubted whether
they should meet sooner than the Time they were once
Prorogued to It was far safer they should be Convened at the
certain Time they were first Prorogued to rather than run any
Hazard of the Legality of the Session

P. 347   After which his Excell ordered the Clerk of the Council to
read what he intended to say to the Assembly. Which being
read all the Gent. of her Majesty's Council being now present
do very well approve thereof as Sufficient & proper on this
occasion

Came Mʳ Henry Coursey Mʳ Robert Gooldsborough Col
Smallwood Mʳ Elias King and Mʳ James Philips to acquaint
his Excell the Governour that there is an appearance of the
majority of the House of Delegates and that they were Come
from them to inform his Excell of the death of Col Wᵐ Dent
their Speaker and desired his Commands to make Choice of
another

To which his Excellency was pleased to answer they might
do so

Came Mʳ Gooldsborough and Mʳ Coursey to acquaint his
Excellency that the House had made choice of a Speaker and
waited his Leave to present him

To which his Excell made answer that he was ready to
receive them

Then came the house of Delegates and presented Col Thoˢ
Smith for their Speaker who formerly acknowledged that
besides his present Inability of Body he well knew. himself
unfitt for that Service and prayed his Excellency would Command the House to make choice of a better

But his Excell was pleased to say he doubted not the
wisdom of the House of Delegates in their Choice of him
who had so fair a Character and would not admitt his Excuse
         to restore him to a good Health of body
the better to Enable him to Discharge his office

Original   Then the Speaker prayed his Exⁿᶜʸ to Grant them the free
Journal.  Exercise of their Rights and Priviledges that they might not
be infringed but suffered freedom of Debate and Access to his
Exⁿᶜʸˢ person & if any mistake should arise it might be Candidly Interpreted

Which his Exⁿᶜʸ was pleased to Assure him of and then
bespake them as followeth.

Mʳ Speaker and you Gentⁿ Delegates.

Your now meeting at this late & unseasonable time of the
year presses your utmost Sedulity in the Dispatch of the

necessary affairs now to be laid before you. The late melancholy Accident might have been prevented, had my often Admonition took place, for I never yet saw any publiq buildings left Solely to Providence but in Maryland. I hope this sad experiment will awaken your Care for the time to come. And in the Interim y$^r$ best consideration to secure the Laws and records of y$^r$ Country, for the Advantage and quiett of ffuture Generations. What is proper to be done in Rebuilding your Statehouse so very necessary for the accomodation of the publiq I Leave Intirely to your own Serious Debates and decision for I have no other ayme than the true Interest and Service of your Country; and shall be heartily sorry to find any here so farr mistaken to Imagine in the Least It can be separate from that of the Crown of England:

This opinion all men of Sence will be ashamed of since I have given you the strictest Assurance of my Constant resolution to Governe you whilst I have the honour to Comand here with a most tender reguard to her Ma$^{tys}$ honour and Service, useing my best endeavour to Advance the Prosperity, and Reputation of this Province, I can never doubt but my Integrity in your Service has been Sufficiently evident by some tryalls since my Administration as you handsomly owned with your thanks the last Session.

Therefore avoiding all heats & misconstructions; I hope you will with me and her Ma$^{tys}$ honble Councill most heartily apply y$^r$selves to the redressing the present Exigencys your Country now lyes under, which will be most acceptable to her Ma$^{ty}$ and very gratefull to myselfe for when you do truly well for yourselves all men will aplaud your Judgement

Gent. the Account of Our Indians giving us a late disturbance shall be laid before you which Realy requires your Consideration, and I heartily Crave your advice and Assistance in this Juncture, th$^t$ for the future, every member of the Province may Enjoy the fruits of his Labour and Industry in peace and Satisfaction.

Never let us be mistaken Gent. in each other but strive Joyntly and heartily, to serve the Country the best & most Judicious way we Cann and oppose whatever may be Imagined prejudiciall to it, in any one Instance w$^t$soever.

The Board ajorned till to morrow morning at nine a Clock.

Wednesday December the 6$^{th}$ 1704.

The Councill in Assembly Sate Present

His Ex$^{ncy}$ the Governour

| Thomas Tench | | | L$^t$ Coll W$^m$ Holland | |
|---|---|---|---|---|
| Thomas Brooke | } | Esq$^{rs}$ | James Sanders Esq$^r$ | } |
| Coll Edward Lloyd | } | | W$^m$ Coursey Esq$^r$ | |

His Ex^ncy being Informed that M^r Thomas Collier Nav^ll
Officer at the Port of W^m Stadt had Cleared the Elizabeth of
Leverpool Edward Ratchdale Ma^r bound for England notwithstanding the Embargoe layd by the Government, advised
that Whereas the said Shipp is still in the Bay that his Ex^ncy as
Vice Admirall will be pleased to Command the said master
to Appear before him before he p^rsumes to Depart this province and thereupon a Warrant was Issued to that purpose
and M^r Tho: Collier being Called in was severely Repre-
manded and Comanded to use his uttmost Dilligence to bring
the said Master before his ^Ex^ncy & prevent his sayling.

The Board adjourned for two hours.

Post Merid.    The Councill Sate present as before

His Ex^ncy is pleased to say that upon many Emergencys
Especially upon the late misfortune of the Court house not
being able to gett any number of the Councill together the
Weather being so hard, he had offten occasion to require the
hon^ble Coll. Hamonds advice and assistance who upon all
Occasion has bin very Ready to undergo the Fatigue of attending being for her Ma^tys Service and good of the Country for which the Gent. of the Councill with his Ex^ncy Give
Coll Hamond their hearty Thanks.

His Ex^ncy purposes to the Board that whereas It is now
time of Warr and the province is but Indifferently provided
with Ammunition the greatest part of the powder being old
and decayed—there being a Considerable sume of money
now in Banck for the purchasing thereof whether it would be
proper to send for a Considerable Quantity of Armes and
Aminision, and to what value, to which the Councill do say
that for the present Service of the Country It will be necessary to send for 200 musquets of high Caliver Boare & 100
Carabines Snapphance & 100 Cuttlaces with Broad Deep
Blades to thrust as well as Cutt with Seale Skinn Scabbards,
200 Catouch Boxes and belts 110 half Barrells of good powder of 56 C weight and 5000 weight of Lead one-halfe in
Bulletts & the other in high Swann shott.

His Ex^ncy says that He observes the Country powder is
dayly decaying, but if there were a Double Store it might be
sold for the full value or more at this tyme.    Therefore proposes that when the Country is so well supplyed that It may
be in the power of the Comander in Chiefe of every County
to sell and dispose thereof rendring an Account to his Ex^ncy
the Governour and the Councill thereof.

Ordered that George Plater Esq^r her Ma^tys Receiver of the
district of patuxent observe his Ex^ncys Directions in Lodging

moneys in England Sufficient to purchase the af<sup>d</sup> Armes and Amunition.

The Councill adjurned till 8 of the Clock to morrow morning

### Thursday December the 7th 1704

#### The Councill Sate present as yesterday

Came the hon<sup>ble</sup> Kenelm Cheseldyn Esq<sup>r</sup> & was added to the Board.

Major Greenberry and five other members from the house bring the following answer to what his Ex<sup>ncy</sup> was pleased to say to them on their meeting

#### By the house of Del December the 7<sup>th</sup> 1704

May it please your Ex<sup>ncy</sup>

Wee have Taken your Ex<sup>ncys</sup> Speech at the opening of this Session into our Consideration and have Resolved with all the unanimity & Dispatch propper to such a Conjuncture to take all possible care proper for the preservation of the Records & Restoring the State house to its former beauty and usefulness by Rebuilding and making Good the Bricks thereof. Wee shall be very sorry to be found in such a mistake as to Imagin that we cann have a Seperate Interest from that of the Crowne of England but hope that constant unanimity of our Debates and Resolutions will shew us to have no other Intentions or Designs then such as may Tend to her Ma<sup>tys</sup> hon<sup>r</sup> and the good of the Country.

And as we shall be att all times very Cearfull to avoid the Entertainm<sup>t</sup> of Jelouscy & Runing Ourselves into heats & misconstructions so we shall very Readily Joyne with your Ex<sup>ncy</sup> and her Ma<sup>tys</sup> hon<sup>ble</sup> Councill in whatsoever shall appear to be for her Ma<sup>tys</sup> hon<sup>r</sup> and the Good of the Country.

As to the Indians business When the Ex<sup>ncy</sup> shall think fitt to Lay it before us we shall not only give our best Advice & Assistance therein but further it with all the unanimity and dispatch which may be proper for that Affaire.

S<sup>r</sup> Wee are very sensible of y<sup>r</sup> Ex<sup>ncys</sup> Good Governm<sup>t</sup> and tender Reguard towards us & doe hope that the same tenderness will be Continued to us: and wee take this opeartunity to assure your Ex<sup>ncy</sup> that as wee cann Entertain no Jealouscys so we shall be Allways ready to make returnes of Gratitude for the Enjoyment of so Great a blessing.

Signed p Order W Taylard Cll house Del.

Esq<sup>r</sup> Tench M<sup>r</sup> Brook and Coll Lloyd
Sent to the house with the following Message.

By his Ex^{ncy} the Governour and Councill in Assembly
Decemb^r 7th. 1704.

Since the unhappy Accident of our Court house and some
of our Laws burnt hath induced this Present meeting of the
Countrye His Ex^{ncy} thought that it might conduce to the obviating the publiq Charge of detaining the Session for the
transcribing them (some being very Long) to have the Bills
which were Read in the house sent for from the late Speakers
house in Charles County and having Ordered them to be
Transcribed ag^t your meeting, They are with the original
Draughts of the said Bills herew^th Recomended to your Consideration for the Reenacting thereof if you see fitt
Signed ꝑ Ord^r W Bladen Cll Councill.

M^r Sanders and Coll Holland sent with the other Message

By his Ex^{ncy} the Govern^r and Councill in Assembly
December the 7th 1704
Gent.
The Misfortune of Ann Arundell County is perticularly
deplorable in the Loss of all their Records being Burnt in the
publiq Court house and Requires Your best thoughts to relieve
the many Confutions & Perplexitys that County lyes now
under. Wherefore we Desire Your Advice & Assistance in
framing some Law which may settle the minds of the Inhabitants there and Confirme the Rights of severall now fresh in
memory which by Length of time may be worne out to the
prejudice of many
Signed ꝑ Ord^r W Bladen Cll Councill

Came Col Smallwood and gave the following Account that
according to his Ex^{ncys} Comand he took sixteen men and an
Indian Interpreter in order to go to the Indians on the Forke
of Potomeck. The first night they lay without the Inhabitants,
And the snow being upon the Ground they saw no footing
untill they came within a mile of the Forte where they heard
an Indian cutting. Then they came to an Hutt whence they
sent two Indians to go see for the Indians & Acquaint them
that the English were come friendly to them & desired to
Speake with them, Also sent Robin the Indian to see for the
Indians who returned the next morning and told him He had
been at one of the Indian Cabbins under the Mountayns but
there were few at home the Chiefe of their greate menn being
gone out a Bear-hunting. Says He. understands there had
been a great Mortality among them, & to the Number of 57 men

Women & Children dead, Supposed of the Small pox. So
that they had left their Forte, where they have a greate deal
of Corne in their Cabbins and all the last Years Corne Standing.

His Ex$^{ncy}$ asks Col Smallwood if he thinks the Inhabitants
on the Eastern Branch may be secure without keeping out
Rangers. Col Smallwood answers that He Cannot say but
believes the matter might be better Settled by further dis-
coursing them.

The Petition of the Inhabitants on the Eastern Branch of
Potowmeck read praying to be better Secured from the Insults
of the Indians. The said Petition with other papers relating
to the Indians sent to the House by Col Hamond & M$^r$ Coursey.

Major Taylor and M$^r$ Dollahyde bring from the House the
following Message Viz.

By the House of Delegates
Dec$^r$ 7$^{th}$ 1704

Upon reading Your Hono$^{rs}$ Message this Day p Col Holland
& James Sanders Esq$^r$ for Assisting in frameing a Bill for
Reliefe of the Inhabitants of Ann-Arundell County in relation
to the Records burnt in the State House. This House have
Considered the Same and in Answer thereto Resolved that
leave is given to the said County to bring in a Bill for their
Reliefe. And Ordered that the Delegates of the said County
prepare a Bill for that Purpose

Signed p Ord$^r$ W Taylard Clk house Del.

Major Taylor & M$^r$ Dollahyde also brought in the Agreem$^t$
of the House with Colonel Dorsey for the Rent of his Greate
House for the Assembly and Courts to Sitt in at twenty pounds
Sterl p Ann : Which was assented to by this Boarde & returned
to the house by M$^r$ Sanders.

It being represented to the Boarde that Col William Dent
Who was the Attorny of S$^r$ Thomas Laurence (her Ma$^{tys}$ Secry
of this Province now in England) is lately dead, and no other
Person in the County impowered thereunto, It is thought
fitting that this Boarde give order to Some person to take care
of S$^r$ Thomas's Interest.

Whereupon the Boarde being informed that the said S$^r$
Thomas Laurence had assigned and made over all the Fees
proffitts and Perquisitts of his Secry's office to William Bladen
for the Satisfaction and payment of two hundred and forty
pounds sterl. 115293 of tob$^o$ The said William Bladen is
thought the properest person to take Care of those ffees And
Whereas it is absolutely necessary that the said S$^r$ Thomas's

Original
Journal. Clerks who mannage the office and the Deputy Secry should be payd their respective Sallarys.

Ordered that the said Bladen take Care and see them payd out of S$^r$ Tho$^{ss}$ Fees.

M$^r$ Eccleston and M$^r$ Hudson with the fol Message. Viz.

### By the House of Delegates
### Dec$^r$ 7th, 1704

The Rebuilding the Stadt house now lying under Consideration this house have resolved their Willingness to rebuild the said house in as Comodious a Manner as before & accordingly treated with M$^r$ Bladen Concerning the Same but his Demands being so great this house will not Concurr

Therefore it is resolved that a Comittee be appointed to treat bargain & agree with such persons as will undertake the said Work & accordingly have appointed M$^r$ Sam$^l$ Young M$^r$ Charles Greenberry M$^r$ Joseph Hill & M$^r$ Rich$^d$ Jones Dell$^s$ of Ann A$^{ll}$ County for that purpose, And likewise that this house pray his Ex$^{ncy}$ to appoint two of the hon$^{rble}$ Councill to Joyne with them & that a bill may be prepared to give them Authority to do the same to which the Concurrence of his Ex$^{ncy}$ & Councill is prayd.          Signed ꝑ Ord$^r$ W Taylard Clk hD.

The Board adjourn'd for an hour.

Post Meridiem.    The Councill Sate P$^r$sent as before.

Proposed that some fitting capable person be appointed Comissary of Warr within this Province to go twice Yearly through the Severall Countys and inspect the Arms & Amunition and see they be in good order. And that such Person take a particular Account thereof in Writing & present the same to his Ex$^{ncy}$ that he may at all tymes know in what order the s$^d$ Arms are & where lodged but that untill he shall be approv'd of in England and his Sallery settled He be payed his Travelling Charges only out of the Duty of 3$^d$ ꝑ h. for purchasing Arms first giving good Security for the Discharge of his Trust & office.

The Boarde do very well approve thereof but cannot propose any propper Person now obvious to their thoughts.

His Ex$^{ncy}$ is pleas'd to aske them what they thinke of M$^r$ Philemon Lloyd of Talbott County.

The Councill are of Opinion there cannot be a properer Person and desire his Ex$^{ncy}$ to comissionate him thereto.

Came Col Smithson and ten other members from the House with the Houses Thanks to his Ex$^{ncy}$ as fol.

By the House of Del Dec<sup>r</sup> 7th, 1704

May it Please Yo<sup>r</sup> Ex<sup>ncy</sup>.

Your sending for those Bills to the late Speakers House in Charles County which You comunicated to this House and the transcribing of them Wee acknowledge have been very advantageous to the Dispatch of Affairs in this House Wee highly applaude Your Care and Prudence therein, and returne Your Ex<sup>ncy</sup> our most hearty thanks for the same.

Signed p Ord<sup>r</sup> W<sup>m</sup> Taylard Cl House Del.

Came M<sup>r</sup> Hill with the proposed Ordinance for erecting the Publique Pews in S<sup>t</sup> Anns Church in Annapolis. Which was assented to & sent to the House by M<sup>r</sup> Coursey.

M<sup>r</sup> Hill brought up a Bill read in the House for Lymitting Officers ffees.

Which was read at the Boarde the first & Second tymes and Sent to the House by M<sup>r</sup> Sanders.

Whereas Richard Clarke of Ann Arundell County stands indicted as well in the Provinciall as that County Court for divers heinous offences as Forgery & uncasing and altering the Quality of Tobacco against whom Sundry Process of Cap<sup>s</sup> & Attachm<sup>t</sup> have at her Ma<sup>tys</sup> suite been awarded; ag<sup>t</sup> which He stands out riding armed to the Terrour of the Sherriffe and other her Ma<sup>tys</sup> Liege People in Contempt of the Law and breach of her Ma<sup>tys</sup> Peace &c.

It is therefore proposed that a peall Act do pass this Session of Assembly to outlaw the said Rich<sup>d</sup> Clarke in case he do not surrender himselfe to Justice within twenty Days after the Copy of the said Act is by the Sheriffe left at his house.

Ord<sup>rd</sup> the said Proposall be carryed to the House by Col W<sup>m</sup> Holland

The Councill adjourn'd untill 8 of the Clock to morrow morning

### Fryday December 8th 1704.

#### The Council Sate P<sup>r</sup>sent as Yesterday

Col Lloyd upon extraordinary Occasions had Leave to go home

The foll<sup>o</sup> message w<sup>ch</sup> Remarques about the Laws sent to the House by M<sup>r</sup> Brooke Col Holland and M<sup>r</sup> Sanders.

### By his Ex<sup>ncy</sup> the Governo<sup>r</sup> & Councill
### Fryday Decemb 8th. 1704.

Since the rising of the late Session of Assembly the following remarqs have been made on some pticular Laws.

Original     1. And first as to the Act prohibiting the Importation of
Journal. bread Bear Flower & Grain from Pensilvania & other parts
of America whether it be in the Legislative Power of this
Province so to do or any otherwise prohibitt trade and if it
were not better to lay a Severe duty thereon which might
serve for a Prohibition

2. That as to the Act obliging Masters of Shipps to publish their Freight before they take tobacco on board It is not
so well worded and ascertained by saying their Certain
ffreight to answer the Intent of the Makers but only serves
to amuse the Merchants at home

3. The Act for laying a Duty of $9^d$ ⅌ Gall on Rum &c
from Pensilvania has not appointed proper Officers for gathering the sayd Impost nor has it given any Power to seize them
in the night time

Of which yo$^r$ Consideration is desired

Signèd ⅌ Order W Bladen Cl Concil

M$^r$ Mackall and M$^r$ Dollahyde bring up the following Bills
being these lately burnt in the Court House & now Engrossed
assented to by the House Viz.

An Act for Limitation of Officers Fees

An Act for Ordering and regulating the Militia &c

An Act for preserving harbours &c.  An Act for Ad-
vancem$^t$ of the Natives &c

An Act. Declaring the Devision of the Countys to be firm
& Stable &c  An Act causing Jurrors &c to Come to the
Provinciall and County Courts

An Act for payment of Fees due from Criminalls

An Act declaring several Laws in force heretofore made.
The said Engrossed Bills were assented to and sent to the
House by M$^r$ Tench & M$^r$ Sanders.  Who had orders to ac-
quaint the House that His Ex$^{ncy}$ had agreed with M$^r$ Evan
Jones of this Towne a Sober Person to looke after the Pub-
lique Buildings at the Rate of tenn pounds ⅌ annum.

Ordered that the Ministers & Readers of every Parish
send an exact List of the parochiall Librarys to his Ex$^{ncy}$ attested by the Vestry.

M$^r$ Taylor and three other members with the Roman Catholique Remonstrance and the houses answer which was endorsed as followeth

By the Governour and Councill December 8th. 1704

This Board are willing a Bill should be brought in to suspend the prosecution of any Romish Priest in Curing the

Penalty of the late Act by executing the function in a private Roman Catholique Family during the Term of Eighteen Months or untill her Ma^{tys} Royall Pleasure shall be knowne therein. Signed ꝑ Ord^r W Bladen Cl Concil.

And sent by M^r Sanders & M^r Cheseldyne

Came M^r Eccleston and M^r Howe with an Ordinance for Removing the Powder House which was assented to they also brought from the House as followeth Viz.^t

### By the House of Delegates Dec^r 8th. 1704

Upon reading the within Message this House do not thinke fitt to prepare a Bill at this tyme ag^t the within named Richard Clarke for that it dos not fully appeare to them that the said Clarks defends himselfe with force and Arms ag^t the Sherriffe.

Therefore this House humbly pray by his Ex^{ncy} that he would please to issue his Proclamacon for the said Clarks rendring himselfe to Justice, And in case he dos not render himselfe according to such Proclamation, then at the next Session of Assembly this House will further consider thereof Signed ꝑ Ord^r W Taylard Cl House Del.

Whereas there is due to Andrew Wellplay for making the Wooden Frame on which the Gunns are mounted the

|  | £ | s. | d. |
|---|---|---|---|
| Sume of | £ 5.. | 19.. | 0 |
| To Thomas Freeborne for the Iron Worke | 5.. | 15.. | 0 |
| To Col John Hamond for Tymber | 1.. | 10.. | 0 |
| And To Willm. Bladen for the Iron | 2.. | 05.. | 0 |
| Am^o in the whole to the Sume of | £15.. | 04.. | 6 |

Ordered that George Plater Esq^r her Ma^{tys} Receiver of the District of Puttuxent pay the said severall sumes to the Severall Persons to whome the same is due as afores^d

Came M^r Frisby and Cap^t Beale with a Bill for dividing S^t Pauls Parish in Prince Georges County which was read and sent to the House by M^r Brooke

The Boarde adjournd for two hours.

### Post Meridiem
#### The Councill Sate p^rsent as before

M^r Colbatch having offered his Ex^{ncy} to preach at Annapolis on the 30th of Jan^ry being the Anniversary of King Charles's martyrdom had the thanks of the Board for his ready Offer.

Original
Journal. Came M<sup>r</sup> Macklaster and M<sup>r</sup> Magrooder with two Bills the
one Declaring the Act ascertayning the Bounds of Lands to
be in force the other for Suspending the Prosecution of
Popish Priests upon the late Act of Assembly &c.

M<sup>r</sup> Dollahyde and M<sup>r</sup> How from the House bring as followeth

By the House of Del Dec<sup>r</sup> 8th. 1704

This House having considered Your Honours Message ꝑ
Thomas Brooke Esq<sup>r</sup> and two other Members of the Hon<sup>ble</sup>
Councill relating to the Bill obliging Ma<sup>rs</sup> of Shipps to publish
their Freight.   The House thinks the Law to be well enough
worded; but the Intention of the House was that it should be a
Temporary Law, but that they find it to be indefinite, And therefore they pray the Concurrence of his Ex<sup>ncy</sup> and her Ma<sup>tys</sup>
hon<sup>ble</sup> Councill that the law be made temporary

And as to the Bill for laying the Duty of 9<sup>d</sup> ꝑ Gall<sup>o</sup> The
house having read and considered the Law they find it to be
Sufficient enough for the purpose to which it was made, It
having appointed a Sufficient Officer for receiving the Impost.

Signed ꝑ Ord<sup>r</sup> W Taylard Cl House Del.

The Board adjournd untill 8 of the Clock to morrow morning

Saturday December 9<sup>th</sup> 1704

The Councill Sate p<sup>r</sup>esent.

The Hon<sup>ble</sup> { Thomas Tench    L<sup>t</sup> Col Holland
M<sup>r</sup> Smith    M<sup>r</sup> Sanders
Col Hamond    M<sup>r</sup> Cheseldyne
& M<sup>r</sup> Coursey

Colonel Hamond sent to the House with the Bill for Suspending the Prosecution of Popish Priests &c.

Came M<sup>r</sup> Collier and brought with him Cap<sup>t</sup> Edw<sup>d</sup> Ratchdale of the Ship Elizabeth of Leverpoole The Said Cap<sup>t</sup> Ratchdale being called in was Cautioned by his Ex<sup>ncy</sup> that He should
not presume to Sayle without his Leave or Lett pass, But is
told that when any Convoy arives at New England New York
or Virginia upon his giving Sufficient Bond to joyne them He
will have leave to go with them.

Ordered that the severall Navall Officers do not cleare any
Shipps which have not his Ex<sup>ncys</sup> Lett pass especially during
the p<sup>r</sup>sent Warr.

Came M<sup>r</sup> Hudson and M<sup>r</sup> Hays and brought from the House
as followeth, viz'.

By the House of Delegates Decemb<sup>r</sup> 9<sup>th</sup> 1704 Original Journal.

This house hath Received all the papers relating to the Ind<sup>ns</sup> by the hon<sup>ble</sup> John Haṁond & W<sup>m</sup> Coursey Esq<sup>r</sup>. Wee have heard all the Informacon that Coll Smallwood & Beale have given from all Which wee cann with no Reasonable Certainty Either Blame or Excuse our Neighbouring Indians the Piscattaways but forasmuch as notwithstanding both our peaceable Carriage towards them and our threatnings have not prevailed upon them to Returne to their Antient dwellings this house hath a good disposicon to make Warr upon them were it not that we have allready undertaken some business of great Charge therefore Wee humbly advise your Excellency to call in the Soldiers & to treat with the said Indians at present in friendly manner and to dissemble the resentm<sup>ts</sup> of the English till they be better Capacitated to carry on a Warr and have more Certainty of their Treachery & Guiltiness

Signed ꝑ Ord<sup>r</sup> W Taylard Clk house Del

By the house of Dell
December 9<sup>th</sup> 1704.

In Answer to the Message as to the Act prohibitting the Importation of Bread Beer Flour &c.

This House are of Opinion that the Legislative power of this Province has Sufficient power to prohibitt Trade in such a Branch of it as that Act Mentions but they are Ready to Concurr Which your hon<sup>rs</sup> Sentiments that its better to lay a Duty on the enumerated Comoditys &c but time will not admitt to Bring in a new Bill therefore they pray the Consideration thereof may be referred to the next Session of Assembly

Signed ꝑ order
W Taylard Clk house Del.

Came M<sup>r</sup> Eccleston and brought up these following Bills viz:

A Bill for better ordering & Regulating the Militia &c.

A Bill for Lymitacon of Officers Fees.

A Bill for preserving Harbours &c.

A Bill for the Advancem<sup>t</sup> of the Natives &c.

A Bill Declaring the Division of Sevrall Countys to be firm & Stable.

A Bill causing Jurors to come to Provinciall and County Courts.

A Bill for paym<sup>t</sup> of Fees due from Criminalls &c.

A Bill declaring Severall Laws heretofore made to be in force.

Original
Journal.
A Bill for suspending the Prosecution of Romish Priests &c.
And a Bill for William Bladen to rebuild the Court House
All which bills were Engrossed were read and Assented to
be her Ma^{tys} hon^{ble} Councill.

M^r King & M^r Hill bring up the Journall of the Comittee
of Accounts

M^r Grey and M^r Jones Bring up the Bill for dividing S^t Pauls
Parish in Prince Georges County,

And a Bill continuing the Land Law in force also four other
Reviving Bills Which were Read and sent to the house by
Colonel Holland and M^r Sanders

Colonel Beale being sent for came and was acquainted that
the House of Delegates desire his Ex^{ncy} to call in the Rangers

He says it will be a great Dissatisfaction to the Inhabitants
on the Frontier of Potomeck and most of. them on the North
side of the Branch will draw off unless they can be Supplyd
with some Amunition.

He is told that upon his sending for it His Ex^{ncy} will order
a Q^r Barrel of Powder and Ball proportionably.

Ordered that Col. Beale discharge the Rangers and take
Care to receive and Secure the Arms belonging to Calvert
County at his owne House untill Colonel Bigger can send for
them.

The Board adjournd for an hour


Post Meridiem
The Councill Sate p^resent as before.

Came Cap^t W^m Watts and M^r Peter Watts & brought the
Bills last sent to the House by Col Holland and M^r Sanders.
Which Bills being assented to by the House were also assented
to by this Boarde and sent againe to the House by M^r Tench
& M^r Coursey.

Then was the Journal of the Comittee of Acc^{ts} read and
assented to & sent to the House by M^r Coursey

Col Smallwood and Ten other members bring up a Bill
imposing 6^d ꝑ hh^d on tob^o for rebuilding the Court House
Which was not thought fitt to be agreed to by this Boarde but
return'd to the House by M^r Tench and Col Hamond

U. H. J.
P. 366
Major Greenberry with the Engrossed Bills for Sanctifying
the Lords Day and Dividing S^t Paul's Parish. Which were
assented to & Returned to the House

Major Greenberry again from the House to acquaint his
Excellency that they having nothing before them wait his
Excellency's Commands to attend him with the Bills of this
Session

Col Holland and M^r Cheseldyne sent to tell them his Excell
Expects them

Came M$^r$ Speaker attended by the Members of the House u. h. j.
& M$^r$ Speaker presented to his Excellency the following Bills
engrossed & Assented to by the Council & House of Delegates viz.

An Act for Limitation of officers Fees.

An Act for ordering & regulating the militia of this Province for the better defence & security thereof

An Act for payment of Fees due from Criminal persons

An Act for causing Grand & petite Jurors & Witnesses to
come to the provincial and County Courts.

An Act for the preservation of the Several Harbours &
Landing Places within this Province

An Act for Rebuilding the Stadt House at Annapolis     p. 367.

An Act declaring the several Divisions of Countys within
this province made by virtue of a former Act Entituled an Act
for the Divisions and regulating the several Countys within
this Province and constituting a County by the name of Prince
Georges County within the same Province to be firm & Stable.

An Act for advancement of the natives of this Province

An Act declaring the several Acts of Assembly formerly
made to be in Force

An Act for suspending the Prosecution of Priests of the
Communion of the Church of Rome Incurring the penalty of an
Act of Assembly Entituled an Act for preventing the Growth
of Popery by Exercising the function in a private family of the
Roman Communication but in no other case whatsoever

An Act for the division of S$^t$ Paul's Parish in Prince George's
County

An Act declaring an Act Entituled an Act for erecting Ann
Arundel & Oxford Towns into ports & Towns made to be in
force

An Act declaring an Act entituled a Act ascertaining the
bounds of Lands to be in force

An Act declaring an Act Entituled an Act for the punishm$^t$
of Suborned Witnesses and Committing wilful & corrupt
Perjury to be in force

An Act declaring an Act Entituled an Act for Sanctifying
and keeping holy the Lord's Day commonly called Sunday to
be perpetual

An Act declaring an Act Entituled an Act concerning Indians
to be in force

# PROCEEDINGS AND ACTS

OF THE

# GENERAL ASSEMBLY

# OF MARYLAND.

*At a Session held at Annapolis, Dec.* 5–9, 1704.

CHARLES CALVERT, LORD BALTIMORE,
*Proprietary.*

JOHN SEYMOUR,
*Governor.*

---

THE LOWER HOUSE OF ASSEMBLY

Jornal of the second Session of Assembly begun and held
at th port of Annapolis the fifth Day of December in the third
year of the Reign of our Sovereign Lady Ann by the Grace
of Gd of England Scotland France and Ireland Queen
Defeder of the Faith &c^ta Annoq Dom. 1704.

Te House met according to Prorogation and being called
over were present.

Gorge Muschamp Esq^r for S^t Mary's City, M^r Thomas
Beak M^r William Watts, M^r Peter Watts, for S^t Mary's County,
M^r Tomas Smith, M^r Elias King, and M^r John Wells for Kent
Couty; M^r Samuel Young, M^r Charles Greenbury, M^r Joseph
Hill and M^r Richard Jones, for Ann Arundel County; M^r
Robct Skinner M^r John Mackall & M^r Thomas Howe,
for Calvert County; M^r James Smallwood, for Charles
Coury; M^r Edward Dorsey, M^r James Maxwell, M^r
Jame Philips, M^r Francis Dallahide, for Baltimore County;
M^r Joseph Gray, M^r John Jones, M^r John Mackalster,
for Smerset County; Col^o Thomas Smithson, M^r Robert
Goldoorough, & M^r Henry Coursey, for Talbot County;
M^r Idward Blay, for Cecil County; M^r Robert Tyler,
and I^r Samuel Magruder for Prince George's County; M^r
Jame Hay, for S^t Mary's City; M^r John Leach, for Calvert
Coury; M^r Gerr^d Fowke, and M^r William Stone, for Charles
Couoy; M^r Nicholas Lowe, for Talbot County; & all Dor-
chestr County, Wanting also M^r Thomas Frisby, M^r William
Peare & M^r William Dare for Cecil County; M^r Thomas
Greefield, M^r William Barton, and M^r John Waters; also
wantig M^r William Aisquith, & M^r William Frisby both sick.

Th House being called over M^r Robert Goldsborough and
M^r Hury Coursey ordered to attend his Excellency to acquaint
him that the Major Part of the House are met but not having
a Speker, Major William Dent, late Speaker, being dead, his
Excelency may be desired to give some Directions how the
Hous shall proceed.

Thy returned and say his Excellency leaves it to the House
of Deegates to proceed to choosing a Speaker.

Threupon the House by Majority of Votes made Choice of
Thoms Smith Esq^r to be their Chairman and accordin

the Chair And afterwards House attended M^r Speaker to
preset him to his Excellency the Governour, where M^r Speaker
was peased to make a short excusatory Speech, disabling

Maryla[...]
  Journ[...]
at the p[...]
year of [...]

Defende[...]

over wer[...]

M.r Tho[...]
County[...]

Robert[...]
for Cal[...]
County:[...]
James [...]
M.r Jos[...]

Goldsb[...]
M.r Edv[...]

James [...]
County[...]
County[...]
chester[...]
Pearce[...]
Greenf[...]
wanting[...]

House [...]
  They[...]
of Dele[...]
  Ther[...]
Thomas[...]
    t[...]

was plea[...]

Maryland Ss<sup>t</sup>

Journal of the second Session of Assembly begun and held
at the port of Annapolis the fifth Day of December in the third
year of the Reign of our Sovereign Lady Ann by the Grace
of God of England Scotland France and Ireland Queen
Defender of the Faith &c<sup>ta</sup> Annoq Dom. 1704.

The House met according to Prorogation and being called
over were present.

George Muschamp Esq<sup>r</sup> for S<sup>t</sup> Mary's City, M<sup>r</sup> Thomas
Beale, M<sup>r</sup> William Watts, M<sup>r</sup> Peter Watts, for S<sup>t</sup> Mary's County,
M<sup>r</sup> Thomas Smith, M<sup>r</sup> Elias King, and M<sup>r</sup> John Wells for Kent
County; M<sup>r</sup> Samuel Young, M<sup>r</sup> Charles Greenbury, M<sup>r</sup> Joseph
Hill and M<sup>r</sup> Richard Jones, for Ann Arundel County; M<sup>r</sup>
Robert Skinner M<sup>r</sup> John Mackall & M<sup>r</sup> Thomas Howe,
for Calvert County; M<sup>r</sup> James Smallwood, for Charles
County; M<sup>r</sup> Edward Dorsey, M<sup>r</sup> James Maxwell, M<sup>r</sup>
James Philips, M<sup>r</sup> Francis Dallahide, for Baltimore County;
M<sup>r</sup> Joseph Gray, M<sup>r</sup> John Jones, M<sup>r</sup> John Mackalster,
for Somerset County; Col<sup>o</sup> Thomas Smithson, M<sup>r</sup> Robert
Goldsborough, & M<sup>r</sup> Henry Coursey, for Talbot County;
M<sup>r</sup> Edward Blay, for Cecil County; M<sup>r</sup> Robert Tyler,
and M<sup>r</sup> Samuel Magruder for Prince George's County; M<sup>r</sup>
James Hay, for S<sup>t</sup> Mary's City; M<sup>r</sup> John Leach, for Calvert
County; M<sup>r</sup> Gerr<sup>d</sup> Fowke, and M<sup>r</sup> William Stone, for Charles
County; M<sup>r</sup> Nicholas Lowe, for Talbot County; & all Dor-
chester County, Wanting also M<sup>r</sup> Thomas Frisby, M<sup>r</sup> William
Pearce & M<sup>r</sup> William Dare for Cecil County; M<sup>r</sup> Thomas
Greenfield, M<sup>r</sup> William Barton, and M<sup>r</sup> John Waters; also
wanting M<sup>r</sup> William Aisquith, & M<sup>r</sup> William Frisby both sick.

The House being called over M<sup>r</sup> Robert Goldsborough and
M<sup>r</sup> Henry Coursey ordered to attend his Excellency to acquaint
him That the Major Part of the House are met but not having
a Speaker, Major William Dent, late Speaker, being dead, his
Excellency may be desired to give some Directions how the
House shall proceed.

They returned and say his Excellency leaves it to the House
of Delegates to proceed to choosing a Speaker.

Thereupon the House by Majority of Votes made Choice of
Thomas Smith Esq<sup>r</sup> to be their Chairman and accordin

the Chair And afterwards House attended M<sup>r</sup> Speaker to p. 2
present him to his Excellency the Governour, where M<sup>r</sup> Speaker
was pleased to make a short excusatory Speech, disabling

Lib. 41. himself by Reason of some Imperfections humbly desired his
Excellency to direct the House to make Choice of some
more able and sufficient Member of that House to
serve in that Station. To which his Excellency replyed
that he very well approved of the Houses Choice; For
which he returned his Excellency humble Thanks for
thinking him worthy for the Execution of a Place of
so great Charge & Trust; promising him to use his
utmost Endeavour, Care and Diligence therein, and so
offered unto him in the Name, and on the Behalf of the whole
House of Assembly, that they might have their accustomed
and usual Privilege, Access to his Person, upon all urgent
Occasions, and free Liberty of Speech ; which was granted;
and then his Excellency was pleased to say to them as followeth.

Mr Speaker & you Gent. Delegates,
    Your now Meeting at this late and unseasonable Time of
the Year presses your utmost Sedulity in the Dispatch of the
necessary Affairs now to be laid before you ; The late melan-
choly Accident might have been prevented had my often
Admonitions took Place, for I never saw any publick Buildings
left solely to Providence but in Maryland.  I hope this sad
Experiment will awaken your Care for Time to come & and in
the Interim your best Considerations to secure the Laws and
Records of your Country for the Advantage and Quiet of future
Generations.   What is proper to be done in rebuilding your
Stadt House so very necessary for the Accomendation of the
Publick I leave entirely to your own serious Debates and Decision
for I have no other Aim than the true Interest and Service of
your Country and shall be heartily Sorry to find any here so
far mistaken to imagine in the least it can be separate from
that of the Crown of England.   Since I have given you the
strictest Assurance of my constant Resolution to govern whilst
I have the Honour to command here with a most tender
Regard to her Majesty's Honour and Service, using my best
Endeavours to advance the Prosperity & Reputation of this
Province, I can never doubt but my Integrity in your Service
has been sufficiently evident by some Trial since my Administration as you handsomely owned with Thanks the last Session.
Therefore avoiding all Heats and Misconstructions I hope you
will with me and her Majesty's Honble Council most heartily
apply yourselves to the present Exigencies your Country now
lies under which will be most acceptable to her Majesty and
very grateful to myself for when you do truly well for yourselves all Men will applaud your Judgments.

Gentlemen,
    The Account of our Indians giving us a late Disturbance
P. 3 shall be laid before you which really requires your Considera-

tion, and I heartily crave your Advice and Assistance in this Lib. 41.
Juncture that for the future every Member of the Province
may enjoy the Fruits of his Labour and Industry in Peace &
Satisfaction.

Never let us be mistaken, Gentlemen in each other, but
strive jointly & heartily to serve the Country the best and
most judicious way we can & oppose whatever may be imagined prejudicial to it in any one Instance whatsoever.

Which being ended Mʳ Speaker & the Members return to
their House, and Mʳ Speaker having taken the Chair he
returned them Thanks for the Honour done him in their
Choice promising them to discharge that great Trust laid
upon him according to the best of his Ability.

Ordered that the Speaker & Delegates of Assembly meet
at the House of Colº Dorsey in Annapolis every Day during
this Session at Eight in the morning & sit till Twelve in the
Afternoon and from two till four. And ordered that Notice
be given by Beat of Drum twice in the Morning and once
in the Afternoon And likewise that Mʳ Wooten the Minister
be desired to attend for Prayers at Eight ºClock in the Morning and at tolling the Bell in the Afternoon.

Nothing else at Present lying before the House they
adjourn till Eight O'Clock to Morrow Morning.

### Wednesday 6ᵗʰ Decemʳ 1704.

The House met again according to Adjournment, being
called over were all present as Yesterday, only Mʳ Henry
Coursey sick.

Mʳ Hugh Eccleston, Mʳ John Taylor, Mʳ John Hudson, &
Mʳ Joseph Ennalls, members for Dorchester County enter the
House and take their Places.

Ordered That his Excellency's Speech made last Night be
read in the House which was done accordingly.

And ordered it be again read and considered of in the
Afternoon.

Mʳ William Dare, Mʳ Thomas Frisby, & Mʳ William Pearce
members for Cecil County enters the House & take their
Places.

Moved by a Member on what Terms the Assembly sit in
Colº Dorsey's House Colº Dorsey informs them it was by an
Agreement wᶜʰ lyes in the Hands of Colº Hammond but
forasmuch as Colº Dorsey, the Landlord being present in the
House offers his House & Lot belonging to it at Rate of
twenty Pounds Sterling Rent for one year certain & so for a
longer Time if the House think fit at the Expiration of the

Lib. 41. first year.   To which this House concurred Nemine contradicente; and ordered an Ordinance be prepared & sent his
Excellency for that Purpose.   Ordered M$^r$ Speaker issue his
Warrant to the Secretary for Writ of Election for a member
to sit in the Room of Col$^o$ W$^m$ Dent, lately deceased.

p. 4    Col$^o$ Thomas Smithson, M$^r$ Henry Coursey, & Major Charles
Greenberry appointed a Committee of Laws; and M$^r$ Elias
King, M$^r$ James Philips & M$^r$ Joseph Hill a Committee ap-
pointed to settle & state the publick Accounts &$^{ca}$

Col$^o$ Edward Dorsey, Col$^o$ James Maxwell, & M$^r$ John
Wells appointed a Committee to enquire into the Aggriev-
auces of this Province &$^{ta}$

Ordered That the Clerk of this House inspect the Journals
of last Sessions & draw off the several References to this
Session and lay before the House in the Afternoon for further
Consideration.

The House adjourns till two of the Clock in the Afternoon

### Post Meridiem

The House met again according to Adjournment, being
called over were present as in the morning.

A Letter from M$^r$ William Stone a Member of Charles
County praying Excuse for his non Attendance being read
the House accepts of his Excuse he being ill & not capable
to travel.

Ordered by the House that his Excellency's Speech be
again read pursuant to the Order in the Morning; which
being done It's resolved it's absolutely necessary that a House
be built as moved in his Excellency's Speech for Accomodation
of the Public &$^{ca}$

Ordered That M$^r$ Edward Dorsey, M$^r$ Samuel Young,
M$^r$ Edward Blay, M$^r$ James Philips, M$^r$ Robert Tyler, M$^r$ John
Taylor, M$^r$ John Wells, M$^r$ Joseph Gray do view & inspect the
Ruins of the Stadt-House & make Report to the House if the
Walls now standing are fit and sufficient to be rebuilt upon
& call any Workman to advise in the Matter.

According to Order of the Morning the Clerk produces
the several References.

The Reference of the publick Post read.   This House conceiving the Weight of Business lying before them and Unsea-
sonableness of the Year, therefore the Consideration thereof
is further referred till next Assembly.   An Article relating to
the Members of the City of Saint Mary's referred to this Session & producing the Charter: This House resolves it does
not properly lie before them.

The Petition of John Nicholls for Sale of Land of William
Edmondson dece'd referred to this Session; Ordered it be

further referred for that the House has not Time to proc
thereupon this Session.

The Proposals made last Assembly, relating to the Ex
iner General's Office & the Fees read; and resolved
same be utterly rejected.

Petition of Cecil County, Petition of Kent County, Peti·
of Talbot County, for Division of their Counties is furl
referred till next Session of Assembly.

The Petition of the Freeholders & Inhabitants of S
Paul's Parish in Prince George's County to ascertain tl
Bounds read, but forasmuch as no Report is yet made of
Order thereon, therefore referred till it be brought into
House.

The Report of the Conference relating to the Land Of
& the Lord Baltimore's Agent referred to this Assembly be
read it's resolved by the House that it be further referred
next Session of Assembly and that an Address be then [
pared to address her Majesty for Relief in the Premises.

The Proposal whether Indians brought from other Co
tries & sold here as Slaves are to be accounted such or
referred, & now again moved it's resolved such Indians as
sold for Slaves shall be so deemed & ordered that the Cc
mittee of Laws prepare a Bill.

The Proposal made last Session for the more Ease in
Administration of Justice to the Inhabitants of this Provi
was here read the further Consideration whereof is refer
till next Sessions of Assembly.

The Proposal of the Clerk of this House for Advancem
of Salary for Support of the said Office referred by last
sembly again read and the further Consideration thereo
referred till next Session of Assembly.

M^r Thomas Greenfield & M^r W^m Barton Members
Prince George's County & M^r James Hay a member for
Mary's City enter the House & took their Places

The Committee appointed to view the Walls of the St;
House enter the House & do report. That the walls are si
cient to be rebuilt upon by sufficient careful workmen. Wl
being read and debated it is put to the Question whether
Stadt House be rebuilt in the same Form as before or
Resolved Nemine Contradicente That the House be buil
the same Form & upon the same Walls as it was before [
suant to Report of the Committee

M^r Speaker produces a Letter from M^r William Blader.
him directed which was read as follows Viz.

Annapolis Decemb⟨r⟩ the 6ᵗʰ 1704
Honour'd Sir,
    I humbly propose to your Honour & the Assembly that in
Case they shall think fit to rebuild the Court House either upon
the Walls as now standing or otherwise I shall undertake the
same to be finished in a very short Time for which I will give
good Security in 4000£ Sterling and be willing to receive such
Pay as they shall think fitt to agree on as Mony comes in &
accrue to the Province all the other publick Buildings having
gone through my Hands, I am ambitious for serving the
Country in this & to approve myself their & your most obliged,
faithful Humble servant.                          W Bladen.


p. 6     Indorsed thus Viz. To the Hoñble Col° Thomas Smith
Speaker of the Gen¹ Assembly Humbly present.
    Which being here read & debated it's resolved by the House
that the Gent. appointed this Day to view the Stadt House
Walls meet the said Mʳ Bladen & treat with him about the
Rebuilding the said House & report the same & his Demands
to the House by all Expedition.
    The House adjourns till to Morrow Morning Eight o'Clock.


### Thursday Xber 7ᵗʰ 1704.

    The House met again according to Adjournment.
    Being called over were all present as Yesterday.
    Mʳ Gerrard Fowlke a member for Charles County enters the
House.
    Was brought into the House Answer to his Excellency's
Speech wᶜʰ was read viz.


### By the House of Delegates December 7ᵗʰ 1704

May it please your Excellency
    We have taken your Excellency's Speech at the Opening
of this Session into our Considerations and have resolved with
all the Unanimity & Dispatch proper to such a Conjuncture to
take all possible Care for the Preservation of the Records &
restoring the Stadt House to its former Beauty & usefulness
by rebuilding & making good the Breaks thereof. We shall
be very sorry to be found in such a Mistake as to imagine
that we can separate Interest from that of the Crown of England
but hope that the constant Unanimity of our Debates & Resolutions will shew us to have no other Intention or Designs than
such as may tend to her Majesty's Honour & the Good of our

Country, and as we shall be at all Times very careful to avoid Lib. 41. the Entertainment of Jealousies & running ourselves into Heats and Misconstructions so we shall very readily join with your Excellency & her Majesty's Hoñble Council in whatsoever shall appear to be for her Majesty's Honour & the Good of our Country.

As to the Indian Business when your Excellency shall think fit to lay it before us we shall not only give our best Advice & Assistance therein but further it with all the Unanimity & Dispatch which may be proper for that Affair.

Sir. We are very sensible of your Ex<sup>cy's</sup> good Governm<sup>t</sup> & tender Regard towards us & do hope that the same Tenderness will be continued to us; and we take this Opportunity to assure your Excellency that as we can entertain no Jealousies so we shall be always ready to make due Returns of Gratitude for the Enjoyment of so great a Blessing.

Signed ꝑ Order   W Taylard Clk. Ho. Del.

Which being read and approved of is ordered to be sent up to his Excellency & Council ꝑ M<sup>r</sup> Charles Greenberry, M<sup>r</sup> Hugh Eccleston, M<sup>r</sup> John Jones, M<sup>r</sup> John Mackall, M<sup>r</sup> George Muschamp & M<sup>r</sup> Robert Skinner. They return & say they delivered the same.

M<sup>r</sup> Thomas Greenfield & others pursuant to an Order of p. 7 last session relating to the Petition of the Parishoners of S<sup>t</sup> Paul's Parish in Prince George's County made Return of their Report & ordered a Bill be prepared.

The Hoñble Thomas Tench & Edward Lloyd Esq<sup>rs</sup> from the Council enters the House and delivers M<sup>r</sup> Speaker the following Message.

By his Excellency the Governor & Council in Assembly December 7<sup>th</sup> 1704.

Since the unhappy Accident of our Court House & some of our Laws burnt has induced this present Meeting of the Country his Excellency thought it might conduce to the obviating the publick Charge of detaining the Session for the transcribing them (some being very long) to have the Bills which were read in the House sent for from the late Speaker's House in Charles County & having ordered them to be transcribed against your Meeting they are with the original Draught of the said Bills herewith recommended to your Consideration for the reenacting thereof if you see fit.

Signed ꝑ Order   W Bladen Clk Council.

Lib. 41.  And likewise brought with them the following Bills, the Laws being burnt.

Bill for Limitation of Officers Fees.

Bill declaring the Division of several Counties of this Province.

Bill for Advancement of the Natives & Residents of this Province.

Bill for regulating the Militia.

Bill for Payment of Criminals fees.

Bill declaring several Acts of Assembly formerly made to be in Force

Bill for causing Grand & Petit Jurors & witnesses to come to Courts

Bill for Preservation of several Harbours in this Province

All indorsed by the Clerk of the Councill & this House the last Session, and likewise the ingrossed Bills sent with them to be read & examined in the House.

Ordered to be read in the Afternoon.

Upon Debate of rebuilding the Stadt House ordered the following Message be sent up to his Excellency & Council Viz.

### By the House of Delegates Dec' 7ᵗʰ 1704

The rebuilding the Stadt House now lying under Consideration this House have resolved their Willingness to rebuild the said House in as commodious a manner as before, and accordingly treated with Mʳ Bladen concerning the same; but his Demand being so great this House will not concur. Therefore it's resolved that a Committee be appointed to treat, bargain & agree with such Persons as will undertake the said work and accordingly have appointed Mʳ Samuel Young, Mʳ Charles Greenberry, Mʳ Joseph Hill, & Mʳ Richard Jones

p. 8 Delegates of Ann Arundel County for that Purpose. And likewise that this House pray his Excellency to appoint two of the Honble Councill to join with them, and that a Bill may be prepared to give them Authority to do the same to which the Concurrence of his Excellency & Council is Prayed.

Signed ꝑ Order W. Taylard Clk Ho. Del.

Sent up to his Excellency & Council by Mʳ Hugh Eccleston & Mʳ John Hudson.

William Holland and James Sanders Esqʳˢ from the Honble Council enters the House & delivers Mʳ Speaker the following Message.

By his Excellency the Governor & Council in Assembly
Decemb<sup>r</sup> 7<sup>th</sup> 1704.

Gent. The Misfortune of Ann Arundel County is particularly deplorable in the Loss of all their Records being burnt
in the publick Court House and requires your best Thoughts
to relieve the many Confusions & Perplexities that County
lies under: Wherefore we desire your Advice and Assistance
in framing some Law which may still the Minds of the Inhabitants there & confirm the Rights of several now fresh in
Memory which by Length of Time may be worn out to the
Prejudice of many.

Signed ꝑ Order  W Bladen Cl Council

Upon reading the foregoing Message it is resolved by the
House that Liberty is given to bring in a Bill for Relief of the
Inhabitants of the said County and that the Gent. Members
of the said County prepare a Bill accordingly and Message
to be prepared for the Council's Concurrence.

Ordered the following Message be sent up to the Council.

By the House of Delegates Dec. 7<sup>th</sup> 1704.

Upon reading your Honors Message this Day by Col° Holland & James Sanders Esq<sup>rs</sup> for Assistance in framing a Bill
for Relief of the Inhabitants of Ann Arundel County in Relation to their Records burnt in the Stadt House this House
have fully considered the same and resolved that Leave is
given the County to bring in a Bill for their Relief and
ordered that the Delegates of the said County prepare a Bill
for that Purpose to which your Hon<sup>rs</sup> Concurrence is prayed.

Signed ꝑ Order  W. Taylard Clk. Ho. Del.

And likewise ordered the following Message be sent Viz.

By the House of Delegates December 7<sup>th</sup> 1704.

This House finding some Agreement has been made about
the House of Col° Edward Dorsey, for Assembly & Provincial Courts to sit in but lies in the Hands of Col° Hammond
which could not readily be laid before the House: Therefore
Col° Dorsey being present proposes to lease the House with
two Lots to the Public for their Use one year certain for
twenty Pounds Sterling & so at that Rate for any longer Time
to which this House concurred and prays the Concurrence of
his Excellency & Council   Signed ꝑ Order

W. Taylard Clk. Ho. Del.

the Governor & Council in Assembly Lib. 41.
Decemb^r 7^th 704.

tune of Ann .rundel County is particu-
: Loss of all teir Records being burnt
House and re uires your best Thoughts
Confusions &Perplexities that County
e we desire yur Advice and Assistance
which may stl the Minds of the Inhab-
m the Right of several now fresh in
ngth of Timemay be worn out to the

ʒned ᵱ Orde W Bladen Cl Council

ɔregoing Mesage it is resolved by the
given to brinʒin a Bill for Relief of the
l County andthat the Gent. Members
epare a Bill ccordingly and Message
Council's Cocurrence.
ng Message e sent up to the Council.

e of Delegate Dec. 7^th 1704.

Honors Messge this Day by Col° Hol-
Esq^rs for Asstance in framing a Bill
itants of AnnArundel County in Rela-
ɔurnt in the Stadt House this House
the same an resolved that Leave is
bring in a ill for their Relief and
ʒates of the sid County prepare a Bill
ch your Hor Concurrence is prayed.
ᵱ Order W Taylard Clk. Ho. Del.

l the followin Message be sent Viz.

f Delegates Lcember 7^th 1704.

ome Agreemnt has been made about
vard Dorsey, or Assembly & Provin-
lies in the lands of Col° Hammond
be laid befo the House. Therefore
ent proposes o lease the House with
ic for their Lse one year certain for
so at that
rred and
Signe

Lib. 41.   Both which Messages were sent up to the Hoñble Council
p. 9 by M⁻ John Taylor M⁻ John Wells & M⁻ Francis Dellahide.
They return & say they delivered their Message.

James Sanders Esq⁻ from the Hoñble Council enters the
House and delivers M⁻ Speaker the foregoing Ordinance
upon the Lease of Col⁰ Dorsey's House, indorsed thus Viz.

Eodem Die   Assented to by her Majesty's Hoñble Council
provided the Public be not obliged to any Repairs of the said
House.          Signed ꝑ Order W Bladen Clk. Council.

Original delivered Col⁰ Dorsey

John Hammond & William Coursey Esq⁻ˢ from the Hoñble
Council enters the House & delivers M⁻ Speaker some Letters
and other Papers relating to the Indians Affairs.   Ordered
the Consideration thereof be referred till to‑Morrow.

The House adjourned till two o'Clock in the Afternoon.

### Post Meridiem

The House met again according to Adjournment, being all
called over were all present as in the Morning.

Ordered by the House that M⁻ Samuel Young provide
Nails, Plank & Scantling for erecting & setting up the Pews
in S᙭ Ann's Church, Annapolis for the Burgesses of the Assembly and that he will provide all other Materials for finishing
the same and that he see the same sufficiently completed.
This House resolved he be paid out of the publick Stock if
his Excellency & Council please to concur therewith·   And
ordered an Ordinance be prepared & sent up for that Purpose.

Ordered the following Message be entered & sent up to
his Excellency & Council Viz.

### By the House of Delegates Dec⁻ 7ᵗʰ 1704.

May it please your Excellency,

Your sending for those Bills to the late Speaker's House in
Charles County which you communicated to this House and
the transcribing of them we acknowledge have been very
advantageous to the Dispatch of Affairs in this House We
highly applaud your Care & Prudence therein and return
your Excy our most hearty Thanks for the same

          Signed ꝑ Order W. Taylard Clk. Ho. Del.

Sent up to his Excellency & Council ꝑ Col⁰ Smithson, M⁻
Muschamp Col⁰ Smallwood M⁻ Tyler, M⁻ Jones, Col⁰ Maxwell, M⁻ Frisby, M⁻ Ennalls, & M⁻ John Jones.

They return & say they delivered their Message.    Lib. 41.
Ordered the following Ordinance be sent up to his Excellency & Council Viz.


By the House of Delegates December 7th 1704.

Upon reading the Proposal for erecting the Pews in S[t] Ann's Church in Annapolis for the Assembly this House resolves that M[r] Samuel Young provide Plank, Nails Scantling & other Materials for erecting setting up & finishing such Pews & he seeing the same finished & compleated this House resolves he be paid & satisfied for the same out of the publick Stock if p. 10 his Excellency & Council please to concur therewith.

Signed ꝑ Order W. Taylard Clk Ho. Del.


Bill for Limitation of Officers Fees read with the Amendment in the last Clause Viz. (after three years) and do pass ꝑ especial Order.

Sent up to his Excellency & Council together with the foregoing Message by M[r] Joseph Hill.  He returns and says he delivered them.

The Honble John Hammond & Kenelm Cheseldine Esq[rs] from the Honble Council enters the House and delivers M[r] Speaker the following Ordinance Viz.


By the Council in Assembly December 7th 1704.

This Board is very ready to agree to any Thing the House proposes but think it for better that you will now agree with an Undertaker who may immediately set about it and since the Cubiloe is not to be built M[r] Bladen, the first proposer is willing on better Advice in Case the Country will give him the Materials saved out of the Fire which appertained to the old Court House to undertake it for a thousand Pounds Sterling to which we desire your Concurrence believing it will Save both Money & Time.

Signed ꝑ Order W Bladen Clk Council


Which being here read & upon further Debate & Consideration this House concur with the Honble Council.

William Coursey Esq. enters the House & delivers M[r] Speaker the Ordinance about the publick Pews indorsed.


Eodem Die.  Assented to by his Excellency & her Majesty's Honble Council

Signed ꝑ Order W Bladen Clk Council

Lib. 41.  Both which Messages ʳere sent up to the Hoñble Council
P.9 by Mʳ John Taylor Mʳ Jan Wells & Mʳ Francis Dellahide.
They return & say they clivered their Message.

James Sanders Esqʳ frm the Hoñble Council enters the
House and delivers Mʳ Speaker the foregoing Ordinance
upon the Lease of Colᵒ Lʳsey's House, indorsed thus Viz.

Eodem Die   Assented o by her Majesty's Hoñble Council
provided the Public be no obliged to any Repairs of the said
House.          Signed · Order W Bladen Clk. Council.

Original delivered Colᵒ )orsey

John Hammond & Willim Coursey Esqʳˢ from the Hoñble
Council enters the House & delivers Mʳ Speaker some Letters
and other Papers relating to the Indians Affairs.   Ordered
the Consideration thereof e referred till to-Morrow.

The House adjourned til two o'Clock in the Afternoon.

### Pos Meridiem

The House met again acording to Adjournment, being all
called over were all present s in the Morning.

Ordered by the House that Mʳ Samuel Young provide
Nails, Plank & Scantling fo erecting & setting up the Pews
in Sᵗ Ann's Church, Annapʋis for the Burgesses of the Assembly and that he will provie all other Materials for finishing
the same and that he see the same sufficiently completed.
This House resolved he be aid out of the publick Stock if
his Excellency & Council piase to concur therewith.   And
ordered an Ordinance be preared & sent up for that Purpose.

Ordered the following Mssage be entered & sent up to
his Excellency & Council Vi

By the House of Clegates Decʳ 7ᵗʰ 1704.

May it please your Excellenc,

Your sending for those Bil. to the late Speaker's House
Charles County which you comunicated to this Hou e
the transcribing of them we acknowledge have be
advantageous to the Dispato of Affairs in this I
highly applaud your Care & Prudence ther ¡
your Excy our most hearty Thnks for thᵉ sarᵐ
          Signed p Ordr W. T

Sent up to his Excellency ⸱ C
Muschamp Colᵒ Smallwood I ᵀ
well, Mʳ Frisby, Mʳ Ennalls, &

The Lower h...

They return & say they ...
Ordered the following ...
lency & Council Viz.


By the House of Delegates ...

Upon reading the ...
Church in Annapolis ...
that Mr Samuel Young ...
Materials for erecting ...
... seeing the same ...

Lib. 41. Engrossed Bill for regulating the Militia &<sup>ta</sup> read & ordered to be indorsed December 7<sup>th</sup> 1704. Compared with the Original. Read & Assented to by the House of Delegates
Signed ꝑ Order W. Taylard Cl. Ho. Del.

Engrossed Bill declaring several Acts of Assembly formerly made to be in force Read & compared by the Original & ordered to be thus indorsed. December 7<sup>th</sup> 1704. Compared. by the original Bill. Read & assented to by the House of Delegates Signed ꝑ Order W. Taylard Clk Ho. Del.

Engrossed Bill causing Grand & Petit Jurors & Witnesses to come to Courts &<sup>cta</sup> Read & compared &<sup>ta</sup> and ordered to be indorsed thus. December 7<sup>th</sup> 1704 Compared by the orig<sup>l</sup> Bill. Read & assented to by the House of Delegates.
Signed ꝑ Order W Taylard Cl. Ho. Del.

Engrossed Bill for Preservation of several Harbours &<sup>ta</sup> Read & compared with the orig<sup>l</sup> Bill & ordered to be indorsed Viz. December 7<sup>th</sup> 1704. Compared & read & assented to by the House of Delegates.
Signed ꝑ Order W Taylard Clk Ho. Del.

James Sanders Esq. enters the House & delivers M<sup>r</sup> Speaker the Bill for Limitation of Officers Fees indorsed By the Council in Assembly December 7<sup>th</sup> 1704. Read the first & second Time & agreed to. W Bladen Clk Council

p. 11 Engrossed Bill for payment of Fees due from Criminals Read compared with the Orig<sup>l</sup>
Ordered to be thus indorsed Viz. Xber 7<sup>th</sup> 1704. Compared with the original Bill & read & assented to by the House of Delegates Signed ꝑ Order W Taylard Clk Ho. Del.

Engrossed Bill for Advancement of Natives &<sup>cta</sup> Compared with the original Bill and ordered to be thus indorsed Viz. December 7<sup>th</sup> 1704. Compared with the original Bill & read & assented to by the House of Delegates
Signed ꝑ Order W. Taylard Cl. Ho. Del.

The ingrossed Bill declaring the Division of several Counties Viz. Compared with the Original & ordered to be thus indorsed December 7<sup>th</sup> 1704 Compared with the Original & read & assented to by the House of Delegates.
Signed ꝑ Order W. Taylard Clk. Ho. Del.

Engrossed Bill for Limitation of Officers Fees compared <sup>Lib. 41.</sup> with the Original ordered to be thus indorsed

December the 7<sup>th</sup> 1704. Compared with the Original & read & assented to by the House of Delegates.

Signed ꝑ Order  W Taylard Cl. Ho. Del.

The House adjourned till to Morrow Morning Nine O'Clock.

Friday the 8<sup>th</sup> December 1704.

The House met again according to Adjournment.

Being called over were all ꝑsent as Yesterday.

Committees ordered to withdraw.

Engrossed Bills for Limitation of Officers Fees.

Engrossed Bill for Preservation of Harbours &<sup>ta</sup>

Engrossed Bill for Advancement of Natives &<sup>ta</sup>

Engrossed Bill for regulating the Militia

Engrossed Bill declaring several Acts to be in Force &<sup>ta</sup>

Engrossed Bill for Payment of Fees due from Criminals & the ingrossed Bill for causing Grand and Petit Jurors & Witnesses to come to Courts; together with their Originals were sent up to the Council by M<sup>r</sup> John Mackall & M<sup>r</sup> Francis Dallahide.

They return & say they delivered the Bills.

Thomas Brooke Esq<sup>r</sup> James Sanders & Col° William Holland Esq<sup>r</sup> enters the House and delivers the following Message to M<sup>r</sup> Speaker. Which was read Viz.

By his Excellency the Governor & Council in Assembly<br>December 8<sup>th</sup> 1704.

Since the rising of the last Session of Assembly the following Remarks have been made on some particular Laws.

1<sup>st</sup>  And first as to the Act prohibiting the Importation of Bread Flour and Grain from Pensylvania and other Parts of America, whether it be in the Legislative Power of this Province so to do, or any otherwise prohibit Trade; and if it were not better to lay a severe Duty thereon might serve for a Prohibition.

2.  Secondly As to the Act obliging Masters of Ships to publish their Freight before they take Tob° on Board it is not so well worded and ascertained by saying their certain Freight to answer the Intent of the Makers but only serves to amuse the Merchants at Home.

Thirdly. The Act for laying a Duty of 9<sup>d</sup> ꝑ Gallon on <sup>p. 12</sup> Rum &<sup>ca</sup> from Pensyl<sup>a</sup> has not appointed proper Officers for

26

Lib. 41. gathering the said Impost nor has it given any Power to seize them in the Night Time of which your Consideration is desired.          Signed ᵽ Order   W Bladen Cl Concil.

Which being read the Consideration whereof is further referred.

Thomas Tench Esqʳ enters the House and delivers Mʳ Speaker the following Messages.

### By the Governor & Council in Assembly
### December 8ᵗʰ 1704.

The Powder House where it now stands so far out of the Town is liable to be easily fired by an Enemy or other evil disposed Person his Excellency does not think it safe there. Wherefore it is proposed that the House be removed within the Town in such convenient Place as his Excellency Shall think fit that it may be under the Care of the Person appointed to look after publick Buildings.
          Signed ᵽ Order   W Bladen Clk Council.

Which was read & ordered by the House to be indorsed thus

### By the House of Delegates December 8ᵗʰ 1704.

Upon reading the within Message the House well approved of the Proposal & does concur with the Hon̄ble Council therein          Signed ᵽ Order   W Taylard Cl. Ho. Del.

And likewise the following Message was read in the House Viz.

### By his Excellency the Govʳ & Council in Assembly
### December the 8ᵗʰ 1704.

Whereas the publick Records are at present lodged in the Free School his Exᶜʸ & this board have agreed with Mʳ Evan Jones a sober careful ᵽson to look after that & all other pub-lick Buildings which now are or hereafter shall be erected in this Town for Fear of Fire at the Rate of £10 Sterling ᵽ Ann. to be paid by the public with which we desire your Con-currence.          Signed ᵽ Order   W Bladen Cl. Council.

Being read was ordered to be indorsed.

By the House of Delegates Dec. 8<sup>th</sup> 1704.

Upon reading this Message this House readily concurred with the Hoñble Council
Signed ℗ Order    W Taylard Cl. Ho. Del.

The aforegoing Messages with their Indorsements were sent up to the Hoñble Council ℗ M<sup>r</sup> Eccleston & M<sup>r</sup> Howe. They return & say they delivered the same.

Proposed by a Member whether it may not be of Service to the Country to raise a Duty of 6<sup>d</sup> ℗ Hhd. on Tobacco towards defraying the Charge of rebuilding the Stadt House.

Resolved it be referred till further Consideration.

M<sup>r</sup> Greenfield shewing that his Wife lying very ill at Home prays Liberty that he may go Home.

Which was granted by the House.

Bill for rebuilding the Stadt House at Annapolis Read the P. 13 first time. Ordered it be read again.

Bill for Division of S<sup>t</sup> Paul's Parish &<sup>ta</sup> and a Message about Masters of Ships publishing Freight &<sup>ta</sup> sent up by M<sup>r</sup> Frisby & M<sup>r</sup> Thomas Beale.

They return & say they delivered the same.

Remonstrance on behalf of the Roman Catholicks being brought into the House was ordered to be read & was thus indorsed, Viz.

By the House of Delegates December 8<sup>th</sup> 1704.

Upon reading the within written Remonstrance in this House the House are inclined to indulge the Roman Catholicks in the private Exercise of their Religion in their own House & Families and therefore they do pray the concurrence of his Excellency the Gov<sup>r</sup> and her Majesty's Council therein that a Bill may be brought in which may allow them such Liberty as they have prayed.
Signed ℗ Order    W Taylard Cl. Ho. Del.

Ordered That Major Taylor, M<sup>r</sup> Joseph Gray, M<sup>r</sup> Francis Dallahide, & M<sup>r</sup> Sam<sup>l</sup> Magruder carry it up to his Excellency & Council. They return & say they delivered the same.

Thomas Tench & James Sanders Esq<sup>rs</sup> enters the House & return the several ingrossed Bills this Day sent up by M<sup>r</sup> Mackall & M<sup>r</sup> Dallahide ; being severally indorsed as follows.

December 7<sup>th</sup> 1704. Assented to by her Majesty's Hoñble Council        W Bladen Cl. Council.

The House adjourned till two of Clock in the Afternoon

Post Meridiem. The House met again according to Adjournment.

Being called over were all present as in the Morning, only M^r Greenfield, who had Liberty to go Home. Col° Bell had Permission to enter the House who gave some Account of the Piscattaway Indians & so was ordered to withdraw.

The Hoñble Thomas Brooke Esq^r enter the House & delivers the Bill for Division of S^t Paul's Parish in Prince George's County indorsed; Eodem Die, Read in Coun^l and will pass.
W Bladen Cl Council.

Ordered That it be ingrossed
The Committee of Laws brought in the following Bills which were read.
Bill declaring the Act ascertaining the Bounds of Lands to be in force, indorsed
Read the first & second Times & by especial Order do pass. W. Taylard Cl. Ho. Del.

p. 14  Bill declaring several Acts to be in force indorsed.
Read the first & second Times by especial Order do pass
W Taylard Clk Ho. Del.

Ordered That M^r John Mackaster & M^r Samuel Magruder carry the aforegoing Bills up to the Council. They retnrn & say they delivered their Bills.
Col° John Hammond and Col° William Holland enters the House and delivers M^r Speaker the Bill declaring several Acts of Assembly to be in force thus indorsed.

By the Governor & Council December the 8^th 1704.

This Bill seems to interfere with her Majesty's Royal Instructions comprising several Laws of different Natures so that if her Majesty Disassents to any one of them the rest will be all repealed thereby Wherefore it is recommended that seperate Bills be prepared to declare the several Laws distinctly in force W Bladen Cl. Council.

Which being read this House concurs therewith & ordered Seperate Bills be ingrossed.
Then the House adjourned till to Morrow Morning Eight O'Clock
Saturday December the 9^th 1704.
The House again met according to Adjournment. Being. called over were all present as yesterday.

Read what was done yesterday

Col° Holland & William Coursey Esq. enters the House & delivers the Bill declaring the Act ascertaining the Bounds of Land in Force indorsed

Eodom Die   Read in Council & past
                                    W Bladen Cl. Council.

Bill for rebuilding the Stadt House indorsed in Council and the Bill for causing Grand & Petit Jurors & witnesses to come to Courts indorsed.

### Decem. 8ᵗʰ 1704.

Assented to by his Majesty's Honble Council.
                                    W Bladen Cl. Council.

Ordered the following Message be entered as follows.

### By the House of Delegates December 9ᵗʰ 1704.

In Answer to the Message as to the Act prohibiting the Importation of Bread Flour &ᶜᵗᵃ this House are of Opinion that the Legislative Power of this Province has sufficient Power to prohibit Trade in such a Branch of it as that Act mentions but they are ready to concur with your Honours Sentiments that 'tis better to lay a Duty on the enumerated Commodities &ᵗᵃ but Time will not admit to bring in a new Bill therefore pray the Consideration thereof may be referred to the next Session of Assembly
                Signed ꝑ Order  W Taylard Cl. Ho. Del.

Col° Hammond enters the House & delivers Mʳ Speaker a Bill relating to the Roman Catholicks with the Bill before p. 15 proposed Ordered it be considered of.

The following Message was read & ordered to be entered Viz.

### By the House of Delegates December 9ᵗʰ 1704.

This House hath received all the Papers relating to the Indians and the Message sent therewith by John Hammond & William Coursey Esqʳˢ and we have heard all the Information that Col° Smallwood & Col° Beale have given us from all which we can with no reasonable Certainty either blame or excuse our Neighbouring Indians the Piscattaways but

Lib. 41. forasmuch as notwithstanding with our peaceable Carriage towards them & our Threatnings have not prevailed upon them to return to their ancient Dwelling this House hath a good Disposition to make War upon them were it not that we have already undertaken some Business of great Charge therefore we humbly advise your Excellency to call in the Soldiers & to treat with the said Indians at present in Friendly Manner and to dissemble the Resentment of the English till they be better capacitated to carry on a War, and have more Certainty of their Treachery & Guiltiness

Signed p Order W. Taylard Cl. Ho. Del.

Ordered That M<sup>r</sup> John Hudson & M<sup>r</sup> James Hey carry up to the Council both the aforegoing Messages.

They return & say they delivered the same.

Bill suspending the Prosecution of Jesuits &<sup>ca</sup>

Bill for rebuilding the Stadt House. Ordered they be indorsed Viz.

December the 9<sup>th</sup> 1704.   Read the first & second Times & by especial Order do pass       W. Taylard Cl. Ho. Del.

Ordered That M<sup>r</sup> Hugh Eccleston carry up the aforegoing Bills to the Council

He returns & says he delivered the same.

Ingrossed Bill for Division of St. Paul's Parish &<sup>ta</sup> indorsed December the 9<sup>th</sup> 1704.

Read & assented to by the House of Delegates

W. Taylard Cl. Ho. Del.

Ingrossed Bill declaring the Act Entituled an Act ascertaining the Bounds of Land to be in force, indorsed by Order December the 9<sup>th</sup> 1704. Read & assented to by the House of Delegates.       W Taylard Cl. Ho. Del.

Bill declaring an Act Entituled an Act for erecting Ann Arundel & Oxford Towns into Ports & Towns formerly made to be in force Indorsed p Order. Read first & second Times & do pass       W Taylard Cl. Ho. Del.

p. 16   Bill declaring the Act for Punishment of Persons suborning witnesses &<sup>ta</sup> to be in force. Read and ordered to be indorsed December the 9<sup>th</sup> 1704.

Read the first & second Times & do pass

W. Taylard Cl. Ho. Del.

Bill declaring an Act Entituled an Act concerning Indians to Lib. 41.
be in force Read & ordered to be thus indorsed. Read the
first & second Times & do pass

W. Taylard Cl. Ho. Del.

Bill declaring an Act Entituled an Act for sanctifying &
keeping Holy the Lord Day commonly called Sunday &ᵗᵃ
Ordered it be read & indorsed. Read the first and second
Times & do pass. W Taylard Cl. Ho. Del.

The two above ingrossed Bills and the other aforegoing
following Bills were sent up to the Council ꝑ Mʳ John Jones &
Mʳ Joseph Gray.

They return & say they deliver the same.

Colᵒ William Holland from the Council enters the House &
acquaints Mʳ Speaker that his Excellency will take Care to
call in the Rangers.

And likewise delivered the Bill for rebuilding the Stadt
House indorsed Read with the Amendments and do pass for
ingrossing. And the Bill Suspending the Prosecution of Priests
& Jesuits &ᵗᵃ Indorsed December the 9ᵗʰ 1704. Read the second
Time in Council & do pass.

W Bladen Cl. Council.

Both ordered to be ingrossed.

The Journal of the Committee of Accounts being read in
the House Ordᵈ Mʳ King carry the same up to the Council for
their Assent.

Mʳ King returns and says he delivered the same.

The Petition of Colᵒ John Cood Read, wherein prays an
Allowance for Imprisonment Fees of two Criminals when
Sheriff.

Ordered the Consideration thereof be referred till next
Assembly.

Ordered That an Indian called Robin be allowed five
Pound Sterling for his Service done the Country and that
it be lodged for him in the Hands of Colᵒ Smallwood.

Ordered That Colᵒ Smallwood be allowed ten Pounds
Sterling for his late Service done the Country.

Whereas William Taylard Clerk of the House have several former years allowed his Salary in remote Counties on
the Eastern Shore therefore now upon his humble Petition it
is ordered that the same shall be allowed & paid him for the
future on the Western Shore unless paid in Money & for
some other extraordinary Service he be advanced & allowed p. 17
more 1200ˡᵇ Tobacco a Journal.

Lib. 41.  Col⁰ William Holland & James Sanders Esqʳˢ enters the
House & delivers the following Bills.
Bill for rebuilding the Stadt House.
Bill suspending the Prosecution of Jesuits &ᵗᵃ
Bill declaring the Act Entituled an Act erecting Ann Arun-
del & Oxford Towns into Ports &ᵗᵃ
Bill declaring the Act for punishing Persons suborning
Witnesses &ᵗᵃ to be in force.
Bill declaring an Act Entituled an Act concerning Indians
to be in force. And the Bill declaring an Act Entituled an
Act for sanctifying & keeping Holy the Lords Day &ᵗᵃ In-
dorsed Eodem Die
Read the first & second Times in Council & do pass
W Bladen Cl. Council.


And likewise the following ingrossed Bills viz.
Ingrossed Bill for Division of Saint Paul's Parish &ᶜᵗᵃ
And Ingrossed Bill declaring an Act Entituled an Act ascer-
taining the Bounds of Land to be in force.
Both indorsed December the 9ᵗʰ 1704.
Read and assented to by her Majesty's Hoñble Council.
W Bladen Cl. Council.


This House being informed by their Clerk that duplicate
Transcripts of the Journals are to be transcribed at his
Charge and forasmuch as there has been one long Assembly
this Year together with this present Sessions that has engaged
him in extraordinary Services for the Public beside what has
been allowed him before this Session it is ordered that he be
allowed three thousand Pounds of Tobacco more.
Put to the Question whether an additional Duty of 6ᵈ ₱
Hhd. shall be raised towards the Charge of rebuilding the
Stadt House or not ? Carried of Majority of Votes that such
a Duty be raised for that Use. And ordered that the Committee of Laws bring in a Bill for that Purpose.
The House adjourned till two o'Clock in the Afternoon.


Post Meridiem. The House met again according to Adjournment. Being called over were present as in the
Morning.
The following ingrossed Bills brought into the House and
ordered to be read viz.
Ingrossed Bill declaring the Act for Punishment of ₱sons
suborning witnesses. Indorsed ₱ Order December the 9ᵗʰ
1704. Read & assented to by the House of Delegates
W. Taylard Cl. Ho. Del.

Ingrossed Bill declaring an Act concerning Indians to be Lib. 41 in force. Read & ordered to be indorsed December the 9ᵗʰ 1704. Read and assented to by the House of Delegates

W Taylard Cl. Ho. Del.

Ingrossed Bill for rebuilding the Stadt House      p. 18
Read and indorsed Decem. the 9ᵗʰ 1704.
Read & assented to by the House of Delegates.

W. Taylard Cl. Ho. Del.

Ingrossed Bill suspending the Prosecution of Jesuits &ᵗᵃ Indorsed ꝑ Order Dec. 9ᵗʰ 1704. Read and assented to by the House of Delegates.      W Taylard Cl. Ho. Del.

Ingrossed Bill for erecting Ann Arundel & Oxford Towns into Ports &ᶜᵗᵃ
Ordered to be indorsed December the 9ᵗʰ 1704 Read and assented to by the House of Delegates

W. Taylard Cl. Ho. Del.

Ingrossed Bill declaring the Act for sanctifying & keeping Holy the Lords Day &ᵗᵃ to be in force. Indorsed ꝑ Order December the 9ᵗʰ 1704 Read & assented to by the House of Delegates      W. Taylard Cl. Ho. Del.

Ordered That Mʳ William Watts & Mʳ Peter Watts carry up the aforegoing Bills to the Hoñble Council.

The Petition of Charles Kilbourn lately publick Gunner praying an Allowance for three Years Salary for the Office; was here read and ordered it be considered of next Assembly.

Moved by the Members of Ann Arundel County that forasmuch as the Stadt House is unhappily burnt so that they are destitute of a Place to hold County Courts in therefore on behalf of the County they humbly pray they may have Liberty to hold Courts in the House where the Provincial Courts are ordered to be held. Which was readily granted by this House.

The Petition of Thomas Bardley complaining against the present Sheriff of Ann Arundel County was here read and debated. The House thereupon referred the Petitioner to the Law for Relief.

Resolved That the Bill for suspending Prosecution of Jesuits &ᵗᵃ And the Bill for Division of Sᵗ Paul's Parish are private Bills and that Fees be paid as follows Viz.

The Bill for suspending Prosecution of Jesuits &ᵗᵃ

To the Hoñble Speaker for his Fees      £5 .. —
To William Taylard Clerk of this House.      2 .. 10

Col° William Holland & ames Sanders Esq^rs enters the House & delivers the followig Bills.

Bill for rebuilding the Stat House.

Bill suspending the Proseation of Jesuits &^ta

Bill declaring the Act Entuled an Act erecting Ann Arundel & Oxford Towns into Pcts &^ta

Bill declaring the Act fc punishing Persons suborning Witnesses &^ta to be in force

Bill declaring an Act Entiiled an Act concerning Indians to be in force. And the Bi declaring an Act Entituled an Act for sanctifying & keepig Holy the Lords Day &^ta Indorsed Eodem Die

Read the first & second 1nes in Council & do pass

W Bladen Cl. Council.


And likewise the followin ingrossed Bills viz.

Ingrossed Bill for Divisin of Saint Paul's Parish &^cta

And Ingrossed Bill declarig an Act Entituled an Act ascertaining the Bounds of Landto be in force.

Both indorsed December 1e 9^th 1704.

Read and assented to by er Majesty's Honble Council.

W Bladen Cl. Council.


This House being informed by their Clerk that duplicate Transcripts of the Journas are to be transcribed at his Charge and forasmuch as thre has been one long Assembly this Year together with this resent Sessions that has engaged him in extraordinary Service for the Public beside what has been allowed him before thi Session it is ordered that he be allowed three thousand Pouds of Tobacco more.

Put to the Question wheier an additional Duty of 6^d p Hhd. shall be raised towars the Charge of rebuilding the Stadt House or not? Carrid of Majority of Votes that such a Duty be raised for that Us. And ordered that the Committee of Laws bring in a Bl for that Purpose.

The House adjourned till wo o'Clock in the Afternoon.


Post Meridiem. The Hose met again according to Adjournment. Being called over were present as in the Morning.

The following ingrossed ¿ills brought into the House and ordered to be read viz.

Ingrossed Bill declaring he Act for Punishment of psons suborning witnesses. Indosed p Order December the 9^th 1704. Read & assented to by the House of Delegates

W. Taylard Cl. Ho. Del.

Act concerning Indians to be Lib. 41
ɔe indorsed December the 9ᵗʰ
ɩy the House of Delegates
    W Taylard Cl. Ho. Del.

the Stadt House          p. 18
he 9ᵗʰ 1704.
louse of Delegates.
    W. Taylard Cl. Ho. Del.

he Prosecution of Jesuits &ᵗᵃ
ɩ4. Read and assented to by
    W Taylard Cl. Ho. Del.

Ann Arundel & Oxford Towns

ːmber the 9ᵗʰ 1704 Read and
ːlegates
    W. Taylard Cl. Ho. Del.

Act for sanctifying & keeping
ː in force. Indorsed ꝑ Order
& assented to by the House of
    W. Taylard Cl. Ho. Del.

Jatts & Mr Peter Watts carry
ɩoñble Council.
lbourn lately publick Gunner
e Years Salary for the Office ;
ː considered of next Assembly.
ɩn Arundel County that foras-
ɩappily burnt so that they are
ounty Courts in· therefore on
ly pray they may have Liberty
ɩere the Provincial Courts are
readily granted by this House.
ɖley complaining against the
l County was here read and
ɩ referred the Petitioner to the

ɩendiʳ ᴾʳᵒˢᵉᶜᵘᵗion of Jesuits
f S          ˋ private

Lib. 41.    And for the Bill for Division of Saint Paul's Parish.

To the Honͤble Speaker for his Fees.                    5 .. —
To William Taylard Clerk of this House              2 .. 10

P. 19    Brought into the House a Bill for laying an Imposition of
6ᵈ ℈ Hhd on Tobacco towards defraying the Charge of building
the Stadt House. Indorsed December the 9ᵗʰ 1704.  By the
House of Delegates.  Read the first & second Times & by
especial Order do pass.               W Taylard Cl. Ho. Del.

Ordered That Colᵒ Smallwood, Colᵒ Maxfield, Mʳ Tyler, Mʳ
Mackall, Mʳ Beale, Mʳ Blay, Mʳ Wells, Mʳ Hill, Mʳ Hudson &
Mʳ Macclaster carry up the Bill to the Council for their Con-
currence.  They return and say they delivered the Bill.

The Petition of William Morington praying a Discharge
of some Goods seized and unjustly detained &ᵗᵃ  Indorsed as
follows.

By his Excellency the Governor & Council
December 9ᵗʰ 1704.

This Petⁿ being read Ordered That the Naval Officer at
Williamstadt discharge the Seizure to which we desire the
Concurrence of the House.
                    Signed ℈ Order W Bladen Cl Council.

Upon reading the said Petition & Order thereupon this
House concurred thereof to discharge the Seizure the Petitioner
allowing the Naval Officer 40s for his Pains & Trouble.  Which
was likewise indorsed & delivered to the Petʳ

The House taking under Consideration these Persons that
were industrious endeavouring to preserve the publick Records
from the Fire of the Stadt House.  Do order That Mʳ Edward
Hancox, Mʳ Richard Dallam, George Hix & three Sailors be
each of them allowed twenty Shillings Sterling as a Present to
buy them Rings.  And that the Sailors Money be lodged for
them in the Hands of Mʳ Elias King.  Allowed to John Beale,
Clerk the sum of five Pounds Sterling for his Service and in
Recompence of his Loss in using his Endeavours to preserve
the publick Records &ᵗᵃ

Thomas Tench Esqʳ enters the House and delivers the Bill
for the Duty of 6ᵈ ℈ Hhd. on Tobᵒ &ᵗᵃ wᵗʰ Indorsᵗ Wᶜʰ being
read the Bill is rejected.  And also the following ingrossed
Bills brought in Viz.

Ingrossed Bill for Division of S<sup>t</sup> Paul's Parish in Prince Lib. 41. George's County, Indorsed by the Council December the 9<sup>th</sup> 1704. Read & assented to by her Majesty's Hoñble Council.

W Bladen Cl. Council.

And the ingrossed Bill ascertaining the Bounds of Land &<sup>ta</sup> to be in force. Indorsed Xber 9<sup>th</sup> 1704. Read & assented to by her Majesty's Honble Council.

W Bladen Cl. Council.

Col<sup>o</sup> William Holland & Kenelm Cheseldine Esq<sup>rs</sup> enters the House & acquaints M<sup>r</sup> Speaker That his Excellency the Governor commands him & the whole House to attend him immediately at the Council Chamber to ccmpleat this Session of Assembly

Thereupon M<sup>r</sup> Speaker and the Members of the House of p. 20 Delegates attended his Excellency's Commands at the Council Chamber, where M<sup>r</sup> Speaker presented his Excellency with the following Bills made this Session Viz.

An Act for Limitation of Officers Fees

An Act declaring the Division of several Counties

An Act for Advancement of Natives & Residents &<sup>ta</sup>

An Act for regulating the Militia.

An Act for Payment of Criminals Fees.

An Act for causing Grand & Petit Jurors & Witnesses to come to Courts

An Act for Preservation of Harbours &<sup>ta</sup>

An Act declaring an Act Entituled an Act ascertaining the Bounds of Land to be in force

An Act for rebuilding the Stadt House.

An Act declaring an Act for erecting Ann Arundel & Oxford Towns & Ports to be in force.

An Act declaring an Act for furnishing ᵱsons Suborning Witnesses to be in force

An Act declaring an Act for sanctifying & keeping holy the Lord's Day to be in force

An Act suspending the Prosecution of Jesuits &<sup>ta</sup>

An Act for Division of S<sup>t</sup> Paul's Parish in Prince George's County

An Act declaring the Act concerning the Indians to be in force

An Act declaring several Acts formerly made to be in force

To which his Excellency was pleased on her Majesty's Behalf to give his Assent by indorsing each separately And being so indorsed his Excellency was further pleased to seal each separate Law, with the broad Seal. And then his Excellency acquainted M<sup>r</sup> Speaker & the rest of the Members that he

Lib. 41. thought it convenient (by Advice of her Majesty's Council) for
her Majesty's Service to prorogue them until     Day of
     next At which Time if there be no Occasion of their
Meeting he would after give them Timely Notice as have been
usually done.   And thereupon M^r Speaker and the rest of the
Members were prorogued accordingly.   So endeth the second
Session of this Assembly on Saturday the Ninth Day of
December Anno Dom. 1704 and the third Year of the Reign
of our Sovereign Lady Ann by the Grace of God of England,
Scotland, France & Ireland Queen Defender of the Faith &^ta
                              W. Taylard Cl. Ho. Del.


     This is a true Record taken from the original Journal lodged
in the Secretary's Office.
     By Order of the House of Delegates.   Recorded & examined
                              p Rich^d Dallam Cl. Ho. Del.
     18^th May 1713.

Maryland ss:
Att a Sessions of Assembly begun and held at the Port of
Annapolis the 5<sup>th</sup> Day of December in the third year of the
Reigne of our Sovereigne Lady Anne by the grace of God
of England Scotland France and Ireland Queen Defender
of the faith &c<sup>a</sup> Annoq Dui.

### 1704

Were enacted the Laws following

### An Act for Limitation of Officers ffees.

Be it Enacted by the Queens most excellent Majesty by
and with the Advice and Consent of her Ma<sup>tys</sup> Governour
Councill and Assembly of this Province and the Authority of
the same that from and after the publication hereof no Officer
or Officers hereafter mencoñd in this Present Act their Ministers Servants or Deputys by reason of Colour of his or
their Office or Offices have receive or take of any Pson or
Psons directly or indirectly any other ffees than by this Act is
hereafter limitted and allowed to the severall Officers hereafter menconñd To the Chancellour or Keeper of the Great
Seale ffor Seale of an Originall Writt six pounds of Tobacco
ffor seale of a Recordari twelve pounds of Tobacco for Seale
of a Subpa ad respondeñd with three Names or under fifteen
pounds of Tob° ffor every Name more than three six pounds P. 182
of Tobacco For seale to a Proclamation of Rebellion three
hundred and Sixty pounds of Tobacco ffor seale of a Comission
of Rebellion three hundred & sixty pounds of Tobacco for
seale of a Grant of Land for one hundred Acres or under One
hundred and twenty pounds of Tobacco ffor every hundred
Acres above one hundred Acres twelve pounds of Tobacco
ffor Seale of a Decree in Chancery ffour hundred and thirty
p<sup>ds</sup> of Tobacco ffor Seale of an Injunction in Chancery two
hundred and forty pounds of Tobacco ffor Seale of an Audita
Querela one hundred and twenty pounds of Tobacco ffor Seale
to an Execucon of a Decree in Chancery one hundred Sixty
and two pounds of Tobacco ffor Seale of a Writt of Covenant
for passing a ffine ffifteen pounds of Tobacco ffor Seale of a
Comission to take Acknowledgm<sup>t</sup> one hundred and twenty
pounds of Tobacco ffor the Councillors hand to a Writt of
Assize two hundred and forty pounds of Tobacco ffor Seale to
Writt of Error to the Councill two hundred and forty pounds
of Tobacco For Seale to Scire facias thereupon two hundred

Lib. 41. and forty pounds of Tobacco ffor Seale of a Super Sedeas thereupon two hundred and forty pounds of Tobacco for the Seale to a Certiorari two hundred and forty pounds of Tobacco ffor the Seale of an Exemplification of Land the same with the patent or Grant ffor the Chancellors hand to a Writt of Covenant two hundred & forty pounds of Tobacco ffor Seale to a Mandamus one hundred and twenty pounds of Tobacco ffor the Seale to a Melius Inquirendum One hundred and twenty pounds of Tobacco ffor the Seale of a Comission of a County Court four hundred and thirty pounds of Tob° ffor Seale of a Dedimus potestatem to swear the Justices two hundred and forty pounds of Tobacco ffor Seale of a Supersedeas to a Comission of Rebellion or Supplicavit two hundred and forty pounds of Tobacco ffor the Seale of Sheriffs patents for his Office four hundred and Eighty pounds of Tobacco ffor the

p. 183 Seale of Posse Comitatus one hundred and twenty pounds of Tobacco ffor the Seale of a Writt of Discharge if any One hundred and twenty pounds of Tobacco ffor Seale of a patent of Denization four hundred and thirty pounds of Tobacco ffor Seale of a ne exeat Provinciam One hundred & twenty pounds of Tobacco ffor Seale of a Writt of Erro$^r$ from any Co$^{ty}$ Court one hundred and twenty pounds of Tobacco ffor Seale of a Scire facias thereupon one hundred and twenty pounds of Tobacco ffor Seale of every other Matter & thing that shall pass the Great Seale and not herein contain'd each one hunbred and twenty pounds of Tobacco To the Comissary Generall or Chief Judge in Testamentary Causes ffor every Letter of Administration or Letter Testamentary one hundred pounds of Tobacco ffor every bond Sixty pounds of Tobacco ffor every oath sixteen pounds of Tobacco ffor a Warrant to Appraisors twenty Eight pounds of Tobacco ffor every Warrant to swear them twenty Eight pounds of Tobacco ffor every Comission to prove a Will or take oath to account or of Administration one hundred pounds of Tobacco ffor Recording Wills Inventarys or Copying the Same or any other Matter out of the Comissarys Office Sixteen pounds of Tobacco per side Computing seven Words to a Line and fifteen lines to a side ffor every order in Testamentary Causes Sixteen pounds of Tobacco ffor every Citation twenty pounds of Tobacco ffor filing every Libell Answer Replication petition &c fforty Pounds of Tobacco ffor Subpœna for Costs Sixteen pounds of Tobacco ffor drawing Definitive Sentence per side sixteen pounds of Tobacco ffor filing of Costs sixteen pounds of Tobacco ffor Copy of Costs Sixteen pounds of Tobacco ffor recording Definitive Sentence Ᵽ side Sixteen p$^{ds}$ of Tob° ffor Execution of Definitive sentence Ᵽ side sixteen pounds of Tobacco ffor Seale to the Definitive sentence four hundred & Eighty pounds of Tobacco ffor Seale

to the Execution of such Definitive sentence two hundred and
forty pounds of Tobacco ffor Copy of every Answer Libell
Replication or Rejoynder as before ᵽ side Sixteen pounds of
Tobacco ffor Drawing Depositions of Witnesses ᵽ side sixteen
pounds of Tobacco ffor filing Interrogatorys forty pounds of
Tobacco for entry of Demand for Administration or probatt of
Wills Eight pounds of Tobacco for entry of every Returne
Eight pounds of Tobacco for every Appearance Sixteen pounds
of Tobacco ffor an Attachment of Contempt fifty six pounds
of Tobacco ffor a Quietus Est one hundred pounds of Tobacco
Secretarys ffees ffor a Recordari twelve pounds of Tobacco for
a Spa ad respondend three names fifteen pounds of Tobacco
ffor every name more than three six pounds of Tobacco ffor
Attachment of Contempt Eighteen pounds of Tobacco ffor a
Proclamation of Rebellion one hundred and twenty pounds of
Tobacco ffor an Injuncon Sixty pounds of Tobacco for an
Audita Querela one hundred pounds of Tobacco For a Writt
of Inquiry of Damages forty pounds of tobacco ffor a Writt of
Covenant to pass a ffine ffifteen pounds of Tobacco ffor a
Comission to take Acknowledgmᵗ One hundred and twenty
pounds of Tobacco ffor a Writt of Assize thirty pounds of
Tobacco ffor a Comission to ffine Officers upon a Melius
Inquirendum or Monstraverunt one hundred and twenty
pounds of Tobacco ffor a Ne exeat provinciam One hundred
and twenty pounds of Tobacco ffor drawing any Instruments
that pass the Seale if it exceed one side Computing seven
words to a line and fifteen lines to a side and so pro rato for
more Sixteen pounds of Tobacco ffor recording the same as
before sixteen pounds of Tobacco ffor entring any other Matter
upon Record if it exceed half a side of a Leaf Eight pounds of
Tobacco If the Matter entred upon Record be above half a
side Computing as before for every side Sixteen pounds of
Tobacco Copying the same with Recording Sixteen pounds of
Tobacco ffor any Wanᵗ or Lycens agᵗ or to one ᵽson only not
under the Seale fifteen pounds of Tobacco ffor any Warrant
or Lycense against or to more than one not under the Seale
then for Each fifteen pounds of Tobacco ffor any other pass or
Discharge not under the Seale fifteen pounds of Tobacco ffor
Search of a Record the first Year nothing ffor Search of a
Record above one Year standing for every Year within the
first five Years ᵽ Annum four pounds of Tobacco & for every
year above five ᵽ Annum two pounds of Tobacco ffor filing
every bill in Chancery forty pounds of Tobacco ffor every
Court the same shall Continue four pounds·of Tobacco ffor
filing every answer thirty six pounds of Tobacco ffor every
oath to the same twelve pounds of Tobacco ffor Writing a
Comission a bond and Recording it for every Sheriffs Office

Lib. 41. two hundred and forty pounds of Tobacco ffor Writt of Posse
Comitatus One hundred and twenty pounds of Tobacco ffor
Writt of Discharge if any One hundred and twenty pounds of
Tobacco ffor Writing and Recording a Comission and dedimus
Potestatem for the County Court three hundred and thirty
pounds of Tobacco ffor every Writt and Return twenty eight
pounds of Tobacco ffor every Subpena and return thirty eight
pounds of Tobacco ffor filing and Recording every Declaration
ꝑ side accounting fifteen Lines to a side and seven Words to
a line Sixteen pounds of Tobacco ffor Copy of the same at the
same rate not to be Charged unless required and delivered ffor
every Appearance entred twelve pounds of Tobacco ffor entry
of an Imparlance Eight pounds of Tobacco ffor a Continuance
or reference Eight pounds of Tobacco for filing a plea if not
Speciall Eight pounds of Tobacco ffor Speciall plea ꝑ side as
before sixteen pounds of Tobacco ffor making up the Issue
thirty two pounds of Tobacco ffor rule to plead for tryall Eight
pounds of Tobacco ffor a Venire facias for Jurors twenty Eight
pounds of Tobacco ffor Copy of Pannell Eight pounds of Tobacco ffor every Verdict Eight pounds of Tobacco ffor entring
Judgment thirty two pounds of Tobacco ffor signing Judgᵗ
twenty four pounds of Tobacco ffor Copy of Judgment thirty
two pounds of Tobacco ffor transcript of the whole proceedings
as before ꝑ side sixteen pounds of Tobacco ffor filing of a bill
of Cost Sixteen pounds of Tobacco ffor Copy of it if Demanded
and Delivered Sixteen pounds of Tobacco ffor every Execution
and return          pounds of Tobacco ffor an Attachment and
scire facias fifty six pounds of Tobacco ffor every Speciall
p. 186 bayle Sixteen pounds of Tobᵒ ffor filing and recording any
Demurrer Sixteen pounds of Tobacco ffor drawing a protest
and recording it two hundred and forty pounds of Tobacco
for drawing any other Matter as publiq Notary attested
under the Seale · fifty pounds of Tobacco if such Matter
exceed one side then ꝑ side sixteen pounds of Tobacco
ffor recording a Patent for Land one hundred and twenty
pounds of Tobacco for proving rights ꝑ poll two pounds of
Tobacco ffor entring Assignmnᵗ not exceeding half a side
sixteen pounds of Tobacco ffor entring Certificate for land
sixteen pounds of Tobacco ꝑ side as before for Warrant for
Land twenty eight pounds of Tobacco for warrant of Resurvey
ꝑ order of Councill fifty pounds of Tobacco ffor Habere
facias Possessionem twenty Eight pounds of Tobacco for a
Replevin twenty Eight pounds of Tobacco ffor a procendo
twenty Eight pounds of Tobacco ffor a Writt of Restitution
twenty Eight pounds of Tobacco ffor Drawing Dedimus
Potestatem to examine Evidences fifty pounds of Tobacco
ffor a habeas Corpus fifty pounds of Tobacco ffor a Certiorari

fifty pounds of Tobacco ffor a Comission to Audite fifty pounds Lib. 41.
of Tobacco ffor an Elegit fifty pounds of tob° ffor a Comission
of Resurvey fifty pounds of Tobacco ffor a Writt of Diminution twenty Eight pounds of Tobacco ffor a Writt of Error to
the County Court fifty pounds of Tobacco for a Scire facias
thereupon fifty pounds of Tobacco ffor a Supersedeas thereupon fifty pounds of Tobacco ffor entring an Acknowledgment
of Land in Court twelve pounds of Tobacco ffor Recording a
Conveyance at Sixteen pounds of Tobacco ꝑ side as before
for taking every Recognizance in Court twenty Eight pounds
ef Tobacco for discharge of every Recognizance twenty
eight pounds of tob° ffor every Venire facias or Warrant to
apprehend Criminalls thirty pounds of Tobacco ffor appearance
sixteen pounds of Tobacco for every respitt and Continuance
twenty Eight pounds of Tobacco ffor every order in Criminall
Cases sixteen pounds of Tobacco ffor Copy of every Recognizance twenty eight pounds of Tobacco For every Indictment
sixteen pounds of Tobacco ffor Allowance of a Writt of Error
twenty eight pounds of Tobacco ꝑ side as before for Copying p. 187
every Indictment the same ffor filing plea to the same eight
pounds of Tobacco for Confession to every Indictment Sixteen
pounds of Tobacco for Allowance of a Writt of Erroʳ twenty
Eight pounds of Tobacco for every Indictment after the first
Name twenty four pounds of Tobacco ffor rule for tryall sixteen pounds of Tobacco ffor Copy of Pannell Eight pounds
of Tobacco for recording Verdict Eight pounds of Tobacco
for Ent Conviccon and signing Judgmᵗ fifty six pounds of
Tobacco for Writt of Execution thereupon fifty six pounds of
Tobacco All other ffees not herein compriz'd belonging to the
Secretarys Office to be Charg'd as Officers do in England pro
rato at one penny ꝑ pound To the Surveyor Generall and his
Deputy To the Survey of one hundred Acres of Land or under
one pound of Tobacco ꝑ Acre for any Quantity above one
hundred Acres and under two hundred Acres for the first
hundred as before and half a pound of Tobacco for the rest ꝑ
Acre If between two hundred Acres and five hundred Acres
then for the first two hundred Acres as before and a Quarter
of a pound of Tobacco for all above ffor five hundred Acres
as before and for all above tenn pounds of Tobacco ꝑ hundred
Acres For every Platt allowing three platts for every Survey
(that is to say) One to the party one to the Examiner Generall
and the other to be entred upon the Surveyors Book Tenn
pounds of Tobacco for the first hundred Acres or under and
after the rate of five pounds of Tob° ꝑ Cent for all above the
ffirst one hundred Acres For Journey ffees if the same be
distant from the Surveyors house twenty Miles or under forty
pounds of tob° if above twenty and under forty miles Eighty

27

Lib. 41. pounds of Tob° if above forty miles and under Sixty then one hundred and twenty p$^{ds}$ of tob° so pro rato ffor every Certificate of Survey be the Quantity more or less five p$^{ds}$ of Tobacco ffor the Resurvey of one hundred and forty Acres of Land or under made with a Circumferenter Chain & other necessary Instruments four hundred pounds of Tobacco ffor Resurvey of any Quantity of Land above One hundred and forty Acres the same ffees that is allowed upon primitive Surveys Computing the said one hundred and forty Acres as a part of the Survey & no more Except it be otherwise Limitted by the Act

p. 188 for ascertaining the bounds of Land Sheriffs ffees ffor serving a Writt and bayle bond thirty five pounds of Tobacco ffor tending on a Prisoner one day twenty four hours in Custody twenty pounds of Tobacco and so pro rato for a longer time ffor Collecting the Publiq dues for every hundred tenn pounds of Tobacco ffor serving an Attachment or Execution tenn pounds of Tobacco And if any Execution be for above one hundred and under five hundred pounds of Tobacco fifty pounds of Tobacco If it exceed five hundred pounds of Tobacco then one hundred pounds of Tobacco If it exceed one thousand then for the first thousand one hundred pounds of Tobacco and every thousand afterwards fifty pounds of Tobacco ffor Comittment and Releasment forty pounds of Tobacco ffor Pillory and Whipping nothing allow'd And after the same rate for mony or Tobacco and it is hereby declared that it is the true Intent and Meaning of this Act the Severall Sheriffs shall have no more ffees that for what shall appear to be Justly due upon such Execution and the same ffees for levying any Attachment for any Sume whatsoever mony or Tobacco or the full value thereof in any Goods or Merchandizes provided the same be Condemned to the use of the Party Plaintiff attaching the same and pro rato for such part thereof as shall be Condemn'd but if no part shall be Condemn'd that shall be attachd that then the said Sheriff shall have only tenn pounds of Tobacco for retaining the Writt afores$^d$ & no more ffor Impanelling a Jury one hundred and twenty pounds of Tobacco ffor serving any Extraordinary Warrant or Comission to be regulated by the Court ffor serving a Scire facias including the persons Sumond thirty pounds of Tobacco ffor Serving a Citation thirty pounds of Tobacco ffor Executing a Comission of Resurvey p Day one hundred pounds of Tobacco ffor Impannelling a Jury two hundred and forty pounds If empowered to swear Jury and Evidences then for every oath twelve pounds of Tobacco ffor every Non est Inventus return'd tenn pounds of Tobacco ffor serving a Subpena thirty pounds of Tobacco ffor Comittment and Releasment forty pounds of Tobacco but for Whipping

and Pilloring nothing allowed. To the Coroner ffor viewing <sub>Lib. 41.</sub>
the body of any person or persons murder'd slain or otherwise
dead by Misadventure to be made out of the Goods and
Chattells of the party so dead if any there be otherwise to be
levyed by the Comissioners of the County where such Accident
shall happen two hundred fifty pounds of Tobacco ffor Arrest- <sub>p. 189</sub>
ing or Sumoning any Sheriff sued or prosecuted in any Court
and for taking security forty pounds of Tobacco ffor arresting
Sumoning or Attaching any other Pson or Psons wherein the
Sheriff is Plaintiff such ffees as are allowed to be taken by the
Sheriff in Such Cases and no more. To the Cryer of the
Provincial Court for swearing every Jury one hundred forty
four pounds of Tobacco ffor swearing every Witness twelve
pounds of Tobacco ffor swearing the bayliff twelve pounds of
tob° ffor every Speciall bayle seventy two pounds of Tobacco
ffor every good Behaviour seventy two pounds of Tob° for
Clearing every Prisoner by Proclamation eighty pounds of
Tob° for the Acquittall of every Prisoner Eighty pounds of
tob° ffor every Appeale from the County Court fifty pounds of
tobacco ffor every Writt of Erro<sup>r</sup> return'd from the County
Court fifty pounds of Tobacco. To the Clerk of the Councill
for every petition in Councill and order in favour of the party
two hundred pounds of Tobacco ffor any Comission or other
Instrument prepard by the said Clark to pass the broad Seale
if for a place of profitt four hundred pounds of Tobacco ffor
every Sheriffs Comission four hundred pounds of Tobacco
ffor every Ranger Surveyor or Comission of Profitt Granted
in Councill two hundred pounds of Tobacco ffor recording any
Matter in Councill ꝑ side for any Private Pson twenty four p<sup>ds</sup>
of tob° and so pro rato for more or less ffor Copy of any
Matter or thing from the Councill Records the same ꝑ side
ffor all searches to the Clerk of the Councill as is to the
honourable Secretary To the Clark of the High Court of
Appeals ffor recording every Writt of Erro<sup>r</sup> Scire facias &
return ꝑ side twenty four pounds of tob° and so pro rato as
before seven words in a line and twelve lines in a sheett. The
like for recording a Transcript the like ffees for recording the
Erro<sup>rs</sup> for Entring and Signing Judgm<sup>t</sup> Eighty four pounds of
Tobacco for filing a bill of Cost twenty four pounds of Tobacco
ffor Copy of the same twenty four pounds of Tobacco ffor all
other ffees as are taken in the Provincial Court Office. To
the Clark of the County Court ffor a Writt and return sixteen
pounds of tob° ffor every declaration of a side Eight pounds
of Tobacco and so pro rato if more ffor Copy of the same if
Demanded as before ffor entring of the Defendants appearance <sub>p. 190</sub>
six p<sup>ds</sup> of tob° ffor every Imparlance four pounds of tob° for
filing every Plea and Demurer if not a Speciall one four pounds

Lib. 41. of tob° If a folio or more pro rato If any Copy Delivered pro-
rato ffor entring any Matter upon Record if half a side four
pounds of tob° If more then pro rato as before ffor a Subpena
if but one name tenn pounds of tob° If two or three Names
sixteen pounds of Tobacco ffor rule to plead or tryall four pds
of Tob° for making up the Issue eight pounds of tob° ffor
Copy if Delivered eight pounds of Tobacco ffor entring
Judgmᵗ sixteen pounds of Tobacco ffor signing Judgᵗ twelve
pounds of Tobacco ffor Venire facias for Jury twelve pounds
of tob° for entring the pannell four pounds of Tobacco for
filing bill of Cost eight pounds of Tobacco ffor Copy of the
same Eight pounds of tob° ffor Execution and return sixteen
pounds of tob° ffor Special bayle six pounds of tob° ffor
Writt of Inquiry of Damages forty four pounds of Tob° ffor
entring an Appeale Eight pounds of tob° for the return of
Certificate Copy of the Record ⱂ side Eight pounds of
Tobacco ffor entring a Writt of Erroʳ Eight pounds of Tobacco
ffor every oath six pounds of Tobacco ffor proving a Deed or
Writing Eight pounds of tobacco ffor Copy of the same if
required ⱂ folio Eight pounds of Tobacco ffor recording the
mark of Cattle and Hoggs four pounds of tob° for taking the
Acknowledgmᵗ of Land in Coʳᵗ twelve pounds of tobacco ffor
recording a Conveyance for Land ⱂ side Eight pounds of
Tobacco ffor Allowance of Habeas Corpus Eight pounds of
tob° ffor search every year after the first till five Years four
pounds of tob° ·P annum and for every Year above five years
two pounds of tob° ⱂ annum ffor Criminalls ffor taking every
Recognizance fourteen pounds of tobacco ffor Discharge of
Recognizance fourteen pounds of tobacco ffor Venire facias or
Warrant fifteen pounds of Tobacco ffor every Appearance
Eight pounds of Tobacco For every respitt or Continuance
Eight pounds of Tobacco ffor every order Eight pounds of
tobb° for Copy of Recognizance fourteen pᵈˢ of tob° ffor
every Indictment ⱂ side Eight pounds of tobacco ffor Copy
p. 191 of the pannell four pounds of tob° ffor recording the Verdict
Eight pounds of tob° ffor entring the Judgment twenty Eight
pounds of Tobacco ffor Execution of the Judgmᵗ twenty Eight
pounds of tobacco for Copy Indictmᵗ ⱂ folio as before Eight
for filing a plea Eight and for Confession of Indictment Eight
pounds of Tobacco.

To the Cryer of the County Court for swearing every Jury
seventy two pounds of Tobacco ffor swearing the bayliff six
pounds of tob° for every Oath six pounds of tob° ffor Speciall
bayle thirty six pounds of tobacco ffor good behaviour thirty
six pounds of tob° for Clearing every Prisoner by Proclamation
or Acquittall forty pounds of tobacco.

And be it further Enacted by the Authority aforesaid by and
with the Advice and Consent aforesaid that the severall Navall
Officers their Sufficient Deputy or Deputy belonging to the
respective Districts next Adjoyning to the Towns and Ports
of Annapolis and William Stad$^t$ shall Constantly reside at the
said Ports for giving Dispatch to all Shipps or Vessells trading
or Coming into them ports.

And it is hereby further enacted and Declared by the
Authority Advice and Consent aforesaid that the severall &
Navall Officers of this Province within their Severall and
respective Districts for the severall Acts and things relating to
their Office by him or them hereby enjoyn'd to be done shall
have and receive the ffees hereafter mencoñd and no more
(that is to say for entring any Shipp or Vessell coming and trading into this Province being under the burthen of one hundred
tonns the Masters thereof shall pay unto that respective Navall
Officer with whom he shall enter such Ship or Vessell as a ffee
for entring thereof the Suñe of five Shill. and no more and
five Shill more for the Clearing thereof and if such ship or
Vessell shall be above the burthen of one hundred tonns the
Master for Entry thereof shall pay to the said Navall Officer
as a ffee tenn Shillings and tenn Shillings for the Clearing
thereof And the said Navall Officers are hereby obliged to
enter all Shipps or Vessells of what burthen soever of the
built of this Province all whose Owners do actually inhabitt
and Reside within this Province and are purchasd held and
enjoy'd by such Owners for the Suñ of two Shill six pence
Sterl which is hereby allowed and ascertained him as a ffee
therefore and for the sume of two shill and six pence shall
Clear the same

And be it further Enacted by the Authority aforesaid that
all small boats belonging to this Province and being under
Eighteen ffoot by the Keele shall pass and repass without any
Lett Hindrance Molestation Seizure of the same unless they
shall Carry and have on board them prohibitted Goods or
goods lyable to pay Custom to her Ma$^{ty}$ not Cocquetted or
Clearing for the same without being obliged to take out permitts for such passing or repassing as aforesaid and that the
Masters of all shallops or open boats trading within this Province do pay to the severall Navall Officers or their Deputy or
Deputys appointed for the granting of permitts the Sume of
two Shillings six pence yearly and no more for the Granting
such permitts as aforesaid and shall give good security to be
taken by such Officers aforesaid or their Deputy or Deputys
in her Ma$^{tys}$ Name that he and they shall and will duly observe
the Acts of trade and Navigation and other Good laws of this
Province relating thereto.

ib. 41.    And be it further Enacted that all and every Collector and
Collectors of this Province shall have and receive such ffees for
entring and Clearing such Ships and Vessells aforesaid as are
above allowed to the Navall Officers and no more And that all
Collectors & Navall Officers shall make a fair table of their
ffees and hang up in their Offices under the penalty of fifty
pounds Sterling to her Majesty her heires and Successors for
the Support of Governm<sup>t</sup> to be recovered in any Court of
Record within this Province by Accon of Debt bill plaint or
Information wherein no Essoyn Protection or Wager of Law
to be allowed.

Provided allways that in Case any Person shall refuse to
pay the same so by this Act Limitted and allowed it shall and
may be lawfull for the Chancellour Secretary Judge for probatt
of Wills &c Surveyor Generall or his Deputys Sheriffs Coroner
p. 193 Clerk of the Councill Clerk of the Court of Appeals the severall
Clerks of the County Courts Cryer of the Provincial Co<sup>rt</sup> and
the severall Cryers of the County Courts to recover the same
by way of Execution against the Goods Tobacco or Chattells
of the Person or Psons so refusing and no other Provided
allways that such person or psons having no tobacco and that
shall refuse to shew unto such Officer or Officers as shall Collect the same such goods and Chattells it shall be lawfull for such
Officer or Officers to take the body or bodys of such person or
Psons in Execution for the same Provided also that no Officer
or Officers in this Act pticularly mencoñd and whose ffees are
hereby settled and Limitted shall by vertue thereof either have
or Cause to be levyed any Execution upon the body Goods or
Chattells of any person or persons whatsoever for any ffees in
this Act Limitted and contain'd without delivering or Causing
to be Delivered a true and Just Account of the ffees to them
due by this Act as aforesaid under the hand or hands of such
Officer or Officers to the Pson or Psons to whom such ffees
demanded are due as aforesaid thirty days at the least before
Execution levyed And in Case any of the said Officer or Officers
as af<sup>d</sup> shall in any wise Act or do contrary directly or indirectly
to this Act he or they so offending shall loose and forfeit to
the party grieved treble damages and shall also forfeit the
sume of six thousand pounds of Tobacco or forty pounds Sterl
the one Moyety thereof to our Sovereign Lady the Queen her
heires and Successors for the Support of Government to be
recovered in her Majestys name the other Moyety to the party
or partys that shall sue for the same to be recovered in any
Court of Record within this Province by action of Debt bill
plaint or Information wherein no Essoyn Protection or Wager
of Law to be Allowed.

And it is further provided that if any ffees for any Matter or Lib. 41. thing hereafter to be done belonging to the Officers aforesaid by the Gov<sup>r</sup> and Councill so allowed and adjudged and not in this Act mencoñ'd Limitted allowed and Adjudg'd it shall be lawfull for such Off<sup>r</sup> To have such ffee or ffees as the said P. 194 Governo<sup>r</sup> & Councill for the time being shall Adjudge and allow of & no more under the Penalty af<sup>d</sup> to be recovered as aforesaid. This Act to endure for three Years or to the end of the next Sessions of Assembly which shall first happen after the three years

<table>
<tr><td>December 7<sup>th</sup> 1704</td><td>December 8<sup>th</sup> 1704</td></tr>
<tr><td>Compared with the originall bill</td><td>Assented to by her Ma<sup>tys</sup></td></tr>
<tr><td>& Read & Assented to</td><td>honble Councill</td></tr>
<tr><td>by the house of Dell</td><td>W Bladen Cl Concil.</td></tr>
<tr><td>Signd p Ord<sup>r</sup> W Taylard Clk hD.</td><td></td></tr>
</table>

December 9<sup>th</sup> 1704

On behalf of her Ma<sup>tys</sup> &c I will this be a Law.

Jo : Seymour

An Act for payment of ffees due from Criminall Persons.    p. 202

Be it Enacted by the Queens most excellent Majesty by and with the Advice and Consent of her Majestys Governour Council and Assembly of this Province and the Authority of the same that from henceforth no Sheriff Goaler Clark Cryer or other Officer shall Charge either their own County to which they belong or the publiq with any ffees for any Criminall Comitted to the Charge of the said Sheriff or Goaler having Sufficient Estate in this Province wherewith to pay the same or being Capable to pay the same by servitude but that such Criminalls being discharged by order and due Course of Law shall pay their Own ffees to Sheriff Goaler Clark and Cryer and other Officers being such as they may demand according to Law either out of his Estate or by Servitude or otherwise.

Provided allways that this Act shall not extend to Malefactors that are Executed or to such other Psons who are banished having no Estate in this Province or to servants Criminalls for whom the County shall pay such ffees as are due by the Acts of Assembly to the sheriff Goaler Clark Cryer or other Officers of such Court where such Criminall shall be Convicted.

And be it further enacted that all Officers ffees due by Law from Criminall Servants shall be paid by the County where the ffact shall be Comitted and that all and every such Criminall servants for whom the County shall pay the ffees due by Law

Lib. 41. to such Officers as aforesaid shall after the end and expiration of his time of Servitude to his Master satisfy and pay unto the Comissioners of the County who payd such his ffees for him to the sheriff & other Officers as aforesaid for the use of the County such sums as they have paid as aforesd and the severall Comissioners of the Severall Countys shall and are hereby empowered to make Inquisition after all such Servants Criminalls for whom the County hath.defrayd the said ffees to
p. 203 the sheriff and other Officers as aforesaid and they the said Comissioners according to their best Discretion shall Cause to be entred rules for the said Servants to make such reasonable satisfaction to the County as they shall think fitt and in such Manner as they shall find Convenient. And for the better security of the County which shall pay such ffees for such Criminall Serv^ts as aforesaid,

Be it Enacted that the Master Mistress or Dame of all such servants be and are hereby enjoyn'd and required at the Expiracon of the time of all such servants servitude to such Master Mistress or Dame to render and deliver up to the Sheriff of the County for the use of the County aforesaid such Servants Criminalls as aforesaid under the penaltys to such Master Mistress or Dame refusing or neglecting to Deliver up such servants as aforesaid of making.Satisfaction to the County all such ffees as by the County aforesaid have been paid for such Criminall as aforesaid and such Sheriff to whom such Criminall Servant shall be delivered as aforesaid is hereby required to receive & secure such servants Criminalls as aforesaid so that he be & appear at the then next County Court to be held for the said County to be disposd of as the said ^Co^rts shall Consider.

Dec^r 7^th 1704.
Compar'd with originall bill and
read and Assented to by
the house of Dell
Sign'd p ord^r W. Taylard Cl hD.

December 8^th 1704
Assented to by her Ma^tys
hon^ble Councill
W Bladen Cl. Concil.

December 9^th 1704.
On Behalf of her Majesty I will this be a Law
Jo. Seymour

An Act for Causing Grand and Petit Jurors and Witnesses to Come to the Provincial & County Courts.

Be it Enacted by the Queens most Excellent Majesty by and with the Advice and Consent of her Majestys Governour Coun-

cill and Assembly of this Province and the Authority of the Lib 41.
same That after the publication hereof the severall and respec- p. 204
tive Sheriffs of the severall and respective Countys within this
Province shall Cause to Come before the Justices of the
Provincial Court two good and lawfull men of each respective
County to serve as Grand Jurors and three good and lawfull
Men of each respective County to serve as Petit Jurors at
every Provincial Court and the said Sheriffs shall return pan-
nells accordingly and twenty days Notice shall be given by the
Sheriffs to the Jurors before the day of their Appearance
(Justices of peace and Delegates Excepted) and such Sheriff
or Sheriffs as shall make Default shall be fined by the Justices
of the Provincial Court One thousand pounds of tob° to her
Majesty for the Support of the Government of this Province.

And be it further enacted by the Authority aforesaid by and
with the Advice and Consent aforesaid that the severall Sheriffs
of the severall and respective Countys af$^d$ shall Cause to Come
before the Justices of the severall County Courts a Competent
and Sufficient Number of the best and most understanding
ffreeholders of their severall and respective Co$^{tys}$ to serve as
Jurors of the severall and respective County Courts And the
severall Sheriffs shall return Pannells accordingly and give
Notice to such ffreeholders ten days before the day of their
Appearance at the said County Courts and such Sheriff or
Sheriffs as shall make default shall be fin'd by the Justices of
the County Courts five hundred pounds of tobacco to her
Majesty for the Support of the Governm$^t$ of this Province.

And be it further enacted that every Person or Psons ffreeholders return'd by the severall Sheriffs to serve as Jurors at
the Prov$^l$ C$^{orts}$ and having such Notice of the day of his or their
Appearance as aforesaid and shall not make his appearance
at the day but make Default shall be fin'd by the Justices of
the Prov$^l$ Court one thousand pounds of Tob° and every Pson
or Psons ffreeholders return'd by the severall Sheriffs to the
severall County Courts to serve as Jurors at the said County
Courts and having such Notice of the day of his or their
Appearance as aforesaid and shall not make his or their
Appearance at the day but make Default shall be fin'd by the p. 205
Justices of the County Courts five hundred pounds of tobacco
to her Majesty both the said ffines to be to her Majesty for
the Support of the Government of this Province.

And be it further Enacted by the Authority aforesaid by and
with the Advice and Consent aforesaid that every Pson that
shall be duly served with process to appear at the Provincial
Court as a Witness to testify in any Matter or thing there
depending and shall not keep his day of Appearance but make
default shall be fin'd by the Justices of the Provincial Court

Lib. 41. one thousand pounds of tobacco and every person that shall be duly served with process to appear in any of the County Coᵗˢ of this Province as a Witness to testify in any Matter or thing there depending and shall not keep his day of Appearance but shall make default shall be fin'd by the Justices of the County Courts five hundred pounds of tobacco both which ffines shall be to her Majesty for the Support of the Government of this Province.

<table>
<tr><td>December 8ᵗʰ 1704</td><td>December 8ᵗʰ 1704</td></tr>
<tr><td>Compar'd with Originall bill<br>Read and assented to by<br>the house of Dell<br>Signd p ordʳ W Taylard Cl hD.</td><td>Assented to by her Majestys<br>honᵇˡᵉ Councill.<br>W Bladen Cl Concil.</td></tr>
</table>

December 9ᵗʰ 1704.

On behalf of her Majesty I will this be a Law.

Jo: Seymour.

An Act for the Preservation of the severall Harbours and landing Places within this Province

Be it enacted by the Queens most excellent Majesty by and with the Advice and Consent of her Majestys Governour Councill and Assembly of this Province And the Authority of the same that from and after the Publication of this Act No person or persons whatsoever whether Inhabitant or fforeigner p. 206 trading with Shipps or Vessells of Greater or lesser burthen having a Deck shall unload or Cast out of their said Shipps or Vessells any kind of Ballast into the Harbours or Creeks where they ride but shall lay the said ballast on the shore above high water Mark and whosoever shall prsume to do Contrary to the Directions of this Act shall for every such default fforfiet and pay two thousand pounds of Tobacco the one half to our Sovereign Lady the Queen to be employ'd for the Support of the Government of this Province and the other Moyety to him or them that shall sue for the same to be recovered by Accon of Debt or Information wherein no Essoyn protection or wager of Law to be Allowed.

And be it further enacted by the Authority aforesaid by and with the Advice and Consent aforesaid that every respective Navall Officer within this Province or Collector for the time being or that shall hereafter be shall at their own proper Cost take out a Copy of this Act from the Office where the Originall Transcript of the body of the Laws shall be kept sign'd by the Keeper of the said Laws and the same affix at theire respective office Doors to the end all Comanders and Masters Lib. 41. of Ships or other Vessells Deckt as aforesaid may have due Cognizance thereof And if such Navall Officer refuse or neg-lect to take out such Copy and affix the same as aforesaid he shall forfeit and pay two thousand pounds of tobacco the one half to our Sovereign Lady the Queen to be employd to the use Intent and purpose aforesaid the other half to the In-former to be recovered as aforesaid.

And be it Enacted by the Authority Advice and Consent aforesaid That if any Pson or Psons that shall presume to build or make any Hedge or Ware a Cross any Creek or River towards the Head or Narrow parts thereof below any Publiq Landing places so as to prejudice and Dam up the Channell shall be lyable to a fine of five hundred pounds of p. 207 tob° to be recovered as aforesaid to the uses aforesaid.

<table>
<tr><td>December 7<sup>th</sup> 1704</td><td>December 8<sup>th</sup> 1704</td></tr>
</table>

December 7<sup>th</sup> 1704

Compar'd by the originall bill
Read and Assented to by the
house of Delegates.
Sign'd p ord<sup>r</sup> W Taylard Clk hD.

December 8<sup>th</sup> 1704

Assented to by her Ma<sup>tys</sup>
hon<sup>ble</sup> Councill
W. Bladen Cl Concil.

December 9<sup>th</sup> ·1704
On the behalf of her Majesty &c I will this be a Law
Jo : Seymour

An Act for Rebuilding the Stadthouse at Annapolis

Whereas William Bladen of Annapolis Esq<sup>r</sup> for himself his Executors & Administrators hath undertaken Covenanted promis'd and agreed to and with the Generall Assembly of this Province for and in Consideration of one thousand pounds Sterl or in Dollars or peices of Eight at four Shillings and six pence as they now pass within this Province to be payd to him the said William Bladen his Ex<sup>rs</sup> or Adm<sup>rs</sup> and of all the old Iron Work Bricks and Timber preserved from the fire when the late Stadt house was burnt at his proper Costs and Charges to Rebuild or Cause to be Rebuilt a New Stadt house upon the Walls and ffoundation of the said late Stadthouse and to Compleat and ffinish all Brick layers Work Carpenters Work Joyners work Plaisterers Work and Glaziers Work and furnish the said Stadthouse with locks and Keys in the same full and ample manner and forme as the said late Stadthouse was built Compleated ffinished and ffurnished at any time before it was burnt the Cubiloe or Terrett only Excepted.

Lib. 41.     Be it therefore Enacted by the Queens most Excellent
Majesty by and with the Advice and Consent of her Majestys
Governour Councill and Assembly of this Province and the
Authority of the same that the said William Bladen may have
p 208 and take to his Owne use to be employd towards the Rebuilding the Stadthouse all the bricks Iron work and timber
aforesaid And that out of the publiq Stock of this Province
shall be payd to the said William Bladen his Ex^{rs} and Adm^{rs}
the sume of one thousand pounds Sterl or in Dollars or peices
of Eight at four and six pence a piece as they now pass within
this Province.

Provided this Act shall not take Effect till the said William
Bladen hath given good security to his Excellency the Governour of two thousand pounds Sterl to perform the same
within Eighteen months.

| December 9^{th} 1704 | December 9^{th} 1704 |
|---|---|
| Read and Assented to by the | Assented to by her Ma^{tys} hon^{ble} |
| house of Delegates | Councill |
| W Taylard Cl hD | W Bladen Cl Concil. |

December 9^{th} 1704

On the behalf of her Ma^{ty} I will this be a Law.

Jo: Seymour.

An Act Declaring the Divisions of Severall Countys within
this Province made by vertue of a former Act Intituled An
Act for the Division and regulating severall Countys within
this Province and Constituting a County by the Name of
Prince Georges County within the same Province to be
firm and Stable.

Whereas by an Act of Assembly made at an Assembly
held at Annapolis the Eighth day of May sixteen hundred
Ninety five Entituled an Act for the Regulating and Division
of severall Countys within this Province and Constituting a
County by the name of Prince Georges County within the
same Province which is now Executed severall Divisions and
Partitions were made And by another Act of Assembly made
p. 209 the third day of Aprill sixteen hundred Ninety Eight Intituled
An Act ascertaining the bounds and Limitts of Ann Arundell
and Baltimore Countys severall other Divisions and Partitions
Lines and Land Marks were made relating to the bounds of
both the said Countys

Be it Enacted by the Queens most excellent Ma^{ty} by and
with the Advice and Consent of her Majestys Governour

Councill and Assembly of this province and the Authority Lib. 41. of the same that such partitions and Divisions Lines and Land Marks as by the Directions of the said Act were made shall remain firm and stable for ever.

And whereas there are severall Countys that are divided by Navigable Rivers and no rule yett made how farr the Iurisdiction of each County shall extend on the River

Be it therefore Enacted by the Authority aforesd that every County lying on any Navigable River in this Province shall extend its Iurisdiction from the shore to the Channell of such River that Divides the County and be divided from the other County by the Channell of the said River And that where any Shipp or Vessell that shall ride at Anchor in the Channell of such River process may be served on board the said Shipp by the Officer of either County that can first serve it But when moved by any hold on the Land shall be supposd to lye in that County to whose shore she is fastned if moved

| December 7ᵗʰ 1704 | December 8ᵗʰ 1704 |
|---|---|
| Compard with the Originall bill & Read and assented to by the house of Delegates Sign'd ꝑ Ordʳ W Taylard Clk hD. | Assented to by her Majestys honᵇˡᵉ Councill W Bladen Cl Concil. |

December 9ᵗʰ 1704.
On behalf of her Majesty I will this be a Law

Joᵒ: Seymour

An Act for Advancement of the Natives and Residents of this p. 210 Province.

Be it Enacted by the Queens most Excellent Majesty by and with the Advice and Consent of her Majestys Governour Council and Assembly of this Province and the Authority of the same that no Pson or Psons whatsoever who have not made this province their seat of Residence for the full Space and term of three Years shall have hold possess or enjoy any place or Office of trust or profitt within the same either by himself or Deputy Except such Pson or Psons as shall have imediate Comission from her Majesty her heires and Successors for any such place or office aforesaid as also such Pson or Psons now possest of any such place or Office as aforesaid But that all and every her Majestys Principall Officers within this Province having or that shall hereafter have Authority by

Lib. 41.    Be it therefore Enactd by the Queens most Exellent Majesty by and with the advice and Consent of her Majestys Governour Councill and Assembly of this Province and the Authority of the same tht the said William Bladen may have
p. 208 and take to his Owne se to be employd towards the Rebuilding the Stadthouse ll the bricks Iron work and timber aforesaid And that out ( the publiq Stock of this Province shall be payd to the sai( William Bladen his Exⁿ and Admⁿ the sume of one thousancpounds Sterl or in Dollars or peices of Eight at four and six pnce a piece as they now pass within this Province.

Provided this Act sha not take Effect till the said William Bladen hath given good ecurity to his Excellency the Governour of two thousand pounds Sterl to perform the same within Eighteen months.

| | |
|---|---|
| December 9ᵗʰ 1704 | December 9ᵗʰ 1704 |
| Read and Assented to by te | Assented to by her Maⁱʸᵗ honble |
| house of Delegates | Councill |
| W Taylard Cl D | W Bladen Cl Conil. |

Deceib r 9ᵗʰ 1704
On the behalf of her Mᵗ I will this be a Law.
                                              Jo : Seymour.


An Act Declaring the Ivisions of Severall Countys within this Province made by ertue of a former Act Intituled An Act for the Division an re,ulating severall Countys within this Province and Coitituting a County by the Name of Prince Georges Couny within the same Province to be firm and Stable.

Whereas by an Act ( Assembly made at an Assembl· held at Annapolis the Ighth day of May sixteen hundre Ninety five Entituled an ct for the Regulating and Divisio of severall Countys withi this Province and Constituting County by the name of rince Georges County within tl same Province which is nw Executed severall Divisions a Partitions were made Ari by another Act of Assembly ma
p. 209 the third day of Aprill si:een hundred Ninety Eight Intitu An Act ascertaining the ounds and Limitts of Ann Arun( and Baltimore Countys sverall other Divisions and Partiti Lines and Land Marks vre made relating to the bound both the said Countys

Be it Enacted by the Queens most excellent Maᵗʸ by with the Advice and Cnsent of her Majestys Gover

Councill and Assembly of this Province and the Authority of the same that such partitions and Divisions Lines and Land Marks as by the Directions of the said Act were made shall remain firm and stable for evr.

And whereas there are several Countys that are divided by Navigable Rivers and no rule yet made how farr the Iurisdiction of each County shall extencon the River

Be it therefore Enacted by the Athority aforesd that every County lying on any Navigable Rivr in this Province shall extend its Iurisdiction from the shor to the Channell of such River that Divides the County and is divided from the other County by the Channell of the said River And that whr any Shipp or Vessell that shall ride at Anchor in the Chanell of such River process may be sered on board the said Shipp by the Officer of either County that can first serve it But when moved by any hold on the and shall be supposd to lye in that County to whose shore sh is fastned if moved

December 7th 1704

Compard with the Originall bill
& Read and assented to by
the house of Delegates
Sign'd p Ordr
    W Taylard Clk hD.

December 8th 1704
Assentd to by her Majestys
onble Councill
W Bladen Cl Concil.

December 9th 1704.
On behalf of her Majesty I will this be a Law

Jo: Seymour

An Act for Advancement of the Natives and Residents of this Province.

p. 210

Be it Enacted by the Queens most Exceent Majesty by and with the Advice and Consent of her Majetys Governour Councill and Assembly of this Province and the Authority of the same that no Pson or Psons whatsoever who have not made this province their seat of Residence for he full Space and term of three Years shall have hold posses or enjoy any place or Office of trust or profitt within the sne either by himself or Deputy Except such Pson or Psons s shall have imediate Comission from her Majesty her heire and Sucsors for any such place or office aforesaid as alsuch or Psons now possesd of any such place or Office But that all and every her Majestys Principall O this Province having or that shall hereafter b

Lib. 41. vertue of any Comission from her Majesty her beires and Successors to him or them Granted to dispose of any Place or Office as afores$^d$ may upon Vacancy of any place or Office whereof they have right to dispose be obliged to make Choice of such Pson or Psons as they shall think most worthy and Capable of executing such place or Office as aforesaid out of the Inhabitants of this Province who have been Resident therein during the time and term aforesaid (Except before Excepted) any Custom or usage to the Contrary notwithstanding.

And be it further Enacted that every Pson or Psons whatsoever having Comission from the Queens Majesty her beires and Successors to exercise any Office within this Province shall actually Inhabitt within this Province and exercise the same in his own proper Pson and not by any Deputy or Deputys without Pticular leave from her Majesty.

December 7$^{th}$ 1704              December 8$^{th}$ 1704

Compar'd with the originall bill   Assented to by her Ma$^{tys}$
and read and Assented to by         hon$^{ble}$ Councill
the house of Dell.                  W Bladen Cl Concil.
Sign'd ꝑ Ord$^r$ W Taylard Cl hD.

Dec$^r$ 9$^{th}$ 1704

On behalf of her Ma$^{ty}$ &c I will this be a Law

                                    Jo: Seymour.

p. 211 An Act Declaring severall Acts of Assembly formerly made to be in force.

Be it Enacted by the Queens most excellent Majesty by and with the Advice and Consent of her Majestys Governour Councill and Assembly of this Province and the Authority of the same that the severall and respective Acts of Assembly heretofore made and Enacted (that is to say) one Act Intituled An Act for Erecting Ann Arundell and Oxford Towns into Ports and Towns One other Act of Assembly Intituled An Act for the punishment of Persons Suborning Witnesses or Comitting wilfull and Corrupt Pjury one other Act Intituled an Act for Sanctifying and Keeping holy the Lords Day comonly called Sunday One other Act Intituled An Act Concerning Indians One other Act Intituled An Act for the present security of the ffrontier Plantations from the Incursions and violence of Indians one other Act Intituled An Act prohibitting trade with the Indians for any fflesh dead or alive

Except Deer and Wild fowle One other Act Intituled an Act Lib 41.
for Quieting Differences that may arise between his Majestys
Subjects within this Province and the severall Nations of Indians of what places soever And every Clause Matter and
thing therein Contain'd is hereby declared to be and remain
in full force and Effect to all Intents Construccons and purposes whatsoever to the end of the next sessions of Assembly
this present sessions not having Leazure fully to Consider
thereof.

| December 7<sup>th</sup> 1704 | December 8<sup>th</sup> 1704 |
|---|---|

December 7<sup>th</sup> 1704     December 8<sup>th</sup> 1704
Compar'd with the Originall bill   Assented to by her Ma<sup>tys</sup>
Read and Assented to by the      hon<sup>ble</sup> Councill
house of Delegates      W Bladen Cl Concil.
Sign'd ꝑ Order
W Taylard Cl hD.

December the 9<sup>th</sup> 1704
On the behalf of her Ma<sup>ty</sup> I will this be a Law
Jo: Seymour.

An Act for Suspending the prosecution of any Priests of the p. 212
Comunion of the Church of Rome incurring the Penaltys
of an Act of Assembly Entituled An Act for preventing
the Growth of Popery by Exercising his ffunction in a private ffamily of the Roman Comunion but in no other Case
whatsoever.

Whereas at the Town and Port of Annapolis in Ann Arundell Co<sup>ty</sup> the third Day of October seventeen hundred and
four was Enacted An Act to prevent the Growth of popery
but forasmuch as the true Intent of the said Act was only to
restrain some exorbitant Accons in the said Popish Bishops
Priests and Jesuits who it is hoped are thereby made sensible
of their Extravagant Demeanour in their Pernicious and Indi-
rect practices It is therefore hereby Enacted & Declared
And be it Enacted by the Queens most Excellent Majesty by
and with the Advice and Consent of her Majestys Governour
Council and Assembly of this Province and the Authority of
the same That no Popish Bishop Priest or Jesuite shall by
vertue of the said Act of Assembly for or by reason of Exercising his ffunction in a private ffamily of the Roman Comunion be prosecuted or Indicted before any her Majestys
Justices impowered to hold plea thereof within this Province
untill the full end and Expiration of the term of Eighteen

Lib. 41. vertue of any Comiss⟩   from her Majesty her heires and
Successors to him or l   n Granted to dispose of any Place
or Office as afores⁴ m     ⟩on Vacancy of any place or Office
whereof they have rig   ⟩ dispose be obliged to make Choice
of such Pson or Psoi   s they shall think most worthy and
Capable of executin₍s. ch place or Office as aforesaid out of
the Inhabitants of ⟩iis Province who have been Resident
therein during the me and term aforesaid (Except before
Excepted) any Cusⁱm or usage to the Contrary notwithstanding.

And be it furtherEnacted that every Pson or Psons whatsoever having Comⁱsion from the Queens Majesty her heires
and Successors to ⁣xercise any Office within this Province
shall actually Inhaltt within this Province and exercise the
same in his own prper Pson and not by any Deputy or Deputys without Pticulr leave from her Majesty.

| December 7 1704 | December 8ᵗʰ 1704 |
|---|---|
| Compar'd with th originall bill | Assented to by her Maᵗʸˢ |
| and read and Asented to by | honᵇˡᵉ Councill |
| the house of l:ll. | W Bladen Cl Concil. |
| Sign'd ꝑ Ordʳ W 'aylard Cl hD. | |

### Decʳ 9ᵗʰ 1704

On behalf of er Maⁱʸ &c I will this be a Law

Jo: Seymour.

p. 211 An Act Declang severall Acts of Assembly formerly made
to be in forc.

Be it Enacid by the Queens most excellent Majesty by
and with the Advice and Consent of her Majestys Governour
Councill and ₍ssembly of this Province and the Authority of
the same tha the severall and respective Acts of Assembly
heretofore mᴅe and Enacted (that is to say) one Act Intituled An Acfor Erecting Ann Arundell and Oxford Towns
into Ports arl Towns One other Act of Assembly Intituled
An Act for te punishment of Persons Suborning Witnesses
or Comittin wilfull and Corrupt Pjury one other Act Intituled an Acfor Sanctifying and Keeping holy the Lords Day
comonly caed Sunday One other Act Intituled An Act
ConcerningIndians One other Act Intituled An Act for the
present searity of the ffrontier Plantations from the Incursions and vlence of Indians one other Act Intituled An Act
prohibittingtrade with the Indians for any fflesh dead or ⸱

Except Deer and Wild fowle One other Act Intituled an Act Lib 41.
for Quieting Differences that may rise between his Majestys
Subjects within this Province and te severall Nations of Indians of what places soever And very Clause Matter and
thing therein Contain'd is hereby aclared to be and remain
in full force and Effect to all Intent Construccons and purposes whatsoever to the end of the next sessions of Assembly
this present sessions not having Lazure fully to Consider
thereof.

December 7th 1704
Compar'd with the Originall bill
Read and Assented to by the
house of Delegates
Sign'd p Order
W Taylard Cl hD.

December 8th 1704
Assnted to by her Ma'tys
hon ble Councill
W Bladen Cl Concil.

December the 9th 170.
On the behalf of her Ma'ty I will this be: Law

Jo: Seymour.

An Act for Suspending the prosecution of ny Priests of the p. 212
Comunion of the Church of Rome incur ng the Penaltys
of an Act of Assembly Entituled An A( for preventing
the Growth of Popery by Exercising his function in a private ffamily of the Roman Comunion but 1 no other Case
whatsoever.

Whereas at the Town and Port of Annapoli in Ann Arundell Co'ty the third Day of October seventeer hundred and
four was Enacted An Act to prevent the Growth of popery
but forasmuch as the true Intent of the said At was only to
restrain some exorbitant Accons in the said Poish Bishops
Priests and Jesuits who it is hoped are thereby ade sensible
of their Extravagant Demeanour in their Pernicius and Indi-
rect practices It is therefore hereby Enacted & Declared
And be it Enacted by the Queens most Excellen Majesty by
and with the Advice and Consent of her Majestys Governour
Councill and Assembly of this Province and the athoity of
the same That no Popish Bishop Priest or Jesui
vertue of the said Act of Assembly f          y
cising his ffunction in a private ffa        
nion be prosecuted or Indict              u-
Justices impowered to h                    st
untill the full end a

Lib. 41. Months from the publication of this Law or until her Majestys
Pleasure shall be declar'd therein.

Provided allways that this Act nor anything therein Contain'd shall in no wise be Construed to extend to defeat
rescind abrogate or Suspend the fforce vigour or Effect of the
said Act for p'venting the Growth of popery in any other
Matter or thing whatsoever or for any longer time than what
is in and by this Present Act expressed and Declared

<table>
<tr><td>December 9<sup>th</sup> 1704</td><td>December 9<sup>th</sup> 1704</td></tr>
</table>

| December 9th 1704 | December 9th 1704 |
|---|---|
| Read and Assented to by the house of Dell | Assented to by her Ma[tys] hon[ble] Councill |
| W Taylard Cl hD. | W Bladen Cl Concil. |

December 9th 1704

On the behalf of her Ma[ty] I will this be a Law

Jo: Seymour

p.213 An Act for the Division of Saint Pauls Parish in Prince
Georges County

Whereas the Parishioners of Saint Pauls parish in Prince
Georges County Have humbly shewn to this Generall Assembly that their Parish being more in length than fifty miles and
uncapable of being Supplyed by one Minister and that the
Great Number of the Inhabitants will afford a Comfortable
Maintenance for two Ministers Have therefore Supplicated
that the said parish may be divided into two parishes.

Be it therefore Enacted by the Queens most excellent
Majesty by and with the Advice and Consent of her Majestys
Gov[r] Councill and Assembly of this province And the Authority of the same that the said parish be divided and is and
shall forever hereafter be divided and the Divisionall Lines
begin and shall be adjudg'd and taken to beginn with the
Dividing branches of Puttuxent River and to run with the
Western branch to a branch called Cabbin branch by the
Plantation of a Certain Edward Willett and so with the Cabbin branch to the head thereof and the Souther most part to
be adjudg'd to be Saint Pauls parish.

And be it further Enacted by the Authority Advice and
Consent af[d] that the said St. Pauls Parish be further bounded
and divided by the Ridge between Puttuxent and Potomack
and the Eastern side of the said Ridge and the Northermost
part of the Western branch and Cabbin branch be adjudged
to be a new and distinct Parish to be called by the name of

Queen Anne's Parish and may Elect and Choose Pper Off$^{rs}$ Lib. 41. and have and enjoy all the Advantages Priviledges and benefitts of a Compleat and intire Pish Any former Act law Division or Ordinance to the Contrary notwithstanding.

<table>
<tr><td>December 9$^{th}$ 1704</td><td>December 9$^{th}$ 1704</td></tr>
<tr><td>Read and Assented to by the<br>house of Dellegates<br>W Taylard Cl h.D</td><td>Read and Assented to by her<br>Ma$^{tys}$ bon$^{ble}$ Councill<br>W Bladen Cl Concil.</td></tr>
</table>

December 9$^{th}$ 1704

On behalf of her Ma$^{ty}$ &c I will this be a Law.

Jo: Seymour

An Act declaring An Act Intituled An Act for Erecting Ann p. 214 Arundell and Oxford Towns into Ports and towns formerly made to be in force.

Be it Enacted by the Queens most excellent Ma$^{ty}$ by and with the Advice and Consent of her Majestys Governour Councill and Assembly of this Province and the Authority of the same that one Act of Assembly heretofore made and Enacted Intituled an Act for Erecting Ann Arundell and Oxford Towns into Ports and Towns & every Clause Matter and thing therein Contain'd is hereby declared to be and remaine in full force and Effect to all Intents Constructions and purposes whatsoever to the end of the next Sessions of Assembly This present Sessions not having leizure fully to Consider thereof

<table>
<tr><td>December 9$^{th}$ 1704</td><td>December 9$^{th}$ 1704</td></tr>
<tr><td>Read and Assented to by the<br>house of Dell<br>W Taylard Clk hD</td><td>Assented to by her Ma$^{tys}$<br>hon$^{ble}$ Councill<br>W Bladen Cl Concil.</td></tr>
</table>

December 9$^{th}$ 1704

On behalf of her Ma$^{ty}$ &c. I will this be a Law

Jo: Seymour.

An Act Declaring the Act Intituled An Act ascertaining the bounds of Land to be in force.

Be it Enacted by the Queens most Excellent Majesty by and with the Advice and Consent of her Majestys Governo$^r$

28

Lib. 41. Councill and Assembly of this Province and the Authority of the same That the Act of Assembly made at a Generall Assembly begun and held at the Port of Annapolis the twenty Seventh day of June in the Year of our Lord Sixteen hundred ninety nine Entituled An Act ascertaining the bounds of Land and every Clause Matter and thing therein Contain'd is hereby declar'd to be and remain in full force and effect to all Intents Construccons and Purposes whatsover to the end of the next Sessions of Assembly this present Sessions not having leizure fully to Consider thereof.

p. 215
|  |  |
|---|---|
| December 9<sup>th</sup> 1704 | December 9<sup>th</sup> 1704 |

December 9th 1704 — Read and assented to by the house of Dell
W Taylard Cl hD

December 9th 1704 — Assented to by her Ma<sup>tys</sup> hon<sup>ble</sup> Councill
W Bladen Cl Concil.

December 10<sup>th</sup> 1704

On behalf of her Ma<sup>ty</sup> &c I will this be a Law.

Jo: Seymour

An Act Declaring the Act Entituled An Act for the Punishment of Persons Suborning Witnesses and Comitting willfull and Corrupt Pjury to be in force.

Be it Enacted by the Queens most excellent Majesty by and with the Advice and Consent of her Majestys Governour Councill and Assembly of this Province and the Authority of the same that the Act of Assembly Intituled An Act for the punishment of persons Suborning Witnesses or Comitting wilfull and Corrupt pjury And every matter Clause and thing therein Contain'd is hereby declared to be and remaine in full force and effect to all Intents Construccons and purposes w'soever to the end of the next Sessions of Assembly This present Sessions not having leizure fully to Consider thereof.

December 9<sup>th</sup> 1704 — Read and Assented to by the house of Delegates
W Taylard Clk hD.

December 9<sup>th</sup> 1704 — Assented to by her Ma<sup>tys</sup> hon<sup>ble</sup> Councill
W Bladen Cl Concil.

December 9<sup>th</sup> 1704

On the behalf of her Ma<sup>ty</sup> &c I will this be a Law.

Jo: Seymour

An Act Declaring An Act Intituled An Act for Sanctifying Lib. 41. and keeping holy the Lords day comonly called Sunday to be Ppetuall.

Be it Enacted by the Queens most Excellent Majesty by and with the Advice and Consent of her Majestys **Governour** Councill and Assembly of this Province and the Authority of the same That one Act of Assembly of this Province Intituled p. 216 An Act for Sanctifying and Keeping holy the Lords day comonly called Sunday and every Clause Matter and thing therein Contain'd is hereby declared to be & remain in full force and effect to all Intents and purposes for ever.

<table>
<tr><td>December 9<sup>th</sup> 1704</td><td>December 9<sup>th</sup> 1704</td></tr>
</table>

December 9<sup>th</sup> 1704      December 9<sup>th</sup> 1704

Read and assented to by the    Assented to by her Majestys
house of Dellegates            hon<sup>ble</sup> Councill
     W Taylard Cl hD.        W Bladen Cl Concil.

December 9<sup>th</sup> 1704

On the behalf of her Ma<sup>ty</sup> &c I will this be a Law.

              J<sub>o</sub> : Seymour

An Act Declaring An Act Intituled An Act Concerning Indians to be in force.

Be it Enacted by the Queens most Excellent Majesty by and with the Advice and Consent of her Majestys Gov<sup>r</sup> Councill and Assembly of this Province and the Authority of the same That one Act of Assembly heretofore made Intituled An Act Concerning Indians and every Matter Clause & thing therein Contain'd is hereby declared to be and remain in full force & effect to all Intents Construccions and purposes whatsoever to the end of the next Sessions of Assembly this present Sessions not having Leizure fully to Consider thereof.

December 9<sup>th</sup> 1704      December 9<sup>th</sup> 1704

Read and Assented by the    Assented to by her Ma<sup>tys</sup> hon<sup>ble</sup>
house of Delegates             Councill
     W Taylard Cl hD        W Bladen Cl Concil.

December 9<sup>th</sup> 1704.

On the behalf of her Ma<sup>ty</sup> &c. I will this be a Law

              J<sub>o</sub>: Seymour

The Seale of the hon<sup>ble</sup> Secretary's office is hereunto affixed on the behalf of S<sup>r</sup> Thomas Laurence Secretary ꝑ me      Th Bordley Clk Secry office.

PRO:

Ala

# PROCEEDINGS AND ACTS

OF THE

# GENERAL ASSEMBLY
# OF MARYLAND.

*At a Session held at Annapolis, May* 15-25, 1705.

CHARLES CALVERT, LORD BALTIMORE,
*Proprietary.*

JOHN SEYMOUR,
*Governor.*

---

THE UPPER HOUSE OF ASSEMBLY.

Marylan
Att a
Port of
of Mary

Day of t
present

The Hor

This c
weather
Board a
Dellegat
the Adv
them ur
Writt of
Great S

rogued :

His E
Intende
of this
thought
To w

Cam
house t
member

Maryland ss<sup>t</sup>.

Att a Councill in Assembly begun & held at the Towne and Port of Annapolis in Ann Arundell County in the Province of Maryland the ffifteenth day of May in the fourth year of her Majesty's Reign &c and there Continued untill the 25<sup>th</sup> Day of the Same month on which s<sup>d</sup> 15<sup>th</sup> Day of May were present

His Ex<sup>ncy</sup> the Governour &c

The Hon<sup>ble</sup> { Col John Addison James Sanders Esq<sup>r</sup>
Coll John Hamond Ken. Cheseldyne Esq<sup>r</sup>
L<sup>t</sup> Col W<sup>m</sup> Holland Col Thomas Enalls

This day being very nigh Spent and by Reason the Rainy weather has so Long Continued many of the members of this Board and the Speaker and many members of the house of Dellegates not being yet arrived his Ex<sup>ncy</sup> is pleased to ask the Advice of the Board if it might be proper to prorogue them untill to morrow morning which was Resolved & a Writt of Proroguation being Accordingly prepared under the Great Seal the same was published by Beat of Drum by which the General Assembly of this Province stands prorogued untill the sixteenth Instant.


Wednesday May the 16th 1705

The Councill Sate Present.

His Ex<sup>ncy</sup> the Governour

The Honble { Thomas Tench Esq<sup>r</sup> Coll Edward Lloyd
Col John Addison L<sup>t</sup> Col W<sup>m</sup> Holland
Robert Smith Esq<sup>r</sup> James Sanders Esq<sup>r</sup>
Col John Hamond Kenelm Cheseldyne Esq
Col Francis Jenkins Col Thomas Ennalls

His Ex<sup>ncy</sup> was pleased to Comunicate to the Board what he Intended to say to the house of Dellegates upon the opening of this present Sessions and desired their Advice what they thought fitt to be omitted therein or Added thereunto.

To which the Several Gentlemen of the Councill say they do think it very proper & Sufficient

Came M<sup>r</sup> Gouldsborough and six other members of the house to Acquaint his Ex<sup>ncy</sup> that the Greatest part of the members of the house were mett at the Court house and had

Original sent them to Acquaint his Ex$^{ncy}$ that their Speaker being
Journal. indisposed they Desired his Ex$^{ncys}$ Directions if they should
Choose another Speaker to whom his Ex$^{ncy}$ was pleased to say
he was much Concerned for Col Smith's Indisposition, But
that he and her Majesty's bon$^{ble}$ Councill having observed his
Good Conduct especially in the last Assembly thought it
Adviseable Especially in Reguard that his Ex$^{ncy}$ is acquainted
the said Col Smith Designs to be here to morrow further to
prorogue the Assembly untill to morrow and therefore would
order a Writt of prorogation to that purpose Accordingly
the said Writt being prepared and sealed with the Great
Seale was published by beat of Drum and thereby the Generall Assembly stands prorogued till Thursday the Seaven-
teenth Instant.

Came M$^r$ Thomas Boardley Clk of the Secretarys and made
oath that he had Examined the Laws of the two last Sessions
of Assembly by him recorded in the Sec$^{rys}$ Office.

### Thursday May 17$^{th}$ 1705

The Councill in Assembly pursuant to her Ma$^{tys}$ Writt of
prorogation of Yesterdays Date mett & Sate p$^r$sent.

His Ex$^{ncy}$ the Gov$^r$ &c.

| | |
|---|---|
| Thomas Tench Esq$^r$ | Col Edward Lloyd |
| Coll John Addison | L$^t$ Coll W$^m$ Holland |
| Thomas Brooke Esq$^r$ | James Sanders Esq$^r$ |
| Robert Smith Esq$^r$ | Kenelm Cheseldyne Esq$^r$ |
| Col John Hammond | Col Thomas Ennalls. |

Maj$^r$ Lowe and three other Members from the house to
Acquaint his Ex$^{ncy}$ of their being mett and Waited his
Comands.

M$^r$ Smith and M$^r$ Sanders sent to the house of Delegates
to Acquaint them his Ex$^{ncy}$ is Ready to Receive them &
Comands M$^r$ Speaker & the Members of the house to attend
him in Councill

Came M$^r$ Speaker and the Members of the house of Dell
to Attend his Ex$^{ncy}$ to whom he was pleased to speak as foll.
viz. M$^r$ Speaker and you Gentlemen Dellegates

Tis very Evident the Treasonable villanous practices of some
Amongst us has encouraged the Indians to Comitt their Bar-
baritys on our fellow Subjects :

Those by their ffrequent Insolencys have put the Country
to the Trouble and Charge of keeping men out to protect the
honest painfull Inhabitants on that frontier : one great motive
these Bold Incendiarys used to Inflame the unthinking Crew
(Who were to Joyne in Concert with 'em) was our Naked-

ness want of Ammunition Ill Arms &c cuñing Specious pretences to bring their Secrett Contrivance to an open Rebellion.

Gent[n] How these necessary matters come to be wanted on this or any other Occasion I hope your Tender Regard for the Countrys Safety will Animate you to a Strict Inquiry, and Cann never Believe any time more proper to Consider of it Then when we are Threatened by all Sorts of Enemys abroad, and Villians within our owne Bowells would enervate and unhinge your Constitution.

Gent[n] her Ma[tys] hon[ble] Councill Advised me to meet you at this time that by the prudent Assistance of your well digested Considerations wee may unanimously Join to Suppress every thing that dares disturbe your peace or the quiet Enjoym[t] of your Fortunes Industry and Care, which a Steady heartiness may now Effectually Establish, to your Lasting honours

I am Resolved Gent[n] During my administration, what her Majesty and her good people here have so prudently sett apart for the Defence of this province shall be disposed of to no other use whatsoever, but for the Safety preservation and Quiett of Every Individuall Member thereof.

And I Doubt not but these frequent Chargeable alarmes will so invigorate your Resolutions, we may be ever in a posture to Crush all Sorts of Disturbances before they are formed into open hostilitys.

And dare Assure you if you'll adhere to some methods I shall presume to lay down, which shall neither be so Burthensome or impracticable as at present your Posterity will be obliged to this present Assembly for their future Tranquility.

I'le transmitt to M[r] Speaker some Lters about the New York Affair & likewise an Account of a Criminall lately condemn'd and Some other Accomplices not Brought on to tryal, by whose Vows & oaths to be Secrett to this horrid Combination, you will be thoroughly Sensible the Scene was Laid to a very Bloody Purpose.

Gent[n] As you very well know the Occasion of this meeting when you have well Considered the Several Instances Contrivances & papers Relating thereto, If we are uneasy for the future blame not a Gentleman who will never be wanting to pform his duty to the Best of Queens, my Sovereign or his strict friendship, & vigilant Care over the Province, her Ma[ty] was Graciously pleased to Constitute me Governour

After which M[r] Speaker & the House of Delegates departed to the house.

The Severall papers and proceedings relating to the Indians &c being Numbered from 1 to numb[r] 24 were sent to the

Original house by Col Lloyd and Col Holland for their perusal &
Journal. Consideration.
    The Board Adjourns 'till 8 of the Clock To morrow morning

Fryday May the 18[h] 1705
The Councill in Assembly Sate present
His Ex[ncy] the Governour &c.

The Hon[ble] {
Thomas Tench Esq[r]      Col Edward Lloyd
Thomas Brook Esq[r]      L[t] Col W[m] Holland
Robert Smith Esq[r]      James Sanders Esq[r]
Col John Hamond          Coll Thomas Ennalls
Col Francis Ienkins      W[m] Coursey Esq[r]
}

Came Panquash & Annotoughk on behalf of Ashquash
Emperour of the Nanticoke Indians
Winnoughquarquo King of the Babcos & Ahatchwoops
Robin Indian Chief of the Indian River Indians on behalf of
his Queen Wyranfconmickonous Queen of the said Indians
and desired to Enter into Articles of Alliance with her most
Sacred Ma[ty] the Queen of Great Britain France and Ireland
and the said Articles being Mutually Concluded on as followeth were interchangeably Signed & Sealed Viz.
    Articles of Peace and Amity concluded and agreed upon
the 19th day of May 1705 in the fourth Year of the Reign of
our Sovereign Lady Anne by the Grace of God of England
Scotland France and Ireland Queen Defender of the Faith
&c By & Between his Ex[ncy] john Seymour Esq[r] Cap[t] Generall & Governour in Chief in and over this her Ma[tys] Province
of Maryland the Lands Islands and Territorys thereto belonging &c. for and on the behalf of her said Ma[tys] Queen of
England all her Subjects as well in this as all other her
Ma[tys] Provinces Collonys and Territorys in America, & Panquash & Annoughtoughk Great men particularly appointed
for and on behalfe of Asquash Emperour of the Nanticoke
Indians & his Indians as followeth.
    Imprimis. The said Panquash and Annoughtoughk on
behalf of the said Ashquash do desire he may be Received &
Acknowledged as Emperour of the Nanticoke Indians to
which his Ex[ncy] the Governour and Councill is pleased to
agree and Accordingly Condescends to treat with the said
Panquash aud Annoughtougk as his Commisioners.
    2.  It is further agreed upon that from this day forward
there be An Inviolable Peace & Amity between her most
Sacred Ma[tys] Queen Ann and the said Ashquash Emperour
of the Nanticoke Indians upon these Articles hereafter mencon'd to Endure to the World's End and that all former Acts

of Hostility and damages whatsoever by either party Sus- Original Journal.
tained be buried in perpetual Oblivion

3. That for preventing Differences between the Indians &
English the said Emperour Ashquash and his Indians shall
Sufficiently ffence in their Corn fields which already are or
hereafter shall be planted by the said Indians at least Seaven
or eight Loggs high.

4. That the said Emperour Ashquash and his Indians
shall Deliver up all Indians that shall Come unto their Gov-
ernm$^t$ or Dominion that are or shall be Enemys to the English
And further if any Indian Subject to the said Emperour
shall kill any Englishman that the said Emperour & his
Indians shall be obliged to deliver such Indians up as a prisoner
to the Governour of this province for the time being.

5. That forasmuch as the English Cannot Easily distinguish
one Indian from another that no Indian shall Come into any
Englishmans Plantation painted and that all the Indians shall
be bound to Call aloud before they Come within Three hundred paces of any Englishmans clear Ground and Lay downe
their Armes whether Gunns Bows or Arrows or other Weapons
for any Englishman that shall Appear upon his Call to Take
up and in Case no man shall Appear that he shall there
Leave his said Arms if he shall Come nearer and afterwards
by Calling aloud shall Endeavour to give notice to the English of his nearer Approaching and if any English man shall
kill any Indian that shall Come unpainted and give such
notice and deliver up his Arms as aforesaid he shall dye
for it as well as An Indian that kills any Englishman and
in Case the Indians and English meete in the Woods Acci-
dentally every Indian shall be bound immediately to throw
down his Arms upon Call and in Case any Indians so
meeting an Englishman and shall Refuse to throw down
his arms upon call he shall be deemed an Enemy.

6. The Priviledge of hunting Crabbing Fishing & fowlling
shall be preserved inviolable to the Indians.

7. That every Indian that killeth a Hogg Calf or other
Beast or any other Goods shall undergo the same punishment that an English man doth for the same Offence.

8. In Case any Servant or Slave Runaway from their
Masters or Children from their Parents or Guardians &
Come to any of the Indian Towns within the Government
and Dominions of the said Ashquash he & his Indians shall
be obliged to Apprehend the s$^d$ fugitives & Bring them to
the Next English Plantation to be Conveyed to their Masters and Guardians aforesaid And in Case any Indians
aforesaid shall Assist any such fugitives in their Flight out
of this Province, That he shall make the Respective Master

Original.
Journâl. or Mistress of such Servant or Slave such Satisfaction as any Englishman ought to do in the Like Case.

9.   That the said Emperour or his Indians shall not make peace with her Ma^{tys} Enemys neither Make any Warr without the Consent of the Governour of this Province for the time being.

10.   In Case the Emperour or any of his Indians shall kill any other Indian in peace & Amity with her Majesty and this Government it shall be Esteemed as Great an Offence as killing an Englishman.

11.   That in Case any Indian or Indians or other Nation or Nations that Come within their dominions or Territorys and shall by them or other Indians under them be Entertained and shall kill any English, and shall kill or Destroy any Hoggs Cattle or horses or shall break any Englishmans house & Steal his or their goods that he the said Ashquash shall be Responsible for the Same and also be Engaged to deliver to the Governour of this province for the time being Murderers and other Criminalls Offenders ag^t these Articles of whom he shall at any time happen to have any Knowledge.

12.   That the said Ashquash shall pay Yearly to the use of her Majesty her heirs & Successors every Year on the Twentieth day of Aprill to Col Thomas Ennalls four Indian Arrows and two Bows to be delivered to his Ex^{ncy} the Governour of this Province for the time being as a Tribute or Acknowledgment to her Ma^{ty} and as a Token of the Continuance of this Peace

The like Articles were Signed & Sealed by his Ex^{ncy} on behalf of her Ma^{ty} on the one part and Winnoughquarquo King of the Babcoes and Ahatchwopps on behalf of his Indians on the other; as also between his said Ex^{ncy} & Robin Indian on behalf of Wyranfconmickonous Queen of the Indian River Indians on the other part.

Robin Chief of the Indians on the Indian River presents to his Ex^{ncy} the following Petition viz^{ts}

To his Ex^{ncy} John Seymour Esq^r Cap^t Gen^{ll} & Gov^r in Chief of the Province of Maryland.

The humble Petition of Robin Indian and Chief of the Indians belonging to the Indian Towne at the head of the Indian River in Somersett County together with the Rest of the Indians thereto belonging,

Humbly Sheweth

That your Ex^{ncys} humble Petitioners being the ancient Inhabitants of Somersett County af^d and a quiett peaceable People towards the English nation have Extremly Suffered

of Late Years by being disturbed & Expulsed from their Original
several Settlements in Towns viz^ts first from Buckingham in Journal.
this County to Assawamem & from thence to the Indian
River and from thence to the head of the said River where
we now are settled in a Town but are Continually Threaten'd
to be Driven from thence likewise although we your Ex^ncys
humble Petitioners have not in the Least Misbehaved our
Selves towards her Ma^tys Liege people and where then to go
we know not unless to the Barrens in the Forest which will
not afford us a living—wherefore your Ex^ncys humble petitioners (absolute necessity urging thereto) Implore your
Ex^ncy to Confirm them their now Settled Town with 1000
Acres of Land thereto next adjoyning which is but a small
Quantity in Respect to what was formerly by us Enjoyed and
grant us a patent for the same wee have already what Rights
the Prop^ry and Governour of Pensilvania     can give and
Surveyed it unto us) and we hope and doubt not but your
Ex^ncy will be so favorable as to Grant the humble Request of
yo^r poor Petitioners and your Petitioners as in duty bound
shall be peaceable Friends & ever pray &c.  Upon the reading whereof it is sent to the house with this Endorsement.
  By his Ex^ncy the Governour & Council in Assembly.  The
within Petition of Robin Indian and other Indians being Read
his Ex^ncy and the Members of this Board are willing to Comply with their desires & Recoḿend to the house of delegates
that they will Consider thereof and by some Act of Assembly
or other means Secure them in the Quiet and peaceable
possession of the one thousand Acres of Land according to
their petition.    Signed ꝑ order W Bladen Cl. Councill.

  Whereas there is a good Law made Restraining the English
Inhabitants of this Province from Carrying any Liquors to
Indian Towns & Cabbins, Notwithstanding which several
English do either by themselves or otherwise by the Indians
for and on their Accounts Carry and send Liquors to the said
Indian Towns and Cabbins to the great Disturbance & Annoy-
ance of the said Indians I do hereby Require all her Ma^tys Subjects Exactly to Comply with the said Law & forbear either by
themselves or others to Carry or send any Liquors to the said
Indian Towns & Cabbins And that the Several Magistrates of
the Several and Respective Countys use their utmost Dilei-
gence in detecting prosecuting and punishing the Offenders
herein, and further I do hereby Empower the Great men at
the Indian Towns upon such Liquors being Brought thither to
break & Stave the Bottles Casqs and Barrells or oversett and
Spill such other Vessells wherein such Liquors shall be without
being Troubled to Answer any Complaint on that Score

Mistress of such Servant or Slave such Satisfaction as any glishman ought to do in the Like Case.

). That the said Emperour or his Indians shall not make ice with her Ma$^{tys}$ Enemys neither Make any Warr without Consent of the Governour of this Province for the time ng.

o. In Case the Emperour or any of ·his Indians shall any other Indian in peace & Amity with her Majesty l this Government it shall be Esteemed as Great an ence as killing an Englishman.

[1. That in Case any Indian or Indians or other Nation Nations that Come within their dominions or Territorys l shall by them or other Indians under them be Enter- ed and shall kill any English, and shall kill or Destroy / Hoggs Cattle or horses or shall break any Englishmans ise & Steal his or their goods that he the said Ashquash ll be Responsible for the Same and also be Engaged to iver to the Governour of this province for the time being irderers and other Criminalls Offenders ag$^t$ these Articles whom he shall at any time happen to have any Knowledge.

[2. That the said Ashquash shall pay Yearly to the use her Majesty her heirs & Successors every Year on the rentieth day of Aprill to Col Thomas Ennalls four Indian rows and two Bows to be delivered to his Ex$^{ncy}$ the vernour of this Province for the time being as a Tribute Acknowledgment to her Ma$^{ty}$ and as a Token of the Con- uance of this Peace

The like Articles were Signed & Sealed by his Ex$^{ncy}$ on half of her Ma$^{ty}$ on the one part and Winnoughquarquo ng of the Babcoes and Ahatchwopps on behalf of his lians on the other; as also between his said Ex$^{ncy}$ & Robin lian on behalf of Wyranfconmickonous Queen of the Indian ver Indians on the other part.

Robin Chief of the Indians on the Indian River presents his Ex$^{ncy}$ the following Petition viz$^{ts}$

To his Ex$^{ncy}$ John Seymour Esq$^r$ Cap$^t$ Gen$^{ll}$ & Gov$^r$ in Chief the Province of Maryland.

The humble Petition of Robin Indian and Chief of the lians belonging to the Indian Towne at the head of the lian River in Somersett County together with the Rest of : Indians thereto belonging,

imbly Sheweth

That your Ex$^{ncys}$ humble Petitioners being the ancient In- bitants of Somersett County af$^d$ and a quiett peaceable ople towards the English nation have Extremly Suffered

of Late Years by being disturbed & Expulsed from their
several Settlements in Towns viz^ts first from Buckingham in
this County to Assawamem & from thence to the Indian
River and from thence to the head of the said River where
we now are settled in a Town but are Continually Threaten'd
to be Driven from thence likewise although we your Ex^ncys
humble Petitioners have not in the Least Misbehaved our
Selves towards her Ma^tys Liege people and where then to go
we know not unless to the Barrens in the Forest which will
not afford us a living—wherefore your Ex^ncys humble petitioners (absolute necessity urging thereto) Implore your
Ex^ncy to Confirm them their now Settled Town with 1000
Acres of Land thereto next adjoyning which is but a small
Quantity in Respect to what was formerly by us Enjoyed and
grant us a patent for the same wee have already what Rights
the Prop^ry and Governour of Pensilvania      can give and
Surveyed it unto us) and we hope and doubt not but your
Ex^ncy will be so favorable as to Grant the humble Request of
yo^r poor Petitioners and your Petitioners as in duty bound
shall be peaceable Friends & ever pray &c.   Upon the reading whereof it is sent to the house with this Endorsement.
By his Ex^ncy the Governour & Council in Assembly.   The
within Petition of Robin Indian and other Indians being Read
his Ex^ncy and the Members of this Board are willing to Comply with their desires & Recom̄end to the house of delegates
that they will Consider thereof and by some Act of Assembly
or other means Secure them in the Quiet and peaceable
possession of the one thousand Acres of Land according to
their petition.      Signed ꝑ order W Bladen Cl. Councill.

Whereas there is a good Law made Restraining the English
Inhabitants of this Province from Carrying any Liquors to
Indian Towns & Cabbins, Notwithstanding which several
English do either by themselves or otherwise by the Indians
for and on their Accounts Carry and send Liquors to the said
Indian Towns and Cabbins to the great Disturbance & Annoy-
ance of the said Indians I do hereby Require all her Ma^tys Subjects Exactly to Comply with the said Law & forbear either by
themselves or others to Carry or send any Liquors to the said
Indian Towns & Cabbins And that the Several Magistrates of
the Several and Respective Countys use their utmost Dilei-
gence in detecting prosecuting and punishing the Offenders
herein, and further I do hereby Empower the Great men at
the Indian Towns upon such Liquors being Brought thither to
break & Stave the Bottles Casqs and Barrells or oversett and
Spill such other Vessells wherein such Liquors shall be without
being Troubled to Answer any Complaint on that Score

or Mistress of such Servant or Slave such Satisfaction as any Englishman ought t do in the Like Case.

9. That the said Emperour or his Indians shall not make peace with her Ma<sup>ty</sup> Enemys neither Make any Warr without the Consent of the Governour of this Province for the time being.

10. In Case the Emperour or any of his Indians shall kill any other India in peace & Amity with her Majesty and this Governmot it shall be Esteemed as Great an Offence as killing a Englishman.

11. That in Cas any Indian or Indians or other Nation or Nations that Coie within their dominions or Territorys and shall by them r other Indians under them be Entertained and shall killany English, and shall kill or Destroy any Hoggs Cattle c horses or shall break any Englishmans house & Steal his ortheir goods that he the said Ashquash shall be Responsible for the Same and also be Engaged to deliver to the Goverour of this province for the time being Murderers and othei Criminalls Offenders ag<sup>t</sup> these Articles of whom he shall at ay time happen to have any Knowledge.

12. That the said Ashquash shall pay Yearly to the use of her Majesty her ieirs & Successors every Year on the Twentieth day of Afill to Col Thomas Ennalls four Indian Arrows and two Bws to be delivered to his Ex<sup>ncy</sup> the Governour of this Pivince for the time being as a Tribute or Acknowledgmento her Ma<sup>ty</sup> and as a Token of the Continuance of this Peac

The like Articles vere Signed & Sealed by his Ex<sup>ncy</sup> on behalf of her Ma<sup>ty</sup> o the one part and Winnoughquarquo King of the Babcoe and Ahatchwopps on behalf of his Indians on the other; as also between his said Ex<sup>ncy</sup> & Robin Indian on behalf of Vyranfconmickonous Queen of the Indian River Indians on theother part.

Robin Chief of th Indians on the Indian River presents to his Ex<sup>ncy</sup> the follovng Petition viz<sup>ts</sup>

To his Ex<sup>ncy</sup> John Seymour Esq<sup>r</sup> Cap<sup>t</sup> Gen<sup>ll</sup> & Gov<sup>r</sup> in Chief of the Province of Maryland.

The humble Petitin of Robin Indian and Chief of the Indians belonging tc the Indian Towne at the head of the Indian River in Somrsett County together with the Rest of the Indians thereto blonging,

Humbly Sheweth

That your Ex<sup>ncys</sup> hmble Petitioners being the ancient habitants of Somersct County af<sup>d</sup> and a quiett ne---
People towards the Inglish nation have Extrerr-

of Late Years by being disturbed & Expulsed from their several Settlements in Towns viz^{ts} fst from Buckingham in this County to Assawamem & fro₁ thence to the Indian River and from thence to the head₃f the said River where we now are settled in a Town but ar₁ Continually Threaten'd to be Driven from thence likewise ₁lthough we your Ex^{ncys} humble Petitioners have not in the Least Misbehaved our Selves towards her Ma^{tys} Liege peop₂ and where then to go we know not unless to the Barrens i the Forest which will not afford us a living—wherefore ₃ur Ex^{ncys} humble peti-tioners (absolute necessity urging ₃hereto) Implore your Ex^{ncy} to Confirm them their now Sttled Town with 1000 Acres of Land thereto next adjoynir₃ which is but a small Quantity in Respect to what was forrerly by us Enjoyed and grant us a patent for the same wee h₃e already what Rights the Prop^{ry} and Governour of Pensilvnia can give and Surveyed it unto us) and we hope ₃d doubt not but your Ex^{ncy} will be so favorable as to Grant the humble Request of yo^{r} poor Petitioners and your Petitioers as in duty bound shall be peaceable Friends & ever pr₃ &c. Upon the reading whereof it is sent to the house wi₁ this Endorsement.

By his Ex^{ncy} the Governour & Coucil in Assembly. The within Petition of Robin Indian and o₁er Indians being Read his Ex^{ncy} and the Members of this Bord are willing to Comply with their desires & Recomend tc the house of delegates that they will Consider thereof and b₁some Act of Assembly or other means Secure them in the Quiet and peaceable possession of the one thousand Acre₁of Land according to their petition. Signed ꝑ order WBladen Cl. Councill.

Whereas there is a good Law made ₁estraining the English Inhabitants of this Province from C₃rying any Liquors to Indian Towns & Cabbins, Notwiths₁nding which several English do either by themselves or o₁erwise by the Indians for and on their Accounts Carry and snd Liquors to the said Indian Towns and Cabbins to the grea Disturbance & Annoy-ance of the said Indians I do hereby Rquire all her Ma^{tys} Sub-jects Exactly to Comply with the said law & forbear either by themselves or others to Carry or send ny Liquors to the said Indian Towns & Cabbins And that the Several Magistrates of the Several and Respective Countys ᵬe their utmost ₁₁₁₁₁. gence in detecting prosecuting and p₁₁₁₁ herein, and further I do hereby F₁₁ the Indian Towns upon such ₁₁₁₁₁ break & Stave the Bottles ₁₁₁ Spill such other Vessells v being Troubled to Ans₁

Original   Ordered that all the papers & Dep° Relating to Richard
Journal.   Clark & his Accomplices be Sent to the house which were
Accordingly sent by M^r Tench & Coll Hamond with this
Message.

By the Gov^r and Councill in Assembly
May the 18, 1705.

Gent^a

The Severall papers herewith sent will Serve to acquaint
Your House what Disturbance has been given the County by
the means of Richard Clark of Ann Arundel County and his
Accomplices with their horrid Projects and Treasonable Contrivances, Which wee desire you will maturely Consider and
Advise how to prevent & Secure the Province from such Disturbances and future Injurys so long Carryed on and so
plainly threaten'd     Signed ᵽ order  W Bladen Cl Councll

Ordered that the two Letters Relating to the New York
Affair be likewise sent to the house of Delegates which were
accordingly sent by Coll Ennalls & M^r Coursey with the
Petition of Robin Indian and the following Message.

By the Governour and Councill in Assembly
May the 18th : 1705

The two Letters herewith sent you are from M^r Perry a
worthy Merchant who wishes this Province Extreamely well if
they give you Sufficient Reason to Believe Your Neighbours
were Apprehensive of any Encrouchment from New York we
hope none will have Reason to think we have been too Vigilant
for Own Security ag^t any such Attempts.

Sign'd ᵽ Ord^r W Bladen Cl Council

Advised that his Ex^ncy for the Ease of the Countys in Their
Levys do grant two Comissions of the Peace in one whereof
only Six Persons to be appointed for hearing & Determining
and one other with a Greater Number only to keep the peace
who not being Obliged to Come from their own homes may
not be paid the Eighty ᵽ Diem for Attendance as a Com^r

The Board adjourns for two hours.

· Post Meridiem   Councill Sate
P^rsent as in the fforenoon

Ordered that the Libel against his Ex^ncy be sent to the House
which is accordingly sent by M^r Tench M^r Smith Coll Hamond
Coll Jenkins Coll Ennalls & M^r Coursey as follows viz.

By his Ex$^{ncy}$ the Gov$^r$ and Councill in Assembly Original Journal.
May the 18th, 1705
To the protestants of Maryland
My friends
I have thought fitt to Advise You to take Care in time to Defend Yourselves from that Wicked Contrivance of Darnall & the Popish Priests in their agreeing with the French and other heathens to destroy You all The Proceedings of Maryland are Easily brought to us over Potowmack River can any people think that the Queen sent a Governour amongst you to be Ruled by Darnall or any other Papists We hear that an Act of Assembly was made ag$^t$ the Popish Priests to blind the people but how long was it before they had their Liberty and the Protestant Ministers silenced, have a Care of a Popish Plott least you have Cause to Repent when it is too late this from a friend is all att present.

The above is a Copy of a Scandalous Seditious Libell published in S$^t$ Mary's County to the great dissatisfaction of her Ma$^{tys}$ Loyal Good Subjects but more especially with a Milicious Intent to render the Administrations of the Govermnt here odious and suspected You cannot but Remember that what was done in Order to checquing & Restraining the Extravagancys of the Popish Priests Came first from Your house and had the Ready Assent of his Ex$^{ncy}$ & this Board so likewise what was done last Sessions in Suspending the Execution thereof for 18 months was first moved in your House and Represented by You as Reasonable to this Board wherefore wee doubt not your Candour in publiqly Resenting so Base and unjust an Abuse and Calumny of his Ex$^{ncy}$ & This Boarde as by the said Libell is Offered ag$^t$ them.
Signed p Order W Bladen Cl Counll

M$^r$ Muschamp and Eleven other Members bring from the house the following Answer to his Ex$^{ncys}$ Speech, viz.

By the house of Dellegates
May the 18$^{th}$ 1705
May it please Your Ex$^{ncy}$
Wee her Ma$^{tys}$ Dutiful and Loyall Subjects the Representatives of the Severall Countys of her Mātys Province of Maryland now Convened in a Gen$^{ll}$ Assembly do give Your Ex$^{ncy}$ our hearty thanks for your Gracious Speech made to us at the Opening of this Session and do Assure Yo$^r$ Ex$^{ncy}$ that wee are now & shall bee at all times ready to the uttmost of Our abilitys to Joyn with your Ex$^{ncy}$ and the hoñ:ble Councill in

Original
Journal. whatsoever shall be Reasonably proposed to prevent Rebellions
and disturbances and to Settle and Establish Peace & Tranquillity which so much Concerns her Ma^{tys} hon^r and Our own
good & welfare And in order thereunto wee are Resolved to
Enquire into the particulars of the Magazine how much Powder
& other Materials has been provided for the publiq use & to
Whom it has been delivered & how & what is become of it.

S^r Wee have allready had aboundent assurance of Yo^r Ex^{ncys}
great Justice & Candour towards us but we begg leave to tell
you that you've created in us new Motives to thank you for the
Promise you've made to us that what is Separated for the publiq
use shall not be disposed of to any other use whatsoever and
we do heartily assure your Ex^{ncy} that there shall not be any
thing wanting in us that may promote her Majesty's Hon^rs the
publiq peace and Tranquility of this her Ma^{tys} Province & the
depression of Imorality & Vice whatsoever.

Signed ꝑ order W Taylard Cl Ho : Del.

The said Gent^n Bring with them likewise

By the House of Dellegates
May 18^{th} 1705

Wee her Ma^{tys} dutifull & Loyall Subjects the Representatives of the Severall Countys within this her Ma^{tys} Province of
Maryland Convened in a Gen^{ll} Assembly do give your Ex^{ncy}
our hearty thanks for the great Care that you have taken
Relating to the Indians and other Matters which so much
disturbed our Peace and Repose and we do Assure Your
Ex^{ncy} that Your prudent Conduct therein has given us an entire
Satisfaction of Your goodness & Generosity towards us which
we hope you will upon all Occasions be pleased to Repeat

Signed ꝑ order W Taylard Cl h. Del.

To which his Ex^{ncy} was pleased to send the following Answer
by M^r Tench M^r Brooke Col Hammond Coll Lloyd M^r Sanders
& Coll Ennalls viz.

Gent. If I have or can do any thing for the Advantage and
wellfare of this her Ma^{tys} province and the Safety and Prosperity of every Individual Member thereof Your kind Acceptance make the fullest Recompence Imaginable to yo^r Assured
Friend                                        Jo : Seymour

M^r Taylard and M^r Walters bring from the house the pet^n of
Robin Indian with the Resolve of the house thereon Endorsed
as follows viz.

By the house of Dell May 18$^{th}$ 1705

Upon Reading the above petition the house Resolves that a warrant be sent to the Queens Surveyor of Somersett County to Lay out one Thousand Acres of Land for the pett$^{rs}$ where they are now Settled and Returne a Certificate of the bounds thereof to this house that it may be Settled upon the peti$^{rs}$ &c if his Ex$^{ncy}$ and Coun$^{ll}$ think fitt to Concurr there with ⸱ Signed ꝑ Order W Taylard Cl ho. Dell

Ordered that the Sherriff of Ann Arundell County take into his Custody Rachell the Wife of Thomas Freeborne so that he have her before his Ex$^{ncy}$ & this board at tenn of the Clock on Monday next to answer to such things as on her Ma$^{tys}$ behalf Shall be Objected ag$^t$ her and to be dealt with According to Law.

The Account of the publiq Armes and Ammunition being ꝑused by this board was sent to the house with the following Message by Coll. Hamond & Col. Lloyd.

### Die Veneris 18° May

By his Ex$^{ncy}$ the Governour and Councill in Assembly.

The Account of the publiq armes & Ammunition now in the Province is herewith sent you for your Inspection & ꝑrusal how it becomes so scanty you will be Informed Upon Inquiry for the publique Satisfaction.

Signed ꝑ ord$^r$ W Bladen Cl. Coun$^{ll}$

The Board adjourns till to morrow morning

### Die Saturni 19° May 1705

### The Councill in Assembly Sate

### P$^r$sent as Yesterday with the addition of M$^r$ Cheseldyn

It being Considered that it is highly Necessary Some ꝑson should lye in or Close to the Goale in this Towne to prevent the Prisoners Breaking the same it is proposed whether it may not be Convenient to have a Little Lodge be Added to one of the doors of the Prison for the Goaler to lye in the which the board do well Approve of and sent the following Message to the house of Dellegates

29

Original
Journal.

Die Saturni 19° May 1705
By the Governour & Councill in Assembly

Wee propose if your House thinks fitt that for the better preventing the Goale at Annapolis being at any time for the future broke or the Prisoners oversetting the Goaler that a small strong wooden lodge be added to one of the Doors wherein the Goaler may and shall be Obliged to lye every Night and this may be done at a Small Charge not Exceeding six pounds Sterl or ffifteen hundred pounds of Tobacco.
Signed ꝑ order W Bladen Cl Coun[ll]

Resolved that the Several Treatys with the Indians be sent to the house for their Perusal & Advice whether they think any thing further necessary to be Added thereto
The said Articles sent to the house with the following Message by M[r] Sanders.

By the Councill in Assembly May 19th 1705

The Several Articles with the nations of Indians on the Eastern Shore are herewith sent you for your Approbation and to Advise what you think further proper to be Added thereto.          Signed ꝑ order W Bladen Cl Coun[ll]

M[r] Frisby and M[r] Stone bring from the house a bill to Confirm a Certain L[re] of Attorney from W[m] Josephs to W[m] Josephs his son which was Read the first time at this Board
M[r] Wells and M[r] Philips bring from the house the Indian Articles approved by the house and assented to.
The Boarde Adjourned for two hours.

Post Meridiem   Council Sate   ꝑrsent as before

Came M[r] Hays & M[r] Jones from the house with a Bill for the Naturalization of Christopher Dangerman of Calvert County which was Read the first time
Major Taylor and four other Members bring from the house as foll :

By the House of Dellegates May 19th 1705

Resolves of the house humbly Offered to his Ex[ncy] and Council as follows
Whereas it Appears to this house that there has been a Treasonable Combination between Richard Clark of Ann

Arundell County and divers other evil ꝑrsons to draw down the Indians upon the Inhabitants of this Province and to Levy Warr ag^t her Majestys Governour & Government

It is Resolved therefore by this house that her Ma^tys Attorney Genll do forthwith prosecute the said Clark and all others his Accomplices for the said Crimes to the uttmost Extent of the Law and the said Attorney is Directed to do the same Accordingly

Resolved that this house will Enter into Examination what Magazine Stores has been provided and Sett apart for the publiq use & defence of this Province during the time that Col Blakiston was Gov^r how and what is become of it &c.

Resolved that this house will upon all Occasions heartily Joyn in Concert with the hon^ble her Majestys Councill to Support her Ma^tys Government here and the hon^r & Reputation of his Ex^ncy the present Governour.

And Resolved that the paper directed to the Protestants of Maryland and which is now laid before this house is a Scandalous Seditious Libell and that the Attorney Genl^l do prosecute the Writer Contriver and Publisher thereof and every of them and the said Attorny is Ord^ed by this house to prosecute the Same to the utmost Extent of the Law accordingly

Signed ꝑ Order W Taylard Cl house Dell.

M^r Macall and five other Members bring from the house the following Message viz^ts.

By the house of Dell May 19th 1705

May it please your Ex^ncy

Wee return you our hearty thanks for Comunicating to us M^r Perry's Letter Relating to the State of New York Affair as to this Province and which is very agreeable to us. S^r this has given us new Assurance of your Care and watchfulness to Improve Every thing that may Tend to our Advantage, And we are sensible of this Great Blessing which We humbly pray upon all such Occasions be Continued to us and do now lay hold on this Oppertunity to Assure yo^r Ex^ncy that as wee can have none so wee will Entertaine none other Interest than such as may promote her Ma^tys hon^r and your Ex^ncys Fame and Reputation.

Signed ꝑ order W Taylard Cl ho. Del.

The members of this Board by the hon:ble Tho^s Tench Esq^r present to his Ex^ncy as followeth.

Original
Journal. May it please your Ex[ncy]
Wee the Members of her Ma[tys] hon:[ble] Councill being
throughly Sensible of your Ex[ncys] most hon:[ble] & dutiful
Regard to her Ma[tys] Interest and your indefatigable Care for
the Safety and welfare of us & other her Ma[tys] Subjects of
this Province upon the many repeated Disturbances of Our
peace as well by the Indians as other Ill disposed persons
and particulary of the many Great Difficultys y[r] Ex[ncys]
unwearied Diligence with so much prudence has lately gone
through without Obliging us in so unseasonable and hard a
Winter to give Our attendance Wee do Return Your Ex[ncy] our
Most Greatefull Acknowledgments for such your Care of and
kind Regard to us and shall ever gladly Approve ourSelves
        Your Ex[ncys]
        Most obliging faithfull humble Servants
May 19th 1705    Coll Edward Lloyd       Thomas Tench
                 W[m] Holland            John Addison
                 James Sanders           Thomas Brooke
                 Thomas Ennalls          Robert Smith
                 Ken: Cheseldyn          John Hamond
                 Will Coursey            Francis Jenkins

The Board adjourns till Monday Morning


Monday May 21st

Councill in Assembly Sate Present

His Ex[ncy] the Governour
Thomas Tench Esq[r]        Coll Francis Jenkins
Coll John Addison          Coll Edward Lloyd
Thomas Brooke Esq[r]       Col W[m] Holland
Robert Smith Esq[r]        James Sanders Esq[r]
Col John Hamond            Ken:[n] Cheseldyne Esq[r]

M[r] Frisby and M[r] John Macall bring from the house the
Petition of M[r] Thomas Collier praying to be Relieved against
a protested Bill of Exchange he tooke by Virtue of his Office
of M[r] William Edmundson who was Owner of the Shipp and
Cargoe upon which the Dutys arose and then a Merchant in
good Credit with the Houses Endorsement on s[d] Petition
Resolving Nemine Contradicente that the said Collier be
Released from the said Debt and whereas Col Thomas Smith-
son publiq Treasurer of the Eastern Shore has upon the said
Endorsement Recovered Judgem[t] ag[t] the said Collier, the s[d]
Collier is only to pay Col Smithson the Costt of Suit of which
the said publiq Treasurer is to Take due Notice and further

the house pray the Concurrence of his Ex<sup>ncy</sup> the **Governour** Original and the hon<sup>ble</sup> Board to their Resolve Which is agreed to by Journal. the Board.

M<sup>r</sup> Goldsborough and Three other Members bring from the house as followeth, Viz.

### By the house of Delegates May 21<sup>st</sup> 1705

May it please Your Ex<sup>ncy</sup>

In Answer to the Message relating to the Libel this house Resolves that the Charging Your Ex<sup>ncy</sup> with any Confederacy or being Ruled or prevailed on by Coll Darnall or any other Papists whatsoever is a most pnicious Scandalous and Seditious Libel Tending to the Destruction of her Ma<sup>tys</sup> Governm<sup>t</sup> here and is a great Scandal to your Ex<sup>ncys</sup> Fame & Reputation this house being very sensible of the Bill ag<sup>t</sup> the Popish Religion and also that Bill to Indulge them or to Suspend the Prosecution of the former Bill began both in this house and were sent from us to your Ex<sup>ncy</sup> and the hon<sup>ble</sup> her Majestys Councill for your Concurrence and Assent thereunto and we do pray your Ex<sup>ncy</sup> to be Assured from us that wee will omitt nothing that may be fitt or proper for us to do to protect & Assert her Ma<sup>tys</sup> Governm<sup>t</sup> and your Ex<sup>ncys</sup> Justice and Innocence in this Matter and to Shew our utmost Resentments ag<sup>t</sup> Such pestilent Disturbances of the Government and Bringing them to Condigne Punishment

Signed ꝑ order W Taylard Cl h. D.

Cap<sup>t</sup> Jones Brings from the house a Bill for Making Valid a letter of Attorney from W<sup>m</sup> Josephs Esq<sup>r</sup> to W<sup>m</sup> Josephs his son which was Read and Assented to the 2<sup>d</sup> time

The Sherriffe of Ann Arundell County in pursuance of an Order of this Board to him directly brought before his Ex<sup>ncy</sup> and this Board Rachel the wife of Thomas **Freeborne** Who being Accused of being an Accessary in letting Benjamine Celie out of Prison denys having any thing to do with Ben<sup>j</sup>: Celie further than Sending him something for his Flux & 18<sup>d</sup> to buy wine and one Shilling she left for him at the Gate house and that She never Induced the Smith to be Aiding or Assisting to lett the said Celie out of Prison

But the Board being very sencible what a pernitious Instrument she has been in this Matter and that she did hire and Induce the Smith to give a file to Benj<sup>n</sup> Celie wherewith he and the Indian filed of their Irons and thereby made way for the said Celie then Comitted as an Abettor to her son Richard Clarke in his Treasonable practices to make his Escape and

Original
Journal. lett out the said Indian Comitted on Suspition of a Barbarous
Murther and Dennis Maccartee comitted for Burglary, Advise
that she be comitted to her Maj^tys Goale in this Town & Port
of Annapolis untill she shall be thence Deliver'd by due Course
of Law.

Whereupon a mittimus ˙ being drawne she was for the
Causes af^d Comitted to the Goale

The Board Adjourns for an hour

Post Meridiem Council Sate ꝑrsent as before

M^r George Vallentine being sent for Received his Ex^ncys
Orders that he should not Suffer any Persons to Converse
w^th or any Messages to be sent to M^rs Rachel Freeborne this
Day Comitted for Treason & Treasonable practices unless
some of her Ma^tys hon^ble Councill be present and Cautiond to
see the said Order put in Execution as he will Answer the
Contrary at his perrill.

The following Message sent to the house by M^r Tench Col
Hamond & M^r Coursey

By the Councill in Assembly May 21^st 1705

His Ex^ncy proposes to the board that whereas upon the late
disturbances he had been obliged to Imploy many ꝑsons to
their Great detriment upon all Emergences he having promised them Reasonable and hon:^ble Satisfaction he finds many
of those Persons much Dissatisfyed to be left so precariously
to the Comittee of Accounts who it is Alledged very often
do not allow them any wise proportionable to their Respective Services How these Persons may be Gratified according
to their Service & Deserts that for the future such persons
may not be discouraged chearfully to serve her Ma^ty and the
Country.

The Board do Resolve that the house of Delegates be
made sincible thereof And that his Ex^ncy be desired by this
Assembly that he will be pleased on such Occasion to direct
and Issue his Orders to the publick Treasurers to pay to Such
persons already or hereafter to be employed on those Occasions or the like What he shall Reasonably think they
Deserves the Councill at their next Meeting approving of the
Disposall of such moneys so Issued and paid.

Signed ꝑ order W Bladen Cl Councll

Humphery Hernaman being sent for Came & being demanded to declare the truth of his Knowledge ag^t M^rs Rachell

Freeborne saith that a Fortnight or three Weeks before M<sup>r</sup>
Benj<sup>n</sup> Cellie Broke prison M<sup>rs</sup> Rachel Freeborne his Mistress
Came down to the Shopp and said It was a pitty such a man
as Celie should lye In prison and Bad him Assist and gett
him Out he says he never saw her in the Shopp before but
afterwards Came down with M<sup>r</sup> Greenberry and urged him to
help Celie out. Owns that he did lay the file in the prison
Window his Mistress said she doubted not to find out Richard
Clarke if Celie was out the Smith Said if he did it should
come to great Damage and his Master would abuse him and
he should lead a life like a dogg She told him if he Could
gett Celie out they would Carry him Safe off that she herself
Intended to leave her husband and go to the New Country
he said he had no mony She bad him never mind it she
would provide for him well enough which she supposed to be
money she urged him not Long before to Sett the Mill on fire
if not by day in the night he further says that when Richard
Clarke was in Prison his Mistress before him Wished he was
out of Prison for she was afraid he would be hanged and
does Verily believe by what she urged him to do for Celie,
She thereby hoped to gett him to Assist him out of prison he
says that his Said M<sup>rs</sup> said that a ffile would gett of his Irons
and then he would gett out of prison well enough, he likewise says his Master Thomas Freeborne is a very honest man
and that when Clarke Came to the house he would gett out
of his Company as soon as he Could and go to bed and leave
him

The said Humphery is Ordered to w<sup>th</sup> Draw

Came M<sup>r</sup> Muschamp and three other Members with the
two following Messages viz.

### By the house of Dellegates May 21<sup>st</sup> 1705

May it please Your Ex<sup>ncy</sup>

This house propose it to be the Consideration of Your
Ex<sup>ncy</sup> and her Ma<sup>tys</sup> hon<sup>ble</sup> Councill as an Expedient for our
future Quiett that Your Ex<sup>ncy</sup> Comissionate such ᵽsons as
many as in Your Wisdom shall seem fitt to Treat with & Renew our former Alliances & Friendshipp with the Seneca and
other Indians on the Western Shore and to use the Best
Methods they Can think on to discover the Murtherers of our
fellow Subjects this being the Most Easy and Ready Method
we Cann think of and therefore we pray Your Excellancys
Concurrence herein &c

Signed ᵽ Order W Taylard Cl h D.

By the house of Dellegates May the 21st 1705

May it Please Yor Exncy

You having Comanded that an hundred men shall be att all times Ready at the Comand of Each Coll in each Respective County to be Raised for the Countrys Service upon any Expedition tis proposed to your Exncy and the honble Councill by this house that a proportionable Quantity of Arms powder and Ball be lodged in the Custody of each Coll out of the Magazine Stores that the men may be Readily furnished therewith upon any Such Expedition. And that Your Exncy will be pleased to give Sufficient Orders to each Respective Coll that upon any mocon or accon of the Indians those men so raised may presently march agt them that no time may be lost this we are of oppinion will Tend much to the Quiett of the Inhabitants & the ffrontier Plantations.

Signed ꝑ order  W Taylard Clk ho. Dell.

Capt Jones & Mr Frisby bring from the house A Bill for the Reliefe of Ann Arundell County.

Purposed by his Exncy that whereas he had Delivered him By Charles Carroll one of the Lord Baltemores Agents a Memoriall in Relation to the Land Law that the same be sent to the House for their Consideration which was Accordingly sent to the house by Mr Tench with the following Message vizt.

By the Councill in Assembly May the 21st 1705

Gentn  Herewith is sent you the Lord Baltemores Agents memoriall or Representation Relating to the Land Law of Which you are Desired to Consider and Returne some Answer thereto.

Sign'd ꝑ Order  W Bladen Cl Councill

Mr Macclaster and Three other Members bring from the house the following Message Vizt.

By the house of Dell
May the 21 : 1705

May it please your Exncy

This house prays leave to represent to Yor Exncy & her Matys hon:ble Council that they are highly Impaired & prejudiced in their Interests and the whole Province much Impoverished by the Tradrs who Come hither by Single Ships one after another before the Generall Fleet appointed to Come hither

& if they are Suffered to depart as soon as they are Loaden they will be in danger of the enemy to be taken and so will feed them thereby p'judicing her Ma^tys^ Interest and if they Gett Safe Serve no other End but their Own but Ruine the Markett as to others and is a Direct P'judice to her Ma^tys^ Subjects here.

Therefore we do humbly pray Yo^r^ Ex^ncy^ that no Shipp or Vessels Bound for Europe with Tobacco may be Cleared untill Sufficient Convoy shall Appear to take Care and Charge of the homeward or untill such time as Yo^r^ Ex^ncy^ in Your Wisdom shall see mett        Signed p Order W. Taylard Cl h Del

In answer whereto the foll° was sent by to the house by M Coursey

### By his Ex^ncy^ the Gov^r^ and Councill in Assembly

In Answer to your Last Message by M^r^ Maclaster & others of Your house his Ex^ncy^ & this Board have allready done what in them lyes to Remedy the evil by Your house Represented in laying a Gen^ll^ Embargo upon all Shipping untill a Sufficient Convoy arrives from England the Strumbilow not being thought Sufficient.

Signed p Order   W Bladen Cl Councill

The Board Adjourns till 8 of the o'Clock To morrow Morning

### Tuesday May the 22^d^ 1705
Councill Sate Present as Yesterday in the Afternoon

His Ex^ncy^ proposes that the house will Appoint some of Their Members to Confer with four of this Board in Relation to the Prisoners now in Goale the present Guard on the publiq Magazine & Prison And the Rangers on the frontiers of the Potomeck.  What shall be done with the said Prisoners whether the Guard on the Magazine and prison & the Rangers on Potomeck shall be longer Continued upon those Services, what Number to be Continued, or be Totally disbanded.

Which Proposal was sent to the house by Col Lloyd & M^r^ Coursey.

Col Addison M^r^ Brooke M^r^ Smith & M^r^ Cheseldyne being Chosen to go on the Conference M^r^ Brooke upon a ffrivolous Occasion ask'd Leave to go home therefore ordered Coll p. 397 Hammond be Appointed in M^r^ Brooks stead

M^r^ Dallahide & M^r^ Fowkes bring from the house the foll Message Viz.

Original
Journal.

By the House of Dell May 22ᵈ 1705

Upon Reading the Memoriall of Mʳ Charles Carroll Relating
to the land Law and Your honʳˢ Message therewith this house
have Considered & Resolved that for as ·Much as this house
at the first opening of this Assembly Continued all References
on their Journall (and whereof this being one) Therefore pray
Your honʳˢ Concurrence therewith & that the Same May be
likewise refered

Signed ꝑ Order  W Taylard Clk house Dell.

Which is agreed to by this Board

The said Gentⁿ bring with them Likewise a Bill for Outlawing Richard Clarke which was Read at this Board the first
time Assented to and sent down to the house by Coll Lloyd
& Mʳ Coursey with Mʳ Thomas Colliers Pettⁿ Assented to by
this Board A Bill Confirming William Josephs Lʳᵉ of Attorney
and A Bill for Relief of Ann Arundell County.

His Exⁿᶜʸ acquaints the Board that he was surprized to hear
that a Gentⁿ of the County here & who bears a post should
tell the Soldiers now appointed to guard the Magazine &
Prison to look well to their Guard for they would be surprized
his Exⁿᶜʸ thereon remarq that if the Gentⁿ had no Reason for
saying so it was very foolish and unaccountable & if he had
Reason to believe any thing of it, It was worse that he did not
acquaint him therewith.

Majʳ Taylor & Mʳ Peter Watts Bring up the four following
Bills

A Bill for punishment of ꝑsons Selling or Transporting any
French Indian or Indians out of this Province.  A Bill Declaring An Act Intituled An Act for Electing Ann Arundˡˡ &
Oxford Towns into Ports & Towns formerly made to be in
force

A Bill Declaring An Act Intituled An Act for the Punishment of ꝑsons Suborning Witnesses, and Committing Willfull
& Corrupt ꝑjury to be in force.

A Bill declaring an Act Intituled An Act ascertaining the
Bounds of Land to be in force

Which were Read and Assented to by this Board & sent to
the house by Mʳ Sanders.

Ordered that the Sherriffe of Ann Arundell County do
Sumons Mʳ John Dorsey to Attend this Board.  And that he
take into his Custody the Body of John Dawling so that
he have him before this Board in the Afternoon.

Came Mʳ Goldsborough & Mʳ Hays from the house with
the following Message viz.

By the house of Dellegates May 22ᵈ 1705.

May it please yoʳ Exⁿᶜʸ

In Answer to Your honours Message by Mʳ Sanders proposing a Conference with four of Yoʳ board this house Concurrs. therewith and have appointed Six Membʳˢ to attend the sᵈ Conference Accordingly Therefore this house desires that you will Appoint the time & Place.

The Board Adjourns for two hours

### Post Meridiem Councill Sate psent as in the Morning

Ordered that the Gentⁿ of the house of Dell appointed on the Conference have notice that the Gentⁿ of this Board appointed on the Same are Ready to meet them at Mʳ Smith's Chamber.

And the said Gentⁿ accordingly withdraw from this Board.

Read the Petition of Richard Young Complaining that the house of Dellegates for the Mast which he had by his Exⁿᶜʸˢ Order sett up on the State house hill had not allowed halffe the Value of his work & Expences which being Considered by this Board the said petʳ was recommended to the house to make him a Better Allowance.

Col Addison Mʳ Smith Col Hammond & Mʳ Cheseldyne from the Conference Report as follows, viz.

By the Conference Appointed to Consider as well Concerning the Prisoners now in Goale as the Guards at the Magazine & Prison & the Rangers on Potomack Frontiers It is Reported as foll vizᵗ.

Proposed that whereas Benjamin Celie stand now Convicted and has Judgment to dye that to Save his life a Bill may be brought in to Transport him to the West Indies and sell him their for Seven years the Produce to be applyed to ease the publiq Charge Expended on him.

Proposed also that whereas Humphrey Hernaman who is now in Prison & has Voluntarily Confesᵗ that he by the Direction and Instigation of his Mistress Rachel Freeborne Conveyed a File to the Prisoners in Prison by which the Prisoners then in prison were Enabled to make their Escape that a bill may be brought in to Convict him of this and to Transport him Considering it will be a great Charge to the province to keep him in Prison till he be Tryed and Convicted according to the Common methods.

That after the proportions of the Magazine Stores are distributed that the Remaining part shall be left at his Exⁿᶜʸˢ Disposal without the Charge of a Guard.

Proposed by the honᵇˡᵉ Councill by way of Enquiry into the State of the Affair relating to the Rangers that they do

Continue their Garison till the Articles ̇c̊ˢ̇/ᴗ5
cluded on and Ratifyed and̥aͷ̊ot Mͬ Charles Carroll Relating
& us.   ̶ ̶ ̶ᵥᵥ·aııa Your honͬˢ Message therewith this house
..ᵥe͞ Considered & Resolved that for as Much as this house
at the first opening of this Assembly Continued all References
on their Journall (and whereof this being one) Therefore pray
Your honͬˢ Concurrence therewith & that the Same May be
likewise refered

> Signed ℗ Order  W Taylard Clk house Dell.

Which is agreed to by this Board

The said Gentⁿ bring with them Likewise a Bill for Outlawing Richard Clarke which was Read at this Board the first
time Assented to and sent down to the house by Coll Lloyd
& Mͬ Coursey with Mͬ Thomas Colliers Pettⁿ Assented to by
this Board A Bill Confirming William Josephs Lͬᵉ of Attorney
and A Bill for Relief of Ann Arundell County.

His Exⁿᶜʸ acquaints the Board that he was surprized to hear
that a Gentⁿ of the County here & who bears a post should
tell the Soldiers now appointed to guard the Magazine &
Prison to look well to their Guard for they would be surprized
his Exⁿᶜʸ thereon remarq that if the Gentⁿ had no Reason for
saying so it was very foolish and unaccountable & if he had
Reason to believe any thing of it, It was worse that he did not
acquaint him therewith.

Majͬ Taylor & Mͬ Peter Watts Bring up the four following
Bills

A Bill for punishment of ℘sons Selling or Transporting any
French Indian or Indians out of this Province.  A Bill Declaring An Act Intituled An Act for Electing Ann Arundˡˡ &
Oxford Towns into Ports & Towns formerly made to be in
force

A Bill Declaring An Act Intituled An Act for the Punishment of ℘sons Suborning Witnesses, and Committing Willfull
& Corrupt ℘jury to be in force.

A Bill declaring an Act Intituled An Act ascertaining the
Bounds of Land to be in force

Which were Read and Assented to by this Board & sent to
the house by Mͬ Sanders.

Ordered that the Sherriffe of Ann Arundell County do
Sumons Mͬ John Dorsey to Attend this Board.  And that he
take into his Custody the Body of John Dawling so that
he have him before this Board in the Afternoon.

Came Mͬ Goldsborough & Mͬ Hays from the house with
the following Message viz.

By the ̣ ̣ ̣ ̣ ̣ there than him and ever since has day <sup></sup>Original
May it please yo<sup>r</sup> Ex<sup>ncy</sup>        ̣ ̣ ̣ his Master to beate & abuse <sup></sup>Journal.

In Answer to Your honours Message by M ̣ ̣ ̣ .
posing a Conference with four of Yo<sup>r</sup> board this house Concu ̣ ̣ ̣
therewith and have appointed Six Memb<sup>rs</sup> to attend the s<sup>d</sup>
Conference Accordingly Therefore this house desires that you
will Appoint the time & Place.

The Board Adjourns for two hours

Post Meridiem Councill Sate psent as in the Morning

Ordered that the Gent<sup>n</sup> of the house of Dell appointed on
the Conference have notice that the Gent<sup>n</sup> of this Board
appointed on the Same are Ready to meet them at M<sup>r</sup> Smith's
Chamber.

And the said Gent<sup>n</sup> accordingly withdraw from this Board.

Read the Petition of Richard Young Complaining that the
house of Dellegates for the Mast which he had by his Ex<sup>ncys</sup>
Order sett up on the State house hill had not allowed halffe
the Value of his work & Expences which being Considered by
this Board the said pet<sup>r</sup> was recommended to the house to
make him a Better Allowance.

Col Addison M<sup>r</sup> Smith Col Hammond & M<sup>r</sup> Cheseldyne from
the Conference Report as follows, viz.

By the Conference Appointed to Consider as well Concerning the Prisoners now in Goale as the Guards at the
Magazine & Prison & the Rangers on Potomack Frontiers It
is Reported as foll viz<sup>t</sup>.

Proposed that whereas Benjamin Celie stand now Convicted and has Judgment to dye that to Save his life a Bill
may be brought in to Transport him to the West Indies and
sell him their for Seven years the Produce to be applyed to
ease the publiq Charge Expended on him.

Proposed also that whereas Humphrey Hernaman who is
now in Prison & has Voluntarily Confes<sup>t</sup> that he by the Direction and Instigation of his Mistress Rachel Freeborne Conveyed a File to the Prisoners in Prison by which the Prisoners
then in prison were Enabled to make their Escape that a bill
may be brought in to Convict him of this and to Transport
him Considering it will be a great Charge to the province to
keep him in Prison till he be Tryed and Convicted according
to the Common methods.

That after the proportions of the Magazine Stores are
distributed that the Remaining part shall be left at his Ex<sup>ncys</sup>
Disposal without the Charge of a Guard.

Proposed by the hon<sup>ble</sup> Councill by way of Enquiry into
the State of the Affair relating to the Rangers that they do

Continue their Garison till the \rticles- ~$₁ Peace are Con-
cluded on and Ratifyed and Conrmed between the Indians
& us.

⌐ame M$^r$ John Dorsey with Cp$^t$ John Young in pursuance
of a Sumons from this Board arl an Oath being Administred
to the said Cap$^t$ Young to dclare the Truth Concerning
what he heard of the Magazine eing besett saith, That since
they were appointed to Guardthe Magazine M$^r$ Dorsey &
he walking together on the Gren in the evening, M$^r$ Dorsey
said we ought to be very watchil to night M$^r$ Young asking
the Reason for it sayd Dorsey aswered that he was credibly
Informed the Magazine was treatned Either that night or
the night following.  Young ased him who told him so M$^r$
Dorsey said he was told by novorse man than Maj$^r$ Greenberry M$^r$ Young said he wonced he did not tell his Ex$^{ncy}$
Dorsey said he would not for tnn pounds he should gett the
Majors ill will, Dorsey said if e thought there was any truth
in it, he would have told himsce.

An Oath being likewise Aministred to M$^r$ Dorsey he
Declares That since the men vere Appointed to guard the
Magazine and Prison he happn'd to meet Maj$^r$ Greenberry
at M$^r$ Ritchmans, Maj$^r$ Greenbrry said he was going home
that night he had some discouse of his going over the Ferry
and the Wind Blowing He aid Brother Dorsey I would
Advise you to be Carefull of te Magazine for said he I have
heard a Story It was threatn'd either That night or the
night following.

He had no further discouse with him at that time but
Comunicated it to M$^r$ Young.

The said M$^r$ Dorsey being \sk'd in what manner Major
Greenberry told him it wheter as an Officer or as a friend
says he thinks as a friend

The said M$^r$ Dorsey be kewise ask'd why he said he
would not have his Ex$^{ncy}$ kno: it for ten pounds says because
Major Greenberry was his (ood Friend and he was afraid
his Ex$^{ncy}$ should be displeasecthat it was done in that manner
to the Guard and further sait not.

The Sherriffe of Ann Arudell County According to Ord$^r$
brought here the body of Joh Dawlin who being demanded
to Declare the Truth of his :nowledge relating to Ben: Ce-
lies breaking Prison & the Siiths Assisting him & what he
knows In relation to M$^{rs}$ Racell Freeborne & in order thereto
having an Oath Administrd to him Declares that his M$^{rs}$
(Rachel Freeborne) that nigr he tooke Benj$^n$ Celie was very
angry at him & said Ratt youor a Whelp how came you to be
so much of a man as to take (elie up It's well yo$^r$ Master keeps
such a pcel of Whelps to tae up men, It's better an hundred

such as you should be there han him and ever since has day and night Endeavoured to Ştt his Master to beate & abuse him.

He ffurther declares that Carles Seevens D$^r$ Hoopers man last night told him and severa others viz. John Pattin & John Kersey that before the prison vas Broke Humphry the Smith ask'd his Advice & told himnis Mistress had been at him several times to assist Benj$^n$ Celie in getting out of Prison But Charles said he advised hm not to do it for it would be his Ruin if he did. About 2 10nths ago he says he saw his Mistress Rachel Freeborn go twice or thrice to the Smiths Shop the first time she Carrie a pair of hinges & then his master and he were in the Shop And Does not know that ever he saw her go to the Shp five times Ever since She has been marryed to his Masterbefore

He says he believes in his Cnscience she went to pswade the Smith to Assist Benjamine ïelie for since Ben: Celie has told him Humphrey and he wee to meet at the Gallows & go together.

Ordered that the Sher. of AnrArundell County do Sum̄ons Charles Steevens to Appear bfore this Board to morrow morning

The Board adjourns till to morow morning

May 23$^d$ 1705 . The Concill Sate prsent

His Ex$^{ncy}$ the Gvernour

| | |
|---|---|
| Thomas Tench Esq$^r$ | Col Francis Jenkins |
| Col John Addison | Cl Edward Lloyd |
| Robert Smith Esq$^r$ | L Col W$^m$ Holland |
| Col John Hamond | Jmes Sanders Esq$^r$ |
| Kenelm Cheseldne Esq$^r$ | |

Benjamin Gather being Brought before this Board by vertue of his Ex$^{ncys}$ Warrant is Demandedto give the best Information he can as well ag$^t$ Richard Clarke of Ann Arundell County as any his Accomplices andbeing Sworne on the holy Evangelist Declares that Richard Clarkes Wife some time in March last Came to his house ona Brown bay horse which she said was Daniel Meriartees her Brother she Importuned him to go up with her to Neal Clark to Carry some things to her husband He went up with hr & lay at Neals house Neale Came home very late in th Night as he told the Dep$^t$ from his mother in Law The next Day the Dep$^t$ & Clarks wife went to Richard Clarkin the lane in sight of the house the Dep$^t$ Ask'd him whyhe lay out & told him

Original
Journal. Col Hamond Advised he should Come in & submitt himself
to his Ex^{ncy}    The said Clark had very Good Cloths on

A Coate he said he had from Edw^d Mariartee & a good
Suite from Topp to Toe at Maj^r Greenberrys & some neates
Tongues and Cheese he had of Maj^r Greenberrys wife he
was mounted on a Black horse with a Bald Face long Dock
and 2 white feet belonging to Edward Meriartee. His wife
brought him two Pistols she not long before bought of James
Lewis.

After Richard Clarke fitted his Pistolls & Saddle upon
Dan͞n Meriartees brown bay horse which he Changed for
Edward Meriartees horse They went in the house upon
which Neale seemed to be Angry at him upon which Richard
went out and they had many Cross words.   While they were
in the house Rich^d Clark ask the Deponent and Neale Clarke
to go with him and Assist him over Potomack River which
they Refused all that Day at night Richard Clarke and his
wife lay on some Straw in an out house belonging to Neale
and the next Day about Twelve of the Clock Clark urged
that he was afraid he should be hanged if he did not make
his Escape prevailed upon the Depon^t & his Brother Neale
to promise and go with and Assist him over Potomack
Accordingly they sett forward and Clark Bad them say if any
p. 404 should ask who he was to say his name was Robert Greenberry—they Came upon M^r Roziers negro Quarter the
Depon^t and Neale Clark Called for a lodging Richard Clark
keeping out of Sight in the Woods they went into the house
after a while Richard Clark Came into the house but tooke
no Notice of his Brother & Depon^t as if he knew them the
Negroes gave them their supper all Three Eat together.
Afterwards went away and Lay in the woods the Negroes
being afraid to entertain them but promised them the Canoe
the next day—then the Negroes endeavoured to secure them.
But Fletchill letting them go they went to Neale Clarks that
night after they had been there an hour Richard Clarke
Came to the pailes brought his Pistolls & his Sword & told
them he had a great Combustion with the Negroes who had
shott his horse but he had escaped

The Next Day he saw him again in the Woods under a
great Tree and he told him he did not know what to do he
feared he should be killed the Depon^t then Departed with him
and has never seen him since but believes he is not quite gone
out but Lurking about.

Came Charles Steevens Servant to D^r Rob^t Hooper according to a Sum͞ons Served on him and being Sworn on the holy
Evangelist to Declare the Truth of his Knowledge in Relation
to Richard Clark or his Abettors Deposes That some time in

the fall he was Carrying in Corn topps into a Tobacco house and
allways observed M^rs Rachel freeborne to be in the Tobacco
house and always as he Came in with a Turn of Corne topps
she pretended to take up and Whittle a piece of Tob° stick
but this Depon^t has very good Reason to believe shee was
Corresponding with her son Richard Clark who hid himself
in the Fodder for that within a Day or Two after he said Clark
told him he was there.

He further says that Thomas Freeborns Daughter Mary
told him this Dep^t that Richard Clark was in the Branch one
night & that she carryed him Victuals.

He says that Humphery Hernam some time after Celie was
Comitted told him He was Advised to lett Ben: Celie out of
Prison & Ask'd this Deponents Advice who told him those
that Advised him so were his Foes & not his Friends After
this M^rs Freeborne Came to the Smiths Shopp & seeing the
Depon^t there went away again only saying Humphery you
are at Work I see.

Not long after that about a Month or five Weeks before the
Prison was broke Humpherey again told this Dep^t he was
Advised to lett the Prisoners out & Run away with them and
so gett shutt of his Slavery but did not tell him neither did
this Depon^t ask him whom but told him those that Advised
him was his Foes about a fortnight before the Prison was
broake the said Humphery told this Dep^t he had altered his
mind and had Resolved to serve out his time honestly and
then the first day he was free he should be as Good a man as
his Master.

Sarah Freeborne on Monday last told this Deponent that
M^rs Rachell Freeborne told old M^rs Story and M^rs Rebeccah
Nicholson that she Asked Humphrey if he Could not Contrive
a way to let the Prisoners out and Humphrey answered Lord
Mistress No I canot do it it's a hanging matter to Which she
Replyed No can't you do it you are a Smith and have Files to
gett their Irons of and may do it that no body may know it.
It will be a means for you to gett Ridd of your Slavery for
Celie and Richard Clarke know all the Country over.

This Deponent veryly believes M^rs Rachel Freeborne Advised Humphery to let out the Prisoners for that before the
Prison was Broke She said in his hearing It was pitty Celie
should be in Prison so long. And ffurther Humphery told him
she was very kind to him in sending or Carrying him Drachms
of the Bottle more than usuall.

One day not long before the prison was broke Celie Called
to this Deponent as he Rodd out of Town and Askd if Humphery was at home to ^Wch the Dep^t said Yes and then he
desired him to tell Humphery he wond^red he did not send the

Original Book he had of his att which this Depon$^t$ ask'd what Booke
Journal. well knowing the said Humphrey could not Read Celie Told
him it was a Story Booke when he Came home he asked
Humphrey for the Booke who told him he Would Carry it
himself at night and would not lett this Deponent see any Book.
The Board Adjourns to the afternoon.

Came M$^r$ Aisquith with Eight Ingrossed Bills viz$^t$.   A Bill
for the Outlawing of Richard Clark of Aund$^{ll}$ County.
A Bill declaring An Act Intituled An Act for Erecting
Aun$^{dll}$ & Oxford Towns into Ports and Towns formerly made
to be in force
A Bill for the Naturalization of Xpher Dangerman of Calvert
County Sadler
A Bill confirming a Certain Lre of Attorney to W$^m$ Josephs
A Bill for punishm$^t$ of Persons Selling or Transporting any
ffriend Indian.
A Bill declaring the Act for punishm$^t$ of ꝑsons Suborning
Witnesses to be in force
A Bill declaring An Act Intituled An Act ascertaining the
bounds of Land to be in force
Which being Read were Severally Assented to by this Board
& were sent down to the house by Coll Lloyd & M$^r$ Coursey.
The following Message sent to the house by Col Addison
and Col Lloyd viz.

### By the Council in Assembly.

Whereas Humphery Hernaman is a principall Evidence
ag$^t$ M$^{rs}$ Rachell Freeborne now Comitted by Aiding and
Assisting her son Richard Clarke in his Traiterous Practices &
Assisting Benj$^a$ Celie to Break the prison wee have Thought
proper to Advertise you thereof and that we do not think
Adviseable the said Hernamans Evidence not fortified with
any Concurrent Testimonys should be Rendered invalid
Signed ꝑ order W Bladen Cl Councll.

The Declarations of Humphery Hernaman & John Dawlin
sent to the house with the above Message
M$^r$ Thomas Frisby M$^r$ Jones & M$^r$ Gray bring from the
house the following Message viz.

### By the house of Dell May 23$^d$ 1705

May it please your Hon$^{rs}$
This house has Considered the Message sent to them by
your hon$^{rs}$ on Monday last Relating to the Satisfying of ꝑsons

Imployed upon Extraordinary Occasions by his Ex^{ncy} the Gov^r Original
in her Ma^{tys} and the Governm^{ts} Service and that to leave them Journal.
to the Comittee of Accounts to make them Satisfaction for
their Services would be too precarious this house have given
particular directions to the Comittee of Accounts to take particular Care of such deserving psons & so to proportion the
Reward as it may in some degree Answer the Expectation of
such psons and this house is very sincible of the Great Care
of his Ex^{ncy} and tender Reguard for the Good and Wellfare
of this Province and as they shall not do any thing detracting
from his Ex^{ncy} So they will at all times be Ready to Make
good such Promises as his Ex^{ncy} shall in the Absence of Assemblys think fitt to make to any Persons who serve her Ma^{ty} or
this Governm^t upon such Extraordinary Occasions

But as to the giving his Ex^{ncy} the Trouble to Issue Ord^{rs} to
the Treasurers this house are of oppinion that that part of the
Message is put too Gen^{ll} & is altogether needless and they
will not Intend that Yo^r Hon^{rs} in your Wisdoms will Insist
Thereon.          Signed p order W. Taylard Clk h D.

Cap^t Jones and M^r Taylor Bring ffrom the house the
following Message viz^t.

### By the House of Dellegates May 25^{th} 1705

Upon Reading the Report of the Confference yesterday the
house proceeded to Debate the same.

1  As to Benj^a Celie this house are of Opinion that the said
Celie being now in the Mercy of the Queen there is no need of
An Act of Assembly to Transport him But leave him Intirely to
the Disposal of his Ex^{ncy} the Gov^r to do with him as he thinks fitt

2  As to the Magazine Stores to be distributed (according
to the former Proposall) and what is left to be at his Ex^{ncys}
Disposall without the Charge of a Guard this house Readily
Concurred therewith.

3  As to the Proposall Relating to the Rangers this house
are willing they be still kept out and proposed that six men
and an Officer be Ordered in Prince Georges County and the
like in Baltemore County.

And this house humbly proposes to his Ex^{ncy} the Gov^r that
the Cap^t of the Rangers in Prince Georges County be Removed
and some other more fitt Person to be put instead to all which p. 409
this house pray the Concurrence of his Ex^{ncys} & Councill
          Signed p Order W Taylard Cl House Dell.

Which being Read is agreed to by this Board
30

Original    M^r Chaseldyne & M^r Coursey are Ordered to Carry to the
Journal     house the foll Message viz^t


### By the Councill In Assembly May 25^th 1705

Your answer this day by M^r Frisby and others to Our pro-
posal on Monday last for the Satisfying psons Imployed by his
Ex^cy on Sundry Exigences is In part well Approved of but
the last paragraph is so abstruse wee must desire yo^r Explana-
tion thereon further we Desire to know how and by whom
the Comissioners to be Appointed to treat with the Senniquis
Indians shall be furnished with mony or Credit to bear their
Charges on that Expedition & purchase Presents for the Ind^ns
It being well known that the French bid as largely for their
Affection as any       Signed p order W Bladen Cl. Counll.


The Board adjourns for an hour.


Post Meridiem Councill Sate present as before.
The following Message sent to the house by M^r Coursey
viz.

### By the Councill in Assembly

Upon Reading the Debates of Your house on the Report
of the Conference Yesterday as to that part Relating to
Benj^a Celle his Ex^cy was pleased to Declare that he is
thankf'll to any that put him in mind of what he may do.
But since that you have not thought fit to Advise how the
said Celle should be disposed of his Ex^cy is not Inclinable
otherwise than according to the sentence pronounced ag^t him
which will be Executed on Fryday next
                     Signed p Ord^r W Bladen Clk Councill


....    The following Petition read att the Board Viz.


### To his Ex^cy the Governour and her
### Ma^ts hon^ble Councill

The humble Petition of Thomas Pitton Comander of the
Shipp factor of Bytheford navigated with 20 Gunns & fifty
men W^m Rock Comander of the Shipp Zant of the same
place mounted with 10 Gunns and navigated with 20 men
Walter Darracott Comander of the Shipp Susan of Barnestaple mounted with six Guns & Navigated with sixteen men
Edward Collins Comander of the Mary and Hannah of By
the ford navigated with sixteen men

M$^r$ Cheseldyne & M$^r$ Coursey are Ordered to Carry to the house the foll. Message viz$^t$.


### By the Councill in Assembly May 25th 1705

Your answer this day by M$^r$ Frisby and others to Our proposal on Monday last for the Satisfying 'psons Imployed by his Ex$^{ncy}$ on Sundry Exigences is In part well Approved of but the last paragraph is so abstruse wee must desire yo$^r$ Explanation thereon ffurther we Desire to know how and by whom the Comissioners to be Appointed to treat with the Senniquis Indians shall be furnished with mony or Credit to bear their Charges on that Expedition & purchase Presents for the Ind$^{ns}$ It being well known that the French bid as largely for their Affection as any    Signed 'p order W Bladen Cl. Counll.


The Board adjourns for an hour.


Post Meridiem Councill Sate 'present as before.

The following Message sent to the house by M$^r$ Coursey viz.

### By the Councill in Assembly

Upon Reading the Debates of Your house on the Report of the Conference Yesterday as to that part Relating to Benj$^n$ Celie his Ex$^{ncy}$ was pleased to Declare that he is thankfull to any that put him in mind of what he may do. But since that you have not thought fit to Advise how the said Celie should be disposed of his Ex$^{ncy}$ is not Inclinable otherwise than according to the sentence pronounced ag$^t$ him which will be Executed on Fryday next

Signed 'p Ord$^r$ W Bladen Clk Councill


p. 410    The following Petition read att the Board Viz.


### To his Ex$^{ncy}$ the Governour and her
### Ma$^{tys}$ hon$^{ble}$ Councill

The humble Petition of Thomas Pitton Comander of the Shipp factor of Bytheford navigated with 20 Gunns & fifty menn W$^m$ Rock Comander of the Shipp Zant of the same place mounted with 10 Gunns and navigated with 20 men Walter Darracott Comander of the Shipp Susan$^a$ of Barnestaple mounted with six Guns & Navigated with sixteen men Edward Collins Comander of the Mary and Hannah of By the ford navigated with sixteen men

Sheweth. That Your Petition$^{rs}$ having Loaden their Shipps Original Journal.
are willing and Desirous to Sayle for Europe in Company
of her Ma$^{tys}$ Shipp Strombulo who your 'pete$^r$ are Informed
is Designed to Sayle about the Tenth of June next. They
therefore humbly pray your Ex$^{ncy}$ and Hon$^{rs}$ Approbation and
Leave to Depart this Province with the said Shipp Strombulo
and An Order to the Severall Nav$^{ll}$ Officers & Coll$^{rs}$ to Clear
Your Petitioners and their Shipps Accordingly and the Rather
that the men under pay on Board the said Shipps are very
Desirous to go for Europe and threaten yo$^r$ Petitioners that
if the said Shipps should be Embargo'd here to Shipp themselves on Board the said Ship Strombulo & Leave Yo$^r$ Petitioners and Travell by Land or otherways to New England
which will be very prejudiciall not only to the Owners of the
Shipps und$^r$ Your peti$^{rs}$ Comand but a Great discouragem$^t$ to
Trade, all Which Your Petiti$^{rs}$ humbly pray yo$^r$ Ex$^{ncy}$ and
Hon$^{rs}$ to take into Consideration & Make such Order therein
as to your Wisdoms shall seem meet

And your Petit$^{rs}$ shall ever pray &c.

Upon the reading whereof the Pet$^{rs}$ are Answered that the p. 411
Gen$^{ll}$ Assembly now sitting have Advised his Ex$^{ncy}$ the Gov$^r$
not to Suffer any of the Shipping to go with the Strumbulo
mann of Warr but to Embargo them untill a Better Convoy
Arrives from England And what is ffarr more her Ma$^{tys}$
Royall Instructions to his Ex$^{ncy}$ on this Point are so Sacred
that he does declare he will not Suffer any of the Shipps to
Sayle without a Sufficient Convoy which may Answer that
Instruc$^{on}$

Came M$^r$ Eliaz King M$^r$ Phillips and M$^r$ Hill with the
Iournal of the Comittee of Accounts upon Reading whereof
it was remarqued that the Comittee have allowed Maj$^r$ John
Freeman for Fire & Candle for the Councill four pounds of
which Article this Boarde desired to be better Satisfyed
having no Grounds to believe the same any ways Just or
Reasonable being sincible no such Charge had ever Occur$^d$
since his Ex$^{ncys}$ arrivall

It is ffurther Remarqd that the Hon$^{ble}$ M$^r$ Tench Col. Addison M$^r$ Brooke M$^r$ Cheseldyn and M$^r$ Coursey are not allowed
for their Attendance in Councill this or the last Sessions of
Assembly neither is there allowed for the Great Seale as
usuall for the two Several Prorogations between Sept$^r$ & December nor any thing for four Copys of the Laws then made
or Seals to the new Laws or the tenn pounds his Ex$^{ncy}$ paid
for the Apprehending of Benj$^a$ Celie & fifty two shill paid to
George Slacomb to put a Stopp to the Members Coming to
the Assembly.

Assembly Proceedings, May 15–25, 1705.

Original Journal. It is further **Remarq'd** that the Allowance to the Secretary for Recording the Laws of the two last Sessions is not any way Equivalent to the Service without due Regulations & Allowance whereof this Board will not Assent to the Journall or Allowances thereon.

Signed ᵱ order   W Bladen Cl Council.

Mʳ Tyler Mʳ Wells Mʳ Hill and Mʳ Macall bring from the house the following Message Viz.

By the House of Dell May 23ᵈ 1705

By the Debates of our house Relating to Benjⁿ Celie the Prisoner Wee did not Intend to put his Exⁿᶜʸ in mind of what he might do but only Asserted the Royal Prerogative but if the Bringing in of a Bill to Transport him or any other thing which may Save his life be thought Necessary if you please to signify to us this house will be very Ready to Concurr with Your honʳˢ in any such Proposal we being very Desirous that his life may be saved.

Signed ᵱ order   W Taylard Cl house Dell.

The Board Adjourns 'till to morrow morning at 8 o'Clock.

Die Jovis 24° May   Councill Sate ᵱrsent as Yesterday.

Advised that Mʳ Philemon Lloyd Mʳ Nathaniel Hynson and Mʳ Thoˢ Addison be Appointed Comissioners to go to Conestoga or further Northward to treat with the Seniquis Indians and that Mʳ Thomas Jones attend them as Clerk to Write what there shall be Occasion for. .

Came Majʳ Contee & nine other Members from the house & bring with them a Bill for Laying a further duty of 6ᵈ ᵱ Hhd on Tob° Exported which being Read at the Board they do not think it Advisable that such Bill do pass especially in this time of Warr when Tobacco is so low for that it will damnify the Trade in Genʰ Deterr the Shipping from Loading
p. 413 in this Province and be a means to Drive them to Virginia Which being so Endorsed was sent to the house by Col Lloyd & Col Hamond

Mʳ Gray and Mʳ How Bring from the house a Bill for Transporting Benjᵃ Celie Which was agreed to by this Boarde notwithstanding the same was not so Regularly brought in the House not having his Exⁿᶜʸ the Govʳ and Councill's Consent thereto.

Mʳ Eccleston and Mʳ How bring from the house a Bill for the selling of Wᵐ Edmonsons Land for payment of the purchase Money to John Nichols the Vender Which were agreed to and sent to the house By Col Lloyd & M^r Coursey

M^r Frisby & M^r Skinner bring from the house the foll Message viz^t.

### By the house of Dellegates May 24^th 1705.

May it please yo^r hon^rs

As to Your Message Relating to the Seniquis Indians the Chief or head men of those five Nations of Indians with whom tis propos'd to Treat they will Come to Susquehannah River where they may be Treated with & as to money to bare the Charges of the Comissioners & to buy Presents for the Indians this house will give directions therein to the Treasurers to Issue money Accordingly.

Signed ꝑ Order W Taylard Clk ho Dell

To which Message this Answer was sent by Coll Lloyd & M^r Coursey.

### By the Councill in Assembly May 24th 1705

Upon Reading Your last message This Board do say they have no Assurance of the Chief menn of five nations Coming down to Susquehannah to Treat with us on failure whereof it will be Absolutely Necessary our Com^rs go to them at Albany that we may be Certainly Assured of their friendship & what Else we may Expect from them having been allready kept too long in the Dark

Signed ꝑ Order W Bladen Cl Councill.

The Board adjourns till the Afternoon.

Post Meridiem    Council Sate  Present as in the Morning

Cap^t Jones Brings up a Bill for the Relief of poor Debtors from Excessive Imprisonm^t & Execution ffees which was Read and Rejected and sent to the house by M^r Coursey

Came M^r Aisquith with the Engrossed Bill to Enable Maj^r Lowe to sell W^m Edmondsons Land to pay the Purchase money w^ch was Read & Assented to and sent to the house by M^r Coursey

M^r Eliaz King Brings up the Journall of the Comittee of Acc^ts which was Read and Assented to as well of Tobacco as Moneys.

Original Journal. Mʳ Grey brings the Engrossed Bill to Banish Benjⁿ Celie Which was Assented to by the Board and sent to the house by Mʳ Coursey.

The Board adjourns till 8 of Clock to morrow morning

### Die Veneris 25° May 1705
### The Councill Sate    Present as yesterday

Came Mʳ Eccleston and others who Brought up a Bill for apportioning the Publick Leavy for the present Year 1705 Which being twice Read & Assented to by this Board Was sent to the house by Mʳ Sanders

Came Mʳ Hill to Acquaint his Exⁿᶜʸ that the house had done all the Business before them & brought up the Bill for appor-p. 415 coning the publick Levy Engrossed & Assented to by the house which was Assented to by this Board and sent to the house by Col Haⁿ̄ond & Mʳ Coursey who is Ordered to Acquaint them that his Exⁿᶜʸ is Ready to Receive them.

Came Mʳ Speaker Attended by the House of Dellegates who presents to his Exⁿᶜʸ the following Bills Engrossed and Assented to as well by the house as her Maᵗʸˢ honːᵇˡᵉ Councill viz.

A Bill for the Relief of Ann Arundell County & all Persons Concerned in the Records thereof lately Burnt.

A Bill Declaring the Act Intituled An Act for the punishmᵗ of ꝑsons Suborning Witnesses & Coⁿ̄itting willful and Corrupt Perjury to be in force.

A Bill for punishment of Persons selling or Transporting any Friend Indian or Indians out of this province

A Bill for Naturalization of Xpher Dangerman of Calvert County Sadler

A Bill for Confirming a Certain Lre of Attorney from Wᵐ Josephs Esq the father to Wᵐ Josephs the son

An Act Impowering Majʳ Nicholas Low Executor of the last will and Testament of Wᵐ Edmondson late of Dorchester County decᵈ to sell a certain Tract of Land in Dorchester County Called Richardsons Choice formerly purchased by the said Wᵐ Edmondson of & from one John Nicholls for payment of a debt due from the said Wᵐ Edmundson to the sᵈ John Nicholls for the Remaining part of the Originall Purchase for the sᵈ Land.

A Bill declaring An Act Entituled An Act Entituled for Erecting Ann Arᵈˡˡ & Oxford Towns into Ports & Towns to be in force
p. 416 An Act Declaring an Act Intituled An Act Ascertaining the bounds of Land to be in force.

# PROCEEDINGS AND ACTS

OF THE

# GENERAL ASSEMBLY

# OF MARYLAND.

*At a Session held at Annapolis, May* 15–25, 1705.

CHARLES CALVERT, LORD BALTIMORE,
*Proprietary.*

JOHN SEYMOUR,
*Governor.*

---

THE LOWER HOUSE OF ASSEMBLY.

# PROCEEDINGS AND ACTS

OF THE

# GENERAL ASSEMBLY

# OF MARYLAND.

*At a Session held at Annapolis, May* 15–25, 1705.

CHARLES CALVERT, LORD BALTIMORE,
*Propriary.*

JOHN SEYMOUR,
*Governor.*

---

THE LOWER HOUSE OF ASSEMBLY.

Maryland s
The thir
& Port of
of May 17
Esqr Cap
Province of
several Wr
May instan
&c Anno 1
At which
the several

For St Ma

Saint Mary

Kent Coun

Ann Arun

Calvert C

Maryland ss.

The third Sessions of Assembly begun and held at the Town & Port of Annapolis in Ann Arundel County the fifteenth Day of May 1705 and from thence by his Excellency John Seymour Esq' Cap' Gen' and Governor in Chief in & over her Majestys Province of Maryland & the Territories thereto bolonging by several Writs of Prorogations prorogued to the 17<sup>th</sup> Day of May instant and in the third Year of Her Majesty's Reign &<sup>ca</sup> Anno Dom. 1705.

At which Time the House being met were called over & the several Members following appeared Viz.

The Hon̄ble Thomas Smith, Esq' Speaker

For S' Mary's City   George Muschamp Esq'  
                M' James Key  
                M' Thomas Beale

Saint Mary's County.   M' William Watts  M' W<sup>m</sup> Aisquith  
                                   M' Peter Watts

Kent County  M' Elias King  
            M' John Wells  
            M' William Frisby

                    Som' County.   M' John Watrs  
                                M' Joseph Gray  
                                M' John Jones  
                                M' John Macklaster

Ann Arundel County.   M' Samuel Young  
                      M' Charles Greenberry  
                      M' Joseph Hill  
                      M' Richard Jones

                    Talbot County   M' Rob' Goldsborough  
                                   M' Nich' Lowe

              Cecil County   M' William Pearce  
                          M' Edward Blay  
                          M' Tho' Frisby  
                          M' William Dare

Calvert County   M' Robert Skinner  
                  M' John Mackall  
                  M' Thomas Howe  
                  M' John Leach

Prince Geo. Co^ty     M^r Tho^s Greenfield
                      M^r William Barton
                      M^r Rob^t Tyler

Charles County   M^r James Smallwood ⎫
                 M^r William Stone    ⎬
                 M^r Gerrard Fowke    ⎭

Dorch^r County   M^r Hugh Eccleston
                 M^r John Taylor
                 M^r John Hudson
                 M^r Jos. Ennalls.

Baltimore County   M^r Edward Dorsey    ⎫
                   M^r James Maxwell    ⎪
                   M^r James Philips    ⎬
                   M^r Francis Dallahide ⎭

Thomas Smithson Esq^r and M^r Henry Coursey for Talbot County and M^r Samuel Magruder for Prince George's County absent.

Col^o Thomas Smithson's Letter of Excuse being read is approved of by the House and his Absence dispensed with

p. 22   M^r Nicholas Lowe, M^r George Muschamp, M^r John Mackall, & M^r John Macklaster ordered to attend his Excellency & Council to acquaint them that the House is met according to Prorogation & ready to receive his Excellency's Commands.

They return & say they have delivered their Message.

The Honble Robert Smith & James Sanders Esq^rs from the Honble Council enters the House & acquaints M^r Speaker that his Excellency commands him and the whole House to attend him immediately at the Council Chamber Whereupon the Speaker and the whole House adjourned to the Council Chamber where his Excellency was pleased to say to them as follows Viz.

M^r Speaker & Gentlemen Delegates,

Tis very evident the treasonable villainous Practices of some among us has encouraged the Indians to commit their Barbarities on Our Fellow Subjects. Those by their frequent Insolences have put the Country to the Trouble & Charge of keeping Men out to protect the honest painful Inhabitants on that Frontier.

One great Motive these bold Incendiaries used to inflame the unthinking Crew (who were to join in Concert with them) was our Nakedness, Want of Ammunition, ill Arms &^ca Cunning Specious Pretences to bring their secret Contrivance to an open Rebellion.

Gent.   How these necessary Matters come to be wanted on this or any other Occasion, I hope your tender Regard for the

Country's Safety will animate you to a strict Enquiry & can <sub></sub>Lib. 41.
never believe any Time more proper to consider of it than
when we are threatned by all Sorts of Enemies abroad & Vil-
lains in our own Bowels which would enervate & unhinge
your Constitution.

Gent. Her Majesty's Hoñble Council advised me to meet
you at this Time that by the prudent Assistance of your well
digested Considerations we may unanimously join to suppress
every thing that dares disturb your Peace or the quiet Enjoyment of your Fortunes, Industry & Care which a steady
Heartiness may now establish to your lasting Honour.

I am resolved Gent. during my Administration what her
Majestys & her good Peopl₂ here have so prudently Set apart
for the Defence of this Province shall be disposed of to no
other Use whatsoever but for the Safety, Preservation and
Quiet of every individual Member thereof.

And I doubt not but these frequent chargeable Alarms will
so invigorate your Resolutions we may be ever in a Posture to
crush all Sorts of Disturbances before they are formed into
open Hostilities, and dare assure you if you will adhere to some
Methods I shall presume to lay down which shall neither be so
burthensome or impracticable (as at present) your Posterity p. 23
will be obliged to this present Assembly for their future
Tranquility.

I'll transmit to Mr Speaker some Letters about the New
York Affairs as likewise an Account of a C. iminal lately condemned & some other Accomplices not yet brought unto Tryal
by whose Vows & Oaths to be secret to this horrid Combination you will be thoroughly sensible the Scene was laid to a
very bloody Purpose.

Gent. As you very well know the Occasion of this Meeting
when you have well considered the several Instances Contrivances & Papers relating thereto if we are uneasy for the future
blame not a Gentleman who will never be wanting to do his
Duty to the best of Queens my Sovereign or his strict Friendship & viglant Care over the Province her Majesty was
graciously pleased to constitute me Governor.

Which being ended Mr Speaker & the rest of the Members
took their Leave & returned to their House where Mr Speaker
having taken the Chair Ordered his Excellency's Speech be
read in the House which was read accordingly, &

Ordered it be read again to Morrow Morning

Mr Thomas Greenfield Colo James Maxwell & Mr Thomas
Frisby ordered a Committee for Election and Privileges

Ordered Mr James Wootton be desired to attend the House
for Prayers in the Church at Seven O'Clock in the Morning &
five in the Afternoon.

Lib. 41.   Ordered That the Clerk of this House inspect the Journal
of the last Sessions of Assembly and draw therefrom all
Referrences to this Session & produce to the next for Consideration

The House adjourns till 7 O'clock to Morrow Morning.


### Friday May 18ᵗʰ 1705

The House again met and being called over were present
as yesterday

A Member of this House informed Mʳ Speaker that Mʳ
Henry Coursey a Member for Talbot County is now under
great Affliction with the Gout whereby he is incapable of
attending the House therefore desires to be excused which is
granted & allowed by the House.

The Committee of Election & Privileges ordered to go out
upon their Committee and was delivered them an Indenture
to enquire into the Election of John Contee Esqʳ a Member
chosen for Charles County to serve in Stead of Colᵒ William
Dent deceased.

Mʳ Elias King Mʳ James Philips and Mʳ Joseph Hill appointed a Committee for stating & examining the publick
Accounts of this Province Ordered to withdraw & repair to
the Committee.

The Committee of Election & Privileges enter the House
& report that the said John Contee is duly elected a Member
for Charles County.

p. 24   And ordered Mʳ Hugh Eccleston & Mʳ Thomas Frisby
attend him to the Council to see him Sworn. They return &
Say they have seen him qualified.

Colᵒ Edward Lloyd & Colᵒ William Holland from the
Honble Council enters the House and delivers Mʳ Speaker
some Letters & Depositions relating to the Indians Affairs
which are ordered to be read and being read the Matters
therein contained are referred for further Consideration

Ordered his Excellency's Speech be again read ; which
being read.

Ordered Mʳ Robert Goldsborough Mʳ Charles Greenberry
and Mʳ Samuel Young prepare an Answer thereto & forthwith lay it before the House for their Consideration.

The Petition of George Symonds & Elizabeth his Wife
praying Leave to bring in a Bill to confirm the Will of Thomas
Knighton deceased being read Ordered Summons issue to
Mʳ Christopher Vernon as prayed & Leave is given the Petʳ
to bring in a Bill the next Sessions of Assembly.

Thomas Tench & John Hammond Esqʳˢ from the Honble
Council enter the House and delivers Mʳ Speaker a Message

relating to Richard Clark & his Accomplices; which being read the Consideration thereof is referred till Afternoon. Lib. 41.

The Petition of Thomas Collier Naval Officer of the Port of Williamstadt being brought into the House was ordered to be read; which follows Viz.

To the Honourable the House of Delegates &ca

The humble Petition of Thomas Collier Naval Officer of Williamstadt

Humbly Sheweth,

That whereas one William Edmondson late of Talbot County deceased in Sept. 1701 delivered to your Petitioner as Naval Officer of Williamstadt three Bills of Exchange drawn by the said Edmondson upon Peregrine Brown Merchant in London for £50 Sterling and was for the Duty of fifty Pipes of Wine imported from the Island of Fiall & at the Time of the drawing & Delivery of the said Bills the said Edmondson was esteemed to be a responsible Person and your Petitioner indorsed the said Bills to the Trearer who sent them to England for Payment The first Bill was lost at Sea & two years after the second came in protested & then Edmondson was dead & so much in Debt that his Estate was not sufficient to pay half his Debts & the Executor had paid as far as Assets & beyond it before the Protest came & the Trearer has sued your Petr upon the Protest as Indorser of the said Bill & got Judgment against him. Therefore your Petitioner prays this Honble House that they will take into their Consideration & relieve him in the Premises by releasing him from the said publick Debt, which if he be enforced to pay will be to his utter Ruin.

And your Petitioner will pray &ca

Which being read was ordered to be indorsed as followeth

By the House of Delegates May the 18th 1705

Upon reading the within Petition the Matter therein contained was taken into Consideration & fully debated in the House. It's resolved Nemine contradicente that the Petitioner Thomas Collier be fully & absolutely released from the Debt & Damages of the Judgment recovered against him in the Petition set forth the said Collier making Satisfaction for the Costs of Suit only whereof Colo Thomas Smithson the Trearer is to take due Notice

Signed ꝑ Order
W Taylard Cl. Ho. Del.

Lib. 41.   The Concurrence of his Excellency the Governor & th
P. 25 Hon^ble Council to the above Resolves of this House i
prayed.          Signed p Order W. Taylard Cl Ho. Del.

The House adjourns till 2 O'Clock in the Afternoon.

### Post Meridiem

The House met again according to Adjournment & Being
called over were all present as in the Morning & John Conte
took his Place.

The Message this Day by Thomas Tench & John Ham
mond Esq^r was read & ordered to be entered Viz.

By his Excellency the Governor & Council in Assembly
Die Veneris 18^th Die May 1705

Gents. The several Papers herewith sent will serve t
acquaint your House with what Disturbance has been give
the Country by the Means of Richard Clarke of Ann Arunde
County & his Accomplices with their horrid Projects & trea
sonable Contrivances which we desire you will maturel
consider & advise how to prevent & secure the Province fror
such Disturbances & future Injuries so long carried on an
so plainly threatned          Signed p Order
                              W Bladen Cl. Council.

Likewise was read Several Papers & Depositions relating t
the said Clarke the Consideration whereof is further referre
Thomas Ennalls & William Coursey Esq^rs from the Counc
enter the House and delivers M^r Speaker a Petition of Robi
Indian & Chief of the Indians belonging to the Indian Tow
at the Head of the Indian River in Somerset County con
plaining of being disturbed and expulsed from their sever
Settlements &^ta and praying a Confirmation of their ow
settled Town; indorsed as follows viz.

By his Excellency the Governor & Council in Assembly

peaceable Possession of the one thousand Acres of Land Lib. 41.
according to their Petition           Signed ꝑ Order
                                W Bladen Cl. Council.

Which being here read Ordered it be thus indorsed viz.

By the House of Delegates May the 18ᵗʰ 1705

Upon reading the above Petition the House resolves that a
Warrant be sent to the Queen's Surveyor of Somerset County
to lay out one thousand Acres of Land for the Petitioners
where they are now Settled and return Cert. of the Bounds
thereof to this House that it may be settled upon the Petitioners &ᵗᵃ if his Excellency & Council think fit to concur
therewith           Signed ꝑ Order  W Taylard Cl. Ho. Del.

Sent up to the Council by Major John Taylor & Mʳ John
Waters.   They return & say they delivered the same.
   The Answer to his Excellency's Speech being brought into
the House was read & approved of and ordered to be
entered Viz.

By the House of Delegates May the 18ᵗʰ 1705.

May it Please your Excellency,                               p. 26
   We her Majesty's dutiful & loyal Subjects the Representa-
tives of the several Counties of her Majesty's Province of
Maryland now convened in a general Assembly do give yʳ
Ex'cy our hearty Thanks for your gracious Speech made to
us at the Opening of this Sessions; and do assure your
Excellency, that we are now, and shall be at all Times ready
to the utmost of our Abilities to join with your Ex'cy & the
Honᵇˡᵉ Council in whatsoever shall be reasonably proposed to
prevent Rebellions & Disturbances and to settle & establish
Peace & Tranquility which so much concerns her Majesty's
Honour & our own Good & Welfare.   And in Order thereunto we are resolved to enquire into the Particulars of the
Magazine how much Powder and other Materials has been
provided for the publick Use & to whom it has been delivered & how & what is become of it.
   Sʳ  We have already had abundant Assurance of your Excellency's great Justice & Candour towards us, but we beg
Leave to tell you that you've created in us new Motives to
thank you for the Promise you've made to us.  What is
seperated for the publick Use shall not be disposed of to any

31

Lib. 41. other Use whatsoever And we do heartily assure your Ex'cy that there shall not be any Thing wanting in in Its that may promote her Majesty's Honour, the publick Peace & Tranquility of this her Majesty's Province & the Depression of all Vice & Immorality whatsoever.                      Signed ꝑ Order
W. Taylard Cl. Ho. Del.

Which being read is ordered to be sent up to his Excellency & Council ꝑ Mr Geo. Muschamp, Mr James Hay, Mr John Contee, Mr Thomas Frisby, Mr John Macclaster, Colo William Pearce, Mr John Jones, Mr William Aisquith, Mr Thomas Beale, Mr Francis Dallahyde, Mr John Leach, & Mr Peter Watts.
They return & say they delivered the same.
Ordered the following Message be read.

### By the House of Delegates May the 18th 1705

We her Majesty's dutiful & loyal Subjects the Representatives of the several Counties within this her Majesty's Province of Maryland do give your Excellency our hearty Thanks for the great Care that you have taken relating to the Indians and other Matters which has so much disturbed our Peace & Repose.  And we do assure your Ex'cy that your prudent Conduct therein has given us an entire Satisfaction of your Goodness & Generosity towards us which we hope you will upon all Occasions be pleased to repeat
Signed ꝑ Order W Taylard Cl. Ho. Del.

Which being read is approved of by the House and ordered that the above Gentlemen (Colo Pearce excepted) carry the same up to his Excellency in Council
They return & say they delivered their Message.
The Honble Thomas Tench, Thomas Brooke, John Hammond, Edward Lloyd & James Saunders and Thomas Ennalls Esqrs from the Council enter the House and deliver Mr Speaker the following Message which being read is ordered to be entered as follows Viz.

### May the 18th 1705

p. 27    Gent.  If I have or can do any Thing for the Advantage & Welfare of this her Majesty's Province & the Safety & Prosperity of every Individual Member thereof your kind Acceptance makes the fullest Recompence immaginable to
Yr assured Friend Jo. Seymour.

The Hoñble John Hammond & Edward Lloyd Esq<sup>rs</sup> from Lib. 41.
the Council enters the House and delivers a Message relating
to the publick Arms.

Read and referred till the Morning for Consideration

The House adjourned till 7 O'Clock to Morrow Morning

### Dies Saturni  May the 19<sup>th</sup> 1705

The House met again according to Adjournment & were
all present as Yesterday

Read what was done Yesterday

The Petition of William Josephs of Prince George's County
praying Leave to bring in a Bill to make Valid a Lre of
Attorney from his Father was read in the House.

Whereupon the said Josephs is ordered to attend the House.

M<sup>r</sup> Josephs appears & produces his Papers Whereupon he
is ordered to withdraw

And ordered M<sup>r</sup> Nicholas Lowe & M<sup>r</sup> John Contee inspect
his Powers & Proofs thereof as is set forth in the Petition and
that they forthwith make Report thereof to the Powers &
Authorities therein given the said Josephs are full, sufficient
& legal.

The Message Yesterday by Col° Ennalls & M<sup>r</sup> William
Coursey Read & ordered to be entered Viz.

### By the Council in Assembly, Die Veneris 18<sup>th</sup> May 1705

The two Letters herewith sent you are from M<sup>r</sup> Micajah
Perry a worthy Merchant who wishes this Province extremely
well; If they give you Sufficient Reason to believe your Neighbours were apprehensive of any Encroachment from New York
we hope none will have Reason to think we have been too
vigilant for our Security ag<sup>t</sup> any such Attempt

Signed ꝑ Order.   W Bladen Cl Council.

Upon which it was ordered the said Letters be read.  A
Letter dated at London Jañry 27<sup>th</sup> 1704 directed to his Excellency Col° John Seymour her Majesty's Lieutenant General &
Governour of Maryland and another of the same Date from
the same Gentleman directed to his Excellency the Governor
of Virginia.

Upon reading whereof the Matters therein contained are
referred for further Consideration.

Moved by a Member that some Work of Window Frames,
Door Cases and other Matters about the rebuilding the Stadt
House are defective; therefore ordered that Col° Edward

Lib. 41. Dorsey, M^r Edward Blay, M^r John Leach, M^r John Wates, and M^r John Jones view and inspect the same and mae Report thereof forthwith that the House may proceed accod-ingly.  A Copy whereof was delivered them.

p. 28   Bill for making valid a Lre of Attorney from William Josehs Esq^r to William Josephs his Son, Read the first and secnd Times and by especial Order do pass.

The Hoñble Thomas Tench, John Hammond, Francis Jn-kins, William Coursey and Thomas Ennalls Esq^s from he Council enters the House and delivers M^r Speaker the fobw-ing Libel and Message therewith viz.

My Friends.  I have thought fit to advise you to take are in Time to defend yourselves from that wicked Contrivance of Darnall and the Popish Priests in their agreeing wit the French & the other Heathens to destroy you all.  Th Pro-ceedings of Maryland are easily brought to us over Patownack River Can any People think that the Queen sent a Govrnor amongst you to be ruled by Darnall or any other Papist We hear that an Act of Assembly was made against the opish Priests to blind the People ; but how long was it befor they had Liberty, and the Protestant Ministers Silenced.  lave a Care of a Popish Plot lest you have Cause to repent wen it's too late.  This from a Friend is all present
To the Protestants of Maryland

By his Excellency the Governor and Council in Assmbly
Die Veneris 18^th May 1705

The above is a Copy of a scandalous & seditious Lrel pub-lished in S^t Mary's County to the great Dissatisfactio of her Majesty's Loyal good Subjects but more especiall with a malicious Intent to render the Administration of the Govern-ment here odious and Suspected.  You cannot but rmember that what was done in Order to checking or restraiing the Extravagances of the Popish Priests came first frm your House, and had the ready Assent of his Excellenc and this Board So likewise what was done the last Sessios in Sus-pending the Execution thereof for 18 Months was fst moved in your House and represented by you as reasonžle to this Board wherefore we doubt not your Candour in publickly resenting so base and unjust an Abuse & Calurry of his Excellency & this Board as by the said Libel is offezd against il^m,m    Signed p Order W Bladen Cl ouncil.

Which being read the House refers it to furthe onsidera-tion.

Proposed whether it be not absolutely necessary to advance [...]
an additional Duty of Six Pence ⅌ Hhd to help defray the
Charge of building the Provincial Court House being a former
vote reassumed?

Put to the Vote whether a Bill shall be brought in for that
Purpose or not

Carryed by a Majority of Votes that a Bill be brought in
for that Purpose.

The Bill to confirm William Josephs Lee of Attorney in his
Son, sent up ⅌ Mr Thomas Frisby and Mr William Stone to
the Council for their Concurrence

They return and say they delivered their Bill

The Hon^ble James Sanders Esq^r from the Council enters
the House and delivers Mr Speaker the following Message Viz.

By his Excellency the Governor & Council
Die Saturni 19^th May 1725

We propose if your House think fit that the better prevent- ... 
ing the Goal of Annapolis being at any time for the future
broke or the Prisoners overreaching the Goaler that a small
strong Wooden Lodge be added to one of the Doors wherein
the Goaler may & shall be obliged to lye every Night & this
may be done at a small Charge not exceeding six Pounds
Sterling or fifteen hundred Pounds of Tobacco
Signed ⅌ Order W Bladen Cl. Council

Which being read was ordered to be thus indorsed

By the House of Delegates May the 19^th 1725

This House having debated the within Message think it
convenient that such an Addition be made to the Prison but
not at the Publick Charge
Signed ⅌ Order W Taylard Cl. Ho. Del.

The Petition of Col^l William Holland read and finding it is
a Matter relating to the Bounds of Land therefore it's referred
to Consideration of next Assembly

William Holland Esq^r from the Honourable Council enters
the House and delivers Mr Speaker the following Message Viz.

By the Council in Assembly Die Saturni 19^th May 1725

The several Articles with the Nations of Indians on the
Eastern Shore are herewith sent you for your Approbation
& Advice what you think further proper to be added thereto
Signed ⅌ Order W Bladen Cl. Council

Lib. 41. Dorsey, M^r Edward Blay, M^r John Leach, M^r John Waters, and M^r John Jones view and inspect the same and make Report thereof forthwith that the House may proceed accordingly.  A Copy whereof was delivered them.

p. 28    Bill for making valid a Lre of Attorney from William Josephs Esq^r to William Josephs his Son, Read the first and second Times and by especial Order do pass.      .

The Hoñble Thomas Tench, John Hammond, Francis Jenkins, William Coursey and Thomas Ennalls Esq^s from the Council enters the House and delivers M^r Speaker the following Libel and Message therewith viz.

My Friends.  I have thought fit to advise you to take Care in Time to defend yourselves from that wicked Contrivance of Darnall and the Popish Priests in their agreeing with the French & the other Heathens to destroy you all.   The Proceedings of Maryland are easily brought to us over Patowmack River Can any People think that the Queen sent a Governor amongst you to be ruled by Darnall or any other Papist.   We hear that an Act of Assembly was made against the Popish Priests to blind the People ; but how long was it before they had Liberty, and the Protestant Ministers Silenced.   Have a Care of a Popish Plot lest you have Cause to repent when it's too late.   This from a Friend is all present
    To the Protestants of Maryland

By his Excellency the Governor and Council in Assembly
Die Veneris 18^th May 1705

The above is a Copy of a scandalous & seditious Libel published in S^t Mary's County to the great Dissatisfaction of her Majesty's Loyal good Subjects but more especially with a malicious Intent to render the Administration of the Government here odious and Suspected.   You cannot but remember that what was done in Order to checking or restraining the Extravagances of the Popish Priests came first from your House, and had the ready Assent of his Excellency and this Board So likewise what was done the last Sessions in Suspending the Execution thereof for 18 Months was first moved in your House and represented by you as reasonable to this Board wherefore we doubt not your Candour in publickly resenting so base and unjust an Abuse & Calumny of his Excellency & this Board as by the said Libel is offered against them          Signed ꝑ Order  W Bladen Cl. Council.

Which being read the House refers it to further Consideration.

Proposed whether it be not absolutely necessary to advance Lib. 41. an additional Duty of Six Pence ȸ Hhd to help defray the Charge of building the Provincial Court House being a former vote reassumed?

Put to the Vote whether a Bill shall be brought in for that Purpose or not

Carryed by a Majority of Votes that a Bill be brought in for that Purpose.

The Bill to confirm William Josephs Lre of Attorney to his Son, sent up ȸ Mr Thomas Frisby and Mr William Stone to the Council for their Concurrence

They return and say they delivered their Bill

The Honble James Sanders Esqr from the Council enters the House and delivers Mr Speaker the following Message Viz.

By his Excellency the Governor & Council
Die Saturni 19th May 1705.

We propose if your House think fit that the better prevent- p. 29 ing the Goal of Annapolis being at any Time for the future broke or the Prisoners oversetting the Goaler that a small strong Wooden Lodge be added to one of the Doors wherein the Goaler may & shall be obliged to lye every Night & this may be done at a small Charge not exceeding six Pounds Sterling or fifteen hundred Pounds of Tobacco

Signed ȸ Order W Bladen Cl. Council.

Which being read was ordered to be thus indorsed

By the House of Delegates May the 19th 1705

This House having debated the within Message think it convenient that such an Addition be made to the Prison but not at the Publick Charge.

Signed ȸ Order W Taylard Cl. Ho. Del.

The Petition of Colo William. Holland read, and finding it is a Matter relating to the Bounds of Land; therefore it's referred to Consideration of next Assembly.

William Holland Esq from the Honourable Council enters the House and delivers Mr Speaker the following Message Viz.

By the Council in Assembly Die Saturni 19th May 1705

The several Articles with the Nations of Indians on the Eastern Shore are herewith sent you for your Approbations & Advice, what you think further proper to be added thereto

Signed ȸ Order W Bladen Cl. Council

Upon reading the Articles of Peace this House ordered the following Message to be prepared & sent up to the Council Viz.

By the House of Delegates  May the 19ᵗʰ 1705.

May it please your Excellency,
  This House does very well approve of the several Articles made with the Indians & sent to this House & they have not to add to the same
                    Signed ꝑ Order  W. Taylard Cl. Ho. Del.

  Sent up to his Excy & Council by Mʳ John Wells & Mʳ James Philips
  .. They return & say they delivered their Message
  Bill for Naturalization of Christ. Dangerman of Calvert County Read ꝑ Order of the House the first & second Time & do pass.
  The Gentlemen appointed to inspect & view some Carpenters Work began upon rebuilding the Stadt House enters the House and reports as follows Viz.

May the 19ᵗʰ 1705

  We appointed as abovesaid do report that the Frame of the
p. 30 Stadt House what is done appears to be done in workman like manner and that the Door Cases are tolerable but a Defect in the Brick work over the Front Porch Doors but that . the Window Frames are so bad & green Timber some with the Bark on & most sham wedged & not one squared and will when shrunk drop to pieces & consequently not fit for that House is the Report of Edward Dorsey, John Leach, Edward Blay, John Waters & John Jones.
  Which Report being read it's ordered that Mʳ William Bladen the Undertaker appear before the House on Monday Morning next.

  The House adjourned till two o'Clock in the Afternoon

Post Meridiem

  The House met again according to Adjournment, & all present as in the Morning
  Bill for Naturalization of Christ. Dangerman sent up to the Council ꝑ Mʳ James Hay and Mʳ John Jones for Concurrence.
  They return and say they delivered the Bill.
  The following Message being prepared ordered to be entered Viz.

By the House of Delegates May the 19<sup>th</sup> 1705     Lib. 41.

Resolves of the House humbly offered his Excellency as follows

Whereas it appears to this House that there has been a treasonable Combination between Richard Clark of Ann Arundel County and divers others evil Persons to draw down the Indi<sup>a</sup> upon the Inhabitants of this Province & to levy war ag<sup>t</sup> her Majesty's Governor & Government; it's Resolved therefore by the House That her Majesty's Attorney General do forthwith prosecute the said Clarke & all other his Accomplices for the said Crimes to the utmost Extent of the Law And the said Attorney is directed to do the same accordingly. Resolved That this House will enter into Examination of what Magazine Stores has been provided and set apart for the publick Use & Defence of this Province during the Time that Col° Blackiston was Governor; how & what is become of it &<sup>ta</sup>

Resolved That this House will upon all Occasions heartily join in Concert with the Honble her Majesty's Council to support her Majesty's Government here and the Honour & Reputation of his Excellency the present Governor

Resolved That the Paper directed to the Protestants of Maryland and which is now laid before this House is a scandalous and seditious Libel and that Att<sup>y</sup> Gen<sup>l</sup> do prosecute the Writer, Contriver & Publisher thereof & every of them. And the said Att<sup>y</sup> is ord<sup>r</sup> by this House to prosecute the same to the utmost Extent of the Law accordingly

Signed ꝑ Order. W. Taylard Cl. Ho. Del.

Which being read was approved of and ordered Major p. 31 Thomas Taylor, M<sup>r</sup> Joseph Grey, M<sup>r</sup> Joseph Ennalls & M<sup>r</sup> John Macclaster carry the same up to his Excellency and Council

They return and say they delivered the same.

Likewise ordered the following Message be prepared Viz. and entered

By the House of Delegates May the 19<sup>th</sup> 1705

May it please your Excellency

We return you our hearty Thanks for communicating to us M<sup>r</sup> Perry's Letter relating the State of New York Affairs as to this Province and which is very agreeable to us Sir, this has given us new Assurance of your Care & Watchfulness to improve every Thing that may tend to our Advantage and we are sensible of this great Blessing which we humbly pray

Lib. 41. may upon all such Occasions be continued to us & do now
lay hold on this Opportunity to assure your Excellency that
as we can have none so we will entertain none other Interests
than such which may promote her Majesty's Honour and your
Excellency's Fame & Reputation.

Signed p Order    W Taylard Cl Ho. Del.

Which being read & approved of Ordered That M^r John
Mackall, M^r John Wells, M^r William Stone, M^r John Waters,
M^r Robert Tyler & M^r Peter Watts carry the same up to the
Council. They return & say they delivered their Message.

The House adjourns till seven O'Clock on Monday Morning next.

### Die Lune May the 24^th 1705

The House again met according to Adjournment And being
called over were all present as on Saturday; only M^r Joseph
Ennalls; gone sick

Read what was done on Saturday

The Report of the Gentlemen appointed to view the Work
on the Court House was again read and lyes under Consideration of the House.

Ordered M^r William Bladen attend the House. He appears and M^r Speaker informs him of the said Report; to
which M^r Bladen made some Answer and desired the House
again to app^t the same Gent. to go with him & make further
Inspection into the Work Which being granted & ordered by
the House they withdrew for that Purpose

M^r Samuel Magruder a Member for Prince George's County
being absent from the House this Session & not sent any
Excuse for the same.

Resolved That the Serjeant attendant immediately go for
him & bring him before this House & that he satisfy the
Messenger for his Charge & Trouble in going

The Business relating to the Indians lying under Consideration of the House It is resolved That M^r Robert Goulds-
p. 32 borough, Major Charles Greenberry and Major Nicholas Lowe
draw up a Message to be sent his Excellency in Answer to
the Message of the Council relating to the same.

Ordered M^r Thomas Frisby and M^r John Mackall carry up
to the Council Thomas Collier's Petition for their Concurrence.
They return and say they delivered the same.

A Message relating to the scandalous Libel being prepared
& brought into the House was here read & ord^d to be entered
as follows Viz.

By the House of Delegates May the 21ˢᵗ 1705

In Answer to the Message relating to the Libel this House resolves that the Charging your Exᶜʸ with any Confederacy or being ruled or prevailed on by Colᵒ Darnall or any other Papist whatsoever is a most pernicious scandalous & seditious Libel tending to the Destruction of her Majesty's Government here & is a great Scandal to yʳ Excy's Fame & Reputation This House being very sensible that the Bill against the Papal Religion and also that Bill to indulge them or to suspend the Execution of the former Bill began both in this House and were sent from us to your Ex'cy and the Honble her Majesty's Council for your Concurrence & Assent thereunto And we do pray your Honour to be assured from us that we will omit nothing that may be fit & proper for us to do to protect and assert her Majesty's Government and your Excellency's Justice & Innocence in this Matter and to shew our utmost Resentment against such pestilent Disturbers of this Government and bringing them to condign Punishment.

Signed ꝑ Order   T. Taylard Cl. Ho. Del.

Mʳ Robert Goldsborough, Mʳ William Frisby and Mʳ John Hudson and Mʳ John Taylor ordered to carry up the said Message to his Excellency & Council

They return & say they delivered their Message

The Gentlemen appointed to view the Stadt House work enter the House and informs them that they cannot recede from their former Report on Saturday. Upon which its Resolved by the House That all those Window Frames already set up be taken down and other good & sufficient Window Frames be set in their Room made of well seasoned Timber.

Mʳ John Taylor sent up to the Council with Journals & Papers relating to the Indians and all Papers about Clarke & Cely.

Bill for Relief of Ann Arundel County read 1ˢᵗ Time

Petition of Alexander Hall on behalf of Sʳ Thomas Lawrence Secretary praying an Allowance for recording the Body of the Laws of Octo. & Decem. Assembly being read.

Ordered twelve hundred Pounds of Tobacco be allowed him next Levy therefor

The Petition of Matthew Beard praying Allowance for looking after & taking Care of the publick Arms & Ammunition for nine Months was read. The Consideration whereof is further referred till some Journals be inspected.

Bill confirming a certain Letter of Attorney from William p. 33 Joseph Esqʳ to William Joseph his Son indorsed in Council 21ˢᵗ May 1705.   Read the first Time

W Bladen Cl. Council.

Lib. 41. Read the first & second Times ꝑ especial Order & will pass
W Taylard Cl Ho. Del.

Ordered the same Bill be carryed up to his Excellency by
Capᵗ Richard Jones
The House adjourns till 2 O'Clock Afternoon

Post Meridiem

The House met again according to adjournment.
Being called over were all present as in the Morning.
It being moved by a Member that it's supposed through the
Negligence of the Sheriff of Ann Arundel County that an
Indian Heathen Enemy and another Criminal made their
Escape out of the Prison of the said County and forasmuch as
this House finds it to be of ill Consequence, therefore Resolved
That the Sheriff of the said County be commanded to give his
Attendance at the Bar of this House tomorrow morning by
Eight O'Clock to answer to what may be objected against
him for such an Escape.

Resolved That Jacob Cole, John Murray, Stephen Ross &
George Hicks be allowed six Shillings a piece for their Service
in going for Mʳ Speaker and ordered That Mʳ Samuel Young
Treasurer for the Western Shore immediately Satisfy & pay
the same for which this Order shall be a Warrant

Major Nicholas Lowe, Mʳ Charles Greenberry, Mʳ William
Stone & Mʳ Hugh Ecclestone are by the House appointed a
Committee of Laws.

The following Message being prepared was read & ordered
to be entered Viz.

By the House of Delegates May the 21ˢᵗ 1705

May it please your Exᶜy.

You having commanded that a hundred Men shall be at all
Times ready at the Command of each Col° in each respective
County to be raised for the Country's Service upon any Expedition 'tis proposed to your Excellency & the Honᵇle Council
by this House that a proportionable Quantity of Arms, Powder
and Ball be lodged in the Custody of each Col° out of the
Magazine Stores that the men may be ready furnished therewith upon any such Expedition and that your Excellency would
be pleased to give sufficient Orders to each respective Col°
that upon any Motion or Action of the Indians those Men so
raised may presently march against them that no Time may
be lost. This we are of Opinion will tend much to the quieting
of the Inhabitants and the Security of the Frontier Plantations
Signed ꝑ Order W Taylard Cl. Ho. Del.

And another Message being approved of by the House was Lib. 41. ordered to be entered as foll. viz.

By the House of Delegates May 21ˢᵗ 1705

May it please your Excellency.

This House proposes to the Consideration of your Excy & her P. 34 Majesty's Honble Council as an Expedient to our future Quiet that your Excellency commissionate such Persons and as many as you in your wisdom shall think fit to treat with and renew our former Alliances & Friendship with the Seneca & other Indians on the Western Shore and to use the best Methods they can think on to discover the Murtherers of our Fellow Subjects this being the most easy & ready Method we can think on and therefore we do pray your Concurrence herein &ᵗᵃ
Signed ꝑ Order W Taylard Cl Ho. Del.

Ordered Mʳ Muschamp, Mʳ Maclaster & Mʳ John Jones carry up the above Messages up to his Excellency.

Bill for Relief of Ann Arundel County read the 2ᵈ Time & do pass.

Ordered Mʳ Richard Jones & Mʳ Thomas Frisby carry up the said Bill up to his Excellency & Council for their Concurrence

They return & say they delivered it.

The Honble Thomas Tench, Esqʳ John Hammond Esqʳ and William Coursey Esqʳ from the Honble Council enters the House and delivers Mʳ Speaker a Petition of the Guards for their Pay together with a Message relating to the same. Referred till to Morrow Morning for Consideration

A Message prepared being read and approved of by the House ordered the same be entered Viz.

By the House of Delegates May 21ˢ 1705

May it please your Excellency

This House prays Leave to represent to your Excy & her Majesty's Honble Council that they are hugely impaired and prejudiced in their Interests and the whole Province much impoverished by the Traders who come hither, by single Ships one after another before the general Fleet appointed to come hither And if they are suffered to depart as soon as they are loaden they will be in Danger of the Enemy to be taken and so will feed them thereby prejudicing her Majesty's Interests, and if they get safe serve no other End but their own but ruin the Market as to others and is a direct Prejudice to her

Lib. 41. Majesty's Subjects here Therefore we do humbly pray your Excellency that no Ships or Vessels bound for Europe with Tobacco may be cleard until a Sufficient Convoy shall appear to take Care & Charge of them homeward or until such Time as y$^r$ Excy in your Wisdom shall seem meet

Signed ꝑ Order W Taylard Cl. Ho. Del

Ordered M$^r$ John Maclaster, M$^r$ John Hudson, M$^r$ John Taylor and M$^r$ Thomas How carry up the foregoing Message to his Excy & Council.

p. 35    The Honble Thomas Tench Esq$^r$ from the Council enters the House and delivers M$^r$ Speaker, Bill for Naturalization of Christopher Dangerman ; Indorsed, Eodem Die

Read in Council the 1$^{st}$ & second Times & do pass.

W Bladen Cl Council.

And likewise delivered M$^r$ Carroll's Memorial relating to the Land Office with a Message relating thereto.    The Consideration whereof is referred till the Morning

The House adjourns till to Morrow Morning Seven O'Clock.

Die Martis May the 22$^d$ 1705

The House met again according to Adjournment.

Being called over were all present as Yesterday only M$^r$ Ennalls gone Home sick

Read what was done Yesterday.

Ordered That John Dally be sent for as Evidence upon Escape of the Indians.

The Representation of M$^r$ Charles Carroll brought into the House last Night was read as followeth.

May the 15$^{th}$ 1705

May it please your Excellency,

I humbly crave Leave to mind your Excy of a Letter writ by the Lords Commissioners of Trade & Plantations to this Governm$^t$ relating to the wrongs done to the Lord Proprietor in and by a Law Entituled an Act for ascertaining the Bounds of Land and that no Answer has been given thereunto as yet to the great Delay of doing his Ldship Justice in Matters so apparently injurious to his Ldships Property I thought this the most proper Time (the Assembly sitting) to give your Excy this Intimation that by the next Return of Ships for England I may be capable of informing his Lordship what shall be done

here in Reference to that Affair.   I beg your Excy's Pardon Lib. 41.
for this Presumption and remain

Your Excellency's Most Hble Serv<sup></sup>
Cha<sup>s</sup> Carroll.

Together with the above came the following Message Viz.

Die Lune 21<sup>st</sup> May 1705

Gents.
Herewith is sent you the Lords Baltimore's Agents Memorial or Representation relating to the Land Law of which you are desired to consider & return some Answer thereto

Signed p Order  W Bladen Cl. Council

Whereupon Ordered it be answered as follows Viz.

By the House of Delegates May 22<sup>d</sup> 1705

Upon reading the Memorial of M<sup>r</sup> Carroll relating to the Land Law & your Honours Message it's considered by the House and resolved that forasmuch as this House at first Opening this Assembly continued all References upon their Journals whereof this being one; therefore this House pray Concurrence & that the same may likewise be referred

Signed p Order  W. Taylard Cl. Ho. Del.

The Petition of the Guards for Allowance read &<sup>ta</sup> Referred to the Committee of Accounts for Allowance.
Bill for outlawry of Richard Clarke &<sup>ta</sup> Read the first & second Times & do pass
And ordered M<sup>r</sup> Francis Dallahyde & M<sup>r</sup> Gerrard Fowlks carry the same up to his Excellency & Council for Concurrence p. 36 and likewise the Message for Referrence of the Land Law. They return & say they delivered the same.
Reviving Bill for Punishment of Persons suborning Witnesses Read the first and second Times & by especial Order do pass.
Reviving Bill declaring an Act ascertaining the Bounds or Land to be in force,  Read the 1<sup>st</sup> & 2<sup>d</sup> Times & do pass
Bill for Punishment of Persons selling or transporting any Friend Indians &<sup>ta</sup> Read the 1<sup>st</sup> & 2<sup>d</sup> Times & do pass
The foregoing Bills were sent up to the Council by M<sup>r</sup> John Taylor & M<sup>r</sup> Watts.
They return & say they delivered their Bills
William Coursey Esq<sup>r</sup> from the Council enters the House & delivers M<sup>r</sup> Speaker the foll. Message Viz.

<sup>Lib. 41.</sup> Majesty's Subjects here Therefore we do humbly pray your
Excellency that no Ships or Vessels bound for Europe with
Tobacco may be cleard until a ufficient Convoy shall appear to
take Care & Charge of them omeward or until such Time as
y<sup>r</sup> Excy in your Wisdom shallseem meet

Signed p Cder W Taylard Cl. Ho. Del

Ordered M<sup>r</sup> John Maclastr, M<sup>r</sup> John Hudson, M<sup>r</sup> John
Taylor and M<sup>r</sup> Thomas How crry up the foregoing Message
to his Excy & Council.

P. 35   The Honble Thomas Tench Esq<sup>r</sup> from the Council enters the
House and delivers M<sup>r</sup> Speake Bill for Naturalization of Chris.
topher Dangerman ; Indorsed Eodem Die

Read in Council the 1<sup>st</sup> & scond Times & do pass.

W Bladen Cl Council.

And likewise delivered M<sup>r</sup> Carroll's Memorial relating to
the Land Office with a Messag relating thereto.   The Consideration whereof is referred Il the Morning

The House adjourns till to Morrow Morning Seven O'Clock.

Die Martis M? the 22<sup>d</sup> 1705

The House met again accorcng to Adjournment.

Being called over were all present as Yesterday only M<sup>r</sup>
Ennalls gone Home sick

Read what was done Yesteray.

Ordered That John Dally e sent for as Evidence upon
Escape of the Indians.

The Representation of M<sup>r</sup> Carles Carroll brought into the
House last Night was read as lloweth.

May the 5<sup>th</sup> 1705

May it please your Excellency,

I humbly crave Leave to mid your Excy of a Letter writ
by the Lords Commissioners c Trade & Plantations to this
Governm<sup>t</sup> relating to the wrong done to the Lord Proprietor
in and by a Law Entituled an At for ascertaining the Bounds
of Land and that no Answer ha been given thereunto as yet
to the great Delay of doing hisLdship Justice in Matters so
apparently injurious to his Ldshos Property I thought this the
most proper Time (the Assemly sitting) to give your Excy
this Intimation that by the next Return of Ships for England
I may be capable of informing hi Lordship what shall be done

here in Reference to that Aïir.  I beg your Excy's Pardon Lib. 41.
for this Presumption and rerain
Your 'xcellency's Most Hble Serv<sup>t</sup>
Cha<sup>s</sup> Carroll.

Together with the above ame the following Message Viz.

Die Lune 21<sup>st</sup> May 1705

Gents.
Herewith is sent you the l)rds Baltimore's Agents Memorial or Representation relatir; to the Land Law of which you
are desired to consider & retrn some Answer thereto
Signed ꝗ Order  W Bladen Cl. Council

Whereupon Ordered it beanswered as follows Viz.

By the House of D:legates May 22<sup>d</sup> 1705

Upon reading the Memo.al of M<sup>r</sup> Carroll relating to the
Land Law & your Honours Message it's considered by the
House and resolved that fcasmuch as this House at first
Opening this Assembly contiued all References upon their
Journals whereof this being ne; therefore this House pray
Concurrence & that the samtmay likewise be referred
Signed ꝗ Order  W. Taylard Cl. Ho. Del.

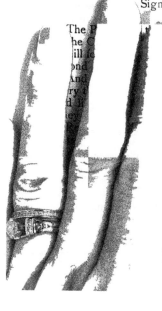

The P ... rds 'or Allowance read &<sup>ta</sup> Referred
he C ... :nt for Allowance.
ill ... iar: Clarke &<sup>ta</sup> Read the first &
ond
And ... s l.llahyde & M<sup>r</sup> Gerrard Fowlks
ry ... ce ;ncy & Council for Concurrence p. 36
d li ... : fc Referrence of the Land Law.
... :livred the same.
... ishn nt of Persons suborning Wit-
... 1 secnd Times & by especial Order

... ȝ an .ct ascertaining the Bounds or
... id thet<sup>st</sup> & 2<sup>d</sup> Times & do pass
... : Persns selling or transporting any
... d the ' & 2<sup>d</sup> Times & do pass
... 'ere set up to the Council by M<sup>r</sup> John

... ney del ered their Bills
... ;q<sup>r</sup> from the Council enters the House
... ' the fol Message Viz.

Die Lune 21ˢᵗ May 1705 By the Council in Assembly
Gent.

In Answer to your last Message by Mʳ Maclaster & other
Members of your House his Ex'cy & this Board have already
done what in them lies to remedy the Evil by your House
represented in lying a general Embargo upon all Shipping
until a sufficient Convoy arrives from England the **Strumbelo**
not being thought Sufficient.

Signed ꝑ Order   W Bladen Cl. Council

Ordered That Mʳ Samuel Young Treasurer immediately
purchase a Roll of Parchment for the publick Service for
which he shall be allowed.

Ordered That John Dalley be called into the House to
declare what he knows about the Escape of Prisoners.
Having so done, it's ordered he withdraw and Mʳ George
Valentine ordered to be called in to show to the House by
what Means he became Keeper of the Prison ; who made it
known & withdrew

The Honble Edward Lloyd & William Coursey Esqʳˢ enters
the House & delivers Mʳ Speaker the Petition of Thomas
Collyer indorsed viz.

By his Ex'cy the Governor & Council in Assembly

May the 21ˢᵗ 1705

This Board do concur with the Resolve of the House of
Delegates that the said Mʳ Collier be eased & released from
the Payment of the said Bill protested.

Signed ꝑ Order   W Bladen Cl. Council

And likewise brought in a Bill confirming a Letter of Attʸ
from Josephs &ᵗᵃ Indorsed.

May 22ᵈ 1705.   Read in Council & past

W Bladen Cl. Council.

James Saunders Esqʳ from the Honble Council enters the
House & delivers the following Bills.

Reviving Bill punishing ꝑsons Suborning Witnesses Indorsed.  Eodem Die Read in Council & agreed to.

W Bladen Cl. Council

Reviving Bill erecting Ann Arundel & Oxford Towns into
Ports & Towns

Eodem Die   Read in Council and agreed to.

W Bladen Cl Council.

Reviving Bill for punishing Persons selling or transporting Lib. 41. any Friend Indians. Indorsed Eodem Die. Read in Coun- P. 37 cil & agreed to. W Bladen Cl. Council.

Reviving Bill for ascertaining the Bounds of Land Indorsed Eod. Die. Read in Council and agreed to
W Bladen Cl Council.

Bill for Relief of Ann Arundel County Indorsed Eod. Die. Read in Council & agreed to ، W Bladen Cl Council.

Bill against Richard Clarke sent up to the Council by M$^r$ Robert Goldsborough and M$^r$ James Hay. They return & say they delivered the same.

The Hoñble James Saunders Esq$^r$ from the Council enters the House and delivers M$^r$ Speaker the following Message Viz. Die Martis 22° Die Maij 1705

Proposed That the House will appoint some of their Members to confer with four of the Board in Relation to the Prisoners now in Goal the present Guard on the publick Magazine and Prison and the Rangers on the Frontiers of Potowmack what shall be done with the said Prisoners whether the Guard on the Magazine & Prison and the Rangers on Potowmack shall be longer continued upon these Services & what Number, or to be totally disbanded.

Signed ꝑ Order W Bladen Cl. Council.

Which being read the following Message was ordered to be returned in Answer to it

By the House of Del &$^{ta}$ 22$^d$ May 1705

Gent.

In Answer to your Honours Message p$^r$ M$^r$ Saunders proposing a Conference with four of your Board this House concurs therewith and have appointed six Members to attend the said Conference accordingly therefore this House desires you will appoint the Time & Place.

Signed ꝑ Order W Taylard Cl Ho. Del.

Major Lowe ⎫ Col° Smallwood ⎫
M$^r$ Contee ⎬ M$^r$ Tyler ⎬ Which was sent up to the
Col° Dorsey ⎭ M$^r$ Goldsborough ⎭ Council by M$^r$ Goldsborough and M$^r$ James Hay. They return & say they delivered their Message. Pursuant to the Order of the House yesterday M$^r$ John Gresham Sheriff made his Appearance and being

Lib. 41. charged for the negligent Escape of the Prisoners &ᵗᵃ he desired some Time to advise with Council in the Matter which was granted by the House and ordered he appear again to Morrow Morning.

Eight Bills deliv'ed Mʳ Charles Greenberry to be ingrossed The House adjourns till two O'Clock Afternoon.

### Post Meridiem

The House again met according to Adjournment

Being called over were present as in the morning

The Hoñble John Hammond Esqʳ from the Council enters the House & acquaints Mʳ Speaker that the Gentlemen of the Conferrence ordered this Day is now at the House of Mʳ Benjamin Fordham and desire that the Gentlemen of this House will attend them immediately.

p. 38    Ordered That Mʳ Robert Goldsborough, Mʳ John Contee, Colº Edward Dorsey, Mʳ Nicholas Lowe, Colº James Smallwood and Mʳ Robert Tyler attend the Conference ordered in the morning  The Petition of Cadwaller Edwards Joyner · praying Allowance for building the publick Pews being indorsed Viz. Die Martis 22º May 1705  The Petition being read at this Board his Excellency is pleased to say that he did order the Petʳ to erect the said Pews for the Accomodations of the Gentlemen of the House of Delegates and doubt not but they will do the Petitioner Justice.

Signed ℗ Order    W Bladen Cl. Council

Which being read and debated in the House it is ordered the same be endorsed as followeth Viz.

### By the House of Delegates May 22ᵈ 1705

The within Petition of Cadwaller Edwards Joyner was here read and this House took the same into Consideration upon which Inspection being made into the public Accounts do find that he has been allowed ten Pounds Sterling for building the Pews which this House conceive to be a sufficient Satisfaction for the Work and therefore this House do resolve he have no further Allowance              Signed ℗ Order

W. Taylard Cl. Ho. Del.

Sent up by Mʳ Joseph Gray to his Excellency & Council.

He returns and says he delivered the Petition

The Gentlemen appointed to attend the Conference enter the House & made Verbal Report thereof to the House.

The House adjourns till to Morrow Morning Seven o'Clock

Die Mercurij May 23ᵈ 1705

The House met again accordᵍ to Adjournmᵗ. Being called over all present as yesterday. Then was read what was done yesterday

Bill declaring the Act for punishing Persons Suborning Witnesses &ᵗᵃ read & assented to by the House of Delegates

W. Taylard Cl. Ho. Del.

Bill for reviving the Act ascertaining the Bounds of Land &ᵗᵃ Read and assented to by the House of Delegates.

Bill for Relief of Ann Arundel County read and assented to by the House of Delegates

Bill for confirming William Joseph's Letter of Attorney, read & assented to by the House of Delegates

Bill for Punishment of Persons selling Friend Indians &ᵗᵃ read and assented to by the House of Delegates

Bill for Utlary of Richard Clarke, Read and assented to by the House of Delegates

Bill declaring the Act for erecting Ann Arundell & Oxford Towns to be in force.

Read and assented to by the House of Delegates

Bill for Naturalization of Xtopher Dangerman, Read and assented to by the House of Delegates.

Which ingrossed Bills were sent up to the Council by Mʳ Wᵐ Aisquith.

He returns and says he delivered the Bills

The Gentlemen of the Conference enter the House and p. 39 deliver their Report in Writing Viz.

The Report of the Conferees with the Honble Council relating to the Message to this House of the 22ᵈ Instant about the Prisoners in Goal the present Guard on the publick Magazine and Prison & the Rangers on the Frontier

1. Proposed That whereas Benjamin Celey stands now convicted and has Judgment to die that to save his Life a Bill may be brought in to transport him to the West Indies to be sold there for seven years and the Produce to be applied to save the publick Charge.

2. Proposed That whereas Humphry Herman who is now in Prison and has voluntarily confest that he by the Direction & Instigation of his Mistress, Rachel Freeborn, conveyed a File to the Prisoners then in Prison who was enabled to make their Escape that a Bill may be brought in to convict him of this and to transport him Considering that it will be a great Charge to the Province to keep him in Prison till he be tryed and convicted according to the common Methods

32

Lib. 41.    3. That after the Magazine Stores are distributed according to the former Proposal of the House what remains of the Powder &ᵗᵃ may be left to his Excellency's Disposal without the Charge of a Guard.

4. That the Rangers be kept out still as a Guard to the Frontiers and Respect is to be had to Baltimore County where the Indians Incursion is to be feared as much as it is on the Branches of Potowmack until a Peace be actually made and the Alliances & Stipulations renewed & affirmed.

1. Upon which the House proceed to debate the same. As to the first Proposal relating to Celey this House leaves him entirely to his Excellency the Governor to dispose of as he thinks fit.

2. Second Proposal read & put to the Question whether Humphry Herman be attainted by Act of Assembly or left to the Course of the Common Law for Tryal. Carryed by Majority of Votes that he receive his Tryal by due Course of Law.

3. This House concurs with the third Article relating to the Powder

4ᵗʰ Article the House concurs with and resolves That six Men & an Officer be appointed out of Prince George's County and six men and an Officer out of Baltimore County Rangers which being read and debated in the House, Ordered That it be answered by a Message from the House.

The following Message was read & ordered to be entered Viz.

By the House of Delegates May 23ʳᵈ 1705

May it please your Honours,

This House has considered the Message sent to them by your Honours on Monday last relating to the Satisfying of Persons employed upon extraordinary Occasions by his Ex'cy the Governor in her Majesty's & the Country's Service and that to leave them to the Com. of Accᵗˢ to make them Satisfaction for their Services would be too precarious this House has given Directions to the Com. of Accᵗˢ to take particular Care of such deserving Persons and to apportion the Reward as it may in some Degree answer the Expectation of such

p. 40 Persons. And this House is very sensible of his Ex'cy's great Care & tender Regard for the Good & Welfare of the Province and as they shall not do any Thing detracting from his Ex'cy's Honour so they will at all Times be ready to make good such Promises as his Ex'cy shall in the Absence of Assemblys think fit to make to any ꝑson who serves her Majesty or this Government upon such extraordinary Occasions. But as to the giving his Excellency the Trouble to Lib. 41. issue Orders to the Treasurers this House are of Opinion that that Part of the Message is put too General & is altogether needless and they will not intend that your Honours in your wisdoms will insist thereon

Signed ꝑ Order   W. Taylard Cl. Ho. Del.

Which being read was approved of by the House & ordered · M<sup>r</sup> Thomas Frisby M<sup>r</sup> John Jones & M<sup>r</sup> Joseph Gray carry the same up to their Honours.

They return & say they delivered the same.

The following Message being prepared in Answer to the Report of the Conferees being read was ordered to be entered as followeth Viz.

By the House of Delegates 23 May 1705

Upon reading the Report of the Conference yesterday the House proceeded to debate the same. As to Celey this House are of Opinion that the said Celey being now in the Mercy of the Queen there is no need of an Act of Assembly to transport him but leave him entirely to the Disposition of his Excellency the Governor to do with him as he thinks fit.

2. As to the Magazine Stores to be distributed according to the former Proposal and what remains to be left at his Excellency's Disposal without the Charge of a Guard to which this House readily concurred.

3. As to the Proposal concerning the Rangers this House are willing to keep still out and Resolves that six men and an Officer be appointed for Prince George's & six men & an Officer for Baltimore County Rangers

And this House humbly proposes to his Ex'cy the Governor

Mem. Page 35 of the Journal wanting
for w<sup>ch</sup> I leave this Blank.

R. D.

They return & say they delivered the same.      ɔ. 41]

William Coursey Esq<sup>r</sup> from the Honble Council enters the House & delivers M<sup>r</sup> Speaker the following Message.

By the Council in Assembly Die Mercurij 23,° Die May 1705

Whereas Humphry Herman is a principal Evidence against M<sup>rs</sup> Rachel Freeborn now committed for aiding & abetting her Son Richard Clarke in his traiterous Practices and assisting Benjamin Celey to break the Prison we have thought it proper

Lib. 41. to advertise you thereof and tha we do not think it advisable
the said Herman's Evidence no fortifyed with many concurrent Testimonies should be rendred invalid

         Signed p Orer  W Bladen Cl. Council.

    Bill apportioning of the public Levy,  Read the first &
second Time & will pass
    M^r John Gresham, Sheriff of ann Arundel County accord-
ing to Order of the House attended & being called in M^r
Speaker was pleased to acquint him that the House was
informed thro' his Neglect the were several Criminal Prisoners, an Indian Enemy & a hite Criminal Servant made
their Escape out of Prison by nich it appeared to the House
the Province was much damnifd.  Upon which M^r Gresham
offered some Matters in his lefence  Ordered he withdraw
    Thereupon the House tok it into Consideration and
debated the same and having so done the said Gresham was
commanded again to appear ad M^r Speaker was then pleased
to ask him some Questions elating to the said Escape &
acquainted him it was an Offace of a high Nature Upon that
M^r Gresham could give no sasfactory Excuse to the House.
Then he was asked what he cmanded from the Public for the
Prisoners Imprisonment Fee; who answered he knew not
certainly but could soon proace his Account.  Afterwards it
was proposed to him by M^r beaker whether he would release
the Imprisonment Fees of Bnjamin Celey & the other two
that made their Escape.  Tcwhich he readily consented and
did declare he was very willg to discharge the same and in
the House did release all thr Imprisonment Fees.  Whereupon the House again toc the Matters into Consideration
and upon the said Gresham Submission this House do acquit
& discharge the said John Gresham from further Damage
that may arise against him or the Escape aforesaid.  Whecy
upon M^r Gresham returnecis most humble & hearty Thamd
to the House for their Favors & so with r            is-
    The Petition of James Siallwood              wancease
an Horse spoiled going o to th                      ng reallar
allowed by Majority of Vots one                   f Tobaard
Ordered the Committee tae t                            uch
    The following brought it                  as ordcy's
to be read & entered as fc                              the
                              from
                              nake

    Die Mercurij 23^d M                 i Assembe of
    Upon reading the                    her
of the Conferrence,               on the R)cca-
                             rt relatin

Benjamin Celey his Excllency was pleased to declare he is Lib. 41.
thankful to any that pu him in Mind of what he may do but
since that you have no thought fit to Advise how the said p. 42
Celey should be disposd of his Excellency is not inclinable
otherwise than according to the Sentence pronounced against
him which will be execud on Friday next.

Signd p Order W Bladen Cl Council

The aforegoing Mess ge from the Honble Council being
here read this House too it into their serious Consideration
and ordered that the sane be answered by the Message following Viz.

### By the Hous of Del. 23ᵈ May 1705

By the Debates of our House relating to Benjamin Celey
the Prisoner we did not irend to put his Excellency in Mind
of what he might do; but nly asserted the Royal Prerogative
but if the bringing in of a Bill to transport him or any other
Thing which may save his Life may be thought necessary if
you please to signifie it ) us this House will very readily
concur with your Honours 1 any such Proposal we being very
desirous that his Life may 2 saved.

Signed p Order W. Taylard Cl. Ho. Del.

Which being read was wll approved of by the House and
ordered it be sent up to te Council p Mr Robert Tyler, Mr
Joseph Hill, Mr John Mack l, & Mr John Wells. They withdrew; and the House adjou ied till to Morrow Morning seven
O'Clock.

### May 24ᵗʰ 1705

The House according to Hjournment again met and being
called over were all present з Yesterday

 Tyler, Mr Hill, Mr Macall & Mr Wells sent up with the
ge last Night enter the House & say they delivered the
 e given them last Niɡt.

 r Sale of a Parcel of and called Richardson's Choice
 ent of a Debt due t John Nicholls, read the second
 ommitted for Amerdmᵗ

 raising an Impost six Pence p Hhd brought by
 e House and was ead the first & second Time &
 And sent up to his Excellency by Mr John Contee,
 ters, Mr George Iuschamp, Mr Francis Dallahyde
& Hill, Mr John Wlls, Mr Thomas Frisby, Major
Jo  Mr Robert Tylr.

 & say they delrered the same.

Us. &c to advertise you thereof and that we do not think it advisable
the said Herman's Evidence now fortifyed with many concurrent Testimonies should be rendered invalid
                            Signed p Order  W Bladen Cl. Council.

    Bill apportioning of the publick Levy. Read the first &
second Time & will pass
    Mr John Gresham Sheriff of Ann Arundel County accord-
ing to Order of the House attended & being called in Mr
Speaker was pleased to acquaint him that the House was
Informed that his Neglect there were several Criminal Prisoners an Indian Enemy & a white Criminal Servant made
their Escape out of Prison by which it appeared to the House
the Province was much damnified.  Upon which Mr Gresham
offered some Matters in his Defence  Ordered he withdraw
    Thereupon the House took it into Consideration and
debated the same and having so done the said Gresham was
commanded again to appear and Mr Speaker was then pleased
to ask him some Questions relating to the said Escape &
acquainted him it was an Offence of a high Nature Upon tha
Mr Gresham could give no satisfactory Excuse to the House
Then he was asked what he demanded from the Public for th
Prisoners Imprisonment Fees: who answered he knew no
certainty but could soon produce his Account.  Afterwards:
was proposed to him by Mr Speaker whether he would release
the Imprisonment Fees of Benjamin Oxley & the other tw
that made their Escape.  To which he readily consented an
did declare he was very willing to discharge the same and s
the House did release all their Imprisonment Fees.  Where
upon the House again took the Matters into Consideratio
and upon the said Gresham's Submission this House do acqu
& discharge the said John Gresham from further Damage
that may arise against him for the Escape aforesaid.  Where
upon Mr Gresham returned his most humble & hearty Thad
to the House for their Favours & so withdrew.                  ar
    The Petition of James Smallwood praying an Allowance
in Horse spoiled going up to the Indian Fort being read
allowed by Majority of Votes one thousand Pounds of Tobac
Ordered the Committee take Notice thereof                  ch
    The following brought into the House this Day was ord's
to be read & entered as followeth                          he
                                                          pm
                                                          ike

    Die Mercurij 23d May 1705 By the Council in Assembly of
                                                          her
    Upon reading the Debates of your House upon the Rea-
of the Conference yesterday, As to that Part relatin

Bejamin Celey his Excellency was pleased to declare he is Lib. 41.
thankful to any that put him in Mind of what he may do but
sine that you have not thought fit to Advise how the said p. 42
Cely should be disposed of his Excellency is not inclinable
othrwise than according to the Sentence pronounced against
him which will be executed on Friday next.

Signed ꝑ Order W Bladen Cl Council

Te aforegoing Message from the Hoñble Council being
hereread this House took it into their serious Consideration
and ordered that the same be answered by the Message followig Viz.

### By the House of Del. 23ᵈ May 1705

By he Debates of our House relating to Benjamin Celey
the Pisoner we did not intend to put his Excellency in Mind
of wht he might do ; but only asserted the Royal Prerogative
but if he bringing in of a Bill to transport him or any other
Thingwhich may save his Life may be thought necessary if
you plase to signifie it to us this House will very readily
concurwith your Honours in any such Proposal we being very
desirou that his Life may be saved.

Signed ꝑ Order W. Taylard Cl. Ho. Del.

Whin being read was well approved of by the House and
orderedit be sent up to the Council ꝑ Mʳ Robert Tyler, Mʳ
Joseph Iill, Mʳ John Mackall, & Mʳ John Wells. They withdrew ; ad the House adjourned till to Morrow Morning seven
O'Clock

### May 24ᵗʰ 1705

The House according to Adjournment again met and being
M‹ called ovr were all present as Yesterday
for     Mʳ Tyer, Mʳ Hill, Mʳ Mackall & Mʳ Wells sent up with the
Message ist Night enter the House & say they delivered the
Messagegiven them last Night.
   ꞁ    Bill forsale of a Parcel of Land called Richardson's Choice
       for Paymot of a Debt due to John Nicholls, read the second
   ꞁ   Time & cmmitted for Amendmᵗ
       Bill for aising an Impost of six Pence ꝑ Hhd brought by
Order of te House and was read the first & second Time &
do pass. And sent up to his Excellency by Mʳ John Contee,
Mʳ John Vaters, Mʳ George Muschamp, Mʳ Francis Dallahyde
& Mʳ Joseph Hill, Mʳ John Wells, Mʳ Thomas Frisby, Major
John Taylc & Mʳ Robert Tyler.
   ꞁ    They retrn & say they delivered the same.

Lib. 41. to advertise you thereof and that we do not think it advisable
the said Herman's Evidence now fortifyed with many concurrent Testimonies should be rendered invalid

Signed ℗ Order  W Bladen Cl. Council.

Bill apportioning of the publick Levy, Read the first &
second Time & will pass

M⁺ John Gresham, Sheriff of Ann Arundel County according to Order of the House attended & being called in M⁺
Speaker was pleased to acquaint him that the House was
informed thro' his Neglect there were several Criminal Prisoners, an Indian Enemy & a white Criminal Servant made
their Escape out of Prison by which it appeared to the House
the Province was much damnified.   Upon which M⁺ Gresham
offered some Matters in his Defence   Ordered he withdraw

Thereupon the House took it into Consideration and
debated the same and having so done the said Gresham was
commanded again to appear and M⁺ Speaker was then pleased
to ask him some Questions relating to the said Escape &
acquainted him it was an Offence of a high Nature Upon that
M⁺ Gresham could give no satisfactory Excuse to the House.
Then he was asked what he demanded from the Public for the
Prisoners Imprisonment Fees; who answered he knew not
certainly but could soon produce his Account.   Afterwards it
was proposed to him by M⁺ Speaker whether he would release
the Imprisonment Fees of Benjamin Celey & the other two
that made their Escape.   To which he readily consented and
did declare he was very willing to discharge the same and in
the House did release all their Imprisonment Fees.   Whereupon the House again took the Matters into Consideration
and upon the said Gresham's Submission this House do acquit
& discharge the said John Gresham from further Damages
that may arise against him for the Escape aforesaid.   Whereupon M⁺ Gresham returned his most humble & hearty Thanks
to the House for their Favours & so withdrew.

The Petition of James Smallwood praying an Allowance for
an Horse spoiled going up to the Indian Fort being read is
allowed by Majority of Votes one thousand Pounds of Tob⁰a⁰.
Ordered the Committee take Notice thereof.              such

The following brought into the House this Day was ord'cy's
to be read & entered as followeth                         the

from
nake

Die Mercurij 23ᵈ May 1705 By the Council in Assemb.ᵉ oʃ
he:
Upon reading the Debates of your House upon the R)cca.t
of the Conferrence, yesterday, As to that Part relatin   >

Benjamin Celey his Excellency was pleased to declare he is Lib. 41. thankful to any that put him in Mind of what he may do but since that you have not thought fit to Advise how the said p. 42 Celey should be disposed of his Excellency is not inclinable otherwise than according to the Sentence pronounced against him which will be executed on Friday next.

Signed ᵱ Order W Bladen Cl Council

The aforegoing Message from the Hoñble Council being here read this House took it into their serious Consideration and ordered that the same be answered by the Message following Viz.

By the House of Del. 23ᵈ May 1705

By the Debates of our House relating to Benjamin Celey the Prisoner we did not intend to put his Excellency in Mind of what he might do; but only asserted the Royal Prerogative but if the bringing in of a Bill to transport him or any other Thing which may save his Life may be thought necessary if you please to signifie it to us this House will very readily concur with your Honours in any such Proposal we being very desirous that his Life may be saved.

Signed ᵱ Order W. Taylard Cl. Ho. Del.

Which being read was well approved of by the House and ordered it be sent up to the Council ᵱ Mʳ Robert Tyler, Mʳ Joseph Hill, Mʳ John Mackall, & Mʳ John Wells. They withdrew; and the House adjourned till to Morrow Morning seven O'Clock.

May 24ᵗʰ 1705

The House according to Adjournment again met and being called over were all present as Yesterday

Mʳ Tyler, Mʳ Hill, Mʳ Mackall & Mʳ Wells sent up with the Message last Night enter the House & say they delivered the Message given them last Night.

Bill for Sale of a Parcel of Land called Richardson's Choice for Payment of a Debt due to John Nicholls, read the second Time & committed for Amendmᵗ

Bill for raising an Impost of six Pence ᵱ Hhd brought by Order of the House and was read the first & second Time & do pass. And sent up to his Excellency by Mʳ John Contee, Mʳ John Waters, Mʳ George Muschamp, Mʳ Francis Dallahyde & Mʳ Joseph Hill, Mʳ John Wells, Mʳ Thomas Frisby, Major John Taylor & Mʳ Robert Tyler.

They return & say they delivered the same.

Lib. 41    Edward Lloyd & William Coursey Esqʳˢ from the Hoñble
Council enters the House and delivers the Eight several
ingross'd Bills, indorsed, Read & assented to by her Majesty's
Hoñble Council.   And the Journal of Accounts with a Message
relating thereto; which being read in the House was recommended to the Comm. of Accounts to make some Amendments in their Journal.
    Bill for Banishment of Benjamin Celey sent up to the Council
by Mʳ Joseph Gray and Mʳ Thomas How for their Concurrence.
They return & say they delivered their Bill.
    Bill for Relief of poor Prisoners, Read in the House the first
Time.

p. 43    The Message Yesterday by Kenelm Chessildine & William
Coursey Esqʳˢ was read and debated in the House & ordered
to be entered viz.


### By the Council in Assembly May 23ʳᵈ 1705

Your Answer this Day by Mʳ Frisby & others to our Proposals on Monday last for the satisfying Persons employed by
his Excellency on Sundry Exigences is in Part well approved
of but the last Paragraph is so abstruse we must desire your
Explanation thereon Further we desire to know how & by
whom the Commissioners to be appointed to treat with the
Seneca Indians shall be furnished with Money or Credit to
bear their Charges on that Expedition and to purchase Presents
for the said Indians it being well known the French bidd as
largely for their affection as any.
                    Signed ᵱ Order W Bladen Cl. Council


    Which being read & debated it's resolved the same be
answered by the following Message Viz.


### By the House of Delegates May 24ᵗʰ 1705

May it Please your Honours.
    As to your Message relating to the Seneca Indians the Chief
or Head Men of those five Nations of Indians with whom it is
proposed to treat they will come to Susquehanah River where
they may be treated with and as to Money to bear the Charge
of the Commissioners & to buy Presents for the Indians this
House will give Direction therein, to the Treasurers to issue
Money accordingly.
                    Signed ᵱ Order W. Taylard Cl Ho. Del.

Which being read & well approved of by the House M<sup>r</sup> W<sup>m</sup> Frisby & M<sup>r</sup> Robert Skinner are ordered to carry the same up to the Council for Concurrence.

Return & say they delivered the same.

Edward Lloyd & William Holland Esq<sup>rs</sup> from the Hoñble Council enter the House and deliver M<sup>r</sup> Speaker Bill for laying Imposition of vi<sup>d</sup> ℣ Hhd for rebuilding the Stadt House. Indorsed as follows. Die Jovis 24° May 1705 By the Co<sup>l</sup> in Ass<sup>y</sup>

This Bill being read this Board do not think it advisable that it pass; especially in this Time of War when Tob° is so low, for that it will prejudice Trade in gen<sup>l</sup> deter the shipping from loading in this Province & be a Means to drive them to Virginia. Signed ℣ Order W Bladen Cl. Council.

The House proceeds now to allow the Fees for private Bills &<sup>ta</sup> pursuant to Act of Assembly.

> Christopher **Dangerman**, Naturalized Dr.
> To the Honble Speaker £ 2 .. 10 .. 0
> To W. **Taylard** Clerk of the House 1 .. 5 .. 0

M<sup>r</sup> William Josephs D<sup>r</sup> for private Bill

To the Hoñble Speaker £ 5. To William Taylard Clerk of the House £ 2 .. 10 .. 0 Ann Arundel County the Private Bill to the Hoñble Speaker 2000 ll Tob° To W<sup>m</sup> Taylard Cl of the House 1000 ll Tob°

The House adjourns till two O'Clock in the Afternoon.

Post Meridiem. The House met again according to Ad- journ<sup>t</sup>

Being called over were present as in the Morning.

Bill for Relief of poor Debtors &<sup>ta</sup> Read with the Amendments. Read the first & second Time and by especial Order do pass.

Col° Edward Lloyd & Col° William Holland from the Council enters the House and delivers M<sup>r</sup> Speaker the following Bills

Bill for Sale of a Parcel of Land called Richardson's Choice. Indorsed in Council thus Eodem Die Read in Council & assented to W. Bladen Cl. Council.

Bill for Exportation of Benjamin Celey Indorsed in Council thus. By his Excy the Governor & Council in Assembly Die Jovis 24° May 1705

The Bill for transporting Benjamin Celey to the West Indies being read this Board are willing the said Bill do pass notwith-

Lib. 41. standing the same was not so regularly brought in your House
not having his Excellency the Governor's Consent thereto.
                    Signed ꝑ Order  W Bladen Cl Council

    Ordered the two Bills be ingrossed
    Likewise ordered the following Message brought in by Col°
Lloyd & Col° Holland be read and entered Viz.


        Die Jovis 24° May 1705   By the Council in Assembly
    In Answer to yours by M^r Frisby & M^r Skinner we say we
have no Assurance that the Chief Men of the five Nations will
come down to Susquehanah to treat with us on failure whereof
it will be absolutely necessary our Commissioners go to them
to Albany that we may be certainly assured of their Friendship
or what else we may expect from them having been already
kept too long in the Dark
                    Signed ꝑ Order  W Bladen Cl. Council


    Which being read in the House the following Message was
ordered to be prepared Viz.


        By the House of Delegates  May 24^th 1705
    The Message by Col° Lloyd & Col° Holland of this Day
being read in the House and in Answer to which the House
humbly conceive that it's more convenient & of less Charge
to the Province first to send a Messenger forthwith up to the
Seneca Forts to invite them down to Conostoga & to know
of a Certainty whether they will there meet or not on their
Failure this House will concur with what is proposed in the
Message         Signed ꝑ Order  W. Taylard Cl. Ho. Del.


    Which being read & approved of was sent up to his Excel-
lency by Cap^t Richard Jones.
    He returns & says he delivered his Message
    Bill for Sale of Edmonson's Land &^ta Ingrossed Indorsed
Read & assented to by the House of Delegates.
    Sent up to the Council by M^r William Aisquith.
    He returns & says he delivered the Bill
    Ingrossed Bill for the Exportation of Benjamin Celey
    Read & assented to by the House of Delegates
p. 45  Ordered M^r Joseph Gray carry the aforegoing Bill up to
their Honours for Assent
    He returns & says he delivered the Bill

Upon motion of the Clerk of this House for Fees to be allowed by M<sup>r</sup> John Gresham of Ann Arundel County for the Accusation laid against him before this House for his Neglect in suffering Criminal Persons to escape &<sup>ta</sup> which was debated and resolved the said John Gresham satisfy & pay the Clerk six hundred Pounds of Tobacco for his Fees.

William Coursey Esq<sup>r</sup> enters the House and delivers M<sup>r</sup> Speaker Bill for Relief of poor Prisoners indorsed.

May 24<sup>th</sup> 1705 This Bill thought to be wholly very ill convenient and therefore wholly rejected

W Bladen Cl. Council.

And the ingrossed Bill for Sale of a Parcel of Land called Richardson's Choice &<sup>ta</sup> Indorsed. May 24<sup>th</sup> 1705. Read & Assented to by her Majesty's Hoñble Council

Ingrossed Bill for Exportation & Banishment of Benjamin Celey Indorsed

May 24<sup>th</sup> 1705 Read and assented to by her Majesty's Hon'ble Council W Bladen Cl. Council

The House adjourns till to morrow morn. seven O'Clock.

Die Veneris May 25, 1705. The House met again accord<sup>g</sup> to Adjournm<sup>t</sup>

Being called over were all present as yesterday

Read what was done yesterday. Bill for apportioning the publick Levy.

Read the first & second Times & do pass

Ordered M<sup>r</sup> John Taylor, M<sup>r</sup> Hugh Eccleston and M<sup>r</sup> John Hudson carry up the Bill to the Council for Concurrence.

They return & say they delivered the Bill.

The Hoñble James Saunders Esq<sup>r</sup> enters the House and delivers the Bill for apportioning the publick Levy Indorsed 25<sup>th</sup> May 1705 Read & agreed to in Council

W Bladen Cl. Council

Ordered to be ingrossed. Which being ingrossed Eodem Die. Indorsed. Read and assented to by the House of Delegates. Was sent up to the Council by M<sup>r</sup> Joseph Hill, and M<sup>r</sup> Joseph Gray for their Assent. And they were ordered to acquaint his Excellency & Council that this House at present has nothing else before them so that if they have any thing to more to impart the House are ready to proceed thereupon. They return & say they delivered their message.

Col° William Holland from the Council and delivers the ingrossed Bill for apportioning the Levy Indorsed 25<sup>th</sup> May 1705 Read & assented to by his Ex'cy the Governor & Council W Bladen Cl. Council

And Col° Holland informs M^r Speaker that his Excellency commands him & the whole House to attend him at the Council Chamber to compleat this Sessions. Thereupon M^r Speaker & the whole House attended his Excellency in the Council Chamber where M^r Speaker presented to his Excellency the several Bills following made this Sessions.

Bill confirming a certain Letter of Attorney from William Josephs the Father to William Josephs the Son.

Bill for Punishment of Persons selling or transporting any Friend Indian &^ta

Bill for Relief of Ann Arundel County and all Persons concerned in the Records thereof lately burnt.

Bill declaring the Act Entituled an Act for Punishment of psons suborning Witnesses &^ta to be in force.

Bill declaring an Act Entituled an Act ascertaining the Bounds of Land to be in force

Bill for the outlawing of Richard Clarke of Ann Arundel County

Bill declaring an Act Entituled an Act for erecting Ann Arundel & Oxford Towns into Ports &^ta to be in force

Bill for Naturalization of Xtopher Dangerman of Calvert County Sadler.

Bill for Sale of Land called Richardson's Choice for Payment of a Debt due from Edmonson to Nicholls.

Bill for Exportation of Benjamin Celey

Bill for apportioning the publick Levy &^ta   To which his Excellency was pleased to give his Assent by indorsing them Severally with these words

"May 25^th 1705.  On Behalf of her most sacred Majesty Queen Ann &^ca I will this be a Law"        Jo. Seymour

Which being done his Ex'cy was pleased to seal the same severally with the broad Seal of this Province.  Which Laws being so signed & sealed his Ex'cy was pleased to acquaint the House that he by the Advice of her Majesty's Council thought it convenient for her Majesty's Service to prorogue them until the 24^th Day of July next and that they were thereby accordingly prorogued.

And so ended this Session of Assembly this 25^th Day of May in the fourth year of the Reign of our Sovereign Lady Queen Ann of England &^ta Anno Domini 1705

W Taylard Clk.

# ACTS.

Maryland Ss:

At a Session of Assembly begun and held at the Town and Port of Annapolis in Ann Arundell County the fifteenth of May 1705 and in the fourth Year of her Majesty's Reigne &c :

### Were enacted the Laws following

An Act for the Relief of Ann Arundell County and all Persons concerned in the Records thereof lately burn'd.

Whereas the Records of Ann Arundell County being lodged in One of the upper rooms of the Publick Court house at Annapolis upon the eighteenth day of October Seventeen hundred and four were burned with the said house to the great loss and detriment of the Inhabitants of the said County and all Other Persons concerned in the Lands Judgments and Records in of and belonging thereunto.

For the redress and relief whereof it is humbly prayed that it may be Enacted and be it Enacted by the Queens most Excellent Majesty by and with the Advice and consent of her Majesties Governour Councill and Assembly of this Province and the Authority of the same that it shall and may be Lawfull to his Excellency her Majesties Governour of this Province for the time being by comission under the great Seal of this Province to Authorize Appoint and Commissionate Seven or more discreet and Sober Persons whereof any three or more of them from time to time to hear and determine all differences claimes and Demands whatsoever between any the Inhabitants or Other Psons interested in the Lands lying within the County af$^d$ at Such places within the said County as they or any three or more of them shall think fitt from time to time with or without any Adjournment Summarily and without the formality and Proceedings in Courts of Law or Equity either upon the verdict or inquisition of Jurors Testimony of Witnesses upon Oath Examination of Parties interested or by all or any the said ways (or otherwise according to their discretions) And that the Judgment or Sentence of the said Commissioners or any three or more of them as af$^d$ shall be finall between the said Parties their heires Executors Administrators & assignes and all claiming by from or

Lib. 64. under them touching the matters and decrees to be made by
the said Commissioners by this present Act thereunto Authorized or any three or more of them the said Commissioners
allways giving timely notice of not less than Sixteen days of
the time and Place of their Sitting Saving the right of all
Persons under age non Sanæ memoriæ Feme coverts and
Persons non resident within this Province during Such time
as they shall continue so who shall & are hereby allowed to
Prosecute their claimes within twelve months after such disability Removed And unless any Party dissatisfyed with Such
a Sentence shall appeall therefrom within thirty days to such
commissioners as his Excy the Governour for the time being
is hereby Impowered to authorize and Appoint by his Commission for that Purpose under the great Seale of this Province
not exceeding five in Number whereof the Maj$^r$ Part If [not] all
such Commissioners meet or two in case only three meet
shall finally determine thereon in Manner aforesaid without
any further Appeall or review.

·And be it Enacted that the said commissioners be & Are
hereby empowered to committ and Punish by fine not Exceeding One thousand Pounds of tobacco all Such Persons who
shall disturb the sitting of the said Commissioners or willfully
refuse to give evidence

And further for the better discovery of Psons rights to
Lands claimed before the said Commissioners. The said
Commissioners or any three or more of them may and are
Empowered to Issue Precepts to the Sher & Survey$^r$ of the
said County to resurvey and make returnes to the s$^d$ Commissioners Pursuant to the ten$^r$ of Such Precepts and warrants
which the said Sher and Surveyor shall and are hereby obliged
to Execute for such reasonable fees as to the said Commissioners shall seem meet and Also the said Commissioners
shall and may make and establish such reasonable table of
p. 219 fees to their Clark whom they are to make Choice of with
the approbation of his Excy for the writing and recording
of any matters before them and to the Sher of the said County
who is hereby Enjoyned by his Sufficient deputy constantly
to attend them and serve and Execute all precepts warrants
orders notices in writing or other Sumons as by the said
Commissioners to the said Sher shall be directed not Exceeding one full moyety in proportion to what is allowed by the
Act of Assembly for limitation of Officers fees to the severall
Sheriffs and Clerks of the County Courts which fees are to
be upon Execution as other fees belonging to Clks and
Sheriffs.

And be it further enacted that the Judgment and determina-
tions which shall be made betwixt Party and Party by Authority

of this Act shall be recorded in a fair book or bookes to be <sup>Lib. 64.</sup> Provided for that purpose at the County charge and every such Judgment and determination shall be signed by three or more of the said Commissioners which book or bookes when Perfected shall be Placed and intrusted in the custody of the Clark of Ann Arundell County among the Records of the said County that all Persons concerned may repair to view the same And further that none of the said Commissioners shall take any fee or reward whatsoever directly or indirectly for any thing to be done by them by virtue or colour of this Present Act Saving the Allowance of eighty Pounds of tobacco p Diem for their Expences during the time as they shall sitt to hear and determine such claimes which charge the Com<sup>rs</sup> of Ann Arundell County are hereby Authorized & obliged to Levy and Assess upon the severall Taxables of the said County and allow unto them in the County levy.

And Provided nevertheless that it shall be lawfull for the Commissioners by this Act Empowered to Assess and Exact Such reasonable charges on all Persons non residents in the said County and making claims before them as in their discretion they shall think fitt accounting therefor to the County levy and that the said Commissioners are hereby empowered to make all necessary rules & orders for the better carrying on all business that shall be brought before them and the good and regular Government of their Court.

And be it further Enacted by the Authority advice and consent af<sup>d</sup> that the Justices and commissioners of Ann Arundell County Co<sup>rt</sup> for the time being be Impowered according to their discretion upon Application to them made and due Proof thereof to Affirm all Judgments heretofore given in the said County Court Now unsatisfyed and award Execution thereon and againe to adjudge and Ascertaine the times of Service of all Orphans by them bound out and Servants According to Act of Assembly heretofore by them adjudged whereof the <sup>p. 220</sup> Record is not Extant but burnt as in their wisdomes they shall think fitt and that for the entries of such Judgments and all matters thereto relating the Clark of the said County be allowed but half fees Any Act Law usage or Custome to the Contrary notwithstanding.

May the 23<sup>rd</sup> 1705          May the 23<sup>rd</sup> 1705

Read and Assented to by the          Read and Assented to by her
house of Delegates          Maj<sup>tcs</sup> hon<sup>ble</sup> Councill.
W Taylard Clk hD.          W Bladen Cl Concil.

May the 25<sup>th</sup> 1705

On the behalf of her most Sacred Maj<sup>ty</sup> Queen Anne &c. I
will this be Law                              ⎧  the great  ⎫
                        Jo : Seymour     ⎨  Seale of   ⎬
                                              ⎩  Maryland  ⎭

An Act Impowering Maj<sup>r</sup> Nicholas Low Executor of the last
will and testament of William Edmondson late of Dorchester County dec'd to sell a certaine tract of Land lying in
Dorchester County called Richardsons Choice formerly
Purchased by the said William Edmondson of and from one
John Nicholls for payment of a debt due from the said William Edmondson to the said John Nicholls for the remaining
part of the Originall Purchase for the said Land.

Whereas the said William Edmondson in his life time Purchased from the said John Nicholls the said tract of Land
called Richardsons Choice lying near the great Choptank
river in Dorchester County but the said William Edmondson
dying before payment of the Consideration of the said purchase
and not leaving Assetts Sufficient to Pay his debts the s<sup>d</sup> John
Nicholls humbly prayed this Generall Assembly that the said
tract of Land might be sold to Satisfy him what remains due
of the s<sup>d</sup> Consideration.

Be it therefore Enacted by The Queens most Excellent
Majesty by and with the Advice and consent of her Maj<sup>ties</sup>
Governour Councill and Assembly of this Province and the
Authority of the same that the said Maj<sup>r</sup> Nicholas Lowe Executor of the last will and testament of the said William
p. 221  Edmondson decd shall be and is hereby Authorized and Empowered to sell Alienate and dispose of the said tract of Land
to the best purchasor or purchasors or him her or them that
will give most for the Same And good form and Authentick
conveyances or Assurances in the Law whatsoever to make
Seale and Execute to such Purchasor or Purchasors which said
Purchasor or Purchasors shall by virtue of such conveyances
or Assurances to be made as aforesaid and of this present Act
be Enabled quietly and Peacably to hold & Enjoy a firm Sure
absolute and indefeazable Estate of inheritance in fee Simple
to them and their heires for ever of in and to the said tract of
Land against all Persons whatsoever.

And be it further enacted by the Authority advice and consent aforesaid that the said Nicholas Low shall out of the
Consideration for which the said Land is to be sold Satisfy
and Pay unto the said John Nicholls his Executors Administrators or Assigns the said debt now due to him from the said

William Edmondson (if the Land af^d shall be sold for so much) Lib. 64.
and that the overplus (if any) shall remaine in the hands
of the said Nicholas Low after Payment of the said Debt and
deduction of his Sallary by him shall be paid and Satisfyed to
the Orphan to whom the said Land was given by the Last will
and testament of the said William Edmondson and shall not
be accounted as Assetts in the hands of the said Executor but
be by virtue of this Act protected from all Attachments and
Condemnations whatsoever any Law Statute usage or Custome
to the Contrary Notwithstanding.

<table>
<tr><td>May the 24^th 1705</td><td>May the 24^th 1705</td></tr>
<tr><td>Read & assented to by the<br>house of Del.<br>W Taylard Clk hD</td><td>Read and Assented to by her<br>Maj^ties hon^ble Councill.<br>W Bladen Cl Concil.</td></tr>
</table>

May the 25^th 1705

On the behalf of her Most Sacred Majesty Anne Queen of
England &c I Will this be a Law

Jo : Seymour   { Great Seale }
               { of Maryland }

An Act confirming a certaine letter of Attorny from William
Joseph Esq^r the father to William Joseph his Son.

Whereas William Joseph of Prince Georges County has
by his humble Petition to his Excellency the Governour and
Council of this Province shewn that his father William Joseph
of this Province Esq^r did by an Instrument under his hand
and Seale Purporting a letter of Attorney which is recorded
in the Secretaries office and thereby Empower him the s^d
William Joseph his Son to sell certaine Lands of his fathers
in order to Pay and discharge certaine Debts of his said
fathers contracted within this Province for and in Payment p. 222
and discharge of which debts the said William Joseph the
Son hath sold certaine Lands of his said Fathers  But in as
much as the Purchasor or Purchasors of the said Lands do
call in question the Authentickness of the af^d letter of Att^ry
involving the said William Joseph the Son in Law Suits
troubles & charges to his great detriment who no ways
doubling of the Sufficiency of his aforesaid letter of Attorny
has allready disbursed Severall Sumes of. mony and Tobacco
in discharge of the said Debts.

It is therefore humbly prayed that it may be Enacted And
be it Enacted by the Queens most Excellent Majesty by and
with the advice and consent of her Majesties Governour
Council and Assembly of this Province and the Authority

Lib. 64 of the same that all or any the said Grantees Bargainees and Purchasers of Any the said William Joseph the eldest Lands within this Province who actually bargained for the same with the said William Joseph the Son before the twelfth day of December in the year of Our Lord Seventeen hundred and three by virtue of the said William Joseph the Elders letter of Attorny shall by the Conveyance or assurance of the To W^m Joseph the Younger Pursuant thereto Notwithstanding any Imperfection or insufficiency of or in the said letter of Attorny or the wording thereof (this Assembly being made Sensible the same was duly Executed) to all intents and Purposes whatsoever have hold and Enjoy the s^d Lands tenements and hereditaments to them their heires and assigns forever any Law Statute Usage or Custom to the Contrary notwithstanding.

<table>
<tr><td>May the 23^d 1705</td><td>May the 23^d 1705</td></tr>
<tr><td>Read and Assented to by the house of Delegates</td><td>Read and assented to by her Maj^tes hon^ble Councill</td></tr>
<tr><td>W Taylard Clk hD</td><td>W Bladen Cl Concil.</td></tr>
</table>

May the 25^th 1705

On the behalf of her most Sacred Maj^ty Anne Queen of England &c^a I will this be a Law.

Jo: Seymour    { Sealed with  
the great Seale of  
Maryland }

An Act for the Exportation and Banishment of Benjamine Cely.

Whereas Benjamine Cely of Prince Georges County within this Province stands convicted & Attainted of felony and
p. 223 Burglary and hath received Sentence of Death Upon the said conviction as appears by the record thereof in her Majesties Provincial Court of this province And for as much as this present Generall Assembly has taken the said Benjamins Cely's case into their consideration and being desirous that the said Benjamine Cely's life may be Saved thereby giving him time and Space for repentance and amendment do humbly pray that it may be Enacted.

And Be it Enacted by the Queens most Excellent Majesty by and with the advice and consent of her Majesties Governour Councill and Assembly of this Province and the Authority of the same that the said Benjamine Cely with all convenient Speed after the end of this Session of Assembly Lib. 64 shall be banished and Exported out of this province into some Island in the West Indies and be there Sold to Serve Seven years and the mony Arising from the Sale shall be Applyed toward the Defraying the publick charge of this Province the Judgment or Sentence of Death af^d given against the said Benjamine Cely in Any wise notwithstanding.

And be it Enacted by the Authority aforesaid by and with the advice and consent af^d That it shall be felony without any Benefitt of clergy for him the said Benjamin Cely to return into this Province within the term of Seven years af^d to commence from the time of his Exportation.

May the 24^th 1705    May the 24^th 1705
Read and Assented to by the    Read and assented to by her
house of Delegates    Maj^ties hon^ble Councill
W Taylard Clk hD    W Bladen Cl Concil.

May the 25^th 1705
On the behalf of her most Sacred Maj^ty Queen Anne of
England &c I will this be a Law

Jo: Seymour

An Act for the Outlawing of Richard Clark of Ann Arundell County.

Whereas it appears to this generall Assembly upon oath that there has been a very wicked and treasonable conspiracy begun and carryed on by Richard Clark of Ann Arundell County and his accomplices to Seize upon the Magazine and upon his Excellency the Governour and overturn her Majesties Government and to bring the heathen Indians together with the said Conspirators to Cutt off and Extirpate the Inhabitants of this Province and for as much as the said Clark flyes from Justice and Dares not Venture himself upon a faire tryall.

Be it therefore Enacted by the Queens most Excellent Ma^ty p. 224 by and with the advice and Consent of her Majties Governour Councill and Assembly of this Province and the Authority of the same that unless the said Richard Clark do within twenty days after the End of this Present Session of Assembly Surrender himself to his Excy the Governour or to any one of her Majesties hon^ble Councill in ord^r to be tryed for his treason af^d that then the said Richard Clark by force and virtue

Lib. 64. of this Act shall be Outlawed and shall forfeit his goods and Chattells Lands and tenements as an out lawed Pson any want of Processe or any Other legall proceedings in any wise notwithstanding.

<table>
<tr><td>May the 23<sup>d</sup> 1705</td><td>May the 23<sup>d</sup> 1705</td></tr>
</table>

May the 23ᵈ 1705

Read and Assented to by the house of Delegates
W Taylard Clk hD

May the 23ᵈ 1705

Read and Assented to by her Majᵗⁱᵉˢ honᵇˡᵉ Councill
W Bladen Cl Concil.

May the 25ᵗʰ 1705

On the Behalf of her most Sacred Majᵗʸ Anne Queen of England &c. I will this be a Law.

Jo : Seymour

An Act for Punishment of Persons Selling or transporting Any friend Indian or Indians out of this Province.

To the end that no breach of Peace may happen between the Neighbouring Indians and the Inhabitants of this Province.
Be it Enacted by the Queens most Excellent Majesty by and with the advice and consent of her Majesties Governour Council and Assembly of this Province and the Authority of the same that any Person or Persons whatsoever that shall take Entice Surprize sell or transport or cause to be Sold or transported out of this province Or Otherwise dispose of Any friend Indian or Indians whatsoever or endeavour or attempt so to do without licence from the Governour for the time being and all Accessaries thereunto shall be fined and Imprisoned at the discretion of the Govʳ and Councill for the time being and that any pson or psons whatsoever that shall inform
p. 225 against or Cause Such Offender or Offenders to be apprehended shall have such Satisfaction therefor as the Govʳ and Councill shall think fitt.

May the 23ʳᵈ 1705

Read and Assented to by the house of Delegates.
W Taylard Clk hD.

May the 23ᵈ 1705

Read and assented to by her Majᵗⁱᵉˢ honᵇˡᵉ Councill
W Bladen Cl Concll.

May the 25ᵗʰ 1705

On the behalf of her Most Sacred Majᵗʸ Queen Anne &cᵃ I will this be a Law.

Jo: Seymour.

An Act For Naturalization of Christopher **Dangerman** of Lib. 64. Calvert County—Sadler.

Be it Enacted by the Queens most Excellent Majesty by and with the advice and consent of her Majesties Governour Councill and Assembly of this Province and the Authority of the Same that Christopher Dangerman Born in the City of Hannover in the Country of Liningburgh under the Dominion of the Emporer of Germany and now Resident in Calvert County within this Province shall be from henceforth adjudged reputed and taken as one of her Majesties Naturall born Subjects of this Province And that he by the Authority af⁴ be Enabled and adjudged to all intents and Purposes to Demand Challenge ask have hold and Enjoy any Lands tenements and hereditaments to which he might anywise be Entituled as if he were a free and Naturall born Subject and also be Enabled to Prosecute maintaine avow Justify and Defend all Manner of Actions Suits Pleas Plaints and Other Demands whatsoever as liberally ffrankly ffreely fully and lawfully as if he had been a Naturall born Subject within this Province Any Law Statute usage or custome to the Contrary notwithstanding.

| May the 23ᵈ 1705 | May the 23ᵈ 1705 |
|---|---|
| Read and Assented to by the house of Delegates | Read and Assented to by her Majᵗⁱᵉˢ honᵇᶦᵉ Councill. |
| W Taylard Clk hD. | W Bladen Cl Concil. |

May the 25ᵗʰ 1705

On the behalf of her Most Sacred Majᵗʸ Queen Anne of England &c. I will this be a Law.     Jo : Seymour [Seal]

An Act declaring the Act Entituled An Act for the Punish- p. 226 ment of Persons Subborning Wittnesses & committing willfull and corrupt Perjury to be in force

Be it Enacted by the Queen most Excellent Maᵗʸ by and with the advice and consent of her Majesties Governour Councill and Assembly of this Province and the Authority of the Same that the Act of Assembly Entituled An Act for the Punishment of Persons Subborning wittnesses or Committing willfull and corrupt Perjury and every Matter clause and thing therein contained Is hereby declared to be and remaine in full force & effect to all intents constructions and Purposes whatsoever.

| By the house of Delegates May the 23ᵈ 1705 Read and Assented to. W Taylard Clk hD. | May the 23ʳᵈ 1705 Read and Assented to by her Majᵗⁱᵉˢ honᵇˡᵉ Councill W Bladen Cl Concil. |
|---|---|

May the 25<sup>th</sup> 1705

On the behalf of her most Sacred Maj<sup>ty</sup> Anne Queen of England &c. I will this be a Law.

Jo Seymour [Seale]


An Act declaring An Act Entituled An Act for erecting Ann Arundell and Oxford Towns into Ports & Towns formerly made to be in force.

Be it Enacted by the Queens most Excellent Majesty by and with the advice and consent of her Majesties Governour Councill and Assembly of this Province & the Authority of the same that one Act of Assembly heretofore made and Enacted Entituled An Act for Erecting Ann Arundell and Oxford Towns into Ports and Towns & every clause matter and thing therein contained is hereby declared to be and remaine in full force and effect to all intents Constructions and Purposes whatsoever to the end of the Next Sessions of Assembly

| May the 23<sup>d</sup> 1705 | May the 23<sup>d</sup> 1705 |
|---|---|
| Read and Assented to by the house of Delegates | Read and attested to by her Maj<sup>tes</sup> hon<sup>ble</sup> Councill |
| W Taylard Cl hD. | W Bladen Cl. Concil. |

May the 25<sup>th</sup> 1705

On the behalf of her most Sacred Maj<sup>ty</sup> Anne Queen of England &c. I will this be a Law

Jo: Seymour { Seale }


An Act declaring An Act intituled An Act Ascertaining the bounds of Land to be in force.

Be it Enacted by the Queens most Excellent Maj<sup>ty</sup> by and with the advice and consent of her Majesty's Governour Councill and Assembly of this Province and the Authority of the same that the Act of Assembly made at a generall Assembly begun and held at the Port of Annapolis the twenty Seventh day of June in the year of our Lord Sixteen hundred ninety nine Entituled An Act ascertaining the bounds of Land and every clause matter and thing therein contained is hereby declared to be and remaine in full force and effect to all intents constructions and purposes whatsoever to the end of ·the next Sessions of Assembly.

May the 23ᵈ 1705

Read and Assented to by the
house of Delegates
W Taylard Clk hD.

May the 23ᵈ 1705    Lib. 64.

Read and Assented to by her
Majesties honᵇˡᵉ Councill.
W Bladen Cl Concil.

May the 25ᵗʰ 1705

On the behalf of her most Sacred Majesty Anne Queen of
England &cᵃ I will this be a Law.

Joᵒ: Seymour  { Seale }

An Act Impowering a Committee to lay assess and apportion
the publick Leavy of this province for this present year
One thousand Seven hundred and five.

Whereas this present Generall Assembly have for the defraying the Publick charge of this province to the twenty third
day of May one thousand seven hnndred and five raised a
certaine Sume of tobacco and mony amounting to the Sum̃e
of two hundred thirty six thousand Six hundred forty seven
pounds of tobacco and two hundred Sixty seven pounds p. 228
Seventeen Shillings and nine Pence half penny in mony But
by reason more publick charges may arise and grow due
before the tenth day of October next which is the usuall and
accustomed time of Payment at which time againe to call &
convene the whole Assembly for that Occasion only considering the great Number of them and the remoteness of their
habitations from the place appointed would be very chargeable and troublesom to the whole Province in generall for
prevention whereof—

Be it Enacted by the Queens most Excellent Majᵗʸ by and
with the advice and consent of her Majesty's Governour
Councill and Assembly of this Province and the Authority
of the same that one Burgess or delegate out of Each county
and one out of the city of Saint Maries be and are hereby
Authorized and appointed a committee to Joyne with some
of her Majesties hoñble Councill to lay and equally assess the
said Publick Levy of this Province (that is to say) of her
Majᵗⁱᵉˢ honourable Councill Thomas Tench Esqʳ Colᵒ John
Hammond Lievᵗ Col William Holland and James Sanders
Esqⁿ And of the house of Delegates Col. Thomas Smyth
Speaker Mʳ George Muschamp Mʳ William Watts Mʳ Charles
Greenberry Mʳ Robert Skinner Mʳ John Contee Mʳ Edward
Dorsey Mʳ John Macclaster Mʳ Robert Gouldesborough Mʳ
Thomas Frisby Mʳ John Taylor and Mʳ Thoˢ Greenfield or

Lib. 64. the Major Part of them shall be and appear at the Town of Annapolis on the tenth day of October next then and there to lay and Assess the said publick levy allready raised and also to Allow levy and Assess what further charges may accrue which to them shall Justly Appear to be due from the Publick not Exceeding two hundred thousand pounds of tobacco and five hundred Pounds currant mony of this Province more than what is allready raised and to apportion order and Pay to the Severall persons to whom the same shall be due and a faire Journall of all their Proceedings to be delivered to the Clark of the Assembly for Satisfaccon of all Persons therewith concerned.

p. 229    But if it shall happen that his Excellency shall please to convene An Assembly before the tenth day of October af^d then this present Act and all and every clause therein contained shall be void and of no effect.

| | |
|---|---|
| May the 25^th 1705 | May the 25^th day 1705 |
| Read and Assented to by the | Read and Assented to by the |
| house of Delegates | Governour and Councill |
| W Taylard Clk hD. | W Bladen Cl Concil. |

May the 25^th 1705

On the behalf of her most Sacred Maj^ty Queen Anne &c. I will this be a Law

Jo: Seymour

The Seale of the Secretary's office is hereunto affixed
On the behalf of the honourable S^r Thomas Laurence Baronet Secretary of Maryland p me

Th Bordley Clk of the Secretaries office

# PROCEEDINGS AND ACTS

OF THE

# GENERAL ASSEMBLY

# OF MARYLAND.

*At a Session held at Annapolis, April* 2–19, 1706.

CHARLES CALVERT, LORD BALTIMORE,
*Proprietary.*

JOHN SEYMOUR,
*Governor.*

---

THE UPPER HOUSE OF ASSEMBLY.

M
of
in

Hi

Th

De
acc

pos
Ses
was

the
to
of
the
the

Mr
S
dou
to
this
to
has
nes

Ger
N
had
ent

Maryland ss<sup>t</sup>

   Att a Session of Assembly held at the Towne and Porte
of Annapolis in Anne Arundell County the 2<sup>d</sup> Day of Aprill
in the 5<sup>th</sup> yeare of her Ma<sup>tys</sup> Raigne &c
   Annoq D<sup>m</sup> 1706

Pr<sup>r</sup>sent in Councill

His Ex<sup>llcy</sup> John Seymour Esq<sup>r</sup> Cap<sup>t</sup> Gen<sup>ll</sup> and Governour in
   Chiefe in and over this her Ma<sup>tys</sup> Province &c.

The hon<sup>ble</sup>
{ Thomas Brooke Esq<sup>r</sup> } Col Francis Jenkins
{ Robert Smith Esq<sup>r</sup> } Col Edw<sup>d</sup> Lloyd
{ Col J<sup>no</sup> Hamond } James Sanders Esq<sup>r</sup>
{ & Col Thomas Ennalls of her Ma<sup>tys</sup> Councill.

   Came M<sup>r</sup> Joseph Hill & M<sup>r</sup> James Hays from the House of
Delegates and acquainte his Ex<sup>ncy</sup> that theire House was mett
according to her Ma<sup>tys</sup> Prorogation
   His Ex<sup>ncy</sup> Says He will Send for them and acquainte them
with what he has to lay before them
   Then his Ex<sup>ncy</sup> advised with the Boarde of what he proposed to say to the Gen<sup>ll</sup> Assembly at the opening of this
Sessions, and the same being reduced into writing and read
was approved of by the whole Boarde
   After which Colonel Hamond was ordered to go downe to
the House and Comand the Speaker and the Members
to attend his Ex<sup>ncy</sup> in Council   Mr Speaker and the Members p. 2
of the House of Delegates being come up, and admitted into
the Councill Roome His Ex<sup>ncy</sup> was pleased thus to bespeake
them.

M<sup>r</sup> Speaker & You Gent<sup>n</sup> Delegates.
   Since our Meeting now, is by her Ma<sup>tys</sup> especiall Comand, I
doubt not but the greate good things So earnestly recomended
to your Serious Consideration for the good and Wellfare of
this Province will be unanimously approved of and assented
to by You it's Rep<sup>r</sup>sentatives; That what her Sacred Ma<sup>tye</sup>
has so wisely & graciously concerted for your future happi-
ness & grandeur may enrich You and Succeeding Generations.

Gent<sup>n</sup>
   Noe Monarch that ever Swayed the English Scepter has
had a more tender reguard for all her Subjects than her present Ma<sup>tye</sup> and though She has been engaged in a great

Maryland ss<sup>t</sup>

Att a Session of Assembly hel at the Towne and Porte Original Journal.
of Annapolis in Anne Arundell Cunty the 2<sup>d</sup> Day of Aprill p. 1
in the 5<sup>th</sup> yeare of her Ma<sup>tys</sup> Raigr &c
Annoq D<sup>m</sup> 1706

P<sup>r</sup>sent in Concill

His Ex<sup>llcy</sup> John Seymour Esq<sup>r</sup> Caj Gen<sup>ll</sup> and Governour in
Chiefe in and over this her Ia<sup>tys</sup> Province &c.

The hon<sup>ble</sup> { Thomas Brooke Esq<sup>r</sup>     Col Francis Jenkins
                  { Robert Smith Esq<sup>r</sup>      Col Edw<sup>d</sup> Lloyd
                  { Col J<sup>no</sup> Hamond          James Sanders Esq<sup>r</sup>
                  { & Col Thomas Ennalls f her Ma<sup>tys</sup> Councill.

Came M<sup>r</sup> Joseph Hill & M<sup>r</sup> James lays from the House of
Delegates and acquainte his Ex<sup>ncy</sup> tha theire House was mett
according to her Ma<sup>tys</sup> Prorogation
His Ex<sup>ncy</sup> Says He will Send for then and acquainte them
with what he has to lay before them
Then his Ex<sup>ncy</sup> advised with the Barde of what he proposed to say to the Gen<sup>ll</sup> Assembly t the opening of this
Sessions, and the same being reduced nto writing and read
was approved of by the whole Boarde
After which Colonel Hamond was orered to go downe to
the House and Comand the Speake and the Members
to attend his Ex<sup>ncy</sup> in Council  Mr Speaer and the Members p. 2
of the House of Delegates being come p, and admitted into
the Councill Roome His Ex<sup>ncy</sup> was plea:d thus to bespeake
them.

M<sup>r</sup> Speaker & You Gent<sup>n</sup> Delegates.
Since our Meeting now, is by her Ma<sup>tys</sup> speciall Comand, I
doubt not but the greate good things So e-nestly recomended
to your Serious Consideration for the gcd and Wellfare of
this Province will be unanimously approv'd of and assented
to by You it's Rep'sentatives; That wha her S        Ma<sup>tye</sup>
has so wisely & graciously concerted for our
ness & grandeur may enrich You and Succe di        lappi-
                                                     .tions.
Gent<sup>n</sup>

Noe Monarch that ever Swayed
had a more tender reguard for all t            pter
ent Ma<sup>tye</sup> and though She ha                her p
                                        n a c

Original chargeable Warr ever since her Accession to the Throne her
Journal. Princely generous Endeavours have not been confined to Brit-
taine alone; but an unwearied tenderness is diffused over all
p. 3 her Ma^{tys} Colonyes & Plantations abroade and more especially
to Us and our Neighbouring Planters; Witness her Ma^{tys}
tymely Interposition with the Zarr of Muscovy; for if that
Grant or Project had not been stopped, You might in good
Measure have bid adieu to the tob° Trade in America; whilst
the divided Interests and Sentiments of the Merch^{ts} at home,
in relation to the Setting up and curing the Circasian Tobaccoes,
had speedily crown'd our Ruine.

Next her Ma^{tys} opening a Trade with Spaine, which has
allready had so very good Success many Spanish Vessells
have been cleared in London, that brought their Wooll and
Comoditys thither, returning thence with our English Manufactures. This Trade mnst prove a certain Advantage to all
our Plantations by the Vicinity & Comerce of the Spanish
West Indies; for I would have You consider tis not the true
Spaniard but a Spanish French King is our Enemy.

Then her Princely Care in passing an Act to encourage the
Transportation of Naval Stores from her Colonyes, that all
her Subjects abroad may truly reape the Benefitt of their
p. 4 Industrye & Labour equall with those soe imediately under
the gracious Influencies of her Royall View and Patronage;
For though Masts, Tarr & Pitch are not to be had here in
Such Abundance, as our Countrymen & Neighbours can furnish; Wee may have as good Flax & Hempe as any in the
World, without any Diminution to our Tobacco Manufacture:
And I hope You will be throughly Sencible This generous
Indulgence to Us & all our fellow Subjects in America, will
certainly occasion the Importations of all necessarys from
England (oftner & cheaper than at present) the want of which
& their extravagant dearness is still very burthensome &
ruinous to the indigent People of this Countrye

These truly Royall endearing Benefactions must ever Sincke
deepe in the Memorys of all loyal good Subjects: Never let
it be sayd that Maryland was ungratefull to so good &
gracious a Sovereigne, Who do's with so much Wisdome
Goodness & Steady Application, endeavour the Prosperity of
England and all it's Dependencys

M^r Speaker. Her Ma^{ty} earnestly recomends the Erecting
p. 5 Towns and Ports which must certainly render You considerable in a very Shorte tyme. I presume as to the Number and
their Scituation Her Ma^{tye} will be advised by You Gentlemen;
Who best know the proper Places for Trade & Busieness; and
as the Advantages naturally proceeding from Such Im-
provem^{ts} are many; and for your owne peculiar good, I hope

there is no Occasion to convince reasonable thinking Men
of it's absolute Necessity; nor can I believe any body will
obstruct this noble generous Designe but a few Gentlemen
at home who have assiduously endeavoured by a certaine
Engrossm$^t$ to make the Produce of your Land & Industrye a
sure Monopolie to themselves; whereby You can never let
the middle and lower Sorte of People reap any thing from a
very hard labour and the Sweate of their Browes but a per-
petuall Indigencye.

Gent$^n$ I am obliged in Justice and good Nature to lay
before you the growing evill of Protested Bills, and with
greate Friendship to recomend it to your best Considerations,
how that fatal Grievance may be removed.

I am obliged to take Notice You make Use of a very unparliamentary Practice which is to Postpone Matters to the last p. 6
Eight or tenn Hours of yo$^r$ rising and then things of very
greate Consequence are naturally hurryed up or so procrastinated that at our next meeting they are forgott, Witness many
of her Maj:tys Royal Instructions layd before you Gent$^n$ at your
first Sitting downe. And though I heartily desired Your Advice and Assistance in a Strict enquiry what became of the
Arms & Amunition of the Province in Tyme of a forreigne
Warr and Intestine Disturbances when We last mett which
Seeme to threaten Us still, You did not then thinke it proper to
enquire into a matter So very necessary for your owne Safety
and Defence.

Give me leave Gent$^n$ to desire You will now applye yourselves heartily to the business before You, that so pernitious
a thing to all wise Councills may not be brought to a Custome
by You Gent$^n$ Delegates And then I can never doubt but by
calme Serious Debates the many greate things under your p. 7
present Care will be in a few days ripened into good wholesome Laws fit for the Royal Sanction.

And as every Body knows this Parte of America was discovered by Englishmen in the Reigne of the famous renowned
Queen Elizabeth; I would have Us of this Province allways
remember noe Prince since (in soe short a tyme) ever applyed
their Royall thoughts and Care more emphatically for your
Wellfare P$^r$servation and Happiness than our present Glorious
Queen Anne.

I have had an Acco$^t$ from the head of the Bay, the Indians
intended Some Motions this Spring and with the advice of
her Ma$^{tys}$ Hon$^{ble}$ Councill have taken proper Measures about
it for the present; but hope Gent$^n$ you will enquire particularly into the truth of this Affaire; For on our last Alarms,
the Severall psons I sent on long and hazardous Journeys to
bring me a Right Intelligence of their Désigne, weer so nar-

Original rowly rewarded, It must be on a very Emergent Occasion I'le
Journal. trouble any Gent$^n$ againe if I may not reasonably be thought
p. 8 a proper Judge w$^t$ such a publiq Service deserves. I have
neither Lands nor Houses to loose here on any Suddaine
fatall Insult, as You Gentlemen Freeholders have; yet my
Reputation, which is dearer to me than any thing in this
World lyes at Stake. But with all the Cheerfull Willingness
imaginable, will expose my life on a true handsome Occasion
for the Defence Service and Peace of this Countrye.

Gent$^n$ I have Severall other materiall things to offer to
your Consideration, but shall p$^r$sume to do it by way of Message.

After which M$^r$ Speaker and the Members of the House of
Delegates took Leave and repair'd to their House.

The Boarde adjourn'd untill nine of the Clock to morrow
Morning.

Wednesday Aprill the 3$^d$ 1706

The Councill in Assembly Sate p$^r$sent as Yesterday.

Then was read Colonel Nathan$^l$ Blakiston Agent for this
Province his Lres of the 20$^{th}$ of Aprill & 8th of September
1705 to his Ex$^{ncy}$ the Governo$^r$ & Councill & Gen$^{ll}$ Assemblye
p. 9    The Petition of M$^r$ John Gresham Jun$^r$ Late Sherriffe of
Anne Arund$^l$ County M$^r$ Tho$^s$ Bordley Clk and Moses Adney
Cryer of the late Speciall Court read praying an Allowance
of Fees to be made them proportionable to their respective
Services in that Court, being read. Ordered that the Petitioners have & receive from the several persons accused such fees
in respect of the Several Services by them done and performed, as are taken & Allowed in the Provinciall Court.

The Petition of the Inhabitants of the Towne and Porte of
Annapolis read praying the Generall Assemblys Consideration
of their greate Loss in the Platt of the Towne being burnt in
the Court House and that they would be pleased to order the
Towne to be resurveyed at the Publick Charge. Which by
this Boarde was thought but reasonable and recomended to
the House of Delegates for their Concurrence thereto.

The Boarde adjourn'd for two Hours

Post Meridiem

The Councill Sate as before

& came L$^t$ Colonel William Holland and was added to the
Boarde

The Councill adjourn'd untill 9 of the Clock to morrow
morning.

The Councill in Assembly Sate present as Yesterday

His Ex^ncy acquainting the Boarde that Cap^t Jno Yoakely who arrived yesterday from Lisbon Assures him that her late Ma^ty Catherine the Queene Dowager of England is lately dead there and that he Saw her carryed in State in Order to her funeral Obsequies. It is advised by the Boarde that his Ex^ncy give Orders to the Clergye that she be left out in the Publick Prayers.

And accordingly the said Ord^r were issued & sent to the Clergye of this Province.

M^r Muschamp and eleaven other Members bring the Houses returne to his Ex^ncys Speech. Viz.

May it please your Ex^ncy

We her Majesty's most Dutiful & obedient Subjects the Representatives of the Inhabitants of the Respective Countys of this Province convened in this Present Generall Assembly Do Give your Excellency hearty thanks for your Gracious Speech to us at the Opening of this Session.

S^r Wee have a Deep sense of the Princely Care And generous Regards that the Best and most Benign of Princes our most Gracious Queen hath upon all Occasions demonstrated to us for our protection and Wellfare and Wee do p. 11 hope that the Royal Care and Benificence will at all times be a motive productive of our Sincere & hearty Allegiance togeather with our assiduous & ffervent Prayers to Almighty God for her Majesty's Long Life & happy Reign over us.

As to the Erecting Ports and Townes we are resolved to take that Affair into our consideration, with all the Speed and Dispatch that a Concerne of such Importance is Capable of and as to all other matters which your Ex^ncy now hath or shall think fitt to lay before us and which may any ways Relate to her Majestys Royal Instructions and to the good and Wellfare of this her Majestys Province Wee will with all Carefullness and assiduity apply ourselves and be Unanimous in our Councills to the Discharging the Dutys incumbent on us.

S^r We want words to Express to your Ex^ncy the great thankfullness and gratitude with which our most Gracious Sovereign by her nobleness & Princely goodness hath filled our hearts but Wee hope that all our present and future actions will demonstrate us to be no other than a dutifull & thankfull people to all those Blessings of favour and Protection with her Majesty of her grace & goodness has bestowed upon us

Original  
Journal. not forgetting that very Eminent one of Placing your Ex<sup>ncy</sup> as her Majestys Representative over us

    Aprill 4<sup>th</sup> 1706

        Signed ꝑ order of the house Dellegates

                W Taylard Cl h D.

p. 12    Ordered that the Papers relating to the Zarr of Muscovys improving the Circasian tob° be sent to the House for their Perusall.

    Colonel Hammond & Colonel Lloyd sent with the said Papers, the Petition of the Inhabitants of Annapolis & the following Message viz<sup>t</sup>

        By the Gov<sup>r</sup> & Councill in Assembly Ap<sup>ll</sup> 4th 1706

    His Ex<sup>ncy</sup> observing that what white Serv<sup>ts</sup> are or have been for some years last past imported into this her Ma<sup>tys</sup> Province are generally Irish Papists Who are induced to come hither by the false 'tho Specious Pretences of the free Exercise of their Superstitious Worship and having lands at the head of the Bay settled on them on the Expiration of their tymes of Servitude, so that many hundreds have been lately import-ed, is pleased to ask the Advice of the Gen<sup>ll</sup> Assembly whether on due Consideration thereof there are not apparent Reasons her Ma<sup>tys</sup> loyal good Subjects here Should be Apprehensive of that growing evil & more especially seing this sort of people are Seated in greate Numbers in Baltemore County and at the head of the Bay frontiers of this Province most

p. 13 lyable to the Invasions of the Common Enimye ; Wherefore in case the Countrye thinke this deserves their Notice, His Ex<sup>ncy</sup> desires they will advise what Measures are to be taken for the prevention thereof; for that the Duty of 30 ꝑ poll is not any Discouragem<sup>t</sup> to that Importation,—And whether it be not reasonable by Some Law to forbid the Sale of Protestant Servants to Ma:<sup>ts</sup> of the Romish Church, they being generally Seduced in their Religion or otherwise misused in their Persons

        Signed ꝑ Order W Bladen Cl Council

    Col Hammond & Col° Lloyd returne & Say they have deliv-ered their Message.

    S<sup>r</sup> Thomas Laurence her Ma<sup>tys</sup> Secry of this Province his Petition to her Ma<sup>tje</sup> and the R<sup>t</sup> Hon<sup>ble</sup> the Lords of Trade & Plantations Letter therewith being read. Ordered that M<sup>r</sup> Sanders go down to the House with the following Message.

By his Ex<sup>ncy</sup> the Gov<sup>r</sup> & Councill in Assembly
Ap<sup>ll</sup> 4th 1706.

His Ex<sup>ncy</sup> thinks fitt to acquaint You that S<sup>r</sup> Thomas Laurence has made his Complaint to her Ma<sup>tye</sup> ag<sup>t</sup> the late Law for Regulating of Ordinarys, Copye of w<sup>h</sup> Complaint is herew<sup>th</sup> sent You that you may assert your Reasons for that Law ; otherwise You cannot expect her Ma<sup>tys</sup> Royall Assent thereto.           Signed ꝑ Order W Bladen Cl Counl. p. 14

Colonel Holland acquainting his Ex<sup>ncy</sup> and the Board that his Wife lay dangerously ill, had leave to go home.
The Board adjourn'd for two hours.

### Post Meridiem.

The Councill Sate ꝑ'sent as before (Save Col Holland)
M<sup>r</sup> Hays & M<sup>r</sup> Jones bring the following Message from the House.

### By the house of Delegates Ap<sup>ll</sup> 4th 1706

Upon that parte of his Ex<sup>ncys</sup> Speech which dos relate to the greate Evill which happens to the People of this Province by Bills of Exch<sup>a</sup> Protested for makeing some Provision of Reliefe therein this House does pray that they may be admitted to confer with her Ma<sup>tys</sup> hon<sup>ble</sup> Councill and that his Ex<sup>ncy</sup> will be pleased to appointe the persons tyme & place of meeting accordingly.     Signed ꝑ Ord<sup>r</sup> W Taylard Cl h Del.

The Boarde adjourn'd untill eight of the Clock to morrow morning.

### Fryday Aprill 5th 1706.
### The Councill Sate Present as yesterday

p. 15

And ordered that Colonel Thomas Ennalls carry the following Answer to the houses message last night.

### By the Council in Assembly Apr<sup>ll</sup> 5th 1706

In Answer to your Houses Message yesterday by M<sup>r</sup> Hays & M<sup>r</sup> Jones desiring a Conference with this Boarde in order to redress the greate Evil of protested Bills of Exch<sup>a</sup> His Ex<sup>ncy</sup> and the Councill are willing to have a Conference with the whole house in the Councill Chamber to morrow morning at ten of the Clock upon the Subject matter at present so pernicious to the Countrye.
          Signed ꝑ order W Bladen Cl Council

M<sup>r</sup> Maccall & M<sup>r</sup> M<sup>c</sup>clester bring the following Message

By the House of Delegates Aprill 5th 1706

May it please Yo<sup>r</sup> Ex<sup>ncy</sup>

This House gives your Ex<sup>ncy</sup> their hearty thanks for putting them in minde to inspect that matter relating to the 3<sup>d</sup> ℔ hh<sup>d</sup> which is given to the Countrye to provide Arms &c And they do humbly pray that Your Ex<sup>ncy</sup> will be pleased to give Order that the Accounts thereof from the tyme the said Grant from

p. 16 the late King tooke place to this tyme, may be layd before them that they may enquire into that matter & what has been payd thereon and what is become of the mony's

Signed ℔ Ord<sup>r</sup> W Taylard Cl House Del.

Resolved that the said Accounts be layd before the House and that Orders issue to her Ma<sup>tys</sup> Receivers to that End.

Came M<sup>r</sup> Robert Keith & M<sup>r</sup> Alexander Adams Ministers of the Church of England in Somersett County with M<sup>r</sup> Francis M<sup>c</sup>cemie a dissenting Minister And the said M<sup>r</sup> M<sup>c</sup>cemie complayns of their Libertye being infringed by a certain Order of Councill prohibiting their building a Meeting House within less than halfe a Mile of any Established Church allready built.

Upon which both partys being heard and it appearing to his Ex<sup>cy</sup> & her Ma<sup>tys</sup> hon<sup>ble</sup> Councill that the House was allready erected on M<sup>r</sup> M<sup>c</sup>cemies own proper Lands. Advised that this matter be layd before my Lord Bishop of London for his Decision And that in the mean tyme M<sup>r</sup> M<sup>c</sup>cemie be at liberty to preach in his house according to the Tolleration.

The Board adjourn'd for an houre

p. 17                    Post Meridiem.

The Councill Sate ℔<sup>r</sup>sent as before.

M<sup>r</sup> How & M<sup>r</sup> Jones bring from the house the following Message.

By the house of Delegates Ap<sup>ll</sup> 5th 1706

May it Please Your Ex<sup>ncy</sup>

Upon reading the Message by Colonel Ennalls this Day relating to the Evill of Protested Bills &c It is resolved that this house attend your Ex<sup>ncy</sup> and Councill to morrow morning to confer upon the Subject matter as desired.

Signed ℔ Ord<sup>r</sup> W Taylard Cl h. Del.

The Board adjourn'd till 8 of the Clock to morrow morning

Saturday Aprill 6ᵗʰ 1706

The Councill Sate Present as Yesterday.

The Petition of Henry Roberts of Anne Arundell County
read praying leave that a Bill might be brought in to illegitimate the issue of Ellinor Roberts Wife of John Roberts decᵈ
upon Sufficient Reasons and Proofs to be given to Such
Comittee or persons as the Generall Assembly shall be pleased
to appoint to inquire thereinto.

The Notorious ill life and Conversation of the sᵈ Ellinor p.18
Roberts being well knowne to sevʳall of this Boarde. They
do recomend it to the House to admitt such Bill to be brought
in upon due sumons served on the said Ellinor & the Petʳˢ
Proofs made It being often practicable in England. And tho'
there has yet been no Example of this kind in this Province;
yet it is conceived it will be fitt to do the Petitioner Justice and
discourage Such Licentious Vicious Women

The said Petition with the aforegoing Endorsement sent to
the house by Mʳ Sanders.

Colonel Lloyd & Col Ennalls ordered to acquaint Mʳ
Speaker & the house that this Boarde wayte the Conference.

The Petition of Capᵗ George Harris praying Leave that a
Bill may be brought in for Sale of Charles Ridgleys Lands
for paymᵗ of his Debts Which being read at the Boarde is
Sent to the house by Colonel Jenkins.

The Petition of Mʳ Thomas Edmondson of Talbott County
Setting forth that he had conveyed nine hundred Acres of
Land to his Broᵗ Wᵐ Edmondson who is dead and the con-
sidʳacon unpayd and praying leave to bring in a Bill to
reinvest the sᵈ Lands in the Petitioner, being read is recomended to the house of Delegates and sent by Mʳ Smith.

The Board adjourn'd till 8 of the Clock on Munday Morning.

Munday Aprill the 8th 1706 p. 19

The Councill Sate pʳsent

{ Mʳ Smith        Col: Lloyd  }
{ Col Hamond      Mʳ Sanders  }
{ Col Jenkins     Col Ennalls }
          and Mʳ Coursey.

It being considered that the pʳsent Session of Assembly
have no prospect of concluding in less than a fortnight or
three weeks; Therefore least the two Courts should interfere,
It is advised that the Provinciall Court be adjourned for a few
days untill the 14th Day of May next. And thereupon His
Exⁿᶜʸ is pleased to order the said Writt of Adjournmᵗ to be

34

Original issued and immediately Sent to the Several Countys that all
Journal. persons may have tymely notice thereof.

Ordered that the following Message be Sent to the house
by Col Lloyd & Col. Ennalls.

### By the Councill in Assembly Ap^ll the 8th 1706

It is recomended to the Consideracon of the Gen^ll Assembly
whether the want of a small runing Cash be not a greate dis-
couragem^t to poor indigent Labourers and Artificers such as
Carpenters Coopers Smiths Brick-layers & Boatmen whose
necessity calls for a present dayly Supply, When as in tob°
p. 20 they cannot receive their pay but at one certaine tyme in the
year which is the greatest Reason such Tradesmen generally
leave the Province & go to the Northward where they are not
under that Difficulty. And therefore in Case your house
thinke this is fitting to be remedyed. Whether it may not be
proper this Gen^ll Assembly should address her Ma^tye to supplye
the Province with some small Copper Coyne which might be
current here according to the Scheme herewith Sent You.

Signed ᵽ Order W Bladen Cl Counl

### Proposall for a running Cash.

That the Assembly address her Ma^tye that she will be most
graciously pleased to grant them a particular Species of Coyne
for this Province (to witt) Small Copper pence Sixpences &
shillings with her Ma^tys Royall Pourtraiture on the one side
Maryland on the other, Which should be only current in this
Province by her royall Proclamation or Act of Assembly.

That her Ma^tye be reimbursed by the Countrye the Value
of the Copper & Charge of Coyning which may perhapps
am° to £700 Sterl. This money may be disposed of by the
p. 21 Publick Treasurers for Bills of Exch^a to £4000 Value That
this money go Current in paym^t of all sumes not exceeding
five pounds. And that no person presume to export any of
it under the Penalty of twenty pounds Sterl. for every twenty
shillings and so pro rato thirty pounds for 30^sh & £40 for
40^s or a greater or lesser quantity by which means it will be
kept in the Countrye.

To make this base Coyne of the intrinsick Value with what
it is designed to pass at. Lett the Publick Faith be engaged
and an Act of Assembly made or other proper Directions
given the Publick Treasurers yearly to sett aside the Value
of one thousand pounds Sterl untill it shall am° to the whole
Creditt so that when any Artificer or Labourer brings him a
Sume of Copper not less than five pounds, he may be able
to give him Bills or other current Coyne for it.

This will effectually answer the End proposed : And the <sub>Original</sub> sume of money thus proposed to be sett aside may remayne <sub>Journal.</sub> a Sacred Treasure never to be touch'd unless on some greate Invasion made on the Country You will by this means keep Tradesmen in the Countrye who will meet with present Reward for their Labour It will greatly promote Towns & encourage Such ꝑsons to reside there Workmens Wages will <sub>p. 22</sub> be considerably cheaper Ordinary Accommodations may well be afforded at halfe the extravagant prices they are now Sold at.

This Cash will keepe the Sherriff out of your tob° Houses, All Officers will be advantag'd thereby, And it will be a trusty Stake for the Country upon any fatall Emergencye to have such a Bancke to make use of which will not only be £4000 but really £7000 when a Violent Incursion of the Enemye might perhaps over run all before the Generall Assemblye could consider how to raise a Sume to answer the pʳsent Exigencye, few being willing to fight even for their owne Countrye much less our Servants unless well incouraged that is payed.

Colonel Thomas Smithson his Letter to his Exⁿᶜʸ the Governour, being read, giving an Account of his pʳsent Indisposition and that he wasted himselfe to no purpose in the publiq Service, having no Allowance proportionable to his Service of attending the Provinciall Court, & desiring his Exⁿᶜʸ to lay his Case before the Generall Assemblye

Ordered that the said Letter be layd before the house of Dᵉˢ & it is recomend if they think fitt to gratifye the said Colonel Smithson.

The sᵈ Lre and Recomendation sent by Colonel Ennalls.

The Boarde being acquainted that there were twenty three <sub>p. 23</sub> very good musquitts, now in Towne to be sold fitt for the Countrys Use. Do advise that they be purchased for the Service of the Countrye they being as good & Cleane as any Arms heretofore bought.

Ordered that George Plater Esqʳ her Maᵗʸˢ Receiver of the District of Pattuxent take Care to buy and pay for the said arms at twenty one Shill ꝑ musquett the risque of the Sea being allready run.

Mʳ John Jones & Mʳ Grey bring up a Bill for the Naturalization of John Baptista Tyler of Prince Georges County, wᶜʰ was read & pass'd wᵗʰ amendment

They also brought up a Bill enabling certain Trustees to sell Lands given to Sᵗ Michaels Parish in Talbott County wᶜʰ was read & the Boarde are desirous to be satisfied whether there be no legall Objections to be made by any person yet unheard agᵗ this Bill, and also to have a Sight of Jones's Will.

The afsᵈ Bills with the Endorsemᵗˢ & the following Message Sent to the house by Col Ennalls & Mr Coursey.

By the Councill in Assembly April 8ᵗʰ 1706

His Exⁿᶜʸ thinks fitt to acquaint You of the late Alarm We
had of one thousand Senequirs Comeing from the Northward
p. 24 with Intent to cut off & carry away our Easterne Shore Indians, And therefore you have the Papers herewith sent you
relating thereto for your perusall.

Signed ᵱ Ordʳ W Bladen Cl Councll

Came Lᵗ Col: Holland & was added to the Boarde
Capᵗ George Harris having been required Severall tymes
by his Exⁿᶜʸ the Govʳ & Councill to come to this Towne &
peruse Several french Letters lately taken in the Prize La
Francois of Rochell this day appeared at the Boarde and
brought two of the said Letters translated into English One
from Monsieur D'Auger the French Governʳ giving an Accoᵗ
of a new Fort at Martinico Called Sᵗ Lewis's Forte expected
to be finished towards the latter end of Febʳʸ last: the other
from Monsʳ D'Patys to Monsʳ D'Casse.

His Exⁿᶜʸ is pleased to take notice of the said Capᵗ Harris's
readiness & Diligence in this Matter and asks the Boarde
what will be fitt to give the said Capᵗ Harris in gratification
of his Service & Trouble.

Advised that he be pay'd the Sume of three pounds Sterl
therefore.

The following Message sent to the house by Mʳ Sanders.


By the Govʳ & Councill in Assembly
Apˡˡ the 8th 1706

p. 25    Gentⁿ Att present the Conveyance of Publiq Letters is
very unsafe as well as tedious, and thereby her Maᵗʸˢ Service
as well as your proper Interests much impaired. It's wished
You would Seriously consider how this may he remedyed.
His Exⁿᶜʸ the Governʳ of Virginia having Comunicated his
Resolution of using his Endeavours with the Assembly of that
Colonye intended to Sitt this month to redress the Evil there

Signed ᵱ Ordʳ W Bladen Cl Coun.


Mʳ Peter Watts and Mʳ Francis Dollahyde bring from the
House the foll Message


By the House of Delegates. Apˡˡ 8ᵗʰ 1706.

This House gives his Exⁿᶜʸ thanks for laying the letter
relating to the Indians before them; but they do not appre-

hend any present Danger from the Indians which may give Original
them any Occasion of entring into any further Considerations Journal.
concerning that matter.  They do also give his Ex$^{ncy}$ thanks
for his Care in that Busieness.  The s$^d$ M$^r$ Watts & M$^r$ Dollahyde bring up the Bill enabling Trustees to Sell Lands given
to the Use of S$^t$ Michaels Parish thus endorsed.


By the house of Delegates. Ap$^{ll}$ 8th 1706

No objection appear'd to this house, only it's sayd there is
a Brother & Sister and likewise have sent a Copy of the Will
as desired.

Signed ꝑ Ord$^r$ W Taylard Cl h. Del.

The said Solomon Jones's Will being read at the Board.
Colonel Ennalls was sent to the house w$^{th}$ the following
Message, Viz$^t$


By the Councill in Assembly, Ap$^{ll}$ 8th 1706 p. 26

The said Solomon Jones's Will being read at this Boarde
as also the Petition of the Vestrye of S$^t$ Michaels Parish
Upon due Consideration had thereof.  The Will do's not
second the Petition.  Which setts forth the said Jones did by
his last Will & Testament in writing bequeath his dwelling
Plantation to be sold and the Proffitts thereof to be appropriated to a Chappel of Ease, but is alltogether uncertaine and
no full Indication of the Testators minde.  Wherefore altho'
this Board will be allways ready to assert the Churches Interest, Yet they will be ever unwilling to do any thing that may
be unlawfull or irregular to the prejudice of any.

Signed ꝑ Ord$^r$ W Bladen Cl Coun.

The Boarde Adjourn'd untill 8 of the Clock to morrow mor. p. 27


Tuesday Aprill the 9th, 1706
The Councill Sate P$^r$sent His Ex$^{ncy}$ the Gov$^r$ &c.

| | | |
|---|---|---|
| ⎧ M$^r$ Smith | ⎧ L$^t$ Colonel Willm. Holland |
| ⎨ Col Hamond | ⎨ M$^r$ Sanders |
| ⎬ Col: Jenkins | ⎬ Col Ennalls & |
| ⎩ Col Lloyd | ⎩ M$^r$ Coursey. |

Advised and resolved that the following persons be comissionated Justices of the Peace and of Oyer and Terminer in
Prince Georges County.  To witt in the Comission of the

Original   Peace.  M^r Robert Bradly, Robert Tyler James Stoddert
Journal.  W^m Tanyhill John Gerrard of the Quor.  Abraham Clarke
Thomas Brooke jun^r Francis Marleborrough Thomas Claggett
Alexander Magrooder & Henry Acton.  Whereof the first
six only in the Comission of Oyer & Terminer & first five
named of the Quor.

Mary Newells Petition read praying leave to Sell a Drame
& Coffee without paying the ordinary Lycence and recom-
ended to the house of Delegates for their Concurrence and
Sent together w^th the following Message by M^r Sanders.

### By the Councill in Assembly Aprill 9th, 1706

Whereas heretofore a lott was layd out for the Rector of
S^t Ann's Parish in the Towne and Port of Añapolis and also
one other Lott for a Vestrye house, now forasmuch as there
is a very good Vestry house built and adjoyned to the Church
there will be no necessity that the former Vestry house should
remayne to that Use but that it may be highly necessary it be
anexed to the Parsons Lott and some further Improvement
p. 28  made thereon, in order to some comfortable provision to be
made of an house for the Reception & Accomodation of a
Minister, to which his Ex^ncy is willing to contribute if the
House thinke fit to give Encouragement thereto.
                    Signed ꝑ Ord^r W Bladen Cl: Concil

M^r Peter Watts brought up a Bill for uniting Newport
Hundred to William & Mary Parish in Charles County.
Which was read the first & second tymes and sent to the
house by M^r Coursey.

Ordered that M^r Evan Thomas of Talbott County cut a
Seale for the Councill Provinciall & severall County Courts
with her Ma^tys Arms & Semper Eadem at the Bottome The
Councill Seale to be inscribed in the Circle Gov^r & Councill.  The Provinciall Seale Provinciall Court & the Sev^rall
County Courts Seals with the Names of the Countys, for
which he will be payed by the Publique and Severall Countys.

M^r Eliaz King and five other Members from the House
brought a Bill for regulating and dividing Several Countys
on the Easterne Shoar & Constituting a County by the name
of Queen Anns County, & the following Message.

p. 29          By the House of Del. Apr^ll 9th 1706

This House prays that his Ex^ncy the Governo^r will be pleased
to name the new County proposed by the Bill herewith Sent.
                    Signed ꝑ ord^r W Taylard Cl h Del.

The af<sup>d</sup> Bill being read the Boarde are willing the same Original should pass And his Ex<sup>ncy</sup> is pleased to name the new Journal. County by the Name of Queene Anns County.

Col Haḿond & Colonel Jenkins were ordered to carry downe the Bill to the House.

{ This Board adjourned untill 8
of the Clock to morrow morning. }

### Wednesday Aprill the 10th 1706
### The Councill Sate present as yesterday

Then was read the Petition of Major Josiah Wilson High Sherriffe of Ann Arundell County, praying reliefe ag<sup>t</sup> the Act of Assembly enjoyning the Sherriffs to execute many Precepts ex Officio.

On Consideration whereof the said Act seems to be very harde on the said Sherriffs there being no Allowance to those tho' to all other Officers in Criminall Causes. And therefore the Petition is recoḿended to the Consid'acon of the House of Delegates that they will by Some Small Additionall Law make such Allowance to the Several Sherriffs of this Province Whereby the execution of Justice may be encouraged & expedited, for as the Law now stands It is a greate impedim<sup>t</sup> to justice

This Pet. so endorsed was sent to the House by Col Lloyd.

The Board adjourned for an hour

### Post Meridiem.   The Councill Sate

M<sup>r</sup> Joseph Ennalls & M<sup>r</sup> Beale brought the Reporte of the Comittee in answer to the Secr<sup>ys</sup> Petition to her Ma<sup>tye</sup> for Ordinary Lycences

Which was read at the Boarde and agreed to by her Ma<sup>tys</sup> honble Councill & is as followeth

### Aprill the 10th 1706

The Report of the Comittee of Laws in Relation to the passing of the Bill for Ordinary Keepers and giving the Fine for the Same to the Countys.

The Comittee have made Diligent Search into the Journalls of the house of Assembly & find that in the year 1662 There was An Act made Intituled An Act for the Encouragement of Ordinary Keepers without any fine given for Lycenses which was but to Continue for three years.

2$^{dly}$   Wee find in the year 1678 An Act made Intituled An Act for Regulating of Ordinarys & Limitting the Number of them within this Province.

wherein the then Assembly for Advancing the Revenue of the Lord Proprietary did give to his said Lordship for every ordinary Lycense in Saint Marys City 2000 pounds Tobacco and in the Countys twelve hundred pounds of Tobacco Which we presume is the first Act of Assembly that gives any Fine for Ordinary Lycenses which was to Continue but for three years.

By Vertue of which Act wee conceive (upon some Discourse had with Colonell Henry Darnall) That the Lord Proprietary out of his Especiall Favour to his Secretarys (they being his Relations) Did give & grant the Profitts Arising from the Ordinary Lycenses by Vertue of that Act to them. But we find no Act of Assembly for Settling the Same on the Secretary during his Lordships Government.

3$^{dly}$   We find in the year 1692 that the then Assembly taking the Profitts arising from Ordinary Lycenses to be noe branch of the Secretarys Office, Did by an Act made the same year give to then Governour Copley for every Lycense to keep Ordinary at Saint Marys two thousand pounds of Tobacco & in the Countys twelve hundred pounds of Tobacco Which Act was to Continue but three years S$^r$ Thomas Laurence being then Secretary of Maryland Who upon passing of that Act & another of the same Sessions Entituld An Act for settling Naval Officers Fees within this Province did go to England & Petition'd his then Majesty King William the third that the said Bills might not pass the Royall Assent under pretence that the same were perquisites belonging to the Secretarys Office.

That upon the said S$^r$ Thomas Laurences Petition the said Act for Navall Officers Fees was Disassented to and ordered to remaine as a Perquisite to the Secretarys Office. But as to Ordinary Lycenses we do not find any order from the King or Councill that it should or ought to be a Perquisite of the Secretarys Office Whereby We Conceive that his Majesty & Councill were of opinion that it was in the power of the Assembly to give such Profits arising from Ordinary Lycenses to whom they pleasd

4$^{thly}$   That true it is The Assembly by an Act made in the time of Governour Nicholson did give the profitts arising from Ordinary Lycenses to the Secretary Which we take to be the first Act of Assembly that ever settled the same on the Secretary or made it a Perquisite of his Office Which Act was but temporary & expired in three years. And altho the Assembly did afterwards by other Acts Continue the Same to the Secre-

tary yet it was always but by Temporary Laws from three Original
years to three years at the Expiration of which Laws it was Journal.
as wee Conceive in the Power of the Assembly to give it to
whom they thought fitt

5$^{thly}$   That as to what S$^r$ Thomas Laurence asserts concern- p. 34
ing his Application to the Comittee of Laws in April 1704.
And their refusal to hear him ag$^t$ the Bill.   We say S$^r$ Thomas
Laurence was not denyed to be heard by that Comittee but
was by them treated with all the Civility & respect and
answered by the Chairman thereof That what they did was
given them in Charge from the House of Delegates & that
that Comittee could not Act Contrary but must proceed
according to their Directions

6$^{thly}$   Upon the Whole Matter wee do not find that any Secry
of Maryland (S$^r$ Tho. Laurence excepted) ever claimed the
Profitts arising by Ord$^{ry}$ Lycenses as a Perquisite belonging to
& inseparable from the Secretarys Office. but when they had
the same it was by the free Donation from the Lord Baltemore
when granted him by the Assembly during his Government
here and since by the Gift of the Assembly w$^{th}$out p'tence of
any other Right thereto so that we are of opinion that unless
S$^r$ Thomas Laurence can make it appear that the same is a
Perquisite incident to the Sec$^{rys}$ Office & inseparable therefrom
Settled by any Act or Acts of Assembly otherwise than as af$^d$
it is & of Right ought to be in the Power of the gen$^{ll}$ Assembly to dispose of the Same as they think fitt.

Neither have we any Reason to believe that our most gracious p. 35
Queene will deny her royal Assent to any Law Enacted
here for the good of this Province upon the bare Insinuation
of private or particular persons whose Interest leads them to
think or say the Contrary Especially where they do not (as the
Act for Ordinary Lycenses does not) lessen her Majestys Officers Just Fees they being limitted by another Act of Assembly
for that purpose

So that upon Consideration had upon the whole matter of
S$^r$ Thomas Laurences Peticon We doe Assert that the Fine for
Ordinary Lycenses is not nor ever was an ancient Fee or Per-
quisite belonging or appertaining to the Secretarys Office of
Maryland          Signed ꝑ Order Rich$^d$ Dallam Cl Conc.


By the House of Delegates Aprill 10th 1706

Upon reading this Report The house concurrs therewith
Sign'd ꝑ Order W Taylard Clk h d.

M$^r$ Jones & M$^r$ Grey bring from the house Viz.          p. 36

By the House of Delegates Apr^ll 10^th 1706

In answer to Your Ex^ncys and Hono^rs Message of the 8th Instant relating to some Gratification to be made to Col° Smithson. This House have considered that it is not long Since that a Gratification was made to the said Col° Smithson of fifty pounds for his Services to the Country: And they are of Opinion that that Gentlemans Services to the Countrye are not so very eminent above all others to deserve a Distinguishment by way of Rewarde

Signed p Ord^r W Taylard Clk h Del.

{ The Board adjourn'd untill 8
{ of the Clock to mor mor.

### Thursday Aprill 11^th 1706

The Councill Sate p^resent as yesterday Saving Colonel Holland who had leave to go home to fetch some Papers necessary for defending his Clayme to some Lands now in dispute before this Assembly

A Bill ascertayning the Navigation of Open Sloops and p. 37 Shallopps in respect of the Enumerated Comoditys being read was approved of and sent to the House by Col Lloyd & M^r Coursey.

The following Memoriall was p^rsented from the Lord Baltimores Agent to his Ex^ncy the Govern^r & read at the Boarde

### Aprill 9^th 1706

May it please Yo^r Ex^ncy

I humbly hope Your Ex^ncy will not take amiss now a second tyme to have rep^rsented to You the Delay of doing the R^t Hon^ble the Lord Baltimore Proprietary of this Province Right & Justice pursuant to the R^t hon^ble the Lords Comission^n for Trade & Plantations Letter in reference to the Law intituled an Act for ascertayning the Bounds of Lands where by the Birth right Propertye and Inheritance of the said Lord Baltimore is palpably invaded, as it was plainly made appeare to the said Lords Comissioners about three years past whereupon the said letter was writt to this Governm^t

The Confidence I have in the Justice of yo^r Ex^ncy and Hon:^ble Councill gives me an Assurance of being rendered Capable to informe his Lordp my Ma^t by this Fleete that his Lordp in this Affaire has had his Share with her Ma^tys Subjects of this Province in the Experience of your Ex^ncys knowne

inclination to do all persons having Occasion to applye them- Original
selves to you equall Right. Journal.

And if it be considered that very few or none besides P. 38
Surveyors Sherriffs Clks and the Promoter of the said Act
have received any Benefitt thereby, but on the contrary a great
many thousand pounds of tob° have been expended to no
purpose by the Inhabitants of this Province in pursuing in
vaine the directions of that Law for reliefe.

It may be hoped that all the Contrivances of a person
knowne to be somewhat Stiff & tenacious of the Conceptions
of his owne Brayne, tho' in the Opinion of others (with respect
to his Character be it Spoken) as well grounded in Knowledge
as himself; Such Conceptions carry little weight may not be
Sufficient to keepe on foot any longer an Act which in
Several Branches thereof is Prejudicial as well to the Lord
Proprietors as the Peoples Right. All which considered I
humbly desire that your Ex^{ncy} will be pleased to reporte
what your Ex^{ncy} shall see fitt in the matter to the Lords
Comissioners of Trade, and that a Copy of Such Reporte
may be for the Proprietarys Perusall delivered to

> Yo^r Ex^{ncys} most humble &
>> most obed^t Serv^t
>>> Charles Carrol

The said Memoriall sent to the house of Delegates who
are desired to give an Answer thereto this Session this p. 39
matter having been so long referr'd & delayed.

Came L^t Col: Aisquith and M^r Joseph Ennalls and brought
up a Bill restrayning Papists from purchassing Protestant or
reputed Protestant Serv^{ts} & for preventing fornication Comitted by white Serv^{ts} working in the Ground &c.

And a Bill for investing certaine Lands in John Whittington and his Heirs which was read & pas't & Sent to
the house by Colonel Hammond & Col Jenkins together with
the other Bill endorsed thus viz^t.

### By the Gov^r & Councill in Assembly
### Apr^{ll} 11^{th} 1706

This Bill being read at the Boarde and observed that
there are two things of different natures couched in one &
the same Law. His Ex^{ncy} in Reguard to her Ma^{tys} Royall
Instructions cannot consent to the passing thereof therefore
It is recommended that these two matters be remedied by
different Laws

> Signed ꝑ Ord^r W Bladen Cl Council.

Original
Journal.     M'. Richard Bennetts Petition read praying leave that a Bill
might be brought in to ascertayne the Bounds of Worton
Mannor in Cecill County.

The Board do not thinke fitt to pass a Bill therefore ; for
that they are of Opinion the Lord Proprietors Grant will be
Sufficient to that End.

[p. 40     M' Grey and M' Ennalls bring up the Bill for preventing
fornication by white Women Serv'' Working in the Ground
which was ordered to lye on the Table.

They also brought up M' Carrolls memoriall endorsed.

### By the House of Delegates Apr'' 11<sup>th</sup> 1706

This house designing to end this Session with what expedition they can do resolve not to enter into any debate about
that matter.  Therefore referr the Same to the Consid'ation
of the next Session of Assembly

Signed ꝑ ord' W Taylard Cl h Del.

{ The Board adjourn'd untill 8 }
{     of the Clock to mor. mor.   }

### Fryday Aprill 12th 1706

The Councill Sate present as yesterday.

Colonel Thomas Ennalls upon urgent Business had the
Leave of his Ex<sup>ncy</sup> & this Boarde to go home.

Then were sent downe to the house The Act of Parliament
prohibiting Comerce with France and that for Encouragement
of Navall Stores to be Imported from these her Majestys
Plantations by Coll Jenkins together with the following Message Viz.

### By his Ex<sup>ncy</sup> the Governour & Councill in Assembly
### Aprill 12th 1706.

p. 41     Some Persons having been presented by the Provinciall &
Ann Arundell County Courts for Bigamy & for suffering a
Quaker Conventicle to be kept in their house, The Justices &
officers of those Courts are at a Stand in the Prosecution the
laws of England providing against those offences seeming
to them to be wholy restraind to her Majestys Subjects residing within the Kingdom of England so that for want of Law
in this Country those offenders expect to escape unpunishd
according to the old saying, Where there is no Law there is
no Offence.

Wherefore It is recom̄ended to the Consideration of this Original
Generall Assembly either to declare those Laws of England Journal.
reach hither (for the better Satisfaction of the several Courts
of Justice) or otherwise by some good Wholesome Laws to
restraine the said Offences.

Signed p order W Bladen Cl Concil.

The Petition of Majʳ Josiah Wilson read as followeth Viz.
To his Exⁿᶜʸ the Governour & her Majestys honʳble Councill
now Sitting

The Petition of Josiah Wilson Sheriff of Ann Arundell
County  Humbly Sheweth

That whereas by an Act of Assembly of this Province for
Limitation of Officers Fees It is provided that any Officers
therein mencon'd having any Fees belonging unto them
which shall be by the Governour & Councill so adjudgd & p. 42
allow'd and not in the Same Act mentioned limitted and
allowed It shall be lawfull for such Officers to have Such Fee
or Fees as the Governour & Councill shall Adjudge & no
more as by the Same Act reference being had thereto may
appear, And there is not any Fee therein allowed the Sheriff
for the severall Services following Viz.

|  | £ tob° |
|---|---|
| For a Declaration with the Writt | 06 |
| For Setting in the Stocks | 12 |
| For Writt of Electing Delegates & Indres | 1500 |
| For only one Delegate | 500 |
| For a habeas Corpus | 10 |
| For Serving a Decl in Ejectment | 200 |
| For Serving a ne exeat Provinciam | 200 |
| For Serving a Writt of Replevin the Same } Fees as for Attachment or Execution. } |  |
| For a Writt of Possession | 250 |

Yoʳ Exⁿᶜʸˢ Petʳ humbly prays yoʳ Exⁿᶜʸ and this honourable
board that whereas he is obligd by his Office to discharge his
Duty in the performance of all and Singular the Premisses,
when lawfully required which cannot be done without Considerable Charge & trouble to your Petʳ he may be allowed for
the above particulars as to yoʳ Exⁿᶜʸ & Honʳˢ it shall seem fitt
and reasonable and yoʳ Petʳ as in Duty bound shall ever pray

Which Petition being read at this board his Exⁿᶜʸ & her
Majestys honourable Councill do think the Fees in this Peti- p. 43
tion rated to be reasonable for the Services to be done and
performed by the severall Sheriffs in this Province and allow
the said Sheriffs to have take & receive the same and no more.

The Councill adjourn'd till to morrow morning eight a Clock.

Original
Journal.

### Saturday Aprill 13th 1706

The Councill Sate present as Yesterday with the addition of Coll Holland

Came George Plater Esq<sup>r</sup> her Majestys Receiver of the District of Puttuxent and laid before his Ex<sup>ncy</sup> and this board his Accounts of the three pence ℈ hogshd given by her Majesty for purchasing Arms & by him rec<sup>d</sup> from the 12th of May 1692 to th 20th of July 1705  On perusall whereof it is observed that the following Sums have been issued viz<sup>t</sup>

| | |
|---|---|
| To Cap<sup>t</sup> Peter Coode | £ 50..00..00 |
| To Cap<sup>t</sup> Nathaniel Bostock | 100..00..00 |
| To allowed Col Blakiston for apprehending } Pyrates & Securing their Effects } | 110..00..00 |

Which the Board thinks the Country ought to be refunded and desire the house will Concurr to represent it to her Majesty and my L<sup>d</sup> Treasurer of England that the Country may be reimbursd.

Also Came George Muschamp Esq<sup>r</sup> & laid before his Ex<sup>ncy</sup> & this board his Acco<sup>t</sup> of the three pence ℈ Hh<sup>d</sup> for Arms arising in Potomack & Pocomoke Districts & by him rec<sup>d</sup> from 1695 to 1703 Ordered the said Acco<sup>t</sup> be also laid before the house of Delegates.  Both which Accounts were sent to the house by Coll Lloyd & M<sup>r</sup> W<sup>m</sup> Coursey.

M<sup>r</sup> James Hay & M<sup>r</sup> Joseph Gray bring from the house the bill for Ascertaining the navigation of open Sloops & Shallops in respect to the enumerated Comoditys with the following endorsement Viz.

### By the house of Delegates Aprill 13th 1706

This bill being read in the house will pass w<sup>th</sup> the following Amendment viz. of Lessening the Security to fifty pounds Sterl.

Which bill together with the Endorsm<sup>t</sup> being read was ordered to be thus endorsd

### By the Councill in Assembly
### April 13<sup>th</sup> 1706

The Board have Considered this bill & think they cannot be too cautious in Securing the Acts of Trade & Navigation duly complyed with and therefore think the Sec<sup>ry</sup> little enough

Sign'd ℈ ord<sup>r</sup> W Bladen Cl Concil.

Came M<sup>r</sup> Frisby & L<sup>t</sup> Coll Aisquith & bring up a Bill for Currency of Coyne

A Bill for making null and void Thomas Edmundsons Con- Original
veyance of Land to W<sup>m</sup> Edmondson Journal.

A Bill declaring the Land law to be in force

A Bill declaring the Law for Erecting Ann Arundell &
Oxford Towns into Ports & Towns to be in Force

A Bill for suspending the Prosecution of Romish Priests &c p. 45

M<sup>r</sup> Skinner & nine other Members bring up the Houses
Address of Thanks to his Ex<sup>ncy</sup> as follows


### April the 13th 1706

May it please Yo<sup>r</sup> Ex<sup>ncy</sup> .

Wee her Majestys most Dutifull & loyal Subjects the Representatives of the Inhabitants of the respective Countys of
this Province now met & convened in a generall Assembly do
give yo<sup>r</sup> Ex<sup>ncy</sup> hearty Thanks for all your kindnesses and generous gratitudes shew'd us from your Accession to the
Government to this time And we do Assure yo<sup>r</sup> Ex<sup>ncy</sup> that as
her Majesty by her royal bounty has filled our hearts with
Thankfullness so she has added one Degree of Joy to our
ffelicity by placing yo<sup>r</sup> Ex<sup>ncy</sup> her Vice Gerent over us which
will highly improve that profound Veneration & Respect which
we now have & shall always desire to retain for yo<sup>r</sup> Ex<sup>cys</sup> Person & Governm<sup>t</sup>. Wee are

May it please yo<sup>r</sup> Ex<sup>ncy</sup>

Yo<sup>r</sup> Ex<sup>ncys</sup> most humble Serv<sup>ts</sup>

| | | |
|---|---|---|
| Samuel Young | W<sup>m</sup> Watts | Robert Tyler |
| Tho<sup>s</sup> Beale | Jo<sup>s</sup> Gray | Ja Smallwood |
| Cha<sup>s</sup> Greenberry | Jn<sup>o</sup> Jones | Gerard Fowke |
| Francis Dollahide | Joseph Hill | Tho<sup>s</sup> Smith Spkr |
| Jn<sup>o</sup> Contee | W<sup>m</sup> Dare | George Muschamp |
| Jn<sup>o</sup> Mackall | Peter Watts | Rob<sup>t</sup> Gouldsbourough |
| Hugh Eccleston | Jas<sup>s</sup> Philips | Ja : Maxwell |
| Jn<sup>o</sup> Leach | Jn<sup>o</sup> Wells | Tho<sup>s</sup> Greenfield |
| Nich<sup>s</sup> Lowe | James Hay | John Macclaster |
| W<sup>m</sup> Stone | Edward Blay | W<sup>m</sup> Frisby |
| Will Aisquith | Rob<sup>t</sup> Skinner | Tho<sup>s</sup> Frisby |
| Tho<sup>s</sup> Howe | Elias King | R<sup>d</sup> Jones ju<sup>r</sup> |
| Sam<sup>l</sup> Magrooder | Jo. Ennalls | |

The Board Adjourns for an hour. p. 46


Post Meridiem the Councill Sate Present as before

The Petition of the Roman Catholicks Signd by Coll Henry
Darnall M<sup>r</sup> Charles Carroll M<sup>r</sup> Richard Bennett & M<sup>r</sup> James
Carroll being this day read at the Board It is observed that

Original the Pet<sup>rs</sup> thô they so stile themselves rather seeme to challenge
Journal. than petition for a Toleration & Freedome & unhandsomely
Charge the Generall Assembly with infringing the same which
they cannot have the least reason to offer seing at the time of
making the Act they had not even the slightest Assurance of
such freedom or Tolleration All which is of the Same piece
with the latter part of the Petition seeming to Insinuate as if
her Majesty would forgett the minutest thing for the ease &
advantage of her Subjects Neither has this board any reason
to be Satisfyed with the Petition<sup>rs</sup> Construction of the houses
Intention which they say was that untill her Majestys Pleasure
should be knowne that they might not be disturb'd in the Intervalls of Assemblys. But we hope we have a better right
and with better reason to Judge it was quite Contrary thereto
for otherwise to what end was the penall Act made or the
p. 47 Suspending one limitted to Eighteen months a certain time
prefix'd

The aforegoing Remarkes on the said Peticon together with
the proposd bill for the Tolleration of the Papists was sent to
the house by Coll Hammond & Coll Jenkins & then

The Board adjourn'd to Munday morning


Munday Aprill 15th, 1706
The Councill Sate P<sup>r</sup>sent

M<sup>r</sup> Smith Col·Hammond Col Jenkins Coll Lloyd Col Holland
M<sup>r</sup> Cheseldyne & M<sup>r</sup> Coursey

Read the Petition of M<sup>r</sup> Samuel Chew & M<sup>r</sup> Nehemiah
Birkheard praying that a bill may be brought in to enable
them to sell Abraham Naylors Estate & dispose the same to
the uses in his will mencon'd.

The said Petition being read & the Board Considering the
Will is to a pious use the Relief of the Poor and that Abraham
Naylor has no heir are willing that a bill may be brought in to
Confirme the Will & recommend the Petition to the house of
Delegates.

Which recommendation was sent to the house by Col Hammond
& Coll Jenkins.

The following Message ordered to be drawn up Viz.


By the Councill in Assembly &c.

Whereas in a late Session there was an order made that the
Powder house should be remov'd within the Towne where the
p. 48 Governour thought fitt But for as much as the Undertakers
aske tenn pounds therefor and will runn no Risq in Case it

should fall in Pieces Wee desire that the house will while they
now Sitt treat with Workmen to do it.
Signed ℗ Ord<sup>r</sup> W Bladen Cl Concll.

Then was read the Petition of M<sup>r</sup> Andr<sup>w</sup> Richmond Master Gunner & Store Keeper at Annapolis praying the payment of his Sallary

Ordered that George Plater Esq<sup>r</sup> pay unto him twenty five pounds Sterling as Master Gunner Store Keeper & Armorer at Annapolis being in full for one years Sallary w<sup>ch</sup> ended the sixth day of February 1705-6

The Board Adjourns for an hour

Post Meridiem   The Councill Sate<br>P<sup>r</sup>sent as in the Morning

M<sup>r</sup> W<sup>m</sup> Frisby & Seven other Members bring from the house a Bill for Advancement of Trade & erecting Ports & Towns in the Province of Maryland

Which was read the first time, endors'd and Sent to the house by Col Jenkins Col Lloyd & M<sup>r</sup> Coursey

Coll Maxwell & M<sup>r</sup> Macall bring from the house their Answer to the Message from this board Concerning Bigamy & Conventicles as follows viz<sup>t</sup>

By the house of Delegates     p. 49<br>Aprill 15th 1706

Yo<sup>r</sup> Hon<sup>rs</sup> Message by Coll Jenkins of the 12th of Aprill Instant this day lay under Debate & Consideration of the house & upon reading of the first branch thereof relating to Bigamy This house resolved that a bill be brought in Declaring the Act of Parliament of England ag<sup>t</sup> Bigamy has been & Still is in force in this Province

And as to the other branch relating to Quakers Conventicles &c This house are of opinion that the Act for Religion has Sufficiently provided that they are punishable according to the Act of Parliament in that Case

Sign'd ℗ Order W Taylard Clk h. D.

Upon reading whereof it is ordered that the following Reply be sent thereunto viz<sup>t</sup>

By the Councill in Assembly<br>Aprill 15<sup>th</sup> 1706

In Answer to part of the house's Message by M<sup>r</sup> Macall & Coll Maxwell Wee have perused the Act of Religion and

35

Original find it no ways Declares the penall laws to be in force here
Journal. but wholy exempts them upon complying with certain Dutys
enjoyn'd.                    Signed ꝑ ord˞ W̅ Bladen Cl Concil.

Came M˞ Young & M˞ Leach from the house to see M˞
George Plater Sworne to his Collection in the Navall Office at
Puttuxent and an oath was accordingly administred to him
for that purpose in his Presence.

p. 50    Came M˞ Jos: Gray & one other Member and brought up
the following bills Ingrossed viz.

A Bill for uniting Newport Hundred to W᷂ & Mary Parish
in Charles County

A Bill declaring the land Law to be in force

A Bill to make null & void a Deed or Convᵃ from Thomas
Edmundson to W᷂ Edmundson

A Bill for Naturalization of Jnº Baptista Tyler of Prince
Georges County

A Bill investing certain lands in John Whittington & his
heires.

A Bill for Division of Severall Countys &c

The Latter whereof being read was recoꝰended to the
house for Amendmᵗ.

But the others were all assented to and sent to the house
by M˞ Sanders

The Councill Adjourns till to morrow morning

Tuesday April 16ᵗʰ 1706

The Councill Sate    Present as yesterday

Came M˞ Jones M˞ Gray & M˞ Mᶜlaster & bring from the
house

A Bill for Advancement of Trade & erecting Towns &
Ports in this Province

. A Bill for Selling Abraham Naylors land to the uses in his
Will mencond

Which being read were agreed to & Sent to the house by
Col Holland & M˞ Cheseldyn

p. 51    Came M˞ Gray and brought up the Ingrossd Bill for Dividing the Countys amended as Recomended which was read &
assented to by this board and Sent to the house by M˞ Coursey.

The Board adjourn'd for an hour

Post Meridiem the Councill Sate

Coll Nathaniel Blakiston Agent for this Province his Lres
Sent to the house

M$^r$ Robert Gouldsborough being heard in favour of the Petition of the Vestry of S$^t$ Michaels Parish in Talbot County and Solomon Jones's Will appearing to be altogether insufficient to make any Estate or Dispose the Land to the uses therein mentiond the Bill is rejected and the partys left to the Coōmon Law.

Came M$^r$ Greenfield Major Lowe & M$^r$ Tyler to present M$^r$ Robert Bradley a new Elected member for Prince Georges County to be Sworne who had the usuall Oaths Administred according to Law and Sign'd the Test & Oath of Abjuration

The Councill adjourns to Eight of the Clock to morrow morning

### Wednesday Aprill 17th 1706
#### The Councill Sate    Present as Yesterday

The Petition of the Roman Catholicks read as followeth Viz. To his Ex$^{ncy}$ the Governour & Councill in Assembly

The humble Petition of her Majestys Dutifull & Loyall Roman Catholiq Subjects of Maryland

Sheweth. That the said Roman Catholicks preferr'd an P. 52 humble Peticon at the Beginning of this Sessions praying that there might be a farther Suspension of the Act Intituled An Act to prevent the Growth of Popery by which they Conceiv'd themselves under Some hardships untill her Majestys Pleasure should be knowne in relation to what her gracious Intensions may be towards them in this Plantation.

That they understand some Expressions in their said Petition have (contrary to their designe) given Offence so as to be a means of hindring their Relief humbly pray'd for

That the giving offence in the least Manner either to her Majesty (by whose Royall pleasure only they must stand or ffall in that Matter) or to the Governm$^t$ here Establish'd under her is a thing they allways have & shall with their utmost industry avoid being as sensible as any her other Subjects of the Happiness they enjoy under the Clemency of her mild & glorious Reigne also hoping that while the Generall blessings that at this Juncture attend her unparallell'd Undertakings make not only her owne Subjects but most of the Christian World rejoyce her said Roman Catholiq Subjects under yo$^r$ Ex$^{ncys}$ prudent Government may not by lying under Hardships in religious Matters till her Majesty Signifys her Pleasure be Depriv'd of sharing the generall Satisfaction which by yo$^r$ p. 53 Ex$^{ncys}$ & Councills concurrence to an Act for the further Suspending the said Law till then they shall fully partake of

And therefore they humbly pray yo$^r$ Ex$^{ncy}$ & Councills Concurrence thereto & they as in Duty bound shall pray.

The following Message Sent to the house

By the Gov<sup>r</sup> & Councill in Assembly
Aprill 17th, 1706

Severall Complaints being made to this board that Persons Sent to the Indians at the head of the bay have been so slightly rewarded for their Extraordinary Services that it will be of ill Consequence & to the Discouragement of others on the like Occasions Wee Desire the house of Delegates will seriously reflect thereon and particularly how M<sup>r</sup> John Hall & a certain Indian by him employed have been gratifyd

Signed ꝑ Ord<sup>r</sup> W Bladen Cl Concil.

Came M<sup>r</sup> Anthony Smith & made Oath that he Saw Col Holland the only Surviving Witness to Thomas Knightons Will prove the Same before M<sup>r</sup> Henry Bonner Deputy Com<sup>ry</sup> of Ann A<sup>ll</sup> County at his the s<sup>d</sup> Antho. Smiths house Col Holland being present Says he believes he did so.

p. 54     The Councill adjourns to the Afternoon

Post Meridiem     Council Sate

Present as in the Forenoon

' Came Major Beale & M<sup>r</sup> Dollahide & bring up

A Bill Declaring the Act for Suspending the ꝑsecution of Romish Priests &c to be in force for 12 months &c.

Which was read & Sent to the house by M<sup>r</sup> Coursey.

The Bill for preventing the Sin of Fornication comitted by white women Servants working in the Ground is Read & Rejected & Sent to the House by M<sup>r</sup> Sanders

Came M<sup>r</sup> Macall & M<sup>r</sup> Hays & brought up the Bill for Advancement of Trade & Erecting Towns & Ports. Engrossd which was assented to & Sent to the house by Coll Holland & M<sup>r</sup> Sanders.

The Comittee of Acc<sup>ts</sup> bring up their Journall

Assented to by the House

M<sup>r</sup> Youngs Account for building the Vestry house to S<sup>t</sup> Ann's Church at Annapolis being read at the Board is thought very unreasonable & is referred to the Perusall & examination of the house.

The Board upon Perusal of the Iournall of the Comittee of Accounts find 3000 lb tob<sup>o</sup> allow'd to M<sup>r</sup> Charles Kilburne &
p. 55 not being Satisfied with the reasonableness thereof order the following Message to be prepared & sent to the house Viz.

By the Councill in Assembly
Aprill the 17th, 1706.

The Journall of the Comittee of Accounts being read it is observ'd that there is 3000 lb tob° allowed to M^r Charles Kilburne for three years Sallary as publiq Gunner

Whereas his Ex^ncy & this board have already allow'd him [twenty] five pounds in full Satisfaction thereof & paid the same out of the Duty of three pence ꝑ hhd. given by her Majesty for Arms &c how this Allowance comes to be now made (Your house having formerly Resolved that he should not be paid out of the Publiq Stock of this Province) seems strange therefore We Desire better Satisfaction therein

Signed ꝑ Ord^r  W Bladen Cl Concll.

M^r Maclaster & M^r Grey bring up a bill Declaring two severall Acts of Parliament to be in force

A Bill Incouraging the Making hemp & Flax &c.

A Bill Suspending the prosecution of Popish Priests

Which were read & Endorsed to pass with the Amendments' & were sent to the House by Col Jenkins

The Bill ascertaining the Damage on ꝑtested bills of Exchange brought by M^r Mclaster & M^r Grey is ordered to lye on the Board

M^r Tho^s Frisby brings from the house the following Answer p. 56 to the Message about 3000 lb tob° allowed M^r Kilburne


Aprill 17th 1706  By the house of Dell.

Read and Debated in the houe & Resolvd that Article of 3000 l tob° be struck off the Journall

Signed ꝑ Order W Taylard Cl ho D.


The Councill Adjourn's till to morrow morning 8 of the Clocke


Thursday April 18th, 1706

The Councill Sate P^rsent as Yesterday.

Read the foll. Memoriall

W^m Bladen on behalf of Coll Natha^l Blakiston Agent for this Province humbly represents that there is due to the said Coll Blakiston from the publiq of this Province for Sallary for his Agency at the rate of 120 £ Sterl ꝑ annum 120 lb for the year ended the 17th of September 1705 for which the s^d W Bladen Attorny in fact for the said Col Blakiston prays an order of this house. And also that the house before they rise

Original will give such Instructions to the Comittee for laying the pub-
Journal. liq Levy that they may allow the s^d Coll Blakiston Sallary of
120^l more w^ch will be due for his Agency 17th of 7ber next
ensuing

Which Memoriall being read at the Board his Ex^ncy & the
Councill recomend it to the house of Dell to take effectuall
Care therein The s^d Coll Blakiston being imployed in buying
& sending in the Arms & Ammunition for this pvince & other
materiall things for the Service thereof.

p. 57   W^ch was sent to the house by Coll Lloyd & M^r Coursey

M^r Fowke brings from the house the following answer to
the Message concerning gratifications made to persons imployed in the publiq Service viz^t

Viz^t            By the house of Delegates
                 Aprill 18th, 1706

Upon reading this Message It is resolved M^r John Hall be
allow'd now for those Services six hundred pounds tobacco &
twenty shillings to the Indian that was with him
                 Signed p order W Taylard Cl h Dell

M^r Jones brings from the House a Bill for Erecting a Parish
on the North side of Elke River which was read & assented
to & sent to the house by M^r Sanders

Came M^r Tyler & M^r Mackall & bring up a Bill prohibiting
the Exportation of European Comoditys out of this Province
w^ch was read & Assented to & sent with the former by M^r
Sanders

M^r Dollahide brings from the house a bill for Encouraging
the making Hemp & Flax & that for suspending the Prosecution of Romish Priests &c both which were read & assented to
& return'd to the house together with the two former by M^r
Sanders.

The Bill ascertaining the Damage on protested bills of Exchange being read at the board It is Remarked that the bill
is so clogg'd in Sev^ll Clauses that it will be complained of as
most unjust & unreasonable and particularly  In the first
p. 58 place the bill is not according to what was concerted at the
Conference for that it was only intended that Persons already
indebted should not be compell'd to give fresh bills of Exchange
under 90 Days Sight but is Detrimentall to trade in that it
Enacts psons both able & willing upon new Contracts shall
not give bills of less than 90 Days sight.

2^dly  All Persons having protested bills already returnd
upon which perhaps they have laid out of their monyes for

above two years are barr'd from recovering the twenty ℗
Cent. to the great Surprize of all Persons.

3<sup>dly</sup> In the bill it is declard Protested bills are to be equal
to Specialtys but by the latter part of that Clause directing
the paym<sup>t</sup> thereof by Ex<sup>rs</sup> or Adm<sup>rs</sup> by a Sort of a Negative
pregnant they are made inferiour.

4<sup>thly</sup> The Security proposd & at the Discretion or perhaps
good will of the Justices is alltogether introductory of an
Arbitrary power to the said Justices to favour whome they
please to the prejudice of many others.

5<sup>thly</sup> Bills of Exchange being the Standard of Trade ought
not to be abasd twenty ℗ Cent being no great advantage
much less a reasonable Recompence in Case of Disappoint-
ment to trading people neither is Currant Coine here answerable to Merchants bills & the growing Interest proposd on p. 59
protested bills in the Country will be very intricate.

6<sup>thly</sup> The house have left out of the bill the making Lands
a Chattle which would be the only means to pay bills & Deter
insolvent Drawers incouraged by their not affecting their
Plantations Wherefore this Board cannot Consent to the bill
as proposd but recomend it to be past with 90 days usance

The aforegoing Remarks sent to the house by Coll Jenkins.

The Board adjourns till the Afternoon

### Post Meridiem  The Councill Sate

#### Present as in the Morning

M<sup>r</sup> Hays & M<sup>r</sup> Howe bring up the Bill declaring several
private Acts to be in force Which was read & past & sent
to the house

The Bill for suspending the Prosecution of Popish Priests
&c—And the Bill for erecting a Parish on the North side of
Elke River being both Ingrossed were read & assented to by
this board & sent to the house by Coll Holland.

Came M<sup>r</sup> Henry Coursey & brought up an Address to her
Majesty & another to the Lord High Treasurer.

Both which are as follows

### To the Queens most excellent Majesty

The humble Address of yo<sup>r</sup> Governour Council & Assembly of this your Majestys Province of Maryland now Convened.

Whereas This your Majestys Province is wholly Destitute p. 60
of any Manner of Coine for want of which we labour under
the greatest difficulties & Inconveniences imaginable Our
Tradesmen for want of prompt payment deserting us Our

Country exposd to every Insult that may be made on us
& for many other weighty Reasons too tedious here to be
inserted Wee Do most humbly Address you' sacred Majesty
that you will be most graciously pleased to grant us a particular Species of a Small Copper Coyne in pence three
pences & six pences with your Maj^{ty's} Royall Protraiture on
the one side & Maryland on the other The Intrinsick value
thereof & yo' Majestys Charge of Coynage amounting to
Seven hundred pounds Sterling·to be remitted by us yo'
Loyall Subjects to your Treasury in England And the said
Coyne to be made only Currant in this yo' Majestys Province
by yo' royall Proclamation The Publiq Faith here Standing
engag'd for the Security of all such who shall receive any the
said Coine which will be a most royall beneficence to

> Yo' Majestys most loyal
> and dutifull Subjects.

p. 61 To the Right hon'ble the Lord high Treasurer of England.

The humble Address of the Governour Councill & Generall
Assembly of the Province of Maryland Humbly Sheweth,
That whereas by an Act.of Assembly made in this her Maj-
estys Province of Maryland Lyonell Copley Esq' Governour
Anno 1692 there was then granted the sume of one Shilling
on every hhd of Tobacco exported out of this Province for a
Supply of our Magazines & Support of Government

And forasmuch as his late Majesty King William by his
royall Instructions bearing date about the year 1691 was
graciously pleasd to appropriate one fourth part thereof for
the Supply of this Province with arms & Ammunition part of
which we most humbly Conceive hath been misapplyed by
these following payments made by our late Governour Col
Nathaniel Blakiston & by Thomas Tench Esq' President of the
Councill before our present Governours Arrivall here viz^t

Imprimis

| By Charges & Disbursements in apprehending the Pyrate Theophilus Turner & Securing him & his Effects sent to the Lord Bellamont by his Majestys order | £ S. D. 60..00..00 |
|---|---|

| p. 62 By Charges & Disbursements in apprehending & discovering securing & sending home the Pyrates taken in the John Hopewell Capt. Munday Com' & Securing their Effects out of which if ever it shall be allow'd me I will againe refund the Country | £ S. D. 50..00..00 |
|---|---|

By an order of Councill to pay Cap<sup>t</sup> Peter Coode
Comand<sup>r</sup> of his Majestys Ship Messenger
Advice Boate one hundred pounds, fifty
pounds w<sup>r</sup>of, was repaid by the said Coode
as by George Plater Esq<sup>r</sup> Rec<sup>r</sup> his account
doth more at large appear

£  S.  D.
50..00..00

By Cash paid Cap<sup>t</sup> Nathan<sup>l</sup> Bostock by order
of the P<sup>r</sup>sident & Councill for the use of her
Majestys Ship the Eagle Advice Boate to
purchase Provisions as ℔ order & Receit

£100..00..00
—————
Totall . . . . . .   260..00..00

The Premisses Considered Wee the Governour Councill &
Generall Assembly now Conven'd do most humbly intreat yo<sup>r</sup>
Lordship favorably to lay this Matter before her most gracious
Majesty that this province may be reimbursd those severall
sums amounting to 260<sup>l</sup> as her sacred Majesty in her Princely
Wisdom shall direct which has been so misapplyed contrary
to his late Ma<sup>ty</sup> King Williams Instructions. Wee her Maj<sup>tys</sup>
Loyal Subjects having only that poor Banke for the Support
of our Country ag<sup>t</sup> all Enemys both foreigne & Domestick
which will now be Sufficiently drain'd when the Arms & Amunition are paid for which his Ex<sup>ncy</sup> our present Governour (our
wants being Considered) hath undertaken to Supply us with.

Your L<sup>dps</sup> favour and Justice in this Matter will for ever
oblige us to be
    My Lord
        Your Lordships most obliged
            faithfull humble Servants

Both which Addresses were Read at the Board & well approv'd of And were Sign'd by his Ex<sup>ncy</sup> the members of the
honourable Councill & those of the house of Delegates

M<sup>r</sup> Wells & M<sup>r</sup> Thomas Frisby bring from the house a Bill p. 64
Incouraging the making Hemp & Flax within this Province
Engross'd which was read and assented to by her Majestys
honourable Councill & was sent to the house by M<sup>r</sup> Coursey

M<sup>r</sup> Ennalls brings up the Engrossd bill for preventing the
Exportation of European Comoditys which was read & assented to & sent to the house by Col Lloyd & Coll Holland
together with the Journall of the Comittee of Accounts
Assented to by the board

M<sup>r</sup> Ennalls brings from the house the foll: Message viz.

Original
Journal.
### By the house of Delegates
### April 18ᵗʰ 1706

May it please yoʳ Exⁿᶜʸ

Upon reading that Paragraph of yoʳ Exⁿᶜ⁾ˢ Speech at opening this Session relating to psons sent on Expedition or any
emergent Occasions

It is Resolved by the house that such psons as shall any
ways be imploy'd by your Exᶜʸ shall be rewarded for such
Services as yoʳ Exⁿᶜʸ shall think fitt This house thinking yoʳ
Exⁿᶜʸ to be a proper Judge of the reward of such Services

Signed p ordʳ W Taylard Cl h D.

p. 65    Mʳ Gouldsborough & Mʳ Coursey bring up the Ingrossd Bill
declaring severall Acts of Parliament of England to be in
force Which was read & assented to by the Board & sent to
the house by Mʳ Sanders.

The said Mʳ Gouldsborough and Mʳ Coursey bring up the
following ordinance of the house vizᵗ


### By the house of Delegates
### Aprill 18ᵗʰ 1706

It being proposd by a member of this house whether it be
not reasonable that Mʳ William Bladen the undertaker of Rebuilding the Court house be not Advanced & paid some part
of the Consideration on his Contract.

It is Resolved that he be paid out of the Publiq Stock at
Assessing of the publiq Levy next the Sume of ffive hundred
pounds being one half If the bon'ble Councill shall think fitt
to Concurr herewith

Signed p Order W Taylard Cl h Del.


Which proposall was Agreed to by the hon'ble Councill.

Mʳ Grey brings up a bill for Apportioning the publiq Levy
which was approv'd of & sent to the house of Delegates by
Lieutᵗ Coll Holland.

p. 66    The Board Adjourns 'till seven of the Clock to morrow
morning


### Friday April 19ᵗʰ 1706
### The Councill Sate

Came Mʳ Stone & Mʳ Jones & brought up the following
Message viz.

By the House of Delegates
Aprill 19<sup>th</sup> 1706

Whereas it has been represented to this house that it is An Aggrievance to this Province that the County Court Comissions are limitted & restrained & with which this house do Concurr & doe therefore pray that his Ex<sup>ncy</sup> will be pleasd to enlarge the said Comissions &c

Signed ℘ Order W Taylard Cl h D.

Which being Debated in full Councill the Board are of opinion the County Courts have sufficient Jurisdiction

M<sup>r</sup> Stone & M<sup>r</sup> Jones brought up the Engrossd bill for laying the Publiq Levy which was read and assented to by this board & sent to the house with the following Message

By the Councill in Assembly
Aprill 19<sup>th</sup> 1706

Upon the houses Representation by M<sup>r</sup> Stone to his Ex<sup>ncy</sup> to inlarge the Jurisdiction of the County Courts Wee have maturely Considered the Same & do Conceive the County Courts have Sufficient Jurisdiction therefore Cannot Advise his Ex<sup>ncy</sup> to make any Enlargement thereof

Signed ℘ Order W Bladen Cl Concll

The Bill Impowering Trustees to Sell Abraham Naylors Land being Ingrossed is assented to by this Board. p. 467

M<sup>r</sup> Wells & M<sup>r</sup> How bring up the Assemblys Order to Coll Blakiston Agent of this Province to Sollicite the severall Addresses to her Maj<sup>ty</sup> & the Lord high Treasurer viz.

Maryland Aprill 18<sup>th</sup> 1706
By his Ex<sup>ncy</sup> the Governour Councill & Assembly

Whereas at this present Sessions we have Addressed her most Sacred Majesty & the right honourable the Lord high Treasurer of England for a Certain Species of Copper Coyne by her Majestys Royal Proclamation to be made Currant in this Province & to have certaine Sums of Money (issued & disbursed by Coll Blakiston when he was Governour of this Province and by the hon<sup>rble</sup> Thomas Tench Esq<sup>r</sup> President, & her Majestys hon'ble Councill of this Province for the Service of the Crowne before his present Ex<sup>ncys</sup> Arrivall out of the three pence ℘ hhd given by her Majesty to Supply the Coun-

Original
Journal.

By the house of Delegates
April 18<sup>th</sup> 1706

May it please yo<sup>r</sup> Ex<sup>ncy</sup>

Upon reading that Paragraph of yo<sup>r</sup> Ex<sup>ncys</sup> Speech at opening this Session relating to psons sent on Expedition or any
emergent Occasions

It is Resolved by the house that such psons as shall any
ways be imploy'd by your Ex<sup>cy</sup> shall be rewarded for such
Services as yo<sup>r</sup> Ex<sup>ncy</sup> shall think fitt This house thinking yo<sup>r</sup>
Ex<sup>ncy</sup> to be a proper Judge of the reward of such Services
Signed p ord<sup>r</sup> W Taylard Cl h D.

p. 65    M<sup>r</sup> Gouldsborough & M<sup>r</sup> Coursey bring up the Ingrossd Bill
declaring severall Acts of Parliament of England to be in
force Which was read & assented to by the Board & sent to
the house by M<sup>r</sup> Sanders.

The said M<sup>r</sup> Gouldsborough and M<sup>r</sup> Coursey bring up the
following ordinance of the house viz<sup>t</sup>

By the house of Delegates
Aprill 18<sup>th</sup> 1706

It being proposd by a member of this house whether it be
not reasonable that M<sup>r</sup> William Bladen the undertaker of Rebuilding the Court house be not Advanced & paid some part
of the Consideration on his Contract.

It is Resolved that he be paid out of the Publiq Stock at
Assessing of the publiq Levy next the Sume of ffive hundred
pounds being one half If the bon<sup>r</sup>ble Councill shall think fitt
to Concurr herewith
Signed p Order W Taylard Cl h Del.

Which proposall was Agreed to by the hon<sup>r</sup>ble Councill.

M<sup>r</sup> Grey brings up a bill for Apportioning the publiq Levy
which was approv'd of & sent to the house of Delegates by
Lieut<sup>t</sup> Coll Holland.

p 66    The Board Adjourns 'till seven of the Clock to morrow
morning

Fryday April 19th 1706
The Councill Sate

Came M<sup>r</sup> Stone & M<sup>r</sup> Jones & brought up the following
Message viz.

Original
Journal.

By the House of Delegates
Aprill 19<sup>th</sup> 1706

Whereas it has been represented to this house that it is An Aggrieveance to this Province that the County Court Comissions are limitted & restrained & with which this house do Concurr & doe therefore pray that his Ex<sup>ncy</sup> will be pleasd to enlarge the said Comissions &c

Signed ⅌ Order W Taylard Cl h D.

Which being Debated in full Councill the Board are of opinion the County Courts have sufficient Jurisdiction

M<sup>r</sup> Stone & M<sup>r</sup> Jones brought up the Engrossd bill for laying the Publiq Levy which was read and assented to by this board & sent to the house with the following Message

By the Councill in Assembly
Aprill 19<sup>th</sup> 1706

Upon the houses Representation by M<sup>r</sup> Stone to his Ex<sup>ncy</sup> to inlarge the Jurisdiction of the County Courts Wee have maturely Considered the Same & do Conceive the County Courts have Sufficient Jurisdiction therefore Cannot Advise his Ex<sup>ncy</sup> to make any Enlargement thereof

Signed ⅌ Order W Bladen Cl Concil

The Bill Impowering Trustees to Sell Abraham Naylors p. 467 Land being Ingrossed is assented to by this Board.

M<sup>r</sup> Wells & M<sup>r</sup> How bring up the Assemblys Order to Coll Blakiston Agent of this Province to Sollicite the severall Addresses to her Maj<sup>ty</sup> & the Lord high Treasurer viz.

Maryland Aprill 18<sup>th</sup> 1706
By his Ex<sup>ncy</sup> the Governour Councill & Assembly

Whereas at this present Sessions we have Addressed her most Sacred Majesty & the right honourable the Lord high Treasurer of England for a Certain Species of Copper Coyne by her Majestys Royal Proclamation to be made Currant in this Province & to have certaine Sums of Money (issued & disbursed by Coll Blakiston when he was Governour of this Province and by the hon<sup>rble</sup> Thomas Tench Esq<sup>r</sup> President, & her Majestys hon<sup>rble</sup> Councill of this Province for the Service of the Crowne before his present Ex<sup>ncys</sup> Arrivall out of the three pence ⅌ hhd given by her Majesty to Supply the Coun-

Original
Journal. try with Arms & Amunition whereby the Same was misapplyed) refunded.

Wee doe desire & direct the said Coll Blakiston our Agent
with all possible Vigour & Diligence to Sollicite our said
Addresses & if not already ship⁺ to hasten away the Arms &
Amunition his Ex^ncy has wrote for which will be to the great
Satisfaction of, &c.

Which said Order was Sign'd as well by his Ex^ncy the
Gov⁺ the Members of her Majestys hon⁺ble Councill as by
the Speaker of the house of Delegates on the behalf & in the
Name of the whole house.

Came Coll John Contee & brought the Severall Addresses
to her Majesty & the Lord high Treasurer from the house &
p. 468  acquainted his Ex^ncy that the house had nothing before them

His Ex^ncy acquaints him that he waits their coming up to
the Councill Chamber.

The Journall of Acc⁺ˢ assented to & Sent to the house

Then Came M⁺ Speaker accompanied with the Members of
the house of Delegates & brought with him the sev⁺ˡˡ bills
following which he presented to his Ex^ncy viz⁺

1    A bill for Advancement of Trade & Erecting Ports &
Towns in the Province of Maryland

2    A Bill Incouraging the making Hemp & Flax

3    A Bill prohibiting the Exportation of European Com̄-
oditys

4    A Bill declaring Several Acts of Parliament of the
Kingdom of England to be in force within this Province

5    A Bill for Dividing & Regulating Severall Countys on
the Eastern Shore & Erecting a new County by the name of
Queen Anns County.

6    A Bill for Erecting a Parish on the North side of Elk
River in Cecill County

7    A Bill for Suspending the Prosecution of Romish
Priests &c

8    A Bill for uniting Newport hundred to W^m and Mary
Parish in Charles County

9    A Bill for Naturalization of John Baptist Tyler

10    A Bill to sell the Freehold of Abraham Naylor applying the money to the uses in his Will &c.

11    A Bill to make null & void a Deed from Thomas Edmundson to W^m Edmundson

12.    A Bill investing certain Lands in J^no Whittington

13.    A Bill declaring the land law to be in force

14.    A Bill for apportioning the Publiq Levy for this present
year, 1706

To Each of which Bills was affix'd the Great Seale of this Original Province & his Ex^{ncy} was pleas'd to enact the Same into Laws Journal. by underwriting every of them thus. p. 469

On behalf of her Sacred Majesty
Queen Anne &c
I will this be a Law

Jo: Seymour

Then his Excellency was pleasd to say to M^r Speaker & the Members of the house of Delegates

Gent^n
With The Advice of her Majestys hon'ble Councill I have thought fitt to prorogue you untill the twentieth of June next ensuing to which time you are accordingly hereby prorogued.
W Bladen Cl Concil

I

# PROCEEDINGS AND ACTS

OF THE

# GENERAL ASSEMBLY

# OF MARYLAND.

*At a Session held at Annapolis, April* 2–19, 1706.

CHARLES CALVERT, LORD BALTIMORE,
*Proprietary.*

JOHN SEYMOUR,
*Governor.*

---

THE LOWER HOUSE OF ASSEMBLY.

Maryland ss.

The fourth Sessions of Assembly begun and held at the
. Town and Port of Annapolis in Ann Arundel County the sec-
ond Day of April in the fifth year of her Majesty's Reign &c.
Annoq Dom. 1706.

At which Time the House being called over met the several
Members following

The Honble Thomas Smith Esqʳ Speaker

Saint Mary's City
George Muschamp Esqʳ ⎱ Balti-
Mʳ James Hay ⎰ more

Col° Edward Dorsey, dead
Mʳ James Maxwell
Mʳ James Philips
Mʳ Francis Dallahyde

Saint Mary's County
Mʳ Thomas Beale
Mʳ William Watts, sick
Mʳ William Aisquith
Mʳ Peter Watts
} Somerset

Mʳ John Waters, Absent
Mʳ Joseph Gray
Mʳ John Jones
Mʳ John Maclaster

Kent
Mʳ William Frisby
Mʳ Elias King
Mʳ John Wells
} Talbot

Col° Thomas Smith Senʳ Absent
Mʳ Robert Goldsborough
Mʳ Henry Coursey
Mʳ Nicholas Lowe

Ann Arundel
Mʳ Samuel Young
Mʳ Charles Greenberry
Mʳ Joseph Hill
Mʳ Richard Jones
} Cecil

Mʳ William Pearce
Mʳ Edward Blay
Mʳ Thomas Frisby
Mʳ William Dare

Calvert
Mʳ Robert Skinner
Mʳ John Mackall
Mʳ Thomas How
Mʳ John Leach
} Dorchester

Mʳ Hugh Eccleston
Mʳ John Taylor, dead
Mʳ John Hudson, sick
Mʳ Joseph Ennalls

Charles
Mʳ John Contee
Mʳ James Smallwood
Mʳ William Stone,
Absent
Mʳ Gerrard Fowlke
} Prince George's

Mʳ Thomas Greenfield,
Absent
Mʳ William Barton, dead
Mʳ Robert Tyler
Mʳ Samuel Magruder

Lib. 41.    Ordered Warrants issue for Election of three Members Viz.
one for Baltimore County in the Room of Col° Dorsey, one
for Dorchester County in the Room of John Taylor one for
Prince George's County in the Room of Major W. Barton.

M^r Joseph Hill & M^r James Hay ordered to attend the Honble Council to acquaint them the House is met according to
Prorogation and are ready to receive his Excellency's Commands.

p. 48    Read in the House the Letter excusatory of M^r William
Watts & his Excuse accepted of M^r Joseph Hill & M^r James
Hay and say his Excellency will send his Message in Answ.
forthwith.

Ordered M^r James Wootton attend the House for Prayers
at Eight O'Clock in the morning and then the House sitt and
in the Afternoon by Adjournment of the House and that Cap^t
Richard Jones acquaint him therewith

The Honble John Hammond Esq^r from the Council enters
the House & acquaints M^r Speaker that his Excy commands
their Attendance at the Council Chamber The House adjourns
to the Council Chamber where his Excellency was pleased to
make the following Speech to them.

M^r Speaker and you Gentlemen Delegates,

Since our Meeting now is by her Majestys especial Command I do doubt not but the great good things so earnestly
recommended to your serious Consideration for the Good &
Welfare of this Province will be unanimously approved of
and assented to by you it's Representatives that what her
Sacred Majesty has so wisely and graciously concerted for
your future Happiness and Grandeur may enrich y^r and succeeding Generations.

Gent.    No Monarch that ever swayed the English Sceptre
has had a more tender Regard for all her Subjects than her
present Majesty and tho she has been engaged in a great
chargeable war ever since her Accession to the Throne her
Princely generous Endeavours have not been confined to
Britain alone but an unwearied Tenderness is diffused over
all her Majesty's Colonies & Plantations abroad aud more
especially to us and our Neighboring Planters witness her
Majesty's Timely Interposition with the Czar of Muscovy for
if that Grant or Project had not been stopt you might in good
Measure bid adieu to the Tobacco Trade in America whilst
the divided Interest & Sentiments of Merchants at home in
Relation to the setting up and curing the Circasion Tobacco's
had speedily crowned our Ruin

Next her Majesty's opening a Trade with Spain which has
already so very good success many Spanish Vessels have been
cleared in London that brought their Wool and Commodities

thither returning thence with our English Manufactures. This Trade must prove a certain Advantage to all our Plantations by the Vicinity and Commerce of the Spanish West Indies for I would have you consider 'tis not a true Spaniard but a Spanish French King is our Enemy.

Then her Princely Care in passing an Act to encourage the Transportation of Naval Stores from her Colonies that all her Subjects abroad may truly reap the Benefit of their Industry & Labour equal with those so immediately under the gracious Influences of her Royal View and Patronage; for tho' Masts Tar and Pitch are not to be had here in such Abundance as our Countrymen & Neighbours can furnish we may have as good Hemp & Flax as any in the World without any Diminution to our Tobacco Manufacture and I hope you will be thoroughly sensible this generous Indulgence to us and all our Fellow Subjects in America will certainly occasion the Importation of all Necessaries from England oftner & cheaper than at present the Want of which and their extravagant Dearness has been and is still very burthensome and ruinous to the indigent People of this Country.

These truly Royal endearing Benefactions must ever strike deep in the Memory of all Loyal good Subjects Never let it be saide Maryland was ungrateful to so good and gracious a Sovereign who does with so much Wisdom Goodness & steady Application endeavour the Prosperity of England and all its Dependencies.

Mr Speaker, Her Majesty earnestly recommends the erecting Towns & Ports which must certainly render you considerable in a very short Time I presume as to their Number and Situation her Majesty will be advised by you Gentlemen who best know the proper Places for Trade & Business And as the Advantages naturally proceeding from such Improvements are many and for your own particular Good I hope there is no Occasion to convince reasonable thinking men of it's absolute Necessity nor can I think any Body will obstruct this so noble generous Design but a few Gentlemen at Home who have assiduously endeavoured by a certain Ingrossment to make the Produce of your Land and Industry a sure Monopoly to themselves whereby you can never let the middle & lower Sort of People reap any Thing from a very hard Labour and the Sweat of their Brows but a perpetual Indigency.

Gent. I am obliged in Justice & good Nature to lay before you the growing Evil of protested Bills and with great Friendship recommend it to your best Considerations how that fatal Grievance may be removed. I am obliged to take Notice you make use of a very unparliamentary Practice which is to

Lib. 41. postpone Matters to the last Eight or ten Hours of your
Rising and then Things of very great Consequence are
naturally hurried up or so procrastinated that at our next
Meeting they are forgot. Witness many of her Majesty's
Royal Instructions laid before you Gentlemen at your first
sitting down and tho' I heartily desired your Advice & Assistance in a strict Enquiry what became of the Arms and
Ammunition of the Province in Time of a foreign War &
intestine Disturbances when we last met which seem to threaten
us still you did not then think it proper to enquire into a
Matter so very necessary for your own Safety & Defence.

Give me Leave Gentlemen to desire you will now apply
yourselves heartily to the Business before yon that so pernicious a Thing to all wise Councils may not be brought to a
Custom by you Gentlemen Delegates, and then I can never
p. 50 doubt but by calm and serious Debates the many great
Things under your present Care will be in a few Days ripened
into good wholesome Laws fit for the Royal Sanction; and
as every Body knows this part of America was discovered by
Englishmen in the Reign of the famous renowned Queen
Elizabeth I would have us of this Province always remember
no Prince since (in so short a Time) ever applied their Royal
Care more emphatically for your Welfare Preservation and
Happiness than our present Glorious Queen Anne.

I have had an Account from the Head of the Bay the Indians intended some motion this Spring and with the Advice
of her Majesty's Honble Council have taken proper Measures
about it for the present but hope Gentlemen you will enquire
particularly into the Truth of this Affair for on our last Alarms
the several Persons I sent on long & hazardous Journeys to
bring me a right Intelligence of their Design were so nar-
rowly rewarded it must be on a very emergent Occasion I'le
trouble any Gentlemen again if I may not be thought a proper
Judge what such a publick Service deserves.

I have neither Lands nor Houses to lose here on any sud-
den fatal Insult as you Gentlemen Freeholders have yet my
Reputation which is dearer to me than any thing in this world
lies at Stake. But with all the chearful Willingness immaginable will expose myself on a true handsome Occasion for
the Defence Service & Peace of this Country.

Gentlemen, I have several other material Things to offer
to your Considᵃ this Session but shall presume to do it by
Way of Message.

Ordered it be read in the Morning and the Speaker and
the Members return to the House where he having taken the
Chair & finding it late, adjourned till 8 o'Clock to morrow
morning.

Wednesday April 3ᵈ 1706

The House met according to Adjournment & were present as yesterday

The Letter excusatary of Colᵒ Thomas Smithson for his Absence read in the House & allowed of as also another Letter as Treaʳ of the Eastern Shore was read as followeth.

Talbot County March 28ᵗʰ 1706

Gent.

I hereby give you Notice that I formerly received from Mʳ Bozman Naval Officer of Potomack District in Payment of his Account and Debt to the Public John Green's first second & third Bills for ten Pounds Eleven Shillings Eight Pence drawn on William Preston in Liverpool indorsed by John Bozman which Bills are all lost and taken as far as I know the Ships being taken by whom sent and I never received the money. I sent to Mʳ Bozman a Copy of the third Bill after first & second last desiring him to procure fourth fifth & sixth but it was not done the Drawer I presume being gone and no Effects. Now I humbly crave Advice and Order of the House whether I shall sue Mʳ Bozman by Reason of his Debt & Indorsement or that you will be content to lose it & discharge me for that sum of ten Pounds Eleven Shillings Eight Pence.

I give you further Notice that in like manner I received from Mʳ Thomas Collier Benjamin Lowes Bills first second & third Bills on John Younger in Whitehaven for five Pounds indorsed by Mʳ Collier &ᶜᵃ I desire Advice & Order of the House about them all Circumstances being the same and to be discharged as of the other always provided that if the Bills can be recovered I will answer for them I had likewise four other sets of Bills lost which by good Providence my Friend lately got from France I had likewise Colⁿ Thomas Brooks first second & third Bills for forty two Pounds payable to Geo. Harris in Somerset County drawn on Isaac Millner in London all lost and taken I have now writ to him to make a fourth fifth & sixth payable as afsᵈ and I shall get them indorsed or to give new Bills to me I desire he may be called into your House and discoursed about it. It is my very great Grief that I am not able to attend even for the adjusting of these Matters. I have accounted for all sums in Payment whereof to myself. I took these Bills in 1704 when all the publick Stock was drawn out of my Hands to less than ten Pounds. I hope you will not put any Damage upon me who am your        Most Humble & diligent Servant

Thoˢ Smithson

p. 51

Lib. 41.    Which being read the House do advise to take such Measures for Recovery as the Law directs.

Ordered That Major Greenberry, M^r Goldsborough, M^r Low & M^r Skinner draw up an Answer to his Excellency's Speech & lay it before the House in the Morning for Consideration.

The Petition of John Baptist Tyler of Prince George's County, a Hollander, read, thereby praying an Act for his Naturalization

Ordered it be recommended to the Committee of Laws to prepare a Bill.

M^r William Dare & M^r Thomas Frisby Members for Cecil County enter the House

Petition of Kent & Cecil Counties read, and ordered that all the Inhabitants of Cecil County on the South Side of Sassafrax River be added to Kent County and that a Bill be prepared therefor.

The Petition of Talbot County Read & ordered it be divided and that a Bill be prepared for Division thereof as prayed.

The Petition of Charles Kilburne being a long Time referred now ordered he have an Allowance of three thousand Pounds of Tob° for his Services &c to be allowed in Ann Arundel or Prince George's County.

The Petition of Col° John Coode for an Allowance for Imprisonm^t Fees for convicted psons read & rejected.

The House adjourns till two o'Clock in the Afternoon.

p. 52                           Post Meridiem

The House met again, and present as in the Morning.

M^r Gerrard Fowlke a Member for Charles County enters the House

A former Ordinance relating to cleaning & fixing the publick Arms read in the House and referred to further Consideration.

Col° Elias King, M^r Joseph Hill, and M^r James Philips are appointed by the House a Committee for stating the publick Accounts &c.

Ordered That Major Charles Greenberry, Major Nicholas Lowe, M^r Hugh Eccleston, Col° John Contee & M^r Thomas Frisby be & are appointed a Committee of Laws &ca.

M^r Thomas Greenfield, Col° James Maxwell, M^r John Wells, and M^r Robert Tyler are by the House appointed a Committee to hear & enquire into the Aggrievances of the Province &c. and report them to the House.

The Representation of Thomas Jones relating to the Land Lib. 41. Records &c. was here read and ordered M$^r$ Samuel Young and M$^r$ John Leach inspect the Land Records in what Condition they are and report the same to the House

The House adjourns till 8 O'Clock to Morrow Morning

### Thursday April 4$^{th}$ 1706

The House again met according to Adjournment, were called over & present as Yesterday and Thomas Greenfield Esq$^r$ enters the House & took his Place.

Upon reading the Ordinance for cleansing & fixing the publick Arms &c. Resolved That the House will address her Majesty that the three pence ꝑ Hhd appropriated for ꝑchasing Arms & Ammunition when the Country is supplied with sufficient the Remainder may be applied for fixing and cleansing such publick Arms as shall be in the Province The Answer to his Excellency's Speech brought into the House and ordered to be read and entered as follows

May it please your Excellency,

We her Majesty's most dutiful & Loyal Subjects the Representatives of the Inhabitants of the respective Counties of this Province convened in this present General Assembly do give your Excellency hearty Thanks for your gracious Speech to us at the Opening of this Sessions.

Sir, We have a deep Sense of the Princely Care and generous Regards that the best & most benign of Princes our most gracious Queen hath upon all Occasions demonstrated to us for our Protection and Welfare and we do hope that the Royal Care and Beneficence will at all Times be a Motive productive of our sincere and hearty Allegiance together with our p. 53 assiduous and frequent Prayers to Almighty God for her Majesty's long Life and happy Reign over us.

As to the erecting Ports & Towns we are resolved to take that Affair into our Consideration with all the Speed & Dispatch that a Concern of such Importance is capable of and as to all other Matters which your Excellency now hath or shall think fit to lay before us and which may any ways relate to her Majesty's Royal Instructions and to the Good and welfare of this her Majesty's Province we will with all Chearfulness and Assiduidty apply ourselves and be unanimous in our Councils to the discharging the Duties incumbent ōn us.

Sir, We want words to express to your Excellency the great Thankfulness and Gratitude with which our most gracious Sovereign by her Nobleness and Princely Goodness hath filled

Lib. 41. our Hearts but do hope that all our present and future Actions will demonstrate us to be no other than a Dutiful and thankful People for all those Blessings of Favour and Protection which her Majesty of her Grace and Goodness had bestowed upon us not forgetting that very eminent one of placing your Ex<sup>cy</sup> as her Majesty's Representative over us.

Signed ꝑ Order of the House of Delegates<br>W. Taylard Clk.

The Petition of Richard Marsden and others Gentlemen of the Vestry of S<sup>t</sup> Michael's Parish in Talbot County praying a Bill for Sale of Solomon Jones his Lands for the use of the said Parish ꝑsuant to the last will of the said Jones was here read & granted.   And ordered a Bill be prepared impowering the said Marsden, M<sup>r</sup> Robert Goldsborough, M<sup>r</sup> James Lloyd, and M<sup>r</sup> Matthew Tilghman Ward, or any two of them, to make Sale thereof as prayed.

M<sup>r</sup> Samuel Young, pursuant to an Ordinance of this House for purchasing Paper and Parchment for the publick use brought into the House Viz. three Rolls of Parchment each containing sixty Skins, two Ream of small writing Paper, two Ream of small Dutch ditto half a Ream of Medium, and half a Ream of Paper Royal which is ordered to be lodged with the Clerk of this House for publick Services only and he to be accountable for it.

Ordered That M<sup>r</sup> George Muschamp, M<sup>r</sup> Peter Watts, M<sup>r</sup> John Wells, M<sup>r</sup> Nicholas Lowe, M<sup>r</sup> Hugh Ecclestone, M<sup>r</sup> John Jones, M<sup>r</sup> Thomas Frisby, Col<sup>o</sup> John Contee, M<sup>r</sup> Robert Tyler, M<sup>r</sup> James Philips, M<sup>r</sup> Joseph Hill, M<sup>r</sup> John Leach attend his Excellency at the Council Chamber with the Answer to his Ex<sup>cy's</sup> Speech.

They return and say they delivered their Message.

Col<sup>o</sup> John Hammond & Col<sup>o</sup> Edw<sup>d</sup> Lloyd from the Hon<sup>ble</sup> Council enter the House & deliver M<sup>r</sup> Speaker the following Message.

By his Ex<sup>cy</sup> the Governor and Council<br>April 4<sup>th</sup> 1706.

p. 54    His Excellency observing what white Servants are or have been for some years last past been imported into this her Majesty's Province are generally Irish Papists who are induced to come hither by the false, tho' specious Pretences, of the free Exercise of their Superstitious Worship, and having Lands at the Head of the Bay settled on them at the Expiration of their Times of Servitude, so that many hundreds have been lately

imported is pleased to ask the Advice of the General Assembly whether on due Consideration thereof, are not apparent
Reasons her Majesty's Loyal good Subjects should be apprehensive of that growing Evil and more especially since these
sort of People are seated in Great Numbers in Baltimore
County and at the Head of the Bay Frontiers of this Province
most liable to the Invasion of the common Enemy; wherefore
in Case the Country thinks this deserves their Notice his Ex<sup>cy</sup>
desires they will advise what Measures are to be taken for
the Prevention thereof for that the Duty of twenty shillings ᵽ
Poll is not any Discouragement to that Importation and
whether it be not reasonable by some Law to forbid the Sale
of Protestant Servants to Masters of the Romish Church they
being generally seduced in their Religion or otherwise misused
in their Persons.

Signed ᵽ Order

W Bladen Cl. Council

Which being read it's resolved that a Bill be prepared to
forbid the Sale of any Protestant Servants to any [master
of the] Romish Church.

The Petition of the Inhabitants of Annapolis read with the
Indorsement from the Hon<sup>ble</sup> Council and resolved that this
House cannot concur with the Indorsment for that they are of
opinion the Inhabitants thereof ought to lay out their Lots at
their own proper Charge.

The Hon<sup>ble</sup> James Saunders Esq<sup>r</sup> from the Council enters
the House and delivers M<sup>r</sup> Speaker the Lords of Trade and
Plantations Letter together with Sir Thomas Lawrence's Pet<sup>r</sup>
relating to Ordinary Licenses.

Referred till Afternoon for Consideration

The House adjourns till two O'Clock Afternoon.

Post Meridiem   The House met according to Adjournment,
and were ᵽsent as before in the Morning M<sup>r</sup> William Stone's
Letter of Excuse read & allowed by the House.

The Paragraph of his Excellency's Speech relating to Ports
and Towns being read & debated  Put to the Question whether
Ports and Towns shall be erected in this Province or not?
Carried in the Affimative and resolved a Bill be prepared and
laid before the House for that Purpose.

The Paragraph in the same Speech relating to protested
Bills &<sup>ca</sup> being also read and debated it's Resolved a Conference with some of the Hon<sup>ble</sup> Council on this Subject be
desired. And ordered the following Message be sent up to
them for that Purpose.

By the House of Delegates April 4<sup>th</sup> 1706.

Upon that P<sup>te</sup> of his Ex<sup>cy's</sup> Speech which does relate to the great Evil which happens to the People of this Province by Bills of Exchange protested for making some Provision for Relief therein this House do pray they may be admitted to confer with her Majesty's Council and that his Ex<sup>cy</sup> will be pleased to appoint the ꝑsons Time and Place of meeting accordingly.     Signed ꝑ Order   W. Taylard Cl. H. Del.

Sent up to his Excellency & Council by M<sup>r</sup> James Hay & M<sup>r</sup> Joseph Gray.
They return & say they delivered their Message.
That Paragraph of his Ex<sup>cy's</sup> Speech relating to ꝑsons sent on Expeditions or emergent Occasions being read & debated ; it's resolved by the House That such ꝑsons as shall any ways be employed by his Excellency the Governor shall be rewarded for such Services as his Ex<sup>cy</sup> shall think fit ; the House thinking him a proper Judge of the Reward for such Services.
The Message by Esq<sup>r</sup> Saunders in the Morning relating to S<sup>r</sup> Thomas Lawrence's Petition about the Law for regulating Ordinaries was read as followeth.

By his Ex<sup>cy</sup> the Governor & Council in Assembly
April 4<sup>th</sup> 1706.

His Ex'cy thinks fit to acquaint you that S<sup>r</sup> Thomas Lawrence has made his Complaint to her Majesty against the late Law for regulating Ordinaries a Copy of which is herewith sent you that you may assert your Reasons for that Law, otherwise you cannot expect her Majesty's Royal Assent thereto.       Signed ꝑ Order   W Bladen Cl. Council.

Which being read is by the House recommended to the Com. of Laws to enquire into the Complaint of the said S<sup>r</sup> Thomas and report to the House what is desired by that Message.
The House adjourns till to Morrow Morning Eight O'Clock.

Friday 5<sup>th</sup> April 1706

The House met again according to Adjournment.
Being called over were present as yesterday.
Read what was done yesterday.
Col° Thomas Ennalls from the Honble Council enters the House & delivers M<sup>r</sup> Speaker the following Message.

By the Council in Assembly April 5<sup>th</sup> 1706.

In Answer to your Message yesterday by M<sup>r</sup> Hays and M<sup>r</sup> Jones desiring a Conferrence with this Board in Order to redress the great Evil of protested Bills of Exchange his Excellency and Council are willing to have a Conferrence with the whole House in the Council Chamber to Morrow Morning at ten of the Clock upon the Subject Matter so pernicious to the Country. Signed ꝑ Order W Bladen Cl. Council.

Which being read is ordered to be read in the Afternoon.
The following Message prepared was ordered to be read and entered.

By the House of Delegates April 5<sup>th</sup> 1706.
May it please your Excellency,
This House gives your Ex'cy their hearty Thanks for putting them in mind to inspect that Matter relating to the three Pence ꝑ Hhd which is given to the Country to provide Arms &<sup>ca</sup> and they do humbly pray that your Excellency will be pleased to give Order that that the Accounts thereof from the Time the said Grant from the late King took place till this Time may be laid before them that they may enquire into that Matter and what has been paid thereon and what is become of the monies.
Signed ꝑ Order W Taylard Cl Ho. Del.

Sent up to his Ex'cy by M<sup>r</sup> John Mackall and M<sup>r</sup> John Macclaster
They return & say they delivered their Message.
The several Committees are ordered to go out on the Com<sup>rs</sup>
M<sup>r</sup> Samuel Young & M<sup>r</sup> John Leach ordered to go out and inspect the Records to make Report thereof in what Condition they are.
The Petition of Cecil County, the Petition of Talbot County, the Petition of Kent County, the Petition of Richard Marsden, the Petition of John Baptist Tyler sent up to the Committee of Laws to prepare Bills on them.
The House adjourns till two o'Clock in the Afternoon.

Post Meridiem
The House met again according to Adjournment.
Being called over were all present as in the Morning.
The Message by Col<sup>o</sup> Ennalls relating to the Conferrence upon Remedy of the great Evil of protested Bills &<sup>ca</sup> Read & resolved that the House concur with the Message by Col<sup>o</sup>

Lib. 41. Ennalls relating to the Conferrence and ordered that a Message be sent up to his Ex'cy & Council in Answer thereto which followeth.

p. 57          By the House of Delegates April 5ᵗʰ 1706

May it please your Excellency,

Upon reading the Message by Col° Ennalls this Day relating to the Evil of Protested Bills it's resolved that this House attend your Ex'cy and Council to Morrow morning to confer upon the Subject Matter as desired.

                    Signed ꝑ Order  W. Taylard Cl. Ho. Del.

     Sent up to his Ex'cy & Council by Mʳ John Jones and Mʳ Thomas Howe.

     They return and say they delivered their Message.

     The Petition of Samuel Dorsey brought into the House and ordered to be read and considered of in the Morning.

     The Committee appointed to enquire into the Aggrievance of this Province enter the House & report as follow.  By the Committee appointed to enquire into the Aggrievances of this Province.  It is reported as follows Viz.

     It's a most oppressive Aggrievance that the Inhabitants of Pensylvania do yearly export out of this Province great Part of those small Quantities of Goods there have been of late imported hither. from her Majesty's Kingdom of England notwithstanding the great Necessity of Goods the Inhabitants of this Province at present lye under and that the constant Practice made of exporting for the Sake of Advantage what sums of Money we have now left in this Province it is adjudged by this Committee that the same ought to be remedied by some Act preventing the Pensylvanians to export hence any manner of Goods (save the Produce of this Province) or by such other Measures as the Honble House of Delegates shall please to think fit It is referred to the Consideration of the House of Delegates as an Aggrievance that the Inhabitants of the whole Province that the Commissioners of Oyer and Terminer in the several County Courts are limitted to ten thousand Pounds of Tobacco or fifty Pounds Sterl. and no more and it's humbly prayed that the House will address his Ex'cy the Governor to take off the Limitation aforesaid

     It is further represented as an Aggrievance that white Women Servants work in the Ground (unless for making Corn for Subsistence) whereby they are generally taken off from Carding, Spinning &ᶜᵃ which is now hoped will be propagated in this Province and moreover thereby the too com-

mon Vice of Whoredom is very much promoted to the great Lib. 41.
Scandal of a Christian Government and Oppression of each
County in maintaining such illegitimate Issue.

Whereas upon the late Revolution the Land Records were
put into the Hands of M<sup>r</sup> William Taylard under the Guard
of Col° John Coode of S<sup>t</sup> Mary's County, who during the
Trust reposed in him by the Governm<sup>t</sup> sent for one of the
Books of the Land Records and never since returned the
same into the Office whereby divers good Gentlemen are in
likelihood of losing very large Quantities of Land and making p. 58
People confused in their Freeholds and particularly M<sup>r</sup> William Josephs. It is therefore referred to the Consideration
of the House and prayed that some Measures may be taken
for the Relief and Ease of the Inhabitants of this Province

Signed ꝑ Order<br>John Collins Cl. Com.

The first Article in the same relating to the Pensylvanians
carrying European Goods out of this Province Read & the
Consideration thereof is referred till to Morrow morning

The second Article relating to Limitation of Actions in the
County Courts Read it is resolved by the House it is an Aggrievance and that his Ex'cy be addressed to relieve it.

As to the other Aggrievance this House refer it till to
Morrow morning for the Consideration of the House.

The House adjourns till to Morrow Morning Eight o'Clock

Saturday April 6<sup>th</sup> 1706.

The House met again according to Adjournment.

Being called over were present as yesterday

Read what was done yesterday.

James Saunders Esq<sup>r</sup> from the Honble Council enters the
House & delivers M<sup>r</sup> Speaker Pet<sup>n</sup> of Henry Roberts of Ann
Arundel County.

Then read Aggrievance of last Night being the first Aggrievance relating to the Exportation of European Goods out
of this Province read and debated; and resolved by the
House that it's no Aggrievance. The third Paragraph in the
Report relating to white women Servants that work in the
Ground, read and debated. Put to the Question whether
white women Servants shall work in the Ground or not?

Carried by Majority of Voices that white women Servants
be excused from working in the Ground and ordered a Bill
be prepared for that Purpose; and resolved the Bill take
Place by Xtmas next.

Lib. 41.    Edward Lloyd and Thomas Ennalls Esq^rs^ from the Honble
Council enter the House and deliver a Letter &^c^ Viz.

Whitehall April 12^th^ 1703

Gent.

The Lord Baltimore having complained to us of some In-
fringem^t^ made upon his Rights by an Act of Assembly of
Maryland ascertaining the Bounds of Land and likewise an
Injury done him by another Act for securing Adm^rs^ & Executors from double Payment of Debts and limitting the Time
for Payment of Obligations within that Province We send
you here inclosed Copies of his Lordship's Observations upon
and Objections against both the said Acts that you may consider thereof with due Regard to his Lordship's Rights and
take such Measures thereupon as may be agreable to Reason
& Justice.  So we bid you heartily farewell

Your very Loving Friends

Dartmouth    ⎫    W. Blaithwait
Rob^t^ Cecill    ⎬    Jn° Pollexfen
Phill Medows    ⎭    Mat. Prior

P. 59    Read and referred till next Sessions of Assembly.  They
likewise acquaint M^r^ Speaker that his Ex'cy desired his Attendance and the whole House upon the Conference.

Upon reading that Paragraph of a Book of the Land
Records &^ca^ Ordered the Serjeant attendant summons Col°
Cood to appear before this House on Monday Morning
next to answer what may be objected against him relating
to that Record.

The Honble Francis Jenkins Esq^r^ from the Council enters
the House and delivers M^r^ Speaker Cap^t^ Harris Petition
which was read and entered as followeth.

To his Ex'cy the Governor, the Honble Council, and the
House of Delegates of the Province of Maryland.

The humble Petition of George Harris, Merchant Creditor
to the Estate late of Charles Ridgeley of Prince George's
County Gent. deceased.  Most humbly complaining, Sheweth
to this Honble Assembly That the said Charles Ridgeley in
his Life time was possessed of a considerable real Estate and
particularly of Eleven hundred Acres of Land in Prince
George's County so that his Credit ran very high and your
Petitioner taking him to be a Person both of Credit and Sub-
stance was encouraged to deal with and credit him for the
Value of sixty nine Pounds five shillings Sterling for most
of which the said Charles gave your Petitioner Bills of Exchange which said Bills not meeting with due Payment have

only increased the Debt and now so it is may it please your Lib. 41. Honours that Deborah the Relict and Executrix of the said Charles Ridgeley hath made up her Account of the Adm'n of her said Husband's Estate and balanced the same to a very small Trifle less than forty shillings so that she alledgeth she hath not wherewith to satisfy your Petitioner unless the real Estate of her said Husband or at least so much thereof be sold to Answer your Petitioner's just Demands. Therefore your Petitioner humbly prays. Leave that a Bill may be brought in to that End, and he shall ever pray.

Indorsed thus. By his Excellency the Gov⟨r⟩ & Council in Assembly April 6ᵗʰ 1706.

The within Petⁿ being read at the Board is thought very reasonable and therefore it is recommended to the House to consider thereof and relieve the Petʳ by admitting such Bill to be brought in the said Deborah Ridgely being duely summoned to make her Objections. Further his Ex'cy is pleased to say that he believes this may serve for a very good Instance for what was urged this Day at the Conference
Signed ⅌ Order W Bladen Cl. Con.

Indorsed by the House of Delegates thus Viz.

By the House of Delegates April 6ᵗʰ 1706.
Upon reading the within Petition and Order thereon It is ᴾ· ⁶⁰ resolved by the House that the Petitioner have Liberty to bring in a Bill next Assembly as prayed and ordered that the widow of the said Deceased and his Heirs if any be summoned to appear before this House to make their Objections if to them it shall seem meet
Signed ⅌ Order W. Taylard Cl. H. Del.

Proposed whether it be not reasonable to contract Lands into Chattels for Payment of Debts &c.
Resolved by the House in the Negative
Henry Roberts Petition read the Consideration whereof is referred till next Assembly and ordered Summons issue
Resolved by the House That a Bill be brought in for Payment of Interest for all Money Debts at Rate of ten ⅌ Cent ⅌ Annum
Thomas Edmondson's Petition read and resolved the Bill be brought in as prayed
The House adjourns till two O'Clock in the Afternoon

Post Meridiem

The House met according to Adjournment.

Being called over were present as in the Morning.

Read the Petition of Samuel Dorsey of Ann Arundel County the Consideration whereof is referred till Monday Morning.

The Petition of M^r Edw^d Hancox praying Preemption of a small House built by the Public at Wapping Wharf read and rejected.

The Petition of Job Evans & Sarah his wife relating to·fifty Pounds Sterling allowed John Perry late constituted Post of this Province read and ordered the Petitioner appear on Monday Morning and produce his Proofs to maintain the Petition Upon the Petition of the Men that guarded the Powder House praying Relief in receiving Pieces of Eight at six shillings for their Services and that the House will grant them Allowance to make up their just Pay Resolved they be advanced Money to make good their Pay according to their Allowance by the Committee of Accounts and that M^r Charles Carroll make good to the Treasurer the money according to her Majesty's Proclamation

The House adjourns till Monday Morning Eight O'Clock

Monday April 8^th 1706

The House met again according to Adjournment.

Being called over were present as on Saturday.

Upon reading the Paragraph of Aggrievances relating to Land Records Ordered M^r Coode and M_r Josephs be called into the House, who appeared and the House having examined fully the matter against Col° Coode relating to that Land Record they are ordered to withdraw and being withdrawn, the House proceed to debate the same but finding no proof therefore dismist.

p. 61    The Petition of Thomas Reading referred till this Day ordered to be read and the Pet^r called into the House, who appeared and the Petition read as followeth.

To the Honble Speaker and the Honble Members of the House of Delegates.

The humble Petition of Thomas Reading constituted Printer of the Province of Maryland, humbly prays

That your Honours will please to order the Laws of this Province to be printed and this House would give him Encouragement for the speedy finishing the same ; and that your Honours would please to settle some Annual Salary for his Support and Encouragement for which he will be obliged to

print all publick Matters as Speeches, Answers, Votes & Proc- Lib. 41.
lamations &c. as your Honours please to direct.

And further whereas there hath been a former Ordinance
of this House to M^r W. Bladen and others that had printing
Presses in the Province obliging all Clerks, Commissarys,
Sheriffs, and other Officers to make use of printed Blanks may
be renewed and settled on your Petitioner

And that there is a small House upon Wapping Wharf
built by the Public, but at present of no use, therefore prays
that the same be granted him that you recommend the same
to his Excy and Council for Concurrence

And your Petitioner as in Duty bound shall pray &^ca

Which being read it is proposed what Encouragement
might be sufficient to give him for his expeditious Printing
the Body of the Laws of this Province.

It is resolved That for his Encouragement he shall be allowed
for each County one and one for this House at the Rate of
twenty Shillings for each Body for which each County is to
make Satisfaction and the Country but is obliged not to exceed
twelve Shillings for the Price of one Body that may be disposed
of by him to any ᵽson. And that for what other Acts shall
be passed in any future Assemblys to be allowed for the same
in Proportion to the present Body of the Laws. Thomas
Reading being present in the House readily agreed to the
Proposal

As to that Paragraph relating to the Country House being
read it's proposed to the Pet^r whether or not he will rent the
said House at the Rate of twelve Pence ᵽ Annum to be paid
to the Treasurer of the Western Shore Annually on Lady
Day; putting it in Repair during the Time of four years to
commence from the 25^th Day of March last past to the which
he readily consented and agreed. Thereupon resolved he
hold the same for the Term afsd on Consideration afsd.

It is further proposed to the said Thomas Reading what he
will require for a Body of Laws to be copyed for the Press.
He offers to make the same for two thousand Pounds of
Tobacco; and this House agrees thereto, and will consider of,
and appoint some ᵽson to examine & correct the same.

The Petition of Mary Newell, of Annapolis, praying Liberty p. 62
for selling a Dram, read and rejected.

Edward Lloyd, and Thomas Ennalls Esq^r from the Honble
Council enters the House and delivers M^r Speaker Proposals
for runing Cash of four thousand Pounds Sterling which was
read and referred for further Consideration

Bill for Naturalization of John Baptist Tyler of Prince
George's County brought into the House Read the first and
second Time and do pass

37

Lib. 41.    Bill enabling certain Trustees to sell Land given to S$^t$ Michael's Parish in Talbot County; Read the first and second Time and do pass.

Sent up to the Honble Council by M$^r$ John Jones and M$^r$ Joseph for their Concurrence

They return and say they delivered the Bills

The Honble Francis Jenkins Esq$^r$ from the Council enters the House and delivers M$^r$ Speaker the Pet$^o$ of George Harris preferred on Saturday last with new Indorsm$^t$ of the Council as followeth.

By the Council in Assembly  April 8$^{th}$ 1706

The Widow Ridgely and her Father Cap$^t$ John Dorsey living but in the two next Counties so that in Eight and forty Hours they may well appear to the Summons we think it very hard to delay the Petitioner to any other Assembly.

W Bladen Cl. Council.

Which being read the House concurs therewith and ordered the Petitioner give Notice to the Persons concerned that they attend this House p$^r$ Thursday next in the Morning by ten o'Clock to make their Objections against passing such a Bill if to them it shall seem meet.

Upon a Motion made in the House by a Member of the House praying Liberty to bring in a Bill on Behalf of the Inhabitants of Charles County to unite New Port Hundred to William and Mary Parish in said County.

It's resolved that a Bill be prepared and brought in for that Purpose so that the Bounds be ascertained.

The House adjourns till two O'Clock Afternoon

Post Meridiem.   The House met, were called over, & present as in the Morning

Moved that whereas M$^r$ Henry Coursey a Member for Talbot County is absent and no Excuse made; Ordered that he have further Time till to Morrow in the Evening and then if no Appearance this House will order he be sent for.

The Committee of Aggrievances enter the House and report that upon Application of a Gentleman of Cecil County it's represented as an Aggrievance that the whole County is now in one entire Parish whereby the Inhabitants of the North Side of Elk River and Susquehannah River cannot possibly travel to Church by Reason of the Breadth of Elk River and

p. 63 for that the said Inhabitants are deprived from receiving any Benefit of the forty p poll by them paid it is prayed that Part·

of the County between Elk and Susquehannah River may be Lib. 41.
divided and made a Separate Parish from the other.

Which being debated in the House Ordered that a Bill be
prepared and brought into the House for the Division thereof
so that the Inhabitants or any for them ascertain the Bounds.

Col⁰ Ennalls and Col⁰ Coursey from the Council enter the
House & deliver Mʳ Speaker the following Message Viz.

### By the Council in Assembly April 8ᵗʰ 1706

His Ex'cy thinks fit to acquaint you with the late Alarm we
had of a thousand Seneca's coming from the Northward with
Intent to cut off and carry away our Eastern Shore Indians
and therefore you have the Papers herewith sent you relating
thereto for your Perusal.

Signed ꝑ Order  W Bladen Cl. Council.

Which being read as also the Papers; Resolved it be
answered.

### By the House of Delegates April 8ᵗʰ 1706

This House gives his Ex'cy Thanks for laying the Letters
relating to the Indians before them but they do not apprehend
any present Danger from the Indians which may give them
any Occasion of entring into any further Consideration of that
Matter   They do also give his Ex'cy Thanks for his Care.

Signed ꝑ Order  W. Taylard Cl. Ho. Del.

Sent up to the Council by Mʳ Peter Watts and Mʳ Francis
Dallahyde.

Bill enabling certain Trustees to sell Land given to Sᵗ
Michael's Parish in Talbot County brought from the Council
by Col⁰ Ennalls & Col⁰ Coursey with Indorsement as follows
Viz.  Eodem Die.   Read in Council and this Board desire to
be fully satisfied whether there be no legal Objections to be
made by any ꝑson yet unheard against the Bill and also to
have a Sight of Jones's Will

Signed ꝑ Order  W Bladen Cl. Council

In Answer to which was thus indorsed

### By the House of Delegates April 8ᵗʰ 1706

No Objections appear to this House; only it's said there is
a Brother and Sister, and have sent up a Copy of the Will as
desired          Signed ꝑ Order   W. Taylard Cl. Ho. Del.

And sent up to the Honble Council by M<sup>r</sup> Peter Watts and M<sup>r</sup> Francis Dallahyde.

They return and say they delivered their Message.

The Petition of John Whittington of Kent County praying Sale of Part of Daniel Toa's Land for Payment of his Debts &<sup>ca</sup>  Read in the House & ordered that Notice be given the Pet<sup>r</sup> to attend the House to Morrow Morning with a Copy of Toa's Will and this House will then further consider of the same.

Bill for Naturalization of John Baptist Tyler brought into the House by Tho<sup>s</sup> Ennalls and William Coursey Esq<sup>rs</sup> indorsed.  Eodem Die.  Read in Council and will pass.

W Bladen Cl. Council.

p. 64    The House adjourns till to Morrow Morning Eight O'Clock.


Tuesday April 9<sup>th</sup> 1706.

The House met according to Adjournment.  Being called over were present as yesterday.  Read what was done yesterday.

The Honble James Saunders Esq<sup>r</sup> from the Council enters the House and delivers M<sup>r</sup> Speaker the following Message which was ordered to be read & entered Viz.


By his Ex'cy the Governor and Council April 8<sup>th</sup> 1706

Gent.  At present the Conveyance of publick Letters is very unsafe as well as your proper Interests much impaired.  I wish you would seriously consider how this may be remedied. His Ex'cy the Governor of Virginia having communicated his Resolution of using his Endeavours with the Assembly of that Colony intended to sit this Month to redress the Evil there.          Signed ꝑ Order  W Bladen Cl. Council

Upon reading the aforegoing Message it is referred to further Consideration till such Time Townes are settled.

The Petition of John Whittington praying the Sale of Lands of Daniel Toas dec'd for paying of a Debt to him due Read, and the Pet<sup>r</sup> ordered to be called into the House; who appearing is ordered to give Account of what Lands there is of the said Toa's undisposed of.  He informs the House there is several Tracts not yet disposed of Viz. one called Honest Dealing containing 400 Acres, Fair Dealing containing 300 Acres and an Addition to Fair Dealing 130 Acres And so

the said Whittington was ordered to withdraw And the House Lib. 41.
having debated the Matter in the afs'd Petition Resolved
That a Bill be brought into the House to invest the said
Whittington and his Heirs in the said Land in Part of Satisfaction of the Debts by him claimed.

Bill for Division of Several Counties Read the first Time
and ordered to be read again.

Col° Thomas Ennalls from the Council enters the House &
delivers, Bill enabling certain Trustees to sell Lands given to
S⁺ Michael's Parish in Talbot County Indorsed thus Viz.

April 8ᵗʰ 1706.   By the Council in Assembly

Solomon Jones's Will being read at this Board, as also the
Petition of the Vestry of S⁺ Michael's Parish upon due Consideration had thereof the Will does not second the Petition
which sets forth the said Jones did by his last will and Testament in Writing bequeath his Dwelling Plantation to be sold
and the Profits thereof to be appropriated to the Use of a
Chapel of Ease, but is altogether uncertain and no full Indication of the Testators Mind.   Wherefore, althô this Board p. 65
will be always ready to assert the Church's Interest yet they
shall ever be unwilling to do any Thing may be unlawful or
irregular to the Prejudice of any      W Bladen Cl Council.

Upon reading the Indorsement aforesaid this House do
find the Will does not second the Petition as is above intimated therefore this House will not further proceed on that
Petⁿ

Bill for uniting New Port Hundred to William & Mary
Parish in Charles County.   Read the first and second Times
and do pass.

Sent up to the Council for Concurrence by Mʳ Peter Watts.
He returns and says he delivered the same.

The Petition of Philemon Hemsley of Talbot County Admʳ
of William Alderne dec'd praying a Bill to vest Lots of Land
in him to enable him to pay Debts &ᶜᵃ   Read and by the
House rejected.

The Petition of Richard Smith relating to the Bounds of
some Land &ᶜᵃ   Read and the Consideration thereof is referred
till Afternoon and ordered the Petʳ have notice then to appear
and the Clerk of the Land Records to attend the House with
the Books in which the Certificates relating to the Petitioner
are recorded.

James Saunders Esqʳ from the Council enters the House and
delivers Mʳ Speaker the following Message.

Lib. 41.        By the Council in Assembly    April 8ᵗʰ 1706

Whereas heretofore a Lott was laid out for the Rector of Sᵗ Ann's Parish in the Town and Port of Annapolis and also another Lot for a Vestry House.  Now forasmuch as there is a very good Vestry-House built and adjoined to the Church there will be no Necessity that the former House should remain to that use but that it may be highly necessary it be annexed to the Parson's Lot & some further Improvemᵗ made thereon in Order to some comfortable Provision to be made of an House for the Reception & Accommodation of a Minister forever to which his Excy is willing to contribute if the House think fit to give Encouragemᵗ thereto

Signed ꝑ Order  W Bladen Cl Council.

Read and referred till the Afternoon
Brought into the House the Petition of Mary Newell which was read and ordered to be entered Viz.

To his Excy the Govʳ her Majᵗty's Honble Council & the Genˡ Assembly.
The humble Petition of Mary Newell of Annapolis, humbly sheweth,

That your Petitioner hath been a very laborious and Painstaking woman for several years in this Province and hitherto hath maintained herself by her Drudgery.  But now may it please your Exey & Honours She finds old Age and Impotency has much impeded her that she cannot longer scuffle in the world so to provide herself with Necessaries as formerly she was able to do Therefore humbly addresses herself to your Excy & Honours humbly requesting Leave to vend Coffee Tea and a Dram   Not that She is in the least desirous to keep a
ꝑ. 66 Tipling House or any Thing tending to Excess and Intemperance but purely to capacitate herself to get an honest Livelyhood without being burthensome to any Body I humbly implore your Excy and Honours out of your Abundance of your Consideration and Pity will be pleased to grant Relief in the Premises   And as in Duty bound will ever pray.
The above Petition was by the Council indorsed thus.

By his Excy the Governor & Council April 9ᵗʰ 1706.

The within Petition being read and the Petitioner's Age and indigent Circumstances considered this Board is willing to give her such Leave.  But in Regard there is an Act of Assembly prohibiting any Person to sell strong Liquors in. or upon their Houses or Plantations without License from the

County Courts and that the Fines of such Licenses are now Lib. 41. vested in the Country we desire you will concur that the poor Woman taking out a License and giving Security according to Law may sell a Dram only without being obliged to pay the Ordinary Fine of 1200 lb Tobacco ꝑ Annum
Signed ꝑ Order W Bladen Cl Council

By the House of Delegates April 9<sup>th</sup> 1706

The within Pet<sup>n</sup> with the Indorsm<sup>t</sup> thereon being read the House readily concurred with the Honble Council &<sup>ca</sup>
Signed ꝑ Order<br>W. Taylard Cl. H. Del.

The House adjourns till two O'Clock in the Afternoon

Post Meridiem. The House met again according to Adjournment. Being called over were present as in the Morning.

The Petition of John Coode late Sheriff of S<sup>t</sup> Mary's County for an Allowance of Imprisonment Fees of two convicted Felons Read & debated &<sup>ca</sup> Resolved he be allowed 15000 lb of Tobacco in full Discharge of all his Accounts to this Time M<sup>r</sup> Coode being called into the House the same is proposed to him which he readily accepted of and returned the House thanks & then withdrew.

M<sup>r</sup> William Coursey enters the House and delivers M<sup>r</sup> Speaker Bill for uniting New Port Hundred to William & Mary Parish in Charles County indorsed thus

By the Council in Assembly April 9<sup>th</sup> 1706

Read the first and second Time and will pass.

Bill prohibiting Protestant Servants being sold to Papists and white Women Servants working in the Ground brought into the House and read the first Time put to the Question whether the Bill be committed for Amendm<sup>t</sup> or not carried by Majority of Votes it be committed for Amendment. p. 67

Bill for Division and regulating several Counties on the Eastern Shore.

Read the first and second Times and do pass. Sent up to the Council by M<sup>r</sup> Elias King, M<sup>r</sup> John Jones, M<sup>r</sup> John Mackall, M<sup>r</sup> James Hay and M<sup>r</sup> John Maclaster together with the following Message Viz.

By the House of Delegates April 9<sup>th</sup> 1706.

This House prays his Excy the Gov<sup>r</sup> will please to name the new County proposed by the Bill herewith sent
Signed ꝑ Order W Taylard Cl. Ho. Del.

Lib. 41.    They return and say they delivered the Message.

The first Part of the Message this Day relating to the adding the Lot of the Vestry to the Lot laid out for a Minister. Read and put to the Question whether it shall be annexed to the Lot or not? Carried by Majority of Votes that the Lot of the Vestry be annexed to the Ministers Lot. And as to the latter Part of the Message relating to Provision for Reception of a Minister this House are unwilling to contribute &ca

The House adjourns till to Morrow Morning Eight O'Clock.

### Wednesday April 10th 1706

The House met again and being called over were all present as yesterday.

Read what was done Yesterday. Message relating to Proposals for Money &ca referred till to Morrow Morning for Consideration.

The Gentlemen appointed to inspect the Land Records enter the House & deliver their Report to Mr Speaker.

Ordered to be read and upon Reading thereof it was debated and referred for further Consideration till the Afternoon

Committee of Aggrievances enter the House and report as follows Viz.

Whereas divers Persons had Money allowed them by the Public for their several Services and Orders have been drawn therefor on the publick Treasurer who denies the Payment any otherways than by Pieces of Eight at six shillings a Piece. (under Pretence of having no other Coin) which they cannot pass away at that Rate; it is represented as a great Aggrievance and prayed the same may be settled by an Act ascertaining at what Rates the several Sorts of Coin of late Current in this Province may pass for the future for the Ease & Advantage of the whole Province. Being read and debated this House resolves it is a Grievance and that a Bill be prepared and brought in to remedy the same by ascertaining the Value of such Coin.

The Honble John Hammond and Francis Jenkins from the Council enters the House and delivers Bill for several Counties indorsed. By the Council in Assembly April 9th 1706.

p. 68    Read the first Time and will pass the new County called Queen Ann's County

Signed ᵽ Order W Bladen Cl. Council

That Bill together with Bill for writing New Port Hundred to William and Mary Parish in Charles County and Bill for Naturalization of John Baptist Tyler &ca Sent up to the Committee of Laws for Ingrossment

Ordered the Committee of Accounts prepare an Address Lib. 41. to her Majesty about cleansing the Arms &<sup>ca</sup>

The House finding M<sup>r</sup> Henry Coursey a Member for Talbot County absent and shewing no sufficient Excuse therefor Resolved unless he appear this Assembly he then to lie under the Censure of the House

Upon reading a former Vote for some Person to examine & correct the Press in Printing the Laws Resolved M<sup>r</sup> Thomas Bordley be appointed to do the same if he think fit to accept thereof

Ordered he be called in who appeared and it being proposed that the House is willing to give him for such Service 3000 ℔ of Tobacco and he accepted thereof and withdrew. Ordered it be allowed.

Brought into the House the Report of the Committee of Laws in Relation to the passing the Bill for Ordinary-Keepers giving the Fine for the same to the Counties. Read and debated in the House Ordered it be endorsed as follows Viz.

By the House of Delegates April 10<sup>th</sup> 1706. Upon reading this Report the House concurs therewith.

Signed ꝑ Order W. Taylard Cl. Ho. Del.

Ordered the following Message be prepared & Sent up with the same Viz.

By the House of Delegates April 10<sup>th</sup> 1706

May it please your Excellency,

This House has transmitted to your Excellency the Report of the Committee of the House containing the Reasons for passing the Act for regulating Ordinaries and therein applying the Fines to the use of the respective Counties and which is the Opinion of this House in Relation to Sir Thomas Lawrence Petition to her Majesty.

Signed ꝑ Order
W. Taylard Cl. Ho. Del.

Ordered the Report be entered in this Journal.

Edward Lloyd Esq<sup>r</sup> from the Honble Council enters the House and delivers M<sup>r</sup> Speaker Petition of Major Josiah Wilson Sheriff of Ann Arundel County read and fully debated in the House is rejected.

M<sup>r</sup> Ennalls and M<sup>r</sup> Beale sent up to his **Excy & Councel** with the Report of the Committee appointed till 2 O'Clock Afternoon

Post Meridiem.

The House met again.  Being called over were all present as in the morning

»»    Mr Watts of Saint Mary's County enters the House and took his place.

Col Smithson's Letter read and his Excellency and Councils Message thereupon Read as follows.

By the Governor and Council in Assembly
Aprl 8th 1700

Gent.  Herewith is sent you Col Smithson's Letter to his Excellency which is referred to your Consideration.  If you think fit to gratify the said Smithson, but it must not be out of the Revenue of the Free School that Law being sanctioned in England
Signed p Order W. Bladen Cl Councill.

Upon reading thereof it's resolved the following Message be sent to the Council in Answer Viz.

By the House of Delegates April 10th 1700.

In Answer to your Exce & Honr Message of the 8th Instant relating to some Gratification to be made Col Smithson this House having considered it is not long since A Gratification was made to the said Col Smithson of fifty Pounds for his Services to the Country and they are of Opinion that that Gentleman's Services to the Country are not so very eminent above all others as to deserve a Distinguishment by way of Reward
Signed p Order W. Taylard Cl Ho. Del.

The Petition of Mrs Marg't Dorsey brought into the House and ordered to be read and entered as follows.

To the Honble House of Delegates

The Petition of Marg't Dorsey Exx of Col Edward Dorsey deceased.

Your Petitioner humbly conceiving That in Right of her Executrixship the Rent now due for the House your Honours now sit in is due to her being twenty Pounds Sterling which she humbly prays may be allowed.
And your Petitioner shall pray.

Which being read in the House and fully debated the Petition is rejected.

And upon rehearing the Petition of Samuel Dorsey it appeared by a former Contract that the same Rent is the Right of the said Samuel Dorsey. Therefore resolved That he be paid the Rent of the House for the year last past by the Treasurer of the Western Shore being £20.

M' Ensalls & M' Beale enter the House and say they delivered their Message of the Morning.

Col' Thomas Smithson's Letter & Message thereupon sent up to Honble Council p M' John Jones and M' Joseph Gray.

They return and say they delivered their Message.

The Petition of M' W. Bladen relating to a Town Lot read & referred till to Morrow Morning for Consideration and ordered that the Clerk procure the foul Draught of the Town Plat for the Inspection of the House.

The Petition of William Sweatnam being brought into the House.

Ordered the Petitioner and M' Bennett be called in ; who appearing and the Matter contained therein being read and argued before the House they withdrew and the same was by the House debated and it's rejected for Incertainty of the Prayer of the Petitioner.

Petition of Col' William Holland praying the Explanation of the Variation of Courses in a Survey of Land. Consideration further referred.

Petition of Cap' Richard Smith read, praying the Explanation of a certain Clause in the Land Law &c' and to be relieved in the Premises.

Col' Holland and Cap' Smith being called into the House and both their Petitions read and the House having heard what they had to say Col' Holland prayed Leave for a Copy to make his Defence and is ordered to withdraw

And then the House resolve on Saturday Morning next to take the same into further Consideration and that Col' Holland and Cap' Smith be ordered then to attend the House.

Bill to invest John Whittington in certain Tracts of Land of Daniel Toas for & towards Satisfaction of Debt due from the said Toas Indorsed Viz.

By the House of Delegates April 10th 1706
Read the first Time and by especial Order to pass.
Signed p Order W. Taylard Cl. Ho. Del

Bill prohibiting the Sale of Protestant Servants to Papists and white women Servants working in the Ground &c' Read

Post Meridiem.

The House met again.   Being called over were all present
as in the morning

p. 69    M<sup>r</sup> Watts of Saint Mary's County enters the House and
took his place.

Col° Smithson's Letter read and his Excellency and Council's Message thereupon Read as follows.


By the Governor and Council in Assembly
April 8<sup>th</sup> 1706

Gent.   Herewith is sent you Col° Smithson's Letter to his
Excellency which is referred to your Consideration.  If you
think fit to gratify the said Smithson, but it must not be out
of the Revenue of the Free School that Law being sanctioned in England

Signed ꝑ Order W. Bladen Cl. Council.


Upon reading thereof it's resolved the following Message
be sent to the Council in Answer Viz.


By the House of Delegates April 10<sup>th</sup> 1706.

In Answer to your Excy & Hon<sup>rs</sup> Message of the 8<sup>th</sup> Instant relating to some Gratification to be made Col° Smithson
this House having considered it is not long since A Gratification was made to the said Col° Smithson of fifty Pounds for
his Services to the Country and they are of Opinion that that
Gentleman's Services to the Country are not so very eminent above all others as to deserve a Distinguishment by
way of Reward

Signed ꝑ Order W. Taylard Cl. Ho. Del.


The Petition of M<sup>rs</sup> Marg<sup>t</sup> Dorsey brought into the House
and ordered to be read and entered as follows.


To the Honble House of Delegates

The Petition of Marg<sup>t</sup> Dorsey Exx of Col° Edward Dorsey
deceased.

Your Petition<sup>r</sup> humbly conceiving That in Right of her
Executrixship the Rent now due for the House your Honours
now. sit in is due to her being twenty Pounds Sterling which
she humbly prays may be allowed.

And your Petitioner shall pray.

Which being read in the House and fully debated the Peti- <small>Lib. 41.</small>
tion is rejected.

And upon rehearing the Petition of Samuel Dorsey it
appeared by a former Contract that the same Rent is the
Right of the said Samuel Dorsey. Therefore resolved That
he be paid the Rent of the House for the year last past by
the Treasurer of the Western Shore being £20.

M$^r$ Ennalls & M$^r$ Beale enter the House and say they
delivered their Message of the Morning.

Col° Thomas Smithson's Letter & Message thereupon sent
up to Honble Council ꝑ M$^r$ John Jones and M$^r$ Joseph Gray.

They return and say they delivered their Message.

The Petition of M$^r$ W. Bladen relating to a Town Lot read
& referred till to Morrow Morning for Consideration and
ordered that the Clerk procure the foul Draught of the
Town Plat for the Inspection of the House.

The Petition of William Sweatnam being brought into the
House.

Ordered the Petitioner and M$^r$ Bennett be called in ; who
appearing and the Matter contained therein being read and
argued before the House they withdrew and the same was by <small>p. 70</small>
the House debated and it's rejected for Incertainty of the
Prayer of the Petitioner.

Petition of Col° William Holland praying the Explanation
of the Variation of Courses in a Survey of Land. Consideration further referred

Petition of Cap$^t$ Richard Smith read, praying the Explanation of a certain Clause in the Land Law &$^{ca}$ and to be
relieved in the Premises.

Col° Holland and Cap$^t$ Smith being called into the House
and both their Petitions read and the House having heard
what they had to say Col° Holland prayed Leave for a Copy
to make his Defence and is ordered to withdraw

And then the House resolve on Saturday Morning next to
take the same into further Consideration and that Col° Holland and Capt. Smith be ordered then to attend the House.

Bill to invest John Whittington in certain Tracts of Land
of Daniel Toa's for & towards Satisfaction of Debt due from
the said Toas Indorsed Viz.

By the House of Delegates April 10$^{th}$ 1706

Read the first Time and by especial Order do pass.
Signed ꝑ Order W. Taylard Cl. Ho. Del.

Bill prohibiting the Sale of Protestant Servants to Papists
and white women Servants working in the Ground &$^{ca}$ Read

Lib. 41. the first Time.    Put to the Vote whether the Bill shall pass or
not?    Carried in the Affirmative that the Bill do pass

Whereas it appears by the Journal of the Committee for
laying the Levy last year that Col° Dorsey in the Right of his
Son Samuel Dorsey was        20℔ Sterling for one years Rent
of the House It's therefore ordered that the Treasurer pay
the same to Samuel Dorsey according to the Vote of this
House and not to the Exx of the said Col° Dorsey.

The House adjourns till to Morrow Morning Eight O'Clock


### Thursday April 11th 1706

The House met again according to Adjournment    Being
called over were all present as yesterday.

Bill investing certain Lands in John Whittington & his
Heirs Bill for restraining Papists or reputed Papists from
purchasing Protestant or reputed Protestant Servants and for
preventing Fornication committed by white Servants working
in the Ground &ca Indorsed April 10th 1706.    By the House
of Delegates.    Read the first Time and put to the Question
whether the Bill pass or not?    Carried in the Affirmative.

Signed ꝑ Order.    W. Taylard Cl. Ho. Del.


April 11th 1706    Read the second Time and do pass.

Both sent up to the Council ꝑ Mr William Aisquith and Mr
Joseph Ennalls for their Concurrence.

p. 71    They return and say they delivered them.

Proposal relating to addressing her Majesty for a particular
Specie of Coin with a Message therewith read and ordered to
be entered in this Journal

Which being debated it is put to the Question whether her
Majesty be addressed therefor or not?

Carried in the Affirmative and ordered an Address be
ppared Col° Hammond & Col° Jenkins enters the House and
delivers Mr Speaker Bill investing Lands in John Whittington.
Indorsed April 10th 1706    By the Council in Assembly

Read the first Time in Council and will pass.

Signed ꝑ Order  W Bladen Cl. Council.


Bill restraining Papists from purchasing Protestant Servants
&ca

Indorsed Viz. April 11th 1706 By the Council in Assembly.

This Bill being read at the Board and considered that there
are two Things of different Natures concluded in one and the
same Law his Excy in Regard of her Majesty's Royal Instruc-

tions cannot consent to the passing thereof.   Therefore recommended to the Committee of Laws to be made Seperate
W. Bladen Cl. Council

Which being read it is recommended as desired
Willian Coursey Esq' enters the House and delivers M'
Speaker M' Carroll's Memorial to his Excellency.
Read and referred for further Consideration.
Read the Petition of M' William Bladen and ordered to be
entered as follows

To the Honble the General Assembly now sitting.
The humble Petition of William Bladen,
Most humbly complaining sheweth That when the Town
and Port of Annapolis was first laid out according to Act of
Assembly Col° Edward Dorsey residing there and undertaker
of the publick Buildings took up two Lots next adjoining to
the publick Place where the Court House was designed to be
built But the said Dorsey failing in his Undertaking turned
a Brick Kilne and other Materials upon the Country as also a
forty Foot House built upon the said Lots which the Country
offered your Petitioner for 3000 ℔ of Tobacco and he agreed
to take the same but in the Afternoon Col° Herman agreeing
to build the Court House for his Convenience and at his Request your Petitioner released his Bargain with the House and
the said Col° Herman actually paid and allowed the Country
therefor 3000 ℔. Tob° and having erected another small thereon
sold the same to M' Gerrard Vansweringen decd for 10000 ℔
Tob° who assigned the said Bargain to your Petitioner for the
very same Consideration of 10000 ℔ Tobacco and all this
before your Petitioner came to live in this Town And further
your Petitioner sheweth That the then Governor Col° Francis
Nicholson without any Privity of your Petitioner (who was so
valuable a Purchaser) caused M' Beard the Surveyor not only
to run a Street out of your Petitioner's Lots but also a Circle
about the publick Buildings wherein most of your Petitioner's
Land is included to his great Detriment especially considering
the said Houses have never gained him the 10th Part of the
Common Interest of his Tobacco he never being heard thereto.
Wherefore he humbly prays your Excellency and this Hon-
ble Assembly to do him Justice and let him have the Land so
dearly bought and honestly paid for and he shall ever pray
Indorsed.   By the Governor and Council in Assembly
April 9th 1706.
We know this Petition to be true think it reasonable and
recommend it to the House of Delegates.
Signed ꝑ Order   W Bladen Cl. Council.

the fifth Time ... Put to the Vote whether the Bill shall pass or
not ... Carried in the Affirmative that the Bill do pass
... it appears by the Journal of the Committee for
... the Levy last year that Col.r Dorsey in the Right of his
Wife ... is Creditor ... 20sh. Sterling for one years Rent
... the House It is hereby ordered that the Treasurer pay
... Bills to Samuel Dyter according to the Vote of this
House and that to the least the said Col.r Dorsey.

The House adjourns till to Morrow Morning **Eight O'Clock**

Tuesday April 11.th 1706

The House met again according to **Adjournment** Being
called ... were all present as yesterday.

... lands in John **Whittington** & his
... Bill for restraint of Papists or reputed Papists from
... ... Protestant Servants and for
... committed by white Servants working
... April 10.th 1706. By the House
... Were ... first Time and put to the Question
... Carried in the Affirmative.

Signed ... W. Taylard Cl. Ho. Del.

... the second Time and do pass
... M.r William Aisquith ...
... Concurrence.

... delivered them.

... addressing her Majesty for ...

... Message therewith read and

... put to the Quest.

... according to Order ...

... Col.r Jenkins ...

... ... ... meeting lands

... By the Cou

... Council and

... p Ord

tions cannot consent to the passinghereof.   Therefore recom
mended to the Committee of Lawso be made Seperate
W. Bladen Cl. Council

Which being read it is recommeded as desired
Willian Coursey Esq' enters th House and delivers '
Speaker M' Carroll's Memorial to ls Excellency.
Read and referred for further Cosideration.
Read the Petition of M' William Bladen and ordered '
entered as follows

To the Honble the General Asseibly now sitting
The humble Petition of William Laden,
Most humbly complaining shewch That when
and Port of Annapolis was first laidbut accordin;
Assembly Col° Edward Dorsey resicng there ana
of the publick Buildings took up tw Lots ne
the publick Place where the Court House was
built But the said Dorsey failing ir his Und
a Brick Kilne and other Materials upn the              Mr
forty Foot House built upon the saic Lot              the
offered your Petitioner for 3000 ℔ of                 the
to take the same but in the Afternoo                  done
to build the Court House for his C
quest your Petitioner released his Ba         cond
the said Col° Herman actually paid a
therefor 3000 ℔. Tob° and havin          Catho-
sold the same to M' Gerrard V
Tob° 'who assigned the said
very same Consideration
before your Petitioner ca                    hereunto
your Petitioner sheweth                      st of the
Nicholson without any
valuable a Purchaser                    said Roman
to run a Street out                     an Act entit-
about the publick                       opery in this
Land is included                        of Conscience
the said Hous                           tation was un-
Common Inte                             mper and out of
                                        n suspended by
                                        Eighteen months
                                        known.   That the
                                        ed and the Queen's
                                        ed as may be ration-
                                        this Juncture intent
                                        ot of more weighty
                                        ou of England offering

Lib. 41.   Upon reading the foregoing Petition it's the Opinion of the
House that M$^r$ Bladen first lay out his Lots and make the
Country sensible of what is set forth in his Petition then this
House will further consider to make him Restitution.

Proposals offered in the House to prepare a Bill to ascertain
the Price of the following Coin

Resolved  That Pieces of Eight pass at          £..4..6
                          Dollars at          —..4..6
                          Duccatoons at        —..5..6

Ordered That a Bill be prepared to ascertain it pursuant to
the Proposal.

The following Message ordered to be prepared and read in
the House Viz.


By the House of Delegates April 11$^{th}$ 1706

In Answer to your Proposal made to this House by his
Excellency and your Honours whether it be not highly necessary to annex the Lot on which the old Vestry House is built
to the Parson's Lot, this House is ready to concur and agree
that the same may be annexed as proposed but they are not
at present inclinable to make any Improvement thereon.
          Signed ꝑ Order   W. Taylard Cl. Ho. Del.


Which being read and approved of was sent up to his
Excellency and Council by M$^r$ Samuel Magruder and M$^r$
Thomas Howe

The House adjourns till two O'Clock in the Afternoon


Post Meridiem.  The House met again according to Adjournment and were all present as in the Morning.

Bill for investing certain Lands in John Whittington sent
to the Committee for Ingrossm$^t$

Bill restraining Papists from purchasing Protestant Servants
&$^{ca}$ Put to the Vote whether Bill shall pass or not?  Carried
in the Negative.

Bill for preventing the sin of Fornication committed by
white women Servants &$^{ca}$

Read the first Time.  Put to the Vote whether the Bill pass
or not?  Carried in the Affirmative and that the Bill do pass.
Ordered it be indorsed.

P. 73   The Petition of Robert Givair and Mary his Wife one of the
Daughters of Edward Day late of Somerset County deceased
praying Relief in a Legacy given by her Father's will lost.
Which being read the House refers the same to Consideration of the next Sessions of Assembly; and ordered that

Notice be given to all Persons concerned to attend the House Lib. 41.
at that Time to prosecute the Petition.

Pursuant to the Order of this House appeared M^{rs} Deborah
Ridgely to make her Objections against a Bill of George
Harris; and the said M^{rs} Ridgely informed the House that
her Father will be here this Night who is assistant to her in
all her Affairs. Therefore prayed the same may be further
referred till the morning which was granted by the House and
she withdrew

Bill preventing the sin of Fornication. Indorsed.

Ordered M^{r} James Hay and M^{r} Peter Watts carry it up to
his Excellency and Council for their Concurrence. They return & say they delivered the Bill.

James Saunders Esq^{r} from the Honble Council enters the
House & delivers M^{r} Speaker Bill for preventing the Sin of
Fornication. Indorsed April 11^{th} 1706. By the Council in
Assembly Read the first Time.

W Bladen Cl. Co.

M^{r} Edward Blay, M^{r} Robert Skinner, M^{r} John Leach, & M^{r}
John Jones, M^{r} William Watts, and M^{r} Peter Watts, view the
work of rebuilding the Stadt House and make Report to the
House in what Condition the same is and if the Work be done
in workmanlike manner.

Bill for preventing the Sin of Fornication read the second
Time & do pass.

Brought into the House a Petition of the Roman Catholicks; which was ordered to be entered as follows.

To the Honble the House of Assembly now sitting.

The humble Petition of the Roman Catholicks hereunto
subscribing on Behalf of themselves and the rest of the
Roman Catholicks of this Province, Sheweth

That upon Application heretofore made by the said Roman
Catholicks to this Honble House for Repeal of an Act entituled an Act to prevent the further Growth of Popery in this
Province whereby the Toleration and Freedom of Conscience
allowed here since the first settling this Plantation was un-
fringed the House moved by a Christian Temper and out of
their commendable Inclination to Moderation suspended by
another Act the Execution of the former for Eighteen months
or until the Queen's Pleasure were further known. That the
said Eighteen months are now near expired and the Queen's
Pleasure not yet signified (being retarded as may be ration-
ably supposed) by her Majesty being at this Juncture intent
upon the Consideration and Settlement of more weighty
Affairs and Opportunities of hearing out of England offering

Lib. 41. but seldom in this war Time: Wherefore they most humbly pray that this Honble House would be pleased further to suspend the Execution of the said act until her Majesty's Pleasure be declared thereon without Limitation of any set Time lest that in the Interval of Assemblys such Time may expire and thereby your Petitioners liable to be disturbed contrary to the Intention of the House and they will pray.   Henry Darnall, Charles Carroll, Richard Bennett, James Carroll

p. 74    Which being read and debated the House granted that Petition.   But put to the Question whether the Execution be suspended 12 or 18 months.

Carried by Majority of Votes 12 Months be allowed.

Ordered the Committee of Laws bring in a Bill to suspend the Execution of that Law for that Time.

Upon reading the Memorial of M$^r$ Charles Carroll relating to the Land Law, being read and debated in the House was ordered to be indorsed as follows Viz.

### By the House of Delegates April 11$^{th}$ 1706.

This House designing to end this Session by what Expedition they can Do resolve not to enter in any Debate upon that Matter.   Therefore refer the same to Consideration of the next Session of Assembly.

Signed ꝑ Order W. Taylard Cl. Ho. Del.

The foregoing Message and the Bill for preventing the Sin of Fornication sent up to the Council by M$^r$ Joseph Gray and M$^r$ Joseph Ennalls.

The House adjourns till to Morrow Morning Eight O'Clock.

### Friday April 12$^{th}$ 1706.

The House met again according to Adjournment.

Being called over were present as yesterday.

Read what was done yesterday.

M$^r$ Joseph Gray and M$^r$ Joseph Ennalls enter the House and say they delivered their Message of last Night

Bill for Advancement of Trade and erecting Ports and Towns in the Province of Maryland, read the first Time and referred to further Consideration.

Message from the Honble Council by Col$^o$ Edw$^d$ Lloyd and William Coursey and delivers M$^r$ Speaker Bill for ascertaining the Navigation of open Sloops &$^{ca}$ Referred to be read and considered of   From the Honble Council Col$^o$ Francis

Jenkins enters the House and delivers M^r Speaker a Message <sup>Lib. 41.</sup>
relating to some Persons presented by Grand Juries with a
Book of the late Acts of Parliam^t   Referred till Afternoon.
   The House adjourns till two o'Clock


   Post Meridiem.   The House met again according Adjournment and present as in the Morning.
   Bill for Advancement of Trade &^ca Read again and committed for Amendments.   Delivered the Committee of Laws
   The House adjourns till to Morrow Morning Eight O'Clock


Saturday April 13<sup>th</sup> 1706.

   The House met again according to Adjournment.
   Being called over were present as yesterday.
   Bill for ascertaining the Navigation of open Sloops & Shal-
lops &^ca   Read the first and second Time and ordered by the
House to be thus indorsed.

By the House of Delegates April 13<sup>th</sup> 1706.

   This Bill being read in the House will pass with Amendm^t
of lessening the Security to 50℔ Sterling
Signed ᵽ Order<br>W Taylard Cl. Ho. Del.


   Sent up to his Excellency & Council ᵽ M^r James Hay and
M^r Joseph Gray.   They return and say they delivered the
same.
   Col° William Holland and Capt. Richard Smith pursuant to <sup>P. 75</sup>
an Order of this House attended and being called in.   The
Petition of Capt. Richard Smith was read and attended and
being called in.   The Petition of Capt. Richard Smith was
read and Col° Holland's Answer to the same and both Parties
being called having offered what they had to say are ordered
to withdraw.   Upon Consideration of the House of the
Premises 'tis thought fit that a Committee be sent out to
enquire into the Premises and make Report &^ca to the Houso.
   Col° John Contee, M^r John Mackall, M^r John Leach, Major
Nicholas Lowe and M^r Hugh Eccleston are appointed a Committee and ordered to go out and enquire in the matter contained in the Petition and to certify and make Report to the
House their opinion in that Matter.   The Gentlemen being
again called in, M^r Speaker informs them that a Committee is
appointed to sit at the George where they must give their
Attendance.

Lib. 41.   Ordered they go out on the Committee and Petition.

Answer and Plat delivered them.

Upon Motion by Col° Holland for Council to be admitted to argue the Petition & Answer before the Committee which is allowed by the House to both Parties if they think fit.

Petition of Nicholas Lowe praying Liberty to bring in a Bill &ᶜᵃ for Sale of Lots of Land of Mʳ ———— for Payment of a Debt read and debated, and by the House rejected.

The Message ⅌ Col° Jenkins of the 12ᵗʰ of April last relating to Presentment of Bigamy &ᶜᵃ

Read and resolved by the House that the Consideration thereof be further referred.

Appeared Capt. George Harris and Mʳˢ Deborah Ridgely pursuant to former Order of this House and being called in were heard by the House and then ordered to withdraw and upon rehearing the Petition of the said Harris, it is-resolved the same be rejected.

A Bill declaring the Act for erecting Ann Arundel and Oxford Towns, Read the first Time and by especial Order do pass.

Bill declaring the Land Law to be in force &ᶜᵃ

Read the first Time and by especial Order do pass.   Bill for Currency of Coin, read the first & second Time & do pass

Bill to make null and void a Deed from Thomas Edmondson to William Edmondson.

Read the first Time and by especial Order do pass.

Bill for suspending the Prosecution of Roman Catholicks within this Province &ᶜᵃ

Read the first and second Time and do pass.

The foregoing Bills sent up to the Council by Mʳ Thomas Frisby and Mʳ Wᵐ Aisquith for their Honour's Concurrence. They return and say they delivered the Bills.

The Gentlemen appointed to view the Work of the Stadt House enter the House and make their Report Which being read was ordered to be entered and Copy delivᵈ Mʳ William Bladen By the Persons for viewing the work about the Stadt House April 12ᵗʰ 1706.

p. 76   1ˢᵗ  We report That the Window Frames in the Lower and Second Stories (accept two) are altogether insufficient and ought to be taken out and new ones made of good season'd Timber put in their Rooms.

2.   That the Shingling is not done in a workmanlike manner being already leaky and in a little will be a means to destroy both the Timber and Plaistering as well as the whole Fabrick.

3.   That the Brick Work over both Porch Doors ought to be taken down and amended and that all the old Plaistering throughout the whole House ought to be pulled down

4. That the moultered Bricks both within and without ought Lib. 41.
to be taken out and new ones put in their Room.

> Edw<sup>d</sup> Blay
> Rob<sup>t</sup> Skinner
> John Leach
> Peter Watts
> W<sup>m</sup> Watts
> John Jones

Which being read in the House is ordered a Copy of the above Report be delivered M<sup>r</sup> William Bladen.

The Honble Edward Lloyd and William Coursey Esq<sup>rs</sup> from the Honble Council enter the House and delivers M<sup>r</sup> Speaker the following Message Viz.

By his Excellency the Governor and Council in Assembly
April 13<sup>th</sup> 1706

George Plater Esq<sup>r</sup> her Majesty's Receiver of the District of Patuxent having laid before his Excy and this Board his Accounts of the 3<sup>d</sup> ℔ Hhd. (given by her Majesty for purchasing Arms) and by him received from the 12<sup>th</sup> of May 1692 to the 20<sup>th</sup> of July 1705. On Perusal thereof we observe that the following Sums have been issued Viz.

| | |
|---|---|
| To Capt. Peter Cood | £ 50 |
| To Capt. Nathaniel Bostock | 100 |
| And to Col° Nathaniel Blackiston for apprehending and Securing Pirates and their Effects | 110 |
| in all | £260 |

Which we conceive the Country ought to be refunded and desire your Advice if it be not fit this Assembly should make to her most Sacred Majesty and the Lord High Treasurer of England to have the Country reimbursed the aforesaid Sums with M<sup>r</sup> Platers Accounts is also sent, M<sup>r</sup> George Muschamps her Majesty's Receiver of the Districts of Potowmack and Pocomoke your Proposal and Inspection

> Signed ℔ Order W Bladen Cl. Council.

Upon reading the foregoing Message resolved that this House will address her Majesty and the Lord Treasurer of England to have the Country reimbursed.

Upon reading the Report relating to the Land Records referred to the Consideration of a full House.

The House adjourns till two O'Clock Afternoon.

Post Meridiem.   The House met again, Present as in the morning, only M^r Richard Jones Leave to go Home,  M^r Robert Tyler Leave to go Home, M^r Samuel Magruder Leave to go Home.

Ingrossed Bill for Naturalization of John Baptist Tyley, Indorsed April 13^th 1706

Read and assented to by the House of Delegates.

Signed ℔ Order<br>W. Taylard Cl. Ho. Del.

Ingrossed Bill for uniting William and Mary Parish to New Port Hundred in Charles County, Indorsed April 13^th 1706.
Read and assented to by the House of Delegates

Signed ℔ Order W. Taylard Cl. Ho. Del.

Petition of Elizabeth Guibert lately called Elizabeth Blackiston for Allowance of Cash paid for Powder and Ball being read in the House and debated and finding it to be of long standing it is resolved it be rejected.

The Petition of Thomas Reading, Printer read and referred till Monday morning

Edward Lloyd and W^m Coursey Esq^rs from the Hoñble Council enter the House and delivers M^r Speaker, Bill to make null and void a Deed of Thomas Edmondson to William Edmondson, Indorsed April 13^th 1706 By the Council in Assembly Read the first Time and will pass.

W Bladen Cl. Council.

Bill declaring the Act for erecting Ann Arundel and Oxford Towns into Ports &^ca

Indorsed Viz.   By the Council in Assembly April 13^th 1706 Read the first Time and will pass

W. Bladen Cl. Council.

Bill declaring the Land Law to be in Force.

Indorsed By the Council in Assembly April 13^th 1706. Read the first Time & will pass.

W. Bladen Cl. Council.

Bill ascertaining the Navigation of open Sloops & Shallops &^ca Indorsed By the Council in Assembly April 13^th 1706. This Board have considered the Indorsement by the House of Delegates on this Bill and cannot consent to the lessening the Securitys especially having so eminent an Example of the great Caution us'd by the Parliament of England to secure this Branch of her Majesty's Revenue and in Case the Condition of the Bonds are designed to be complyed with what Lib. 41. signifies the Value of the Security given.

Signed ꝑ Order W. Bladen Cl. Con<sup>l</sup>

Bill for Currency of Coin &<sup>ca</sup> with Indorsement of the Council is rejected.

Bill for Advancement of Trade &<sup>ca</sup> brought into the House and ordered to be read on Monday morning.

Ingrossed Bill for settling Land in John Whittington of Kent County Indorsed April 13<sup>th</sup> 1706. Read and assented to by the House of Delegates.

Signed ꝑ Order W. Taylard Cl. Ho. Del.

Ingrossed Bill for Division of several Counties. Indorsed April 13<sup>th</sup> 1706.

Read and assented to by the House of Delegates

Signed ꝑ Order W. Taylard Cl. Ho. Del.

Petition of M<sup>rs</sup> Jane Crofts read in the House and rejected. p. 78
The House adjourns till Monday Morning Eight o'Clock.

Monday April 15<sup>th</sup> 1706.

The House met again according to Adjournment.

Being called over were present as on Saturday.

Read what was done a Saturday

Upon reading a Scheme of what Laws of England were held to be in force in this Province reported to the House by Col° Thomas Smithson pursuant to a former Order the House find it not to be so perfect as they expected.

Therefore Resolved That M<sup>r</sup> Rob<sup>t</sup> Goldsborough and M<sup>r</sup> Nicholas Low inspect the said Scheme of those Acts and report the same more amply to the next Session of Assembly.

John Hammond and Francis Jenkins Esq<sup>rs</sup> from the Honble Council enter the House and deliver M<sup>r</sup> Speaker the Bill for suspending Prosecution of Popish Priests &<sup>ta</sup> Indorsed. By his Excellency the Governor and Councill in Assembly April 13<sup>th</sup> 1706

The Petition of the Roman Catholicks signed by Col° Henry Darnall, M<sup>r</sup> Charles Carroll, M<sup>r</sup> Richard Bennett, and M<sup>r</sup> James Carroll being this Day read at the Board it is observed that the Petitioners tho' they so stile themselves rather seem to Challenge than petition for a Toleration and Freedom and unhandsomely charge the General Assembly with infringing the same which they cannot have the least Reason to offer seeing at the Time of making the Act they had not even the

Lib. 41. slightest Assurance of such Freedom or Toleration All which is of the same Piece with the latter Part of the Petition seeming to insinuate as if her Majesty would forget the minutest Thing for the Ease & Advantage of her Subjects.

Neither has this Board any Reason to be satisfied with the Petitioners Construction of the Houses Intention which they say was until her Majesty's Pleasure should be known that they might not be disturbed in the Interval of Assemblies.

But we hope we have a better Right and with better Reason to judge it was quite contrary thereto for otherwise to what End was the Penal Act made or the suspending one limitted to Eighteen Months a certain Time perfix'd

Signed ꝑ Order  W Bladen Cl. Council.

Which being read in the House the Bill was ordered to be laid aside.

Col° William Holland from the Hoñble Council enters the House and delivers M^r Speaker a Petition of Samuel Chew and Nehemiah Birkhead praying Liberty to bring in a Bill to confirm the will of Naylor late of Ann Arundel County deceased.  Read and ordered a Bill be prepared.

Bill for Advancement of Trade read the first Time with Amendments and committed again for further Amendment.

Col° William Holland from the Council enters the House & delivers M^r Speaker the following Message Viz.

By the Council in Assembly, April 15^th 1706.

Whereas in a late Session there was an Order made that the Powder House should be removed within the Town where the Governor thought fit but forasmuch as the Undertakers ask above ten Pounds therefor and will run no Risque in Case it should fall in Pieces we desire the House will while they now sit treat with workmen to do it.

Signed ꝑ Order  W Bladen Cl. Council.

Which being read its ordered that M^r Samuel Young and Major Charles Greenberry treat and agree with some Undertaker for removing the said House and make their Report thereof to the House in the Afternoon

Ordered That Col° John Contee and M^r Henry Coursey draw up and prepare an Address to her Majesty on the Proposal for Copper Coin and also for an Allowance to refund Money made use of out of the 3^d ꝑ Hhd. &^ca

The House adjourns till two O'Clock Afternoon.

Post Meridiem. The House met again according to Ad- Lib. 41. journment.

Being called over were present as in the Morning.

The Message from the Council of the 12th Instant by Colº Jenkins was read this Day and ordered to be entered Viz.

By his Excellency the Governor and Council in Assembly
April 12th 1706.

Some Persons having been presented by the Grand Juries in the Provincial and Ann Arundel County Courts for Bigamy and for suffering a Quaker Conventicle to be kept in their House the Justices and Officers of those Courts are at a Stand in the Prosecution. The Laws of England providing against those Offences seeming to them to be wholly restrained to her Majesty's Subjects residing within the Kingdom of England so that for want of Law in this Country those Offenders expect to escape unpunished according to the old saying where there is no Law there's no Offence Wherefore its recommended to the Consideration of this General Assembly either to declare those Laws of England reach hither for the better Satisfaction of the several Courts of Justice or otherwise by some good wholesome Laws to restrain the said Offence.      Signed p Order W Bladen Cl. Council.

Upon reading that Part relating to Bigamy the House resolve that a Bill be brought in declaring that the Act of Parliament against Bigamy has been & still is in Force within this Province. And as to the second Branch of the said Message relating to Quaker Conventicles this House are of p. 80 opinion that the Act for Religion has sufficiently provided that they are punishable according to the Act of Parliament in that Case.

Ordered a Message be drawn up and sent to the Governor & Council in Answer to their Message.

Bill for Advancement of Trade &ca Read second Time with Amendment and do pass.

Sent up to the Council for their Concurrence by Mr William Frisby, Mr Robt Tyler, Mr William Watts, Mr Francis Dallahyde, Mr John Macclaster & Mr Joseph Ennalls Mr John Jones & Mr Gerrard Fowlke. They return and say they delivered the Bill.

Mr Samuel Young, Mr Robert Skinner, and Mr John Leach ordered to attend the Council with Mr Plater Navall Officer for Patuxent District to see him prove his Acots

They return and say they have seen it done.

Lib. 41.    Upon reading Capt. Richard Smith's Petition and considering the matters therein contained the House think fit to refer the further Consideration thereof till next Assembly

Ingrossed Bill declaring the Land Law to be in force.

Ingrossed Bill to make null & void Edmondson's Conveyance.

Ingrossed Bill for Naturalization of John Baptist Tyler.

Ingrossed Bill uniting New Port Hundred & W^m & Mary Parish.

Ingrossed Bill investing Lands in John Whittington.

Ingrossed Bill for Division of several Counties, sent up to the Council by M^r Joseph Gray & M^r Tho^s Beale together with the Original

They return and say they delivered their Message

Francis Jenkins, Edward Lloyd, James Saunders, and William Coursey Esq^rs from the Council enter the House and bring with them Bill for Advancement of Trade Indorsed April 15^th 1706 By the Council in Assembly This Bill read & will pass with the Amendments remarked.

Signed ꝑ Order W Bladen Cl. Council.

Ordered the following Message be entered viz.

By the House of Delegates, April 15^th 1706.

Your Honour's Message by Col° Jenkins of the 12^th of April Instant this Day lay under debated and Consideration of the House and upon reading the first Branch thereof relating to Bigamy this House resolved that a Bill be brought in declaring that the Act of Parliament of England against Bigamy has been and still is in Force in this Province.

And as to the other Branch relating to Quaker Conventicles this House are of Opinion that the Act for Religion has sufficiently provided that they are punishable according to the Act of Parliament in that Case

Signed ꝑ Order
W. Taylard Cl. Ho. Del.

Which being read was approved of by the House and sent up to the Council by Col° James Maxwell and M^r John Mackall.   They return and say they delivered their Message

The House adjourns till Eight o'Clock to Morrow.

p. 81    Tuesday April 16^th 1706

The House met again according to Adjournment.

Being called over were all present as yesterday.

Bill for advancement of Trade &<sup>ca</sup> Read with the Amend- <sub>Lib. 41.</sub>
ments remarked & do pass

Bill to sell the Freehold of Abraham Naylor applying the
money to the uses in the will   Indorsed April 16<sup>th</sup> 1706.   By
the Council in Assembly Read the first Time and will pass
W. Bladen Cl. Co.

And the Bill for Encouragement of Trade &<sup>ca</sup> assented .

James Saunders Esq<sup>r</sup> enters the House & delivers M<sup>r</sup>
Speaker the following Message Viz.

By the Council in Assembly April 15<sup>th</sup> 1706.

In Answer to Part of the Houses Message by Col° Maxwell
and M<sup>r</sup> Mackall we have perused the Act of Religion and find
it no Ways declares the Penal Laws to be in force here but
wholly exempts the Dissenters upon complying with certain
Duties therein injoined.
Signed ꝑ Order W. Bladen Cl. Co.

Upon reading the foregoing Message,  Resolved That a Bill
be prepared declaring the Act of Parliament against Dissenters
to be in force in this Province

Bill for appointing Itinerant Judges for the Ease and
Security of this Province.

Read the first Time and referred for further Reading till
Afternoon.

Bill declaring the Statute against Bigamy to be in force.

Read the first Time and committed for Amendments.

Col° Edward Lloyd from the Honble Council enters the
House & delivers M<sup>r</sup> Speaker Ingrossed Bill for dividing
several Counties &<sup>ca</sup> with some Remarks which were amended
and sent up by M<sup>r</sup> Joseph Grey.

James Saunders Esq<sup>r</sup> enters the House from the Honble
Council and delivers the following Bills

Bill to make void Edmondson's Deed.

Bill for Naturalization of John Baptist Tyler

Bill declaring the Act ascertaining the Bounds of Land to
be in force.

Bill uniting New Port Hundred to William and Mary Parish.

Bill settling certain Lands on John Whittington,

All severally indorsed thus

By the Council in Assembly April 16<sup>th</sup> 1706  Bill for Division <sub>p. 82</sub>
of Several Counties &<sup>ca</sup>

Indorsed Viz.   April 16<sup>th</sup> 1706.   Her Majesty's Honble
Council have read and assented hereto.

The House adjourns till two O'Clock Afternoon
W Bladen Cl. Council.

Lib. 41.    Post Meridiem. The House met again according to Adjournment. Being called over were all present as in the Morning

The Account of Rent claimed by the Rector of the.Free school brought into the House which was ordered to be entered Viz.

The Public is D$^r$ to the Rectors and } Visitors of the Free schools &$^{ca}$ }

| | £. s. d. |
|---|---|
| To Rent of the Library Room at £12 p Annum as p Agreement from the 3$^d$ of May 1700 to the 3$^d$ of May 1706 being 6 years } | 72..0..0 |
| To the Rent of the Council Room and the rest of the House for the same at £18 p Annum. } | 108..0..0 £180..0..0 |

Per            Contra                         C$^r$

| | £. s. d. |
|---|---|
| By Money allowed in the publick Levy Anno Dni. 1704 } | 52..0..0 |
| Ballance due | 128..0..0 |
| | £180..0..0 |

April 16$^{th}$ 1706
Errors Excepted p
W Bladen Reg$^r$ of the
Free School

The Governor and Visitors of the Free School desire this Account may be allowed in the publick and that the House will give Orders therefor.

Signed p Order W Bladen Reg$^r$ Free School.


Which Account was here read and debated and by the House thought fit and ordered that the first Article in the said Account of the £72 be allowed and the other Article of the Account being examined debated and regulated its resolved that thirty Pounds Sterling be allowed for the Use of the Council Room and the Rooms where the Commissary's and Secretary's Offices are held and that the same be in full to this Day.

The Report of the Gentlemen appointed to inspect the Land Records was again read in the House and ordered to be entered Viz.

By the Committee appointed for Inspection of the Land Records it's humbly reported as followeth, That the Major Part of the Records are much worn and decayed and want Amendment but more immediately these following Viz.

A. and B. lately transcribed to be examined.

F. containing Wills Inventories Court and Assembly Proceedings such Part as relates to Land therein to be transcribed.

J. and K. a small Paper Book in 3 Pieces much torn but for the present will serve with the Alphabet transcribed and Book stitched together.

H. the Alphabet and some Part of the Book to be transcribed.

X. The Letter M. in the Alphabet to be transcribed

Q. The first Leaf out and to be new bound.

R. Part of the 4ᵗʰ Leaf torn off the Remainder to be tran- p. 83 scribed and the Book bound.

A. A. To be mended and new covered.

C. C. To be mended and covered as before.

D. D. To be mended in the Binding and the Alphabet and covered as before.

E. E. To be mended and covered as before.

F. F. To be new bound.

G. G. To be new bound

H. H. The Alphabet from the Letter P. to be transcribed 3 Leaves of the Alphabet being wanting.

I. I. To be mended and covered as before.

K. K. To be covered the Alphabet mended and Book

W. S. Two Leaves the Letters H. I. K. L. and M. to be transcribed the Alphabet fastned, the Book mended and new covered,

M. M. To be mended and covered.

L. L. To be mended in the Binding of the Alphabet and new covered

W. C. To be mended in the Alphabet and new covered

W. C. N° 2. To be new sewed and covered

W. C. N° 3. To be new covered

W. C. N° 4. To be new covered

N. S. N° 2. Wants little but covering

D. S. N° B. To be mended in the Alphabet

W. C. N° 5. To be mended in the Binding and covered.

D. N° A. To be mended in the Alphabet, examined from the Letter I. to Q. and that Part to be transcribed.

N. S. N° B. To be new covered.

D. S. N° F. The Letters N. O. and Part of P. in the Alphabet being torn to be examined and transcribed

C. B. N° 2. To be covered and the Alphabet mended. Those two Books are wanting and supposed to be lost Viz.

Liber L. for the Years 1656 and 57 and Liber R. M.

Lands at the Herekill for the Year 1670

It's further shewed to the Honᵇˡᵉ House of Delegates that many others are in a very mean Condition and want to be transcribed but we are of Opinion that with good Usage and

Lib. 41. the above Amendments made they may endure for a small
Time till Books may be had to transcribe them. All which
is humbly referred to the Consideration of the House
                              Signed ꝑ Order Thoˢ Jones Clk.

And its further represented to the House that of our own
Observation we find the Records in General are not so carefully looked after as they ought to be being made Use of for
Seats for the Clerks and laid upon and used instead of Desks
and Tables to write on And we humbly offer to the House
that as for the Transcripts made into new-Books and others
repaired we think it highly necessary that the Secretary main-
p. 84 tain the Records both in Transcripts and Repairs at his proper
Cost & Charge and that this House appoint a Committee to
inspect the same every Session of Assembly or as often as
the House shall seem meet   All which we humbly submit to
the House                              Samuel Young
                                       John Leach

Which being again read and debated this House think it
highly necessary the Records aforesaid be repaired and transcribed.  And thereupon its resolved by the House that Mʳ
Samuel Young and Mʳ Charles Greenberry be and are appointed to treat and agree with some Person to transcribe
and put such Records in Repair as they shall see necessary to
be done and examine and see the same perfect as intimated
in the said Report and likewise examine such other Transcripts of Records that shall be transcribed anew : For which
this House will make Satisfaction according to Agreement
by them made.

Mʳ Joseph Hill, Mʳ James Hay, and Mʳ William Aisquith
are appointed a Committee for Elections and Privileges and
ordered to withdraw upon that Committee and was delivered
to them an Indenture returned by the Sheriff of Prince
George's County.

Proposed by a Member whether Mʳ Bordley be satisfied for
his Services on a Committee appointed to hear and report
the Difference between Colᵒ William Holland and Capt. Richard Smith by the Country or not?  And resolved the said
Parties satisfy the same

The Committee of Elections & Privileges make their Report indorsed on the Back of an Indenture for Election of a
Delegate for Prince George's County as follows

April 16ᵗʰ 1706  By the Committee of Elections and Privileges.

It is reported to the House of Delegates that upon Examination of the within Indenture the within mentioned Robert

Bradley appears to be duly elected to serve as a Delegate for Lib. 41.
Prince Georges County.

Signed ꝑ order.   Thoˢ Bordley Cl. Com.

Ordered Mʳ Thomas Greenfield desire Mʳ Bradley to walk
into the House.

Mʳ Bradley appears in the House and took his Place.

Ordered Mʳ Thomas Greenfield, Mʳ Robert Tyler and Mʳ
Nicholas Lowe attend him to the Council Chamber to see him
qualified

They return and say they have seen him sworn

Bill for Advancement of ten ꝑ Cent Interest.

Read the first Time and committed for Amendment.

The House Adjourns till to Morrow Morning Eight O'Clock

Wednesday April 17ᵗʰ 1706.

The House met again according to Adjournment & were
all present as yesterday

Read what was done yesterday.

Upon the further Petition of Thomas Reading its ordered
he be allowed more ten Shillings by each County and 10/ ꝑ
the Country for his further Encouragement in printing the
full Body of the Laws.

Bill for Advancement of Interest of Money at 10 ꝑ Cent
read the second Time and committed for Amendment.   Bill
appointing Itinerant Judges &ᶜᵃ.   Read the first Time and put
to the Question whether the Bill shall pass or not?   Carried
in the Negative.

Journal of Accounts read in the House and assented to. p. 85
Indorsed and sent up to the Council by the Gentlemen of the
Committee for their Honours Concurrence

They return and say they delivered their Journal.

Mʳ Elias King by Favour of the House has Liberty to go
Home.

Ingrossed Bill to impower Trustees to sell Naylor's Freehold &ᵗᵃ Read and assented to.

The following Memorandum brought into the House and
ordered to be entered Viz.

Memorandum To renew the Order for sending for a Sufficient Quantity of Free Stone to pave the Church and Piaza
the former not mentioning enough To prime and paint the
Piaza and Vestry House and the Back Door of the Church
within and without Indorsed April 17ᵗʰ 1706.

His Excellency desires to know if the Free Stone for paving
the Church be included in Mʳ Samuel Young's Account or if

Lib. 41. not the House will renew the Order to the Treasurer to send
for it as also give an Order to the Treasurer for the painting
the Piaza Vestry House and Back Door of the Church.

Signed p Order W Bladen Cl. Council

Which being read in the House readily concurred and
ordered That M<sup>r</sup> Sam<sup>l</sup> Young employ some Person for painting the Piaza Vestry House & Back Door of the Church and
likewise to send for the Paving of the Church & Satisfaction
will be made by the Country.

The House adjourns till two o'Clock Afternoon

Post Meridiem.  The House met again according to Adjournment and were present as in the Morning.

Proposed whether it be not for the Good and Advantage of
this Province to make Hemp and Flax approved of & resolved
a Bill be prepared for that Encouragement and to be rated
Hemp at 6<sup>d</sup> and Flax at 9<sup>d</sup> p ll.

This House being informed that the Roman Catholicks had
this Day preferred a Petition to his Excellency and Council
wherein they have given his Excellency & that Honble Board
Satisfaction to their Objections on the former Petition and that
the Governor and Council were inclinable to give way to the
Bill for suspending Execution of Popish Priests.

Ordered That Major Thomas Beale and M<sup>r</sup> Francis Dallahyde carry the same up to his Excellency and Council

They return and say they delivered the Bill.

William Coursey Esq. from the Council enters the House
and delivers M<sup>r</sup> Speaker Bill suspending the Prosecution of
Popish Priests indorsed April 16<sup>th</sup> 1706.

By the Council in Assembly Read the first Time

Signed p Order.   W. Bladen Cl Con<sup>l</sup>.

John Saunders Esq: from the Honble Council enters the
House and delivers M<sup>r</sup> Speaker Bill for preventing Fornica-
p. 86 tion &<sup>ta</sup> Indorsed By the Council in Assembly April 17<sup>th</sup> 1706
This Bill being read is thought very unreasonable and rejected.

Signed p Order W Bladen Cl. Council.

And Message was referred till the morning.

Ingrossed Bill for Encouragement of Trade &<sup>ta</sup> read and
assented to by the House of Delegates.

Sent up to the Council for their Concurrence by M<sup>r</sup> James
Hay and M<sup>r</sup> John Mackall.

They return and say they delivered the Bill

Bill ascertaining Damages on Protested Bills,

Read the first Time and put to the Question whether the Lib. 41.
Bill pass or not? Carried in the Affirmative

Bill for encouraging making Hemp and Flax

Read the first Time & put to the Question whether the Bill
pass or not? Carried in the Affirmative & do pass.

Bill suspending the Prosecution of Popish Priests &ᵗᵃ read
again & do pass.

Bill declaring several Acts of Parliament to be in force,
Read the first Time and by especial Order do pass.

Bill encouraging the making Hemp & Flax &ᵗᵃ read the
second Time & do pass

The foregoing 4 Bills sent up to the Council by Mʳ Joseph
Grey & Mʳ John Maclaster for their Honours Concurrence.

They return and say they delivered the Bills

William Holland and William Coursey Esqʳˢ enter the House
& delivers Mʳ Speaker Ingrossed Bill for Encouragement of
Trade &ᵗᵃ

Bill for confirming the last Will and Testament of Thomas
Knighton late of Ann Arundel County deceased Read the
first Time & referred till next Assembly and ordered all Persons concerned have Notice then to give their Attendance if
to them it shall seem meet.

William Coursey Esq; enters the House and delivers Mʳ
Speaker the following Message

Maryland April 17. 1706. By the Hoñble the Rector Governor
and Visitors of the ffree Schools.

Whereas the Hoñble the House of Delegates upon the
Account yesterday by us exhibited for the Rent of the School
House in Annapolis made so very inconsiderable an Allowance for the Council Chamber & publick Offices its that House
that it will not answer the half of the common Interest of the
money expended in Building thereof we do hereby represent
unto the General Assembly that altho' we shall not gainsav
the Bargain about the Library yet we are not willing the
House should be held and used for a Council Room or other
publick Services on such precarious Terms any longer Therefore propose that you will either make a particular Agreement
for the Rent of the Council Room or otherwise ᵱchase the
whole House which we are willing to offer the Public at à very
reasonable Rate.

Signed ᵱ Order W Bladen Cl. Lib: School.

To the Hoñble the Genˡ Assembly.

Which being read this House say they will not purchase
but are willing to take the whole House one year at Rent of

Lib. 41. £12 Sterling or £6 for the Council Room if the Visitors concur therewith.

Proposed whether it be not necessary that a Bill be brought in to prohibit the Pensylvanians to carry European Goods out of this Province?

p. 87 Put to the Question whether a Bill be brought in for such Prohibition or not?

Carried in the Affirmative and ordered a Bill be brought in.

Message by William Coursey Esq' relating to Charles Kilburn's Petition of an Allowance of 3000₹ Tob° read and debated

This House have resolved that the same be struck off. The Journal of the Committee of Accounts indorsed and sent up to the Council ꝑ M' Thomas Frisby

He returns and says he delivered the same.

The House adjourns till to Morrow Morning Eight o'Clock.


### Thursday April the 18ᵗʰ 1706

The House met again. Being called over were all present as yesterday

Read what was done yesterday. And upon reading the Petition of Job Evans and his wife Adm'ˢ of John Perry deceased Inspection was made in the Journal of Accounts. Feb'ʸ 19ᵗʰ 1697/8 wherein & by M' Mason's Letter and his Account it is found that in the year there was lodged in the Hands of M' Robert Mason then Treasurer of the Western Shore the Sum of £50 Sterling payable to the said John Perry but does not appear to this House that the same or any Part thereof has been since satisfied. Therefore ordered that M'ˢ Susannah Mason Exa of the said Robert Mason appear before the House next Session of Assembly and that She has Notice to bring her Books Accounts and Papers & Receipts if any to shew if the Debts aforesaid be satisfied or not or otherwise to pay the same to the said Administrators.

Message by James Saunders Esq' of Yesterday read in the House viz.


### By his Excellency the Governor and Council in Assembly
### April 17ᵗʰ 1706.

Several Complaints being made to this Board that Persons sent to the Indians at the Head of the Bay have been so slightly rewarded for their extraordinary Services that it will be of ill Consequence and to the Discouragement of others on the like Occasions. We desire the House of Delegates will

seriously reflect thereon and particularly how Mʳ John Hall Lib. 41. and a certain Indian by him employed have been gratified
Signed p Order W Bladen Cl. Council.

Read and resolved Mʳ John Hall be allowed more 600ˡˡ Tobᵒ and the Indian 20ˡˡ.

Indorsed and sent up to the Council ᵱ Mʳ Gerrard Fowlks.

Andrew Welpley Carpenter being called into the House to treat and agree with him to bring the Powder House into the Town of Annapolis; he appeared and it was proposed to him whether he would undertake the Work and to remove the House & place it where his Excellency shall please to appoint and to run all Risque and Hazard and settle the same House in such Place in as good condition as it now stands for £ 15 Sterling which he agreed to and obliged himself to have it done by the Middle of July next to all which this House likewise agreed.

Francis Jenkins Esqʳ enters the House and delivers Mʳ p. 88 Speaker Bill for declaring 2 several Acts of Parliament to be in force. Indorsed April 17ᵗᵃ 1706 By the Council in Assembly read and will pass with the Amendments.
Signed ᵱ Order W Bladen Cl. Council.

Bill for suspending the Prosecution of Popish Priests. Indorsed Eodem Die Read in Council and will pass with Amendmᵗ    Signed ᵱ Order W Bladen Cl. Council.

Read in the House with Amendments and do pass with Amendment

Bill for encouraging the making Hemp and Flax &ᵗᵃ Indorsed April 17ᵗʰ 1706 By the Council in Assembly. This Bill with the Amendment proposed, and being made Temporary for and during the Term of 3 years and to the End of the first Session of Assembly next ensuing and will pass.
Signed ᵱ Order W. Bladen Cl. Co.

Bill prohibiting the Exportation of European Goods put to the Question whether it pass or not?

Carried in the Affirmative and do pass. Sent up to the Hon̄ble Council by Mʳ Robert Tyler and Mʳ John Mackall for their Concurrence

They return and say they delivered the Bill

Bill encouraging making Hemp and Flax read again with Amendment proposed and will pass.

Bill declaring several Acts of Parliament in Force &ᵗᵃ Read in the House and committed for Amendment

39

Lib, 41.    Bill for suspending Prosecution of Popish Priests

Bill for encouraging the making Hemp & Flax.    Sent up to the Council for their Honour's Concurrence by M<sup>r</sup> Francis Dallahyde and M<sup>r</sup> Samuel Magruder

They return and say they delivered the Bills

M<sup>r</sup> George Plater's Petition praying an Allowance for sending several publick Letters and Packets to Annapolis &<sup>ta</sup> with the Indorsment thereon, Read in the House and debated.    It is the opinion of the House that the Petitioner ought to have sent such Letters and Packets to the next Sheriff who is obliged to dispatch them away according to the Act of Assembly and therefore his Petition is rejected.

Bill for erecting a new Parish in Cecil County

Read the first Time & by especial Order do pass Sent up to the Council by M<sup>r</sup> John Jones for their Concurrence

Ordered by the House that George Plater Esq<sup>r</sup> pay unto Samuel Young Esq<sup>r</sup> 200£ Sterling within ten Days before the Fleet go out of the Province.

Copy delivered him.

M<sup>r</sup> Bladen's Memorial brought into the House ꝑ Edward Lloyd and W<sup>m</sup> Coursey Esq<sup>rs</sup> relating to Col<sup>o</sup> Blakiston's Agency and Salary for the same

Which being read and debated the House finds there is now to Col<sup>o</sup> Blackiston for his Agency from the 17<sup>th</sup> Day of Sept. 1704 to the 17<sup>th</sup> Day of Sept. 1705 120ł Sterling which is ordered to be paid M<sup>r</sup> Bladen by Col<sup>o</sup> Thomas Smithson Treasurer for the Eastern Shore for the use of the said Col<sup>o</sup> Blackiston

As to the other Year's Agency Resolved to refer Payment thereof till the year expire

p. 89    James Saunders Esq<sup>r</sup> enters the House and delivers M<sup>r</sup> Speaker Bill for erecting a new Parish in Cecil County, Indorsed By the Council in Assembly.    Read the first Time and will pass.        Signed ꝑ Order W Bladen Cl Council.

Bill for suspending Prosecution of Popish Priests Indorsed Eodem Die Read in Council and past with Amendment
        Signed ꝑ Order  W Bladen Cl. Council

Bill prohibiting European Goods to be exported Indorsed April 18<sup>th</sup> 1706 By the Council in Assembly Read in Council and passed                    W Bladen Cl. Con.

Sent to the Committee to be ingrossed.

M<sup>r</sup> Samuel Young's Account together with a Message brought into the House which Message was ordered to be entered Viz.

By the Council in Assembly April 17ᵗʰ 1706.

This Account being perused at this Board we cannot approve thereof therefore refer it to the Examination of the House of Delegates it seeming to be very unreasonable.

Signed ꝑ Order<br>
W. Bladen Cl. Co.

Read and referred by the House for further Consideration

Francis Jenkins Esqʳ enters the House and delivers Mʳ Speaker Bill ascertaining Damages on protested Bills with Indorsment of the Hoñble Council.

Upon reading thereof this House thought fit no further to proceed thereon

Colᵒ John Contee, Mʳ John Jones and Mʳ Thomas Greenfield is appointed to inspect & regulate the Account of Mʳ Samuel Young sent to the House from the Hoñble Council and to make Report of their Regulation to the House.

The House adjourns till two O'Clock Afternoon

Post Meridiem.

The House met according to Adjournment.

Being called over were present as in the Morning.

Message from the Visitors of the Free School brought into the House was here read and fully debated and ordered to be indorsed Viz. By the House of Delegates Apˡ 17ᵗʰ 1706.

Upon reading the within Message this House offer £20 for one whole Year's Rent of the School-House if the Visitors of the Free School please to concur therewith.

Bill declaring several Acts of Parliament to be in force &ᵗᵃ Read the first and second Time and by especial Order do pass.

Ingrossed Bill erecting a Parish on the North Side of Elk River &ᶜᵃ Indorsed April 18ᵗʰ 1706.

Read and assented to by the House of Delegates.

Ingrossed Bill suspending the Prosecution of Popish Priests &ᵗᵃ Indorsed April 18ᵗʰ 1706

Read and assented to by the House of Delegates. These two ingrossed Bills and Bill declaring several Acts of Parliament to be in force sent up to the Council by Mʳ James Hay and Mʳ Thomas Howe

They return and say they delivered the same.

Address to her Majesty and to the Lord High Treasurer &ᵗᵃ to reimburse the Country some Money misapplied &ᵗᵃ and the Address for Copper Coin both read and sent to his Excellency and Council to be Signed ꝑ their Honours

Ordered to be entered at the End of this Journal

p. 90

Lib. 41.   Ingrossed Bill encouraging making Hemp and Flax Indorsed April 18th 1706.

Read and assented to by the House of Delegates.

Sent up to the Council by M[r] John Wells & M[r] Thomas
Frisby. They return and say they delivered the same.

The following Message prepared and sent up to his Excellency and Council by M[r] Joseph Ennalls Viz.


May it please your Excellency,

Upon reading that Paragraph of your Excellency's Speech
relating to Persons sent on Expeditions on any emergent
Occasion it is resolved by the House that such Persons as
shall any ways be employed by your Excellency shall be
rewarded for such Services as your Excellency shall think fit.
This House taking your Excellency to be a proper Judge of
the Reward for such Services.

Signed ᵱ Order W. Taylard Cl. Ho. Del.


William Holland Esq[r] from the Hoñble Council enters the
House and delivers M[r] Speaker Bill declaring several Acts
of Parliament to be in force. Indorsed April 18th 1706 By the
Council in Assembly read & past.

Sign'd ᵱ Order W Bladen Cl. Co.


The ingrossed Bill for suspending the Prosecution of Popish
Priests Indorsed April 18th 1706. Her Majesty's Hoñble
Council have read and assented hereto.

Signed ᵱ Order W Bladen Cl. Co.


Ingrossed Bill for erecting a Parish on the North Side Elk
River Indorsed April 18th 1706 Her Majesty's Hoñble Council have read & assented hereto.

Signed ᵱ Order W Bladen Cl. Co.


The Gentlemen appointed to examine the Accounts of M[r]
Samuel Young relating to the Building the Vestry House
enter the House and inform M[r] Speaker and the House of
what Objections they make to the Account and upon Debate
thereof its put to the Question whether there shall be any
Abatement or not?

Carried in the Negative that there be no Abatement and
ordered the Acc[t] be allowed and sent up by way of Message.

The following Message sent up to the Council ᵱ M[r] Henry
Coursey & M[r] Rob[t] Goldsborough

By the House of Delegates April 18<sup>th</sup> 1706

It being proposed by a Member of this House whether it ꝺe not reasonable that M<sup>r</sup> W. Bladen the Undertaker of re-ꝺuilding the Stadt-House be not advanced and paid some Part of the Consideration on his Contract. It is resolved he ꝺe paid out of the publick Stock at assessing the next publick ⌐evy the sum of one hundred Pounds being one half if the Hoñble Council shall think fit to concur therewith.

Signed ꝑ Order W. **Taylard** Cl. Ho. Del.

Ingrossed Bill to prohibit the Exportation of European Ꝼoods Indorsed Read and assented to by the House of Ɔelegates. Sent up to the Council by M<sup>r</sup> Joseph Gray
He returns and says he delivered it.
William Coursey Esq enters the House and delivers M<sup>r</sup> Ꝼpeaker Ingrossed Bill for encouraging making Hemp and Ꝼlax Indorsed April 18<sup>th</sup> 1706. Her Majesty's Hoñble Coun-ːil have read and assented hereto.

Signed ꝑ Order W Bladen Cl. Co.

Col° Lloyd and Col° Holland enters the House and delivers Ꙇ<sup>r</sup> Speaker the Bill prohibiting the Exportation of European Ꝼoods &<sup>ta</sup> Indorsed April 18<sup>th</sup> 1706
Read and assented to by the Council.

Signed ꝑ Order. W. Bladen **Cl. Co.**

M<sup>r</sup> William Coursey enters the House and delivers M<sup>r</sup> Ꝼpeaker the Addresses
James Saunders Esq<sup>r</sup> enters the House and delivers M<sup>r</sup> Ꝼpeaker ingrossed Bill declaring several Acts of Parliament ꝺ be in Force. Indorsed April 18<sup>th</sup> 1706
Her Majesty's Hoñble Council have read and assented ereto. Signed ꝑ Order W Bladen **Cl. Co.**

Bill apportioning the publick Levy Read the first and sec-nd Time & do pass.
Sent up to the Council by M<sup>r</sup> Joseph Grey. He returns nd says he delivered the Bill.
Col° William Holland enters the House and delivers M<sup>r</sup> peaker the Bill for apportioning the publick Levy Read and greed to in Council.
The House adjourns till two o'Clock Afternoon

Post Meridiem. The House met again according to Ad-ᴉurnment. Being called over were all present as in the **ꙇorning**

Lib. 41.    The House now will proceed on settling Fees for private
Bills past this Session

|  |  | £ | s. | d. |
|---|---|---|---|---|
| Resolved That M^r Speaker's Fees for the private Bill for uniting William and Mary Parish to New Port Hundred be settled at 1200^ll Tob° |  | 5.. | 0.. | 0 |
| And to William Taylard Clerk 600^ll Tob° or |  | 2.. | 10.. | 0 |
| Thomas Edmondson for the Bill to make Edmondson's Deed void M^r Speaker's Fees |  | 4.. | 0.. | 0 |
| To William Taylard for his Clerks Fees ꝑ ditto |  | 2.. | 0.. | 0 |
| M^r John Whittington to M^r Speaker for the Bill settling Lands on him &^ta |  | 4.. | 0.. | 0 |
| To William Taylord Clk House his Fees for the same |  | 2.. | 0.. | 0 |
| M^r Ch^r Vernon to M^r Speaker Fees for the Bill to sell the Freehold of Naylor |  | 5.. | 0.. | 0 |
| To William Taylard Clerk for the same his Fees, |  | 2.. | 10.. | 0 |
| Talbot County to M^r Speaker for the Bill for Division of the Counties 5^ll. Kent County Ditto 5^ll. and Queen Anne's County Ditto 5^ll. |  | 15.. | 0.. | 0 |
| To William Taylard ꝑ Clerks Fees in Ditto |  | 7.. | 10.. | 0 |
| Saint Ann's Parish on North Side Elk for their private Bill allowed to M^r Speaker for Fees 1000^ll Tob. |  |  |  |  |
| To William Taylard for his Fees in Ditto 500^ll Tobacco |  |  |  |  |
| Col° Darnall and all that signed that Petition for Bill to suspend the Prosecution of Popish Priests &^ta for their Bill ordered to M^r Speaker |  | 6.. | 0.. | 0 |
| To William Taylard Clerk of the House ꝑ Ditto |  | 3.. | 0.. | 0 |

The House adjourns till to Morrow Morning Eight o'Clock.


p. 92                    Friday April 19^th 1706.

The House met again according to Adjournm^t
Being called over were present as yesterday.  Read what
was done yesterday.
Ingrossed Bill ꝑ apportioning the publick Levy Indorsed
April 19^th 1706 Read & assented to by the House of Dele-
gates            Signed ꝑ Order W Taylard Cl Ho. Del.


Which Bill was sent up to the Council by M^r William Stone
& M^r John Jones together with the following Message Viz.

By the House of Delegates April 19<sup>th</sup> 1706

Whereas it has been represented to this House that it is an Aggrievance to this Province that the County Court Commissioners are limitted and restrained and with which this House do concur and do therefore pray that his Excellency and be pleased to enlarge the said Commissions &<sup>ta</sup>

Signed ꝑ Order W. Taylard Cl. Ho. Del.

They return and say they delivered their Message and the Bill

Kenelm Chesildine and William Coursey Esq<sup>rs</sup> enters the House & delivers M<sup>r</sup> Speaker a Letter to Col<sup>o</sup> Blackiston Agent for the Province which being read was by Order of the House

Signed by M<sup>r</sup> Speaker on Behalf of the whole House and sent up again to the Council by M<sup>r</sup> John Wells & M<sup>r</sup> Tho<sup>s</sup> Howe. They return and say they delivered the same

Col<sup>o</sup> Edward Lloyd enters the House and delivers M<sup>r</sup> Speaker the Bill for apportioning the publick Levy

Indorsed April 19<sup>th</sup> 1706 Her Majesty's Hon̄ble Council have read and assented hereto.

Signed ꝑ Order W Bladen Cl. Co.

And the following Message was brought into the House Viz.

By the Council in Assembly April 19<sup>th</sup> 1706.

Upon the Houses Representation by M<sup>r</sup> Stone to his **Excy** to enlarge the Jurisdiction of County Courts we have maturely considered the same and do think the County Courts have sufficient Jurisdiction. Therefore cannot advise his **Excy** to make any Enlargement.      Signed ꝑ Order
W Bladen Cl. Co.

And likewise was again brought into the House the Hon̄ble Rector and Governors &<sup>ta</sup> Reply with Indorsment thereon. Ordered to be entered Viz :

By the Hon̄ble the Rector, Governor and Visitors of the Free School April 18<sup>th</sup> 1706.

In Reply to the House of Delegates Answer to our Proposal yesterday about the Rent of the Council Room or purchasing the whole House out and out we do hereby represent to the Hon̄ble House that we cannot concur therewith in leasing the Council Room on the Terms proposed; and altho' we do not

Lib. 41. think it reasonable to turn the publick Records out of the House whereby they may be exposed yet we are obliged to give you warning to provide an House for her Majesty's Council to sit in for we are resolved on the 3ᵈ of May next to lock up the Doors of the said Council Chamber and seeing we have made you the first Offer and given you such fair Caution we hope neither you nor any others will think the Country anywise unhandsomely dealt with by us.

Signed ꝑ Order W. Bladen Cl. Libˡ School.

Indorsed By the House of Delegates.   April the 18ᵗʰ 1706.

Upon reading the within Message this House proposes and do offer 20lɬ Sterling for one Years Rent of the whole School House if the Visitors of the Free School please to concur therewith.        Signed ꝑ Order  W. Taylard Cl. Ho. Del.

p. 93   Which was returned back and this Day was again brought into the House with the following Indorsment.   By the Rector Governor & Visitors of the Free School April 19ᵗʰ 1706.  We do agree to the Offer of the House of Delegates

Signed ꝑ Order.  W. Bladen Cl. Libˡ School.

Mʳ John Contee sent up to the Council with the Addresses and is likewise ordᵈ to acquaint his Excellency that this House having no Matters of Moment before them so that the House is ready to wait of his Excellency and her Majesty's Hoñble Council to conclude this Session when his Excy shall please to command them.   He returns and acquaints Mr Speaker that his Excellency says he waits their coming up to the Council Chamber.   Upon which Mʳ Speaker and the whole House attended his Excellency and Council at the Council Chamber and carried with him the several Bills following which he presented to his Excellency Vizᵗ.

Bill for Advancement of Trade and erecting Ports and Towne in the Province of Maryland

2.   A Bill encouraging the making Hemp and Flax

3.   A Bill prohibiting the Importation of European Commodities.

4.   A Bill declaring several Acts of Parliament of the Kingdom of England to be in force in this Province.

5.   A Bill for dividing and regulating several Counties on the Eastern Shore and erecting a new County by the Name of Queen Ann's County.

6·   A Bill erecting a Parish on the North Side of Elk River in Cecil County.

7. A Bill for suspending the Prosecution of Romish Lib. 41. Priests &ᵗᵃ

8. A Bill uniting New Port Hundred and William and Mary Parish in Charles County.

9. A Bill for Naturalization of John Baptist Tyler.

10. A Bill to sell the Freehold of Abraham Naylor applying the money to the uses in the Will.

11. A Bill to make null and void a Deed from Thoˢ Edmondson to Wᵐ Edmondson

12. A Bill investing certain Lands in John Whittington.

13. A Bill declaring the Land Law to be in force.

14. A Bill for apportioning the publick Levy for this present Year 1706.

To each of which said Bills was affixed the great Seal of this Province and his Excellency was pleased to enact the same into Laws, by underwriting every of them thus. On Behalf of her Sacred Majesty Queen Ann &ᵗᵃ I will this be a Law.

John Seymour

Then his Excellency was pleased to say to Mʳ Speaker and P. 94 the Members of the House of Delegates.

Gentlemen. With the Advice of her Majesty's Honbel Council I have thought fit to prorogue you until the 20ᵗʰ Day of June next ensuing. To which Time you are accordingly prorogued.

ꝑ Order   W. Taylard Cl. Ho. Del.

The Houses Address of Thanks to his Excellency the Governor sent up by Mʳ Skinner and nine other Members. Ordered to be entered. April 13ᵗʰ 1706.

May it please your Excellency.

We her Majesty's most Dutiful and Loyal Subjects the Representatives of the Inhabitants of the respective Counties of this Province now met and convened in a General Assembly do give your Excellency hearty Thanks for all your Kindnesses and generous Gratitudes shewed to us from your Accession to this Goverment to this Time and we do assure your Excellency that as her Majesty by her Royal Bounty have filled out Hearts with Thankfulness so she has added one Degree of Joy to our Felicity by placing your Excellency her Vicegerent over us which will highly improve that profound Veneration and Respect which we now have and shall always desire to retain for your Excellency's Person and Government.

Lib. 41.    May it please Your Excellency Your Excellency's most Humble Servants

| | | |
|---|---|---|
| Sam¹ Young | Joˢ Grey | Robᵗ Tyler |
| Thoˢ Beale | Joⁿ Jones | James Smallwood |
| Charles Greenberry | Joˢ Hill | Ger'd Fowke |
| Fraˢ Dallahyde | Wᵐ Dare | Thoˢ Smith, Speaker |
| Joⁿ Contee | Peter Watts | Geo. Muschamp |
| Joⁿ Mackall | Wᵐ Stone | Robᵗ Goldsborough |
| Hugh Eccleston | Ja. Philips | Ja : Maxwell |
| John Leach | Joⁿ Wells | Thoˢ Greenfield |
| Nichˢ Lowe | James Hay | John Macclaster |
| Wᵐ Aisquith | Edwᵈ Blay | Wᵐ Frisby |
| Tho. Howe | Robᵗ Skinner | Thoˢ Frisby |
| Sam¹ Magruder | Elias King | Richᵈ Jones Jʳ |
| Wᵐ Watts | Jos. Ennalls | |

# ACTS.

Maryland ss;

Att a Session of Assembly Begun and held at the Town
and Port of Annapolis in the county of Ann Arundell on the
second day of Aprill in the fifth year of the Reigne of our
Sovereign Lady Queen Anne of England, Scotland, France
and Ireland Defender of the Faith &c^a Annoq Dni 1706—
his Excellency John Seymour Esq^r being Governour were
Enacted the following Laws.

An Act Declareing An Act Entituled An Act Ascertaining
the bounds of Land to be in force

Be it Enacted by the Queens most Excellent Majesty by
and with the Advice and Consent of her Majesty's Governour
Councill and Assembly of this Province and the Authority of
the same That the Act of Assembly made att a Generall
Assembly begun and held att the Port of Annapolis the
twenty seaventh day of June in the year of our Lord One
thousand six hundred Ninety Nine and Every Clause matter
and thing therein contain'd is Hereby Declared to be and
Remain in full full force and Effect to all Intents Constructions and Purposes whatsoever to the end of the next Sessions of Assembly.

Aprill the 15^th 1706

Read & Assented to by the house of Delegates
Signed ᵱ ord^r W Taylard Clk h D.

Aprill the 16^th 1706

Her Majesty's hon^ble Councill have read and Assented
hereto Signed ᵱ ord^r
W Bladen Cl Concll.

Maryland Aprill the 19^th 1706

On behalf of her most Sacred Majesty Queen Anne &c. I
will this be a Law.

Jo: Seymour

Lib. L. L. An Act for Naturalization of John Baptist Tyler of Prince Georges County, Planter.

Be it Enacted by the Queens most Excellent Majesty by and with the advice and consent of her Majesty's Governour Council and Assembly of this Province and the Authority of the same that John Baptist Tyler borne under the Dominions of the States Generall of the united Provinces now resident in Prince Georges County in this Province shall from henceforth be adjudged reputed and taken as one of her Majesty's Naturall borne Subjects of this Province and he is by force and virtue of this Act Adjudged to all intents and purposes within this Province to Demand challenge ask have hold and Enjoy any Lands tenements and hereditaments within the same to w^{ch} he might anywayes be Entituled as if he was a free and naturall borne Subject and also be Enabled to Prosecute mainetaine avow Justify and Defend all manner of Actions suits pleas Plaints and other Demands whatsoever or howsoever within the said Province as liberally ffranckly, freely fully and Lawfully as if he had been a Naturall borne Subject any Law Statute usage or custome to the Contrary notwithstanding.

P 233      Aprill the 13^{th} 1706.            Aprill the 16^{th} 1706
        Read and Assented to by the   Her Maj^{tys} hon^{ble} Councill have
           house of Delegates          read and assented hereto
           Signed p ord^r                  Signed p ord^r
             W Taylard Clk h D.              W Bladen Cl Concil.

Aprill the 19^{th} 1706.
On the behalf of her Sacred Maj^{ty} Queen Anne &c. I will this be a Law.

Jo Seymour


An Act for the dividing and regulating Severall Counties on the easterne shore of this Province and Constituting a County by the name of Queen Anns County within the same Province.

Forasmuch as diverse the Inhabitants of Talbot Kent and Cecill counties within this Province have by their Petitions to this Present generall Assembly complained of the Irregular Scituation of their Counties and the seats of Judicature within the same to the great Illconveniencys of the suitors thereunto for redress whereof for the future

Be it Enacted by the Queens most Excilent Maj^{ty} by and Lib. L. J. with the advice and consent of her Majesty's Govern^r Councill and Assembly of this province and the Authority of the same that from and after the first day of May which shall be in the year of our Lord One Thousand seven hundred and seven The bounds of Talbot County shall Containe Sharps Island Choptank Island and all the Land on the North side of Great Choptank river and Extend itself up the said River to Tuckahoe bridge and from thence with a streight line to the mill Commonly called and known by the name of Swetnams mill and from thence down the south side of Wye river to the Mouth thereof and from thence Down the Bay (including Poplar Island) to the first Beginning also Bruffs Island in Wye River

And that from and after the said First day of May one thousand seven hundred and, seven the Island called Kent p. 234 Island and all the Land on the south side of Chester river to a branch called Sewells Branch and with the said branch to the head thereof and from thence with an east line to the extent of this Province, & bounded on the South with Talbot County to Tuckahoe bridge and from thence with Tuckahoe Creek and Choptank river to the mouth of a branch falling into the said river called or known by the name of the White March branch and from thence with a north east line to the extent of this Province and bounded on the East with the Exteriour bounds of this Province shall be and is hereby constituted Founded and incorporated into a County of this Province and shall be Denominated called and known by the name of Queen Ann's County & shall and may after the said first day of May One Thousand Seven hundred and Seven as afores^d have and enjoy all rights benefitts and Privilidges Equall with the other Countys of this Province such as sending Burgesses to the generall Assembly having County Courts Sheriffs Justices and other Officers and Ministers requisite and necessary and as used in other Counties of this Province

And that from and after the said first Day of May one thousand seven hundred & seven Kent County shall begin at the South Point of the easterne Neck and from thence run up Chesapeak bay to Sarsafrax river and up the said river to the South end of the Long horse bridge lying over the head of the said River and from thence with a line Drawn East and by south to the Exteriour bounds of this Province and with the Exteriour bounds of this province untill it intersect p. 235 the line of Queen Anns County and with the said County down Chester river to Eastern Neck where it first begun and shall contain all the Land within the said bounds.

Lib. L. L. An Act for Naturalizatio of John Baptist T)'
Georges County, Plantr.

Be it Enacted by the ʃueens most Excel
and with the advice and onsent of her Maj
Council and Assembly o this Province  n
of the same that John hptist T)ler borɪ
minions of the States Geerall of the  un t
resident in Prince Geores County in
from henceforth be adjdged reputed
of her Majesty's Natura borne Subj
and he is by force and 'rtue of thiʅ
intents and purposes witin this Pr
lenge ask have hold and Enjoy an
hereditaments within th  same t
be Entituled as if he wa a free
and also be Enabled to 'rosecut
and Defend all manner f Act
other Demands whatsoeer or
Province as liberally ffrackly,
if he had been a Naturɩl  b
usage or custoɪne to theCoɪ

P 233      Aprill the 1 3ᵗ 1 7oͼ

Read and Assented to bybѧ
house of Delegates
Signed ⅌ ordʳ
W Taylard Cl

.\pri
On the  behalf of  h
will this be a Law.

An Acʈ .
on the
Coun:
same .

Foras:
Cecill c:
this Pr:
Scitua:
the saɪ:
for red:

Be it Enacted by the Governor ... hall by and ... with the advice and consent ... ... Councill and Assembly ... ... authority of the
same that from and after the ... ... May which shall be
in the year of our Lord, One Thousand seven hundred and
seven The ... ... ... contains Sharps
Island Choptank Island ... ... ... on the North side of
Great Choptank river ... ... ... the said River to
Tuckahoe bridge ... ... ... a streight line to the
mill Commonly called ... ... ... name of Swetnams
mill and from ... ... ... side of Wye river to
the Mouth thereof ... ... ... from the Bay (including
Poplar Island ... ... ... after Broffs Island in
Wye River

And that from and after the said First day of May one
thousand seven hundred and seven the Island called Kent
Island and all the Land on the south side of Chester river in
a branch called Sewells Branch and with the said branches
the head thereof and from thence with an east line to the
extent of this Province, & bounded to the South with Tuckahoe
County to Tuckahoe bridge and from thence with Tuckahoe
Creek and Choptank river to the mouth of a branch falling
into the said river called or known by the name of the North
March branch and from thence with a north east line to the
extent of this Province and bounded on the East ... ...
Exterieur bounds of this Province shall be and is hereby
constituted Founded and incorporated into a County of this
Province and shall be Denominated called and known by
the name of Queen Ann's County & shall and ... from the
said first day of May One Thousand Seven hundred and
Seven as aforest have and enjoyll rights ... and
Priviledges Equally with the other Cuntys of this Province
such as sending Burgesses to the generall Assembly holding
County Courts Sheriffs Justices and ther Officers and Ministers requisite and necessary and caused ... ...
of this Province

And that from and after the said first day of May one
thousand seven hundred ... ... Point C ...
at the South Point of ... ... Nk ... ...
up Chesapeak bay to ... ... ... ...
the South end all the ... ... ...
of the said River ... ...
and by south ... ...
with the East ...
the line of ...
down Ch ...
shall contain ...

Lib. L. L.     And that trom and after the said first day of May One
thousand seven hundred and seven Cecill County shall Containe all the Land on the north side of Sarsafrax river and
Kent County aud shall be bounded on the east and north
with the Exteriour bounds of this Province on the west with
Susquehanna river and Cheseapeak bay and on the South
with Sarsafrax river and Kent County.

And Be it further Enacted by the Authority afores^d by and
with the advice and Consent aforesaid that the severall Persons herein after mentioned nominated and appointed shall
be and are hereby Authorized Impowered and required to
call to them the Surveyors of the severall and respective
County's aforesaid and cause them to run out the lines bound
and Divisions of the said County's according to the directions
in this Act before mentioned (where they are not by naturall
bounds divided One from the other that is to say for Talbot
County Col° Thomas Smithson M^r Robert Gouldesburry Maj^r
John Hawkins M^r Matthew Tilghman Ward M^r Thomas Em-
merson M^r Robert Grundy M^r Daniel Sherwood, M^r Thomas
Robins M^r James Lloyd and M^r John Dawson.   For Queen
Anns County M^r Philemon Lloyd M^r Richard Tilghman  M^r
Philemon Hemsley M^r William Turloe M^r Arthur Emmery
M^r John Salter M^r John Whittington M^r Edward Chetham
M^r Nathaniel Wright M^r John Coppidge M^r William Elliot
Valentine Carte and Edward Browne.   For Kent County Col
p. 236 Thomas Smyth M^r Elias King M^r William Frisby M^r John
Wells M^r Edward Blay M^r Phillip Hopkins M^r William Com-
egies and M^r William Harris  And for Cecill County M^r
Thomas Frisby M^r William Dare M^r John Hynson M^r John
Dowdell M^r Francis Mauldin Nicholas Highland M^r John
Mall M^r William Parsons and M^r John Jawart which said
Persons are hereby required and Enjoyned on or before
the first day of September next after the end of this Present
Sessions of Assembly to cause the said lines and bounds of
the said Counties as af^d to be marked & lined by a Double
line of Marked trees that the same may be known and perceived by all Persons and shall returne Certificates of the Due
Courses thereof one to Each County Concerned to be recorded in the County records and one for Each County to the
Governour and Councill to be recorded in the Councill
records And that from and after the said First Day of May
one Thousand seven hundred and seven the s^d Counties nor
either of them being as aforesaid Divided shall not Containe
any other bounds or quantitys of Land than what is herein
before mentioned any Law statute usage or custome to the
Contrary notwithstanding.

And be it further Enacted by the Authority aforesaid by Lib. L L. and with the advice and consent aforesaid that the severall and respective Psons before in this Act mentioned or the Major Part of them shall be and are hereby authorized Empowered and required on or before the last Day of September next Ensuing to meet together in their severall and respective Counties to Consult and agree of the most Convenient Place in Each of the said Counties whereon to build their Courthouse for the Ease and Conveniency of the Inhabitants and suitors and then and there to treat and Agree with the Owners and all psons interested in such Lands and buy and Purchase of such Owners & others interested therein to her Majesty her heires and Successors for the use of their Counties whereon to build their Courthouses two acres of the said Land at the discretion of the Persons least Prejudiciall to the Owners thereof and shall Cause the same to be surveyed and Layd out and after such Survey so made shall p. 237 Cause the same to be marked staked out and Divided from the other Lands adjacent, and if in case any Person or Persons shall willfully refuse to make sale of any such Lands herein before mentioned or be disabled to do the same thro' nonage Coverture non sane memorie or other Impediment or disability whatsoever that then the said Psons herein before mentioned and nominated for each respective County or the major part of them are hereby Authorized by Virtue of this Act To Issue out Warrants to the Sheriffes of the said County's to Impower them to Impannell and returne a Jury of Freeholders to Appeare before the Persons herein before mentioned at such days and times as by them shall be Thought Convenient which Jury upon their oaths to be administred by the said Persons or the major part of them in each respective County are to and shall Enquire and assesse what damage and recompence they shall think fitt to be awarded to the Owners and all psons interested in such Lands according to their severall and respective Interests therein and what sume of tobacco the sayd Jury shall Adjudge the sayd Land to be worth shall be returned by the said Psons under their hands and seales and under the hands and seales of the s^d Jurors to the severall County Courts where such Land shall lye to be payd and allowed by the Commissioners of the severall County Courts to the Party or Party's Owner of such Land or Lands.

And Be it further Enacted by the Authority Advice and consent aforesaid that for satisfaction and Payment of all Charges and Expences whatsoever arising or becoming due to any Pson or Psons for any thing to be Done by Virtue of this Act they shall be satisfyed and Payd by the Severall and

Lib. L. L. respective Inhabitants of the said severall & respective Counties wherein the same shall become due and shall be Levyed
raised and Assessed by the Commissioners of Each respective County Courts by a due and Equall Assessment upon
Each Taxable Pson within the said severall Counties.

p. 238    And be it Enacted by the Authority aforesaid by and with
the advice and consent aforesaid That for Talbot County Col.
Thomas Smithson for Queen Anne's County M^r Richard
Tilghman.  For Kent County Col^o Thomas Smyth for Cecill
County M^r John Hynson or in default of them or any of them
or any of them the next named to them in this Act are required
to give notice to the Sheriffs of the severall respective Counties mentioned in this act who upon such notice given to them
are required to give notice unto the severall Psons mentioned
in this Act of the time & place that such Persons shall meet
for the Executing the severall things in this Act contained
who upon such Notice to them given are hereby required to
Attend accordingly.

Aprill the 13^th 1706.  Read and Assented to by the house
of Delegates.  Signed ꝑ ord^r W Taylard Cl house Del.

Aprill the 16^th 1706  Her Majesty's honble Councill have
read and Assented hereto  Signed ꝑ ord^r
W Bladen Cl. Concil.

Aprill the 19^th 1706

On the behalf of her most sacred Majesty Queen Anne &c^a
I will this be a Law                                    Jo. Seymour

An Act for Erecting a Parish on the North Side of Elk River
in Cecill County.  ·

Forasmuch as it hath been represented to this present General Assembly tha^t by the Ill Situacon of the Parish Church in
Cecill County being built on the South side of Elk River
within the said County the Inhabitants on the north side of Elk
p. 239 River Cannot come to that Church & are thereby Deprived
of the Great Blessing of having the Gospell preached among
them for remedy whereof It is prayed That it may be Enacted;
And be it Enacted by the Queens most Excellent Majesty
by and with the Advice and Consent of her Majestys Governour Councill and Assembly of this Province and the Authority of the same That from and after the first day of May
One thousand Seven hundred and Six all that part of Cecill
County lying on the North side of Elk River being Bounded

as followeth (That is say) Beginning at Turkey point on the Lib. L. L. North side of Elk River aforesaid and running with the said river to Smiths Mill at the head thereof then east to the Exterior bounds of this Province to Susquehanna River thence with the east side of the said River and the bay of Chesepeak to the first Beginning shall be and is by this Act Constituted Erected and made into a parish to be called by the name of North Elk Parish Seperated and Divided as aforesaid from the Parish Already made in the said County & shall be and is hereby adjudged deemed and Taken to be a Separate and distinct parish and shall have hold and Enjoy all previlledges and Advantages that are held and Enjoyed by other Parishes in this Province.

Aprill the 18<sup>th</sup> 1706 : Read & Assented to by the house of Delegates   Sign'd p Ord<sup>r</sup>   William Taylard Cl house Del

Aprill the 8<sup>th</sup> 1706 Her Majestys Hon<sup>ble</sup> Councill have read & assented hereto ; Sign'd p Ord<sup>r</sup>
W Bladen Clerk Councill

Maryland Aprill the 19<sup>th</sup> 1706

On behalf of her most Sacred Majesty Queen Anne &c I will this be a Law Jo : Seymour

An Act for Vesting and Settleing Certain Lands In John Whit- p. 240 tington and his Heires Late the Estate and Inheritance of a Certain Daniell Toaes for and towards Sattisfication and payment of a debt Due from the said Toaes and paid by the s<sup>d</sup> Whittington.

Whereas John Whittington of Kent County Gent: by his petition to this Present Generall Assembly hath sett forth that a Certain Daniell Toaes late of the said County Deceased being in his Life time Indebted to a certaine Richard Swetnam Late of Talbott County Deceased in the sume of thirty five Thousand pounds of Tobacco & being Willing & Desirous to have the same Satisfied and payed by his last will and Testament in writing did leave severall tracts of Land to be sold for the payment of his Debts and of his said will did Constitute and appoint his son Daniell Toaes the son & Executor suffered himself to be sued for the said Debt Due to the said Swetnam and being taken in Execution for the same did prevail w<sup>th</sup> the said John Whittington and a Certain Michaell Miller since Deceased to become security for payment of the said Debt &

40

Lib. L L. Cost that the said Dan[ll] Toaes the Son & Executor in some
short time after dyed Leaving the said Debt & Cost wholly
unsatisfied & payed and not Leaving behind him sufficient
psonall Estate to Sattisfy the same whereby the said John
Whittington after the death of the said Miller & Toaes the
son & Executor became wholly Lyable to Answer the said
p. 241 Debt of Thirty five thousand pounds of tobacco and therefore
humbly prayed that he might be Releived in the premisses by
this Generall Assembly & that An Act might pass to settle &
Invest him the said John Whittington and his beires and Assigns into such lands of the said Daniell Toaes the son as to
this Generall Assembly should seem sufficient to Satisfy pay
and reimburse the said John Whittington the said Debt of
thirty five Thousand pounds of tob[o] & his Costs `& damages
sustained by reason of his the said Whittingtons being security
for the same as aforesaid.

Be it therefore Enacted by the Queens most Excellent Majesty by and with the Advice and Consent of her Majestys
Governour Councill & Assembly of this Province and the
Authority of the same That from and after the End of this
present Sessions of Assembly the said John Whittington his
beires & Assigns shall stand & be seized of a good Estate of
Inheritance in fee simple to him his heires and Assignes for
ever of in and unto the lands & premisses hereafter mentioned
being parte of the Estate and Inheritance of the said Daniell
Toaes the Son (that is say) One tract of land Called by the
name of Honest Dealing Containing four hundred acres; one
other tract of Land Called fair Dealing Containing three hundred acres, one other tract Called Addition to fair Dealing
Containing one hundred & thirty acres, all which said Three
tracts of land are sittuate Lying & being in Kent County afd
and also one other tract of land lying in Cecill County Called
by the name of Cross Saile Containing five hundred seventy
five acres and that the said John Whittington by force and
Vertue of this Act shall have hold use Occupy Possess and
p. 242 Enjoy the Lands and premisses afs[d] to him his heires & Assigns
for Ever against any the right title Claimes or demands of the
beires of the said Daniell Toaes the ffather or Daniel Toaes
the Son any law Statute usage or Custom or any Deed of
Gift will or Bequest made or Executed by the said Daniell
Toaes the ffather or Daniell Toaes the son to the Contrary
Notw[th]standing.

Provided allways and it is hereby Enacted and Declared by
the Authority advice and Consent af[d] that if In case the heires
Executors or Administrators of the said Daniell Toaes the
ffather or Daniell Toaes the son shall or do w[th]in twelve months
to Comence from the End of this Sessions of Assembly satisfy

& pay unto the said Jn° Whittington his heires Executors Lib. L. L. Administrators or Assignes the said sume of thirty five thousand pounds of tobacco w<sup>th</sup> Costs of suite and all other cost Damages and Expences whatsoever that the said Jn° Whittington hath or shall sustaine or be putt unto by Reason or means of his the s<sup>d</sup> Whittingtons being bound for the said Daniell Toaes the Son as af<sup>d</sup> that then & from that time the said Lands and premisses shall revert and returne to such heir Execu<sup>r</sup> or Adm<sup>t</sup> of the said Dan<sup>ll</sup> Toaes the ffather or Daniell Toaes the son as shall sattisfy and pay the same in as full and ample a manner as if this Act had never been made anything in this Act to the Contrary Notwithstanding.

By the house of Delegates Aprill 13<sup>th</sup> 1706 Read & As- p. 243 sented to.     Sign'd p ord<sup>r</sup> William Taylard Cl house Del.

### Aprill 16<sup>th</sup> 1706.

Her Maj<sup>tys</sup> hon<sup>ble</sup> Councill have read & Assented hereto
Sign'd p ord<sup>r</sup>
William Bladen Cl Council.

### Maryland Aprill 19<sup>th</sup> 1706.

On Behalf of her most Sacred Majesty Queen Ann &c I will This be a Law                         Jo: Seymour

An Act to make Null & Voyd a Certaine Deed or Conveyance made by Thomas Edmondson to William Edmondson & remaining upon Record in Dorchester County Court

Whereas Thomas Edmondson of Talbott County by his petition to this present Generall Assembly hath Complained that heretofore he did for the Consideration of fforty Thousand pounds of tobacco by Deed Indented Sell Alienate Confirm and make over & in Dorchester County Co<sup>rt</sup> acknowledge unto his brother William Edmondson a certain tract of Land Sittuate upon Great Choptank River in Dorchester County Called or known by the name of William borrough containing Seven hundred acres as also the moiety of one other tract of land sittuate on the said River and County containing about two hundred acres Called or known by the name of Richardsons ffolly formerly by the last will and Testament of John Edmondson Deceased Bequeathed to the said Thomas Edmondson being all that tract part of the said Tract Called Richardsons folly not included in that part of the said tract formerly Given and granted by the said John Edmondson to

Lib. L. L. the said William Edmondson as by the Record of Dorchester
p. 244 County Court Relation being thereunto had may appear and
for that the said Petitioner doth further sett forth that the
said sume of forty thousand pounds of tobacco the Consideration aforesaid nor any part thereof was not Sattisfied and
payed to the said Thomas Edmondson by the said William
Edmondson in his Life time and that there is not any asetts
remaining in the hands of the Executor of the said William
Edmondson or any thing of the Estate of the said William
Edmondson whereby to Sattisfy and pay his Just Debt the
truth of which petition Evidently appearing to this Generall
Assembly they pray that it may Enacted.

And be it Enacted by the Queens most Excilent Majesty by
and with the advice and Consent of her Majestys Governour
Councill and Assembly of this Province and the Authority of
the same that from and after the End of this present sessions
of Assembly the said Deed or Conveyance so as af$^d$ made and
Executed by the said Thomas Edmondson to the said William
Edmondson and recorded in Dorchester County Court shall
to all Intents and purposes be Deemed adjudged and taken
and is hereby Declared to be null and void and of no Vallidity
or Effect whatsoever and that the said Thomas Edmondson
by force and Vertue of this act shall be and is impowered into
and upon the said Lands or premisses or any part thereof in
the name of the whole to reenter and the same againe to have
hold possess and Enjoy to him his heires and assigns forever
as in his first and former Estate in as Large ample and Bene-
p. 245 ficiall manner to all Intents and purposes as if the said Deed
Conveyance sale or allienation had never been had or made
anything in the said Deed Conveyance or record of Dorchester
County Court Law Statute usage or Custom to the Contrary
Notwithstanding.

Aprill 15$^{th}$ 1706.   Read and assented to by the house of
Delegates.   Sign'd ꝑ ord$^r$ William Taylard Clk house Del.

By the Councill in Assembly Aprill 16$^{th}$ 1706.

This bill read and assented to.        Sign'd ꝑ ord$^r$
                                   W$^m$ Bladen Clk Council.

Maryland April 19$^{th}$ 1706.

On Behalf of her most sacred Majesty Queen Anne &c I will
This be a Law                              Jo : Seymour

An Act for uniting Newport Hundred now part of King <small>Lib. L. L.</small> and Queens Parish to William & Mary Parish in Charles County.

Whereas It is represented to this present Generall Assembly by the Inhabitants of William and Mary parish that the said parish is so small that the fforty pounds of tobacco per poll is not sufficient to Maintaine a Minister in the said parish the same not Exceeding ten Thousand pounds of Tobacco per Annum and that the said Hundred of newport is by the Division of Charles and S$^t$ Maries County's Left in the said Charles County and that the said Parish Called King and Queens Parish without the said Hundred Called New Port hundred is sufficient to maintain a Minister being of Greater Vallue then the said William and Mary Parish & the said Hundred Called Newport Hundred to the same adjoyned & therefore Humbly prayed that the said Hundred Called newport Hundred might be united to and made parcell of <small>p. 246</small> the said William and Mary parish.

Be It therefore Enacted by the Queens most Excellent Majesty by & with the advice and Consent of her Majestys Governour Councill and Assembly of this province and the Authority of the same that from and after the first day of June next Ensuing after the end of this p$^r$sent session of Assembly the said Hundred of Newport shall be divided and taken from the said Parish Called King and Queens Parish in St. Mary's County and be added and united unto W$^m$ And Mary Parish in Charles County in which the same lyes and shall from and after the time aforesaid by Vertue of this Act be deemed adjudged reputed and taken as part and parcell of the said W$^m$ and Mary parish and not as parte or parcell of King and Queens parish in S$^t$ Maries County and that the Inhabitants thereof shall have and Enjoy all benefitts and previlledges Equall w$^{th}$ any other the Inhabitants of the s$^d$ Parish any Law statute usage or Custom to the Contrary Notwithstanding.

Aprill 13$^{th}$ 1706 : Read and Assented to by the house of Delegates.  Sign'd p ord$^r$ W$^m$ Taylard Cl house Del.

### Aprill 16$^{th}$ 1706

Her Majestys Honorable Councill have read & Assented hereto.  Sign'd p ord$^r$ W Bladen Clk Councill.

### Aprill 19$^{th}$ 1706

On the Behalf of her most Sacred Majesty Queen Anne &c. I will this be a Law.  Jo: Seymour

An Act Declaring Severall acts of Parliament made in the
Kingdom of England to be in force within this Province.

Be it Enacted By the Queens most Excellent Majesty by
and with the advice and Consent of her Majestys Governour
Councill and Assembly of this province and the Authority
of the same that the act of Parliament made at the Parliament
begun and held at Westminster the nineteenth Day of March
in the first year of the reigne of our Late Sovereigne Lord
King James the first Intituled an Act to restraine all persons
from marriage untill their former wives and former husbands
be Dead and the severall penall acts of parliament of England
mentioned in the act of parliament made att the parliament
held att Westminster in the first year of the reigne of our
late Sovereign Lord and Lady King William and Queen
Mary Entituled an Act for Exempting their Majestys Protest-
tant Subjects Dissenting from the Church of England from
the Penaltys of Certain Laws together with the said Last
mentioned Act of Parliament Exempting their Majestys Protestant Subjects Desenting from the Church of England from
the penaltys of the said Laws & Every article Clause matter
and thing in the said Acts contained shall be & are in full
force to all Intents & purposes within this Province.

Aprill 18ᵗʰ 1706   Read and assented to by the house of
Delegates          Sign'd ℗ ordʳ Wᵐ Taylard Cl house Del.

p. 248   Aprill the 18ᵗʰ 1706. Her Majestys Honorable Councill
have read & Assented hereto.
Sign'd ℗ order Wᵐ Bladen Cl Councl.

Maryland Aprill 19ᵗʰ 1706

On behalf of her most Sacred Majesty Queen Anne &ᶜᵃ I
will this be a Law.                              Jo: Seymour

An Act Declaring An Act Entituled An Act Entituled An Act
for Suspending the prosecution of any Priests of Communion
of the Church of Rome incurring the penaltys of An Act of
Assembly Entituled An Act for preventing the Growth of
Popery by Exercising their ffunction in a private Family of
the Roman Communion but In noe other Case Whatsoever
to be in force.

Be it Enacted by the Queens most Excellent Majesty by and
with the advice and Consent of her Majestys Governour Council and Assembly of this province and the Authority of the

same that the Act of Assembly made att A Sessions of Assem- Lib. L. L.
bly begun and held att the towne and Port of Annapolis the
fifth Day of December one thousand seven hundred & four
Entituled An Act for Suspending the Prosecution of Any
Priests of the Communion of the Church of Rome incurring
the penaltys of An Act of Assembly Entituled An Act for
preventing the Growth Popery by Exercising their ffunction
in a private ffamily of the Roman Communion but in noe other p. 249
Case whatsoever & Every Article matter clause and thing
therein Contained shall be & Remain in full force and Effect
to all Intents and purposes for and during and unto the full
End & term of twelve months next after the End of this Sessions of Assembly or her Majestys Pleasure first knowne.

April 18ᵗʰ 1706. Read & Assented to by the house of
Delegates: Sign'd ⅌ Ord'
Wᵐ Taylard Cl house Del.

Aprill 18ᵗʰ 1706 : Her Majestys honorable Council have read
& Assented hereto ; Sign'd ⅌ ord'
Wᵐ Bladen Cl Council.

Maryland Aprill 19ᵗʰ 1706 :

On behalf of her most Sacred Majesty Queen Anne &c I
will This be a Law. Jo : Seymour

An Act to prohibitt the Exportation of European Comodity's
out of this Province.

Be it Enacted by the Queens most Excellent Majesty by
and with the advice and Consent of her Majestys Governour
Councill and Assembly of this Province and the Authority of
the same That no goods or Comoditys of the product or
Manufacturs of Europe now or att any time after the End of
this Session of Assembly Imported into this Province by Land
or Water to any other place whatsoever on pain of forfeiting
to her Majesty her heirs and Successors all such goods or
comoditys so exported or attempted to be Exported out of p. 250
this province or the full Value thereof one half thereof to her
Majesty her beires and Successors for the Support of the Government of this province and the other half to the Informer or
him or them that will informe or sue for the same to be recovered against such Exporter by action of Debt bill Plaint or
Information in any court of Record within this Province
wherein noe Essoyne protection or wager of Law to be
Allowed

Lib. L. L.     Provided Always that this Act nor anything therein Contained shall Extend or be Construed or. taken to Extend to goods and Merchandizes Imported into this Province which are bona fide consigned or belonging to any ꝑson or ꝑsons actually residing in the Collony of Virginia or province of Pensilvania or goods and merchandizes imported in order to be shipt of for the coast of Guinea; This Act to Indure for three years and from thence to the End of the next Sessions of Assembly which shall Happen next after the end of the said three year.

Aprill 18ᵗʰ 1706   Read and assented to by the house of Delegates.     Sign'd ꝑ ordʳ Wᵐ Taylard Cl house Del.

Aprill 18ᵗʰ 1706.   Her Majestys honorable Councill have read & Assented hereto.   Sign'd ꝑ ordʳ
Wᵐ Bladen  Cl Council.

Aprill 19ᵗʰ 1706.   On the behalf of her most Sacred Majesty Queen Anne &c I will this be a Law.
Jo: Seymour

p. 251 An Act Incouraging the making Hemp & Flax within this Province.

The Inhabitants of this Province being in a great measure incouraged by our most Gracious Queens Royall Assent to an Act of Parliament made in the third and fourth years of her said Majesty's Reigne Intituled. An Act for Incorageing the Importation of Navall Stores from her Majestys plantations In America to make Hemp within this province and this present Generall Assembly being willing and Desirous that the said Incouragement should not prove Ineffectuall but that soe Good and great an advantage to this Province should be furthered and promoted for further Incouragement thereof Doe pray that it may be Enacted.

And be it Enacted by the Queens most Excellent Majesty by and with the advice and Consent of her Majestys Governour Councill & Assembly of this Province and the Authority of the same That if any person or Persons Living or Inhabiting wᵗʰin this Province shall hereafter make by him her or Themselves or by his her or their servants or workmen upon any the Lands or Plantations within this Province any Quantity or Quantitys of Hemp or fflax and Cause the same to be Water Rotted bright and Clean and made merchantable and that such person or persons making such hemp or flax be

indebted to any person or persons Residing or trading into Lib. L. L.
this province in any sume or sumes of mony or Tobacco that p. 252
then such Person or 'psons to whome the same are or shall be
Due shall be and are hereby obliged to take and receive of
and from such his her or their Debtor or Debtors tendring in
some Port or Town within this Province such Hemp or fflax
water Rotted bright Cleane and made merchantable One
fourth part of such Debt Due from such debtor or Debtors
that Can and will tender and pay the same after the rate of
six pence per pound for Hemp; and nine pence per pound
for flax & so proportionably for any greater or Lesser quantity and according to the same rate in tobacco att one penny
per pound and if any Creditor or Creditors shall refuse to
accept and take such quantity of Hemp or fflax att the Rates
aforesaid when to them tendred towards satisfaction of his
Debt and shall after such Tender bring any accon att Law
against the Debtor for the same that then such Debtor pleading a tender of such Hemp or fflax & proving the same to
Effect the plaintif shall be non suite and shall pay Costs to
the Defendant.

Aprill 18ᵗʰ 1706. Read and Assented to by the house of
Delegates. Sign'd 'p order Wᵐ Taylard Cl house Del.

Aprill 18ᵗʰ 1706. Her Majestys Honorable Councill have
Read and Assented hereto
Sign'd 'p ordʳ W Bladen Clk Councill.

Aprill the 19ᵗʰ 1706. p. 253
On the behalf of her most sacred Majesty Queen Anne &cᵃ
I will this be a Law. Jo: Seymour

An Act to Impower trustees to sell the freehold and Demesne
Land of Abraham Naylor Late of Ann Arundell County
Deceased & apply the money to the uses mentioned in his
Last Will and Testament.

Whereas Abraham Naylor late of Ann Arundell County
planter Deceased was in his Lifetime seized in ffee of One
Plantation & one hundred acres of Land or their abouts with
the appurtenances lyeing on or near Herrin Creek in Ann
Arundell and by his last will and testament in writing he Did
Devise that the said Plantacon and Land should be sold by
Samuell Chew & Nehemiah Birkhead of Ann Arundell' County his trustees and Overseers by him nominated and appointed
by that his Last will and Testament and what Remained of

Lib. L. L. the purchase money after his Debts and Legacys were paid
he did appoint to be Disposed of to the use and relief of
Poore people of the Quarter of Ustone In the parish of Dran-
feild in Darby Sheire in the Kingdom of England for ever
and whereas the said trustees in order to performe the said
will have agreed to Bargaine and sell the said Plantacon and
p. 254 land to Christopher Vernon of Ann Arundell County In Consideration of a Sume of money by him to Be payd to the said
trustees to the uses in the sayd will mentioned.

Be it therefore Enacted by the Queens most Excellent
Majesty by and with the advise and Consent of her Majestys
Governour Councill and Assembly of this province and the
authority of the same that the last will and Testament of
Abraham Naylor late of Annarundell County Deceased shall
be adjudged to be good and sufficient in Law to all Intents
and purposes whatsoever to vest and settle the lands therein
mentioned in Samuell Chew and Nehemiah Birkhead the
Trustees to the uses in the said will menconed and all such
grants bargains and sales of those premises w$^{th}$ the appurtenances hereafter to be made and Executed by them the said
trustees or by Either of them to Christopher Vernon and his
heirs accordiug to the agreement made between them shall
be adjudged to be good and Effectuall in the Law and shall
sufficiently Vest and Execute a good and Indefeisible Estate
of Inheritance in him the said Christopher Vernon his heires
& Assigns forever any Defect Omission or Imperfection in
the said Last will and Testament or any thing in this present
p. 255 act or any other Law Statute use or Custom to the Contrary
thereof in any wise Notwithstanding.

Aprill the 17$^{th}$ 1706.   Read & Assented to by the house
of Delegates   Sign'd ꝑ ord$^r$   W$^m$ Taylard Clk house Del.

### Aprill 19$^{th}$ 1706.

Her Majestys Honorable Councill have read and Assented
hereto.   Sign'd ꝑ ord$^r$          W Bladen Clk Councill.

### Aprill 19$^{th}$ 1706.

On the behalf of her most sacred Majesty Queen Anne &c
I will this be a Law.                       Jo: Seymour

An Act Impowering a Committee to lay assess and apportion
the publick levy of this Province for this present year One
thousand seven hundred and six.

Whereas this present Generall Assembly have for the Defraying the Publick Charge of this Province to the Eighteenth

Day of Aprill One Thousand seven hundred and six r
certaine Sume of tobacco and mony amounting to the s
two hundred Sixty one thousand seven hundred twe
pounds of tobacco and the sume of One hundred Ninet
pounds eleven Shillings and four pence Currant mony
province as by the Journall of the Comittee of accounts a

But by reason more publick charges may arise anc
Due before the tenth day of October next which is the
and accustomed time of payment att which time againe
and Convene the whole Assembly for that occation onl
sidering the great number of them and the remoteness (
habitation from the place appointed would be very cha
and troublesome to the whole province in Generall for p
tion whereof.

Be it Enacted by the Queens most Excellent Maje
and with the advice and Consent of her Majestys Gov
Councill and Assembly of this province & The Autho
the same that one Burgess or Delegate for each res
County & one for the Citty of S' Marys be and are
Authorized and appointed a comittee to Joyne with some
Majestys honorable Councill to lay and Equally Asse
said publick Levy of this province—(That is to say)
Majestys Honorable The Honorable Thomas Tencl
Robert Smith Esq' Collonel John Hamond and Lieu
Collonel William Holland and of the house of Delega
S' Marys Citty M' George Muschamp for S' Maries (
M' William Watts Thomas Smith Esq' for Kent Coun
Ann Arundell County M' Charles Greenberry for (
County M' John Leach for Charles County Collonel
Contee for Baltemore County M' James Maxwell for Son
County M' John Maclaster for Talbott County M' N
Lowe for Cecill County M' Edward Blay for Dor(
County M' Hugh Ecclestone & for Prince Georges (
M' Thomas Greenfield; or the Major part of them sl
and appear at the Towne and port of Annapolis the fir:
day of October next then and there to lay and assess tl
publick Levy already Raised and also to allow Levy and
what further Charges may accrue which to them shall
appear to be Due from the publick not Exceeding tw
dred thousand pounds of tobacco and one thousand p
Currant mony of this Province more then what is a
raised & to apportion order and pay the same to the S
persons to whome the same shall be due and a fair Jou
all their proceedings Deliver to the Clerk of the Assem
satisfaction of all persons therew'h Concerned.

But if it shall happen that his Excellency shall pl(
Convene an Assembly before the first Tuesday of C

Lib. L. L. afᵈ then this present Act & all and Every Clause therein Contained shall be void and of noe Effect.

p. 258     Aprill 19ᵗʰ 1706.   Read and Assented to by the house of Delegates   Signed ⅌ ordʳ       ·Wᵐ Taylard Cl house Del.

### Aprill 19ᵗʰ 1706

Her Majestys honorable Councill have Read and Assented hereto.   Sign'd ⅌ Ordʳ         Wᵐ Bladen Cl Counl.

### Aprill 19ᵗʰ 1706

On the behalf of her most Sacred Majesty Queen Anne &ᶜᵃ I will this be a Law.                         Jo : Seymour

An Act for advancement of trade and erecting Ports & Towns in the Province of Maryland.

Be it enacted by the Queens most excellent Majesty by and with the advice and consent of her Majesty's Governour Councill and Assembly of this Province and the Authority of the same that from and after the end of this present Session of Assembly the Towns Ports and Places herein after mentioned shall be the Ports and Places where all Ships and Vessells trading into this Province shall unlade and put on shoare all Negroes Wares goods merchandizes and Comodities whatsoever (That is to say)

In St. Maries County Saint Maries Town Saint Clements Town and a Town on Beckwiths Island in Petuxent river

In Kent County, In Chester river on a plantation of Mʳ Joce's between Mʳ Willmores and Edward Walvins Plantation In Warton Creek on a Tract of Land where ffrancis Barne lives formerly laid out for a Town and at Sassafrax river where Shrewsberry Town was

p. 259     In Ann arundell County, The Town and Port of Annapolis, London Town on the south side of South river a Town in West river where the Town was formerly And at Herring Creek where the Town was formerly laid out And a Town to be laid out in Maggotty river on the Plantation late in the Possession of Thomas Harrison On the south side of the said River.

In Calvert County at the head of Saint Leonards Creek on both sides of the mill branch at the Mouth of the said Branch at the head of Hunting creek on both sides of the said Creek and in the freshes of Petuxent river at the Plantation of George & Thomas Hardisty

In Charles County at Port Tobacco and New Port where Towns were formerly laid out and at Benedict-Leonard Town in Petuxent river where the Town was formerly Erected

In Baltemore County at Whetstone neck in Patapsco river, Upon the Land called Chillberry in Brush river and a Town on Forster neck on Gun Powder river

In Somersett County on the Northwest side of Wicomoco river on the wood land Reach below Daniel Hast creek, At Rehoboth In Pocomoke river, and at Snow hill where the Towns were formerly Erected and on a point of Land lying in the fork of Monokin river where Captain Henry Smith formerly lived sometime called the White house and at Colebournes Creek in Annamessex.

In Talbot County at Oxford formerly Erected into a port & Town and at Doncaster in Wye river and at Kings Town in Great Choptank.

In Cecill County At Captaine Johns Creek where a Town was formerly laid out In Elk river and the Land belonging to Isaac Calk in Sassafrax river.

In Dorchester County at Cambridge in Great Choptank and at Islington In little Choptank and Little Yarmouth in Transquaking River where Towns were formerly laid out and at the Emperours Landing in Nanticoke river.

In Prince Georges County at the Land of William Mills in Petuxent river at Mattapany Landing on the Land of Thomas Brooke Esq$^r$ at Mount Calvert where the Court house stands and at the upper Landing in the Western branch Comonly called Col Belts Landing at the upper Landing in the Northern branch on the West side of the said branch Comonly called Andersons Landing and at broad Creek in Potomack river on the south side of the said Creek at Thomas Lewis's Landing.

In Queen Anns County in Courseca Creek upon the Plantation where Robert Smith Esq$^r$ now lives at Broad Creek on Kent Island where the same Town was formerly laid out.

Out of which the following Places and No others shall be and are by this Act reputed and appointed Ports (that is to say) Annapolis in Ann Arundell County Saint Maries Town in Potomack at Chester Town Upon Joces Land in Chester river Green hill Town In Somersett County below Daniel Hast Creek in Wiccomoco At The Town of Oxford in Great Choptank and at Beckwicks Island In Petuxent river

And be it further Enacted by the Authority Advice and Consent af$^d$ that the severall and respective psons herein after named shall be and are hereby appointed Commissioners of in and for their Severall and Respective Counties and they and every of them shall Execute the Powers and Au-

Lib. L. L. thorities hereby to them given according to the rules and directions hereafter in this Act mentioned and prescribed as well for the buying and Purchasing of the Aforesaid Town Lands Ports and Places aforesaid as for surveying the same and marking and staking Out the severall Lotts to be laid out in the said Towns to the end that the length breadth & Extant of every Town Port and Place and the lotts therein

p. 261 may the better be known and Observed That is to say for Saint Mary's County Mr Thomas Beale Col Henry Lowe Majr William Aisquith Mr Joshua Guybert Mr James Hay Mr Henry Jowles Mr George Muschamp Mr William Watts and Mr Peter Watts  For Kent County Col Thomas Smyth Mr Elias King Mr John Wells Mr William Frisby Mr William Harris Mr Edward Blay Mr William Potts Mr Thomas Ringgold and Mr Philip Hopkins.  For Ann Arundell County Mr Samuel Young Mr Charles Greenberry Mr Joseph Hill Mr Richard Jones Mr Seth Biggs, Mr John Price Mr Josias Lowgood Mr Robert Eagle Mr John Hammond Mr William Hammond and Thomas Homewood for Calvert County Mr Robert Skinner Mr John Mackall Mr John Leach, Mr Thomas Howe Colo John Rigger Colo Walter Smith Capt Richard Smith Mr Samuel Holdsworth Mr George Parker Mr Henry Cox Mr John Smith of Halls Creek and Mr James Heighe for Charles County Mr James Smallwood Mr John Contee Mr Gerard Foulkes Mr William Stone Capt. William Barton Mr Joseph Manning Mr William Herbert Mr William Wilkinson Mr Richard Harrison and Mr Phillip Lynes.  For Baltemore County Mr James Maxwell Mr James Phillips Mr Francis Dollahide Mr John Hall Mr Thomas Ball Mr Aquila Paca Mr John Dorsey Mr William Talbott Mr James Crook and Majr Thomas Hammond  For Somersett County Mr Joseph Gray Mr John Jones Mr John McClester Mr John Waters Mr John West Mr James Dashield Mr John Cornish Mr John Francklin Mr Arnold Elzey and Mr Joseph Venables  for Talbot County Mr Robert Gouldesborough Mr Nicholas Low Mr Thomas Robbins Mr Matthew Tilghman Ward Mr Daniel Sherwood Majr John Hawkins Mr Robert Grundy Mr John Dawson and Mr Thomas Emmerson  For Cecill County Mr Thomas Frisby Mr William Dare Mr John Hinson Mr Matthias Vanderheyden Mr John Dowdall Mr John Hall Mr John Jeaurt Mr Thomas Kelton Mr Matthias Vanbibber for Dorchester County Mr Hugh Eccleston Mr Joseph Ennalls Mr John Hudson Colo Jacob Loockerman Mr Walter Campbell Mr John Kirk Mr Richard Owens Mr John Rawlings

p. 262 Mr Tobias Pollard Mr Francis Howard & Mr Thomas Hickes. For Prince Georges Mr Thomas Greenfield Mr Robert Tyler Mr Samuel Maggruder Mr John Browne Mr Alexr Maggruder Mr Fredrick Clodius Mr Robert Bradley Mr Thomas Sprigg

M<sup>r</sup> Thomas Odell M<sup>r</sup> William Tanyhill and M<sup>r</sup> Robert Wade, Lib. L. L. for Queen Anns County M<sup>r</sup> Henry Coursey M<sup>r</sup> Philemon Lloyd M<sup>r</sup> Richard Tilghman M<sup>r</sup> William Turloe M<sup>r</sup> Nathaniel Wright M<sup>r</sup> John Salter M<sup>r</sup> John Coppige M<sup>r</sup> Edward Brown M<sup>r</sup> John Whittington and M<sup>r</sup> Edward Chetham

And be it further Enacted by the Authority Advice and Consent afores<sup>d</sup> that the Commissioners herein before nominated and appointed for each respective County or the Maj<sup>r</sup> Part of them are hereby Empowered some time before the first day of September in the year of our Lord one thousand seven hundred and six to meet together upon the respective lands and Places in this Act before mentioned or at some other Convenient place near thereabouts and shall then and there treat & Agree with the Owners and Persons interested in the s<sup>d</sup> Lands for One hundred Acres of Convenient Land at the discretion of the said Commissioners least Prejudiciall to the Owners thereof And after purchase thereof shall Cause the same to be survey'd and layd out and after the same so survey'd and layd out shall cause the same One hundred Acres of Land to be marked staked out and Divided into Convenient streets lanes and Allys with Open Spare places to be left on which May be Erected Church Chappell and Markett house and other publick buildings and the remaining part of the s<sup>d</sup> One hundred Acres of Land as near as may be into One hundred Equall Lotts marked on some Posts or Stakes towards p. 263 the Streets or Lanes with Number one two three four and so forward to One hundred to be divided and laid out, Out of which lotts the Owner of the said Land shall have his first Choice for one Lott and after such Choice the remaining lotts may be taken up by others but no ꝑsons shall Presume to Purchase more than One lott in a Town or Port during the first four Months after the laying Out such Port or Town and the lotts shall be purchased by the Inhabitants of the County where such Ports or Towns shall lye and in Case the Inhabitants of the Countys shall not take up the lotts within the time of four months after such laying out as af<sup>d</sup> It shall then be free for any Pson or Psons whatsoever to take up the said Lott or lotts paying the Owner Proportionable for the same And in case any ꝑson or ꝑsons shall Willfully refuse to make sale of any such Lands herein before mention'd or any ꝑson or ꝑsons that thro' Nonage Coverture Non Sanæ Memoriæ or any other disability or Impediment whatsoever be or are disabled to make such Sales as aforesaid that then the Commissioners aforesaid nominated and Appointed in Each respective County or the Maj<sup>r</sup> Part of them shall and are Virtue of this Act Authorized empowered and required to Issue out Warrants under their hands and Seales to the Sheriffs of their severall and

640    *Assembly Proceedings, April* 2–19, 1706.

Lib. L. L. respective Counties which said Sheriffs are allso hereby
required upon receipt of such Warrants to Impannell & returne
a Jury of the most Substantiall freeholders inhabitants within
the said County to be and appear before the said Commissioners at a Certaine day & time by them to be limited which
Jury upon their oaths to them to be Administred by the said
Commissioners or the Maj$^r$ Part of them shall enquire Assess
and returne what Damages & Recompence they shall think
fitt to be awarded to the Owners of such Lands and all Persons
interested therein according to their severall and respective
Interests and what sume of tob° the s$^d$ Jury shall adjudge the
p. 264 said Land to be Worth shall be paid to the owners and all
Psons interested therein by such Pson or Persons as shall take
up the said Lotts proportionably to their Lot or lotts.

And the said Commissioners the Major part of them are
hereby Empowered by Warrant under their hands and seales
to sumons the Queens Surveyor of Each respective County to
survey and lay out one hundred acres of Land in the Places
herein before mentioned and appointed in manner and form
af$^d$ and the same to Divide into One hundred equall Lotts as
the said Commissioners or the Maj$^r$ Part of them shall Direct
with Convenient Streets lanes and Allys as af$^d$ as near as may
be to the benefitt of the taker up of Each respective Lott and
when the said One hundred acres of Land is so surveyed laid
out Valued and Divided as af$^d$ that then whosoever shall make
Choice of any Lott and make Entry thereof with such pson as
by the said Commissioners or the Maj$^r$ Part of them shall be
Appointed to keep the book for Entry of such Lotts and pay
or give security for the payment of such sume of tobacco as
shall by the Direction of the said Commissioners or Jury be
rated upon such Lott & payable to the Owner of such Land
and on such Lott so as aforesaid taken up build one sufficient
twenty square house at the least within twelve months after
taking up such lot or lotts each respective Lott to be held of
the Lord Proprietary of this Province his heires & Assignes
to such taker up and builder his her or their heires or Assignes
forever at and under the Yearly rent of One farthing Currant
Mony of this Province for Each respective Lott the Land being
old rents and half Penny of each Lott where the Lands was
taken up by new rents and the same or any other building or
p. 265 manner of settling upon such Lott according to the Direction
of this Act shall invest the said Taker up and builder upon
such Lott his heires and Assignes of a good indefeazable Estate of Inheritance to him and his beires forever and shall bar
the Owner or Owners or any pson or persons interested in
the said Lands whether living within or without this Province
and even the Lord Proprietary of this Province his heires and As-

signes saving the rents in and by this Act reserved to be paid
to his said Lordship his heires and Assignes and the Tobacco
to be paid by such Taker up and builder as af^d to the Owner
of such Land and likewise upon tender of payment and refusall
with Proof of the Tender and refusall of such Tobacco as aforesaid such building as af^d shall be binding to all intents and
purposes against the said Parties their heires & Assignes so
as aforesaid refusing or others Clayming any title or Interest
in the said Lands and grounds and shall be full Authority to
the s^d Commissioners or the Major Part of them in Each
respective County shall Nominate and appoint a Person qualifyed to keep a book to Enter Down the proceedings of the
said Commissioners & Each Persons Choice of any respective
Lott That thereby It may Appeare what Lotts are taken up
and what remaine undisposed of and the Commissioners proceedings therein Likewise And in Case any difference happen
to arrise in or about the taking up the s^d Lotts or the particular Dividents hereby allotted or any other Matter referring to
the Execution of this Act the said Commissioners in Each
respective County or the Major Part of them shall Immediately
without any formality of Law (Ore tenus) hear and Determine
the Matter of Difference according to their discretions and
their Judgments therein shall be finall.

And be it further Enacted by the Authority afores^d by and
w^th the Advice and Consent af^d that the Surveyors shall have
& receive for surveying and laying out each respective
Towne into Streets & Lotts as af^d the sume of One Thousand
Pounds of tobacco and no more to be paid and allowed him
by each respective County in the County levy where such
Towne shall be laid out.

And in case the taker up of such Lott or Lotts refuse or
neglect to build upon such Lott or Lotts within the time
afores^d by this act appointed that then it shall and may be
lawfull for Any Other Person or Psons whatsoever to Enter
upon the s^d Lott or Lotts so as afores^d not built upon paying
such sume of tobacco as shall be first sett and assest upon
such Lott to the Commissioners af^d or such other ꝑson as the
Commissioners in Each respective County or the Maj^r Part
of them shall Nominate and appoint to receive the same for
the publick use and benefitt of such Towne wherein such
lotts shall lye and be taken up the second time.

Provided allways that such second taker up or Purchaser
build and finish within one yeare after such his Entry made
such house as in this act is before limitted and appointed to
be built by the first taker up which house shall give and settle
as good estate to all intents and Purposes to such second
taker up and builder as af^d his beires and Assignes as is in

41

Lib. L. L. and by this Act before limitted and settled upon the first
taker up and builder subject to the same rents and reserva-
tions in and by this Act before limitted and appointed.

And in Case any the said Lotts shall be neglected to be
taken up in any the Ports or Towns aforesaid in any County
of this Province for and during the term of Seven Years next
after the publication of this Act that then & in such case the
Owner or ᵖsons interested at the first in such Land shall after
such time Expired be possessed and interested in the said
Lott or Lotts as in their first or former Estate anything in
this Act Contained to the Contrary notwithstanding.

And Be it further Enacted by the Authority advice and
Consent aforesaid that from and after the first day of January
seventeen hundred and seven all Masters of Ships and Ves-
p. 267 sells trading into this Province shall unlade and put on Shoar
all goods and merchandizes in such ships and Vesells Imported
to be sold here by Any merchants or goods consigned to
their factors at such Towns Ports and places as are before
sett down and appointed in this Act for unlading goods and
merchandises and at No other Place or Places whatsoever on
paine of Loosing and forfeiting all such Goods and merchandizes by them Landed or put on Shoar at any other Place or
Places whatsoever than as aforesaid one third part thereof to
her Majesty beires and Successors for the Support of the
Government of this Province one other third Part to the use
of the County where such goods shall be put on Shoare for
and toward Defraying the County charge and the other third
part to the informer or him or them that will inform or sue
for the same to be recovered in any court of record of this
Province by Action of Debt bill Plaint or information wherein
No Essoyn Protection or wager of Law to be Allowed.

And be it further Enacted by the Authority afᵈ by and
with the Advice and consent aforesaid that from and after the
first day of January one thousand seven hundred and seven
no merchant factor or Mariner trading into this Province shall
traffick sell or barter away any goods or **Comodities** Imported
or brought into this Province and not Really & bona fide
wholly Owned by and upon the Proper account & risq of the
Inhabitants of this Province but at some of The Towns Ports
or Places before in this Act Appointed to be Ports or Towns
under Paine of forfeiting to her Majesty her heires and Successors all such goods and merchandizes sold Or Bartered
away at Any other Place or Places within this Province or the
full Value thereof to the uses afᵈ to be recovered as aforesaid
wherein No Essoyne protection or Wager of Law to be allowed any Law statute usage or custome to the Contrary
Notwithstanding.

And be it further Enacted by the Authority afores[d] by and with the Advice and consent aforesaid that there shall be Allowed to all Debtors whatsoever owing any tobacco to any Pson or Psons whatsoever or howsoever such Debtor bringing his tobacco to the Ports towns or Places aforesaid & there Paying the same to his Creditor or Creditors or his or their Receivers the sume of tenn pounds of tobacco p Centum for every hundred pounds of tobacco so brought to the Places af[d] and there paid as aforesaid to be deducted out of such Debtors said Debt or allowed of in bar or discount of any Action to be brought against any Debtor or Debtors by any Creditor or Creditors in any Court within this Province.

Lib. L. L. P. 268

And Be it further Enacted by the Authority Advice and consent af[d] that any Person or psons that shall dwell and inhabit in any of the said Ports towns or places such pson or psons shall or may contract for Barter buy and Purchase any quantity or quantities of goods or Merchandizes whatsoever any Law Statutes or usage to the Contrary notwithstanding Provided Nevertheless that such pson or psons buying or Contracting Or any ways purchasing bartering or Engrossing such goods wares or merchandizes shall likewise sell or barter away the said goods and merchandizes in the same Town or port or Place where they were Brought or in some other Port or Town w[th]in this Province and not Else where.

And be it further Enacted by the Authority Advice and Consent afores[d] that from and after the first day of January One thousand seven hundred afores[d] all sheriffs Clarks of the County Courts Navall Officers and Collectors, The Lord Baltemores Collectors and Receivers of his Lordships Revenues shall be and are hereby Obliged Actually to dwell and inhabit in some of the said Ports or towns or there keep their Sufficient Deputy or Deputies for the necessary and quick Dispatch of all business to their severall Offices appertaining and that the Deputy Com[ry] in Each respective County be Obliged actually to dwell & inhabit in the most Convenient Town or Port in each respective County for the Ease and Conveniency of the Inhabitants thereof

p. 269

And for Encouragement of all Tradesmen and Artificers to live and inhabit in the aforesaid Ports or towns Be it Enacted by the Authority advice and Consent af[d] that all tradesmen and Artificers or other persons whatsoever following or using any Manuall Occupation trade or Calling in Any the Ports towns or Places af[d] and there Actually living and residing with their families and using their trades and callings shall be and are by force and Virtue of this Act Exempted and discharged from paying any Publick or County levies for themselves Journeymen and servants during the first four years of their residing in such Ports or Towns

Lib. L. L.    And for the better Encouragement of forreigners Aliens merchants or tradesmen to come and Inhabit In such Ports or Towns be it Enacted by the Authority Advice and Consent af$^d$ that any Alien or forreigner that shall Come and reside in Any of the Ports Towns or Places af$^d$ and their Exercise or follow merchandize or Any trade or Manuall Occupation for the term of four years such aliene or forreigner shall by Virtue of such his Residence and of this Act be Deemed p. 270 adjudged and accounted to be a free Denizon and have hold and Enjoy all benefitts Privileges and advantages that any free Denizen hath or ought to have and Enjoy within this province.

And Be it allso Enacted by the Authority Advice and Consent af$^d$ that the severall and respective Justices of the severall and respective County Courts within this Province shall from and after the end of this Present Session of Assembly be Obliged to put out all Male Orphan Children apprentices to some of the tradesmen & Inhabitants in the said Ports or Towns (if such tradesmen and Inhabitants Can be found and will take such Orphans) And not to any other ꝑson or ꝑsons whatsoever which said Tradesmen and Inhabitants of Ports and Towns shall be Subject to the Conditions and Agreements to be made with them by the Comⁿ of the County Courts on behalf of such Male Orphans as other ꝑsons that take Orphans have or ought to be and shall & are hereby obliged to ꝑforme the same.

And be it further Enacted and Declared by the Authority Advice and Consent aforesaid that Nothing in this Act shall Oblige or be Construed to Oblige any ꝑson or ꝑsons whatsoever his her or their heires or Assignes that formerly hath taken up and built upon any Lott or Lotts in the Ports towns or places aforesaid by Virtue of any former Law or Act of Assembly Againe or anew to take up such Lott or lotts so as af$^d$ formerly taken up and built upon but that they their heires and Assignes shall & may have hold and Enjoy the same as if this Act had never been made.

p. 271    And be it likewise Enacted by the Authority Advice and Consent af$^d$ that Any ꝑson or ꝑsons whatsoever that shall Offend Act or Do Contrary to this present Act or the true intent and meaning thereof in Any Case for which No fine or forfeiture is before in and by this Act Imposed he she or they so Offending shall forfeit and pay to our Sovereign Lady the Queens Majesty her heires and Successors the severall sumes of tobacco following (that is to say) Every Sheriffe or his Deputy five thousand Pounds of tobacco Every Clark of the County Court or his Deputy five thousand Pounds of tobacco Every Navall Officer and Collector or their Deputies tenn

Thousand Pounds of tobacco the Collectors and receivers of the Lord Baltemores Revenues or their Deputies Tenne Thousand pounds of tobacco to be recovered as aforesaid wherein No Essoyne Protection or Wager of Law to be Allowed.

And be it further Enacted and Declared by the Authority advice and Consent aforesaid That if any of the places by this Act Appointed for Ports or Towns shall happen to be upon the dwelling plantation or plantations of any ꝑson or ꝑsons Whatsoever whereon there is Erected any Dwelling house or other Houses or whereon there is Planted any Orchard or garden and the Lott or quantity of Land by this Act allowed to the Owner thereof for his Choice will not include such houses orchards or gárdens that then it shall be in the Power of the said Com꜠ in Each respective County or the Majʳ part of them either to Allow to such Owner or Owners of such houses Orchards or Gardens what Other or more recompence or lotts such Commissioners or the Majʳ part of them or the p. 272 Jury afᵈ shall Conceive such houses Orchárds or Gardens may be worth over and above the Value of the Land so as afᵈ to be Assessed by the said Commissioners or Jury Any thing in this Act to the Contrary notwithstanding.

Apŕill the 17ᵗʰ 1706
Read and Assented to by the house of Delegates
Signed ꝑ ordʳ   W Taylard Clk house Del.

Aprill the 17ᵗʰ 1706
Her Majesty's honourable Councill have read & Assented hereto   Signed ꝑ ordʳ          W Bladen Cl Concil.

Aprill the 19ᵗʰ 1706.
On the behalf of her most Sacred Majᵗʸ Queen Anne &cᵃ I will this be Law                    Jo : Seymour

The Seale of the Secretary's Office is hereunto Affixt this fifteeth day of June Anno Dni 1706
On behalf of the honᵇˡᵉ Sʳ Thomas Laurence Baronᵗ Secretary of Maryland.
                    ꝑ me
                        Th Bordley Clk of the Secʳʸˢ office

# INDEX TO NAMES OF PERSONS AND PLACES.

# INDEX TO ACTS.

42